The Routledge Companion to Education

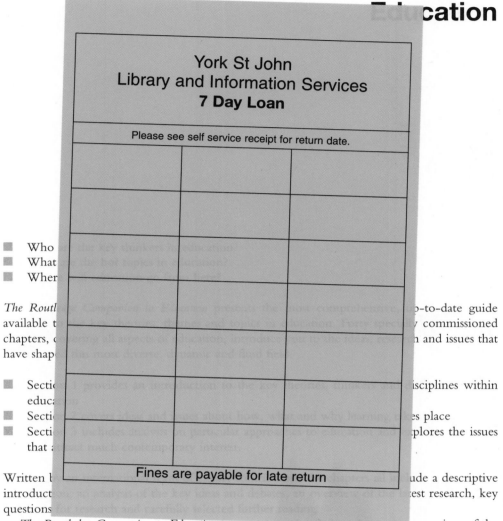

- Who are the key thinkers in education?
- What are the hot topics in education?
- Where are the key thinkers in education?

The Routledge Companion to Education presents the most comprehensive, up-to-date guide available to the key themes, debates and topics in education. Forty specially commissioned chapters, covering all aspects of education, introduce the reader to the ideas, research and issues that have shaped the most diverse, dynamic and fluid field of study.

- Section 1 provides an introduction to the key disciplines within education
- Section 2 contains ideas and facts about how, when and why learning takes place
- Section 3 includes analyses of particular approaches to education and explores the issues that attract much contemporary interest.

Written by experts in the field, all of the chapters include a descriptive introduction, an analysis of the key ideas and debates, an overview of the latest research, key questions for research and carefully selected further reading.

   The Routledge Companion to Education is a succinct, detailed, authoritative overview of the topics which are at the forefront of educational research and discourse today. This classic collection is a bookshelf essential for every student and scholar serious about the study of education.

James Arthur is Head of the School of Education at the University of Birmingham, UK.

Andrew Peterson is Senior Lecturer in Education at Canterbury Christ Church University, UK.

The Routledge Companion to Education

Edited by
James Arthur and
Andrew Peterson

Routledge
Taylor & Francis Group

NEW YORK AND LONDON

First published 2012
by Routledge
2 Park Square, Milton Park, Abingdon, Oxon OX14 4RN

Simultaneously published in the USA and Canada
by Routledge
711 Third Avenue, New York, NY 10017

Routledge is an imprint of the Taylor & Francis Group, an informa business

British Library Cataloguing in Publication Data
A catalogue record for this book is available from the British Library

Library of Congress Cataloging in Publication Data
The Routledge companion to education/[edited by] James Arthur
and Andrew Peterson.
  p. cm.
  1. Education.   I. Arthur, James, 1957–.
  II. Peterson, Andrew, 1976–.
  LB14.7.R685 2012
  370—dc22   2011014097

ISBN: 978-0-415-58346-6 (hbk)
ISBN: 978-0-415-58347-3 (pbk)
ISBN: 978-0-203-80224-3 (ebk)

Typeset in Galliard, Optima and Helvetica Neue
by Florence Production Ltd, Stoodleigh, Devon

MIX
Paper from
responsible sources
FSC® C004839
www.fsc.org

Printed and bound in Great Britain by
TJ International Ltd, Padstow, Cornwall

Contents

ethnicity

social class

Illustrations

Figures

Tables

Author biographies

Professor James Arthur, Head of School of Education, University of Birmingham. He has written widely on the relationship between theory and practice in education, particularly the links between communitarianism, social virtues, citizenship, religion and education. He is Director of citizED, sits on the executive of the *Society for Educational Studies* and is editor of the *British Journal of Educational Studies*.

Professor Tina Besley, University of Illinois at Urbana-Champaign, Research Professor in Educational Policy Studies. She is co-editor of *E-Learning & Digital Media* and associate editor of *Educational Philosophy and Theory*. She has had works published in philosophy of education, educational politics and policy, globalisation, research assessment in higher education, subjectivity, youth studies, e-learning, social networking and entrepreneurial studies in education.

Emeritus Professor Tom Bisschoff, University of Birmingham, Senior Lecturer. Joint Editor of the Commonwealth Council for Educational Administration and Management (CCEAM) journal, *International Studies in Educational Administration* (ISEA). He has written widely on school finances, project management and school marketing. He is interested in leadership for school improvement.

Dr Douglas Bourn, Institute of Education, University of London, Director of Development Education Research Centre. Editor of *International Journal of Development Education and Global Learning*. Chair of Earth Charter UK and Humanities Education Centre, Tower Hamlets, London, and author of numerous articles on global citizenship, internationalisation in higher education and education for sustainable development.

Dr Marion Bowl, University of Birmingham, Senior Lecturer and Director of Studies for Continuing Professional Development. Researches in the field of post-compulsory, adult and community education, particularly in the UK and Aotearoa, New Zealand.

Dr Hazel Bryan, Canterbury Christ Church University, Head of Department, Centre for Enabling Learning. She is head of the CEL Department at Canterbury Christ Church, which runs a Masters course in Enabling Learning, teaching those who work with young people who have difficulties engaging and/or learning. She has an interest in primary education and has given papers on the ways Religious Studies is taught in schools.

Professor Orison Carlile, Waterford Institute of Technology, Waterford, Course Coordinator MA in Management in Education. His research interests are in educational management and reflective practice and he is co-author of the best-selling text *Approaches to Learning* (McGraw-Hill/OU Press, 2008).

Dr Theodore Michael Christou, University of New Brunswick, Assistant Professor of Education. He has written widely on the history of education and educational philosophy in teacher education. His research concerns conceptual history, as well as the reconciliation of humanist and religious thought in teaching and learning.

Professor Michael Connelly, University of Toronto, Professor Emeritus in the Department of Curriculum, Teaching and Learning at the Ontario Institute for Studies in Education. He has written on curriculum studies, science education, teacher education and narrative inquiry and is an international educational consultant.

Dr Robin L. Danzak, University of South Florida Sarasota-Manatee, Visiting Assistant Professor of Speech-Language Pathology. Her research focuses on language and literacy learning of bilingual children and adolescents.

Professor Ian Davies, University of York, Professor in Education. He is the editor of the citizED and CiCea journal *Citizenship Teaching and Learning*. Publications include the *Sage Handbook of Education for Democracy and Citizenship*.

Professor Jon Davison has been professor of teacher education in four universities including the Institute of Education, University of London where he was also Dean. His research interests include sociolinguistics, the teaching and learning of English and Media, citizenship education and the professional formation of teachers.

Professor Kathryn Ecclestone, University of Birmingham, Professor of Education and Social Inclusion. Her research explores the interplay between policy, practice and attitudes to learning and assessment in post-compulsory education, with focus on the rise of a 'therapeutic ethos' in curriculum content, teaching and assessment across the education and welfare system.

Simon Ellis, Canterbury Christ Church University, Senior Lecturer in the Centre for Enabling Learning. He is actively involved in teaching and research in the areas of SEN and inclusion and has a specific interest in pupil behaviour.

Richard Farnan, Harrogate Grammar School, Teacher of Science and Psychology. He studied BA(Hons) Psychology at the University of Leeds, and completed his PGCE at the University of Sunderland.

Michael Hammond, Associate Professor in New Technologies, University of Warwick. He has written for both academic and practitioner audiences on the use of ICT to support teaching and learning. His interests include the past use of ICT, technology and curriculum reform and online communication.

John Huckle, University of York, ESD consultant and visiting fellow in the Department of Educational Studies. Further information concerning his interests and publications can be found on his website at http://john.huckle.org.uk.

Emeritus Professor Peter Jarvis, University of Surrey, Professor of Continuing Education, Department of Politics. He is widely accredited, holding a number of honorary visiting professorships at universities worldwide, as well as honorary memberships to various international professional associations. He is also a frequent speaker on all aspects of adult education, distance learning and lifelong learning.

Professor Anne Jordan, Waterford Institute of Technology, Waterford, Course Coordinator of Masters in Learning and Teaching. Her research interests are in postgraduate supervision, and she is co-author of the best-selling text *Approaches to Learning* (McGraw-Hill/OU Press, 2008).

Dr Dina Kiwan, Birkbeck College, University of London, Academic Fellow/Senior Lecturer in Citizenship Education. Co-Director of the International Centre for Education for Democratic Citizenship (ICEDC), she writes on theories of citizenship in multicultural societies, migration and nationality, and in citizenship and education.

Professor Chris Kyriacou, University of York, holds a personal chair in Educational Psychology in the Department of Educational Studies. He has written extensively on aspects of teaching in schools. His publications include two widely used textbooks, *Effective Teaching in Schools* and *Essential Teaching Skills*, and a large number of research papers. His current research focuses on helping pupils whose behaviour, attitudes or circumstances have given rise to serious concerns within a school.

Ralph Leighton, Canterbury Christ Church University, Principal Lecturer in Education, Course Leader for 11–18 PGCE Citizenship. Current research centres on radical approaches to citizenship education.

Professor Terence Lovat, The University of Newcastle, Australia, Professor of Education. He was chief investigator on the multiple research projects of the Australian Values Education Program, 2003–2009. His major research interests are in values education and Islam's relations with the Western politick.

Julie McLeod, Associate Professor of Curriculum, Equity and Social Change, University of Melbourne. Her research interests lie in interdisciplinary and sociocultural studies of education, identity, equity/inequality and social change. She is beginning a study on the cultural history of adolescence in Australia, 1930s–1970s.

Professor D.G. Mulcahy, Central Connecticut State University. He has written widely on the theory of a liberal education, the ideal of the educated person, the school curriculum, and educational policy.

Dr Alis Oancea, University of Oxford, Lecturer in research policy and philosophy. She is an elected Executive Council member of the British Educational Research Association, Secretary of the Philosophy of Education Society of Great Britain (Oxford branch), and member of the Peer Review College of the Economic and Social Research Council. She has published widely in the fields of philosophy of research, research policy and governance – including research evaluation – and post-compulsory and lifelong education and training.

Dr Nick Peim, Senior Lecturer in Education, University of Birmingham. He teaches theories of education and learning, philosophy of research and supervises research students. He has a forthcoming book on ontology, education and improvement.

Professor Michael A. Peters, University of Illinois at Urbana-Champaign, Professor in the Department of Educational Policy, Organisation and Leadership and Director of the Global Studies in Education. He is the editor of *Educational Philosophy* and *Theory, Policy Futures in Education* and co-editor of *E-Learning and Digital Media* and the author of some 50 books and 500 articles and chapters.

Dr Andrew Peterson, Senior Lecturer in Education, Canterbury Christ Church University. He works in the field of the education of citizenship teachers and has published in the field of civic and moral education. He sits on the executive of the *Society for Educational Studies* and on the editorial board of the *British Journal of Educational Studies*.

Dr Sacha Powell, Canterbury Christ Church University, Principal Lecturer in the Research Centre for Children, Families and Communities. Her primary research interests are within the broad field of Early Childhood Studies with a particular focus on children's rights and voices.

Dr Deirdre Raftery, University College Dublin, Deputy Head of the School of Education and Lifelong Learning. She was appointed Visiting Research Fellow at the University of Oxford in 2010, where she worked on new research for her history of Irish missionary sisters 1860–1960. She is joint editor of the *History of Education* journal.

Dr Christopher Rhodes, University of Birmingham, Senior Lecturer in Educational Leadership. Joint editor of the Commonwealth Council for Educational Administration and Management (CCEAM) journal, *International Studies in Educational Administration* (ISEA). His research interests include leadership for learning, the student experience, professional development, coaching and mentoring and leadership succession management.

Dr Michele Schweisfurth, University of Birmingham, Reader in Comparative and International Education, Director of the Centre for International Education and Research, and lead tutor for Masters in International Studies in Education. She is editor of the journal *Comparative Education*, and Chair of the British Association for International and Comparative Education. Her research interests include global citizenship education, university internationalisation, and learner-centred pedagogy in comparative perspective.

Professor Alan Sears, University of New Brunswick, Professor in the Faculty of Education. His research interests include citizenship education, history education and educational policy.

Dr Robina Shaheen, European Business School London (Regent's College), Lecturer in business research methods and business communication. She has conducted research and written on subjects including life-skills in primary school children, education for sustainable development, 14–19 education reforms, creativity and universal primary quality education. Her research interests are in developing material and teaching for creativity and ways this can be used in improving individual and business performance.

Dr Elaine R. Silliman, University of South Florida, Professor of Communication Sciences and Disorders. She is internationally recognised in the areas of oral and written language disability in school-age children, including bilingual children.

Dr Emma Smith, University of Birmingham, Reader in the School of Education. She is the executive editor of *Educational Review* and has written extensively on issues of education policy and inequality. She is the author of *Key Issues in Inequality and Social Justice* (Sage, 2011).

Dr Vanita Sundaram, University of York, Lecturer in Education, Director of Undergraduate Studies. She is interested in gender studies, inclusion, violence (and gender), inclusive methodologies and inequalities in education.

Emeritus Professor Janet Tod, Canterbury Christ Church University. She is a chartered educational and clinical psychologist and has been engaged for many years in teaching, research and publication in the areas of SEN and inclusion.

Dr Jodi Tommerdahl, University of Texas in Arlington, Associate Professor of Education. She has received postgraduate degrees from the University of London, the École des Hautes Études en Sciences Sociales and the Sorbonne. She is on the editorial board of the journal *Child Language Teaching & Therapy* and carries out research on language development, language impairment and the relationship between language and cognition.

Professor Anna Vignoles, Institute of Education, University of London, Professor of Economics of Education and Deputy Director of the Centre for the Economics of Education. She has written widely on the subject of the quantitative evaluation of education policy, the economic value of education and skills and the use of longitudinal data in education research.

Dr Paul Warwick, University of Leicester, Leader of PGCert in Citizenship Education. He also holds a variety of teaching and tutorial roles across the PGCE, Masters, BA and Foundation Degree programmes, and has previously served as the Deputy Director of the Centre for Citizenship Studies in Education.

Professor Anne West, London School of Economics and Political Science, Professor of Education Policy in the Department of Social Policy. She is also Director of the Education Research Group. Her research focuses on education policy reform, in particular the impact of market-oriented reforms on equality and social justice, and the financing of school-based education.

Dr Louise C. Wilkinson, Syracuse University, Distinguished Professor of Education, Psychology, and Communication Sciences. She is an internationally recognised educational leader. She serves on the boards of the *British Journal of Educational Studies*, *Journal of School Connections,* and *Linguistics and Education*. Her focus of research is on students' language/literacy learning.

Dr Shijing Xu, University of Windsor and Beijing Foreign Studies University, Assistant Professor at the Faculty of Education, University of Windsor and Affiliated Research Associate at the National Research Center for Foreign Language Education, Beijing. She works on cross-cultural Chinese immigrant family education and narrative inquiry. With Michael Connelly, she is establishing a Sister Schools Network between China and Canada.

Editors' introduction

As the chapters presented in this companion demonstrate, education is a diverse, dynamic and fluid discipline. It is at once theoretical and practical, and has many themes and interests (not all of which we have been able to include in this compendium). In considering the areas which this companion could cover, we sought to recognise not only those ideas which are at the forefront of educational research and discourse in Western nations today, but also those which cut across local and national boundaries. The overall aim of this companion is to provide an overview and exploration of these key educational issues, ideas and concepts, and we have sought to do this in an informed and accessible way. Our intention has been to bring together experienced and early-career researchers from a range of nations to contribute their ideas by way of presenting an introduction, review and synthesis of the major theories and topics in education in Western nations today.

Following this short introduction, the companion is divided into three sections. Section 1, 'Educational foundations', introduces readers to key theories, thinkers and disciplines within education. It comprises chapters on liberal education (Mulcahy), communitarianism (Arthur), civic republicanism (Peterson), postmodernism (Peters and Besley), feminism (McLeod), history of education (Raftery), sociology of education (Leighton), philosophy of education (Oancea), educational psychology (Farnan) and economics of education (Vignoles). Section 2, 'Teaching and learning', covers ideas and issues about how, what and why learning takes place. It comprises chapters on learning (Carlile and Jordan), teaching (Kyriacou), curriculum and curriculum studies (Connelly and Xu), language (Wilkinson and Silliman), motivation and behaviour (Ellis and Tod), creativity (Shaheen) and assessment (Ecclestone). Section 3, 'Organisation and issues in education', includes analysis on particular approaches to education and to the main substantive educational issues within Western nations today. It comprises chapters on early childhood education and care (Powell), education and schooling 5–11 years (Bryan), education and schooling 11–16 years (Peterson and Leighton), post-compulsory, higher education and training (Bowl), lifelong learning (Jarvis), alternative education (Warwick), citizenship education (Davies), social class (Davison), comparative education (Schweisfurth), development education (Bourn), cultural-linguistic diversity and inclusion (Danzak, Wilkinson and Silliman), education and neuroscience (Tommerdahl), gender (Sundaram), globalization (Peim), well-being and education (Ecclestone), leadership and school effectiveness (Rhodes and Bischoff), multicultural education (Kiwan), education policy (West), religion and education (Sears and Christou), social justice and inequalities in education (Smith), sustainable development (Huckle), technologies and learning (Hammond) and values education (Lovat).

We have a number of people to thank for their help and support in the production of this companion. First, our sincere thanks and gratitude go to the authors of its chapters, who have been faultless in their cooperation. Second, we would like to thank the publishers, Routledge, and in particular Helen Pritt and Claire Westwood for their help from initial idea through to publication. Third, we owe a particular debt of thanks to Aidan Thompson for his coordination and administration of this project. He has provided outstanding service to this project and without his assistance this text would not be of the standard that it is. We hope that readers will find the chapters here of interest and that their content will provoke further critical thought and dialogue.

Dr Andrew Peterson, Canterbury
Professor James Arthur, Birmingham

Section 1

Educational foundations

Liberal education

D.G. Mulcahy
Central Connecticut State University

Overview

The idea of a liberal education is so central to educational discourse that it is almost necessary to grasp what it means in order to understand the concept of education itself. Predating schools and universities as we now know them, its beginnings are usually traced back to classical Greece. There it is associated with the education Plato envisioned for his idealized ruler, the philosopher king, for whom it was considered essential, and with the philosophy of Aristotle (Hirst, 1971; Carr, 2009). With the rise of the university in the Middle Ages, studying the liberal arts and sciences which had become the recognized content of a liberal education was seen as both worthwhile in itself and foundational to further studies. Although it lost some favor over time, liberal education is still widely viewed as the measure of what it means to be an educated person and as the best preparation for employment and further studies. Yet, while the contrary impression exists, what is now variously termed 'liberal education,' 'liberal arts education,' and 'general education,' is a contested concept that continues to evolve (Kimball, 1995). It is as such that I shall treat of it here.

Introduction

The historian Sheldon Rothblatt wrote of Cardinal Newman's *Idea of a University* that it "remains the singlemost influential book on the meaning of a university in the English language" (Rothblatt, 1997, p. 7). One might add that by virtue of the issues it addressed and the justification it presented, it also provides the basic language of the conversation surrounding liberal education. It is, accordingly, an appropriate point at which to begin examining the idea in its more recent evolution. Here one detects several differing points of view. The general position adopted by Newman remains widely held, and I shall treat of that first. Second, I shall treat departures from this view, ranging from those that reject the idea entirely to those that seek a reconceptualization. Of special interest here is the question of how current thinking on wider educational issues impacts the idea. Consideration of this, and of theorizing possibly at odds with sometimes romanticized idealizations of liberal education, comprise the final section of the chapter.

Liberal education as cultivation of the intellect

Cardinal Newman

For Newman, stated succinctly, liberal education was "cultivation of the intellect," its object "nothing more or less than intellectual excellence" (1947, p. 107; see also Arthur and Nicholls, 2007, pp. 120–149; and Mulcahy, 2008a, pp. 35–69). Fundamental to this stance is Newman's theory of the nature and structure of knowledge and the mind's capacity for intellectual development. For him, following Aristotle, knowledge is a true account of reality. It is one unified whole of which the various subjects constitute the parts. By studying these subjects (which, strictly speaking, were literature, science, and theology) and their interrelations, one can gain an understanding of the world and of the relative value of things. With the assistance of intensive tutorial work it is possible, according to Newman, to develop a philosophical habit of mind, combining with a broad knowledge the ability to engage in critical analysis and reflection. This it is that constitutes cultivation of the intellect and that defines intellectual excellence. It is this formation that fortifies for Newman the belief that liberal education is foundational to further studies and engagement in the world, and why it is ultimately the most useful education even if it seeks no such end. Moral or religious formation has no place in liberal education; although in the university as he envisioned it, Newman insisted – overly so in the opinion of some (McClelland, 1973, *passim*) – that liberal education should be accompanied by such moral and religious formation.

Mortimer Adler

Newman's insistence on intellectual excellence as a defining characteristic of liberal education caused him, as it did Aristotle, to distinguish it sharply from professional or mechanical education, just as he viewed it as distinct from moral and religious formation. He also remained largely silent on a central feature of liberal education as it took form in the United States, namely, education for democratic citizenship, one emphasized in the so-called Western Civilization courses on many campuses in the mid-twentieth century. At the University of Chicago during the presidency of Robert Hutchins, this took the shape of a Great Books program (Carnochan, 1993). Working closely with Hutchins on that project and others, including the editing of *Encyclopedia Britannica*, was Mortimer Adler. Adler later adapted this idea for schools in *The Paideia Proposal*.

Adler represents well the view that basic schooling should be "general and liberal," "nonspecialized and nonvocational" (1982, p. 18) while simultaneously providing an education for democratic citizenship. Based on the principle attributed to Hutchins, that "the best education for the best is the best education for all" (Adler, 1982, p. 6), basic schooling would, in addition, educate the young for personal development and even for work (Adler, 1982, p. 18). It would also remain true to core principles of democracy, namely, that all citizens are equal, democracy depends upon an educated citizenry, all are educable, and democracy demands that all should have the same quality of education.

4 > Gove's argument

As laid out in programmatic terms in *The Paideia Proposal*, students would be presented with organized knowledge, namely, language and literature, mathematics and science, and the social studies. Students would also acquire the basic intellectual skills of learning. For Adler, these consisted first of reading, writing, speaking, and listening; second, calculating, problem-solving, observing, estimating, and measuring; and third, exercising critical judgment. Basic schooling in the shape of liberal education would also require students to gain an enlarged understanding of ideas and values through the study of great books and involvement in creative activities. Finally, so as to avoid tracking students, Adler was adamant that since everyone is considered to be essentially equal, all should follow the same course of study.

Paul Hirst

The emphasis on intellectual formation in Adler is consistent with Newman. But as in Newman, the perception of education for citizenship as a feature of liberal education remained less pronounced in England throughout much of the twentieth century. Of particular importance here is the position of Paul Hirst for whom, in line with Newman and along with his colleague R.S. Peters, a liberal education lies in knowledge and understanding in depth and breadth (Hirst and Peters, 1970). According to Hirst, over time the human race constructed seven forms of knowledge as ways of understanding reality: mathematics, physical science, interpersonal experience as found in history for example, moral judgment, aesthetic experience, religion, and philosophy (Hirst and Peters, 1970, pp. 63–64; Hirst, 1974, pp. 30–53). The forms express how humans think and know, and the young need to be initiated into such thinking and knowing. According to Hirst, moreover, since each of the forms corresponds to a way in which people attempt to understand the world, liberal education is to be focused on the study of all of the forms. As with Newman and Adler, such an education is highly rationalist in character. It is directed at intellectual formation and does not include moral or religious formation any more than vocational or professional preparation.

Departing from tradition

Rejections and modifications of liberal education

Hirst's commanding theory of a liberal education dominated the philosophical discussion of curriculum at the level of schooling for over a quarter century. In 1993, however, Hirst retracted his position, saying that experiential knowledge trumps theoretical knowledge in important ways. In a manner reminiscent of Newman's own retreat from liberal education (Mulcahy, 1973; Mulcahy, 2008b), he now believed that "education may at many stages turn out to be best approached through practical concerns," and considered "practical knowledge to be more fundamental than theoretical knowledge, the former being basic to any clear grasp of the proper significance of the latter" (Hirst, 1993, p. 197). Moving beyond Hirst, John White characterized general education as concerned to promote "a person in the round," as one "who lives the life." Highlighting "the primacy of the practical," he argued that we ought to "begin our thinking about the curriculum with the human being as agent, not the human being as knower." This, he believed, may lead us to "a more practically-oriented curriculum" of general education as distinct from one premised on the acquisition of knowledge and a consequent neglect of "thinking about ends and means" (2004, p. 184).

As intimated earlier, the idea of a liberal education has not been without its critics. Throughout the nineteenth century it faced persistently sharp attack in the *Edinburgh Review*. More recently, Richard Pring (1993) raised questions regarding the premature dismissal of so-called vocational subjects from the idea, and Nel Noddings went so far as to argue that "liberal education is a false ideal for universal education" (1992, p. 28). Hirst's remarkable retraction of his theory of a liberal education, moreover, followed along lines of criticism brought against his original position by Jane Roland Martin. It is the sharply focused analysis of Martin made in 1981 in "Needed: A New Paradigm for Liberal Education" (Martin, 1994, pp. 170–186) that is considered here the most compelling of critiques.

Seeking a new way forward: Jane Roland Martin

Believing her criticism of Hirst's theory to be applicable to contemporary curriculum theorizing in general, Martin argued that philosophical investigation of curriculum was stuck in a rut and "endorsed a theory of curriculum that is seriously deficient" (1994, p. 171). Of particular concern to Martin was its exclusion of values of practicality, feelings, and emotions, and what she termed the '3Cs' of care, concern, and connection. Traditional thinking about the school curriculum such as that found in Hirst's theory, she believed, "ignores feelings and emotions and other so-called 'non-cognitive' states and processes of mind." It also ignored "knowledge how," it excluded education for action (1994, p. 173), and it relied on a conception of education that divorced mind from body (1994, pp. 170–186).

Given Martin's critique, the question arises if alternative conceptions of liberal education ought to be considered. Reflecting a forthright attempt to create a new conceptualization reflecting a well-articulated feminist perspective, here, too, Martin provides a starting point by adding a new goal for liberal education. The new goal is preparing the young for the 3Cs, that is, for the reproductive and productive processes in society (1994, 2000). In this, Martin does not overlook academic studies long associated with liberal education. She sees them as but one part of a broader education, however, one that "integrates thought and action, reason and emotion, education and life" in a reconceived idea of liberal education (1994, p. 183).

Seeking a new way forward: innovative theory and practice

While these are directions about which Martin theorizes (see Mulcahy, 2002), innovative practice especially in higher education is making headway in bringing them into being. Given the growing force of marketplace considerations in redefining education as largely utilitarian in character, and the particular challenges it presents to liberal education, this may be welcome. Innovative theorizing may be even more important, however. This includes educational theorizing not directly linked to but holding out new possibilities for reconceptualizing the idea of a liberal education and bringing to fruition Martin's call for a new paradigm. Such innovative theorizing includes, for example, perspectives from critical pedagogy, learning theory, and constructivist theory. Drawing on case studies from a range of liberal arts subjects and areas of professional study, the recent work of William Sullivan and Matthew Rosin (2008) brings a sense of urgency and possibility regarding the promise of practical knowledge and practical reason for liberal education, as does the work of Raelin (2007) and Marquez (2006). Pertinent, too, is the earlier work of DeVitis, Johns, and Simpson (1998) in relating service-learning to liberal education. Building on Ernest Boyer (1983, 1987) and reflecting the critical pedagogy of Paulo Freire (1971) and Ira Shor (1992), they "envision a rich linkage between liberal and service-learning that will permit students to be critically reflective participants in whichever settings or callings they choose to enter" (DeVitis, Johns, and Simpson, 1998, p. 13). In their opinion, the key values of autonomy and service to community are not taught through didactic methods alone because one must experience citizenship at a deep level of involvement and participation for such learning to occur, a point supported by Eyler and Giles (1999) and Tonkin (2004) regarding service-learning and by Baxter Magolda (2004, 2006) and King and Baxter Magolda (2005) regarding self-authorship and intercultural learning.

Although historically absent in the tradition, DeVitis and his colleagues are committed to introducing an element of action learning to liberal education. The related idea of knowledge production by school students is elaborated in dramatic terms vis-à-vis the reform of liberal education by Carl Bereiter. Drawing on cognitive science and the growth of knowledge-based organizations, Bereiter (2002) suggests that if liberal education is to survive, it will require a careful synthesis of new ideas and enduring principles. This "would mean enlarging liberal education so as to encompass both the grasping of what others have already understood and the sustained, collective effort to extend the boundaries of what is known" (2002, p. 25). The boundaries of what others have already understood are largely represented by academic disciplines which Bereiter, like Martin, wishes to retain without believing that on their own they constitute a complete liberal education. As for knowledge production, Bereiter sees schools, like research laboratories, becoming knowledge-building organizations where daily activities of the classroom undergo a cultural shift "from classroom life organized around activities to classroom life organized around the pursuit of knowledge" (2002, p. 18).

Towards a new paradigm for liberal education

The foregoing review of the theory and practice of liberal education and of more broadly based educational theorizing identifies important points of the debate and new departures. It also indicates that the idea of liberal education is in flux. But if the certitude that once was present no longer exists, new possibilities have appeared. Before considering the implications of these for the ongoing evolution of liberal education in the twenty-first century, a word about purpose and organizing principles is needed.

When Hirst presented his theory of a liberal education, he made clear that it was erected upon the nature and structure of knowledge itself, a feature that provided a supporting organizing principle for the theory. Martin viewed this as unacceptable, however, because it assumed that the exclusive purpose of liberal education was to promote knowledge and, second, because the focus was upon theoretical knowledge. A principle based on an alternative set of assumptions but one not fully developed by Adler is the idea of education as grounded in what he called the vocations or callings of life. In *The Educated Person* (Mulcahy, 2008a), I adopted a modification of Adler's stance and relied upon it as the organizing principle of a reformed theory of liberal education. Unlike Hirst's original theory, this principle is grounded in a moral commitment aimed at enabling one to define and pursue one's own vision of the good life in a spirit of communitarianism and respect for others (see Arthur and Bailey, 2000). As such, it provides liberal education (as distinct from liberal learning with which it may be confused) with both moral purpose and justification.

Liberal education as a preparation for life

Liberal education viewed as a preparation for life or for meeting the vocations of living may be conceived around the work, recreational, practical, and philosophical callings or demands of living that are largely universal and persistent in kind. Such a preparation does not mean preparation for some distant future, a charge sometimes leveled against it. To do this successfully, however, as I have argued (Mulcahy, 2008a, pp. 147–196), a clarification of the nature of these demands is needed in order to gauge the kinds of curriculum and teaching that may be necessary. From this clarification it becomes evident that education for both thought and action, that is, theoretical and practical knowledge, is necessary. Such an education embraces education for doing and making, education of the emotions, and education for interacting with other people where care, concern, and connection come into focus. Understood in this way, liberal education provides for the many-sided development of the individual, not mere cultivation of the intellect in a narrowly rationalist sense. As a consequence, questions of curriculum and teaching need to be approached in a way that reflects this broader aspiration.

Given the value attributed to practical knowledge in this view, research suggesting the traditional aversion to practical knowledge in liberal education is unfounded takes on an added significance. This includes research on service-learning, for example, which bears out the claim that service-learning and civic engagement not only promotes the capacity to engage in action but also heightens understanding and develops caring towards others (Davis and Dodge, 1998; Tonkin, 2004). It also includes the work of Sullivan and Rosin (2008) on the contribution of practical reason to liberal education. Stated differently, practical knowledge and practical reasoning may be at least as necessary as theoretical knowledge for approximating the most traditional goal of liberal education, that of increased understanding of ideas and values. If widely accepted, a practical as distinct from a narrowly vocational dimension could breathe new life into liberal education.

Curriculum and pedagogy

So what, more specifically, is the proper content and methodology of liberal education and who decides? These questions become especially vexing if, as constructivist theory and critical pedagogy suggest, students ought to be involved in answering them and if, as others such as Adler believe, there are permanent studies to which all should be exposed. The position adopted here, following Dewey (1897), is that there are both sociological and psychological perspectives —the needs of society and the needs of the individual—that ought to be borne in mind in deciding these questions and that it is the role of the teacher, through mutual communication involving the student, to decide on implementation at the point of teaching (see Mulcahy, 2008a, pp. 177–196; Biesta, 2006, pp. 23–26; Shor, 1992; and Freire, 1971). Two important implications emerge from this. The first is that it calls for a teacher who is a well-educated professional (meaning he or she has the necessary knowledge, skills, and attitudes) capable of making and implementing informed teaching decisions. Given the association between liberal education and community action envisaged here, this may call for new forms of teacher preparation (Peterson and Knowles, 2009). This view of the teacher is a point that needs to be made explicit given the marked eagerness of state authorities to determine the contents of the curriculum and dictate the manner of teaching through official directives, certification requirements, and external assessments of learning. The second implication is that, contrary to the long-standing view, there can be no universally prescribed content of a liberal education. Content is a matter to be decided by students and teachers, in consultation with others if needs be, partly on the basis of the aspirations, experience, capacities, and general circumstances of each student. To assist in this, general parameters or curriculum guidelines may be helpful but they cannot on their own be decisive.

Questions for further investigation

1   How suitable is the idea of a liberal education for guiding curriculum and educational policies in the twenty-first century at the local and national levels?
2   Can you justify a form of liberal education that includes practical reasoning along with theoretical reasoning?
3   Contrary to the widespread interpretation of the idea, should liberal education embrace emotional and moral formation? Why or why not?
4   Historically, liberal education was dominated by the view that the nature and structure of knowledge ought to determine the contents to the curriculum. But what weight do you believe ought to be given to the following two considerations in drawing up the curriculum: a) the interests and capacities of the learner and b) the academic disciplines?

Suggested further reading

Barrow, R. and White, P. (Eds.) (1993) *Beyond liberal education*. London: Routledge. Marks an important evolution in contemporary theorizing on liberal education.
Kimball, B.A. (1995) *Orators and philosophers: a history of the idea of liberal education*. New York, NY: College Entrance Examinations Board. A comprehensive historical examination of the evolution of the idea of a liberal education over the centuries.
Martin, J.R. (1994) *Changing the educational landscape: philosophy, women, and curriculum*. New York, NY: Routledge. A collection of essays reflecting an important feminist perspective on the idea of a liberal education and related concepts.
Mulcahy, D.G. (2008) *The educated person: toward a new paradigm for liberal education*. Lanham, MD: Rowman and Littlefield. Presents a new paradigm for liberal education shaped by emergent themes in contemporary educational thought.
Sullivan, W.M. and Rosin, M.S. (2008) *A new agenda for higher education*. San Francisco, CA: Jossey-Bass. Argues the case for including practical reasoning in liberal education.

References

Adler, M.J. (1982) *The paideia proposal: an educational manifesto*. New York, NY: Macmillan.
Arthur, J. with Bailey, R. (2000) *Schools and community: the Communitarian agenda in education*. London: The Falmer Press.
Arthur, J. and Nicholls, G. (2007) *John Henry Newman*. London: Continuum.
Baxter Magolda, M.B. (2004) 'Evolution of a constructivist conceptualization of epistemological reflection,' *Educational Psychologist, 39*, 1, pp. 31–42.
Baxter Magolda, M.B. with Crosby, P. (2006) 'Self-authorship and identity in college: an interview with Marcia B. Baxter Magolda', *Journal of College & Character*, 7, 1, pp. 1–2.
Bereiter, C. (2002) 'Liberal education in a knowledge society', in Smith, B. (Ed.) *Liberal education in a knowledge society*. Chicago, IL: Open Court, pp. 11–33.
Biesta, G. (2006) '"Of all affairs, communication is the most wonderful": The Communicative Turn in Dewey's Democracy and Education', in Hansen, D.T. (Ed.) *John Dewey and our educational prospect*. Albany, NY: State University of New York Press, pp. 23–26.

Boyer, E.L. (1983) *High school*. New York, NY: Harper & Row.

Boyer, E.L. (1987) *College: The undergraduate experience in America*. New York, NY: Harper & Row.

Carnochan, W.B. (1993) *The battleground of the curriculum: liberal education and American experience*. Stanford, CA: Stanford University Press.

Carr, D. (2009) 'Revisiting the liberal and vocational dimensions of university education', *British Journal of Educational Studies*, *57*, 1, pp. 1–17.

Davis, O.W. with Dodge, J. (1998) 'Liberationist theology through community service-learning at Trinity College of Vermont', in DeVitis, J.L., Johns, R.W. and Simpson, D.G. (Eds.) *To serve and learn: the spirit of community in liberal education*. New York, NY: Peter Lang, pp. 92–101.

DeVitis, J.L., Johns, R.W. and Simpson, D.G. (Eds.) (1998) *To serve and learn: the spirit of community in liberal education*. New York, NY: Peter Lang.

Dewey, J. (1897) *My pedagogic creed*. New York, NY: E. L. Kellogg & Co.

Eyler, J. and Giles, D.E., Jr. (1999) *Where's the learning in service-learning?* San Francisco, CA: Jossey-Bass.

Freire, P. (1971) *Pedagogy of the oppressed* (trans. M. Bergman Ramos). New York, NY: Herder & Herder.

Hirst, P.H. (1971) 'Liberal education', in Deighton, L.C. (Ed.) *The encyclopedia of education, Vol. 5*. New York, NY: Macmillan, pp. 505–509.

Hirst, P.H. (1974) *Knowledge and the curriculum*. London: Routledge and Kegan Paul.

Hirst, P.H. (1993) 'Education, knowledge and practices', in Barrow, R. and White, P. (Eds.) *Beyond liberal education*. London: Routledge, pp.184–199.

Hirst, P.H. and Peters, R.S. (1970) *The logic of education*. London: Routledge and Kegan Paul.

Kimball, B.A. (1995) *Orators and philosophers: a history of the idea of liberal education*. New York, NY: College Entrance Examinations Board.

King, P.M. and Baxter Magolda, M.B. (2005) 'A developmental model of intercultural maturity', *Journal of College Student Development*, *46*, 6, pp. 571–592.

Martin, J.R. (1994) *Changing the educational landscape: philosophy, women, and curriculum*. New York, NY: Routledge.

Martin, J.R. (2000) *Coming of age in academe: rekindling women's hopes and reforming the academy*. New York, NY: Routledge.

Marquez, I. (2006) 'Knowledge of being v. practice of becoming in higher education: overcoming the dichotomy in the humanities', *Arts and Humanities in Higher Education*, *5*, 2, pp. 147–161.

McClelland, V.A. (1973) *English Roman Catholics and higher education, 1830–1903*. Oxford: The Clarendon Press.

Mulcahy, D.G. (1973) 'Newman's retreat from a liberal education', *Irish Journal of Education*, 7, 1, pp. 11–22.

Mulcahy, D.G. (2002) *Knowledge, gender, and schooling: The feminist educational thought of Jane Roland Martin*. Westport, CT: Bergin and Garvey.

Mulcahy, D.G. (2008a) *The educated person: toward a new paradigm for liberal education*. Lanham, MD: Rowman and Littlefield.

Mulcahy, D.G. (2008b) 'Newman's theory of a liberal education: a reassessment and its implications', *Journal of Philosophy of Educaton*, *42*, 2, pp. 219–231.

Newman, J.H. (1947/1873) *The idea of a university defined and illustrated* (Ed. C.F. Harrold). New York, NY: Longmans, Green and Co.

Noddings, N. (1992) *The challenge to care in schools*. New York, NY: Teachers College Press.

Peterson, A. and Knowles, C. (2009) 'Active citizenship: a preliminary study into student teacher understandings', *Educational Research*, *51*, 1, pp. 39–59.

Pring, R. (1993) 'Liberal education and vocational education', in Barrow, R. and White, P. (Eds.) *Beyond liberal education*. London: Routledge, pp. 49–78.

Raelin, J.A. (2007) 'The return of practice to higher education: resolution of a paradox', *Journal of General Education*, *56*, 1, pp. 57–77.

Rothblatt, S. (1997) *The modern university and its discontents: the fate of Newman's legacies in Britain and America*. Cambridge: Cambridge University Press.

Shor, I. (1992) *Empowering education: critical teaching for social change*. Chicago, IL: University of Chicago Press.

Sullivan, W.M. and Rosin, M.S. (2008) *A new agenda for higher education*. San Francisco, CA: Jossey-Bass.

Tonkin, H. (Ed.) (2004) *Service-learning across cultures: promise and achievement*. New York, NY: The International Partnership for Service-Learning and Leadership.

White, J. (Ed.) (2004) *Rethinking the school curriculum: values, aims and purposes*. London: RoutledgeFalmer.

2

Communitarianism

James Arthur
University of Birmingham

Overview

There are a great diversity of beliefs and policy positions adopted by those who describe themselves as communitarians. Communitarianism, like twentieth-century liberalism, can be an ambiguous term. It is increasingly used by both radical and conservative thinkers and hence it is not surprising that it means different things to different people (Arthur, 2000).

Introduction

The use of the term 'communitarianism' can certainly be ambivalent and yet the central contemporary debate in political philosophy has been that between liberalism and the communitarians (Daleney, 1994). Within this debate Patrick Neal and David Paris (1990, p. 421) observe that:

> The competing positions are often difficult to characterise (or, sometimes, even to distinguish) and it is often unclear what would be the theoretical and or practical significance of affirming one position over the other.

This is further complicated by the fact that some of those typically identified as communitarians have not identified themselves either with the term or with the so-called communitarian movement. Communitarians are an extremely heterogeneous group of philosophers and social scientists.

Communitarianism is a philosophical stance originating from academia and developed from a critique of liberal individualism by such people as Michael Sandel, Alasdair MacIntyre, Charles Taylor, Michael Walzer and John Gray. Communitarianism is therefore a rather loose grouping which holds that the community, rather than the individual or the State, should be at the centre of our analysis and our value system. There are to two distinct groups that are normally referred to as communitarians. The first group, the 'communitarian theorists', engage in debate with liberalism, but do not generally advocate specific public policy statements. The second group, the 'public philosophy communitarians', are similarly critical of liberalism and other dominant political stances, and seek a communitarian agenda perspective on legal, social and educational public policies. Whilst there is a general connection between these two groups, there are also important differences and so it is worthwhile to distinguish between them.

The communitarian theorists

In the 1970s, three central texts advanced the liberal cause: John Rawls' *A Theory of Justice* (1972), Ronald Dworkin's *Taking Rights Seriously* (1978) and Robert Nozick's *Anarchy, State and Utopia* (1977). These texts have largely defined the agenda for the debate between liberalism and communitarianism (Wallach, 1987). These books placed an emphasis on individual liberty, on rights and on distributive justice which caused some commentators to refer to them as 'rights theorists'. For these liberal authors, society should provide a framework for its members to choose their own values and ends. The function of the state is simply to promote the capacity of each and every individual to decide for him or herself what is good or worthwhile. Society does not choose in advance what the common good would be, since in a liberal conception society is not intended to have a vision of the good. The state should, therefore, not reward or penalise particular conceptions of the good life held by its members. The state simply provides a neutral framework within which potentially conflicting conceptions of the good can be pursued.

Rawls, in particular, attempted to establish a philosophical method that would help us adjudicate moral and political conflict in our democratic methods so that we can preserve individual rights. This is the liberal thesis of the primacy of the right over the good. In other words, the pursuit of the good by individuals has only to be constrained by the impartial principles of justice that everyone finds reasonable. The response of the communitarian theorists has been to argue that Rawls and the others have constructed a liberal theory which is too abstract and individualistic, ignoring the moral and social nature of human beings. Two major attacks are made against these liberals by communitarian theorists which are summarised by Avineri and De-Shalit (1992, p. 2) in the following way: first, that the premises of individualism such as the rational being who chooses freely are wrong or false and that the only way to refer to individuals is in their social context; second, that the premises of individualism give rise to morally unsatisfactory consequences. Communitarians make it clear that our attachment to communities is not voluntary, that social attachments are not normally chosen ones (e.g. family, nationality, etc.), and that our upbringing and the values we adopt and live by are often acquired involuntarily rather than being a matter of rational choice by the individual.

For Michael Sandel, liberalism, in so far as it is individualistic, is the politics of rights, while communitarianism is the politics of the common good. He rejects the liberal view of man as a free and rational being in favour of the Hegelian conception of man being historically conditioned. For him, there is no such thing as an unencumbered self since the self is always constituted through community. Sandel (1984) claims that we should give up the politics of rights in favour of a politics of the common good. Mary Anne Glendon (1991) has also challenged the rights-based thinking of liberals and has detailed the limits of its resulting 'legalism' in her book *Rights Talk*, calling for a moratorium on the manufacturing of new rights. She believes that the liberal position on human rights has shifted from: 'I can do what I want as long as I do not hurt others', to 'I can do what I want because I have a right to do so'. Another contribution to the debate has been the publication in 1985 of *Habits of the Heart*, in which Robert Bellah and his colleagues attempt to challenge liberal conceptions of community. Drawing heavily upon the framework provided by MacIntyre's *After Virtue* (1981), these writers are convinced that individuals have become increasingly detached from their social and cultural contexts, and they seek to reverse this trend through the renewal of community.

The public philosophy communitarians

A new dimension to the communitarian debate emerged in 1990 as a result of a meeting of 15 social philosophers, ethicists and social scientists in which they discussed the establishment of a group to explore a number of social matters affecting society. This group included Amitai Etzioni who in January 1991 launched, as editor, a communitarian journal entitled *The Responsive Community: Rights and Responsibilities*. The group did not wish to describe themselves either as liberals or conservatives since they believed these terms had become outdated. By November the group had issued a communitarian platform in the form of a 14-page document summarising their approach and listing their basic objectives (Etzioni, 1995; 1997). Community was to be the central concept in their new movement, supported by traditional conceptions of the family, values and education. It was an attempt to spread the message from academia by turning theoretical communitarianism into a public philosophy.

Compared to theorists such as MacIntyre and Sandel, the public philosophy communitarians have greatly expanded the policy implications dimension. The communitarian theorists challenge the individualistic liberal opposition to the common good, whilst this new movement has expanded this notion by adding questions about the balance between individual and social responsibility and promoting the idea of pluralism bounded by a core of shared values. Etzioni's particular version of communitarianism is essentially a political movement with himself firmly established as the party leader seeking to effect public opinion and policy. In order to distinguish his movement clearly from claims that he is a liberal in conservative clothes, Etzioni has modified the name of his movement – 'responsive communitarians'. Etzioni has made it clear that his communitarianism is responsive to all members of a community and that it definitely was not the same as being majoritarian. In a sense Etzioni has presented communitarianism as an ally of liberalism against state coercion.

The role of the state in this communitarian liberal model is essentially one of umpire, maintaining the peace between conflicting groups and creating the structures necessary for an on-going public conversation that generates a shared sense of fairness and reciprocity by ensuring that the values underpinning society are respected. The traditional liberal idea of state neutrality with regard to individual action is rejected in favour of a more positive contributory policy of actively developing the structures within the community necessary for its own continued existence. The most obvious of these structures is education, but they might also include policies to protect the weak and reintegrate the excluded members of the community. The communitarian liberal position is one that values both individual choice and action, but places it within the context of a rich and worthwhile common culture. As such, it seeks to avoid the pitfalls of excessive and illusory individualism and reactionary conservatism. Fundamental to this view is the transmission of values and traditions from one generation to the next, so the institutions of the family and the school take a paramount position, without both of which the community would end.

Education

In the educational context there has been an emerging field of educational literature which draws on communitarianism (Keeney, 2006). This limited but growing field has largely focused on the implications of communitarianism for education in schools. This is not surprising considering that all versions of communitarianism have important communal norms which are significant for educational theory, policy and practice. Within the liberal–communitarian debate this limited discussion of education to date centres on the contrast between schooling for the fulfilment of individual life plans against schooling to meet the collective needs of the community. Communitarians have argued that Western notions of education encourage individuals to compete against each other for material and symbolic advantages and therefore schooling promotes individualism and generally ignores the moral claims that communities have on their members. This individualistic view of education, which promotes independence over loyalty, is also potentially subversive to the relationship between the child and the child's initial community: the family. There is often little sense in which the child is encouraged to limit their individual choices for the good of the community or develop choices which serve the communal need. Some communitarians would also say that the State and market have failed to cultivate essential virtues and have undermined the moral underpinning once provided by the family and local community. They believe that the school can help by attempting to solve these tensions between individualism and community by promoting an education in, of and by the local community for participation in democracy. However, there is a problem with this idea since as Walter Feinberg (1995, p. 51) says: 'There are too many communities with too many different conceptions of the good, some of which are conflicting or mutually exclusive, to enable a pluralistic society to adopt a communitarian perspective as its only educational foundation'. He rejects the idea of a communitarian education, preferring instead to combine elements of communitarian understanding with the liberal view of education.

John Haldane (1995) regrets the fact that education in Britain has suffered as a result of the neglect of trying to understand communitarianism and he says that the British philosophy of education will not improve unless it engages with the challenges of recent debates in moral philosophy. Haldane advocates a moderate form of communitarianism which is both 'pre-social nature' and 'intra-social self determination'. He believes that a person is both an individual and a social being and that education 'is a matter of conserving bodies of knowledge, sentiment and conduct, as these are incarnate in traditional practices' and that education is a 'social practice concerned with the transmission of certain traditional values'. His language is unmistakably of the communitarian theorist. He says (1995, pp. 83ff):

> Since learning . . . is the correlative of being taught, what one learns is to a greater or lesser degree ways of seeing, understanding, valuing, imagining and behaving that are antecendently possessed by the teacher who is thereby authoritatively qualified with respect to them.

He makes clear that he does not aim to produce a system of social cloning or dent the critical capacity of children to think. Paul Theobald and Dale Snauwaert (1995, p. 2) provide us with a short summary of the difference between the liberal and communitarian purpose of education:

> The fundamental purpose of communitarian education is the transmission of the cultural heritage, and with it enculturation into an ethic of association wherein there are fundamental obligations to the common good. In contrast, the fundamental purpose of

liberal education is preparation for defining and pursuing one's own conception of the good life and with it enculturation into an ethic of tolerance wherein there is respect for the equal rights of others.

John Gray (1996) offers us a communitarian liberal perspective of education and argues that the marketisation of education should be ended. He believes that real diversity within and between cultures, which would include the existence of faith-based schools, should be actively promoted. He believes that the State should have a clear commitment to the family, in all its diversity today, and that the State should ensure that the obligations of parenthood, including the responsibility to educate, are understood and accepted. He believes that access to good quality education should not be contingent on income and that as a vital aid to equal opportunity the allocation of opportunity should be meritocratic.

Schools are seen by public philosophy communitarians as the 'second line of defence' after families, and within the American context communitarianism has contributed to the debate in education through its followers calling for the restoration of civic virtues. Indeed, the American communitarian movement in its 1991 statement included the following point: 'We *hold* that schools *can* provide essential moral education – without indoctrinating young people' (Etzioni, 1995, p. 8). As Etzioni (1997, p. 92) says: 'schools are left with the task of making up for under-education in the family and laying the psychic foundations for character and moral conduct'. He believes that the purpose of education is the reinforcement of values gained in the home and the introduction of values to those children whose parents neglected their character formation. Etzioni calls for moral reconstruction within education which means the development of basic personality traits in pupils. He recognises the dangers of authoritarianism and the reluctance of teachers to engage in this process. Nevertheless, he insists that children who learn poor values within families and schools will become poor students and deficient workers.

Etzioni effectively believes that the State should teach virtue and he claims that proper values are not being taught in schools. He does not tell us what proper values are, nor does he offer any rational principles for the source of these values. It is also ironic that as Hyland (2002) says communitarian policies often involve more State intervention rather than less. Many communitarians believe that educational professionals should train children in democratic decision-making. The aim is no less than developing a sense of equality, democracy and social justice in the young by removing racism, sexism and homophobia. Bruce Frohnen (1996, p. 175) argues that much of the communitarian thought on education meshes perfectly with the thoughts of John Dewey who advocated democratic education and emphasised the egalitarian character of community. Some communitarians believe that the State school is still heavily dominated by 'values neutrality' and they recommend that we should train the young to develop the habits of acting morally.

Much of the communitarian appeal is essentially directed at State/public schools where there has been a renewed emphasis on character education and notions of good citizenship. In England and Wales there does appear to be the basis of a communitarian approach within the education system. Education is not value-free and whilst children would not learn morality by learning maxims or clarifying values, they do have their moral sense enhanced by being regularly induced by friends, family and schools to behave in accord with the most obvious standards of right conduct. These standards would include honesty, fair dealing, reasonable self-control and a set of core values which would more than likely correspond to the statement of values which the National Forum for Values in Education and the Community produced. The Forum identified a number of values on which members believed society would agree and four general value areas were identified consisting of self, relationships, society and the environment. Each of these areas has a general statement followed by a list of objectives for value-orientated behaviour and thinking. These value statements have formed part of the guidelines for schools, but each school community needs to decide how to interpret them within their own context. Golby (1997) believes that schools in the UK are ill equipped to fulfil communitarian aims in education.

Citizenship education and the common good in schools are two key concepts in the communitarian agenda in education. Citizenship is concerned with the social relationships between people and the relationships between people and the institutional arrangements afforded by the State and society. Citizens therefore need, in many communitarian views, a society with a degree of common goals and a sense of the collective common good. Within this thinking, the citizen earns the right of citizenship through their participation in society by attending to their duties and responsibilities which are the defining characteristics of the practices of citizenship. The difficulty with this notion of citizenship is that it is a status which needs to be earned and therefore can be lost. Communitarians say that the State should create opportunities to empower citizens and that the local community should encourage participation through example. Nevertheless, the problem of how to motivate people to become active citizens with a concern for the collective good is daunting, especially for teachers.

The core ideas in the communitarian agenda for education in schools are reduced to eight basic themes. All of them have policy implications for the way we educate young people (Arthur, 1998). They are:

1   *The family should be the primary moral educator of children.*
    The role of the family in education is at the core of the communitarian perspective. The focus lies with parenting, rather than with marriage per se. Families headed by single parents, communitarians claim, experience particular difficulties. A communitarian perspective generally places the primary duty on the moral education of children on both parents and, in various degrees, on their extended family. Schools are seen, theoretically at least, as secondary moral educators, but since many children actually spend more time consistently in school than they do with their parents, schools are increasingly seen in the front line.

2   *Character education includes the systematic teaching of virtues in schools.*
    Communitarians of all persuasions have been extremely critical of values clarification methods in schools and have instead advocated that schools should teach a common set of values or morals as a way of dealing with social fragmentation. They do not offer any explicit set of moral values as they leave this to the community to devise. However, they do give greater emphasis to the concept of a virtue-centred education which is based on tradition. They generally reject ideas of values which can mean anything to any individual or group, at any time.

3   *The ethos of the community has an educative function in school life.*
    A central theme in communitarian thinking is the stress that it places on community as a human good; in particular, the importance of certain types of obligations and communal commitments and values which form the ethos of a school. A genuine community from a communitarian perspective is therefore one which is more than a mere association of individuals. It is rather a community which has common ends, not congruent private interests, but shared goals and values.

4   *Schools should promote the rights and responsibilities inherent within citizenship.*
    Almost all communitarian thinking emphasises the duties we owe to the community in return for the rights we enjoy as citizen members of the community. To claim certain rights within a community involves reciprocal duties which together integrate you into

the community itself. Ideally, communitarians prefer that individuals feel responsible for others in the community for its own sake rather than out of feeling obliged to reciprocate. Nevertheless, communitarians are strongly supportive of citizen education programmes which aim to enhance social and moral responsibility in young people and above all educate them to be committed to full participation as citizens.

5 *Community service is an important part of a child's education in school.*

Some prominent communitarians have campaigned for mandatory community service for all young people as a formal part of the school curriculum. The key to understanding this kind of communitarian thinking is to focus on the experiential learning which is being advocated. Schools are expected to provide young people with opportunities to work within their local community in order to build their characters and encourage them to form the habits to participate beyond school in community-involvement projects.

6 *A major purpose of the school curriculum is to teach social and political life-skills.*

Communitarians would say that education should above all be directly concerned with the development of reflective thinking and social action through informed civic participation. That the abilities for making socially productive decisions do not develop by themselves; rather, they require that the content of the school curriculum, skills and attitudes be introduced early and built upon throughout the years of schooling. The school curriculum should therefore promote those skills which are necessary for social and political literacy so that young people can make reasoned judgements, considering others' views and acting for the benefit of society.

7 *Schools should promote an active understanding of the common good.*

Another central theme in communitarian thinking concerns the idea of the 'common good'. Many communitarians believe that there exists a collective or public interest which can be promoted by individuals within communities. Education is one of these collective interests. Within schools, communitarians advocate that children should be encouraged to participate together in some shared processes by which they can experience creating the 'common good' for themselves. An education to understand the common good needs to encourage practices of cooperation, friendship, openness and participation.

8 *Religious schools are able to operate a strong version of the communitarian perspective.*

Many religious schools of all faiths are communities of place and memory and exhibit many of the features of the communitarian perspective on education. Many religious leaders also appear to support communitarian efforts and adopt aspects of communitarian thinking in explaining their own practices in education.

Conclusion

The term 'communitarianism' can be both ambiguous and used ambivalently. There are thus a number of tensions and unresolved issues within the communitarian perspectives on education. The first is that there is no comprehensive theory of education from a general communitarian perspective. Communitarian thinking on education has not advanced far enough to provide either a coherent 'end' for education or concrete 'means' by which we can achieve this end. This is not surprising when there are distinctly two schools in communitarian thinking: one which believes that communitarianism simply offers liberalism some assistance in reforming itself, and the other which believes that communitarianism is a distinctive philosophy or approach in itself.

Questions for further investigation

1   Is communitarianism a liberal political philosophy?
2   What are the implications of communitarianism for schools as communities?
3   In what ways can a communitarian perspective assist teachers in the classroom?

Suggested further reading

Arthur, J. with Bailey, R. (2000) *Schools and Community: The Communitarian Agenda in Education*. London: Falmer Press. A review of the implications of communitarian theory for education in schooling.

Golby, M. (1997) 'Communitarianism and Education', *Pedagogy, Culture and Society*, 5, 2, pp. 125–138. A good starter article addressing communitarianism and education.

Keeney, P. (2007) *Liberalism, Communitarianism and Education: Reclaiming Liberal Education*. Aldershot: Ashgate Publishing. An introduction to communitariansm and liberal theory in relation to education.

References

Arthur, J. (2000) *Schools and Community: The Communitarian Agenda in Education*. London: Routledge.

Arthur, J. (1998) 'Communitarianism: What are the implications for education?', *Educational Studies*, 24, 3, pp. 353–368.

Avineri, S. and De-Shalit, A. (Eds.) (1992) *Communitarianism and Individualism*. Oxford: Oxford University Press.

Bellah, R.N., Madsen, R., Sulliva, W.M., Swidler, A. and Tipton, S.M. (1985) *Habits of the Heart: individualism and commitment in American life*. Berkeley, CA: University of California Press.

Daleney, C.F. (1994) *The Liberalism – Communitarian Debate*. Lanham, MD: Rowman and Littlefield Publishers.

Dworkin, R. (1978) *Taking Rights Seriously*. Harvard, MA: Harvard University Press.

Etzioni, A. (1995) *The Spirit of Community: rights, responsibilities and the communitarian agenda*. London: Harper Collins.

Etzioni, A. (1997) *The New Golden Rule: community and morality in a democratic society*. New York, NY: Basic Books.

Feinberg, W. (1995) 'The Communitarian Challenges to Liberal Social and Educational Theory', *Peabody Journal of Education*, 70, 4, pp. 34–55.

Frohnen, B. (1996) *The New Communitarians and the Crisis of Modern Liberalism*. Lawrence, KN: University Press of Kansas.

Glendon, M.A. (1991) *Rights Talk: the impoverishment of political discourse*. New York, NY: Free Press.

Golby, M. (1997) 'Communitarianism and Education', *Curriculum Studies*, 5, 2, pp. 125–139.

Gray, J. (1996) *After Social Democracy – politics, capitalism and the common life*. London: Demos.

Haldane, J. (1995) 'Educating: Conserving Tradition', in Almond, B. (Ed.) *Introducing Applied Ethics*. Oxford: Blackwells.

Hyland, T. (2002) 'Third Way Values and Post-School Education Policy', *Journal of Education Policy*, 17, 2, pp. 245–258.

Keeney, P. (2006) *Liberalism, Communitarism and Education: Reclaiming Liberal Education*. Wiltshire: Ashgate.

McIntyre, A. (1981) *After Virtue: A Study in Moral Theory*. London: Duckworth.

Neal, P. and Paris, D. (1990) 'Liberalism and the Communitarian Critique: A Guide for the Perplexed', *The Canadian Journal of Political Science*, *23*, 3, pp. 419–439.

Nozick, R. (1977) *Anarchy, State and Utopia*. New York, NY: Basic Books.

Rawls, J. (1972) *A Theory of Justice*. Harvard, MA: Harvard University Press.

Sandel, M.J. (1984) *Liberalism and its Critics*. Oxford: Basil Blackwell.

Theobald, P. and Snauwaert, D.T. (Eds.) (1995) 'Education and the Liberal Communitarian Debate', *Peabody Journal of Education*, *70*, 4.

Wallach, J.R. (1987) 'Liberals, Communitarians and the Tasks of Political Theory', *Political Theory*, *15*, 4, pp. 581–611.

3

Civic republicanism

Andrew Peterson
Canterbury Christ Church University

Overview

This chapter introduces civic republican political thought and draws out its educational importance and relevance. The educational ideas which have found expression within civic republicanism are explained and explored. In the conclusion, which also acts as a summary of the chapter's main themes, some further issues for the relationship between civic republican ideas and education are briefly considered.

Introduction

At the time of writing there does not exist a clear and concise civic republican theory of education. This does not mean, however, that those who subscribe to versions of civic republicanism are silent on the matter of education, nor does it mean that civic republican ideas have no relevance for educators. Indeed, and as this chapter seeks to demonstrate within its confines, educators have a great deal to gain from critically engaging with the theoretical and public policy issues raised by contemporary civic republican political thought. In order to facilitate this, it is necessary to consider what civic republican political theory is and what its educational implications are. This is the aim of this chapter.

Civic republicanism is a broad political theory which has found increasing expression within Western political theory and public policy over the past two decades. Drawing on what has been termed a civic republican 'tradition' which is viewed as including scholars such as Aristotle, Cicero, Niccolò Machiavelli, James Harrington, Jean-Jacques Rousseau and James Madison (see Honohan, 2002, for a clear and detailed consideration of the civic republican tradition), contemporary proponents of civic republican have sought to reintroduce particular republican concepts and ideas in order to critique what they perceive to be the negative effects of liberal dominated Western political theory and political systems. In lamenting the prevalence of individualising (as opposed to communal) tendencies in public life, including the perceived large-scale retraction of individuals into private life, civic republicans call for an active citizenry who engage in public life, and have identified a key role for formative and educative processes in securing this end. The following eloquent consideration of the current state of civic engagement in Italy from one of the leading proponents of civic republicanism, Maurizio Viroli, highlights well the civic republican concern. Viroli (1999, p. x) suggests that there are two Italys:

> One is comprised of people who are concerned only with their families and their own personal successes, the other of people who have a strong civic awareness and are actively engaged in commitments to their community, to the needy, to the environment, even at the cost of sacrificing their own interests. As in any country, the boundaries between these two groups are not rigid: civic Italians may become uncivic; uncivic Italians may discover the dignity of a life informed by ideals of democratic citizenship. And there are also significant overlaps, inasmuch as one and the same person can be a fervent opponent of certain social rights and yet be active in the community. The problem is that uncivic Italy is far stronger than civic Italy, and this is true for many other countries as well.

These sentiments have much in common with the views of civic republicans more generally who call for an active, practice-based conception of citizenship and who have suggested that people have much to gain from pursuing a political life. This does not mean, however, that civic republicans necessarily concur as to why the politically active life is one worth living. Indeed, civic republicanism can be an amorphous political theory.

Some political theorists have advanced what we might consider to be clear and detailed civic republican theories. In addition, certain republican ideas (as distinct from whole-scale theories) can also be found within the work of a wide range of political scientists over the last three decades, including Benjamin Barber, Hannah Pitkin and Stephen Macedo. Furthermore, over the last decade, civic republicanism has found increasing expression in the discourse of political leaders; most notably the leader of the governing Spanish Socialist Workers' Party in Spain, José Luis Rodrìguez Zapereto, who has identified the civic republican ideas of Philip Pettit as heavily informing his political outlook and his approaches to public policy (see Martí and Pettit, 2010, for a detailed analysis). In the United Kingdom, civic republicanism was also explicitly referred to as an influencing agenda behind the work of David Blunkett (2003a, 2003b) during his time as secretary of state for education and employment and, even more so, in his role as secretary of state for the Home Department. The American political sociologist Robert Bellah (2008) also identified a civic republican element in the public rhetoric of Barack Obama in his (successful) campaign to become president.

Understanding civic republicanism

I have written elsewhere that, in general terms, contemporary civic republican theories are best understood as incorporating a 'commitment to four, inter-related principles. First, that citizens possess and should recognise certain *civic obligations*; second, that citizens must develop an awareness of *the common good*, which exists over and above their private self-interests; third, that citizens must possess and act in accordance with *civic virtue*; and fourth, that civic engagement in democracy should incorporate a *deliberative* aspect' (Peterson, 2009, p. 57). Underpinning and influencing these four commitments are two particularly civic republican conceptions of freedom or liberty, both of which seek to counter (or at least supplement) the dominant liberal understanding of liberty which casts it in terms of freedom from interference. This liberal position is classically explained by Berlin in terms of negative freedom. According to Berlin (1998, p. 194), negative freedom conceives that an individual is 'free to the degree to which no man or body of men interferes with [his] activity'.

The first civic republican conception of liberty, drawn from Hellenic roots and in particular the work of Aristotle, conceptualises freedom in terms of participation in self-government. To be free is to play an active part in public life. From this understanding of freedom, we can understand active engagement in the public life of our political communities as having intrinsic benefit and as relating to a particular conception of the good life (either in the sense that the political life *is* the good life or that it is *one form* of the good life amongst many). It is this first form of civic republican freedom that can be found within, for example, Adrian Oldfield's (1990) *Citizenship and Community: Civic Republicanism and the Modern World* and in Michael Sandel's (1996) *Democracy's Discontent: America in Search of a Public Philosophy*. A second form of civic republican liberty has been identified as stemming from the Roman strand of the republican tradition, as expressed in the writings of Cicero and Machiavelli. Like the liberal notion, this conceives freedom in negative terms but is concerned with the absence of arbitrary domination rather than interference. In other words, true freedom consists in the extent to which individuals are able to follow their own lives (and conception of what the good life may be) free from arbitrary domination by the state (*imperium*) or by fellow citizens (*dominium*) (Pettit, 1999, p. 52). Such arbitrary domination can be avoided (or at least reduced) through the active participation of citizens in political life. In this sense, the practice of citizenship is of instrumental benefit, worthwhile not in and of itself but for the freedom it ultimately provides individuals to follow their own goals in life. The extraction of this second form of republican liberty owes much to Quentin Skinner's (see, for example, 1990, 1998) exploration of historical republican ideas, and has found its clearest contemporary expression in Philip Pettit's (1999) *Republicanism: A Theory of Freedom and Government*, Maurizio Viroli's (1999) *Republicanism*, and John Maynor's (2003) *Republicanism in the Modern World*.

Because they understand freedom in different ways, civic republicans do not necessarily understand the four main commitments cited above in unified terms. Whilst there is not sufficient space to explore these differences in detail here, a couple of examples serve to illustrate this point. First, whilst republicans who stress the intrinsic benefits of political participation typically understand civic obligations as deriving from deeply held moral bonds, those who stress the instrumental importance of civic engagement ground civic obligation in terms of reciprocity and common interests and as such do not seek to ground their ideas on the communitarian idea of embedded social relationships. Second, intrinsic republicans typically present civic virtue in terms of deeply held internalised character traits, whilst instrumental republicans present civic virtue in terms of civility, which includes 'an ability to listen and articulate responses and the willingness and courage to accept decisions that are opposed to an individual's own view' (Maynor, 2002, p. 54). On this second account, civic virtues can be understood as less deeply held capacities central to the practice of citizenship which are not necessarily internalised within one's individual character. To note these differences within the field of civic republicanism is important and, at least as far as education and schooling are concerned, remind us that to talk of a 'civic republican model' of citizenship or of education is overly simplistic. We should be careful as well to remember that even if it is possible to identify differences in emphasis between civic republican standpoints, it is not always simple to delineate what the practical implications of these may be.

Civic republicanism is, then, a political theory which permits differences in spirit between its main proponents. Such differences notwithstanding, and whatever their variations concerning the deeper basis and nature of their main claims, civic republicans today are committed to active and practice-based forms of citizenship, which require citizens to possess the requisite civic virtue necessary to engage in public life in a considered and deliberative way. These ideas bear some similarity to the civic aims of education and schooling which find expression in the education systems of a number of nations. In both England and Australia, for example, the national education goals include the development of active and responsible citizens, who participate in a socially and morally responsible way and who look to beyond their own individual interests towards the common good (QCDA, 2007; MCEETYA, 2008). Moreover, in many nations, including the United States, Australia, Canada, the four nations of the United Kingdom, France, Spain, Japan, Hong Kong, Singapore and a number of nations in Eastern Europe, there has been renewed interest in the importance of civic education (see Davies, Chapter 24 in this volume for a more detailed exploration of citizenship education; for collected editions which cover the scope of civic education in the nations cited here as well as others, see Arthur *et al.*, 2008; and Reid *et al.*, 2010). This interest across nations is not necessarily homogeneous in nature. The precise curricular approaches vary according to a number of factors, including traditional and historical approaches to civic education, the context and identified present needs of the particular nation, whether jurisdictional responsibility for educational curricular is at a national or state/territory/provincial level and the extent to which civic learning operates as a distinct subject (as in the case of citizenship education in England) or comprises part of a larger subject grouping, alongside other humanities-based subjects such as History (as in the case of social studies in a number of nations). Nevertheless, and particularly in terms of Western democratic nations, there has been enough congruence between the respective curricular aims and content for civic education for some commentators to identify the influence of a civic republican model of citizenship education to be a common feature of such initiatives (Hughes *et al.*, 2010, p. 295). This model is one which, as the ideas explored above suggests, focuses on the combination of knowledge, skills, dispositions and participative practice (or service-learning). In some nations (such as England and Spain) the influence of a civic republican model of citizenship on civic education has been explicitly noted, whilst in others (such as the United States and Australia) this influence remains largely implicit. The question remains, however, as to what civic republicans themselves have said about education and schooling within their wider political theories. This is the focus of the next section.

Civic republicanism and education

This section considers how contemporary civic republicans have conceptualised education as an important element of their formative project. In order to understand civic republican ideas on education more fully, it is important to appreciate that civic republicans typically have a developmental view of human nature. For civic republicans (in both the historical and the contemporary sense), the knowledge, skills and dispositions required for active and effective civic engagement require cultivation within citizens (and indeed within pupils during their schooling). According to Adrian Oldfield (1990, p. 152) the desire and character necessary for the practice of citizenship may not necessarily be inherent within humans, it has to be 'inculcated and maintained'. He reminds us that '[I]n some sense citizens are *in statu pupillari* for the whole of their lives'. Michael Sandel (1996, p. 319) would be sympathetic to these sentiments, suggesting that the formative state becomes necessary 'when the natural bent of persons to be citizens can no longer be assumed'. As such, education for citizenship is a lifelong and continual process which has an important place within the schooling, but extends beyond this into the community and across political life itself. Indeed, we should also note that education and schooling represents just one element of the formative processes which produce republican citizens. Republicans are quick to remind us that the laws, institutions and political processes within a democracy also have an educative function in cultivating the capacity for civic engagement. This recognition that civic engagement is of itself of educative value is significant in terms of education and schooling. Oldfield (1990, p. 155) explains the educational benefits of political participation as follows:

> Not only is the process educative in itself – the more one participates, the more one develops the attitudes appropriate to a citizen: largeness of mind and an appreciation that the interests of the community are one's own – but the example set by the initial participators will draw ever-widening groups of individuals into the political arena.

According to Benjamin Barber '[T]he taste for participation is whetted by participation: democracy breeds democracy' (1984, p. 265). Similar arguments to these are often used to support the inclusion of service-based forms of learning within the curricular of both pupils in schools and students in further and higher education.

As was suggested in the introduction, it is generally the case that civic republicans refer to their educational objectives, especially those which concern children and young adults, in a general way. Oldfield (1990, p. 164), for example, states his case in strong terms. He suggests that the requisite capacities for effective citizenship need to be 'authoritatively inculcated' and that this may involve 'minds [being] manipulated'. In adopting this viewpoint Oldfield, as indeed have most contemporary civic republican theorists, makes reference to the Tocquevillian idea of 'habits of the heart'. In other words, the desire and character inimical to an active political life must be *internalised* by individuals: '[N]o amount of political participation and economic democracy, no level of civic education or national service, will suffice for the practice of citizenship in a political community – unless and until the external covenant becomes an internal one' (Oldfield, 1990, p. 172). For this reason these broadly stated educational aims found within certain civic republican positions invite comparison with the fields of character education and communitarian education. Perhaps more importantly, they also invite a concern over the indoctrination of an exclusive and dominant culture (in terms of values, norms and characteristics) in a way which oppresses minority groups.

Two notable attempts to provide a clearer picture as to the civic republican requirement for the development of citizens through the education and schooling process are provided by John Maynor (2003) and Iseult Honohan (2006), both of whom point to a pluralistic account of republican education (and in doing so seek to counter the charge of exclusion and indoctrination). Considering the general and civic aims of education in the United States, Ireland and France, Honohan (2006, p. 205) argues for what she terms a 'plural republican' approach which 'aims to foster solidarity without giving priority to the dominant culture in a way that oppresses and alienates minorities'. The solidarity which Honohan has in mind can be understood as a commitment to commit to, and engage within, deliberative forums through which different, and at times opposing, interests can be discussed with a view to finding 'some collective direction' (p. 199). With this in mind, Honohan (2006, pp. 205–206; emphasis in the original) details three strands to her plural republican approach to education: (i) the development within students of an '*aware[ness] of multiply reiterated interdependencies*'; (ii) the development within students of '*civic self-restraint*' – the central civic republican idea that citizens should have a mind towards the common good (understand in terms of public interest); (iii) the development within students of the abilities necessary for '*deliberative engagement*'. Honohan locates her plural republican educational ideas as going beyond liberal approaches to the civic aims of education, whilst stopping short of the inculcation of 'more specific values' and the desire to 'transform them [citizens] into altruists or to require constant engagement in political activity' found within 'some models of communitarian education' (2006; see Arthur, Chapter 2 in this volume for an analysis of communitarian approaches to education). Honohan makes clear that she does not have in mind a form of education which presupposes allegiance to a static and dominant national identity or shared culture. She argues instead for an education aimed at developing a commitment to civic life animated by the principles of recognising plural interests and reciprocity, as well as an awareness of interdependence between citizens.

John Maynor (2003) has presented similar ideas regarding education from a civic republican perspective. Maynor establishes a number of underpinning elements of his modern republican approach to civic education: (i) that civic education must start from an understanding of freedom in terms of non-domination; (ii) that civic education must aim at cultivating a 'rich sense of citizenship and civic virtue'; (iii) that civic education should enable young people to share their own interests, and to come to learn and understand the interests of others, through deliberative practices (for more on the connections between republican deliberative practices and civic education, see Peterson, 2009, 2011). Similarly to Honohan, Maynor rejects the idea that a republican form of education need necessarily involve the inculcation of a fixed and common culture. He suggests that any 'modern republican account of civic education will teach individuals how to engage constructively with others who have made incompatible life choices . . . it does not require that they accept or adopt these alternative ends' (2003, p. 186).

Both Honohan and Maynor are, then, committed to a civic republican informed educational agenda which ultimately aims at the creation of citizens who are able, when necessary and in an appropriate way, to engage in deliberation with others in order that interests become known and discussed in public life. This is underpinned by a commitment to paying attention to the public interest (over and above one's own private and individual interests). This sentiment has much in common with the stated aims of a number of civic education initiatives across the world. This connection is most notable in England where the Advisory Group on the *Education for Citizenship and the Teaching of Democracy in Schools* (QCA, 1998, pp. 7–8), chaired by Professor Bernard Crick and which heavily informed the statutory teaching of citizenship education in state schools for pupils aged 11–16, cited the following in arguing for the introduction of the subject:

> We aim at no less than a change in the political culture of this country both nationally and locally: for people to think of themselves as active citizens, willing, able and equipped to have an influence in public life and with the critical capacities to weigh evidence before speaking and acting; to build and to extend radically to young people the best in existing traditions of community involvement and public service, and to make them individually confident in finding new forms of involvement and action among themselves.

Indeed, Maynor (2003, p. 186) points to the inclusion of statutory classes in citizenship education, which he categorises as a 'robust form of civic education'. He praises in particular the requirements that pupils be taught through a combination of political, moral and social education to engage with others and with their political communities, to share their own interests and to listen and learn about the views of others, and to be taught to practise these capacities through participative activities. For Maynor, 'by asking them [pupils] to consider other people's experiences and to be able to recognize another's interests, it [citizenship education] moves in the direction that any modern republican approach to civic education should take' (2003, p. 187).

Conclusion

As the exploration here hopes to have suggested, civic republicanism is an important field of political theory which is finding increasing reference within the public policy discourse of a number of nations and which has resonance for the civic aims of education and schooling. At the time of writing, it would not be a mis-characterisation to suggest that the explicit educational agenda within civic republicanism is (at least in its contemporary form) in its infancy and is likely to burgeon over the next decade. For this to occur, those seeking to draw on civic republican ideas will need to show, as Honohan and Maynor have started to do, the ways in which republican goals can be applied to education and schooling in a way which accepts the critical cultivation of the knowledge, skills and dispositions required by citizens, but which stops short of the uncritical and homogenous inculcation of fixed values and cultures. Concurrently, those within education have much to benefit from paying closer attention to civic republican ideas and to the issues they raise for the civic aims of schooling. Perhaps most important among these is the notion that education has an important role to play in the cultivation of an engaged and active citizenry and that this role is one which is mutually interdependent with a range of other formative processes within democratic political communities. This idea, still I believe under-explored in educational discourse, is at the very least worthy of our attention.

Questions for further investigation

1   How do the ideas of civic republicanism introduced in this chapter appear similar and/or different to other theories explored in this volume?
2   How are the civic aims of education and/or civic education itself comprised within different nations and what similarities/differences are there between these and the civic republican commitments detailed in this chapter?
3   What criticisms may there be of civic republican approaches to education?

Suggested further reading

Honohan, I. (2002) *Civic Republicanism*. Abingdon: Routledge. A clear, detailed and accessible analysis of civic republican political theory which traces its traditional roots, its development and its contemporary form.

Peterson, A. (2011) *Civic Republicanism and Civic Education: The Education of Citizens*. Basingstoke: Palgrave. An exploration of the central ideas of contemporary civic republican theorists which seeks to raise important issues and implications for the aims and purposes of civic education in Western democratic nations.

Viroli, M. (1999) *Republicanism*. New York, NY: Hill and Wang. An eloquent and engaging exposition of a particular civic republican theory which details the Italian influence on the republican tradition and which considers the application of republican ideas in the contemporary context.

References

Arthur, J., Davies, I. and Hahn, C. (2008) *Sage Handbook of Education for Citizenship and Democracy*. London: Sage.

Barber, B. (1984) *Strong Democracy. Participatory Politics for a New Age*. Berkeley, CA: University of California.

Bellah, R. (2008) 'Yes he can: the case for Obama', in *Commonweal*. 14th March.

Berlin, I. (1998) *The Proper Study of Mankind: An Anthology of Essays*. Hardy, H. and Hausher, R. (Eds.). London: Pimlico.

Blunkett, D. (2003a) *Active Citizens, Strong Communities: Progressing Civil Renewal*. London: Home Office.

Blunkett, D. (2003b) *Civil Renewal: A New Agenda*. London: CSV/Home Office.

Honohan, I. (2002) *Civic Republicanism*. Abingdon: Routledge.

Honohan, I. (2006) 'Educating citizens: nation-building and its republican limits', in Honohan, I. and Jennings, J. (Eds.) *Republicanism in Theory and Practice*. Abingdon: Routledge.

Hughes, A., Print, M. and Sears, A. (2010) 'Curriculum capacity and citizenship education: a comparative analysis of four democracies', *Compare, 40*, 3, pp. 293–309.

Martí, J.L. and Pettit, P. (2010) *A Political Philosophy in Public Life: Civic Republicanism in Zapatero's Spain*. Princeton, NJ: Princeton University Press.

Maynor, J.W. (2003) *Republicanism in the Modern World*. Cambridge: Polity Press.

MCEETYA (2008) *Melbourne Declaration on Educational Goals for Young Americans*. MCEETYA.

Oldfield, A. (1990) *Citizenship and Community, Civic Republicanism and the Modern State*. Abingdon: Routledge.

Peterson, A. (2009) 'Civic republicanism and contestatory deliberation: Framing pupil discourse within citizenship education', *British Journal of Educational Studies, 57*, 1, pp. 55–69.

Peterson, A. (2011) *Civic Republicanism and Civic Education: The Education of Citizens*. Basingstoke: Palgrave.

Pettit, P. (1999) *Republicanism: A Theory of Freedom and Government*. Oxford: Oxford University Press.

Qualifications and Curriculum Authority (1998) *Education for Citizenship and the Teaching of Democracy in Schools* (Crick Report). London: QCA.

Qualifications and Curriculum Development Authority (2007) *The National Curriculum for Citizenship* (Key Stages 3 and 4). Available at: http://curriculum.qca.org.uk/subjects/citizenship/index.aspx (accessed 10 August 2010).

Reid, A., Gill, J. and Sears, A. (Eds.) (2010) *Globalization, the Nation-State and the Citizen*. Abingdon: Routledge.

Sandel, M. (1996) *Democracy's Discontent: America in Search of a Public Philosophy*. London: Belknap Harvard.

Skinner, Q. (1990) 'The republican ideal of political liberty', in Bock, G., Skinner, Q. and Viroli, M. (Eds.) *Machiavelli and Republicanism*. Cambridge: Cambridge University Press, pp. 291–309.

Skinner, Q. (1998) *Liberty Before Liberalism*. London: Cambridge University Press.

Viroli, M. (1999) *Republicanism*. New York, NY: Hill and Wang.

4

Education and postmodernism

Michael A. Peters and A.C. (Tina) Besley
University of Illinois

[T]he only absolute truth is that there are no absolute truths.
(Paul Feyerabend, On Truth and Reality: Postmodernism (online))

I define postmodern as incredulity toward metanarratives.
(Jean-François Lyotard 1984, p. xxiv)

[P]ostmodernism is born at the moment we discover that the world has no fixed center.
(Umberto Eco, in Hutchens and Suggs, 1997, p. 117)

Overview

This chapter charts postmodernism as a broad term that describes a philosophical movement, a style in architecture and the arts, and a critical re-evaluation of modernism, modernity, and modernization uncovering its Enlightenment assumptions of historical progress and its industrial society as a broad backdrop for assessing both the industrial model of education and its current globalization.

Introduction

This chapter begins by providing a brief characterization of 'postmodernism.' It examines its historical origins, providing a comparative context for viewing similar claims for the concept of 'post' as 'something that comes after' as well as an analytical schema that pictures modernity in relation to its past (the pre-modern) and its future (the postmodern). This schema is a device for connecting all the issues concerning modernity in its cultural, political, and historical aspects and understanding its significance in relation to education. The next section presents the main cluster concepts and themes characterizing postmodern/post-structuralist philosophy and discusses them in relation to the critical tasks that face education in the contemporary world today.

Characterizing postmodernism

The term 'postmodernism' has a rich and complex history with roots in Western skepticism and more recently in Romanticism and the counter-Enlightenment. Briefly, skepticism is the questioning attitude to any taken-for-granted claims. Philosophical skepticism is a form of inquiry or method that emphasizes the limitations of knowledge and the importance of continually testing our beliefs. Romanticism was an intellectual and literary movement originating in eighteenth-century Europe as a reaction against the Industrial Revolution and the scientific rationalization of culture. Romanticism in education places the imagination as the supreme faculty of the mind and emphasizes the subjective self.

Postmodernism was first used in the late nineteenth and early twentieth centuries to describe a style of painting and music, a critique of religion, and, following Friedrich Nietzsche, a philosophical analysis of the concept of modernity. Nietzsche's critique of modernity in his terse statement "God is dead, God remains dead! And we have killed him," focuses critique on many of the institutions and values of modern society highlighting the life-negating aspects of modern culture (Nietzsche, 1974, orig. 1882, Sec. 125). He railed against modernity's excessive rationalism, egotistical individualism, mass society, and the fragmentation of culture. He wanted to transcend modernity in order to develop a healthy culture where everyone could become more fully human. An educational ideal was the self-overcoming individual, one who can question old values and create new ones.

Postmodernism was later used by historians such as Arnold Toynbee to describe a stage of history following the First World War and the decline of Christianity and the West. Since the 1950s, postmodernism has been increasingly applied to movements in art, architecture, music, literature, history, and philosophy. In philosophy, postmodernism has been associated with the works of Nietzsche, Martin Heidegger, and Ludwig Wittgenstein and French 'post-structuralist' philosophers (including Jean-François Lyotard, Michel Foucault, Jacques Derrida, Jean Baudrillard), philosophers of science (Thomas Kuhn and Paul Feyerabend), neo-Marxist thinkers such as Fredric Jameson and David Harvey, and American neopragmatists such as Richard Rorty.

The term also emerged at a time when many scholars in different disciplines were trying to name the transitional period of a profound shift in philosophy, the arts, economics, sociology, science, political economy and, indeed, the history of the world. Charles Jencks (1996, pp. 14–15) has recorded 70 related uses, including "post-industrial," "post-minimalism," "post-Marxism," and "post-liberal era," and charted a genealogy of "postmodernism" in terms of its pre-history (1870–1950), its positive definition (1950–1980), and its final phase characterized by attacks upon it and its anthologization (1980–present). We have a somewhat different list from Jencks (Table 4.1). Our list contains both positive and negative characterizations of what we might call 'the transition period' – a network of terms that bear a family resemblance to one another. Postmodernism exemplifies apocalyptic thinking – the end of modernism, the completion of European modernity, the beginning of a new globalism – but it is not special in this regard and shares this feature with many other intellectual movements that share some common characteristics.

This list clearly shows the kinds of transitions hypothesized by scholars from different disciplines. What nature and role will education play in a world characterized by these alternative descriptions? The range outlined points to some ways of answering the question.

Table 4.1 Post (isms) and new globalisms

post-minimalism	the post-industrial society
post-performance	media society
post-civilization	society of the spectacle
post-logical positivism	consumer society
post-Kantian	mass society
post-empiricist	post-structuralism
post-analytic philosophy	post-colonialism
post-bourgeois society	*postmodernismo*
post-scarcity society	postmodernism
the knowledge society	postmodern era
the personal service society	the postmodern condition
the service class society	globalization
the technetronic society	the knowledge economy

The list also suggests a simple analytical schema, that, for the sake of clarity and simplicity, contrast postmodernism with pre-modernism and with modernism (or modernity) not necessarily to suggest invariant and sequential historical stages but more as a heuristic device for understanding an emerging set of global forces (Table 4.2).

The schema in Table 4.2 indicates that there are alternative descriptions or vocabularies for analyzing the modern or modernity – that we can contrast it with various forms of the premodern and we can prefigure the transition to future states. In this respect then modernism/postmodernism might be regarded as 'philosophy of culture' and modernization/postmodernization might be regarded as 'philosophy of development' whereas modernity/postmodernity might be seen as a 'philosophy of history and politics'. The schema, while simple, really only provides an ideal typical model and a way of recognizing the multiple layers and complexity when coming to talk about modernity. The hinge concept here is 'modernity' that we understand by contrasting it with the past and with the future. However, we should avoid a simple representation of the past or the future in terms of a universal history (or political

Table 4.2 Analytical schema – alternative vocabularies

Pre-modern	*Modern*	*Postmodern*
Classicalism	Modernism	Postmodernism
Traditionalism	Modernization	Postmodernization
Medievalism	Modernity	Postmodernity
Scholasticism	Reflexive Modernity	Postcolonialism
Communalism	Alternative Modernities	Globalization
Tribalism	Multiple Modernities	New globalisms
Feudalism	Industrialism	Postindustrialism
	Structuralism	Post-structuralism

economy) that relies on modern (and Enlightenment) concepts of 'progress', linear time and development, and progressive moral and political stages that then describes the apex of historical development as the current stage of development of Western liberal democracies. This would be to repeat the mistakes of modern German historiography beginning with Hegel's teleological universal world history as the dialectical progress of Reason toward unity with Absolute Spirit. Hegel's view of world history represents the manner in which the Spirit develops into its purest form, ultimately attaining its own essential freedom, and thus, world history is the unfolding of Spirit in time and the history of freedom. Hegel's philosophy of history is the most developed philosophical theory that attempts to find meaning in history and his theory has been hugely influential, serving as a basis for Marx's analysis of political economy of capitalism and also for liberal political theory, including the work of Francis Fukuyama. Hegel's philosophy of history also provides an encapsulation of the mainspring of a Eurocentric concept of development and as the historical roots of modernization and development theory.

Education has tended to play a central role in this philosophy of history because education in the broadest sense is pictured as the 'education of reason' which provides the platform for development as freedom. World history, as the development of reason, became the basis for its re-articulation at the level of the individual and the basis of modern educational theory. Hegelian phenomenology became the basis for a theory of culture (*Bildung*) and education focusing on the cultivation of categories of the mind and 'stages of development' in psychology and cognitive theory. In much liberal and Marxist theory drawn from a Hegelian conception of history, education becomes the motor for progressive change, emancipation and ultimately also national economic development. It is not too much of a generalization to say that the Nietzschean attack on Hegel underwrites much of what we regard as postmodernism and post-structuralism. Indeed, positioning themselves against the totalizing narrative of Hegel, we find the source of Lyotard's definition of postmodernism as 'suspicion toward metanarratives', Deleuze's attack on the dialectic, Foucault's and Derrida's demonstrations of the myth of the unitary subject and their joint re-evaluation of the other main feature of Hegelian modernity: abstract universality, the quest for the ultimate foundations of rationality and an essentialist conception of social reality.

Postmodernism/Post-structuralism

New forms of criticism emerged in education in the 1990s as theorists began to develop accounts of postmodern education in relation to the trilogy of race, class and gender (e.g. Aronowitz and Giroux, 1991); or investigated the relationship of postmodernism and education to speak of 'many voices in different worlds' (e.g. Usher and Edwards, 1994); or examined the significance of Lyotard's (1984, orig. 1979) *The Postmodern Condition* for education (Peters, 1995). After this initial introduction in education, scholars began to focus on post-structuralism and its significance for education (Peters, 1996, 1998; Blake *et al.*, 1998) and on individual post-structuralist thinkers (Marshall, 1996; Besley and Peters, 2007; Peters and Besley, 2007; Peters and Biesta, 2008; Peters and Marshall, 1999).

Post-structuralism can be characterized as a mode of thinking, a style of philosophizing, and a kind of writing. Yet the term should not be used to convey a sense of homogeneity, singularity and unity. More generally, it is a label used in the English-speaking academic community to describe a distinctively *philosophical* response to the structuralism characterizing the work of Roman Jacobson, Claude Lévi-Strauss, Louis Althusser, Jacques Lacan, and Roland Barthes. As a French and predominantly Parisian affair, first-generation post-structuralism is inseparable from the immediate intellectual milieu prevailing in postwar France. A history dominated by diverse intellectual forces: the legacy of Alexander Kojéve's and Jean Hyppolite's 'existentialist' interpretations of Hegel's (1977, orig. 1807) *Phenomenology of Spirit/Mind*; Heidegger's phenomenology of Being and Jean-Paul Sartre's existentialism; Jacques Lacan's rediscovery and structuralist 'reading' of Freud; the omnipresence of Georges Bataille and Maurice Blanchot; Gaston Bachelard's radical epistemology and Georges Canguilhelm's studies of science; and, perhaps, most importantly, the French reception of Nietzsche. It is also inseparable from the structuralist tradition of linguistics based upon the work of Ferdinand de Saussure and Roman Jacobson, and the structuralist interpretations of Claude Lévi-Strauss, Roland Barthes, Louis Althusser and (early) Michel Foucault. Post-structuralism, considered in terms of contemporary cultural history, can be understood as belonging to the broad movement of European formalism, with explicit historical links to both formalist and futurist linguistics and poetics, and the European avant-garde.

Post-structuralism, then, can be interpreted as a specifically *philosophical* response to the alleged scientific status of structuralism – to its status as a mega-paradigm for the social sciences – and as a movement which, under the inspiration of Nietzsche, Heidegger, and others, sought to de-center the 'structures,' systematicity, and scientific status of structuralism, to critique its underlying metaphysics, while at the same time preserving central elements of structuralism's critique of the humanist subject. Post-structuralism challenges scientism in the human sciences, the rationalism and realism that structuralism continues from positivism, with its faith in scientific method, progress, and in the capacity of the structuralist approach to discern and identify universal structures of all cultures and the human mind. Post-structuralism is anti-foundational in epistemology, and allows a new emphasis upon perspectivism in interpretation.

Table 4.3 provides a shorthand account of the main cluster concepts of postmodern philosophy as they inform developments across the disciplines. The pattern that emerges allows us to both criticize and revaluate conceptions of modernity and modern education that accompany it and also to posit and experiment with alternative conceptions that we can call 'postmodern education' and postmodern society.

Post-structuralism encourages a *critical* history through a re-emphasis on diachronic analyses, on the mutation, transformation, and discontinuity of structures, on serialization, repetition, 'archeology' and, perhaps most importantly, what Foucault, following Nietzsche, calls genealogy. With genealogical narratives, questions of ontology become historized. Through Foucault, Nietzsche's work provides a new way to theorize and conceive of the discursive operation of power and desire in the constitution and self-overcoming of human subjects.

Much of the history of post-structuralism can be written as a series of innovative theoretical developments of or about Heidegger's notion of technology. Heidegger's philosophy of technology is related to his critique of the history of Western metaphysics and the disclosure of being. The essence of technology is a *poiesis* or 'bringing forth' which is grounded in disclosure (*aletheia*). He suggests that the essence of modern technology shows itself in what he calls *enframing* and reveals itself as 'standing reserve', a concept that refers to resources that are stored in the anticipation of consumption. As such, modern technology names the final stage in the history of metaphysics (nihilism) and the way in which being is disclosed in this particular epoch: a stockpiling in principle completely knowable and devoted entirely for human use. He suggests that the essence of technology is nothing technological; it is rather a system (*Gestell*), an all-embracing view of technology, described as a mode of human existence that focuses upon the way machine technology can alter our mode of being, distorting our actions and aspirations. Heidegger sees his own work as preparation for a new beginning that will enable one to rescue oneself from nihilism and allow the resolute individual to achieve an authenticity.

Table 4.3 Postmodern philosophies

(I) Cluster Concepts

1　Anti-essentialism
2　Anti- or post-epistemological standpoint
3　Anti-realism about meaning and reference
4　Anti-foundationalism
5　Suspicion of transcendental arguments and viewpoints
6　Rejection of the picture of knowledge as accurate representation
7　Rejection of truth as correspondence to reality
8　Rejection of canonical descriptions and final vocabularies
9　Suspicion of metanarratives
10　The rejection of universal or world history

(II) Themes

1　Perspectivism
2　The diagnosis and critique of binarism
3　The critique of the metaphysics of presence
4　Substitution of genealogical narratives for ontology
5　The diagnosis of the power/knowledge connection
6　Exposure of structures of ideological domination
7　Erasure of boundaries between literature and philosophy
8　The disarticulation of the self
9　The self-deconstructing character of postmodern discourse
10　The non-referentiality of language
11　The cultural construction of subjectivity
12　The diffusion of power in communication
13　The notion of ideology as pervasive
14　The naturalizing tendency in language

Source: adapted from Magnus, 1989.

Post-structuralist accounts criticize the ways that modern liberal democracies construct political identity on the basis of a series of binary oppositions (e.g. 'we'/'them', 'citizen'/'non-citizen', 'responsible'/'irresponsible', 'legitimate'/'illegitimate') which has the effect of excluding or 'othering' some groups of people. Countries grant rights to citizens but regard non-citizens, that is, immigrants, asylum-seekers, and refugees, as 'aliens'. Some strands of post-structuralist thought examine how these boundaries are socially constructed, how they are maintained and policed. In particular, the deconstruction of political hierarchies of value comprising binary oppositions and philosophies of difference are seen as highly significant for currents debates on multiculturalism and feminism, and as issuing from the post-structuralist critique of representation and consensus.

Foucault's later work based on 'governmentality', coined in relation to an analysis of liberalism and neo-liberalism, has initiated a substantial body of contemporary work in political philosophy which deals directly with political reason. Foucault views liberalism as originating in a doctrine concerning the critique of state reason. For Foucault, governmentality means the 'art of government' and signals the emergence of a distinctive type of rule that became the basis for modern liberal politics. He maintains that the art of government emerged in the sixteenth century, motivated by diverse questions: the government of oneself (personal conduct); the government of souls (pastoral doctrine); the government of children (pedagogy). Around the same time 'economy' is introduced into political practice as part of the governmentalization of the state. What is distinctive in Foucault's approach is the question of *how* power is exercised and, implicitly, he is providing a critique of contemporary tendencies to overvalue problems of the state, reducing it to a unity or singularity based upon a certain functionality. The notion of governmentality is particularly pertinent to education as elaborated in a recent collection by Peters, Besley, Olssen, Maurer and Weber (2009) *Governmentality Studies in Education*. Both Foucault and Derrida, returning to Kant's cosmopolitical writings, have addressed the prospect for global governance and Derrida has talked about both deepening democracy and – entertaining developments of new technologies – a 'democracy to come.'

One element that distinguishes post-structuralism is the notion of *difference* which various thinkers use, develop, and apply in different ways. The notion of difference comes from Nietzsche, from Saussure, and from Heidegger. Gilles Deleuze (1983, orig. 1962), in *Nietzsche and Philosophy*, interprets Nietzsche's philosophy according to the principle of difference and advances this interpretation as an attack upon the Hegelian dialectic. Derrida's notion of difference can be traced back to at least two sources: Saussure's insight that linguistic systems are constituted through difference; and Heidegger's notion of difference. From the first mention of the notion of difference (in 1959) to its development as *différance* takes nearly a decade. *Différance*, as Derrida (1981, pp. 8–9) remarks, as both the common root of all the positional concepts marking our language and the condition for all signification, refers not only to the 'movement that consists in deferring by means of delay, delegation, reprieve, referral, detour, postponement, reserving' but also and finally to 'the unfolding of difference' of the ontico-ontological difference, which Heidegger named as the difference between Being and beings. As such, *différance* is seen as plotting the linguistic limits of the subject. Lyotard (1988), by contrast, invents the concept of the *différend* which he suggests establishes the very condition for the existence of discourse: 'that a universal rule of judgment between heterogeneous genre is lacking in general' (p. xi), or again, 'there is no genre whose hegemony over others would be just' (p. 158). A *différend*, as Lyotard (1988) defines it 'is a case of conflict, between (at least) two parties, that cannot be equitably resolved for lack of a rule of judgment applicable to both arguments' (p. xi). Post-structuralist notions of difference, pointing to an anti-essentialism, have been subsequently developed in relation to gender and ethnicity: the American feminist philosopher Iris Marion Young (1991) writes of *Justice and the Politics of Difference* and the African-American philosopher Cornel West (1993) speaks of 'The New Cultural Politics of Difference'.

Lyotard's definition of the 'postmodern condition' characterizes a feature of post-structuralism that we can call the suspicion of transcendental arguments and viewpoints, combined with the rejection of canonical descriptions and final vocabularies. In particular, 'suspicion towards metanarratives' refers to the question of legitimation with reference to the *modern* age in which various grand narratives have been advanced as a legitimation of state power. There is no synthesizing or neutral master discourse that can reproduce the speculative unity of knowledge or adjudicate between competing views, claims or discourses. The 'linguistic turn' of twentieth-century philosophy and social sciences does not warrant the assumption of a metalinguistic neutrality or foundational epistemological privilege.

Conclusion

In a variety of publications over the last couple of decades, we have attempted to chart the significance of post-structuralism, post-structuralist thinkers (e.g. Peters, 1996; 2001; Besley and Peters, 2007; Peters and Besley, 2007) as well as to adopt post-structuralist theory as a matrix for entertaining critical histories of postindustrial knowledge economies and the influence they exert on education systems – a kind of critical cultural political economy of education and knowledge (Peters and Besley, 2006; Peters *et al.*, 2009; Peters, 2007, 2010a, 2010b, 2010c; Araya and Peters, 2010). The new production of knowledge and the global knowledge economy, together with classical assumptions of rationality, individuality and self-interest, are important construction sites for knowledge deconstruction and critique and for developing alternative conceptions.

Questions for further investigation

Postmodernism and post-structuralism provide intellectual resources for educational theorists and practitioners to unpick the ruling assumptions of modern industrial education, the dominant neo-liberal paradigm of globalization where education serves the interests of capitalism in the global economy and to hypothesise and invent new forms of postmodern education.

1   How does the emerging political economy of global education and knowledge with its technical development of global knowledge and learning systems and new media networks shape new global systems of education?
2   In what ways does the dominance of a global informational cybernetic capitalism provide the architecture for global education systems and influence educational standards and curricula?
3   What are the new forms of openness based on open source and open access models that encourage the redesign and reconfiguration of global publics and global public spaces?

Suggested further reading

Best, S. and Kellner, D. (1997) *The Postmodern Turn.* New York, NY: The Guilford Press. This book presents a groundbreaking analysis of the emergence of a postmodern paradigm in the arts, science, politics, and theory.

Peters, M.A. (2010) *The Last Book of Postmodernism: Apocalyptic Thinking, Philosophy and Education in the Twenty-First Century.* New York, NY: Peter Lang. Further book from the co-author of this chapter on the relationship between education and postmodernism.

Peters, M.A. and Burbules, N. (2003) *Poststructuralism and Educational Research.* Boulder, New York and Oxford: Rowman & Littlefield. This book explores the impact of post-structuralism in language that makes the basic issues at stake accessible for a broad readership and attempts to answer what post-structuralism means for authors such as Foucault, Lyotard, Cixous, Derrida, and Haraway, and what significance does it have for educational inquiry?

References

Araya, D. and Peters, M.A. (2010) (Eds.) *Education in the Creative Economy*. New York, NY: Peter Lang.

Aronowitz, S. and Giroux. H. (1991) *Postmodern Education: Politics, Culture and Social Criticism*. Minneapolis. MN: University of Minnesota Press.

Besley, A.C. and Peters, M.A. (2007) *Subjectivity and Truth: Foucault, Education and the Culture of Self*. New York, NY: Peter Lang.

Blake, N., Smeyers, P., Smith, R. and Standish, P. (1998) *Thinking Again: Education After Postmodernism*. Westport, CN: Bergin and Garvey

Deleuze, G. (1983[1962]) *Nietzsche and Philosophy* (trans. H. Tomlinson). New York, NY: Columbia University Press.

Derrida, J. (1981) *Positions* (trans. A. Bass). Chicago, IL: University of Chicago Press.

Hegel, G.W.F. (1977 [1807]) *The Phenomenology of Spirit [Mind]* (trans. A.V. Millar). Oxford: Clarendon Press.

Hutchens, J. and Suggs, M. (1997) *Art Education: Content and Practice in a Postmodern Era*. Reston, VA: The National Art Education Association.

Jencks, Charles (1996) *What is Post-Modernism?* (4th Ed.). New York: St Martins Press.

Lyotard, J.-F. (1984 [1979]) *The Postmodern Condition: A Report on Knowledge* (trans. G. Bennington and B. Massumi). Minneapolis, MN: University of Minnesota Press.

Lyotard, J.-F. (1988) *The Differend: Phrases in Dispute* (trans. G. Van Den Abbeele). Minneapolis, MN: University of Minnesota Press.

Marshall, J.D. (1996) *Michel Foucault: Personal Autonomy and Education*. Dordrecht: Kluwer.

Murphy, P., Peters, M.A. and Marginson, S. (2010) *Imagination: Three Models of Imagination in the Age of the Knowledge Economy*. New York, NY: Peter Lang.

Nietzsche, F. (1974 [1882]) *The Gay Science* (trans. W. Kauffmann). New York, NY: Vintage.

Peters, M. (1995) (Ed.) *Education and the Postmodern Condition*. London and Westport, CN: Bergin & Garvey.

Peters, M. (1996) *Poststructuralism, Politics and Education*. London and Westport, CN: Bergin & Garvey.

Peters, M. (1998) (Ed.) *Naming the Mutiple: Poststructralism and Education*. London and Westport, CN: Bergin & Garvey.

Peters, M.A. (2007) *Knowledge Economy, Development and the Future of Higher Education*. Rotterdam: Sense Publishers.

Peters, M.A. (2010a) 'Critical historiographies: retemporalizing experience "after" the spatial turn'. Paper given at *Time, Space, and Education*, University of Bergen and Norwegian Teacher Academy, 29–30 September.

Peters, M.A. (2010b) 'Three forms of knowledge economy: learning, creativity, openness', *British Journal of Educational Studies*, 58, 1, pp. 67–88.

Peters, M.A. (2010c) 'Creativity, openness and the global knowledge economy: the advent of user-generated cultures', *Economics, Management and Financial Markets*, 5, 3, pp. 15–36.

Peters, M.A. and Besley, A.C. (2006) *Building Knowledge Cultures: Education and Development in the Age of Knowledge Capitalism*. New York, NY: Rowman & Littlefield.

Peters, M.A. and Besley, A.C. (2007) (Eds.) *Why Foucault? New Directions in Educational Research*. New York, NY: Peter Lang.

Peters, M.A. and Biesta, H. (2008) *Derrida, Politics and Pedagogy: Deconstructing the Humanities*. New York, NY: Peter Lang.

Peters, M.A. and Marshall, J.D. (1999). *Wittgenstein: Philosophy, Postmodenism, Pedagogy*. London and Westport, CN: Bergin & Garvey.

Peters, M.A., Murphy, P. and Marginson, S. (2009) *Creativity and the Global Knowledge Economy*. New York, NY: Peter Lang.

Peters, M.A, Besley, A.C., Olssen, M., Maurer, S. and Weber, S. (Eds.) (2009) *Governmentality Studies in Education*. Rotterdam: Sense Publications.

West, C. (1992) 'The new cultural politics of difference', in West, C. (Ed.) *Keeping Faith: Philosophy and Race in America*. London and New York, NY: Routledge.

Usher, R. and Edwards, R. (1994) *Postmodernism and Education*. London, Routledge.

Young, I.M. (1991) *Justice and the Politics of Difference*. Princeton, NJ: Princeton University Press.

5

Feminism

Julie McLeod

Melbourne Graduate School of Education, University of Melbourne

Overview

This chapter maps the contribution of feminist ideas and politics to educational research and practice, focusing on the period since the beginnings of what is called the second-wave of feminism in the 1970s to the present. It predominantly addresses feminism and school education, with brief reference to the sectors of early childhood and higher and further education.

Introduction

Feminism has had a major impact on educational ideas and provision, making gender a central category of scholarly and policy analysis and consequently reframing understandings about knowledge, curriculum and pedagogy. This, in turn, has brought new perspectives and questions to enduring debates about the social and individual purposes of education. In the following discussion, key strands and shifts within feminist approaches to education are identified, alongside discussion of examples of feminism's impact in educational practice and research. First, political typologies are examined to show the differences among feminist traditions and their significance for education; second, an historical account is offered that maps shifts in feminist educational ideas and policy over the last three to four decades, noting some persistent as well as new future challenges. Running through both accounts is a focus on shifting conceptions of gender identity, in large part because 'identity' has been a much contested and theorised topic in feminist education. Much debate in feminist education is characterised by struggles over how to recognise claims to difference and claims to equality; this encompasses differences between genders, and differences within gender groups. Does recognition of gender differences weaken claims for equality? Does equality demand sameness, or can equality accommodate difference? Such questions have fuelled extensive theoretical and philosophical debate (Scott, 1988); but they have also shaped feminist educational reforms, which the following discussion of debates and examples of interventions shows.

Scope and influence

At a very broad level, feminism is a political movement for social change to improve the position of women (Walters, 2006): it has also generated a substantial body of ideas and ways of looking at and analysing social, political and cultural practices. Education has been a central focus of feminist activity, examined as a site both for (re)producing gender-based inequalities and for promoting changes in attitudes to gender roles and relations (Arnot and Mac An Ghaill, 2006; Skelton *et al.*, 2006). Gender differences in educational experiences, pathways and experiences existed long before feminism brought them to public and political attention. One of the most significant legacies of early feminist interventions was to interrupt common sense and accepted views about gendered experiences and futures, by naming some differences as not natural and acceptable but as social problems and inequalities that demanded redress. Thus, for example, gender differences in subject preference, post-school aspirations, classroom interactions, informal social and inter-personal practices, or the relative position of women and men in educational leadership, were noticed and identified as problems and as manifestations of systematic and widespread disadvantage (McLeod, 2004). How such disadvantages were to be tackled, and their causes and effects explained, continue to be the source of considerable debate and dispute among feminist educators. Nevertheless, feminism – understood in the above broad terms –has had a significant impact at systems, institution and classroom levels across many parts of the world. While one might reasonably hesitate before claiming feminism's influence as universal, its reach certainly extends beyond the 'global north' (Connell, 2007), informing, for example, the development of gender equity policies and strategies in developed and developing countries and in the goals of international agencies such as the United Nations (Unterhalter, 2007). The *United Nations Millennium Goals* include the target to: 'Eliminate gender disparity in primary and secondary education, preferably by 2005, and in all levels of education no later than 2015' (United Nations, 2010).

Improving gender equity and access has been an important component of feminist educational reforms, but it does not represent the full extent of feminist activity. Feminism has had a profound and far-reaching impact on epistemological, ethical and relational dimensions of education. In scrutinizing curriculum and pedagogical practices, feminists have made problematic what has counted as worthwhile knowledge, questioning the supposed gender-neutrality of curriculum texts, or the exclusions of women and girls from history, or the salience of gender relations and representations across curriculum areas. Feminism has not been alone in its assessment of the sociological context of knowledge but it has brought to the fore the ways in which gender difference and women's position have often been neglected or silenced in mainstream curriculum as well as in other critical accounts of the exclusionary norms of dominant knowledge forms and curriculum subjects (Arnot, 2002). The content of history curriculum offers an example of rethinking what counts as valuable knowledge. Throughout the 1970s and 1980s, developments in women's history, which sought to bring the experiences of women – both ordinary and extraordinary – into the historical picture and to name gender relations as phenomena with a history that needed to be investigated, informed developments in school-based history curriculum. Instead of national history curriculum focused predominantly on political history or achievements in the public sphere, feminist educators argued that the history of family life, or women's role in political movements, or struggles for women's enfranchisement, were examples of topics that warranted inclusion in school history. In many countries new textbooks and syllabi were developed that reflected women's presence in stories and images about the past, and contributed to the growing attention to gender relations as a legitimate topic for curriculum to address (McLeod, 2004).

Reframing what matters

Along with other social movements, feminism has helped transform how the purposes and expectations of education are debated, understood and experienced. Results, outcomes and pathways remain important, but feminism has helped advance a focus on the interpersonal and emotional aspects of education, looking to how processes of inclusion and exclusion operate at micro, local levels as well as systemic, macro levels. Feminists have also been at the forefront in exploring the ways in which educational institutions help shape and construct identities. This has influenced all sectors of educational provision, drawing attention to the ways in which matters such as the hidden and the explicit curriculum, teacher and peer attitudes, and interactions in and outside the classroom actively shape gender identities and gender relations. Schools, or early childhood settings, or universities and colleges are not neutral grounds on which pre-existing gender differences are acted out; rather, they are sites that contribute to the production and regulation of gender difference (McLeod and Yates, 2006; MacNaughton, 2000; Walkerdine *et al.*, 2001; Kehily, 2002).

The influential work of feminist scholars, including philosophers and psychologists (for example, respectively Jane Roland Martin and Carol Gilligan) introduced new frameworks for judging what education should be offering, bringing forcefully into the picture qualities and dispositions such as care and inter-personal skills, and exposing the gendered nature of ostensibly neutral curriculum and norms of the 'good student' (Martin, 1986; Gilligan, 1982). What Roland Martin called the '3Cs' of 'care, concern and connection' represent gendered qualities typically associated with the private sphere – women's domesticated space, the world of emotional labour, of reproduction, of interpersonal relations. Feminists argued that the knowledge, insights and experience valued, required and produced in this part of life were relegated to an inferior status against the knowledge typically aligned with the abstractions and individualism of the (male) public sphere. The critique here was not only about content knowledge – what was or was not included in the syllabus, what was represented in textbooks, although this is significant – but was also about forms of interactions and dispositions – which ways of being and knowing were valued, and what types of ways of approaching and living in the world were disrespected, or denigrated or ignored. Such critiques informed many pedagogical and curriculum innovations, often under the banner of girl-friendly or sexually inclusive schooling, which sought to incorporate, for example, more collaborative and group-based learning or topics from personal and domestic life (Yates and McLeod, 2010). In science classes, for example, topics on machines and gears were taught using domestic appliances rather than cars or factory machinery; or more group-based, problem-solving activities were developed instead of a reliance on individual science reports on experiments. The latter example reflects a focus on project-based pedagogy that derived as well from the influence of progressive education, which co-incided with elements of feminist critiques and reforms of pedagogy and curriculum.

Whose feminism?

There has also been substantial disagreement with feminist educational agendas, evident since the 1970s, but gaining ground throughout the 1990s onwards. This dissent comes from a range of quarters, including those who are sceptical of feminist claims, or who see feminism as having achieved its aims and is therefore no longer a salient force for educational reform, or who view feminism as a somewhat more pernicious movement that has advantaged girls' education at the expense of neglecting, or even disadvantaging boys. Concerns about the education of boys, and the so-called 'boy turn' in gender equity, have produced a rather blunt polarization between pro- and anti-feminist educators (Weaver-Hightower, 2003; Epstein *et al.*, 1998; Lingard and Douglas, 1999). Regardless of the merit or need for addressing boys' education within gender equity programmes, this movement has tended to demonise and caricature feminism, and at the same time, to borrow and adapt some of the reform strategies – inclusive curriculum, gender-specific learning – that feminists initiated to improve the educational experiences and outcomes for girls (Keddie and Mills, 2007). One further consequence of the so-called 'boy turn' has been an implicit characterization of feminism as a homogenous political and educational movement, with common goals and strategies – yet this misrepresents the theoretical and political diversity within education feminism.

There are many different political categories of feminism (e.g. socialist, black, liberal, radical and lesbian) classified according to their analysis of inequality and views on how social change can be achieved. There are also feminists who have been influenced by particular theoretical and interpretative traditions, such as post-structuralist and psychoanalytic feminism (St Pierre and Pillow, 2000). And increasingly, as second-wave feminists grow older, there is more and more discussion of generational differences between feminists, between 'baby-boomers' and Gen X, or Y, between second, third and post-third feminism (Woodward and Woodward, 2009). There are, then, many ways of being a feminist, and feminism itself deploys a wide range of political and analytical strategies to achieve its goals. Indeed, it is now quite common to refer to feminisms, rather than feminism, to dramatise the plurality of perspectives that fall within this political and identity category. The following section provides a map of the different political types and categories of feminism and indicates the kind of educational reforms that each tends to favour.

Types of feminism/s

While this overview is necessarily selective and brief, it nevertheless attempts to highlight the distinguishing features of the major categories of feminism and the striking points of comparison and contrast among them.

Liberal feminists are characterised as having faith in the process of legislative reform and in being able to 'change the system from within'. Framed by the political and philosophical tradition of 'liberalism', liberal feminism 'asserts that individual women should be as free as men to determine their social, political and educational roles, and that any laws, traditions and activities that inhibit equal rights and opportunities should be abolished' (Weiner, 1994, p. 54). Liberal feminists have advocated reforms such as equal opportunity legislation or strategies to improve the education of girls within the existing education system and to make that system more equitable – for example, increasing overall participation and retention rates of girls, encouraging women teachers to seek promotion and to occupy senior positions, and ensuring that schools have non-discriminatory practices.

In contrast, radical feminists are characterised as wanting to achieve far more fundamental change. While in the short-term radical feminists may settle for reforming the patriarchal state or making male-dominated bureaucracies more equitable, their long-term political goals are more revolutionary. To use a much-quoted metaphor, liberal feminists want women to have more pieces of the existing social 'pie', whereas radical feminists want to change the way the pie is made and put together – to change social and power relations and the way in which existing social institutions perpetuate the subordination of women. Patriarchy is a central concept for radical feminism and refers to a social structure in which men as a group systematically have power over women as a group, and for radical feminists, this is the fundamental division of power in societies (Hughes, 2002). Radical feminists address the distinctive needs and experiences of women as a strategy for empowering them and working against women's structural subordination. Educational strategies advocated by radical feminist include single-sex schooling or women- and girls-only classes and spaces within co-educational settings; pedagogies which are inclusive of girls' alleged different styles of learning; and curricula which include and value the experiences and histories of women and girls (Skelton and Francis, 2009).

Like radical feminists, socialist feminists believe that changes in the position of women will only be achieved through the fundamental transformation of society. Socialist feminists do not reject the concept of patriarchy, but see the relative structural inequality of women as also linked to their economic position within capitalist social and economic systems; that is, they believe that the fundamental division in society is not only between women and men, but also between socio-economic classes. For socialist feminists, the task is to work against both capitalism and patriarchy (Whelehan, 1995; Lorber, 2009). The dilemma is working out how class and sexual inequality intersect and how one analyses the relative effects of each structure and experience. A persistent question is whether economic and class differences are more fundamental than sexual inequality or vice versa. Educational strategies influenced by socialist feminism include industrial and work campaigns for equal employment opportunity and affirmative action for women teachers (Blackmore, 1999), and addressing the impact of class on girls' and women's educational experiences and outcomes (Walkerdine *et al.*, 2001; McLeod and Yates, 2006; Reay *et al.*, 2005).

A further set of political groupings within feminism addresses the intersection of race and ethnicity with gender and the ways in which social and educational institutions are racist as well as sexist (Tsolidis, 2001; Mirza and Joseph, 2009; Reay *et al.*, 2005). This grouping is often described as postcolonial feminism or black feminism (Weedon, 1999). Central to this political analysis is the argument that feminism itself has been racist, assuming and addressing the ideal of a white, Western, middle-class woman, and silencing or erasing the experiences of indigenous, ethnic-minority women and women of colour (Moreton-Robinson, 2000; Mohanty, 1988; Hill Collins, 1990). Building from recognition of diversity and differences between women, black and ethnic-minority feminists challenge social institutions and feminists to recognise the ways in which race and ethnicity structure social and political life. In education, this form of feminism examines, for example, the attitudes to, and hidden assumptions held by teachers and pupils about girls from culturally and linguistically diverse backgrounds, the content of the curriculum and whether it reflects racial and ethnic diversity, and the factors influencing the participation and outcomes of girls from indigenous and ethnic-minority cultures (Tsolidis, 2001; MacNaughton and Davis, 2009). Feminist critiques that focus only on gender difference have been criticised for producing one-dimensional concepts of identity and for neglecting the salience of intersecting identity categories that shape women's experience. Described as 'intersectional analysis' (Yuval-Davis, 2006), such insights have been very influential in education feminism, fuelling a wide range of studies and interventions that address, for example, how race, class, gender and sexuality intersect to shape identities and educational outcomes and experiences (Ali *et al.*, 2010)

Post-structuralist feminists take their name from a set of ideas (post-structuralism) about language, discourse, subjectivity, power and the production of meaning (Weedon, 1999). According to post-structuralists, language, or the wider term 'discourse', does not simply reflect social reality or convey pre-existent meanings; rather, meanings are produced in and by discourses. For example, the meaning of gender differences, or of masculinity and femininity, is understood as not being constant and pre-given. Instead, it is argued that these meanings are historically and culturally specific. A focus for many feminist post-structuralists has been on understanding the different discourses and practices that shape and produce gender identities and define femininity and masculinity.

In the field of gender and schooling, feminists taking up post-structuralism have commonly explored the ways in which schooling practices and discourses shape gender identity (Davies, 1989; MacNaughton, 2000). They argue that gender identity is constructed by multiple and contradictory discourses and that gender identity itself is not fixed, pre-given or unitary. Such work examines, for example, the different ways in which schooling positions and constructs girls compared to boys and asks questions about the extent to which schooling replicates conventional forms of masculinity and femininity or allows the possibility for new forms of identity to be fashioned. Post-structuralism has been very influential among many feminist researchers in education (Skelton *et al.*, 2006; Hey, 1997) and has also had a significant impact on the orientation of gender equity policies (McLeod, 2001).

These typologies and descriptions – and this is not an exhaustive list – can only provide a beginner's guide to the range and types of feminisms. The point of outlining some of these differences is to show that feminism is a complex and diverse social and political movement, that there are significant differences in the ways in which feminists think and that these differences have an impact on the kinds of feminist educational reforms they are likely to advocate. This typological mapping of the field, however, tends to convey a rather static picture of feminism, as if there are stable and consistent ways of enacting feminist principles and politics in education. In the next section, a more historical account is provided of feminism in education, with a view to presenting a more dynamic picture of shifts in emphases, strategies and theoretical orientations. Some of the examples in this narrative are drawn from developments in Australian education, but similar shifts in feminist education and feminist theory occurred more widely (Arnot and Mac Anh Gaill, 2006), and the examples serve to show how feminist ideas translate into educational policies, practices and debates.

Shifting concerns and narratives of change

In constructing the following historical account of feminism in education, key concepts and theoretical debates within feminism more broadly are noted, before discussion of how these were then taken up in education. In order to build a coherent story from an abundance of issues, concepts and programmes, I have focused on changing feminist conceptions of 'identity' and how these, in turn, shaped feminist educational practices.

Taking as a beginning point the rise of the second-wave of feminism in the late 1960s and 1970s, we can identify the strong influence of sex-role and social learning theory on feminist and non-sexist educational programmes. In the 1970s, gender identity was understood through the concept of the 'sex role' and policy and programme language was more likely to refer to non-sexist or equal opportunity education rather than feminist education, even though the links to feminism were self-evident. A strategic focus for equal opportunity programmes was to expose the negative effects on pupils of stereotypical sex-role attitudes and behaviours. An understanding of identity (that of both children and adults) as formed by 'sex-role socialisation' underpinned much second-wave feminist discussion. As US feminist Kate Millet argued, 'sexual politics obtains consent through the "socialization" of both sexes to basic patriarchal politics with regard to temperament, role and status' (Millet, 1972, p. 26). For Millet, and for many other feminists writing in the late 1960s and early 1970s, women's sex role was narrow and confining in comparison to the diverse and rich roles available to men. Women were entrapped by their biology: if women were to overcome their subordination, they needed to transcend their biology.

For second-wave feminists, the 'sex role' was a foundational analytic category and was pivotal to their liberatory project: liberation from oppressive sex roles, from patriarchal expectations and from the destiny of anatomy. The 'sex role' enabled feminists (and others) to conceptualise the possibility of new ways of being, disconnected from biological imperatives and ingrained cultural habits. The appeal of the sex-role concept was twofold: it provided a critique of patriarchy, and it made clear and possible the ways in which one could challenge and resist patriarchy and build a new form of politics. In the 1970s, the 'personal was political' in many ways.

The influential 1975 Australian Commonwealth Schools Commission report, *Girls, School and Society*, argued that 'Until recently there has been little questioning of sex roles and so people have tended to adopt their sex roles without attempting at any stage to analyse the stereotype so formed in a rational way' (p. 16). Through, for example, values clarification exercises and role plays, checklists and quizzes, teachers and pupils were encouraged to examine their stereotypical values and opinions, urged to abandon traditional and sexist ways and to overcome the poverty and limits of conventional and rigid gender differences.

From same to different

In such feminist initiatives, identity was understood as unitary and as an artefact of culture or of socialisation. In the 1980s, however, gender identity was more likely to be represented through discourses of difference. Difference had two sets of meaning here. In feminist debates, 'difference' denoted differences among and between women as well as the intrinsic difference (embodied, affective, ontological, epistemological) of women from men. A view of gender identity as composed of a constellation of intrinsic capacities and dispositions became very influential in feminist education during the 1980s (Yates, 1998). This understanding fostered many gender equity and curriculum programmes that celebrated intrinsic gender 'difference' and, following a combination of influences, embraced a belief in women's and girls' distinctive 'ways of knowing' (Belenky *et al.*, 1986). Accompanied by 'common-sense' assertions about women's and girls' special capacity for collaboration, conversation and cooperation, the attention to difference generated much curriculum and professional development based on presumed gender differences in learning styles (Yates, 1998; McLeod, 1998). In Australia and elsewhere, this approach to reform was described as promoting 'girl-friendly' schooling, or 'gender-inclusive' curriculum (Office of Schools Administration, 1990). The role of schools was to create learning environments that would facilitate the unfolding of these inherent and immutable capacities: gender difference was valorised and girls' learning styles were held to be superior to boys' and as representing a preferred mode of learning for all students. The purpose of feminist education was thus to transform teaching and learning so that they became 'girl-friendly' and more sympathetically matched to the inherent qualities of girls. In this respect, femininity (and inversely and negatively, masculinity) was a kind of projection, one that essentialised and fixed gender identity, and children and teachers were encouraged to conform to its normative demands. Interestingly, much work influenced by the 'boy turn' in education elevates gender differences as intrinsic – evident in discussions of 'learning styles'– in ways similar to how some feminists have characterised 'women's ways of learning'; that is, as arising from inherent dispositions, and bestowing a commonality of experience and orientation on 'all boys' or 'all girls'.

The focus on difference has also brought a more complex understanding about gender and the differences, not only between girls and boys, but also within the genders. The 1987 Australian *National Policy for the Education of Girls* declared that 'Girls are not a homogenous category'. In feminist theory and politics more broadly, the attention to differences within the category 'women' registered a critique of the hegemony of essentialism and of gender universalism. On the one hand, the turn to 'difference' in education promoted the circulation of relatively conventional ideas about masculinity and femininity and of gender difference (even if inflected positively). On the other hand, it encouraged a more nuanced account of the heterogeneity of gender identity. In both readings, important feminist debates were being exercised, and having a definite effect on policies and programmes.

The view of gender identity as intrinsic difference was destabilised in the 1990s by a sustained focus on gender not as natural but as a 'construction'. (We can observe some resonances here with the earlier socialisation models, despite strenuous attempts on the part of post-structuralists to distance themselves from the 1970s.) Such a discursive shift was made possible by the political and theoretical attention to 'differences among women' – as discussed above – and by the increasing interest among many feminist researchers in post-structuralist ideas, and especially ideas about the relation between subjectivity and discourse.

During the 1990s, post-structuralism offered a new way of conceptualising identity and working towards educational and gender reform. For feminist educators, one of the most significant aspects of this body of theory was that it enabled a turn to how identity was constructed in and by educational processes and practices (Collins *et al.*, 2000; Davies, 1989). Since then, much feminist educational research and many educational policies have foregrounded 'identity' as an object of enquiry and a target for reform (Youdell, 2010; Dillabough *et al.*, 2008). Against views of natural gender difference, the call has been to investigate how subtle as well as overt interactions, practices and discourses produce masculinity and femininity and the 'gender order'. And this work has had a significant impact on gender equity policies and on professional practice – particularly across schools and early childhood settings (Collins *et al.*, 2000; Ailwood and Lingard, 2001; Keddie and Mills, 2007). In turning attention to the processes that shape gender identities, this work has animated initiatives to examine the construction of masculinity and femininity – at school, system and classroom levels – to promote pedagogies that challenge constraining and rigid gender norms, and question homophobia and heteronormative views of gender relations.

Conclusion

The recent history of feminism and education reveals a complex and dynamic engagement with competing ideas about gender equality and gender difference. And this is not abating in the present. Many fear that feminist agendas have been eclipsed by both the 'boy-turn' and a narrow outcomes-based focus on testing and ranking. This is not to say that feminism is no longer necessary or that girls and women do not face any problems or inequalities in relation to education. Feminism, it is argued here, continues to offer a powerful perspective on educational experience, one that needs to be re-asserted in the current times when education is at risk of being subsumed by instrumental and outcomes-only agendas. Feminist agendas have helped expand understandings about what matters in education, and made gender relations and gender identity categories of analysis that matter for policy and for practice. As the discussion above indicates, the challenges confronting feminism in education today encompass a greater attention to the 'intersectionality' of identity categories and to translating recognition of difference *and* equality into educational practices. A further challenge for feminism in education is how it recognises, remembers and records its own achievements, including understanding the processes and outcomes that have changed, as well as the patterns of inequality, disrespect and disadvantage that persist, and the kind of new or rejuvenated feminist response that this may require.

Questions for further investigation

1   In your view, is feminism relevant to educational reform and practices today; if so, in what ways, and if not, why? How would you argue and justify your case?
2   Feminist philosophers questioned the gendered norms of the 'good student', proposing a focus on 'care, concern, connection'. Is this a reasonable and defensible proposition? What impact has this critique had on educational systems and practices? What do you think are the important qualities of the 'good student'?
3   Struggles over recognition of difference and calls for gender equality have been a long-standing feature of feminist politics and educational reforms. What weight do you think these matters have in your own educational and cultural context? How important do you think these issues are in terms of 1) curriculum design and practice; 2) teacher interactions with pupils?

Suggested further reading

Berger, M.T. and Guidroz, K. (Eds.) (2010) *The Intersectional Approach: Transforming the Academy through Race, Class and Gender*. Chapel Hill, NC: University of North Carolina Press. A collection of key and re-issued articles by leading international scholars on the development and application of intersectional analyses in education and other fields of higher education.

McLeod, J. and Yates, L. (2006) *Making Modern Lives: Subjectivity, Schooling and Social Change*. Albany, NY: State University of New York Press. A longitudinal qualitative study of young people aged from 12 to 18, exploring the influence of feminism on changes in gender identity and gender relations.

Skelton, C., Francis, B. and Smulyan, L. (Eds.) (2006) *The Sage Handbook of Gender and Education*. London: Sage. An important collection of chapters addressing diverse aspects of feminism, gender and education; it provides a sound overview of major issues and debates in the recent past and emerging challenges.

Unterhalter, E. (2007) *Gender, Schooling and Global Social Justice*. London: Routledge. This book provides an important analysis of feminist goals and reforms in relation to non-Western countries and an accessible examination of theories of social justice and capability approaches.

Weiler, K. (Ed.) (2001) *Feminist Engagements: Reading, Resisting, and Revisioning Male Theorists in Education and Cultural Studies*. New York: Routledge. In this collection of essays, leading feminist researchers reflect on the personal and scholarly impact of influential male theorists and offer illustrations of how feminist engagements have transformed the practice of theorising.

References

Ailwood, J. and Lingard, B. (2001) 'The endgame for national girls' schooling policies in Australia', *Australian Journal of Education*, 45, 1, pp. 9–22.

Ali, S., Mirza, H., Phoenix, A. and Ringrose, J. (2010) 'Intersectionality, Black British feminism and resistance in education: a roundtable discussion', *Gender and Education*, 22, 6, pp. 647–661.

Arnot, M. (2002) *Reproducing Gender; Essays on Educational Theory and Feminist Politics*. London: RoutledgeFalmer.

Arnot, M. and Mac An Ghaill, M. (Eds.) (2006) *The RoutledgeFalmer Reader in Gender and Education*. New York, NY: Routledge.

Belenky, M.F., McVicker, B.C., Goldberger, M.R. and Tarule, J.M. (1986) *Women's Ways of Knowing: The Development of Self, Voice, and Mind*. New York, NY: Basic Books.

Blackmore, J. (1999) *Troubling Women: Feminism, Leadership and Educational Change*. Buckingham: Open University Press.

Collins, C., Kenway, J. and McLeod J. (2000) *Factors Influencing the Educational Performance of Males and Females at School and their Initial Destinations after Leaving School*. Canberra, ACT: Department of Education, Training and Youth Affairs.

Commonwealth Schools Commission (1987) *The National Policy for the Education of Girls in Australian Schools*, Schools Commission, Canberra.

Connell, R. (2007) *Southern Theory: The Global Dynamics of Knowledge in Social Science*. Cambridge: Polity.

Davies, B. (1989) *Frogs and Snails and Feminist Tales: Pre-school Children and Gender*. St Leonards, NSW: Allen & Unwin.

Dillabough, J., McLeod, J. and Mills, M. (2008) 'In search of allies and others: "Troubling" gender and education', *Discourse: Studies in the Cultural Politics of Education*, 29, 3, pp. 301–310.

Epstein, D., Elwood, J. and Hey, V. (1998) *Failing Boys? Issues in Gender and Achievement*. Buckingham: Open University Press.

Gilligan, C. (1982) *In a Different Voice: Psychological Theory and Women's Development*. Cambridge, MA: Harvard University Press.

Hey, V. (1997) *The Company She Keeps: An Ethnography of Girls' Friendships*. Buckingham: Open University Press.

Hill Collins, P. (1990) *Black Feminist Thought: Knowledge, Consciousness, and the Politics of Empowerment*. New York: Routledge.

Hughes, C. (2002) *Key Concepts on Feminist Theory and Research*. London: Sage.

Keddie, A. and Mills, M. (2007) *Teaching Boys: Developing Classroom Practices that Work*. Crows Nest, NSW: Allen & Unwin.

Kehily, M.J. (2002) *Sexuality, Gender and Schooling: Shifting Agendas in Social Learning*. London: Routledge.

Lingard, B. and Douglas, P. (1999) *Men Engaging Feminisms: Pro-feminism, Backlashes and Schooling*. Buckingham: Open University Press.

Lorber, J. (2009) *Gender Inequality: Feminist Theories and Politics*. New York, NY: Oxford University Press.

MacNaughton, G. (2000) *Rethinking Gender in Early Childhood Education*. St Leonards, NSW: Allen & Unwin.

MacNaughton, G.M. and Davis, K. (Eds.) (2009) *Race and Early Childhood Education: An International Approach to Identity, Politics, and Pedagogy*. London: Palgrave MacMillan.

Martin, J.R. (1986) 'Redefining the educated person: rethinking the significance of gender', *Educational Researcher*, 15, 6, pp. 6–10.

McLeod, J. (1998) 'The promise of freedom and the regulation of gender – feminist pedagogy in the 1970s', *Gender and Education*, 10, 4, pp. 431–445.

McLeod, J.(2001) 'When poststructuralism meets gender,' in Kenneth Hultqvist and Gunilla Dahlberg (Eds.), *Governing the Child in the New Millennium*. Routledge, New York, pp. 259–289.

McLeod, J. (2004) 'Which girls, which boys? Gender, feminism and educational reform', in Allen, J. (Ed.) *Sociology of Education: Possibilities and Practices* (3rd Ed.). Southbank, VIC: Social Science Press/Thomson Learning Australia, pp. 165–196.

McLeod, J. and Yates, L. (2006) *Making Modern Lives: Subjectivity, Schooling and Social Change*. Albany, NY: State University of New York Press.

Millet, K. (1972) *Sexual Politics*. London: Abacus, Sphere Books.

Mirza, H.S. and Joseph, C. (Eds.) (2009) 'Black feminisms and postcolonial paradigms: Researching educational inequalities', *Special Issue Race Ethnicity and Education*, 12, 1.

Mohanty, C.T. (1988) 'Under western eyes: Feminist scholarship and colonial discourses', *Feminist Review*, 30, Autumn, 61–68.

Moreton-Robinson, A. (2000) *Talkin up to the White Woman: Indigenous Women and Feminism*. St Lucia, QLD: Queensland University Press.

Office of Schools Administration (1990) *A Fair Go For All: Guidelines for Gender-inclusive Curriculum*, Ministry of Education, Victoria.

Reay, D., David. M. and Ball, S. (2005) *Degrees of Choice: Social Class, Race, Gender and Higher Education*. Stoke-on-Trent: Trentham Books.

Schools Commission (1975) *Girls, School and Society: Report by a Study Group to the Schools Commission*, Canberra, Australia.

Scott, J. (1988) 'Deconstructing equality-versus-difference: or the uses of poststructuralist theory for feminism', *Feminist Studies*, *14*, 1, pp. 32–50.

Skelton, C., Francis, B. and Smulyan, L. (Eds.) (2006) *The Sage Handbook of Gender and Education*. London: Sage.

Skelton, C. and Francis, B. (2009) *Feminism and the Schooling Scandal*. London: Routledge.

St Pierre, E. and Pillow, W. (2000) *Working the Ruins: Feminist Poststructural Theory and Methods in Education*. New York, NY: Routledge.

Tsolidis, G. (2001) *Schooling Diaspora and Gender: Being Feminist, Being Different*. London: Open University Press.

United Nations (2010) *United Nations Millennium Goals: Goal 3 Promote Gender Equality and Empower Women*. Available at: www.un.org/millenniumgoals/gender.shtml (accessed 15 November 2010).

Unterhalter, E. (2007) *Gender, Schooling and Global Social Justice*. London: Routledge.

Walkerdine, V., Lucey, H. and Melody, J. (2001) *Growing up Girl; Pyscho-social Explorations of Class and Gender*. Basingstoke: Palgrave.

Walters, M. (2006) *Feminism: A Very Short Introduction*. New York, NY: Oxford University Press.

Weaver-Hightower, M. (2003) 'The "boy-turn" in research on gender and education', *Review of Educational Research*, *73*, 4, pp. 471–498.

Weedon, C. (1999) *Feminism, Theory and the Politics of Difference*. Oxford: Blackwell.

Weiner, G. (1994) *Feminisms and Education: An Introduction*. Buckingham: Open University Press.

Whelehan, I. (1995) *Modern Feminist Thought: From the Second Wave to 'Post-feminism'*. New York, NY: New York University Press.

Woodward, K. and Woodward, S. (2009) *Why Feminism Matters: Feminism Lost and Found*. London: Palgrave.

Yates, L. (1998) 'Constructing and deconstructing "girls" as a category of concern', in MacKinnon, A., Elgvist-Saltzman, I. and Prentice, A. (Eds.) *Education into the 21st Century: Dangerous Terrain for Women*. London: Falmer Press.

Yates, L. and McLeod, J. (2010) 'Gender and learning', in Peterson, P., Baker, E. and McGaw, B. (Eds.) *International Encyclopedia of Education*, 5 (3rd Ed.). Oxford: Elsevier, pp. 432–437.

Youdell, D. (2010) *School Trouble: Identity, Power and Politics in Education*. London: Routledge.

Yuval-Davis, N. (2006) 'Intersectionality and feminist politics', *European Journal of Women's Studies*, *13*, 3, pp. 193–209.

6

History of education

Deirdre Raftery
University College Dublin

Overview

This chapter provides an introduction to research in the field of the history of education. It discusses the legacy of the history of 'ideas' in education, gives an overview of developments in historiography, and identifies some methodological issues of interest to the historian of education. Due to the limits of time and space, the chapter concerns itself principally with Western education of the modern period. However, a wide range of reading is suggested in the chapter to facilitate researchers.

Introduction

Bowen (1981), in his three-volume study of Western education, refers to the 'interplay' between the history of ideas and their institutionalisation in the process of education. This interplay is central to the history of education and will be explored in this chapter. We will see that the field of history of education has points of contact with other disciplines, such as philosophy and social history, but it is nonetheless a distinct discipline with specific *foci*. For example, Plato's writing on education in the *Republic* may be of interest to both the philosopher and the historian of education, but for different reasons. While the philosopher may locate Plato's discourse within the development of Western ideas, the historian of education may look within the *Republic* for evidence of education practices.

Because the history of 'ideas' is so central to the history of education, the published work of a number of prominent thinkers has had an influence on the field of history of education, and the 'grandmasters of educational thought' such as John Locke and Jean Jacques Rousseau, are points of reference for many scholars. Lockean theory permeates discussions of Enlightenment education, while Rousseau's *Émile* is a well-documented point of reference in histories of childhood education. The chapter will outline the contribution of some education theorists to discourse in the history of education, and will explore historiography in the field of the history of education, which has generated research that has contributed to our understanding of social history while also stimulating theoretical and methodological innovations. It will be seen that without jettisoning the legacy of the history of education 'ideas', the field of history of education has, from the second half of the twentieth century, widened to embrace the study of institutions, practices, teaching, learning, systems and individuals. Ways of 'doing' history of education, for all of these areas of interest, have developed. The chapter will note shifts in areas of scholarly interest, and approaches to research and writing.

Finally, the chapter will comment briefly on research culture, outlining the contribution of some scholarly publications and learned societies to the development of a vibrant research field.

Educational ideas and history of education

Western education came to assume its modern character by the sixteenth century, stimulated by the writings of Erasmus and Luther who had argued that both religious beliefs and political loyalty could be controlled through education. Increasingly from this time, Catholics and Protestants harnessed schooling in support of their aims. By the seventeenth century, religious dissent and non-conformity resulted in some conflict about the nature and content of education. A further 'purpose' to education was articulated by those who believed that education should have a wider social purpose.

Research in the history of education has explored this period, acknowledging the extraordinary impact of the development of printing, and drawing on sources such as schoolbooks which appeared in very significant numbers from the printing presses of Europe. At that time, many prominent sixteenth-century scholars were interested in developing the best methods for instruction. Erasmus, for example, produced his treatise on classroom practices, *On the Right Method of Instruction (De ratione studii)*. It presented a graded progression of studies, from elementary grammar through to the study of classical and Christian literature. The process of education in Europe was transformed by the widespread production of such school textbooks, which took the form of anthologies, grammar texts and graded readers. Some of these were adopted by schools as 'set texts', and the practice of studying a text had a shaping influence on the organisation of teaching and learning in the classroom. Programmes of instruction were developed, and perhaps the most celebrated of these was the Jesuit *Ratio studiorum*, which became a definitive 'correct method' of studies from 1599.

Throughout contintental Europe, movements spread to develop schooling on organised principles. The growth in the number and types of schools, and developments in literacy are just some of the concerns of the historian of education. Scholars recognise that sources for this early stage in formal schooling are often problematic; documents can be unreliable or incomplete, and indeed some were deliberately destroyed. For example, Bowen (1981, p. 9) comments on, 'the most dramatic [destruction of sources] being the burning of Huguenot educational records . . . in the seventeenth century when those French Protestants were bitterly suppressed by a resurgent and vindictive Catholicism'.

Education in England also changed significantly in the sixteenth century. Henry VIII harnessed schooling in support of his movement to anglicise the Church, dissolving the monasteries and chanteries, enforcing education at schools run by clergy who were subordinate to the Crown, and introducing the use of mandatory textbooks. Tudor policy on education in Ireland was articulated in a series of penal laws, which proscribed Catholic education and suppressed the Irish language. There is a wealth of research on education in this period, and on the 'Protestantisation of the nation' under Elizabeth I (1558–1603). Equally, the area of Catholic recusancy and the growth of clandestine schools has been examined by scholars.

Scholarship on the seventeenth and eighteenth centuries demonstrates the breadth of the field, with researchers working on the relationship between education and culture, science, museums and collectors, Enlightenment ideas, and informal agencies such as societies and learned groups. Dick and Watts (2008, p. 509) have written about the importance of schoarship that examines 'the way industrial and technological advances combined with the fruits of discovery, science, art, literature and culture', noting that Enlightenment education took place 'not only in formal institutions of schooling and higher education, but also through the variety of informal agencies and discourses whereby culture is transmitted'. Dick and Watts (2008) bring together important new scholarship on areas as varied as medical education, dance and travel, while other researchers have examined the eighteenth-century imagination and the educational value of travel (Brewer, 1997; Porter, 2000, 2001; Sloan, 2003; McGregor, 2007). The role of women in education at this time has also been the subject of a considerable *corpus* of work (Raftery, 1997; Weiller and Middleton, 1999; Watts, 2007).

Women's education in the ninteteenth century has also been an area that has attracted significant interest. Drawing on the doctrine of 'separate spheres' that has informed much scholarship in women's history, scholars have been interested in the different forms of educational provision for women and men. In England, for example, there has been particular interest in the 'unexpected revolution' in female education in the second half of the nineteenth century, which was marked by the widening of education oportunities to females, and the opening up of public examinations, and by higher education for middle-class women (Bryant, 1979; Burstyn, 1980; Hunt, 1987; Spencer, 2004; Goodman and Martin, 2004). In the mid-nineteenth century, education had been made available to middle-class women through cultural and scientific societies, the mechanics institutes, and the working men's college movement. As Purvis (1991) noted, this was like a type of 'adult education'. Speaking at society meetings was an important outlet for women involved in the organised women's movement; for example, at the London Working Men's College a number of women read papers in the 1890s, including Millicent Garrett Fawcett and Emily Penrose, Principal of Bedford College for women. Bedford College and Queen's College London were founded in 1848 and 1849 respectively, providing lectures for many women who hoped to work as teachers or governesses. Indeed the education of governesses, which has attracted scholarly interest, has been shown to have had a direct influence on the eventual opening up of higher education opportunities to women. The Governesses Benevolent Institution (GBI), founded in 1841 to provide support to unemployed governesses, quickly developed into Queen's College London, providing tuition for both girls and women. Bedford College equally provided both school and college tuition to females, and by 1909 it had become part of the University of London. The question of university education for women was pursued vigorously by those who wanted to see degrees awared to women, and scholarship has paid attention to how universities, including those at Cambridge, Oxford, Aberdeen and Dublin, eventually opened their doors to females (Kaye, 1972; Raftery, 1997; MacWilliams Tullberg, 1998; Parkes, 2004).

The other major development in nineteenth-century education was the spread of popular education. In England, society had been shaken by the effects of the French Revolution, and there was fear that the working classes might be receptive to Jacobin ideas. It was felt that education could be the means whereby the upper ranks could exercise control on the poor, making them law-abiding. In addition, there was growing middle-class interest in religion, and Evangelicals pursued their aim to make society more pious and moral. Again, education was harnessed in pursuit of this aim. The Society for the Establishment and Support of Sunday Schools

(1785) had nearly a quarter of a million children enrolled by 1795, and by 1803 this number had risen to 844,728 pupils. There was a huge growth in the publication of moral tracts and pious lesson books for children and young adults, which encouraged the poor to be content (Altick, 1957; Goldstrom, 1972; Raftery, 1997). Following the success of the Sunday schools, interested parties examined the possibility of providing day schools. The work of the Rev Andrew Bell and Joseph Lancaster paved the way for mass education in Britain, as they developed cost-effective systems for providing schooling for the poor. The Anglican National Society for Promoting the Education of the Poor (known as the National Society) and the Nonconformist British and Foreign School Society used their techniques, respectively. For example, Bell showed the National Society how to use the 'monitorial system' of education to organise schooling with little expense. His system did not require a well-educated teaching force, rather a large school could be managed by one teacher who would delegate work to older pupils who acted as 'monitors'. Bell produced a manual, *Instructions for Conducting Schools*, which the teacher was to follow exactly, and there were lesson books for the children's use in the 'national' schools.

In Ireland, with the founding of the Kildare Place Society (Society for Promoting the Education of the Poor of Ireland) in 1811, the ideas of Lancaster and Bell spread. French liberals also showed interest in the monitorial system, and the Society for the Encouragement of National Industry sent a deputation from France to study the way Lancaster's Borough Road School was run. The monitorial system was subquently used, albeit to a modest degree, in both Ireland and France for several decades. The system which became more widespread in schools by the mid-nineteenth century was the 'simultaneous' method, whereby the teacher taught all the children at the same time. Researchers in the history of education have examined not only the systems that brought about the spread of literacy in the nineteenth century, but also innovations in pedagogy and in the production of education materials, such as textbooks and charts. Historiography on the education reforms of the nineteenth century, at all levels, points to the complex and rapidly changing learning environment at that time.

Some themes in recent research in history of education: religion, colonialisms, social change, gender

The British historian of education Brian Simon (1966) argued in the 1960s that 'the relation between educational and social change' should be central to historical study, a perspective echoed by the social historian Asa Briggs (1972) who considered that the history of education should be 'part of the wider study of the history of society, social history broadly interpreted with the politics, the economics and . . . the religion put in'. The influence of these and other historians of education, particularly in Britain, was significant; in the decades that followed, the field gained its own status within the study of history. Lowe (2000) has argued that the history of education is now clearly identified as a full and proper element in the study of history more generally, and that it has a central role to play in the development of social, economic and political history. While gender remains an area of interest, discourse in the history of education engages with aspects of social change, colonialisms and – almost in response to Briggs' appeal – the 'religion' is 'put in'.

Catholic education, for example, has been scrutinsed from many perspectives, and historians of education have demonstrated an interest in the contribution of particular religious orders, the role of missionaries in schooling, and the relationship between church and state over issues of control in educational provision and curriculum. For example, Whitehead (2007) has done research into Jesuit archives as resources for educational and cultural history, while Raftery and

Nowlan-Roebuck (2007) have examined the relationship between convent schools and the National Board in nineteenth-century Ireland. O'Donoghue (2001, 2004) has done considerable research on religious orders and education in nineteenth- and twentieth-century Australia and Ireland. Smyth (2007) has worked on Canadian sources, and a volume of important research has been generated by researchers in Belgium (Depaepe *et al.*, 1992; Hellinckx *et al.*, 2009). Historiography has also been well served in France (Rogers, 1998, 1991, 1995, 2005), in the USA (Coburn and Smith; Hoy, 2002, 2006) and in the UK (Mangion, 2005, 2008). Most recently, a particularly useful tool for researchers is a substantial historiographical essay with sources appended, *The Forgotten Contribution of the Teaching Sisters* (2009), edited by Bart Hellinckx, Frank Simon and Marc Depaepe. Adding to an existing body of work on Anglican education, there is also research on missionaries who worked in education (Garvey, 1994; Allen, 2008; O'Connor, 2000).

Some of the research on missionaries and education is located in the discourses of colonialisms and race. This kind of work provides a stimulating example of ways in which theoretical approaches are brought to bear on sources in the history of schooling. Examples include work on colonial schooling and missionary evangelism in north-eastern Zambia (Garvey, 1994), on Anglican mission education in Zanzibar and Northern Rhodesia (Allen, 2008), and on mission infant schools in India, Canada and New Zealand (Prochner *et al.*, 2009).

Other recent historical research on education in colonial contexts examines North India (Allender, 2007), and while Kallaway (2005, 2009) has worked on British colonial Africa and South Africa in the 1930s and 1940s, Omolewa (2008) has examined 'the colonial factor in the mass literacy campaign in Nigeria, 1946–1956'. Utilising print culture as a source, Walsh (2008) explores education and the 'universalist' idiom of empire through his work on the use of Irish National School books in both Ireland and Ontario, while Montgomery (2005) also uses textbooks to explore issues of 'race-thinking' and 'ethnic nationalism'.

An equally robust *corpus* of research into the relationship between education and social change exists. Some of this has been utilised and analysed by historians of education who participated in an ESRC Seminar Series on social change in the history of education, which ran in parts of the UK between 2004 and 2006. Some researchers focused on change and the teacher, while others have scrutinised systems (see McCulloch and Richardson, 2007).

Many reseachers have looked closely at education traditions. For example, Hendrie (1997) explores ways in which the dominie was the embodiment of the educational tradition that was distinctive to Scotland, while McManus (2002) has written a detailed study of the evolution of indigenous education in the Irish 'hedge schools'. Exploring education, national identity and social change in Ireland, Scotland and Wales, Raftery *et al.* (2007) draw together a substantial body of work, directing researchers to key texts in the field. Scottish education has been scrutinised in a special issue of *History of Education* (2009), which will be of use to researchers interested in education and citizenship in modern Scotland.

Scholars, particularly in the last 30 years, have had an increased interest in recovering the voices of 'women of ideas', with the result that educational works by women such as Mary Astell and Mary Wollstonecraft form part of the discourse on the gendered nature of education in the late seventeenth and eighteenth centuries. A substantial volume of research on female education has been published, looking at 'learned women', print culture, curriculum, schooling and preparation for life and work (Myres, 1990; Hunt, 1987; Bakker and van Essen, 1999; Raftery and Parkes, 2007; Meyer, 2007). Research has also been done on women teachers in international contexts (Theobald, 1984, 1991; Strober and Langford, 1986; Middleton, 1987; Rogers, 1995; Cunningham and Gardner, 2004; van Drenth and van Essen, 2008), and on women in education policy (McDermid, 2009; Goodman and Harrop,

2000; Goodman and Martin, 2007). Because of the 'revolution' in nineteenth-century female education as noted earlier, there is also a substantial body of work on women in higher education (Raftery, 2002; Spencer, 2004; Murphy and Raftery, 2004; Dyhouse, 1976, 1981; Hunt, 1987), and there is also work on gender and colonialism (Goodman and Martin, 2002).

Historiography, methodologies and sources

Historians of education continue to engage with changes and developments in scholarship (Raftery et al., 2007; Richardson, 2007; Mattingly et al., 2008). Work on sources and methodologies has been invigorated by McCulloch and Richardson (2000) and Goodson and Sikes (2001). Scholars have challenged the historian of education to gather data in a variety of methods, including using quantitative data (Carpentier, 2008), and through creating oral archives (Cunningham and Gardner, 2004; Raftery and KilBride, 2006). Scholars have also used sources such as images (Burke and Ribiero, 2007; Spencer, 2007) and material culture to write the social history of the classroom (Grosvenor et al., 1999). In much of this kind of work, the impact of technologies on the history of education is evident.

Collections of important work spanning a range of themes and areas have also been published in recent years, and these volumes not only bring together some groundbreaking research but also facilitate new researchers. Roy Lowe (2000) has edited a four-volume collection, *History of Education: Major Themes*, comprising 111 contributions that examine teaching, learning, the social context of education and – importantly – historiographical debates within the field. Changing trends in scholarship, and the range of methodologies embraced by researchers in Europe, Australia and North America, are also evident in articles collected in *The RoutledgeFalmer Reader in History of Education* (McCulloch, 2005). These articles examined higher education; informal systems of education; the relationship between schooling and the State; education and social mobility; curriculum; teachers and pupils; education, work and the economy; and education and national identity.

Conclusion

The study of education from a historical perspective is a broad field, embracing research on education ideas and practices, institutions and individuals, policies and traditions. In Britain alone, as Richardson (2007) demonstrated, there has been a huge growth in scholarly output in the history of education since the mid-twentieth century. With the exception of the history of medicine, 'the historical development of education in Britain has become as well charted as any of the "sub-fields" of social history that emerged in the early 1960s' (Richardson, 2007, p. 569). The intellectual vibrancy of the field internationally is reflected in the range and growth of publications. International journals such as *History of Education, History of Education Researcher, Paedagogica Historica, The Journal of Education Administration and History* and *History of Education Quarterly* publish the work of established scholars, as well as that of newly emerging researchers. Historians of education also publish in journals outside their field, but within areas of theoretical interest, such as *Gender and Education*.

The field is vivified by academic societies, international conferences and colloquia, all of which contribute to published research. International meetings of scholars in the field include the annual International Standing Conference of the History of Education (ISCHE), the annual conference of the History of Education Association (USA) and the annual conference of the

History of Education Society (UK). In the UK, the History of Education Society was established in 1967, and in 1972, the Society published the first issue of its journal, *History of Education*. Historians of education also partake in networks and groups at international conferences of associations such as the European Education Research Association (EERA) and the American Education Research Association (AERA).

It is likely that future research in history of education will engage increasingly with theorists from other disciplines, reconsidering interpretations and using different methodologies to illuminate our understanding of the past. Technologies will play a crucial role in data gathering and archiving, and creative ways of interrogating different types of sources will continue to be central to the work of the historian of education.

Questions for further investigation

1   Oral histories are a potentially rich source of data for the historian of education. In what way might oral history projects be designed to gather data on teachers' lives and pupils' experience of schooling? Useful reference tools here are *The Oral History Reader,* by Robert Perks and Alistair Thompson (Eds.) (1998, London and New York, NY: Routledge), and Ivor Goodson and Pat Sikes, *Life History Research in Educational Settings* (2001, Buckingham and Philadelphia, PA: Open University Press).

2   Of what 'value' are images in researching the history of education? Does the artifical 'constructedness' of images of schooling mitigate against their use in research, or can they be interpreted in meaningful ways? Helpful reading: *Silences and Images, the Social History of the Classroom*, by Ian Grosvenor *et al*. (Eds.) (1999, New York, NY: Peter Lang).

Suggested further reading

Goodman, J., McCulloch, G. and Richardson, W. (Eds.) (2008) *Social Change in the History of British Education.* London and New York, NY: Routledge. This book examines ways in which education has contributed to social change in Britain. Formal and informal types of education are examined, and contributors engage with questions concerning theory and methodology. The chapters span a wide period, from the sixteenth century to the present, including research on England, Scotland, Ireland and Wales, and the book is a major contribution to the history and historiography of education.

McCulloch, G. (Ed.) (2005) *The RoutledgeFalmer Reader in History of Education.* Oxford and New York, NY: Routledge. This volume comprises some of the leading recent research in the field, and is a useful tool for students and academics. It is divided into eight parts: Higher Education; Informal Agencies of Education; Schooling, the State and Local Government; Education and Social Change and Inequality; Curriculum; Teachers and Pupils; Education, Work and the Economy; and Education and National Identity.

References

Allen, J. (2008) 'Slavery, colonialism and the pursuit of community life: Anglican mission education in Zanzibar and Northern Rhodesia, 1864–1940', *History of Education*, 37, 2, pp. 207–226.

Altick, R. (1957) *The English Common Reader*. Chicago, IL: Chicago University Press.

Bakker, N. and van Essen, M. (1999) '"No matter of principle". The unproblematic character of coeducation in girls' secondary schooling in the Netherlands, c. 1870–1930', *History of Education Quarterly*, 39, pp. 454–475.

Beales, A.C.F. (1965) *Education Under Penalty*. London: University of London.

Bowen, J. (1981) *A History of Western Education* (Vol. 3). London: Methuen.

Brewer, J. (1997) *The Pleasures of the Imagination: English Culture in the Eighteenth Century*. London: HarperCollins.

Briggs, A. (1972) 'The study of the history of education', *History of Education*, 1, 1, pp. 5–22.

Burke, C. and de Castro, H.R. (2007) 'The school photograph: portraiture and the art of assembling the body of the schoolchild', *History of Education*, 36, 2, pp. 213–226.

Carpentier, V. (2008) 'Quantitative sources for the history of education', *History of Education*, 37, 5, pp. 701–720.

Cressy, D. (1976) *Education in Tudor and Stewart England*. New York, NY: St Martin's Press.

Cunningham, B. and Kennedy, M. (Eds.) (1999) *The Experience of Reading: Irish Historical Perspectives*. Dublin: ESHSI.

Curtis, B. (1983) 'Schoolbooks and the myth of cultural republicanism: the state and the curriculum in Canada West, 1820–1850', *Histoire Sociale – Social History XVII*, 32, pp. 305–29.

Depaepe, M., Debaere, F. and Van Rompaey, L. (1992) 'Missionary education in the Belgian Congo during the colonial period (1908–1960)', *Neue Zeitschrift für Missionswissenschaft/Nouvelle Review de science missionaire*, 48, 4, pp. 265–280.

Dick M. and Watts, R. (2008) 'Editorial', *History of Education*, 37, 4, pp. 509–512.

Freeman, M. (Ed.) (2009) 'Special Issue: Education and citizenship in modern Scotland', *History of Education*, 38, 3, pp. 327–332.

Garvey, B. (1994) 'Colonial schooling and missionary evangelism: the case of Roman Catholic educational initiatives in north-eastern Zambia, 1895–1953', *History of Education*, 23, 2, pp. 195–206.

Goldstrom, J.M. (1972) *The Social Content of Education, 1808–1870: a Study of the Working Class School Reader in England and Ireland*. Shannon: Irish University Press.

Goodman, J. and Martin, J. (2004) *Women and Education, 1800–1980: Educational Reform and Personal Identities*. London: Palgrave.

McCulloch, G. and Richardson, W. (Eds.) (2007) 'Special Issue: Social change in the history of education: the British experience in international context', *History of Education*, 36, 4–5.

Goodson, I. and Sikes, P. (2001) *Life History Research in Educational Settings*. Buckingham and Philadelphia, PA: Open University Press.

Goody, J. (1968) *Literacy in Traditional Societies*. Cambridge: Cambridge University Press.

Grosvenor, I., Lawn, M. and Rousmaniere, K. (Eds.) (1999) *Silences and Images: the Social History of the Classroom*. New York, NY: Peter Lang.

Hendrie, W.F. (1997) *The Dominie: a Profile of the Scottish Headmaster*. Edinburgh: John Donald.

Hoy, S. (2006) *Good Hearts: Catholic Sisters in Chicago's Past*. Urbana, IL: University of Illinois Press.

Hunt, F. (Ed.) (1987) *Lessons on Life: the Schooling of Girls and Women, 1850–1950*. Oxford: Basil Blackwell.

Jones, G.E. and Roderick, G.W. (2003) *A History of Education in Wales*. Cardiff: University of Wales.

Kallaway, P. (2005) 'Welfare and education in British colonial Africa and South Africa during the 1930s and 1940s', *Paedagogica Historica, XLI*, III, pp. 337–356.

Knowles, D. (1955) *The Religious Orders in England*. Cambridge: Cambridge University Press.

Lawn, M. and Grosvenor, I (Eds.) (2005) *Materialities of Schooling*. Oxford: Symposium Books.

Lowe, R. (2000) 'Writing the history of education', in Lowe, R. (Ed.) *History of Education: Major Themes* (Vol. I.) Oxon and New York, NY: Routledge.

Mattingly, P., Jarausch, K., Craig, J., Kett, J. and Turner J. (2008) 'Universities in Europe: North American perpsctives on European historiography', *History of Education*, 37, 3, pp. 469–490.

McCulloch, G. and Richardson, W. (2000) *Historical Research in Educational Settings*. Buckingham and Philadelphia, PA: Open University Press.

McCulloch, G. (Ed.) (2005) *The RoutledgeFalmer Reader in History of Education*. Oxon and New York, NY: Routledge.

McGrath, P. (1967) *Papists and Purists under Elizabeth I*. London: Blandford Press.

McGregor, A. (2007) *Curiosity and Enlightenment: Collectors and Collections from the Sixteenth to the Nineteenth Century*. New Haven, CT and London: Yale University Press.

McManus, A. (2002) *The Irish Hedge School and its Books, 1695–1831*. Dublin: Four Courts Press.

Meyer, C. (2007) 'The struggle for vocational education and employment possibilities for women in the second half of the nineteenth century in Germany', *History of Education Researcher*, 80, pp. 85–89

Middleton, S. (1987) 'Schooling and radicalization: life histories of New Zealand feminist teachers', *British Journal of Sociology of Education*, pp. 169–189.

Montgomery, K. (2005) 'Banal Race-thinking: ties of blood, Canadian history textbooks, and ethnic nationalism', *Paedagogica Historica*, XLI, III, pp. 313–336.

Myres, S.H. (1990) *The Bluestocking Circle: Women, Friendship and the Life of the Mind in Eighteenth Century England*. Oxford: Clarendon Press.

O'Connor, D. (Ed.) (2000) *Three Centuries of Mission: The United Society for the Propagation of the Gospel*. London: Continuum.

O'Donoghue, T. (2001) *Upholding the Faith: the Process of Education in Catholic Schools in Australia 1922–1965*. New York, NY: Peter Lang.

O'Donoghue, T. (2004) *Come Follow Me and Forsake Temptation: the Recruitment and Retention of Members of Catholic Teaching Orders, 1922–1965*. Bern: Lang.

Omolewa, M. (2008) 'Programmed for failure? The colonial factor in the mass literacy campaign in Nigeria, 1946–1956', *Paedagogica Historica*, 44, 1–2, pp. 107–121.

Patterson, L. (2003) *Scottish Education in the Twentieth Century*. Edinburgh: Edinburgh University Press.

Paedagogica Historica (2008) Vol. XLVI, 1 & 2.

Porter, R. (2000) *The Creation of the Modern World: The Untold Story of the British Enlightenment*. New York, NY and London: W.W. Norton.

Porter, R. (2001) *Enlightenment: Britain and the Creation of the Modern World*. London: Penguin Books.

Purvis, J. (1991) *A History of Women's Education in England*. Milton Keynes: Open University Press.

Raftery, D. (1997) *Women and Learning in English Writing, 1600–1900*. Dublin: Four Courts Press.

Raftery, D. and Nowlan-Roebuck, C. (2007) 'Convent schools and national education in nineteenth-century Ireland: negotiating a place within a non-denominational system', *History of Education*, 36, 3, pp. 353–365.

Raftery, D., McDermid, J. and Jones, G.E. (2007) 'Social change and education in Ireland, Scotland and Wales: historiography on nineteenth-century schooling', *History of Education*, 36, 4–5, pp. 447–463.

Raftery, D. and Parkes, S.M. (2007) *Female Education in Ireland, 1700–1900: Minerva or Madonna?* Dublin and Portland, OR: Irish Academic Press.

Richardson, W. (2007) 'British historiography of education in international context at the turn of the century', *History of Education*, 36, 4–5, pp. 569–593.

Rogers, R. (1995) 'Boarding schools, women teachers, and domesticity: reforming girls' secondary education in the first half of the nineteenth century', *French Historical Studies*, 19, 1, pp. 153–181.

Rogers, R. (1995) *From The Salon to the Schoolroom: Educating Bourgeois Girls in Nineteenth Century France*. University Park: Penn State University Press.

Rogers, R. (1998) 'Retrograde or modern? Unveiling the teaching nun in nineteenth-century France', *Social History*, 23, 2, pp. 146–164.

Simon, B. (1966) 'The history of education', in Tibble, J.W. (Ed.) *The Study of Education*. London: RKP.

Sloan, K. (Ed.) (2003) *Enlightenment: Discovering the World in the Eighteenth Century*. London: British Museum.

Smyth, E. (Ed.) (2007) *Changing Habits: Women's Religious Orders in Canada*. Montreal: Novalis.

Smyth, E. (2008) 'Canonizing the text: readers, teaching manuals and Ontario women religious, 1867–1920', in Van Gorp, A. and Depaepe. M. (Eds.) (2008) *Auf der Suche nach der wahren Art von Textbüchern* (Beiträge zur historishchen und systematischen Schuchbuchforschung 7), Bad Heilbrunn: Verlag Julius Klinkhardt, pp. 119–127.

Spencer, S. (2007) 'A uniform identity: schoolgirl snapshots and the spoken visual', *History of Education*, 36, 2, pp. 227–246.

Stowe, A.M. (1908) *English Grammar Schools in the Reign of Queen Elizabeth*. New York, NY: Teachers College, Columbia University.

Strober, M.H. and Langford, A.G. (1986) 'The feminization of public school teaching: cross-sectional analysis, 1850–1880', *Signs: Journal of Women in Culture and Society*, 11, pp. 212–235.

Theobald, M. (1984) '"Mere accomplishments?" Melbourne's Early Ladies' Schools reconsidered', *History of Education Review*, *13*, pp. 15–28.

Theobald, M. (1991) *Women Who Taught: Perspectives on the History of Women and Teaching*. Toronto, ON: University of Toronto Press.

Van Drenth, A. and Van Essen, M. (2008) 'The ambiguity of professing gender: women educationists and new education in the Netherlands, 1890–1940', *Paedagogica Historica*, *44*, 4, pp. 379–396.

Walsh, P. (2008) 'Education and the "universalist" idiom of empire: Irish national school books in Ireland and Ontario', *History of Education*, *37*, 5, pp. 645–660.

Watts, R. (2007) *Women in Science: a Social and Cultural History*. London: Routledge.

Weiler K. and Middleton, S. (Eds.) (1999) *Telling Women's Lives: Narrative Enquiries in the History of Women's Education*. Buckingham: Open University Press.

Whitehead, M. (2007) '"To provide for the edifice of learning": researching 450 years of Jesuit educational and cultural history, with particular reference to the British Jesuits', *History of Education*, *36*, 1, pp. 109–143.

7

Sociology of education

Ralph Leighton
Canterbury Christ Church University

Overview

If not for academic convention, this chapter would be entitled 'sociologies of education', as we are not here concerned with a single approach or interpretation. The sociology of education comprises numerous theories and perspectives, supported by an ever-widening range of research methodologies, which seek to understand and explain education within social and/or personal contexts. A historical account of the nature and development of these would not be particularly illuminating as differing and often conflicting insights often arise contemporaneously, while a list of key concepts and terms without appropriate theoretical contexts would limit the reader's understanding of them and of their interrelationship.

This chapter therefore briefly examines the nature of sociology, including some of its conceptual divisions. It then considers the sociology of education in four subsections: the purpose of education, the organisation of education, the experience of education, and what students learn. Subsections should not be regarded as exclusive categories as people in school will encounter purpose, organisation, and content simultaneously to their learning; they are therefore interconnected. The chapter concludes with a brief commentary on current and possible future areas of research interest in the sociologies of education, followed by some questions for consideration by the reader, and some recommended reading to consolidate the brief outlines presented.

Introduction

To isolate the sociological study of education from the study of other aspects of human society and personal experience would obscure more than it would clarify. Education does not exist for and of itself. Even if we each make sense of our experiences of formal education in different ways – and it is formal education with which we are concerned – we do not arrive at that sense without experiencing other social circumstances or processes, nor without having been exposed to particular social conventions regarding how one can or should make sense of processes and circumstances.

Children experience families or other units of primary socialisation before they experience schooling, and it is there that their informal education begins. They are inculcated into others' perceptions of gender roles and introduced to a range of socially and ethnically determined values as interpreted by those who raise them. Simultaneous to their schooling they will continue to experience family, a range of peer groups and, increasingly, the mass media. Their experiences of social phenomena such as politics and religions are also likely to vary in both nature and extent. They will encounter these in different ways, and interpret them differently, because their parents/carers are different, their friends are different, the media they access will vary, the range of faiths they might encounter is wide, as are available political allegiances, and all can change. Therefore, to fully understand the sociology of education it is necessary to understand the rudiments of sociology which the next section briefly outlines.

An overview of sociology

Sociology developed from the positivist approach established by Comte, which considered society to be analogous to an organism. From this perspective, social institutions have interdependent functions which, when performed to their full potential, combine to produce a healthy and evolving society; when they are not performing as they should, the society which they comprise will become dysfunctional and stagnate. The relationship between institutions reflects and reinforces the nature of social structure to bring about commonly held objectives and desired outcomes. Education is viewed as that social institution which transmits knowledge and reinforces the familial function of socialisation into prevailing conventions, norms, and values; education trains people to 'fit in', giving them the skills necessary for employment which meet the demands of the social institution of work. The more complex a society's structures, the more complex is the nature of its institutions and relationships between them. This is sometimes referred to as a functionalist or consensus perspective and can be further investigated in the writing of, for example, Durkheim and of Merton.

Often contrasted to this is the critical approach typified by, but not exclusive to, Marxist analysis. Here, social institutions are again considered to reflect the nature and structure of the society in which they exist, but it is argued that these institutions do not evolve but are created and controlled. Rather than commonly held objectives and desires agreed through consensus, it is argued that social institutions are formed and controlled in and by the interests of a dominant class. Thus, under capitalism all social institutions reflect, legitimise, and perpetuate an unequal distribution of wealth and opportunity; in a patriarchal society, the dominance of men will be legitimised and perpetuated. Adherents of critical sociology view education under capitalism as preparing a compliant workforce with the skills demanded by those who own and control the means of production, reinforcing obedience to authority, and perpetuating false perceptions of equality and opportunity. The works of Gramsci and of Althusser offer insight into some of the premises underlying this approach.

While there is a long and strong tradition in sociology of studying social structures and institutions, there developed awareness that people are influenced by each other and by their perceptions and behaviour, as well as by organisations and processes. This gave rise to an emphasis on agency rather than structure as emphasised by Mead and by Goffman. The focus of study moved from what structures do to what people do, identifying the multiplicity of roles people play and the complex interaction between these and between them and people's interpretations of them. These sociologists are concerned with interaction within the classroom, with how teachers and students perceive themselves and each other.

More recently, postmodernism has had a significant impact on sociological understanding, with particular relation to identity, commodity, and consumerism. Often a more concept-based approach rather than a research-based one, insights offered by Bauman and by Bourdieu illustrate this perspective for the determined student.

Readers are best served by considering the evidence and arguments put forward in each case and coming to their own conclusions; there is no obligation to adhere to any one of these perspectives. At times the broad sweep of positivist or structural data and interpretation might serve one's purpose, at others it might be more helpful to consider social interaction or shared or conflicting interpretations and meanings. Sociology is a tool – perhaps more accurately a toolbox – not a set of off-the-shelf answers.

Sociologies of education

The purposes of education

Responses to the question 'what is education for?' vary, depending upon who is asking and who is being asked. Advocates of a biological analogy propose that education functions for the well-being and development of society. Durkheim (1956) argued that education served three main functions:

1   Reinforcing social solidarity through subject content and through shared rituals.
2   Transmission of norms and values, social roles and social stability are reproduced through replication of hierarchies and social expectations.
3   The young are exposed to a variety of skills, the extent to which they show aptitude in these directs them towards suitable employment and maintains the social division of labour.

Similarly, Parsons (1965) proposed that the classroom is a microcosm of society in which the young are prepared for their adult roles. They are introduced to social norms and values which are internalised in order that social equilibrium is maintained. Education therefore serves to integrate and to produce conformity. Further, it plays key economic roles in both transmitting technical skills and stratifying the potential workforce, institutionalising and justifying inequalities of reward.

Conflict theorists' responses to the same question are similar in some ways, but differ in tone and substance. They argue that the curriculum – in particular, according to Bowles and Gintis (1976), the hidden curriculum – serves to reinforce the status quo and engender an unquestioning acceptance of authority. Bowles and Gintis also put forward a theory of role allocation – further demonstrated in the research of Willis (1980) in relation to working-class boys and by Spender and Sarah (1980) in relation to women both as students and as teachers – that schools ensure that social inequality is reproduced through education. Far from the egalitarian model put forward by consensus theorists, conflict theorists argue that access to education is differentiated by ethnicity (Gillborn, 1990), gender (Spender and Adler, 1989), and social class (Ball, 2006) and that the social inequalities of access result in the continued social inequalities of outcomes. Thus, from this perspective, while there is an illusion of differential success and rewards based on merit and application, the reality is that education is managed so that those with power –

in many societies, white and financially powerful men – ensure that other white men are recruited from amongst their children to inherit that power, ensuring the self-perpetuation of the elite.

The organisation of education

Consensus and conflict theorists agree that the organisation of education reflects the organisation of society. The more complex the social structures and interrelationships, the more complex the organisation of those structures will appear to be. For consensus theorists this means that schools in modern industrial societies will have hierarchies which reflect other social hierarchies, some subjects will be deemed more important than others, and some personnel will be deemed more important, the relative worth in each case reflecting the worth which society places upon that subject or position. Through experiencing ranking in this way, students are prepared for the hierarchies in wider society and learn to accept the authority which goes with them (Davis and Moore, 1953).

This apparently increasing complexity is seen as an illusion by conflict theorists, who argue that the relationship between structure and authority is a constant – those with power do all that they can to retain it. Therefore the hierarchies in schools – whether of subjects or of personnel – simply reflect the ruling class imperative to justify inequality by making it an everyday occurrence, acting as part of what Althusser (1971) terms 'the Ideological State Apparatus' to control how we think, what we think, and what we think about.

This hierarchy of personnel is not only one of head teacher/principal, subject leaders, teachers in a variety of formats. It also refers to hierarchies between students, and between students and staff. A critic of what he perceived as the increasing domination of professionals in all spheres of life, Illich (1973) was less concerned with the indoctrination of learners into capitalist modes of behaviour than with teachers' exercise of power in managing the process and content of learning to suit their own needs and interests rather than those of their students. Freire (1978) shared this concern but primarily in relation to education and with more emphasis on education as a toll of oppression. From a more conventionally Marxist viewpoint, Bowles and Gintis (1976) indicated that teachers are also victims of oppression, reduced to 'Jug and Mug' rote teaching, where the teacher as expert pours her/his knowledge into the pupil as empty vessel; we can be sure that they were well aware of the more colloquial meaning of 'mug'.

The experience of education

As indicated in the overview to this chapter, some of the references above to the purposes and organisation of education could justifiably have been included in this subsection. After all, part of the experience of education is its organisation and every element relates to its purpose. Despite claims that education is a meritocracy (Young, 1961) – a term often now misused in education and wider discussion in this way to imply that everyone has an equal chance of success and therefore those who are the most successful are also the most talented – there is a wealth of sociological evidence to the contrary.

While largely adhering to a functionalist perspective, Merton (1968) identified latent as well as manifest functions – that there can be hidden and unintended as well as stated or intended consequences of structures. He also noted that not all outcomes are good or beneficial, describing these as dysfunctions. One of the latent dysfunctions he identified in streamed, set or otherwise stratified classrooms is the self-fulfilling prophecy, a concept further developed by the social psychologists Rosenthal and Jacobson (1968), and which extends Becker's (1963) work on

61

deviance. Although Merton was a structural theorist, many of those who have developed this concept have been more concerned with interaction and social relationships than with institutions.

Labelling theory states that those with power – for example, teachers – attach labels to what they deem to be acceptable/unacceptable, which could be behaviour or social category. Pupils are then allocated that label so that it becomes their 'dominant status' (Goffman, 1990). While it is possible to negotiate labels, such negotiation is often reduced to what Merton described as conformity or rebellion; conformists would accept their label, while rebels might (unintentionally?) exchange one negative label for another. Behaviour might be in regard to punctuality, presentation, language, or other social aspects which can be changed, even if the teacher does not recognise the change. Social categories such as ethnicity, gender, and social class are clearly much harder to change and therefore the label is more likely to be permanent. That is not to say that having different expectations of people on the basis of their behaviour or social category is justified, but that teachers do this, then treat their students according to the label. When the students who are given unchallenging work because they are perceived as lacking application fail to make progress, the teacher regards this as evidence that their perception was correct. Students who are excluded for disruptive behaviour might fail to understand the work covered in their enforced absence; when they return from exclusion and therefore fidget and distract their peers, the teacher's perception is that they are continuing to misbehave, that they have literally not learned their lesson. In both cases there has been a self-fulfilling prophecy.

The perception of many teachers that if they have taught the same lesson to all, then all have had the same opportunity to learn is further challenged by postmodernist analyses found in the work of Bourdieu and Passeron (2000) on what they term 'cultural capital'. Pupils from households with values such as respect for authority, conformity, deferred gratification, and diligence, who recognise and use particular speech patterns and who aspire to gaining particular (or any) qualifications, come to school with a distinct advantage over their peers. Such values might be considered middle class, but this concept can be equally applied to gendered or ethnically located social perceptions. Jackson and Marsden's (1970) much earlier study illustrated how the conflict between home/class values and school values can have a significant impact on learning and academic progress, and on familial and class relationships and allegiances. In turn, Giddens' (1978) description of structuration ascribes different value systems to different social classes. As Florio-Ruane (2001) puts it, schools operate a 'culturalectomy' in their assumption that all learning takes place without awareness or recognition of the varied cultural experiences of pupils and staff.

What students learn

Class and ethnicity inequalities of access to learning and learner status can be identified in the identification of language structures and codes developed by Labov (1969) and by Bernstein (1973). Labov demonstrated that the non-standard English of a pupil designated as having learning difficulties was highly complex and capable of dealing with abstract notions in a rational manner, but that it was educators' inability to deconstruct and understand such usage which resulted in the pupil's negative label. Using a totally different approach, Bernstein identified that teachers and middle-class pupils used what he called an elaborate code while working-class pupils' code was restricted. These indicated different ways of explaining and understanding so that teachers might not be aware of pupils' meanings, and vice versa. Despite their different approaches, both studies show that the language brought to and used in the classroom has a significant effect on what is learned and known to be learned.

As identified above, there is a surface agreement between consensus and conflict theorists that education is organised to serve the needs of society. However, for consensus theorist this means that the curriculum is structured so that pupils learn what society needs them to learn, while conflict theorists argue that the curricula – both overt and hidden – ensure that pupils learn what the exploiting class requires them to learn. While consensus theorists indicate the employability facilitated by literacy and numeracy, they do not ignore that skills such as understanding one's place in the social hierarchy are also learned in school.

A Marxist analysis is rather more complex. Mannheim (1991) argued that knowledge does not simply consist of a body of absolute truths but is created by social and economic relationships. It reflects the position in society of those who generate or receive that knowledge as well as the corresponding events and dominant ideas of specific historical periods. In other words, 'knowledge' does not exist in some separate sphere of truth but is the product of social, historical and economic circumstances. For Mannheim and other conflict theorists, 'ideology' constitutes the systems of thought – as well as the ideas and 'facts' which these produce – which obscure the reality of social conditions and which therefore serve to reinforce the status quo. Therefore, what schools teach as 'true' is one more aspect of the exploitation and proletarian false consciousness upon which capitalism depends.

Current and possible future interests

As societies change – whether as a result of political or economic influences, population migration and the resultant adjustments to mores, or simply time moving on – sociologists are interested to find out whether what they thought they knew at one time remains true at another, and the extent of and reasons for change/no change. In particular, access to education and the nature and effects of the hidden curriculum remain at the forefront of research, with new and wider foci. Among the more significant additional areas of interest are the professional competences of teachers within what is known as the standards agenda, education as a commodity, and an increasing awareness of international dimensions to all aspects of education; as ever, these research fields often overlap.

Access to education continues to relate to differential success, and measures of success, by social class, gender, and ethnicity. In addition, sociologists are becoming increasingly aware of and interested in adult education and lifelong learning, examining rates of participation and the life stories of those who participate (David, 2008). It is also recognised that higher education is not always available or perceived as appropriate for and by those seeking skills for employment, leading to considerable research and theorising about the purpose and efficacy of vocational training and qualifications.

There continues to be a focus on processes of role allocation, particularly the increasing emphasis given to qualifications which – for some – is creating an image of education as something to be bought and consumed; this is the commodification of education. Educational credentials are considered to have replaced the social stratification role formerly performed by family networks and resources, and by social background. Again, social variables such as class, ethnicity, and gender are scrutinised. Similarly, the debate on organising education by students' perceived ability levels also continues, examining whether comprehensive schooling in its various international forms has created equality of opportunity or whether it has inhibited the raising of attainment. One area of interest which brings together opportunity and commodification is discussion around the extent of, reasons for, and implications for themselves and for society, of those who either leave formal education without adequate qualifications or who fail to complete their schooling.

Education in non-Western societies has traditionally been measured against what is defined by Anglo-Saxon countries, and this largely continues to be the case in the context of global society (Kibera and Kimokoti, 2007). What is different is the increasing awareness of the distinctive voices of sociologists and other researchers and theorists from countries other than those in Europe and North America. Recent research has considered how education might assist the disadvantaged, and the effects of the spread of liberalisation and the development of globalisation on the purposes, quality, and regulation of, and access to, education in regional and global contexts. It is likely that future research will continue to reconsider current and established theories and interpretations of the role of education in everyday lives. Innovations will be scrutinised and new social relationships examined. There can be no doubt that, as research continues to be more multidisciplinary and society more complex, there will always be a need for the diverse insights provided by the sociologies of education.

Questions for further investigation

1   What are the benefits and limitations of looking at education as a social system rather than as a social experience?
2   Can education be understood in its own right, or must it be viewed in relation to other aspects of society?
3   What is the relationship between formal and informal education, and which has the greater influence?
4   To what extent do our social circumstances influence the education we experience?

Suggested further reading

Bourdieu, P. and Passeron, J-C. (2000) *Reproduction in Education, Society and Culture.* London: Sage. An intellectually challenging and densely argued text, the authors demonstrate the complexity of postmodern relationships and cultural commodities. Education is not seen as 'out there' or separate from the common experience, but part of the everyday as both cause and effect of social reproduction.

Mills, C.W. (1980) *The Sociological Imagination.* Middlesex: Penguin. This classic text goes beyond describing sociology to clarifying its potential for social analysis and to reinvigorate one's 'capacity for astonishment' (p. 14). The final chapter 'On Intellectual Craftsmanship' should be required reading for all aspiring social scientists.

Spender, D. and Sarah, E. (Eds.) (1980) *Learning to Lose: Sexism and Education.* London: The Women's Press. While this text is over 30 years old, it is less dated than the editors might have hoped it would be by now. Education is scrutinised from a clear and radically feminist perspective, simultaneously raising awareness that gender, age, class, sexuality, and ethnicity are not separate spheres of existence but are overlapping and interdependent experiences.

White, R. with Brockington, D. (1983) *Tales Out of School: Consumers' Views of British Education.* London: Routledge & Kegan Paul. Unlike many researchers into education, the authors explicitly invited and considered the views and insights of children who experience it. This text is an outstanding example of sensitive research methodology and highly significant responses.

References

Althusser, L. (1971) *Lenin and Philosophy and Other Essays*. New York, NY: Monthly Review Press.

Ball, S.J. (2006) *Education Policy and Social Class: the selected works of Stephen J. Ball*. London: Routledge.

Becker, H.S. (1963) *Outsiders: Studies in the Sociology of Deviance*. Glencoe: Free Press.

Bernstein, B. (1973) *Class, Codes and Control Vol. 1: Theoretical studies towards a sociology of language*. London: Paladin.

Bourdieu, P. and Passeron, J-C. (2000) *Reproduction in Education, Society and Culture*. London: Sage.

Bowles, S. and Gintis, H. (1976) *Schooling in Capitalist America*. London: Routledge & Kegan Paul.

David, M.E. (2008) 'Social inequalities, gender and lifelong learning: A feminist, sociological review of work, family and education', *International Journal of Sociology and Social Policy*, 28, 7/8, pp. 260–272.

Davis, K. and Moore, W. (1953) 'Some principles of stratification', *American Sociological Review*, 18, 4, pp. 394–397

Durkheim, E. (1956) *Education and Sociology*. Glencoe: Free Press.

Florio-Ruane, S. (2001) *Teacher Education and the Cultural Imagination: Autobiography, Conversation, and Narrative*. London: Lawrence Erlbaum.

Freire, P. (1978) *Pedagogy of the Oppressed*. Middlesex: Penguin.

Giddens, A. (1978) *The Class Structure of the Advanced Societies*. London: Hutchinson.

Gillborn, D. (1990) *Race, Ethnicity and Education: teaching and learning in multi-ethnic schools*. London: Unwin Hyman.

Goffman, E. (1990) *Stigma: Notes on the Management of Spoiled Identity*. Middlesex: Penguin.

Illich, I. (1973) *Deschooling Society*. Middlesex: Penguin.

Jackson, B. and Marsden, D. (1970) *Education and the Working Class*. Middlesex: Penguin.

Kibera, L.W. and Kimokoti, A.C. (2007) *Fundamentals of Sociology of Education: with reference to Africa*. Nairobi: Nairobi University Press.

Labov, W. (1969) 'The logic of Non-Standard English', in Keddie, N. (1978) (Ed.) *Tinker, Taylor . . . The Myth of Cultural Deprivation*. Middlesex: Penguin.

Mannheim, K. (1991) *Ideology and Utopia: an introduction to the sociology of knowledge*. London: Routledge.

Merton, R.K. (1968) *Social Theory and Social Structure*. Glencoe: Free Press.

Parsons, T. (1965) *Politics and Social Structure*. New York, NY: Free Press.

Rosenthal, R. and Jacobson, L. (1968) *Pygmalion in the Classroom*. New York, NY: Holt, Reinhart and Winston.

Spender, D. and Adler, S. (1989) *Invisible Women: the schooling scandal*. London: Women's Press.

Spender, D. and Sarah, E. (Eds.) (1980) *Learning to Lose: Sexism and Education*. London: The Women's Press.

Willis, P. (1980) *Learning to Labour: How working class kids get working class jobs*. Farnborough: Gower.

Young, M. (1961) *The Rise of the Meritocracy, 1870–2033: an essay on education and equality*. London: Thames and Hudson.

8

Philosophy of education

Alis Oancea
University of Oxford

Overview

This chapter will attempt to define what 'philosophy of education' is and means, as well as detailing the methods and scope of it, in conjunction with rationalising the purpose and reasons for philosophising for education, and putting forward a case for a philosophy which works with educational practice.

Introduction – what is philosophy of education?

Definitions

Somewhat ironically, most dictionary definitions of philosophy of education are circular. Philosophy of education is what philosophers of education do; or, in a slightly different sense, it is what philosophers do when they apply themselves to the complex field of education. A major problem of such definitions is that they clump together a wide range of activities and texts, some of which (despite being undertaken by people publicly or professionally recognised as philosophers) may not amount to much in terms of depth of educational inquiry. Another problem is that they exclude work by people not commonly (or mainly) identified as philosophers, but who may raise and explore philosophical issues in education in thoughtful and original ways.

Another set of definitions of philosophy of education describe it as a way of thinking, being, or acting. Dewey's (1916) famous definition of philosophy as 'the generalised theory of education' is based on a mix of the three, although with the emphasis firmly on thinking: philosophy is a form of thinking, originated in perplexity, and framing hypotheses to be tested in action. This does not imply that philosophising is necessarily a solitary activity. The social relations, in which philosophical activity is embedded, are often antagonistic; serious engagement in philosophising may be a matter of study and scholarship, but also one of embracing a particular way of being in the world, as well as one of becoming adept at crossing argumentative swords over bridges of tradition.

However, what differentiates 'philosophers' from other reflective scholars may be difficult to explicate solely in terms of attitudes, depth of thinking, or rigour of argumentation. The boundaries here are porous at best. So perhaps the least controversial way to define the territory of philosophy of education would still be in disciplinary terms. Philosophy of education is the disciplined philosophical study of problems in the field of education. 'Philosophical' here points to three things: first, that philosophical methods and ways of argumentation are used; second, that the questions asked and arguments proposed are related back to debates in different branches of philosophy; and third, that the problems raised may themselves be philosophical in nature. 'Disciplined' means both that the study is systematic or methodical and that it is subject to critical scrutiny in the particular disciplinary community of philosophy of education. This community has its own infrastructure of (in universities) chairs, societies, journals, funding programmes, networks, and conferences. It also is engaged in meta-level reflection about its own structure, context, and development, and about its relationships with mainstream philosophy and education research. Contributors to philosophy of education are accountable to that community, as well as to the wider community of education scholarship and practice.

Scope

Philosophy of education is an 'essentially contested' field with 'diffuse topography' (Phillips, 2008, p. 4). The problems explored in philosophy of education may be educational problems amenable to philosophical treatment (e.g. the achievement differential between boys and girls in particular subjects, levels, and environments), or philosophical problems of relevance to the field of education (e.g. the different views of human flourishing and of good social life underpinning discussions about what the aims of education should be). The particular issues of interest may change over time and across the contexts in which they are raised. Many of the examples used in this chapter will be drawn from Anglophone contexts, with particular reference to the UK context. The chapter will, however, also emphasise the historical rootedness of much Anglophone philosophy of education in international philosophical traditions, as well as the richness of contemporary exchanges across geographic and linguistic borders. There is still much more work to do in articulating and describing these complex connections.

Over the past two decades, in Anglophone contexts, issues explored by contributors to philosophy of education included:

- the nature, aims, and values of education (including issues of autonomy, self-determination, and well-being);
- the nature and possibility of learning and of teaching;
- the development of learners and of their mind;
- knowledge, discourses, and the curriculum (e.g. selection of what should be taught, assessment and evaluation, and cognition, but also issues of differentiation and control, the role of emotions and art in education, and different forms of education, including aesthetic, religious, physical, science, environmental, etc.);
- ethics and moral education;
- social and political aspects of educational institutions, learning environments, educative practices, and education reform (such as liberal and vocational education, the common school, democracy and citizenship, power, authority, parents' and children's rights, equality, diversity, inclusion, fairness and justice, caring, oppression, accountability, quality, and the role of education in social change);

67

■   communication, intersubjectivity and the role of language;

■   philosophical underpinnings of research methodologies, and philosophical disputes about education research and about the kinds of evidence that may inform policy and practice in education;

■   meta-philosophy (reflection on the sources and purposes of philosophy of education, on its relationships with other fields, and on its meta-narratives).

This snapshot of topics is incomplete, but still it provides an indication of the richness of the field, of its rootedness in long-standing philosophical traditions, and of its strong links with education research, practice, and policy.

Methods

There is very little explicit discussion in philosophy of education publications of the methods and processes through which they, and the arguments within, were constructed. Oancea and Bridges (2009) used selective data about the philosophy of education publications submitted to two successive UK Research Assessment Exercises (RAE) to gather information about how philosophers of education described their approach or 'methodology'. (The RAE is a peer review-based national exercise carried out in the UK every five to seven years to assess the research outputs, outcomes, and environment of higher education departments in all disciplines.) The greatest proportion of philosophers submitting their work to the latest two RAEs (2001 and 2008) identified their methods as 'analysis' (34 per cent in 2001), 'critique' (11 per cent), and 'review and synthesis' of literature and evidence (10 per cent). 'Applied philosophy' and philosophical 'argument' accumulated 7 per cent each; 'theorizing' and 'interpretation and reflection', 3 per cent each; and 'evaluation' and 'comparative philosophy', 1 per cent each. The proportions were similar in 2008.

A further 9 per cent of the total papers submitted to RAE 2001 combined one of the above 'philosophical' approaches with empirical work (including textual/documentary analysis, discourse analysis, case study, ethnography, action research, and mixed methods – in this order). Some 14 per cent described their work as 'cross-disciplinary' in approach. This category includes work that was described as philosophical, but was rooted in an approach drawn from, in order of frequency, history, policy studies and political theory, sociology and social theory, cultural and media studies, literary studies and linguistics, psychology and psychoanalysis, and hermeneutics and theology. The remaining 8 per cent of the papers described their main approach by reference to named authors or schools of thought, including post-structuralism, deconstruction, constructivism, gender theory and feminism, critical theory, and the work of A. MacIntyre, K. Popper, and L. Wittgenstein.

Why philosophise about education and why does it matter?

Many lament the recent state of philosophy of education as a discipline, particularly in the Anglophone contexts that experienced what is often described as a 'golden age', roughly overlapping with the 1960s–1970s, when the field was characterised by strong growth in infrastructure and by wide public recognition as one of the foundation disciplines of educational studies, and a central component of teacher training programmes. Once the external conditions – such as the ubiquity of philosophy in teacher training curricula across the country – were changed, the fear was there that philosophy of education as a field may wither away. Talk about philosophy of education since the 1970s has been in terms of loss and signs of revival. However, despite the golden age narrative, philosophy of education seems to be thriving these days, if the activity of philosophy societies in the UK and internationally, or the volume and quality of publications, are anything to go by. There is no doubt a serious danger that the waning of funding and the increased demands for performative accountability in universities may affect drastically the future of the discipline, in particular as an academic subject. But I would suggest that external conditions are only one factor among several that can contribute to the health and long-term prospects of the field. I would rate highly two other factors, which make the continuous contemporary development of the field seem less of a paradox. One is the perennial character of the sources of philosophy; the other is the ongoing contribution of philosophy and philosophers of education to disciplinary and interdisciplinary knowledge, to social and political developments, and to educational practice. Let us look at each of these factors in turn.

Sources of philosophising

Philosophising begins in source experiences. Thinking about the source experiences of philosophy of education may help explain its ongoing attraction to individual new students, practising teachers, and researchers, and the persistence of current interest in philosophy of education at disciplinary level. Like for all philosophy, in generic terms these source experiences may include wonder, doubt, anxiety, or alienation and suppression. Each major philosophical tradition, including those in philosophy of education, has in some way reflected on one or all such core experiences and explored views of human nature and existence that accounted for (or took into account) their generative power.

One motive to philosophise may be puzzlement and awe:

Wonder is the only beginning of philosophy.

(Plato, *Theaetetus*, 155d)

It is through wonder that men now begin and originally began to philosophize.

(Aristotle, *Metaphysics*, 982b)

The above quotes point to subjective perplexity (whether directed at trivia or at more worthy objects) in front of unexplained or contradictory things, which can be quenched with acquiring knowledge through philosophical investigation. But there is more to the ancient sense of *philosophical wonder* than informed perplexity; Plato himself speaks elsewhere of a kind of wonder that is a culmination, rather than merely a trigger, of philosophical investigation. Such wonder is reverential and accompanies, rather than being superseded by, knowledge, or the contemplation of essences – the essence of beauty (*Symposium*, 210e), or of the good (*Republic*).

These senses of wonder have been carried through philosophical thought to this day. On the one hand, wonder has been mistrusted, as a lower-order response to novelty: losing oneself in wonder was deemed detrimental to deep enquiry and scientific explanation. Wonder was seen as 'broken knowledge', to be displaced by proper knowledge (Bacon, *The Advancement of Learning*, I.3; also, Descartes). Much of the early 'educational thought' literature, which is often described as philosophy of education (including works on education by mainstream philosophers), exhibits this transient sense of wonder in front of the complexities of human nature and of social and individual human development ('the Child'). This kind of wonder ends in the search for more, truer, clearer, more accurate, more comprehensive, or deeper knowledge.

On the other hand, however, wonder has been described by philosophers as the experience which keeps science from lulling us into a false sense of certainty and justice. Rather than *ending* in successful enquiry, wonder sustains and challenges it. Heidegger spoke of ontological wonder (wonder before the Being of beings); Wittgenstein, of 'awakening' to wonder at the contact before language and reality; Levinas, of wonder (*étonnement*) as the traumatic 'sobering up' of the self to the Other. In all these cases, philosophy can no longer postulate science as superseding wonder, but has to come to terms with wonder's persistence as an often traumatic but enduring experience of mystery that can be a source, condition, and climax of philosophy.

Philosophising can also arise from *doubt*, in its many guises: from the suspended judgement of the ancient sceptics; to constructive methodical doubt that ultimately clears itself (Descartes); to dissatisfaction about the abundance of false problems generated by confusing uses of language (analytic philosophy); to beliefs unsettled through confrontation with a situation where expectations for action are disappointed (Peirce, Dewey); or to pervasive postmodern incredulity towards given presumptions and promises. Living with doubt can take radical shapes. Lyotard's famous 'definition' of postmodernism as 'incredulity towards metanarratives' (1984, p. xxiv) points to doubt as a persistent loss of faith, not something to be outgrown or replaced when a 'truer' account is constructed, but just that – 'an inability to believe [metanarratives] any longer even if we once could' (Burbules, in Siegel, 2009, p. 525).

In a pragmatic view, one 'doubts because he has a positive reason for it, and not on account of the Cartesian maxim' (Pierce, *The Fixation of Belief*, 5.265 – a view shared, among others, by Habermas). Unlike Cartesian or analytic doubt and confusion, which ultimately get cleared away through inquiry and analysis, justified pragmatic doubt persists. Beliefs that do not yield the expected consequences – such as the belief that the recent expansion of higher education in the UK would accelerate upwards social mobility among the most disadvantaged – are strong reasons to question the assumptions on which to build programmes of reform, such as those about the role of education in social change and the conditions within which that role may be realised. Pragmatic doubt arises in situations of ambiguity and controversy and it works as a stimulus for continued inquiry, debate, and action; 'to maintain the state of doubt and to carry on systematic and protracted inquiry – these are the essentials of thinking' (Dewey, 1971, p. 3).

Like wonder, doubt can border on terror and trauma (e.g. Cavell's discussion of scepticism as a recoiling impulse originated in terror about the thinness of language and the precariousness of human identity – 1979). These are *extreme experiences* that, alongside other, equally powerful ones (passion, anxiety, despair, nausea), may compel philosophers to struggle towards expressing the limits of the human condition. Philosophising may thus become an unavoidable expression of the dizzying consciousness of the contingency of one's existence and of the freedom and responsibility that come with it (Kierkegaard, Sartre) – not just living *with* extreme experiences, but living *as* them.

There is also a more political sense of alienation at play here. Social and political oppression and the domination of instrumental rationality form a 'disenchanted' (Weber) world, in which the philosophical experience of *suppression* may be a more powerful driver than wonder (Marx). Education is a site where domination and suppression, and the struggle to enact change, may take particularly poignant expressions. Weber's analysis of rationality and domination, Marxist and neo-Marxist revolutionary critiques, critical theorists' emancipatory principles, and feminist philosophy have all drawn on such source experiences to generate strong programmes of inquiry in the field of philosophy of education.

Purposes and contributions of philosophy of education

Why is philosophy of education important? The following text captures well a great part of the range of purposes to which philosophers of education have over the years declared commitment:

> To be reflective about our practice, to avoid inconsistencies in our beliefs, to be aware of what we are committed to as a consequence of holding the principles we claim to hold, and to expand our horizon of possibilities by considering alternative goals or ideals that might never have occurred to us if it were not for the work of some philosopher of education.
>
> (Phillips, 2010, p. 18)

I will use several examples to illustrate this judgement.

Philosophers of education have traditionally aimed to *analyse and clarify* the meanings of words, concepts, conceptual schemes, and propositions, and their logical implications. Analytic philosophy of education flourished in the 1960–1970s – for example, the work of Israel Scheffler, in the North American context; and that of Richard Peters and Paul Hirst, in the UK context – and has been continued and developed to this day; for example, through the work of John White, Patricia White, Terence McLaughlin, Graham Haydon, Michael Hand, Andrew Davis, and Christopher Winch, again in the UK context. Analytic philosophers of education have seen the construction of analysis, critique, and argument as a powerful tool in settling disputes based on conceptual confusion, but also as groundwork or conceptual framing for empirical research. In their efforts to act as 'consultants to researchers proper' they deliberately resisted the temptation to create theory (Wilson, 1998, p. 31), partly because they saw philosophy as having a major 'therapeutic' role in 'free[ing] one's thinking from the mental cramps which . . . erroneous theories have inflicted on it' (White, in Heyting *et al.*, 2001, p. 14). It was precisely this resistance that gave analytic philosophy much of its strength as a methodology, but also some of its limitations as a programme of inquiry. Early analytic philosophy was accused of lacking practical relevance and privileging traditional values and particular powerful discourses. It is important, however, to note that in the more recent decades analytic philosophy has engaged with these objections and has developed in ways that retain the careful attention to rigour and precision in the argument, whilst drawing on sources from the wider traditions of philosophical writing to contribute to 'the understanding of philosophically interesting concepts and their interrelationships' (White, ibid., p. 16).

Many pragmatists and contemporary neo-pragmatists shared with analytic philosophy the concern for clear and distinct ideas and arguments, and for the ways in which they can be methodically sought and constructed, while directing their efforts towards testing the consequences for action of the concepts and beliefs with which they engaged. With a view to action, philosophy and philosophical thinking may permeate research and practice (including policy) in education not only by developing critical analysis and argument, as described above, but also in ways that are possibly more organically connected to the worlds of practice and practitioners (be they educators, researchers, or policy-makers). As argued elsewhere (Oancea and Bridges, 2009), they may contribute to *nurturing democratic conversation* about education – including responsible critique, public reasoning and dialogue, engagement with multiple forms of evidence, and the development of humanity-enhancing relations. In addition, philosophy may *support practical deliberation* at all levels and on all aspects of educational practice, including support for practitioners in their efforts to 'expose and examine the taken-for-granted presuppositions implicit in their practice in order that they may reflectively reconstruct their understanding of their practice and of how its internal good may, in their own practical situation, be more appropriately pursued' (Carr, 2004, p. 62). For some, this role is a *phronetic* rather than technical one, to be fulfilled by 'practical' rather than 'theoretical' philosophy; but recent neo-Aristotelian work in the philosophy of education has been putting forward arguments for a synergy, rather than opposition, of 'practice' (*praxis and poiesis*) and 'theory' (see Oancea and Bridges, 2009, for fuller elaboration of the points summarised in this paragraph).

Philosophers of education may also engage in more *constructive work*; for example, by using empirical data and other sources, such as literature, to make substantive points, by introducing new language and asking new questions with the specific purpose of stimulating deeper reflection on substantive educational problems (Noddings, 2007, p. xiv), or by engaging in theory creation and refinement. Such work is clearly facilitated by collaborations with researchers in the full range of sub-fields of education and in other disciplines. In some cases, it has already become difficult to identify a particular individual as a 'philosopher of education' or as an 'empirical researcher' (unless one goes only by formal criteria such as initial degrees and job titles). The boundaries between the two have always been permeable, but there seems to be more mutual acceptance in the current context, both of the contribution that a philosopher is likely to make to an empirical research project and of the importance of such engagement for philosophy of education itself.

Finally, as 'muckrakers of the presumptions of thought' (Oksenberg-Rorty, 2008, p. 14), philosophers of education are engaged in asking difficult questions, challenging beliefs and assumptions, and subjecting received views to *critical scrutiny*. Exposing presumptions of thought to the light of critique is, again, an aim to which philosophers of many traditions would subscribe, although in different ways, from contemporary analytic philosophers and neo-pragmatists, to philosophers in the critical tradition, and to those embracing postmodern attitudes. The point of philosophising about education, from a critical perspective, is 'to call into question any views taken for granted' (Biesta, in Heyting *et al.*, 2001, p. 10) by researchers, practitioners, policy-makers and philosophers alike, as well as any received practices, power relations, institutions, and narratives that are constitutive of educational environments and systems. The different traditions do, however, differ strongly in how effective (and in what ways) they want critique to be. Analytic philosophy aspires to settle disputes by clearing confusion. Critical theory aspires to effect political and practical change and is imbued with emancipatory aims for fairer, better education, with all, and for each of all. By contrast, as in the case of some writing with a postmodern outlook, critical dialogue, informed by awareness of difference, contingency, transience, and power, may itself become the very aim of philosophising.

What seems to be in store for the future of philosophy of education?

Any integrative account of philosophy of education is inevitably tentative. Attempting to speculate on the future of the discipline, given its diffuse topography, is even more difficult. Thus the commentary below is a very personal account of some signposts that seem to me to indicate the current direction of travel in the discipline.

First, I believe that the diversity of approaches and traditions, including cross-disciplinary linkages, is likely to be even more strongly recognised and valued. Philosophy of education has become a pluralised field where the academic monopoly of any one particular tradition is possibly less likely to take hold now than ever before. Once-dissident voices are now situated at the core of disciplinary infrastructures. Once-powerful traditions find themselves working alongside their earlier opponents and needing to legitimise themselves for future generations of philosophers, researchers, and practitioners. To use Oakeshott's metaphor, the 'conversation' of philosophy of education has not only been transformative, but has also been transformed and is transformable yet.

Second, there seems to be increasing acceptance of a more modest, though quietly confident, attitude relative to the purposes and possibilities of philosophy in education. After decades of neo-Marxist, feminist, and postmodernist critique, philosophy of education as a field has been deconstructed and destabilised, and then meshed together again in ways that are perhaps more than ever wary of absolute certainty, authority, and disciplinary monopoly. As a consequence, many philosophers of education now describe themselves as striving to ask more challenging questions *with*, rather than *for*, or *on behalf of*, others. Philosophers of education hold themselves answerable to their own professional community, rooted in philosophical traditions, but also to other practitioners and researchers in education – valid and legitimate contributions and criticisms are expected and acceptable from all these groups.

Third, it seems likely that the future may bring more collaborative work with other relevant groups – including education researchers, other philosophers, scholars in other disciplines, but also teachers and students, civil servants, government researchers, and politicians. The blurring of the philosophical/empirical divide among projects of enquiry looks set to continue. One implication of this development may be that growing attention will be given to issues in the philosophy of education research. Judging from the distribution of topics covered in philosophy of education publications over the past decade in a wide range of countries, there are signs that this is already happening.

Fourth, and perhaps in answer to external pressures (such as the demands for performative accountability in universities, the tighter definition of 'research' in the public policy space, now explicitly including work in the arts and the humanities, and the increasingly detailed specification of research impact), it is likely that philosophers of education and their networks and professional associations are likely to continue paying increasing attention to the disciplinary infrastructure for their work. This infrastructure includes chairs and job titles, teaching courses, funding for study and inquiry, the awarding of higher degrees, publication outlets, associations, events, and so forth. More formalised programmes, networks, and relationships with other parts of the public domain are to be expected.

And fifth, philosophy of education seems to be moving, like virtually all disciplines, towards increased internationalisation (which does not have to mean convergence) of the debates about its substantive topics, language, and methodological approaches, and of its disciplinary dynamics. There already is an abundance of international and regional associations in the philosophy of education, whilst formerly national ones are becoming increasingly international. Multilingual publications and conferences are no longer a rarity. International institutional exchanges and collaborations are becoming common; philosophers of education themselves are becoming international professionals, moving easily from one national context to another.

Conclusion

There is still an important place for over-flowing, stand-alone philosophy bookcases in education libraries; but it is also possible that the field is becoming more fluid, open, and in many ways closer to educational practice. If this account is mistaken, wiser readers will set it right, and the new generation of philosophers of education will show it to be wrong.

Questions for further investigation

1 How can philosophy of education contribute to empirical educational research?
2 Is philosophy of education important for the education of teachers? In what ways?
3 What does philosophy of education have to offer to educational policy?
4 How is philosophy of education currently developing in non-Anglophone contexts?
5 What can be learned from international collaborations in philosophy of education?

Suggested further reading

Bailey, R., Barrow, R., Carr, D. and McCarty, C. (2010) (Eds.) *The Sage Handbook of Philosophy of Education*. London: Sage. Wide-ranging overview of the field; the chapter by D.C. Phillips ('What is philosophy of education?' pp. 3–19) outlines the aims and scope of philosophy of education.

Carr, W. (Ed.) (2005) *The Routledge/Falmer Reader in Philosophy of Education*. London: Routledge. Useful map of substantive issues in education addressed by contemporary philosophers of education.

Heyting, F., Lenzen, D. and White, J. (Eds.) (2001) *Methods in Philosophy of Education*. New York, NY: Routledge. One of the very few publications around that engages directly with how philosophers of education approach their disciplined enquiry.

Noddings, N. (2007) *Philosophy of Education* (2nd Ed.). Boulder, CO: Westview. Very accessible, informative and engaging introduction to the field. Start here!

Pring, R. (2004) *Philosophy of Educational Research* (2nd Ed.). London: Continuum. Highly readable introduction to the major problems in the philosophy of education research.

References

Carr, W. (2004) 'Philosophy and education', *Journal of Philosophy of Education*, *38*, 1, pp. 55–73.

Dewey, J. (1971) *How We Think*. Buffalo, NY: Prometheus Books.

Dewey, J. (1916) *Democracy and Education: An introduction to the philosophy of education*. New York, NY: Macmillan.

Heyting, F., Lenzen, D. and White, J. (Eds.) (2001) *Methods in Philosophy of Education*. New York, NY: Routledge.

Lyotard, J.-F. (1984) *The Postmodern Condition: A report on knowledge* (trans. G. Bennington and B. Massumi). Minneapolis, MN: University of Minnesota Press.

Noddings, N. (2007) *Philosophy of Education* (2nd Ed.). Boulder, CO: Westview.

Oancea, A. and Bridges, D. (2009) 'Philosophy of education – its contribution and status since 1988', *Oxford Review of Education*, *35*, 5, pp. 553–568.

Oksenberg-Rorty, A. (2008) 'The dramatic sources of philosophy', *Philosophy and Literature*, *32*, 1, pp. 11–30.

Phillips, D.C. (2008) 'Philosophy of education', *Stanford Encyclopedia of Philosophy*. Available at: http://plato.stanford.edu/entries/education-philosophy.

Phillips, D.C. (2010) 'What is philosophy of education?', in Bailey, R., Barrow, R., Carr, D. and McCarty, C. (Eds.) *The Sage Handbook of Philosophy of Education*. London: Sage, pp. 3–19.

Siegel, H. (ed.) *The Oxford Handbook of Philosophy of Education*. Oxford: Oxford University Press.

Wilson, J. (1998) 'Philosophy and educational research: a reply to David Bridges *et al.*', *Cambridge Journal of Education*, *28*, 3, pp. 129–133.

9

Educational psychology

Richard Farnan
Harrogate Grammar School

Overview

The following chapter will introduce the use of psychology within education. The field of educational psychology is vast and comprises many subsections, theories and contradictions. The chapter will introduce the main theories within educational psychology and will illustrate ways in which they seek to explain behavioural and cognitive development in children. These ideas will then be explored with reference to their use in education, and in particular the relationship between educational psychology and effective classroom practice. Finally, possible new directions of educational psychology will be explored.

Introduction

Educational psychology has risen to prominence rapidly over the past century and now plays an important role in the education of children of all ages. It can be defined as 'the application of psychology and psychological methods to the study of development, learning, motivation, instruction, assessment and the related issues that influence the interaction of teaching and learning' (Elliott, 2000). It is a topic which spans 'human development, individual differences, measurement [and] learning' (Glover and Ronning, 1987). Psychology and education are irretrievably linked as the study of the brain will always be married to how the mind develops and is educated. The close connections between psychology and education can be evidenced in the written format at least as far back as the eighteenth-century thought of Swiss educator Johann Pestalozzi's theories of educational development. Pestalozzi's ideas were underpinned by 'love, work and social interaction' (de Guimps, 2008) and the basis that children's 'innate faculties should be developed in accordance with nature' (Pound, 2005). A further early link between the study of the brain and intelligence came through the pseudo-science of phrenology. German physician and anatomist Franz Josef Gall (1758–1828) proved that the brain was split into two sections, interconnected by commissures to opposing sides of the spinal cord. Amongst his sound biological findings he made the erroneous link between intelligence with the shapes and sizes of people's heads (Finger, 1994), reminding us that connections between psychology and education are not always unproblematic.

The idea of separate faculties for separate categories of intelligence is something which has been heavily investigated within education in recent years. Individual learning styles, such as the VAK (visual, auditory and kinaesthetic) model, have been suggested as having a role to play in education, although their application has been critiqued through the suggestion that over rigidity is prohibitive as it can allow for pupils to refuse to try to explore other methods of learning. Work by Gardner (1993) suggested that there are multiple facets of intelligence (linguistic, logic–mathematical, musical, spatial, bodily kinaesthetic, naturalist, interpersonal and intrapersonal), supporting a multi-modal method of understanding pupil intelligence in a way which can inform the planning of lessons. This is something exemplified by Dr Jonathon Sharples from York University (2009), who emphasises the importance on learning of strengthening neural pathways through a rich tapestry of different activities designed to accommodate all intelligence strengths.

Theories of development: cognitive, behaviourist and psychoanalytical

The most commonly referenced theories regarding intellectual development are based around a cognitive view of psychology, the branch of psychology which concerns itself with how people think, perceive and remember. Jean Piaget used the idea of different mental processes to establish a set of developmental stages through which we all move at approximately the same ages as we mature intellectually. Previous to this, the idea had been that the child's mind was the same as the adult's, only smaller and thus less effective at carrying out multiple tasks. Binet and Piaget's work suggested that the intelligence of a child 'is not simply a miniature replica of the adult's, but something that grows and develops through a series of stages that originally bear little obvious similarity to the finished result' (Fancher, 1979). Piaget's stages of cognitive development are shown in Table 9.1

Piaget's sequential stages of mental progression have been broadly incorporated into the way education and curricula are structured in a number of nations. The National Curriculum in England provides an illustrative prime of this framework. Looking at how the physics topic 'Forces and Motion' is broken down in the National Curriculum, at Key Stage 1 (children aged 5–7, at the end of Piaget's pre-operational stage), pupils are taught: *'pushes and pulls'*, *'how to recognise changes in speed and direction'* and to *'describe the movement of familiar things'* (Weblink 1 – The National Curriculum). The topics shown above are very basic, dealing with concrete objects the child can see and act upon themselves, in control of their own 'pulls' and 'pushes'. Describing the movement of familiar things, for example, can allow the child to use examples from their life and marries with Piaget's view of the child being an experimenter, a valuable skill well within their grasp. The investigative methods also prescribed in the curriculum at this Key Stage also do not overstretch the child, simply playing on existing schemata, such as *'explore, using the senses of sight, hearing, smell, touch and taste as appropriate'*, allowing the child to assimilate and accommodate new schemata. Moving on to Key Stage 3 (ages 12–16, the formal operational stage) the topic includes; *'how the forces acting on a falling object change with velocity'*, *'why falling objects may reach a terminal velocity'* and *'the quantitative relationship between force, mass and acceleration'* (Weblink 2 – The National Curriculum). These abstract concepts are only understood by

Table 9.1 Piaget's stages of cognitive development

Stage	Age	Sophistication of thought
Sensorimotor Stage	0 to 2 years	Infant only knows the world via its immediate senses and the actions it performs. The infant cannot distinguish between itself and its environment.
Pre-operational Stage	2 to 7 years	Still dominated by external world, can only focus on one aspect of an object or situation at one time and lacks the mental sophistication necessary to carry out logical operations on the world.
Concrete Operational Stage	7 to 11 years	Can carry out mental operations on the world and can de-centrate (can account for more than one aspect of an object or situation at the same time). Mental operations need a physical aid, however, hence being named the *concrete* operational stage.
Formal Operational Stage	11+	Ideas can be manipulated in the head without the aid of physical/concrete examples, problems are approached using a systematic and organised method and novel hypothetical and abstract concepts can be understood.

children in the formal operational stage, as they are physically and mentally equipped to be able to resolve the disequilibrium provided by new situations not fitting in with their already existing schemata.

Piaget's is not the only cognitive theory of intellectual development with important application within education. Both Jerome Bruner (1915–present) and Lev Vygotsky (1896–1934) developed cognitive theories which agreed in part with Piaget's views. Where they differed somewhat was their incorporation of social factors in cognitive development. Bruner's theory of cognitive development was focused more on social factors necessary for learning, with an extra emphasis on the role of language and how it is intrinsically linked with mental processes. Vygotsky's theory similarly developed the idea that cognitive development was a tiered process and that social interaction and language were major influences on the rate of intellectual development, suggesting we 'become ourselves through others' (Vygotsky, 1993). The gradual grasp of language allows the child to internalise their thoughts and, as such, the child can start to compute higher order mental processes. Vygotsky suggested a 'zone of proximal development' (ZPD from here on) whereby the child's potential intellectual ability is accelerated when placed in proximity of a more expert person.

Bruner and Vygotsky both advocated the link between language acquisition and intellectual development. This view was shared by Italian teacher Loris Malaguzzi (1920–1994), who believed in a strong focus on children acquiring different sort of 'languages' (i.e. a child may observe a cat then draw the cat, move like a cat and then discuss the cat's actions) in an environment where the education is a shared experience between the child and not just the teacher, but the whole community (Hall *et al.*, 2010). Malaguzzi set up early years schools in Reggio Emilia, in Northern Italy, using these ideas and the schools were extremely successful in promoting development both intellectually and socially. The success of such schools are said to have influenced Bruner himself, as well as the famed cognitive psychologist Howard Gardner (1943–present), who has set up a similar project in conjunction with Harvard University in the United States (Guidici *et al.*, 2001).

Language acquisition is something which does not reach a peak as the child enters the final stages of mental development. The ability to reach higher levels of literacy allows 'new worlds to be opened in [their] mind and imagination' (Bettelheim and Zelan, 1981). Working within the framework of Vygotsky's ZPD, the teacher is the 'facilitator' for language development and, as such, mental development. The importance of literacy in education is highlighted by Postman and Weingartner (1971) as:

If you do not know the meanings of history words or astronomy words you do not know history or astronomy. This means, of course, that every teacher is a language teacher: teachers, quite literally, have little else to teach, but a way of talking and therefore seeing the world.

The importance of a strong link between language and higher order mental operations (something which demonstrates reaching the formal operational stage in Piaget's staged theory of cognitive development) is again stressed by Haas Dyson (1993), who views literacy learners as 'social negotiators'. Another higher order operation, according to Piaget, is the ability to carry out reasoning with regard to abstract concepts and mental manipulations. Studies by Byrne *et al.* (1994) have led him to claim that 'difficulty with language causes difficulty with reasoning'. A more recent study found that an increase in literacy levels, driven by a 'key words strategy', led to a significant increase in attainment levels within Science (Farnan, 2010).

A further example of the importance of the ZPD can be illustrated through the early years strategy implemented initially in the United States by Dr David Weikart called 'The High/Scope Approach'. This approach centres around the child being an 'active learner' and making sure the '*adults and children share control*' (Holt, 2007), focusing on support of inquisitiveness and a problem-solving approach to social conflict (Hohnmann and Weikart, 1995). The scheme has been highly successful; its graduates are shown to have higher earnings, increased levels of employment and fewer crimes than others not in the scheme, and is now used in more than 20 countries including the UK, Mexico, the Netherlands, Korea and South Africa. The implementation of supported 'play' time has been accredited with making a contribution to the development of problem-solving, creativity, communication and developing understanding of social rules (Bruce, 2001), something linked not only with cognitive theories but also underlined by current work in developmental psychology and also neuroscience (Jenkinson, 2001).

Theories of cognitive development are the most readily linked to educational psychology. Yet there are also a selection of different approaches which can relate to teaching and learning. The behaviourist approach, most commonly associated with John Watson (1878–1958) and Burrhus Skinner (1904–1990), offers a simplified approach to learning and mind development through classical conditioning (of which Pavlov's experiment with salivating dogs is an example), focusing on rewards and punishments. This learning theory, despite being simple, has shown successes when applied to teaching children with special educational needs and to behaviour management (Wertsch, 1991). The punishment must be chosen carefully, however, be it introducing something to the child (such as running laps or extra homework) or the removal of something from them (privileges such as play-time or access to a TV in free periods). A week-long suspension may be considered a tough punishment by one pupil yet considered a week's holiday by another. Similarly with the use of behaviourist strategies within effective teaching and learning, it is important that when praise and rewards are used as part of an outcome-led assessment that the child does not simply use the work as a tool to get the reward, as when the rewards stop so will the work and, thus, the understanding (Kohn, 1993). Behaviourist strategies will only become an effective, and permanent, cause of intrinsic motivation and learning when the rewards are complemented with information about their growing mastery of a subject or when praise of good work leads to an increase in confidence and subsequent enjoyment of a task, which is most common in academically weaker pupils and those with special educational needs. There are several theories which can be applied to educational and emotional development, as shown above. Cognitive development theories are the ones most commonly referenced in educational psychology, but they have their limitations, which will be discussed later.

Understanding and managing behaviour

One of the most important attributes in a teacher is their ability to manage a classroom and develop a safe and successful learning environment. This can be aided by using educational psychology to learn more about the motivation and behaviour of pupils, their causes, as well as strategies to improve these. The main focus here will be the strategies which can be used to create a positive learning environment which stem directly from educational psychology and provide a brief case study into its practical application within classrooms.

First, it is important to establish rules and procedures within the classroom. Weinstein and Mignano (1997) suggest rules and procedures should cover the following, at minimum:

- *Administrative routines* – e.g. taking attendance;
- *Student movement* – e.g. entries and exits;
- *Housekeeping* – e.g. watering plants or storing personal items;
- *Routines for accomplishing lessons* – e.g. how to collect assignments;
- *Interactions between teacher and student* – e.g. how to get the teacher's attention;
- *Talk among students* – e.g. giving help or socialising.

Evidence shows that it is important to choose rules carefully. For instance, a rule forbidding pupils from helping each other with work may prevent the teaching pupil from reinforcing his own knowledge and learning more as they teach. A 'No erasing writing mistakes' may make students focus more on preventing mistakes than on effective communication (Burden, 1995). It is also important that the rules are explained with reference to why they are in place, as put by Weinstein (1999):

> Teaching children that something is wrong because there is a rule against it is not the same as teaching them that there is a rule against it because it is wrong, and helping them to understand why this is so.

Culturally, classroom behaviour and behaviour management strategies vary drastically. There are no hard and fast rules to good behaviour management. There are cross-cultural shifts in behaviour management, from the more Western 'classroom rules' approach to the Japanese approach, which states that success 'does not depend on many rules, but on a sense of trust and interdependency between the classroom teacher and his or her students and among the students' (Shimahara and Sakai, 1995).

One way to control behaviour problems, 'is to prevent them in the first place' (Woolfolk, 2001). A classic study by Kounin (1970) showed that both teachers with good working environments and those with poorly controlled classrooms had the same methods of handling behaviour, yet the better classrooms were as a result of the teacher being able to prevent problems more effectively. Kounin (and more recently confirmed by Evertson, 1988) went on to suggest four key areas in prevention of poor behaviour:

1   *Withitness* – communicating to students that you are aware of everything that is happening in the classroom.
2   *Overlapping* – keeping track of and supervising several activities at a time.
3   *Group focusing* – keeping as many students as possible involved in appropriate class activities and avoiding narrowing in on just one or two students.
4   *Movement management* – keeping lessons and the group moving at an appropriate, and flexible, pace, with smooth transitions and variety.

The importance lies in making sure the pupils are engaged and stimulated in the lesson and subject content, meaning that they are on task. Research has shown that, as teacher supervision increases, students' engagement time also increases. One study showed that when pupils are working under teacher supervision they are on task 97 per cent on the time, compared to 57 per cent of time on task when working without supervision (Frick, 1990). When children are on task, they are not being disruptive or being badly behaved. However, engagement alone does not ensure good learning is occurring, as pupils may be struggling with the work or implementing the wrong learning strategies for the task. The pupil must be provided with worthwhile, appropriate learning activities. Research by Weinstein and Mignano (1997) showed that of the 1,000 hours of mandated instruction per child, they will only be engaged in worthwhile tasks for 300–400 hours. Pupils will only learn when they are thinking about and practising their new knowledge, it is up to the teacher to ensure that the allocated time is maximised to encourage greater engaged academic learning time.

Inclusion

The study of inclusive education is extremely relevant to education, as good teaching requires a high proportion of time differentiating and personalising work for all children and teaching according to each child's needs. Inclusive education is a broad construct, and encapsulates a vast range of pupil needs, as well as pupils with accentuated creativity, giftedness and talent. A text on learning disabilities by Hallahan, Kauffman and Lloyd (2000) lists several definitions of learning difficulties, with The National Joint Committee on Learning Disabilities defining a learning disability as:

> a general term that refers to a heterogeneous group of disorders manifested by significant difficulties in the acquisition and use of listening, speaking, reading, writing, reasoning or mathematical difficulties.

The term 'learning disability' covers a large amount of disorders, from common problems such as dyslexia and dyspraxia to behavioural and emotional disorders. It is not important here to detail each type of problem. What is important is detailing how educational psychology can be used to assist and enable pupils to access and engage with learning. A school and teacher's job is to ensure that their teaching caters for all. Inclusive education sets about 'rejecting exclusion and encouraging participation for all'. Here, early identification is incredibly important. Reading, writing and speech difficulties should be noted as early as possible. As well as this it is important to take note of behavioural problems such as inattention, impulse control and hyperactivity as indicators for behavioural disorders, such as ADHD. One common problem resulting in the lack of identification occurs through 'learned helplessness' where pupils with learning disabilities may come to believe that they cannot control or improve their own learning (Seligman, 1975). Early identification is essential and can then allow the child's needs to be taken into account when tailoring their education to suit their needs.

In England (and Wales), inclusive education is a high status field and has been promoted through legislation. Before 2001 the law required that all state-educated children should attend mainstream schools, provided three conditions were met:

1   The child must receive the special provision that he or she requires.
2   The child's placement must be compatible with the 'efficient education' of other children in the same school.
3   The child's placement must be compatible with efficient use of available resources.

With the 2001 Special Educational Needs and Disability Act, however, came notable reform. Instead, and in addition to a range of other measures, a child with special educational needs must now be educated in mainstream school unless this would be incompatible with the wishes of the child's parents or the provision of efficient education of other children. We should remember, however, that inclusive education is not an uncontentious field, and it is generally accepted that a fine balance must be struck between competing needs and tensions, something noted in the questioning of Norwich (2008):

> When does treating people differently emphasize their differences and stigmatise or hinder them on that basis? And when does treating people the same become insensitive to their difference and likely to stigmatise or hinder them on that basis?

It is important that pupils with a special educational need are allowed access to the opportunities that a mainstream school provides, without being to the detriment of their education or social well-being. Strategies must be in place to enable the child with special educational needs to be able to function well in a mainstream school. Examples of these include individual support, differentiated lesson resources, regular meetings and assessments and the production of individual education plans (IEPs).

Differentiation for more able pupils is something much less contentious but something equally important not to ignore. Pupils falling within this category also have special educational needs and face may problems such as boredom, frustration and becoming impatient with friends, parents and even teachers, with problems being more prevalent in those within the highest range of academic ability (Robinsin and Clinkenbeard, 1998). They also need differentiated work so as to reach their full potential. Gifted students 'tend to learn more when they work in groups with other high ability peers' (Fuchs et al., 1998). This has been sought by way of several educational practices, either by streaming classes by ability (best done when in larger schools so that the most gifted students are around their peers) or by using acceleration techniques to move children up year groups, either a full year change or just for several specialist subjects ('a logistical nightmare' (Eyre, 1997)). All of these methods of acceleration have their drawbacks, however, especially acceleration by year group as it can isolate the gifted child when amongst pupils of the same advanced intellect but of a differing social maturation. It is the schools' and teachers' jobs to ensure that there is enough stimulation and encouragement in the child's specific educational programme to ensure the child makes the very most of their giftedness.

Looking towards the future

Educational psychology is moving at an incredibly fast pace, yet to a large extent the ideas in place remain located within the theoretical ideas of cognitive psychologists over half a century ago. The work of Piaget and Vygotsky require more scrutiny, despite the theoretical import-ance of the work. Demand characteristics were evident in Piaget's methodologies, ignoring the child's social understanding of the test, as well as neglecting the importance of cognitive factors accounting for individual differences in development. Modifications to the theories are common and will continue to be made. There are currently a number of important develop-ments and particular directions for educational psychology, of which three seem to me to be the most pertinent.

First, technological advancements, most notably within the field of neuroscience, now mean that the brain can be analysed in even more detail and mapping of brain function with activities can lend us even more knowledge regarding how the brain works and evolves through education. Neuroscience studies have already shown us how our brain is used for memory. Further investigation into aspects of memory, such as long-term potentiation (increasing the responsiveness of a neuron and the potential for firing over days or weeks, thus increasing memory) show clear links to how neuropsychology can provide possible methods of improving memory and recall within education (Gleitman *et al.*, 1999).

Second, the role of educational psychologists and their links with schools, and teachers in particular, is constantly changing. The importance of educational psychology is undoubted, but it is unclear as to how this is best transported into the classroom itself. The educational systems' links with educational psychology can be particularly fragmented: educational psychologists in the United Kingdom, for example, are trained by universities, then employed by governments and local education authorities, who then allocate budgets to schools, who then apply for educational psychologists' support. The psychologist can only work effectively when they have a knowledge of the school and the pupils, which takes time they may not be afforded. Some educational psychology is now taught within teacher preparation courses, but whether that is enough or not to be fruitful unaided by educational psychologists is not clear. The increasing emphasis on diagnosing children (and all the bureaucracy that goes with it) means that educational psychologists are prevented 'from getting out and applying psychology in ways that they believe would have more impact upon individual pupils, their teachers, school managers and policy-makers in both local and central government' (Lyons, 1999), with Poulou (2005) going further by arguing that 'through a productive dialogue between educational psychology and education, educational psychology provides the knowledge defined by its field to be utilised by teachers, whereas at the same time, teachers gain a wider reconceptualisation of their practice'.

A third area of further interest is the way in which the educational psychology profession's impact can be measured and evaluated, Mackay (2002) arguing 'there must still be fundamental re-examination of the position and role of the profession'. Can educational psychologists be doing and achieving more? Somewhat hamstrung by the emphasis on diagnosing and working within special educational needs, are there enough educational psychologists to ensure that 'research that educational psychologists are uniquely qualified to carry out' (Mackay, 2002) is being conducted out and filtered into the classroom? The importance of continued research into educational psychology is highlighted by a survey that showed 98 per cent of headteachers believed research to be 'important' or 'very important', that their top research priorities were in areas at the heart of educational psychology, and that they wanted research as part of the core service delivery to their schools (Mackay, 1997). Yet educational psychology is not an area of psychology which is thriving, registered clinical psychologists outnumbering educational psychologists three to one in 2000, despite being equal in number in 1970. It is clear that educational psychology has a strong future, whichever direction it evolves to take. Mackay (2002) states the profession's capabilities succinctly:

> The influence the profession could have on society is unlimited – higher achievement levels, lower levels of disruptiveness in schools, lower incidence of crime, a more skilled workforce, a stronger economy.

Questions for further investigation

1   What stage of cognitive development is most applicable to your age range? Can Piaget's and Vygotsky's theories be used to enhance your teaching in your subject?
2   Thinking about your personal career development, are there any aspects of educational psychology which you need to become more familiar with in order to enhance your classroom management?
3   How can you improve literacy in your classroom? What strategies can be used to ensure that literacy problems are not a roadblock to cognitive development and how important is a subject-specific vocabulary within your specialist subject?
4   How can the multi-modal approach to intelligence be best used to enhance the effective planning of lessons and subsequent learning?
5   How will the gathering promotion of inclusion affect pupils who are gifted and/or talented? And how will pupils with learning or health problems adapt to an inclusive school in the future? What advantages and disadvantages could arise?

Suggested further reading

Armstrong, A.C., Armstrong, D. and Spandagou, I. (2009) *Inclusive education: international policy and practice*. London: Sage Publications Ltd. A comprehensive evaluation of the value of inclusion in education with international examples.

Child, D. (1986) *Psychology and the teacher*. London: Cassell Educational Ltd. Covers all the bases of educational psychology theory.

Emner, E.T., Evertson, C.M. and Worsham, M.E. (2000) *Classroom management for secondary teachers* (5th Ed.). Boston, MA: Allyn & Bacon. Classroom management strategies for secondary teachers, with reference to the psychology behind behaviour and behaviour management.

Eyre, D. (1997) *Able children in ordinary schools*. London: David Fulton Publishers, Ltd. A guide to effective education for gifted and talented students. The book gives expert analysis of identification, classroom planning and differentiation in both primary and secondary schools, using a case study framework.

Sharples, J. (2009). *Brain, mind and education: an emerging science of learning (Unit 5.6)*. The Institute of the Mind. York University

References

Bettelheim, B. and Zelan, K. (1981) *On learning to read: the child's fascination with meaning*. London: Thames and Hudson.

Bruce, T. (2001) *Helping young children to play*. London: Hodder and Stoughton.

Burden, P.R. (1995). *Classroom management and discipline: Methods to facilitate cooperation and instruction*. White Plains, NY: Longman.

Byrne, M., Johnstone, A.H. and Pope, A. (1994) 'Reasoning in Science: A language problem revealed?', *School Science Review*, 75, pp. 103–107.

de Guimps, R. (2008) *Pestalozzi: His life and work*. Charleston, SC: BiblioBazaar.

Dyson, A.H. (1993). *Negotiating a permeable curriculum: On literacy, diversity and the interplay of children's and teachers' worlds, or the mystery of Eugenie and Mr. Lincoln*. Concept Paper Series. Urbana, IL: National Council for the Teaching of English.

Elliott, S.N. (2000). *Educational psychology: Effective teaching*. Colombus, OH: McGraw-Hill College.

Evertson, C.M. (1988) 'Managing classrooms: a framework for teachers', in Berliner, D. and Rosenshine, B. (Eds.) *Talks to teachers*. New York, NY: Random House, pp. 54–74.

Fancher, R.E. (1979) *Pioneers of psychology*. London: W.W. Norton and Company, Inc.

Farnan, R.R.W. (2010) *Improving literacy skills in science* (unpublished Masters paper). Sunderland: University of Sunderland.

Finger, S. (1994) *Origins of neuroscience: A history of explorations into brain function*. New York, NY: Oxford University Press.

Frick, T.W. (1990). 'Analysis of patterns in time: A method of recording and quantifying temporal relations in education', *American Educational Research Journal*, 27, pp. 180–204.

Fuchs, L.S., Fuchs, D., Hamlett, C.L. and Karns, K. (1998) '"High achieving students", interactions and performance on complex mathematical tasks as a function of homogenous and heterogeneous pairings', *American Educational Research Journal*, 35, pp. 227–268.

Gardner, H. (1993) *Frames of mind* (2nd Ed.). Fontana, CA: Fontana.

Gleitman, H., Fridlund, A.J. and Reisberg, D. (1999). *Psychology* (5th Ed.). New York, NY: W.W. Norton & Company, Inc.

Glover, J.A. and Ronning, R.R. (1987) *Historical foundations of educational psychology: Perspectives on individual differences*. New York, NY: Springer.

Guidici, C. *et al*. (2001) *Making learning visible: Children as individual and group learners*. Reggio Emilia: Reggio Children Publications.

Hall, K. *et al*. (2010) *Loris Malaguzzi and the Reggio Emilia experience (Continuum Library of Educational Thought)*. London: Continuum International Publishing Group, Ltd.

Hallahan, D.P., Kauffman, J.M. and Lloyd, J.W. (2000) *Introduction to learning difficulties* (4th Ed.). Boston, MA: Allyn and Bacon.

Hohmann, M. and Weikart, D.P. (1995) *Educating young children*. Ypsilanti, MI: High/Scope Press.

Holt, N. (2007) *Bringing the high/scope approach to your early years practice*. Abingdon: Routledge

Jenkinson, S. (2001) *The genius of play*. Stroud: Hawthorn Press.

Kohn, A. (1993) 'Rewards versus learning: A response to Paul Chance', *Phi Delta Kappan*, 72, pp. 496–506.

Kounin, J.S. (1970) *Discipline and group management in classrooms*. New York, NY: Holt, Rinehart and Winston.

Lyons, J. (1999) 'A framework for educational psychology device delivery', *Educational Psychology in Practice*, 15, 3, pp. 158–166.

Mackay, T. (1997) 'Psychological service delivery to primary schools: do head teachers want research?', *Educational Psychology in Practice*, 13, pp. 165–169.

Mackay, T. (2002) 'The future of educational psychology', *Educational Psychology in Practice*, 18, 3, pp. 245–253.

Norwich, B. (2008) *Dilemmas of difference, inclusion and disability: International perspectives and future directions*. London: Routledge.

Postman, N. and Weingartner, C. (1971) *Teaching as a subversive activity*. London: Penguin/Pitman Publishing.

Poulou, M. (2005) 'Educational psychology within teacher education', *Teachers and Teaching*, 11, 6, pp. 555–574.

Pound, L. (2005) *How children learn*. London: Step Forward Publishing Ltd.

Robinsin, C.S. and Clinkenbeard, P.R. (1998) 'Giftedness: An exceptionality explained', in Spence, J.T., Darley, J.M. and Foss, D.J. (Eds.) *Annual Review of Psychology*. Palo Alto, CA: Annual Reviews, pp. 117–139.

Seligman, M.E.P. (1975) *Helplessness: On depression, development and death*. San Francisco, CA: Freeman.

Sharples, J. (2009). *Brain, mind and education: an emerging science of learning*. The Institute of the Mind, York University.

Shimahara, N.K. and Sakai, A. (1995) *Learning to teach in two cultures*. New York, NY: Garland.

The National Curriculum (1999) *Science*. Available at: http://curriculum.qca.org.uk/uploads/Science%201999%20programme%20of%20study_tcm8–12062.pdf?return=/key-stages-1-and-2/subjects/science/keystage1/index.aspx (accessed 23 October 2010).

The National Curriculum – Key Stage 1 Science. Available at: http://curriculum.qcda.gov.uk/key-stages-1-and-2/subjects/science/keystage1/index.aspx (accessed 23 October 2010).

Vygotsky, L.S. (1993) *The collected works of L.S. Vygotsky: Volume 2* (trans. J. Knox and C. Stevens). New York, NY: Plenum.

Weinstein, C.S. (1999) 'Reflections on best practices and promising programs: Beyond assertive classroom discipline', in Freiber, H.J. (Ed.) *Beyond behaviourism: Changing the classroom management paradigm*. Boston, MA: Allyn and Bacon, pp. 147–163.

Weinstein, C.S. and Mignano, A.J., Jr. (1997) *Elementary classroom management: Lessons from research and practice* (2nd Ed.). New York, NY: McGraw-Hill.

Wertsch, J.V. (1991) *Voices of the mind: A sociocultural approach to mediated action*. Cambridge, MA: Harvard University Press.

Woolfolk, A. (2001) *Educational Psychology* (8th Ed.). Boston, MA: Allyn and Bacon.

10

Economics of education

Anna Vignoles
Institute of Education, University of London

Overview

Economists bring a unique, though not always welcome, perspective to the study of education. They recognise that the world does not have infinite resources to spend on education and therefore hard decisions have to be made about where spending would best be directed. Economists use a set of theoretical and empirical tools to provide answers to a wide range of pressing questions in the field of education, such as:

1   How can we improve educational outcomes and produce education more efficiently?
2   Why do some individuals acquire less education than others?
3   What is the impact of education on individuals and the wider economy?
4   Why should the state invest in education?

This chapter describes how the economics of education helps address these four key issues, highlighting the contribution of both economy theory and the wealth of empirical evidence produced by education economists. Looking to the future, the key economic challenges in the field of education are then identified.

Introduction

Economics is about understanding the problem of scarcity. There are never enough resources to go around. Ask a headteacher or a university vice chancellor and they will always talk of the need for more resources, as will of course the hospital manager and the social worker. Economists ask how we might best distribute the scarce resources that we have, to produce more of the things that we genuinely value in society, including education. Economists provide a useful perspective on some of the key education questions that we, as a society, need to address.

First, economic analyses can help us determine how best to produce education. Economists model the production of education in a manner analogous to other forms of production, identifying what inputs into the education process appear to have most impact on the amount and quality of education produced. This aspect of economic enquiry is about efficiency. Although economists are primarily concerned about efficiency, they also study a second set of issues relating to equity, and why some individuals get more education than others. Third, economists evaluate the long-run impact of education on individuals and society. They measure the financial return to education for individuals, in the form of better employment prospects, and the wider economy, in the form of higher economic growth. A fourth issue is the optimal role of the state. We all agree that up to a certain age compulsory education is vital and should be free at point of use. However, not everyone agrees about the extent to which the state should provide all forms of education, such as higher education. Economists can help explain why, from an economic perspective, state involvement in education is desirable due to the market failures that exist.

We consider these four sets of issues in turn after a brief historical overview of key theoretical developments in the economics of education.

Main section

The famous economist Adam Smith in his *Wealth of Nations* treatise (1776) first discussed education as an investment: previously education was viewed as a pastime for the privileged. It was not until the 1960s, however, that Becker formalized the notion that individuals invest in education to earn a return on their investment, a theory known as *human capital theory* (Becker, 1964). In other words, individuals invest their money (e.g. tuition fees) or their income foregone (e.g. what they could have earned if they had not been in education) and they do this in the expectation that in the future they will earn a return. Originally Becker envisaged the return to education as being financial, i.e. higher wages or better employment prospects. Recently the notion of a return to education has been broadened to include non-pecuniary returns which are arguably as important, such as job satisfaction.

Of course human capital theory is not the only theoretical model used in education economics. Alternative paradigms exist, such as signalling or screening theory, which sees education as a sorting device, enabling employers to identify high and low productivity workers (Spence, 1973; Blaug, 1976). However, human capital theory dominates education economics today and has had a huge impact on the way that policy-makers conceive of education. The questions we address below are therefore largely framed from a human capital perspective.

How can we produce education more efficiently?

Economists model the production of education, relating inputs, such as teachers, to outputs, i.e. academic achievement (Todd and Wolpin, 2007; Haveman and Wolfe, 1995). Economists recognise that education production differs from other types of production but argue that it is nonetheless useful to understand which inputs into the education process are important.

To illustrate the usefulness of the education production function approach, consider first the resources that are spent on education. As educators, we would like to spend more on education. However, as our health colleagues would also like to spend more on health – we are in a constant tussle for resources. It is therefore crucial that we understand which resources are particularly important in producing high levels of education achievement. There is a large literature which has, for instance, studied the relationship between expenditure and children's achievement. This literature has also considered the impact of other resource measures, such as class sizes. Empirically, it has been found that whilst increased expenditure does have a positive impact on educational achievement, this effect is surprisingly small (Burtless, 1996; Hanushek, 2003). Additional spending also appears to have a greater impact on child outcomes in the early years of education (Angrist and Lavy, 1999; Dearden et al., 2002; Machin et al., 2007). Smaller class sizes also make a difference largely in the early years (Card and Krueger, 1992; Slater et al., 2009).

How do we interpret the fact that resources per se do not appear to have a major impact on educational achievement? The literature suggests that small differences in per pupil funding do not make a major difference to pupil achievement in countries which have relatively high levels of per pupil funding. If a country was to move from class sizes of 50 to class sizes of 30, this might make more of a difference. This literature also tells us that school systems are not necessarily efficient: increasing inputs does not automatically generate benefits. As every teacher knows, good education and high pupil achievement are not only determined by class sizes but also by many factors that are not so easily quantified, such as school culture and behaviour policy. This is an important point that is often lost in the debate about how much we should spend on schooling.

What has also been found to matter a great deal in the education production function literature is teacher quality (Rivkin et al., 2005). However, identifying the characteristics of good teachers is difficult. The number of years of experience that a teacher has and their qualification level is not related to the educational progress made by their students, although very new teachers are less effective. So we cannot improve teacher quality just by hiring better qualified teachers. We do know, however, that teacher quality is linked to how well teachers are paid: higher wages attract more and potentially higher quality people to the teaching profession. Hence teacher pay is an important potential policy lever to improve teacher quality (Lavy, 2002).

Most importantly, the evidence suggests that families are the major determinant of a child's educational achievement not schools (Coleman, 1966; Teddlie and Reynolds, 2000; De Coulon et al., 2011). Despite the emphasis on schools, in many developed countries only around 10–20 per cent of the variation in education achievement between different pupils is down to the school attended. The importance of early family background is also confirmed by the finding that cognitive skills at least are primarily developed during the early years and improving students' cognitive skills in the late teen years and adulthood is much harder (Heckman, 2007). We cannot understate the importance of early family environment in the production of education and skill.

How can we improve the equity of educational outcomes?

We have said that family background is an important determinant of educational achievement. What this means in practice is that the gap between socio-economically advantaged and disadvantaged children in terms of their educational achievement emerges very early indeed (Carneiro and Heckman, 2003; Feinstein, 2003). A parents' level of cognitive skill and their educational achievement are strong predictors of their child's level of skill and education (Ermisch and Francesconi, 2001; Chevalier et al., 2007; Plug 2004; Sacerdote, 2002). The fact that family background influences pupil achievement to such a great extent means that education is not the great leveller that people once hoped it would be. There was an expectation that expanding educational opportunities would necessarily improve social mobility but in some countries, such as the UK, expanding educational opportunities has meant expanding opportunities to the more advantaged families (Blanden *et al.*, 2005). Socio-economic inequalities in education achievement are globally persistent and this remains a key challenge for economic researchers and government.

What is the impact of education on individuals and the wider economy?

Economists have undertaken a huge amount of research evaluating the impact of education on individuals' wages, using Mincer's (1958, 1974) famous earnings function (see Psacharopoulos, 1973 as an early example). The Mincer earnings function enables economists to model the relationship between schooling and earnings. The consensus is that education does causally increase individuals' wages (Card, 1999; Harmon and Walker, 1995; Dearden *et al.*, 2002; Blundell *et al.*, 2005), although there is debate about a) the extent to which education increases productivity or just provides a signal of existing ability (Weiss, 1995) and b) the contribution of education to economic growth (Sianesi and Van Reenen, 2003; Krueger and Lindahl, 2001).

Across developed countries, the private economic return to education, i.e. the benefit to the individual in the form of higher earnings, is around 5–10 per cent per year of schooling (Carnoy, 2007). The private return varies by level of education and across countries, and depending on the level of state subsidy (Psacharopoulos and Patrinos, 2002). Where state subsidy of education is greater, the private return is also higher as individuals pay less for their education. Economists are also interested in the social return to education, i.e. the benefit to the economy as a whole. Krueger and Lindahl (2001) found that education investment makes a similar contribution to a country's economic growth as it does to individuals' wages though it is not simply the average education level of the workforce that matters for economic growth but rather the quality of education acquired and the actual skills gained by workers (Hanushek and Woessmann, 2007).

Economists have also started to think about the wider non-economic benefits of education. Education clearly benefits individuals and societies in ways that go beyond increases in productivity and wages. For example, education can alter individuals' behaviour, encouraging them to adopt healthier life styles. Recent work has tried to quantify these wider benefits, putting monetary values on the health gains or reductions in crime associated with more education (Lochner and Moretti, 2004; Brehm and Rahn, 1997; Dee, 2004). Whilst this is a fruitful area for future research, we must be mindful that putting a monetary value on all the benefits of education is unlikely to be possible or even desirable. Instead, we need to acknowledge that education has wider benefits that are not easily quantified but that policy-makers do need to take account of.

Why should the state invest in education?

We also need to consider why we need state intervention in education. We could leave education to the market and let individuals wishing to send their children to school pay for it themselves. This would give them choice in the provision they use. Some parents would spend a lot, some a little. Some might choose not to send their children to school. Clearly it is the latter problem that causes us all to agree to compulsory and free schooling up to a minimum level. Beyond a certain point, however, we do need to debate the role of the state, in terms of both funding education (e.g. universities) and providing it (e.g. state schools).

State intervention is necessary for equity reasons. Clearly if some parents do not send their children to school, this will disadvantage them permanently. The second reason for state intervention is market failure. If there are benefits of education that accrue not just to the individual but to society as a whole (externalities), individuals will not take these altruistic benefits into account when deciding how much education to acquire. These externalities cause individuals to under-invest in education from society's perspective. The state can overcome this by boosting investment in education.

Even if the case for state investment in education is clear, the case for state provision is less obvious. State-provided services are arguably less efficient since they are not subject to market pressures. One option is to give everyone a certain amount of money and allow them to spend it on a private school of their choice. This leads to equity concerns as richer parents top up the state funding and purchase better schooling. An alternative is a quasi-market, where parents have a free choice of any state school, potentially leading to competition between schools for pupils and higher standards. Many countries, such as the UK, New Zealand and parts of the US, have pursued quasi-markets as a way to solve the apparent trade-off between efficiency and equity (Epple and Romano, 1998, 2003; Hoxby, 2000; Le Grand, 1991, 1993).

In the UK, school competition does not appear to have had a major impact on pupil achievement (Bradley *et al.*, Johnes and Millington, 2001; Gibbons *et al.*, 2008). The US evidence (e.g. Hoxby, 2000, 2003a, 2003b) shows that while increased competition among schools and moves to decentralise school finance *can* enhance attainment, it can also increase inequality because richer parents are better able to take advantage of a more market-oriented system. The trade-off between efficiency and equity therefore has not been solved by the introduction of market forces into education.

So why might quasi-markets not work? Economic theory, specifically principal-agent theory, suggests an explanation (Besley and Ghatak, 2003). The incentives facing principals (headteachers) and agents (teachers) may not be aligned. The teacher may, for example, want to focus on low-achieving children, whilst the headteacher wants to attract as many pupils to the school as possible and hence wants to maximise average test scores. A key requirement for competition to impact on pupil achievement is for the main agents in the system (teachers) to respond to competitive pressures and yet in practice teachers may have no incentive to do so. Recognition of this problem has lead to many countries and US states to develop performance-related pay and incentive schemes for teachers with mixed results (Tomlinson, 2000).

Future developments

Going forward there are a number of issues that the economics of education is particularly well placed to help tackle. Many of the questions posed above still need to be fully answered. We need to develop our understanding of what works in schools. Using quantitative evaluation methodologies, economists can determine whether an intervention or a policy has had genuinely causal impact on children's achievement. This is crucially important in an era of global resource scarcity. As public spending is cut, we need to identify where resources are being currently wasted. In education we need to identify policies that have genuine positive impacts on child achievement and keep investing in them. We need to drop the burdensome, costly policies that do not work. Economists need to do more cost benefit analyses of specific programmes and influence policy by telling policy-makers what does not work as much as what does.

Another crucially important area for further research is the role of teachers. Economists have shown the crucially important role that teachers play in determining pupil achievement but we are still some way off being able to identify what makes a good teacher and how we can improve the effectiveness of existing teachers.

Conclusion

Economists have made a major contribution to the study of education, largely by highlighting efficiencies and inefficiencies in the education system and helping policy-makers understand the long-run economic value of education. Economics also helps us understand the incentives facing schools, teachers and parents and thus why we end up with the system that we have. Economics has its limits of course. Education has both non-economic and potentially unquantifiable benefits – we cannot ignore these benefits just because we cannot measure them. Further, those motivated to go into teaching may have other non-economic factors that influence their decision, such as vocational inclination and care for others, that are not easily factored into economic models. Again we forget this at our peril.

Questions for further investigation

1   How do we improve teacher quality in an era of scarce resources?
2   Does increasing access to education just lead to qualification inflation, whereby jobs that previously needed a degree now need a Masters degree?
3   What is the global effect of education on economic growth?

Suggested further reading

Gorard, S., Taylor, C. and Fitz, J. (2003) *Schools, Markets and Choice Policies*. New York, NY: RoutledgeFalmer. This book provides a different perspective on marketisation of education.
Blanden, J., Gregg, P. and Machin, S. (2005) 'Educational Inequality and Intergenerational Mobility', in Machin, S. and Vignoles, A. (Eds.) *What's the Good of Education? The Economics of Education in the United Kingdom*. Oxford: Princeton University Press. This book discusses the role of education in promoting social mobility (or otherwise) (see especially chapter by Blanden et al[v1].).

References

Angrist, J. and Lavy, V. (1999) 'Using Maimonides' Rule To Estimate the Effect of Class Size of Scholastic Achievement', *Quarterly Journal of Economics*, *114*, pp. 533–76.
Becker, G. (1964) *Human Capital: A Theoretical Analysis with Special Reference to Education*. New York: Columbia University Press.

Besley, T. and Ghatak, M. (2003) 'Incentives, Choice, and Accountability in the Provision of Public Services', *Oxford Review of Economic Policy*, 19, pp. 235–249.

Blanden, J., Gregg, P. and Machin, S. (2005) 'Educational Inequality and Intergenerational Mobility', in Machin, S. and Vignoles, A. (Eds.) *What's the Good of Education? The Economics of Education in the United Kingdom*. Princeton, NJ: Princeton University Press.

Blaug, M. (1976) 'The Empirical Status of Human Capital Theory: A Slightly Jaundiced Survey', *Journal of Economic Literature*, 14, pp. 827–855.

Blundell, R., Dearden, L. and Sianesi, B. (2005) 'Evaluating the Impact of Education on Earnings: Models, Methods and Results from the NCDS', *Journal of the Royal Statistical Society Series A*, 168, 3, pp. 473–512.

Bradley, S., Johnes, G. and Millington, J. (2001) 'School Choice, Competition and the Efficiency of Secondary Schools in England', *European Journal of Operational Research*, 135, pp. 527–544.

Brehm, J. and Rahn, W. (1997) 'Individual-Level Evidence for the Causes and Consequences of Social Capital', *American Journal of Political Science*, 41, pp. 999–1023.

Burtless, G. (1996) *Does Money Matter? The Effect of School Resources on Student Achievement and Adult Success*. Washington, DC: Brookings Institute.

Card, D. (1999) 'The Causal Effect of Education on Earnings', in Ashenfelter, O. and Card, D. (Eds.) *Handbook of Labor Economics*, Volume 3A. Amsterdam: Elsevier.

Card, D. and Krueger, A. (1992) 'Does School Quality Matter? Returns to Education and the Characteristics of Public Schools in the United States', *Journal of Political Economy*, 100, F1–F40.

Carneiro, P. and Heckman, J. (2003) *Human Capital Policy*, NBER Working Papers 9495, National Bureau of Economic Research, Inc.

Carnoy, M. (1997) 'Recent Research on Market Returns to Education', *International Journal of Educational Research*, 27, 6, pp. 483–490.

Chevalier, A., Denny, K. and McMahon, D. (2007) 'A multi-country study of inter-generational educational mobility', UCD Geary Institute Working Paper 2007/25, Dublin.

Coleman, J. (1966) *Equality of Educational Opportunity*. The Coleman Report.

Dearden, L., Ferri, J. and Meghir, C. (2002) 'The Effect of School Quality on Educational Attainment and Wages', *Review of Economics and Statistics*, 84, pp. 1–20.

De Coulon, A., Meschi, E. and Vignoles, A. (2011) 'Parents' Skills and Children's Cognitive and Non-cognitive Outcomes', *Education Economics*, 1469–5782 (online). Accessed January 2011.

Dee, T. (2004) 'Are There Civic Returns to Education?', *Journal of Public Economics*, 88, pp. 1697–1720.

Epple, D. and Romano, R.E. (1998) 'Competition between Private and Public Schools, Vouchers, and Peer-group Effects', *American Economic Review*, 88, 1, pp. 33–62.

Epple, D. and Romano, R.E. (2003) 'Neighbourhood Schools, Choice, and the Distribution of Educational Benefits', in Hoxby, C.M. (Ed.) *The Economics of School Choice*. Chicago, IL: University of Chicago Press.

Ermisch, J. and Francesconi, M. (2001) 'Family Matters: The Impact of Family Background on Educational Attainment', *Economica*, 68, pp. 137–156.

Feinstein, L. (2003) 'Inequality in the Early Cognitive Development of British Children in the 1970 Cohort', *Economica*, 70, pp. 73–97.

Gibbons, S., Machin, S. and Silva, O. (2008) 'Choice, Competition and Pupil Achievement', *Journal of the European Economic Association*, 6, pp. 912–47.

Hanushek, E.A. (2003) 'The Failure of Input-based Schooling Policies', *Economic Journal*, 113, pp. F64–F98.

Hanushek, E. and Woessmann, L. (2007) 'The Role of Education Quality for Economic Growth', in The World Bank/Policy Research Working Paper Series. *RePEc:wbk:wbrwps:4122*.

Harmon, C. and Walker, I. (1995) 'Estimates of the Economic Return to Schooling for the United Kingdom', *American Economic Review*, 85, 5, pp. 1278–1286.

Haveman, R. and Wolfe, B. (1995) 'The Determinants of Children's Attainments: A Review of Methods and Findings', *Journal of Economic Literature*, 33, pp. 1829–1878.

Heckman, J.J. (2007) 'The Economics, Technology and Neuroscience of Human Capability Formation', *Proceedings of the National Academy of Sciences*, 104, 3, pp. 13250–13255.

Hoxby, C. (2000) 'Does Competition Among Public Schools Benefit Students and Taxpayers?', *American Economic Review*, 90, pp. 1209–1238.

Hoxby, C. (2003a) *The Economics of School Choice*. Chicago, IL: Chicago University Press.

Hoxby, C. (2003b) 'School Choice and School Competition: Evidence From the United States', *Swedish Economic Policy Review*, 10, pp. 9–66.

Krueger, A.B. and Lindahl, M. (2001) 'Education for Growth: Why and for Whom?', *Journal of Economic Literature*, *39*, 4, pp. 1101–1136.

Lavy, V. (2002) 'Evaluating the Effect of Teacher Group Performance Incentives on Students Achievements', *Journal of Political Economy*, *110*, 6, pp. 1286–1317.

Le Grand, J. (1991) *Equity and Choice*. London: Harper Collins.

Le Grand, J. (1993) *Quasi-markets and Social Policy*. London: Macmillan.

Lochner, L. and Moretti, E. (2004) 'The Effect of Education on Criminal Activity: Evidence from Prison Inmates, Arrests and Self-Reports', *American Economic Review*, *94*, pp. 155–189.

Machin, S., McNally, S. and Meghir, C. (2007) 'Resources and Standards in Urban Schools', *Centre for the Economics of Education Discussion Paper 76*. London: London School of Economics.

Mincer, J. (1958) 'Investment in Human Capital and Personal Income Distribution', *Journal of Political Economy*, *66*, pp. 281–302.

Mincer, J. (1974) *Schooling, Experience and Earnings*. New York, NY: Columbia University Press, NBER.

Plug, E. (2003) 'Schooling, Family Background, and Adoption: Is it Nature or is it Nurture?', *Journal of Political Economy*, *111*, pp. 611–641.

Psacharopoulos, G. (1973) *Returns to Education: An International Comparison*. New York, NY: Jossey-Bass, Elsevier.

Psacharopoulos, G. and Patrinos, H.A. (2004) 'Returns to investment in education: a further update', *Education Economics*, *12*, 2, pp. 111–134.

Rivkin, S.G., Hanushek, E.A. and Kain, J.F. (2005) 'Teachers, Schools, and Academic Achievement', *Econometrica*, *73*, 2, pp. 417–458.

Sacerdote, B. (2002) 'The Nature and Nurture of Economic Outcomes', *American Economic Review*, *92*, pp. 344–348.

Sianesi, B. and Van Reenen, J. (2003) 'The Returns to Education: Macroeconomics', *Journal of Economic Surveys*, *17*, pp. 157–200.

Slater, H., Davies, N. and Burgess, S. (2009) 'Do teachers matter? Measuring the variation in teacher effectiveness in England', *CMPO Discussion Paper 09/212*, Bristol: University of Bristol.

Spence, M. (1973) 'Job Market Signalling', *Quarterly Journal of Economics*, *87*, pp. 355–374.

Teddlie, C. and Reynolds, D. (2000) *The International Handbook of School Effectiveness Research*. London: Reynolds, Falmer Press.

Todd, P. and Wolpin, K. (2007) 'The Production of Cognitive Achievement in Children: Home, School, and Racial Test Score Gaps', *Journal of Human Capital*, *1*, pp. 91–136.

Tomlinson, H. (2000) 'Proposals for Performance Related Pay for Teachers in English Schools', *School Leadership and Management*, *20*, pp. 281–298.

Weiss, A. (1995) 'Human Capital vs. Signalling Explanations of Wages', *The Journal of Economic Perspectives*, *9*, 4, pp. 133–154.

Section 2

Teaching and learning

11

Learning

Orison Carlile and Anne Jordan
Waterford Institute of Technology

Overview

This chapter illustrates learning as a dynamic co-construction of meaning, and derives a set of implications for educationalists which can be used to guide pedagogy and practice. Consider the following example: a young boy playing with water sees that hard toys sink. When he notices that hard wooden toys float, his understanding is deepened. An older sister can challenge his understanding by showing him how a hard non-wooden bowl floats. By undertaking joint activities to see what does, and does not float, they acquire a shared, more sophisticated understanding of flotation theory. This is an example of the co-construction of meaning.

Introduction

Figure 11.1 illustrates the co-construction of meaning and the interdependence of learning and teaching. The right-hand circle symbolises the role of a learner – the young boy – in constructing meaning. The left-hand circle indicates the role of a more knowledgeable peer – the sister – in guiding learning. In a formal context, she would be the teacher; in peer-learning, a person may be learner at one moment and a teacher at another. The top circle represents the shared understanding constructed by mutual feedback mechanisms of affirmation or challenge. There are a number of further points which are useful to consider:

1   At the heart of the diagram is a set of mutual learning and teaching behaviours: explication, dialogue, questioning, discussion, argument, demonstration or performance.

2   These activities generate mental processes: attention, perception, retention and encoding which are interpreted as the meaning of the activities.
3   This meaning either confirms or challenges previous understandings, leading to a deeper understanding of the constructs.
4   The more sophisticated participant will be attentive to the activity of the other person, through observing, listening or questioning. This will lead to an evaluation of the learner's understanding.
5   It may also lead to changes in the teacher's personal understanding which is more sophisticated than that of the learner, and draws on wider sources and experience.
6   The teacher's feedback challenges or reinforces the understanding of the learner.
7   The culmination is a shared understanding, shown in a further set of mutual activities such as celebration and joint iterative performances.

The only distinction between the children playing with water in our example and the formal educational process is a greater sophistication of teachers and their pedagogical interventions. The pedagogical interventions illustrated in Figure 11.1 are described by, three major theories of learning developed in the twentieth century – behaviourism, cognitivism and constructivism. We now discuss these in turn.

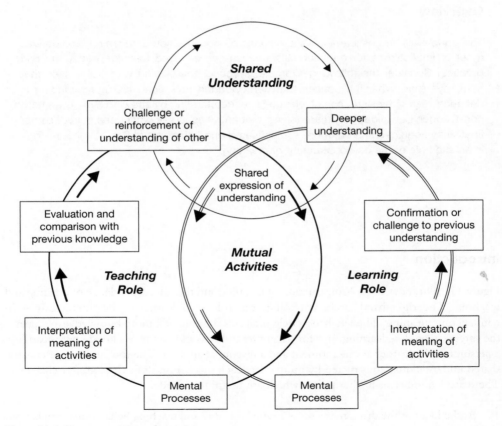

Figure 11.1 Co-construction of meaning

Behaviourism

The main claim of behaviourism is that there are scientific laws governing stimulus and response associations in the behaviour of all organisms. Using these laws, a trainer can steer natural associations in a preferred direction to cause learning. Although behaviourists initially ignored unobservable mental processes – due in part to the limitations of animal experimentation – they later admitted purposeful behaviour in animals and humans (Tolman, 1948). All the interactions between a learner and teacher are behaviours, and this first major learning theory offers advice on types of stimulus, response and reinforcement in the structuring of learning and teaching activities. These feature in Figure 11.1 in the form of 'mutual activities', 'challenge or reinforcement of understanding of other' and 'shared expression of understanding'.

Behaviourism offers practical advice to teachers, trainers and curriculum planners rather than to learners. It suggests that teachers need to consider existing learner competencies in planning the curriculum. For example, the learning intentions should be explicit, based on the desired observable learner behaviours, and aligned with assessment. Close attention should be paid to varied stimuli and the sequencing of teaching activities. Constant feedback should be provided with rewards for behaviour that is appropriate rather than punishment for what is not. Finally, the extent to which learning outcomes have been achieved should be used in evaluating the effectiveness of a curriculum in order to refine it. Although the emphasis on the nature, sequencing and repetition of stimuli, response and feedback gave behaviourism a prominent role in instructional design, and educational technology (Skinner, 1958), several factors contribute to its poor estimation today. Its association with animal training has led to its perception as de-humanising. The learner is presented as a passive entity, with little input into learning intentions. All power is placed into the hands of the teacher or curriculum designer. However, the continuing relevance of behaviourism is shown by calls for structure and practice in foundational learning and by demands for accountability and quality control measured by the achievement of learning outcomes.

Cognitivism

The field of cognitivism grew out of the increasing recognition of the significance of mental activity in human learning. Initially, the brain was considered as a 'black box', and cognition could only be inferred. However, recent developments in brain imaging have led to a more direct detection of cognitive activity in learning. The cognitivist perspective features in Figure 11.1 in the form of 'mental processes' such as attention, perception, memory, encoding and concept-formation. For example, a classic article by Miller (1956) pointed out the limitations of short-term memory paving the way for the concept of 'chunking' learning materials to facilitate storage and retrieval.

Unlike behaviourism, cognitivism offers insights to the learner in the self-regulation of learning, as well as to the teacher. Models drawn from information processing have identified many learning preferences and styles. For example, shallow encoding, based on repetition, and deep encoding, based on connections and patterns, led to an identification of surface and deep learning styles (Craik and Tulving, 1975; Marton and Säljö, 1976).

It has been suggested that material not suiting a particular learner's cognitive style may be more difficult to learn, so teachers are advised to carry out formative assessment of students' learning styles and vary their teaching styles. However, learning style theories have attracted much criticism on the grounds that they are based on dubious theoretical foundations and have not been shown empirically to make any significant difference to learning (Curry, 1990; Stahl, 2002; Coffield *et al.*, 2004).

According to cognitivists, teachers should promote active learning methods, use multi-sensory stimuli to facilitate attention and encoding, and emphasise structure and concepts. Learners should use metacognitive strategies such as pre-organisers, concept-maps and diagrams to identify pattern, structure and relationships, 'chunking' material and revision schedules to aid retention. Neuroscience now enables a dynamic view of brain activity and shows the huge capacity for cognitive growth, and critical developmental periods. For example, children acquiring a second language can develop accent-less speech if they learn before the age of 12, but not after (Richards *et al.*, 1992). Recent research demonstrates the ongoing creation of new neurons – especially in the hippocampus – a brain structure important for learning (Byrne, 2008). The popular saying 'cells that fire together, wire together' summarises Hebb's idea (1949) that the simultaneous firing of neurons increases associations in learning. The view that neurons, once damaged, were thought to be irreplaceable has been supplanted by the knowledge that brain connective tissue can increase with activity. The famous US 'Nuns Study' demonstrates that learning in old age reduces cognitive decline (Snowdon, 2001).

Although modern imaging techniques can be used to diagnose learning potential and address a range of learning problems, disorders such as ADHD remain obstacles because formal educational settings require students to attend and conform. Dyslexia is particularly problematic because so much learning is dependent on reading and writing. Chapter 29, 'Neuroscience and education', in this volume cites a reliable study of newborns which assessed 'within the first 36 hour of infants' lives whether they would later fit into one of three reading groups: normal, poor or dyslexic readers'. However, educators should be sceptical of the simplistic claims of dubious commercial neuro-scientific theories such as *Brain Gym* (Hyatt, 2007). A weakness of the cognitivist approach is its emphasis on individual mental processes overlooking the pervasive social factors increasingly recognised as central to learning. Moreover, knowing which areas of the brain light up when a certain learning event occurs is not the same as the meaning which the learner ascribes to an event. This requires a constructivist approach.

Constructivism

While cognitivism focuses on information-processing, constructivism concentrates on what learners do with that information to create meaning. Figure 11.1 contains many constructivist concepts such as 'interpretation', 'meaning' and 'understanding'. Personal constructivism claims that individuals actively construct knowledge based on personal experience in an effort to make sense of the world (Jordan *et al.*, 2008, p. 57). The resulting differentiation in learning is exemplified in the Multiple Intelligences theory developed by the US psychologist Howard Gardner (Gardner, 1999) which posits a range of individual 'intelligences', giving learners a 'jagged intelligence profile' of differing strengths and weaknesses.

At an extreme level, personal constructivism would make learning a totally private mental act. However, social constructivism claims that learning occurs in contexts that are both social (Vygotsky, 1978) and cultural (Bruner, 1996). The philosopher Wittgenstein argued that 'understanding goes on, not in the head, but in perfectly public contexts of teaching and learning' (Carr, 2010). Such contexts draw on dialogic communication in the co-construction of meaning through 'conversations' between learners and teachers, with the learner engaging in 'teachback', making explicit to the teacher what has been learned (Pask, 1975).

According to social constructivists, learning occurs within a social context and 'decontextual-ized learning activity is a contradiction in terms' (Lave, 2009, pp. 201–202). The contextual nature of learning is emphasised in 'communities of practice' where individuals engage as 'active participants in the practices of social communities and construct identities in relation to these communities' (Wenger 1998, p. 4). Socially constructed knowledge is the most sophisticated stage described by Baxter Magolda (1992) in her research which identified four stages of epistemological development in students. At the initial stage, knowledge is considered absolute. This progresses to a transitional stage where knowledge is seen as uncertain. This is followed by a stage of independent knowing when students rely on personal opinion. The final stage is more integrative, with an awareness that knowledge is socially constructed and based on knowledge claims in context.

Social interactions also shape personal qualities such as self-esteem – feeling good about oneself – and self-efficacy – feeling capable (Bandura, 1977). This is a dynamic, reciprocal process as shown in Figure 11.2. The meaning of the behaviour is socially constructed, and modifies the social environment. The influences are reciprocal as shown by the double-headed arrows. The diagram shows how the social environment influences self-perception which in turn influences behaviour. Learning is driven by these perceptions, together with values, motivation, determination and resilience. The emotional dimension of learning is also important as learners relate knowledge to previous experiences, interests and assumptions since 'emotions and feelings are represented in the process of meaning-making' (Bruner, 1996). Emotional reactions and critical reflections on beliefs and attitudes have been identified by Mezirow (1990, p. 167) as critical factors in adults' transformative learning which involve changes in self-awareness and learner identity. As Jarvis points out 'It is the whole person who learns' (Jarvis, 2006, p. 50). However, people may not be fully aware of their attitudes, emotions or even what they know. In 'tacit knowledge' our preliminary intuitions are underpinned by unconscious feelings or 'passions'; 'we can know more than we can tell' (Polyani, 1967, p. 4). This iceberg in Figure 11.3 illustrates how unconscious passions and intuitions lead to the emergence of conscious meaning.

An increase in consciousness also figures in the movement from unconscious pre-motivation to conscious volition or the will to learn as shown in Figure 11.4. Barnett (2007) identifies the will to learn as an important topic in modern educational discourse, since it relates to the task of engaging new types of learners and social groups in the drive towards mass participation in education.

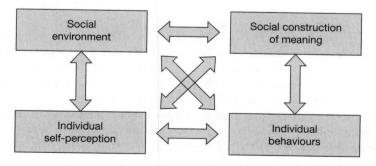

Figure 11.2 Reciprocal interaction of the social and individual

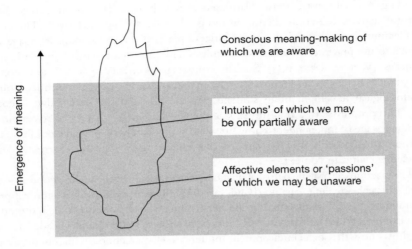

Figure 11.3 Emergent meaning

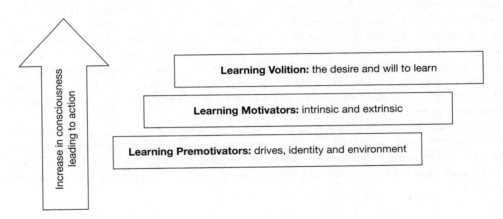

Figure 11.4 Emergence of the will to learn

Learner engagement is fostered in situations and spaces where all learners are stimulated and motivated by relevant and useful knowledge which they interpret and evaluate actively. This requires a community of enquiry in which learners discuss, re-evaluate and construct new meanings and understandings (Fisher, 2005). For example, Knowles (1980) claims in his theory of Andragogy that relevance and usefulness is particularly important to adult learners who differ significantly from children in self-concept, wealth of experience, motivation to learn and a problem-solving approach to learning. Though widely adopted by adult educators, it has been criticised for its Western assumptions of self-direction in learning and its view that children may not also be self-directed.

In retrospect, early constructivist expectations for 'discovery learning' have proven unrealistic in school settings because of its diminution of the important role of the teacher in scaffolding learning by explanation. Constructivism reminds the teacher, however, that explanations may be differently interpreted by learners. For example, if new material to be learned conflicts with existing mental constructs, it may be rejected, ignored or misinterpreted as in the case of a creationist's response to evolutionary theory. Learners' misinterpretations provide a valuable teaching opportunity to explore their mental constructs which can then be challenged by offering alternative explanations. Such misinterpretations are only one example of the way in which learners may 'misconstruct' knowledge. There may also be dispositional obstacles such as non-engagement, alienation and low motivation, as in the case of adult learners with literacy problems who may be loathe to engage with formal education since it may threaten their self-esteem. Similarly, there may be psychosocial obstacles such as emotional disturbance and family problems. A classic text *Kids Don't Learn from People They Don't Like* (Aspy and Roebuck, 1984) describes how poor interpersonal relationships in the classroom – one of the characteristics of incompetent teaching (Carlile, 1999) – can be an obstacle to learning. Although we have not yet gained sufficient distance to identify its legacy or to be more authoritative about its future directions, social constructivism today remains the most generally accepted theory of learning.

Context of learning

The emphasis of the theories discussed above has been on the psychology of individual learners and their interactions. We move now to the sociocultural factors that influence learning both positively and negatively and to the various sites of learning that throw light on the different purposes of learning.

Social-cultural factors

The non-learning described earlier can be attributed not simply to individual psychology but to external social forces. Dominant social groups may perpetuate their advantage through the investment of social and cultural capital in the learning of their offspring. This 'capital' takes the form of books, cultural artefacts and lifestyles which can lead to improved learning (Bourdieu, 1977). Similarly, Bernstein argues that more successful social groups employ 'extended' language codes containing abstraction and generalisation. Less successful ones utilise 'restricted' codes requiring physical presence and gestures to convey meaning (Bernstein, 1977). Recent empirical studies (Marks *et al.*, 2010, pp. 98–119) confirm that learners' possession of cultural capital are critical factors in successful academic achievement.

The purposes, content and style of learning are also strongly influenced by the surrounding culture. Stereotypically, eastern cultures see learning as an induction into their traditional values, norms, experiences and ways of thinking whereas modern Western cultures place more value on self-development and self-actualisation and the resulting self-esteem. Despite their academic success – attributable to the value their culture place on effort – it has been claimed that Asian youths have low self-esteem, whereas 'The self-esteem of African-American students tends to be higher than that of . . . Asian students – in inverse proportion to their academic achievement' (Csikszentmihalyi, 1996, p. 425).

Furthermore, changes in the nature of knowledge and society have impacted on learning, and can lead to a number of tensions for learners.

Democratisation versus commodification

The internet and World Wide Web enable a much greater democratisation of, and access to, the kinds of knowledge that would only have been available to specialists in the past. The ready availability of medical information to the layman is an example. There are clear benefits to the learner in such access to knowledge, including that of greater empowerment. On the other hand, there is a greater appropriation of learning, including what was informal learning, by formal institutional and commercial providers. This may lead to what has been termed the 'totally pedagogised society' (Bernstein, 2001) in which every aspect of life and learning becomes fodder for the market in education, and pedagogy becomes a bastion against the unpredictability of modern life.

Personalisation vs. regulation

Another move, in line with constructivist philosophy, is in the personalisation of learning. This is facilitated by the new technologies which can deliver learning materials directly to the individual. In theory, learners can choose what they personally want to learn, how they might learn it and when they learn it. Countering this is the greater regulation of formal learning by external agencies, with a significant increase in the number of regulatory bodies responsible for, and evaluating, the quality of what is learned. The quality agenda – a feature of many Western societies over the last decades – threatens personalisation with its control and standardisation of learning.

Learning vs. teaching

A recent change in linguistic usage is the way that 'learning' has been prioritised over 'teaching' or 'education'. This small reversal signals a change in emphasis away from teaching and the transmission of knowledge towards learning as a process. For example, one of the Education Masters courses at the Waterford Institute of Technology is in learning and teaching, rather than teaching and learning. Confusingly, 'learning' is also used as a noun to describe the provision of learning opportunities, as in the term 'formal learning', in preference to 'formal education' (Jarvis, 2006). This ties in with a recent discourse of 'learner-centredness' and 'self-directed learning'. Yet Sue Cross claims that identifying any given experience as entirely learner centred is 'an arbitrary judgement' (Cross, 2009, p. 6). The role of the teacher in demonstrating key skills or elucidating difficult 'threshold' concepts is increasingly deliberated (Meyer and Land, 2006). The constructivist distrust of the teacher and teaching as an obstacle may give way to a better appreciation of the role of teaching in facilitating understanding.

Conclusion

This chapter offers several modern perspectives on learning and on its social context. It offers insights into the way in which people learn and suggests some implications for pedagogical policy and practice. It has not been possible within this chapter to cover the many sites and spaces in which learning takes place, nor has it been possible to deal with issues in great depth. However, we hope that this chapter may provide a starting point from which readers may explore further and develop their own learning.

Questions for further investigation

1   What is the balance between learning for the purpose of individual personal development, learning for enculturation or for economic reasons?
2   Do people learn in different ways for different purposes or at different stages in their life?
3   In your view, how does new media and social network use influence learning?
4   Has the emphasis on student-centred learning marginalised the teacher?

Suggested further reading

Bruning, R.H., Schraw, G.J., Norby, M. and Ronning, R.R. (2004) *Cognitive Psychology and Instruction* (4th Ed.). New Jersey, NJ: Pearson Merrill Prentice Hall. This is a comprehensive account of the ways in which a knowledge of cognitive psychology is important in understanding learning. It utilises American terminology and references to school practice.

Illeris, K. (2009) *Contemporary Theories of Learning: Learning theorists . . . in their own words.* Abingdon: Routledge. This is a collection of readings from key learning theorists, themed around dimensions of learning such as the environment, the person and the content. It omits cognitivist, behaviourist and sectoral approaches.

Jordan, A., Carlile, O. and Stack, A. (2008) *Approaches to Learning: a Guide for Teachers.* London: McGraw-Hill/Open University Press. This is an integrated overview of theoretical perspectives drawn from philosophy, psychology, sociology and pedagogy. The chapters offer a summary of key principles, examples and illustrations from contemporary research and practice.

References

Aspy, D. and Roebuck, F. (1984) *Kids Don't Learn from People They Don't Like* (2nd Ed.). Amherst, MA: HRD Press.

Bandura, A. (1977) 'Self-efficacy: towards a unifying theory of behavioral change', *Psychological Review*, *84*, pp. 191–215.

Barnett, R. (2007) *A Will to Learn: Being a Student in an Age of Uncertainty.* SRHE Series, Berkshire: OU Press & McGraw Hill Education.

Baxter Magolda, M. (1992) 'Students' epistemologies and academic experiences: implications for pedagogy', *Review of Higher Education*, *15*, 3, pp. 265–287.

Bernstein, B. (1977) *Class Codes and Control* (Vol. 3). London: Routledge and Kegan Paul.

Bernstein, B. (2001) 'From pedagogies to knowledges', in Morais, A., Neves, I., Davies, B. and Daniels H. (Eds.) *Towards a Sociology of Pedagogy.* New York, NY: Peter Lang, pp. 363–368.

Bourdieu, P. (1977) 'Cultural reproduction and educational reproduction', in Karabell, J. and Halsey, A.H. (Eds.) *Power and Ideology in Education.* London: Oxford University Press, pp. 487–511.

Bruner, J. (1996) *The Culture of Education.* Cambridge MA: Harvard University Press.

Byrne, J. (Ed.) (2008) *Learning and Memory, a Comprehensive Reference.* Oxford: Elsevier.

Carlile, O. (1999) *Incompetent Teachers in Irish Voluntary Secondary Schools: Principals' Assessments, Attitudes and Reactions.* PhD thesis, University of Hull.

Carr, D. (2010) 'Learning: meaning, language and culture', in Arthur, J. and Davies, I. (Eds.) *The Routledge Education Studies Reader.* London: Routledge.

Coffield, F., Moseley, D., Hall, E. and Ecclestone, K. (2004) 'Learning styles and pedagogy in post-16 learning. A systematic and critical review'. London: Learning and Skills Research Centre.

Craik, F.I. and Tulving, E. (1975) 'Depth of processing and the retention of words in episodic memory', *Journal of Experimental Psychology: General, 104,* 3, pp. 268–294.

Cross, S. (2009) *Adult Teaching and Learning: Developing Your Practice.* London: Open University Press McGraw-Hill Education.

Csikzentmihalyi, M. (1996) *Creativity: Flow and the Psychology of Invention.* New York, NY: Harper Collins.

Curry, L. (1990) 'One critique of the research on learning styles', *Educational Leadership, 48,* pp. 50–56.

Fisher, R. (2005) *Teaching Children to Think.* Cheltenham: Nelson Thornes Ltd.

Gardner, H. (1999) *Intelligence Reframed: Multiple Intelligences for the 21st Century.* New York, NY: Basic Books.

Hebb, D.O. (1949) *The Organization of Behavior.* New York, NY: Wiley

Hyatt, K.J. (2007) '"Brain Gym" Building stronger brains or wishful thinking', *Remedial and Special Education, 28,* 2, pp. 117–124.

Jarvis, P. (2006) *Towards a Comprehensive Theory of Human Learning.* London: Routledge.

Jordan, A., Carlile, O. and Stack, A. (2008) *Approaches to Learning: a Guide for Teachers.* London: McGraw-Hill/Open University Press.

Knowles, M. (1980) *The Modern Practice of Adult Education* (Rev. Ed.). Englewood Cliffs, NJ: Prentice Hall Regents.

Lave, J. (2009) 'The practice of learning', in Illeris, K. (Ed.) *Contemporary Theories of Learning: Learning theorists . . . in their own words.* London: Routledge

Marks, G., Cresswell, J. and Ainley, J. (2010) 'Explaining socioeconomic inequalities in student achievement: the role of home and school factors', in Arthur, J. and Davies, I. (Eds.) *The Routledge Education Studies Reader.* London: Routledge.

Marton, F. and Saljö, R. (1976) 'On qualitative differences in learning 1 – outcome and process', *British Journal of Educational Psychology, 46,* pp. 4–11.

Meyer, J.H.F. and Land, R. (Eds.) (2006) *Overcoming Barriers to Student Understanding: Threshold concepts and troublesome knowledge.* London: Routledge.

Mezirow, J. and Associates (1990) *Fostering Critical Reflection in Adulthood: A Guide to Transformative and Emancipatory Learning.* San Francisco, CA: Jossey-Bass.

Miller, G.A. (1956) 'The magical number seven, plus or minus two: some limits on our capacity for information processing', *Psychological Review, 63,* pp. 81–97.

Pask, G. (1975) *Conversation, Cognition and Learning.* New York, NY: Elsevier.

Polyani, M. (1967) *The Tacit Dimension.* New York, NY: Anchor/Doubleday & Co.

Richards, J.C., Platt, J. and Platt, H. (1992) *Longman Dictionary of Language Teaching and Applied Linguistics.* London: Longman.

Skinner, B.F. (1958) 'Teaching machines', *Science, 128,* pp. 969–977.

Snowdon, D. (2001) *Aging with Grace: What the Nun Study Teaches Us About Leading Longer, Healthier And More Meaningful Lives.* New York, NY: Bantam Books.

Stahl, S.A. (2002) 'Different strokes for different folks?', in Abbeduto, L. (Ed.) *Taking Sides: Clashing on Controversial Issues in Educational Psychology.* Guilford, CT: McGraw-Hill, pp. 98–107.

Tolman, E.C. (1948) 'Cognitive maps in rats and man', *Psychological Review, 55,* pp. 189–208.

Vygotsky, L.S. (1978) *Mind in Society.* M., John-Steiner, V., Scribner, S. and Souberman, E. (Eds.) Cambridge, MA: Harvard University Press.

Wenger, E. (1998) *Communities of Practice: Learning, Meaning and Identity.* Cambridge: Cambridge University Press.

12

Teaching

Chris Kyriacou
University of York

Overview

This chapter explores our understanding of the notion of teaching in the context of policy initiatives and research on practice.

Introduction – what do we mean by teaching?

For centuries the basic process of teaching has involved a three-stage sequence which begins with a teacher 'informing, describing, explaining, demonstrating' something to a pupil. The pupil is then required to demonstrate what they have learnt to the teacher. The teacher then provides feedback to the pupil, in the form of an evaluation and/or further teaching. These three stages constitute what is commonly referred to as a didactic, teacher-centred, direct, or transmission style of teaching. In essence the teacher is viewed as an expert in the topic at hand, and the act of teaching involves the teacher using this expertise to foster pupil learning. Teaching a topic may involve many cycles of this process. Teaching someone a discrete piece of learning could take a few minutes, whilst teaching someone an in-depth understanding of a complex topic could take months or years.

Didactic teaching can work very well if the pupil is highly motivated and the teacher is able to conduct the process skilfully. However, it has the drawback that the pupil can spend too much time simply listening to a teacher and monotonously practising what they have learnt. In these circumstances pupils' attention and interest can easily lapse. A further drawback is that the pupil's role in the process is essentially a passive one, as a receiver-and-repeater of knowledge, and many pupils find it hard to develop and sustain an engagement in learning in such a passive context. Nevertheless, a number of writers have argued that the skilful use of didactic teaching is still the most efficient way of teaching (Good and Brophy, 2007).

In contrast many educationists have advocated a style of teaching in which pupils can play a more active role where they can take centre stage and where the teacher's role becomes more one of setting up stimulating activities through which pupils learn. This can involve individualised project work based on investigative tasks; small group discussion; collaborative activities; role-play activities; and the imaginative use of materials and technologies (including ICT). This style of teaching is commonly referred to as student-centred or indirect teaching. Advocates of this approach highlight the motivational aspects of such activities, and the educational benefits that accrue to pupils in having greater self-directed control over organising their work and engaging in a dialogue with others (both the teacher and other pupils) about their work. In recent years innovative developments in the use of ICT (Daly and Pachler, 2010) and in providing opportunities for pupil dialogue (Mercer and Hodgkinson, 2008) have led to a number of exciting initiatives to improve the quality of teaching in schools.

In most countries the dominant style of teaching can be described as didactic (OECD, 2009). This is particularly the case in developing countries. In Western (developed) countries such as the UK, however, a balanced mix of didactic and student-centred teaching is typical, and some teachers can indeed be described as adopting student-centred teaching as their dominant style. A look at reports and policy documents produced by the Training and Development Agency for Schools (TDA), the Office for Standards in Education (Ofsted) and the Department for Education (DfE), for example, provide an important overview of how teaching is currently viewed in England. In particular, these include the TDA's description of the teaching standards expected of newly qualified teachers, Ofsted's annual report on the quality of teaching evident in schools, and the DfE's vision of the future direction of national strategies for classroom practice. However, in order to avoid adopting an insular view of the key issues addressed by such publications, it is helpful to consider publications which consider practices in other countries and those which have drawn on research evidence to evaluate the relative success of different classroom practices (e.g. Hattie, 2008; Muijs and Reynolds, 2010). Looking at the wider picture serves to highlight the extent to which teaching is embedded in a particular sociocultural setting, and how views about the nature and purpose of teaching not only differs between countries, but also between different settings within a country (Anderson, 2009; Leach and Moon, 2008). In addition, it also highlights that the attempt to identify classroom practices that unequivocally 'work best' (which has given rise to a discourse of 'what works' as a foundation for evidence-based teaching) is problematic and needs to be treated with caution (Issitt and Kyriacou, 2009).

Teaching in context

Teaching needs to be seen at a macro-level within the context of the aims of education as whole, and at a micro-level in terms of how these educational aims can be applied to a particular lesson (or sequence of lessons) by addressing specific learning outcomes. Moreover, such aims are also framed by a social context containing a wide range of competing expectations and demands from pupils, school managers, parents, examination boards, and governmental bodies and agencies (Cullingford, 2009; Skinner, 2010). In addition, we also need to take account of the way teaching takes place in a personal context for the teacher – how do teachers view teaching, and moreover sustain their motivation and passion for teaching (Day and Gu, 2010; Morgan et al., 2010)?

Schooling as a whole and the particular details of the curriculum being followed both occur within this wider framework of educational aims. As such, all teaching needs to locate itself within this wider framework. Such aims cover not only academic matters, but also wider aspects of education, such as personal and social development, and how a pupil is better placed as a result of their educational experiences to make a positive contribution to society and to lead happy and fulfilling lives. In many countries a formal statement of the aims of the education system that relate to schooling can be found in appropriate legislation or other types of governmental documentation. Whilst the prose used is often grandiose and flowery, this can serve as an important reminder of the wider picture that teaching at the classroom level is intended to serve. Slight changes in the wording of official documentation can serve to highlight a shift in emphasis and priority in government policy regarding teaching, and for this reason it is important to revisit from time to time how educational aims and the classroom practices advocated are formulated in official policy publications.

The wider framework of educational aims, however, needs to be translated into specific learning outcomes in order for teaching to be purposeful in its focus and to enable teachers to assess whether their intended learning outcomes are being achieved. There are four key types of learning outcomes that teaching needs to address: knowledge, understanding, skills and attitudes.

Knowledge refers to pieces of information; for example, the capital of France, the chemical formula for water, how to copy and paste material in creating a PowerPoint slide. Knowledge relates essentially on the swift and accurate recall of facts and procedures, and can be consolidated by frequent use. *Understanding* refers to meaningful connections between pieces of knowledge. One can 'know' the chemical formula for water, or the procedure for dividing one fraction by another. Understanding, however, requires such knowledge to be meaningful – in essence to understand the nature of atomic structure and chemical bonding which requires water to have the molecular structure that it does, or to understand the mathematics which equates to the procedure of inverting the second fraction and then multiplying. Knowledge can be subject to faulty recall, whereas understanding helps to secure knowledge. As such, teaching needs to ensure that what is learnt has an appropriate level of meaningfulness for pupils. Questioning and conversational dialogue are effective methods of securing meaningfulness. A *skill* can be defined as activity performed with expertise. This can cover examples such as how well pupils can set up apparatus for an experiment, solve an equation, write an abstract of a story, or draw a diagram. The two key qualities of a skill are speed and precision. Teaching a pupil to develop skills requires repeated practice with corrective feedback.

Teachers also need to promote two key types of positive *attitudes*: first, a love and enjoyment of the subject or activity (e.g. Science or Reading); and second, positive attitudes towards themselves as learners (in particular their self-belief that making an intellectual effort will lead to successful learning). Learning is a high-risk activity and failure is painful. As such, repeated failure can easily lead to a lowering of confidence, disaffection and a withdrawal of effort. One of the major challenges facing teaching is to teach in a way that will elicit and sustain positive self-beliefs in pupils, particularly if these have already been damaged by pupils' prior experiences. Ensuring that the work is adequately differentiated so that it caters for the different interests and levels of ability within the class, and ensuring the teaching is supportive rather than hostile in tone (particularly when a pupil has got something wrong) are key aspects of the type of teaching needed.

Each of these four types of learning outcomes warrants a conceptual analysis in their own right (Newton, 2000; Wilen *et al.,* 2008) and the issues underpinning the need for conceptual clarity become very evident whenever learning outcomes need to be assessed (Gardner, 2006).

Teaching skills

Teaching is a skilled activity. Skilled performance involves a clear purpose which is characterised by expertise. There are three stages involved in skilled performance where such expertise is displayed. First, the teacher needs to have knowledge (expertise in knowledge) about a range of possible actions concerning what to do in a particular situation. Second, the teacher needs to be able to make the right choice (expertise in decision-making) about which of these possible actions is the one to select. Third, the teacher needs to carry out the action (expertise in action) with a high level of competence.

For example, let us take a situation in which a pupil has been asked to explain how many times a dice thrown 36 times is likely to come up as a 6, and the pupil is unable to offer an answer. The teacher needs to know that there are a variety of things to do next – such as giving the pupil a hint, asking them to relate the question to a previous activity, asking the pupil to discuss the question in a small group, demonstrating how to approach the question, simplifying the question, or asking another pupil the same question. The teacher then needs to take account of the topic, the pupil's ability, whether the pupil seems confident or anxious, how difficult the question is in the light of the lesson activities, in order to decide what to do next; let us assume the decision made by the teacher is to give the pupil a hint. The teacher then needs to give a hint which is clear, appropriate, helpful and supportive.

When an episode of teaching goes badly (or in this context is handled unskilfully), we need to identify whether the problem involved poor expertise in knowledge, poor expertise in decision-making, or poor expertise in action. It is only on this basis that the teacher (through self-reflection and/or through helpful feedback from an observer) can address how best to improve their teaching skills in situations where problems are apparent.

Attempts have been made by many writers to produce a descriptive list of the different types of teaching skills that underpin teaching and to relate these to a knowledge base about teaching (Kyriacou, 2007; Stronge, 2007). Some of these lists have formed the basis for the initial and in-service training of teachers (for an example drawn from the English context see TDA, 2008). A particularly useful framework for considering the notion of teacher expertise has been developed by Pollard (2010), which is presented in terms of key principles derived from research on effective teaching and learning. Pollard notes that the exercise of high-level teaching skills (i.e. teacher expertise) lies in the way in which an expert teacher's behaviour is very sensitive to their context and situation. An expert teacher is able to make well-informed choices and adjustments to what and how they teach so that pupil engagement and learning is maximised.

The tasks of teaching

Turning our focus onto the lesson, teaching can be viewed in terms of three key tasks (Kyriacou, 2009):

- Planning and preparation: What do I need to do before the lesson starts?
- Presentation and monitoring: What do I need to do during the lesson?
- Reflection and evaluation: What do I need to do after the lesson?

Much has been written about planning and preparation. One essential feature of this task is to have a clear idea about the learning outcomes the lesson is designed to foster. The most audacious attempt to categorise educational objectives was carried out by Bloom et al. (1956). Bloom's taxonomy of educational objectives has had a major influence on the planning of educational courses. Although the precise details of his taxonomy are less used now, his central message still remains a powerful one: there is a complex range of learning outcomes that a teacher may have in mind, and successful planning requires a careful identification of how pupils' experiences in a lesson will effectively foster these. It is now common practice in many educational contexts for a teacher to be expected to state which learning outcomes a lesson (or course of lessons) is designed to foster. Indeed, this approach has now been adopted by many textbook writers who list learning outcomes at the start of each chapter.

The heart of a lesson involves issues concerning presentation and monitoring. The teacher plays a key role in making sure that all the learning activities operate as smoothly as possible and are effective in fostering the intended learning outcomes. Such activities can include explaining, asking questions, setting up group-work discussion and making use of ICT. One of the most important aspects of teaching is how the teacher makes use of language (through both teacher–pupil and pupil–pupil interaction) to monitor and extend pupils' learning. Indeed, many writers have argued that how language is used in the classroom is perhaps the most important of all factors in promoting pupil learning (Mercer and Hodgkinson, 2008). One widely advocated technique is the use of 'scaffolding', which derives from the writing of Vygotsky. Scaffolding refers to the way in which a teacher through the use of hints, prompts and shaping the focus of a pupil's attention can help a pupil successfully carry out the task in hand by building upon the pupil's existing knowledge and understanding (Cowie et al., 2010).

Another key issue relates to one of the most famous statements in educational psychology: Ausubel's (1968) call to teachers to ascertain what pupils know already and teach them accordingly. Ausubel is highlighting here the importance of tailoring new learning to pupils' previous learning. This idea builds upon Piaget's work on the cognitive development of the child and his characterisation of how children 'actively construct' new understanding – teaching which adopts this approach is referred to as a 'constructivist approach' (Cowie et al., 2010). A dialogue with pupils at the start of a lesson which explores what pupils already know and understand about a topic can play an essential part in helping to ensure that the learning activities prepared for the lesson are appropriate in terms of both content and level of difficulty.

There are two types of monitoring which needs to occur during a lesson. The first is logistical:

- Are pupils doing what they should be doing?
- Are pupils working at the right pace?
- Do any adjustments need to be made to the lesson to ensure the lesson engages pupils?

The second type of monitoring is learning focused:

- How well is each pupil's learning progressing?
- Are pupils having any problems in their understanding?
- Do pupils need help to cope with the current task or to be set a more challenging task?

Learning-focused monitoring underpins two key developments in recent thinking about teaching and learning in the classroom. The first is 'personalised learning' – the need to adjust learning experiences to take account of each particular pupil's learning needs (Courcier, 2007); and the second is 'assessment for learning' – the need to use feedback from assessment to promote each pupil's learning (Black et al., 2003).

After the lesson, the task of reflection and evaluation has two facets. The first concerns thinking about and evaluating pupils' learning, and the second concerns thinking about and evaluating one's own teaching. Regarding the first facet, the practice of marking pupils' work in recent years has moved from a dominance on 'summative assessment' (the scoring or grading of a pupil's work in order to record the standard achieved) to a dominance on 'formative assessment' (writing comments on pupils' work designed to fostering learning and to help them improve their future work) (Gardner, 2006).

Regarding the second facet, teachers are increasing encouraged to reflect and evaluate their teaching with a view to considering how they can improve their practice (Jones *et al.,* 2006). Such reflection also includes more emphasis on how teachers should use the assessment of pupils' learning to guide their planning of future lessons. In order to facilitate and support teacher development through reflection, teachers are regularly observed teaching by a colleague as part of teacher appraisal and performance management schemes, and are also encouraged to improve their practice by taking account of evidence about good practice channelled through government policy initiatives such as national teaching strategies, school-based in-service training sessions, or engagement in small-scale research activities. In addition, the TDA's (2008) 'professional standards for teachers' also provide an important framework for thinking about and evaluating teacher development.

Relationships and discipline

Underpinning teaching is the need to establish a sound and positive relationship between the teacher and the taught. Within the context of schooling this can be problematic as teachers often have to teach pupils who are disaffected, lack interest in the subject, or may have serious personal problems that interfere with them being able to deploy appropriate effort at school (Beaman *et al.,* 2010; Kyriacou, 2002). There are two main facets to such relationships. First, the teacher needs to create a classroom climate within which the relationship between the teacher and pupils is based on mutual respect and rapport and where pupils accept the authority of the teacher to organise and run the lesson. Second, the teacher needs to exert discipline to deal with any pupil misbehaviour that occurs.

It is not possible to describe the ideal relationship between teachers and pupils as both teachers and pupils differ in their personal needs and their personalities. Teachers also have preferred ways of teaching (teaching styles) and pupils also have preferred ways of learning (learning styles). As such the type of relationship that might work best for one teacher or pupil might not work well for another teacher or pupil. However, research on classroom management (Evertson and Weinstein, 2006) indicates that there are two generic characteristics which seem to apply well for most teachers and most pupils most of the time.

First, pupils need to have confidence in their teacher's ability to teach well. This will be characterised by a teacher who behaves in a confident manner, and displays to pupils that they have the appropriate skills to organise learning activities that engage pupils. Indeed, the essence of a teacher's authority needs to lie in the pupils' recognition of the teacher's expertise rather than in feeling intimated by the teacher. One of the major shifts in the nature of teaching in schools has been one from seeing the teacher as strict and authoritarian in their dealings with pupils towards seeing the teacher as being more personal and humane.

Second, pupils need to have confidence in their teacher's ability to exercise discipline. Exercising discipline seems to be most effective when it involves the use of staged strategies. Most misbehaviour can be minimised pre-emptively by making sure the teaching engages pupils and by careful monitoring and action for pupils who appear to be disengaged. This may include directing questions at pupils who appear to be inattentive, circulating around the room to check that pupils are working appropriately, and maintaining a task-focused climate. The next stage of action involves using a mixture of reprimands, rule-reminders and conversing with a pupil to investigate whether there is a problem that underpins why the pupil has misbehaved (for example, the pupil may be unable to do the task that has been set). Such actions are best dealt with quietly on a one-to-one basis, rather than publicly (where other pupils can hear what is being said). The third stage involves threatening to take matters further, which can include the threat of a punishment. The final stage involves taking matters further, such as involving more senior teachers, parents, carrying out punishments, and in the most serious cases, exclusion from the school. Skilful teachers will normally be able to deal with most problems within stages one and two. Indeed, one of the key features in schools which have comparatively lower rates of exclusions (compared to schools with similar pupils) is that the teachers more frequently adopt classroom practices which are effective in exercising discipline within the classroom level and avoid recourse to 'taking matters further'.

Conclusion

There is little doubt that teaching is a complex activity. Nevertheless, research has enabled us to gain an understanding of the key features of teaching and the relative effectiveness of different classroom practices. Moreover, a number of publications have sought to establish as clearly as possible how research findings can provide an evidence base to inform teaching in schools (e.g. Pollard, 2010). However, the interplay between the different aspects of any given situation continues to present teachers and policy-makers with major challenges in their attempts to initiate changes that will lead to improvements in the learning experience for pupils. What seems to be increasingly apparent is that the socialisation function of teaching (helping to prepare pupils to lead to satisfying and fulfilling lives) needs to go hand in hand with a more exclusive focus on promoting academic attainment. Moreover, developing practices that are more successful in meeting the needs of disaffected pupils remains a major issue facing educationists. As such, when looking at the nature of teaching and effective classroom practice, it is crucially important to bear in mind the wider picture regarding the purposes of education and the personal and social context within which the teaching occurs.

Questions for further investigation

1   Is it possible to identify teaching practices that will work best?
2   How far can teaching be personalised?
3   What role does dialogue play during teaching?

Suggested further reading

Cullingford, C. (2009) *The art of teaching: Experiences of schools.* London: Taylor and Francis. This excellent book provides an insightful analysis of how pupils experience teachers and teaching by drawing extensively on their perceptions.

Kyriacou, C. (2009) *Effective teaching in schools: Theory and practice* (3rd Ed.). Cheltenham: Nelson Thornes. In this book I have drawn on key insights provided by conceptual and research-based writings on teaching to develop a conceptual framework for understanding and promoting sound classroom practice.

> Mercer, N. and Hodgkinson, S. (Eds.) (2008) *Exploring talk in schools: Inspired by the work of Douglas Barnes.* London: Sage. This book addresses how and why the quality of talk that takes place in the classroom, particularly through the use of high-quality dialogue, has a major impact on promoting and sustaining pupil learning.

References

Anderson, P.M. (2009) *Pedagogy.* New York, NY: Peter Lang.

Ausubel, D.P. (1968) *Educational psychology: A cognitive view.* New York, NY: Holt, Rinehart and Winston.

Beaman, R., Wheldall, K. and Kemp, C. (2010) 'Recent research on troublesome classroom behaviour', in Wheldall, K. (Ed.) *Developments in educational psychology* (2nd Ed.). Abingdon: Routledge, pp. 135–152.

Black, P., Harrison, C., Lee, C., Marshall, B. and Wiliam, D. (2003) *Assessment for learning: Putting it into practice.* Maidenhead: Open University Press.

Bloom, B.S., Engelhart, M., Furst, E., Hill, W. and Krathwohl, D. (1956) *Taxonomy of educational objectives: The classification of educational goals, Handbook 1: Cognitive domains.* New York, NY: Longmans Green.

Courcier, I. (2007) 'Teachers' perceptions of personalised learning', *Evaluation and Research in Education,* 20, 2, pp. 59–80.

Cowie, H., Smith, P.K. and Blades, M. (2010) *Understanding children's development* (5th Ed.). Chichester: Wiley.

Cullingford, C. (2009) *The art of teaching: Experiences of schools.* London: Taylor and Francis.

Daly, C. and Pachler, N. (2010) 'E-learning: The future?', in Arthur, J. and Davies, I. (Eds.) *Routledge Education Studies Textbook.* Abingdon: Routledge, pp. 216–226.

Day, C. and Gu, Q. (2010) *The new lives of teachers.* Abingdon: Routledge.

Evertson, C.M. and Weinstein, C.S. (Eds.) (2006) *Handbook of classroom management: Research, practice, and contemporary issues.* Mahwah, NJ: Lawrence Erlbaum.

Gardner, J. (Ed.) (2006) *Assessment and learning.* London: Sage.

Good, T.L. and Brophy, J.E. (2007) *Looking in classrooms* (10th Ed.). Boston, MA: Allyn and Bacon.

Hattie, J. (2008) *Visible learning.* London: Routledge.

Issitt, J. and Kyriacou, C. (2009) 'Epistemological problems in establishing an evidence base for classroom practice', *Psychology of Education Review,* 33, 1, pp. 47–52.

Jones, J., Jenkin, M. and Lord, S. (2006) *Developing effective teacher performance.* London: Paul Chapman.

Kyriacou, C. (2002) *Helping troubled pupils.* Cheltenham: Nelson Thornes.

Kyriacou, C. (2007) *Essential teaching skills.* (3rd Ed.). Cheltenham: Nelson Thornes.

Kyriacou, C. (2009) *Effective teaching in schools: Theory and practice* (3rd Ed.). Cheltenham: Nelson Thornes.

Leach, J. and Moon, B. (2008) *The power of pedagogy.* London: Sage.

Mercer, N. and Hodgkinson, S. (Eds.) (2008) *Exploring talk in schools: Inspired by the work of Douglas Barnes.* London: Sage.

Morgan, M., Ludlow, L., Kitching, K., O'Leary, M. and Clarke, A. (2010) 'What makes teachers tick? Sustaining events in new teachers' lives', *British Educational Research Journal,* 16, 2, pp. 191–208.

Muijs, D. and Reynolds, D. (2010) *Effective teaching: Evidence and practice* (3rd Ed.). London: Sage.

Newton, D.P. (2000) *Teaching for understanding: What it is and how to do it.* London: RoutledgeFalmer.

Organisation for Economic Cooperation and Development (2009) *Creating effective teaching and learning environments: First results from TALIS.* Paris: OECD.

Pollard, A. (Ed.) (2010) *Professionalism and pedagogy: A contemporary opportunity. A commentary by TLRP and GTCE.* London: TLRP.

Skinner, D. (2010) *Effective teaching and learning in practice.* London: Continuum.

Stronge, H. (2007) *Qualities of effective teachers* (2nd Ed.). Alexandria, VA: Association for Supervision and Curriculum Development.

Training and Development Agency for Schools (TDA) (2008) *Professional standards for teachers in England.* London: TDA.

Wilen, W., Hutchinson, J. and Ishler, M. (2008) *Dynamics of effective secondary teaching* (6th Ed.). New York, NY: Pearson.

13

Curriculum and curriculum studies

Michael Connelly and Shijing Xu
University of Toronto and University of Windsor

Overview

This chapter describes the range of definitions and meanings associated with the terms "curriculum" and "curriculum studies." We describe the main debates in the field and adopt a particular stance useful for newcomers to the field, especially for those concerned with curriculum in the schools and with how curriculum is viewed in public and political discourse. The chapter concludes with a brief look into the not too distant future.

Introduction

Definition: curriculum and curriculum studies

The word "curriculum" points to two related matters, formal and informal things and activities (in schools, other institutions, and in life) and the study of these things and activities. Curriculum is studied in curriculum studies. This relationship is established in the field's two Web of Science journals, *Curriculum Inquiry* and *Journal of Curriculum Studies*. The titles of both define a close relationship between curriculum and curriculum studies. But what is done in curriculum and in curriculum studies often appear in the literature as separate things, hence the two part title of this chapter.

Definition of curriculum

When the word "curriculum" is used in educational institutions, it is commonly understood to refer to the content of what is taught, often including extracurricular activities. This broad common-sense notion of curriculum is refined and interpreted in many different ways. Some think of content in terms of disciplinary subject matter, others in terms of student abilities, experiences, and learning, others in terms of social needs and purposes, and still others in terms of particular teacher-based programs. The result is that curriculum is notorious for its diversity of definitions. Introductory textbooks (Marsh, 2008) and encyclopedic overviews (e.g. Connelly and Xu, 2010) invariably begin with descriptions of the variety of definitions. Most of these definitions reflect interpretations of the everyday meaning of the word as referring to what is taught and point to curriculum practicalities, that is, to subject matter, students, teachers, and social context, and to various mixes of these matters vertically and horizontally through the years of education.

There are two complications associated with this range of what might be called practical curriculum definitions. First, "curriculum" is not an internationally common term and may not be part of the educational lexicon in certain countries while in others the term may have been borrowed from the English-speaking West but may have subtly different meanings in these national contexts. Second, in university curriculum departments where curriculum studies is normally done, "curriculum" often means something quite different than the practical use of the word described above. Common referents are "curriculum theory," "reconceptualism," "criticism of curriculum practices," and "the avoidance of curriculum for reasons of the 'status quo'." The tension currently splitting the field into disparate groups is that while one of the principal purposes of curriculum studies is to critique existing practices, criticism and its products must take root in, and change, the practices critiqued. But critical curriculum theory has become an abstract textual exercise disconnected from practice. Criticism is based on imagined practice and proposals for action are mostly abstract suggestions found in books and journals with little practitioner readership. It is important to note that by practical we mean a theoretically derived *way of thinking* about curriculum in which *action* is the subject matter and outcome of deliberations.

Definition of curriculum studies

The range of definitions of "curriculum studies" is less than that of "curriculum." Four recent definitions follow. Schubert (2008) retains the relationship of curriculum studies to curriculum by defining curriculum in terms of "experiential journeys" and implying that curriculum inquiry is the study of these journeys. He organizes curriculum inquiry into four "paradigms," (e.g. critical inquiry), nine "emergent eclectics" (e.g. practical inquiry), and eight "contemporary venues" (e.g. intended curriculum).

Pinar (2008) lists three "moments" which structure contemporary curriculum theory: curriculum development, curriculum reconceptualism, and internationalization. Pinar collapses the distinction between curriculum and curriculum studies by defining curriculum as "a highly symbolic concept" and "an extraordinarily complicated conversation" in which curriculum studies, which emerged in the second moment, is aimed at theoretical understanding.

Reid (1992) defines curriculum studies in terms of *ways of thinking* about curriculum: curriculum as plan, curriculum as cultural reproduction, curriculum as personal experience, curriculum as practical art. Reid positions himself in the practical art tradition which follows from Schwab's language of the practical described below.

Our own way of thinking about curriculum inquiry is to divide it into three areas based on curricular studies subjects: curriculum subject matter, curriculum topics and preoccupations, and curriculum theory. We use this breakdown below in the section "Structure of curriculum studies."

Making sense of diverse thought in curriculum and curriculum studies

Schwab, one of the field's leading thinkers, developed two foundational concepts for helping make sense of curriculum and curriculum studies: *commonplaces of curriculum* (Schwab, 1962) and *language of the practical* (Schwab, 1969, 1971, 1973, 1983).

The first, *commonplaces*, provides an analytic structure for analyzing and assessing different definitions, different proposals for curriculum reform, and different policies for overall school curriculum and for specific curriculum subjects. Without advancing a definition, Schwab suggested that all comprehensive curriculum statements, documents, and activities dealt with subject matter, learner, teacher, and milieu, that is, dealt with the commonplaces. Two useful activities for readers interested in commonplaces as a way of sorting out diversity in the field are to search the literature for two or more definitions or two or more curriculum policies and then ask, of each, "What does the author make of subject matter? . . . of milieu? . . . of teacher? . . . of learner?" *and* "Which of these is the starting point of the argument and how do the others fit in?" Inevitably, different concepts of subject matter, teacher, learner, and milieu will be revealed by the first question while the second will establish the text's logical priorities. For instance, a curriculum designed with international competition (milieu) in mind might proceed from there to the idea that subject matter needed to be strengthened. In such a case, milieu is the curricular starting point and subject matter is the key commonplace while the learner and teacher are derived in terms of milieu and subject matter. On the other hand, a curriculum developed on the basis of a concern that student interests and abilities were being sidetracked by a subject matter-oriented curriculum might begin with the learner. In this case, learner is the starting point with subject matter, teacher, and milieu derived in terms of learners. In this way Schwab's idea of the commonplaces provides an analytic tool for readers and evaluators interested in assessing curriculum documents.

For those interested in the theoretical origins of Schwab's idea of the commonplaces, it is worth noting that his idea is based on Aristotle's Topica devoted to discourse fields or areas, which lack fixed theoretical structures and accepted facts. Such fields are, accordingly, based on arguments revolving around widely held opinion. Arguments change as accepted opinions change. The range of opinions is not infinite and is organized by certain types which Aristotle called "topics." For practical fields like curriculum, there is no theoretically fixed, true nor best way for all time, only the best way under the circumstances as determined by an argument based on the topics. This helps explain why curriculum issues are never solved. They are always with us, taking different solution paths depending on time and circumstance in which different commonplaces assume prominence and relate in particular ways to other commonplaces.

Schwab's second concept, *language of the practical*, establishes a theoretical perspective for thinking about curriculum, for researching curriculum, and for curriculum studies in general. Again, drawing on an Aristotelian distinction found in the Metaphysics between the theoretical and practical disciplines, Schwab argued that curriculum is a practical field concerned with *making curriculum* – for example, making policies, courses, learning activities, and workshops – and with *doing curriculum* – for example, teaching, implementing curriculum, evaluating curriculum. Curriculum, said Schwab following Aristotle, is a practical field with the *actions* of making and doing as its ends whereas the basic disciplines in the theoretical fields are aimed at *knowledge* and *understanding*. Thus, with this concept of the language of the practical, Schwab provided a way of thinking about the kind of research that might be done in curriculum studies, and he provided a way of thinking about the purpose of teaching undergraduates and graduates in curriculum. The publication of the language of the practical marked a turning point in the nature of curriculum studies (Null, 2008). The main issue in the field of curriculum studies is between those who think, in terms of "practical" ends vs. those who think in terms of "theoretical" ends.

Structure of curriculum and curriculum studies

In this section we describe both the structure of curriculum as found in educational institutions and the structure of the field of curriculum studies.

Structure of curriculum

There are five main factors that determine the structure of curriculum: institutional structure, subject matter structure, available instructional time (horizontal factor), age/grade divisions (vertical), and student interest and ability.

Institutional structure

The school is the main institutional structure. Though found in different cultures and countries, schools are surprisingly similar worldwide. The fact that schools are physical places with walls and have at least one teacher and a group of students with a fixed day length and fixed operating times through the year, shapes the structure of curriculum. Schools, however, exist in many different forms ranging from one-room schools with few students and multiple grades to comprehensive high schools with large numbers of students. There are academic schools focused on specific subjects – for example, science; there are vocational schools focused on the practical work world; and there are special interest alternative schools oriented to student interests and abilities. There are schools within schools aimed at creating a sense of community in large comprehensive schools, and there are schools based on student achievement standards. Most of these institutional arrangements retain recognizable horizontal and vertical structures although there are alternative schools with specially structured curricula.

Subject matter structure

The, almost, universal way of organizing content is by subjects. The subject matter structure of secondary schools often closely mimics the structure of the academic disciplines (e.g. science, mathematics, literature), while subject matter in the elementary school is normally divided into broader interdisciplinary areas (e.g. reading, arithmetic, language). The specific breakdown into different subjects yields a visibly obvious structure of the curriculum. When a person asks for a description of a school's curriculum, they are normally asking for content structure.

Available instructional time (horizontal factor)

Given a specific amount of available time arising from the institutional structure – for example, 315 instructional minutes per day – each subject is allocated specific amounts of time, normally assigned in terms of "periods." A period normally has a fixed time – for example, 45 minutes – allocated to it for a specific school, or age/grade group in a political jurisdiction. An important source of discussion within curriculum is competition over how much time to allocate to each subject. Should mathematics in grade 10, for example, have the same amount of allocated time as does art? When there are budget cuts, "soft" subjects such as art and physical education tend to be given reduced time. This discussion occurs both for disciplinary subjects in the secondary school and for the broader more interdisciplinary subjects at the elementary school level. The horizontal structure of curriculum generates debates with labels such as "the overloaded curriculum" and "time on task."

Age/grade divisions (vertical)

Here, the sequence of content to be taught throughout the grades is the structuring issue. The main concerns are what should be taught at what level and how to bring about smooth transitions and sequences from one age/grade level to another and across subjects at a given level. Many possibilities exist. Sometimes one subject is seen as prerequisite to another; for instance, based on disciplinary knowledge considerations, chemistry may be a grade 10 subject and biology a grade 11 subject. Or, biology may precede chemistry based on considerations of student interest and maturity. Sometimes a specific set of subjects are specified as core subjects and each is offered every year, each year building on the preceding years. Still other situations may arise where a subject or topic is said to be so important it needs to be built in to all subjects; for example, language across the curriculum. The vertical structure of curriculum is often the target of curriculum critics when it is said that one political jurisdiction has higher standards than another because of more advanced content concepts at the same age/grade level; for example, "Country 'x' has a weak educational system compared to country 'y' because grade 12 students in 'x' study the same content as grade 10 students in 'y'." Comparative achievement studies conducted by organizations such as the International Association for the Evaluation of Educational Achievement and the Programme for International Student Assessment (PISA) contribute to such debates.

Student interest and ability

Different student interests and abilities yield one of the ongoing sources of discussion over curriculum organization. Two broad curriculum structure issues arise. The first is how to certify and give graduating diplomas to students. Some systems specify a core curriculum which must be achieved at a certain level. In jurisdictions where a core curriculum is specified, it is possible to specify what is taught in all schools at specific times throughout the year. Other systems define progress in terms of credits which may be achieved in different ways as students choose courses of interest. Comprehensive high schools in North America and Europe tend to work on a credit system with the result that students may acquire the required certificate credits and graduate with quite different curriculum backgrounds. Combinations of core and elective subjects are possible. Some systems, such as China's, use a national examination modified in various ways at provincial and other local levels to select and stream students following high school.

The second structuring feature based on student interest and ability is the creation of special routes and programs. One expression of this is "tracking" in which students of different interest and ability choose, or are required to study, different sequences of courses called tracks. The extreme version of tracking is found where special schools exist. Vocational schools are an example as is the creation of special schools such as an arts school or a science school. There has been an expansion of *alternative schools* within large school boards. The Toronto District School Board (TDSB) for example lists 19 elementary and 22 secondary alternative schools on their website (Toronto District School Board, 2010). The existence of alternative schools within a larger system may generate public debate. The creation of the most recent TDSB alternative school, the Afrocentric Alternative School, generated impassioned debate over a several-year period.

Structure of curriculum studies

Curriculum studies structure refers to the organization of school board, university, and other organizations devoted to the study of curriculum. The above discussion of the definition of curriculum and of Schwab's ideas for organizing diverse curriculum thought is an example of curriculum studies at work. Curriculum studies is organized into three main components: curriculum subject matters, curriculum topics and preoccupations, curriculum theory.

Subject matters

Subject matter is the most visible, and the largest, structure in curriculum studies. This follows from the fact that content subject matters are the primary way of organizing school curriculum (described above). The structure of faculties of education often mirrors school curriculum structure. Almost all faculties of education have, for example, several elementary school and secondary school mathematics teacher educators. Each of these areas has one or more professional associations with their own conferences, journals, and other networking professional methods. In science, for example, there are many organizations such as the Science Teachers Association of Ontario (STAO), the National Association for Research in Science Teaching (NARST), *The Journal of Research on Science Teaching*, *Science Education* and so forth. Depending on the purpose of these organizations, they may have somewhat different, though overlapping, membership. NARST membership is primarily drawn from universities whereas STAO is more local with a broader membership drawn from school boards, teacher associations, universities, and government.

Curriculum topics and preoccupations

Following Schwab's idea of the *language of the practical* and the importance of *making* and *doing*, there are a wide range of curriculum topics and preoccupations; for example, curriculum policy-making, curriculum policy analysis, curriculum evaluation, curriculum and gender, curriculum and race, etc. These pursuits cut across the subject matter areas, although some writers speak in general whereas others write specifically in the context of subjects. For example, gender in the curriculum may be written about as a general topic cutting across the curriculum horizontally and vertically or it may be written about in the context of a specific subject matter at a specific age/grade level; for example, gender and mathematics in eighth grade (Hanna, 1986).

Historically, curriculum studies was preoccupied with curriculum development and the associated preoccupations of curriculum implementation and curriculum evaluation. These traditional preoccupations faded as the limited success of curriculum reform efforts became evident (Fullan, 2008). These historically important *curriculum preoccupations* dealt explicitly with curriculum. The expanding array of recently introduced *curriculum topics* occupies a different position in curriculum studies. For instance, gender in the curriculum is focused on a specific curriculum topic, is connected to societal critique, and is pursued with an emotive and moral voice. Many writers on the topics are found in university departments other than ones called "curriculum and instruction." At one end of the scholarly continuum this literature is more concerned with social science thought in general than it is with curriculum matters. Others write in a curriculum vein but do so "in general," that is, they are concerned with the topic across the curriculum, and still others write explicitly with respect to a specific age/grade level and/or a specific subject matter. In general those writing in the *topics* argue that the topic in question should be dealt with horizontally and vertically across all subjects in the curriculum.

Curriculum theory

Curriculum theory and general curriculum studies were at one time interdependent. People who wrote what could be called curriculum theory did so in the context of the curriculum structures noted above. There was a close relationship between practice and theoretical writing. Recently curriculum theorists have taken a "wrong turn" to text (Westbury, 2007) and are separated from those doing research on curriculum practices. Currently, the literature of curriculum theory falls under the rubric of "reconceptualism," a self-defined label designed to reflect the rich, abstract, theoretical literature of the curriculum theory part of curriculum studies. This engaging literature is currently cut off from curriculum and the broad base of curriculum studies. There is potential in the curriculum theory literature for connecting with, and making a difference to, curriculum. To do so will require a re-direction in what is now called curriculum theory and a rededication to improving curriculum practice.

Ongoing and future developments

Curriculum, as noted above, is a practical field characterized by shifting opinion on what should be taught, to whom, by whom, and for what purpose. The debates surrounding the impact of modern technologies on education are illustrative. Moreover, in complex multicultural societies, and in an age of global communication, opinion rarely coalesces around any particular desirable curriculum content, practice, or end. The result is continuing public political debate over curriculum in deliberative forums: school staff meetings, school councils, teacher organizations, administrative and government committees, television, newspapers, books, blogs. Politicians and political parties commonly prepare political platforms which are used to gain public support during elections and which are used to justify actions following elections. Curriculum functions as the basis for narratives of persuasion and justification in public political discourse.

The word "curriculum" tends not to be used in public debate where the more expansive word "education" is used. But an analysis of educational debates, and associated educational policies, using either intuitive good sense or, more analytically, Schwab's commonplaces, reveals that this debate is curricular. The No Child Left Behind (NCLB) Policy in the United States, for example, is called an educational policy. When analyzed, the arguments are seen to be curricular and have to do with what should be taught to equalize opportunity for socially and culturally diverse groups of students. The heated criticisms of the student achievement testing measures introduced to evaluate the success of the NCLB curriculum reform revolve around what is or is not taught in schools and the effect this has on students and society.

China is a contrasting political system with a contrasting achievement testing history. There has been a long tradition in China where achievement testing is used nationally to stream students based on test results. However, in recent years China has been moving in an opposite direction to North America, in that efforts are being made to reform the testing system. The arguments and reasons given for this change are curricular and have to do with the impact of testing on student lives, the limitation of test scores as an indicator of workforce ability, competition with other countries, and the limitations testing places on what is taught. Zhao (2009) points out that Americans admire models of excellence in countries such as China, while China appears to emulate American education as it moves toward more local autonomy, more flexibility, more choice, less testing, less content, and less standardization. Our personal view is that reciprocal learning is important to the future. Reciprocal learning is based on the idea that each system acknowledges and retains its cultural strengths while adopting valuable features in other systems. Furthermore, we may keep in mind the Chinese saying, 他山之石，可以攻玉 (literally, "The stones of other hills may be used to polish gems"), meaning that "By others' faults, wise people correct their own."

Conclusion

The point we wish to make relative to the future of curriculum and curriculum studies is that the place to look for future directions is public discourse surrounding policy changes. There we currently see vibrant debate over achievement testing and, when this debate is analyzed in curriculum terms, we see subject matter content, equality of student opportunity and national needs at work. In China this matter is expressed in debates over rural education, the education of children of migrant workers, and the education of minority group children. In America and in other parts of the world there are equivalent debates over multiculturalism, race, social class, gender and the effects of globalization, migration and circular migration. To return to Aristotle and Schwab, it would appear that variable opinions on these matters will likely mark the future of curriculum and curriculum studies.

Questions for further investigation

1 What is the curriculum policy in a political jurisdiction (province, state, country) of interest to you? Describe the stated purpose of the policy, the main areas covered and the terms used to structure the policy (e.g. subject matter, goals, behaviors, rubrics etc.).
2 What is the curriculum of a school, and of a classroom in that school, found in your choice of jurisdiction in Question #1?
3 Analyze the curriculum policy and the curriculum described in Questions #1 and #2 using Schwab's commonplaces. Write a short paragraph summary of each.
4 Identify a recent curriculum debate found in the media. Collect statements and arguments about this debate and then analyze the debate from a curriculum point of view.

Suggested further reading

Curriculum statements in a local administrative jurisdiction; for example, a school board. Begin with the website, for example, the website for the Toronto District School Board. Many items will not be labeled curriculum that are, in fact, curricular. You will need to use Schwab's commonplaces and the structure of curriculum above in your search. You might extend your search by interviewing the curriculum coordinator or superintendent, sometimes called a program person.

Connelly, F.M. (Ed.) with He, M.F. and Phillion, J. (Assoc. Eds.) (2008) *The Sage Handbook of Curriculum and Instruction.* Thousand Oaks, CA: Sage Publications, Inc. The *Handbook* summarizes the literature of curriculum studies between 1992, the publication date of Jackson's *Handbook of Research on Curriculum,* and 2008. The *Handbook* is organized around the concept of the curriculum as practical. It is divided into three parts: Curriculum in Practice, Curriculum in Context, and Curriculum in Theory. The parts are broken down into "curriculum action" sections: Making Curriculum, Managing Curriculum, Diversifying Curriculum, Teaching Curriculum, Internationalizing Curriculum, and Inquiring into Curriculum.

Marsh, C.J. (2008) *Key Concepts for Understanding Curriculum* (4th Ed.). New York, NY: Routledge. This is the most recent comprehensive textbook introduction to curriculum studies. The book is divided into six parts: Introduction: Definitions and Concepts, Curriculum Planning and Development, Curriculum Management, Teaching Perspectives, Collaborative Involvement in Curriculum, and Curriculum Ideology.

Westbury, I. and Wilkof, N.J. (1978) *Joseph Schwab. Science, curriculum, and liberal education: Selected essays.* Chicago, IL: The University of Chicago Press. The book reprints Schwab's "practical" papers as well as other writings by Schwab on science education and general education. The set of papers, combined with the interpretive introduction by Westbury and Wilkof, provides a comprehensive introduction to Schwab's practical theory of curriculum.

References

Connelly, F.M. and Xu, S.J. (2010) 'An overview of research in curriculum inquiry', in McGraw, B., Baker, E. and Peterson, P. (Eds.) *Elsevier International Encyclopedia of Education* (3rd Ed.). Amsterdam: Elsevier Inc, pp. 324–334.

Fullan, M. (2008) 'Curriculum implementation and sustainability', in Connelly, F.M. (Ed.) with He, M.F. and Phillion, J. (Assoc. Eds.) (2008) *The Sage Handbook of Curriculum and Instruction.* Thousand Oaks, CA: Sage Publications, Inc.

Hanna, G. (1986) 'Sex differences in the mathematics achievement of Eighth Graders in Ontario', *Journal of Research in Mathematics Education,* 17, 3, pp. 231–237.

Jackson, P.W. (1992) *Handbook of Research on Curriculum: A Project of the American Educational Research Association.* New York, NY: Macmillan.

Marsh, C.J. (2008) *Key Concepts for Understanding Curriculum* (4th Ed.). New York, NY: Routledge.

Null, W. (2008) 'Curriculum development in historical perspective', in Connelly, F.M. (Ed.) with He, M.F. and Phillion, J. (Assoc. Eds.) (2008) *The Sage Handbook of Curriculum and Instruction.* Thousand Oaks, CA: Sage Publications, Inc.

Pinar, W.F. (2008) 'Curriculum theory since 1950: Crisis, reconceptualization, internationalization', in Connelly, F.M. (Ed.) with He, M.F. and Phillion, J. (Assoc. Eds.) (2008) *The Sage Handbook of Curriculum and Instruction.* Thousand Oaks, CA: Sage Publications, Inc.

Reid, W.A. (1992) *The Pursuit of Curriculum: Schooling and the Public Interest.* Norwood, NJ: Ablex Publishing Corporation.

Schubert, W.H. (2008) 'Curriculum inquiry', in Connelly, F.M. (Ed.) with He, M.F. and Phillion, J. (Assoc. Eds.) (2008) *The Sage Handbook of Curriculum and Instruction.* Thousand Oaks, CA: Sage Publications, Inc.

Schwab, J. (1983) 'The practical, 4: Something for curriculum professors to do', *Curriculum Inquiry,* 13, 3, pp. 239–265.

Schwab, J.J. (1973) 'The practical 3: Translation into curriculum', *School Review,* 81, pp. 501–522, in Westbury, I. and Wilkof, N.J. (1978) *Joseph Schwab. Science, Curriculum, and Liberal Education: Selected Essays.* Chicago, IL: The University of Chicago Press.

Schwab, J.J. (1971) 'The practical: Arts of eclectic', *School Review,* 79, 4, pp. 493–542.

Schwab, J.J. (November, 1969) 'The practical: A language for curriculum', *The School Review*, 78, 1, pp. 1–23.

Schwab, J.J. (1962) 'The teaching of science as enquiry (The Inglis Lecture)', in Schwab, J.J. and Brandwein, P.F. (Eds.) *The Teaching of Science*. Cambridge, MA: Harvard University Press.

Toronto District School Board (2010) 'Alternative Schools'. Available at: www.tdsb.on.ca/_site/ViewItem. asp?siteid=122&menuid=490&pageid=379 (accessed 2 July 2010).

Westbury, I. (2007) 'Theory and theorizing in curriculum studies', in Forsberg, E. (Ed.) *Curriculum Theory Revisited*. Uppsala, Sweden: Uppsala University, Studies in Educational Policy and Educational Philosophy, Research Reports, pp. 7, 1–19.

Zhao, Y. (2009) *Catching Up or Leading the Way: American Education in the Age of Globalization*. Alexandria, VA: ASCD.

14

Language

Louise C. Wilkinson and Elaine R. Silliman
Syracuse University and University of South Florida

Overview

The primary purpose of this chapter is to describe the language proficiency requirements for students' achievement in school. In addition, this chapter reviews the current policy context for research on academic language proficiency, including the European Union and the United States. Also examined is the relationship of academic language proficiency to successful participation in the academic discourse requirements across disciplines and in specific content areas. As defined by Bailey (2010), academic language proficiency "is a formal register ... used in school settings for instructional and procedural/navigational purposes that includes the vocabulary, syntax, and discourse associated with classroom talk, textbooks, tests, and other curricular materials" (p. 234). The discussion also includes a review of trends, issues, and how future research is likely to develop on academic language proficiency.

Introduction – the European context: the current policy context of language diversity

Because of the common borders created by the European Union, as well as other immigration patterns related to socio-economic or political factors, language diversity in western European schools is now a fact. For example, according to Extra and Yagmur (2002), the largest Turkish and North African communities reside in Germany and France, respectively. Of the 27 EU countries, Germany has the greatest number of Turkish immigrants (Treffers-Daller *et al.*, 2010), while the Netherlands ranks second as an immigration country for those with Turkish and Moroccan nationality. In contrast, immigration to the United Kingdom since 1991 primarily consists of individuals from the Indian sub-continent (India and Pakistan) (Migration Policy Institute, 2010), followed by those of Afro-Caribbean origin, with Cantonese-speaking Chinese and their British-born children constituting the third largest immigrant community (Hua, 2008).

Extra and Yagmur (2002) also point out that reliable demographic information on immigrant groups to the 27 EU countries is difficult to obtain due to wide variations on how data are collected, updated, or even collected at all.

As might be expected, under current economic conditions, many EU schools are struggling with various degrees of success, much less financial support, on how to embed the understanding of language diversity into the educational curriculum. To illustrate the challenges that many are facing, Lyons and Little (2009) report that in Ireland 7 percent of primary grade students and 5 percent of post-primary students have a first language that is neither English nor Irish. Furthermore, a number of obstacles were identified in the failure to provide these students with sufficient access to and support in the mainstream curriculum: (1) English language support is not coordinated and more often is disorganized; (2) the tendency to hold a "deficit" perspective about non-English/Irish speaking children; and (3) the absence of appropriate teacher preparation on either pre- or in-service programs. Similar situations exist elsewhere. In the Catalan region of Spain, the majority of immigrant students are from North Africa and Central and South America and progress in bilingual education has been slow (Bochaca, 2006). Even within a single country, such as Morocco, children who speak various Berber dialects (i.e., Moroccan Arabic dialects) are at a distinct disadvantage when they enter school where the language of instruction is Modern Standard Arabic and French (Daniel and Ball, 2010).

Academic language proficiency

Little research has been conducted on the short- and long-term consequences of inadequate educational programs for immigrant students, an inadequacy that significantly impacts on their ethnic, linguistic, and religious identity (García-Sánchez, 2010). In a similar manner, there has been only modest research on the oral language and literacy practices of bilingual low-income immigrant families as well as the development of academic language proficiency in emerging bilinguals. Most of this small research base involves students whose first languages were Turkish, Moroccan Arabic, or Berber.

For example, in a preliminary study of the home language input of 3-year-old children from Moroccan-Dutch, Turkish-Dutch, and monolingual Dutch families in The Netherlands, Scheele et al. (2010) selected a representative sample according to socio-economic status (SES) (Moroccan-Dutch families overall had the lowest SES). Mothers were interviewed in their preferred language by researchers who shared the same cultural membership. Mothers were asked to rate how often they read picture books to their children, told stories, engaged children in conversations about daily events, sang songs together, and allowed their children to watch educational TV. Rating choices ranged from daily to never. Children's nonverbal cognitive ability was assessed. In addition, their vocabulary recognition, a measure of vocabulary breadth, was evaluated in the two languages (L1 and L2) experienced in the home. Although children across the three groups did not differ in nonverbal cognition, as might be predicted, the Turkish-Dutch and Moroccan-Dutch children experienced significantly less oral and literate language experiences in both L1 and L2 than did the monolingual Dutch children. This pattern of maternal input was also reflected for the most part in their children's lower L1 vocabulary scores. Given the limitations of a self-report study, the authors interpret these findings as evidence that young children from low-income bilingual immigrant families are at dual risk: first, limited oral and literate interactions "have to be divided over two languages" (Scheele et al., 2010, p. 137) and, second, the restricted extent of interactions reduces L1 support for the acquisition of L2.

Obviously, more studies are needed, in both Europe and North America, on the quality, not just the quantity, of early L1 interactions and subsequent linkages to academic language proficiency. In one of the few studies on academic language proficiency, Droop and Verhoeven (2003) focused on the oral language and reading skills in grades 3 to 4 of low SES Turkish and Moroccan children contrasting their performance with monolingual Dutch students from both high and low SES families. Oral language knowledge of vocabulary, morphosyntax, and story comprehension were assessed with Dutch language instruments that had been validated on students culturally similar to the sample in the study. Decoding and reading comprehension abilities in Dutch were also examined. Results indicated that children from the linguistic minority groups lagged behind both SES groups of Dutch children. Between the start of grade 3 and the end of grade 4, the knowledge gap increased the most for oral vocabulary knowledge, an extension into the primary years of the preschool findings by Scheele *et al.* (2010) just reviewed. This vocabulary gap significantly contributed to problems in reading comprehension, a finding also consistent with the gap patterns of Spanish-English-speaking bilingual students in the United States (see Chapter 28, "Cultural–linguistic diversity and inclusion," in this volume).

A third study focused just on oral narratives. Treffers-Daller *et al.* (2010) examined the complex syntax of young adults who were Turkish-German bilinguals and were born either in Germany or in Turkey and were recent returnees to that country from Germany. They were compared with monolingual Turkish young adults. All groups came from working-class families. The German born and raised bilinguals evidenced a smaller range of complex Turkish syntax as spoken in Turkey than did the returnees, suggesting that attrition had taken place in the abilities of the German-born group to utilize complex Turkish grammar; hence, this group would not meet Grosjean's (2010) standard for bilingualism as the regular use of two or more languages in everyday lives.

The policy context of education in the United States

Three interrelated trends define contemporary education in the United States at the beginning of the twenty-first century: (1) the achievement gap among students of varied cultural and linguistic backgrounds, which, to a large extent, mirrors current achievement gaps in the European Community as just discussed; (2) the emphasis on accountability in public education, with a particular focus on teacher efficacy; and (3) the move toward a uniform set of curriculum standards. The achievement gap and accountability trends make clear the critical need in the coming years for better teacher preparation and continuing professional development, while the trend toward a uniform set of curriculum standards marks the first time in the educational history of the United States that core national standards have taken center stage.

The achievement gap

As it is for the EU countries, but in a more complex way because of the heterogeneous population in the US, the achievement gaps among groups of children with varying socio-economic status, first language preference, and race and ethnicity is the major challenge for American education in the early twenty-first century. In 2008, according to US government data, approximately 5.1 percent of kindergarten to grade 12 students spoke another language at home and had difficulty speaking English (ChildStat.Gov, 2010). In the past three decades, the number of these "language minority," children, 75 percent of whom speak Spanish as their home language (Fry, 2007), increased from 3.8 to 10.8 million. Overall, the Hispanic school-age population in the US increased by 11 percent from 1988 to 2008, from 11 percent to 22 percent, while the percentage of school-age children who were native African Americans decreased over the same period, from 17 to 16 percent (National Center for Education Statistics (NCES, 2010a). Other federal government statistics (NCES, 2010b) show that 17.4 percent of children, ages 5 through 17 years old, live at or below the poverty line, a percentage that has not changed since 1990.

For decades, the gaps among students appear early and become amplified from first grade through high school, especially for many Hispanic and African American students. On the 2009 National Assessment of Educational Progress (NAEP) (NCES, 2010c), a national measure administered to representative samples of students at grades 4 and 8, 71 percent of fourth-graders and 74 percent of eighth-graders identified as English language learners (ELLs) scored below the basic level in reading. In contrast, among non-ELL students, 33 percent of fourth-graders and 25 percent of eighth-graders were below the basic level in reading. The picture for mathematics achievement is similar. On the 2009 NAEP, 43 percent of fourth-graders and 72 percent of eighth-graders identified as ELLs scored below the basic level in mathematics, compared to 18 percent of non-ELL fourth-graders and 27 percent of non-ELL eighth-graders.

Notably, students in the United States have not fared well on international comparisons as shown by the Program for International Student Assessment (PISA) and Progress in International Reading Literacy Study (PIRLS) assessments, where the number of countries outperforming the US is large. PISA is a system of international assessments that measures 15–year-olds' performance in reading literacy, mathematics literacy, and science literacy every three years. The most recent report (2006) shows that the average mathematics literacy score in the US was lower than the average score in 23 of the other 29 Organisation for Economic Cooperation and Development (OECD) countries. In science literacy, the average score of 15–year-olds in the US was lower than the average score in 16 of the other 29 OECD countries. PIRLS is an international comparative study of the reading literacy of fourth-grade students. The most recent results show that the average reading comprehension score of US fourth-grade students in 2006 was higher than the average score of students in 22 of the 44 other countries and educational jurisdictions that participated in the PIRLS assessment. Ten countries and educational jurisdictions had average scores higher than the scores of US students. The average scores of students in the remaining 12 countries and educational jurisdictions were not significantly different from the scores of US students.

The negative consequences of the gaps extend well past high school to higher education, where, according to a recent Brookings Institution's report (Haskins *et al.*, 2009), the widening gaps in higher education between rich and poor, and between whites and minorities, may lead to a downturn in economic mobility, making it harder for today's low-income students to move up the economic ladder.

Teacher accountability

In the US, educational standards and the actual content taught, as well as standards for teacher credentialing, are determined by individual states. Since the passage of the No Child Left Behind (NCLB) Act in 2001, however, the federal government has assumed a major role in the setting of educational standards and in the call for teacher accountability. School districts are under pressure to guarantee a skilled teacher in every regular education classroom. However, teachers designated under NCLB standards as "highly qualified" are not necessarily the most effective teachers in the classroom. Effective teachers have students who learn and can demonstrate that learning in a variety of venues including standardized tests. Students with effective teachers will also be capable of achieving at each grade level, be ready to learn the curriculum at the next level, and, eventually, graduate from high school, having completed the required curricula. Simply demanding that teachers, even "highly qualified" ones, be more accountable for student achievement on standardized testing is not enough to overcome the achievement gaps. Teachers require the essential skills to assist all students to achieve to their potential. This goal presents certain challenges. Students who speak social dialects that are different from the Standard English, such as some students of African American heritage (see Chapter 28, "Cultural–linguistic diversity and inclusion," in this volume), might be more likely to succeed in the Standard American English academic language register of their core content areas if their teachers enhanced linguistic flexibility in code switching. This aim can be achieved by altering teachers' preconceptions about social dialect variations (Fogel and Ehri, 2006) and teaching students to (Horton-Ikard and Pittman, 2010): a) engage in contrastive analyses of their social dialect and Standard American English in order to more explicitly highlight similarities and differences and b) enhance their dialect awareness through developing a broader understanding of sociolinguistic concepts underlying different ways of speaking. All teachers, regardless of the content area or grade level they teach, or even if they teach in the European Community or the US, should have knowledge about a) social variations in how a specific language is pronounced and b) research-based instructional strategies that will assist all students, including students who are second language learners, to comprehend and produce content information (Silliman and Wilkinson, 2010).

Common educational standards

Many European Community countries (e.g. England, Ireland, France, Norway, etc.) have national curriculum standards. However, as noted in the US, academic standards have always been the preserve of the individual 50 states. Recently, there has been a press by the Council of Chief State School Officers and the National Governors Association toward the adoption of national standards for core content areas that meet four criteria (Common Core State Standards Initiative, 2010). These standards must be: (1) research and evidence based, (2) aligned with college and work expectations, (3) rigorous, and (4) internationally benchmarked. Academic language proficiency is at the heart of these national standards.

The proposed Common Core State Standards (CCSS), which must be voluntarily adopted by individual states, encompass the English Language Arts and Literacy in History/Social Studies, Science, and Technical Subjects from kindergarten to grade 12. The CCSS specify the fundamental content that students are expected to know and be capable of demonstrating in each grade as they progressively reach toward college and career readiness. However, the CCSS: a) do not specify how teachers should teach grade level content, b) do not guide states on how to support students who are significantly below or above grade level expectations, or c) restrict states from developing more rigorous core standards. To date, 35 states have adopted the CCSS for the English language arts and mathematics (Lewin, 2010).

Survey and analysis: academic language proficiency

Cultivating academic language proficiency in oral comprehension, speaking, reading and writing is the process stressed at each grade level in the CCSS for students to meet the foundational standards. For example, grade 1 literature expectations are that students can explain differences between books that tell stories (or are constructed as narratives) and books that provide information (a type of expository genre) as well as integrate story events using a compare-contrast strategy. In terms of informational text expectations in grade 1, the anticipation is that students have sufficiently emerging metalinguistic awareness so that they can ask and answer questions about the meaning of words and sentences in order to interpret the text. It is also expected that students will display integrated interpretations to describe reasons that an author provides to support the relevant points in an informational text.

Students' school achievement depends upon their being proficient in academic language – the language of classroom instruction, textbooks, and a great deal of "teacher talk." Academic language refers to the vocabulary, syntax, and discourse associated with classroom talk, textbooks, tests, and other curricular materials (Bailey, 2010) as well as the specific linguistic features associated with academic disciplines (content areas) (Hakuta *et al.*, 2001; Wilkinson and Silliman, 2010). Mastery of advanced oral and written English-language skills that enable students to formulate and express their ideas well enough to participate fully in classroom activities is the most important skill for success in school. Cummins (2000, pp. 66–67) asserts that:

> Academic language proficiency refers not to any absolute notion of expertise in using language but the degree to which an individual has access to and expertise in understanding and using the specific kind of language that is employed in educational contexts and is required to complete academic tasks [and] to function effectively in the discourse domain of the school.

Three negative outcomes are likely when students lack proficiency in understanding and using the academic language of content areas. First, students are less likely to learn the skills they need from daily classroom experiences, such as how to use reading and writing to engage in new ways of thinking. Second, because their participation in classroom activities is significantly reduced, they do not benefit as they should from interactions with peers and teachers (Wilkinson and Silliman, 2008; Francis *et al.*, 2006). Third, this reduction in participation subsequently interferes with the development of identity formation as a student in school learning communities (Christian and Bloome, 2004; Danzak and Silliman, 2005.)

The distinction between the everyday oral language register and the more specialized register of academic language is a critical one; these differences are shown in Table 14.1.

These discourse registers, each of which is characterized by its own vocabulary, syntax, degree of formality, and social context, are simultaneously interdependent and independent (Cummins, 2000). While it is possible to "code switch" from one register to the other in a relatively seamless

Table 14.1 Academic language register and everyday oral language register

Everyday oral language register	*Academic language register*
Vernacular discourse varieties that are more oral	Specialist discourse varieties that are more literate
Primary language abilities	Secondary language abilities and advanced literacy-related language abilities
Typical of face-to-face conversation	Typical of the discourse of schooling, including: textbooks, standardized tests, composition, and selected teacher-talk
Not sufficient for academic achievement	Necessary for academic achievement

(Adapted from Wilkinson and Silliman, 2008)

manner (the interdependent dimension), each register can be used separately (the independent dimension) in both the oral and the written domains (Reyes and Ervin-Tripp, 2010). For example, in talking with close friends, individuals probably would use a more oral, or informal register; people are more likely to activate the academic language register when giving a class presentation or writing a research report on the negative environmental consequences of the recent "oil spill" in the US Gulf of Mexico.

Developing academic language proficiency is similar, in some respects, to learning a second language. Primary-language ability means knowing "how to talk" in the situations of everyday life. As such, it encompasses the language socialization processes of a child's culture. Learning the academic language register, however, is not regarded as an automatic process. The fact that learning this register is not automatic, as the previous discussion on social dialect variations indicated, appears to be a major educational challenge for second language learners and monolingual-speaking children who come from less literate households in both the US and the European Union. There is a substantial body of research revealing that the vocabulary, syntax, and discourse features of the academic language register must be taught (e.g. Bowers and Kirby, 2010; Gersten et al., 2007; Hakuta et al., 2001), if not with multiple experiences during the preschool years, such as shared storybook reading, then in elementary school, middle, and high school. In particular the interface between vocabulary and syntax begins to change around ages 9 to 10 years old and continues through adolescence, as found in the increasing linguistic density of expository writing (Berman and Nir, 2010). Berman (2007) contends there is a difference between being a fluent native speaker of a language, as indicated by command of the everyday oral language register, and becoming a proficient user of language for school learning, which is intertwined with literacy learning well into adolescence and beyond. In contrast to the oral language register, the academic language register represents a new tool for thinking and communicating in more literate ways (Short and Fitzsimmons, 2007; Verplaste and Migliacci, 2008). Finally, each content area, whether it is literature, mathematics, history, geography, science, or social studies, uses its own specialized academic language register (see, for example, Ravid et al., 2010; Schleppregrel, 2007). Each calls on students to learn new ways of thinking and communicating.

Trends and issues: academic language proficiency

One of the most salient issues in US schools is that many students cannot read at the professional levels of the required school texts, due to density of the language, particularly at the levels of vocabulary and syntax. A related issue is that students do not have as much experience and practice with traditional text-based writing of both expository and narrative texts. With many of the new technologies (e.g. Twitter, instant messaging, etc.) students' writing has become telegraphic. Many do not have or do not practice the strategies of elaborated discourse to apply to written language, which involves greater text density. At the same time, students do need to develop skills with the new literacies. This includes how students learn online. To do so, students must develop the literacy skills of: a) locating online information with reputable search engines and other tools, b) critically evaluating information they locate; and c) synthesizing competing points of view, or the reading and writing skills of communicating ideas online (Anders et al., 2010).

A second issue is that many teachers in the US find themselves under-prepared to serve optimally the diverse student population (see also teacher preparation in Ireland; Lyons and Little, 2009). While teachers should be prepared to teach all students, many are not always able to state why certain aspects of classroom language may be challenging for many students (Bailey, 2008, 2010; Gersten *et al.*, 2007). Although the passage of NCLB in 2001 put pressure on states and school districts to guarantee a skilled teacher in every regular education classroom, this does not appear to have led to improvement in the achievement of under-represented groups of students: the achievement gap has been stable for decades. Even though teachers may meet the requirements to be classified as "highly qualified" under national standards, they may not be effective in the classroom with all students. In particular, content area teachers face the challenge of teaching subject matter to students who struggle with the comprehension and production of English academic language. As used in instruction, English academic language is a tool that offers a solution for increasing student achievement in core subject areas. A critical research question is whether students who are taught strategies to comprehend and use effectively academic language in their core content areas will score higher on achievement tests and will function better in school and college. All teachers, regardless of the content area, grade level, or where they teach, should be knowledgeable of the research-based instructional strategies that will assist all students to comprehend and produce content information in academic English or, in the European Community, the academic form of the particular language of the classroom.

Finally, the impact of the current press for Common Core State Standards (CCSS), which are to be adopted voluntarily by individual states, is unclear. The current US administration has allocated funds on a priority basis to states adopting the CCSS in the "Race to the Top" competition. With the consequent performance on national test results, teachers may find that the stakes of these "high stakes" tests have increased enormously and be tempted to dedicate disproportionate instructional time to test preparation at the expense of teaching authentic core knowledge and developing academic language proficiency in their students.

How academic language proficiency research will develop in the future

We see five prominent research strands on academic language.

1 Since content knowledge and language knowledge are intertwined, we need to better understand the nature of that complex issue. We need more research on social dialect and language variation across content areas, including teaching and reading and writing in the content areas. Such information for each core content area could provide the basis for how best to teach students; for example, "the language of science."

2 Research should not be narrowly focused. Programs of inquiry should be coordinated such that language and literacy elements are understood as they interact synergistically.

3 We must develop comprehensive conceptual models of how to integrate content area language with the general knowledge of language that students bring to school, especially for students who are ELLs and/or who come to school from homes that are not high literacy homes (Shatz and Wilkinson, 2010). This includes integrating the continuum of students' everyday oral language knowledge with the academic language they encounter in school learning activities.

4 We know little about how teachers can implement relevant formative assessments in classrooms as a major tool for obtaining authentic information about how and what students learn.

5 We need better understandings of how content area teachers should provide integrated language support using resources of other staff, such as speech-language specialists, especially (but not limited to) vocabulary and syntax. This will guide effective instruction for all knowledgeable teachers.

Conclusion

This chapter presented the educational policy context on language diversity in the European Community and the US and described the language proficiency requirements for students' achievement in school. The discussion suggested that policy, teaching, and learning issues in relation to cultural and linguistic minorities do not differ between many of the EU countries and the US. What does differ is how various countries are responding to the diversity of their school-age populations as critical resources for a global world. The review also provided an overview of the current policy context for research on academic language proficiency and its relationship to successful participation in the academic discourse requirements across disciplines and in specific content areas. The discussion included a review of trends, issues, and how future research is likely to develop on academic language proficiency.

Questions for further investigation

1 How does the academic language register vary across content areas, as well as across languages and cultures?
2 How best can we integrate content area academic language with the language(s) that students bring to school?
3 For students who must first acquire academic language when they enter formal schooling, to what extent does the metalinguistic ability to code switch flexibly (between languages or dialects) predict academic success? Is code switching ability more predictive of success in one content area versus another?
4 How best can content area teachers provide integrated language resources by working with other school personnel such as speech-language specialists?

Suggested further reading

Grosjean, F. (2010) *Bilingual: life and reality*. Cambridge, MA: Harvard University Press. This volume defines who bilinguals are and the psychological ramifications of knowing and using more than one language. It presents an accessible introduction to linguistic idiosyncrasies, attitudes toward bilingualism, how to support learning two languages, and the challenges in raising bilingual children.

Shatz, M. and Wilkinson, L. (2010) *The education of English language learners: Research to practice*. New York, NY: Guilford Press. This volume describes evidence-based strategies for supporting English language learners (ELLs) by promoting meaningful communication and language use across the curriculum. Topics include assessment and instruction for typically developing ELLs and those with language disabilities and disorders.

Wilkinson, L. and Silliman, E.R. (2008) 'Academic language proficiency and literacy instruction in urban settings', in Wilkinson, L., Morrow, L. and Chou, V. (Eds.) *Improving literacy achievement in urban schools: Critical elements in teacher preparation*. Newark, DE: International Reading Association, pp. 121–142. This chapter defines and elaborates the key concept of academic language proficiency, which is the foundation of all school learning; links to reading and writing are emphasized.

References

Anders, P., Chou, V., Lenski, S., Lewis, J., Mason, P., Morrow, L. and Wilkinson, L. (2010) *Improving teacher preparation and development for promoting literacy achievement in high poverty urban schools: A systemic approach: A White Paper of the IRA LLUTE Commission*. Newark, DE: International Reading Association. Available at: www.reading.org/Libraries/Resources/LLUTE_WhitePaper_Final.sflb.ashx or the Executive Summary available at: www.reading.org/Libraries/Resources/LLUTE_WhitePaper_ExecutiveSummary.sflb.ashx. Accessed August 2010.

Bailey, A. (Ed.) (2008) *The language demands of school: Putting academic English to the test*. New Haven, CN: Yale University.

Bailey, A. (2010) 'Implications for assessment and instruction', in Shatz, M. and Wilkinson, L. (Eds.) *The Education of English language learners: Research to practice*. New York, NY: Guilford.

Berman, R. (2007) 'Developing linguistic knowledge and language use across adolescence', in Hoff, E. and Shatz, M. (Eds.) *Blackwell handbook of language development*, Malden, MA: Blackwell, pp. 347–367.

Berman, R.A. and Nir, B. (2010) 'The language of expository discourse across adolescence', in Nippold, M.A. and Scott, C.M. (Eds.) *Expository discourse in children, adolescents, and adults: Development and disorders*. New York, NY: Taylor and Francis, pp. 99–121.

Bochaca, J.G. (2006) 'Ethnic minorities and the Spanish and Catalan educational systems: From exclusion to intercultural education', *International Journal of Intercultural Relations*, 30, pp. 261–279.

Bowers, P. and Kirby, J. (2010) 'Effects of morphological instruction on vocabulary acquisition', *Reading and Writing Quarterly*, 23, 5, pp. 515–537.

Child Stats.Gov (2010) *America's Children In Brief: Key National Indicators Of Well-Being, 2010*. Available at: www.childstats.gov/americaschildren/tables/fam5.asp? popup=true (accessed 10 September 2010).

Christian, B. and Bloome, D. (2004) 'Learning to read is who you are', *Reading and Writing Quarterly*, 20, pp. 365–384.

Common Core State Standards Initiative (2010). Available at: www.corestandards.org/the-standards (accessed 3 June 2010).

Cummins, J. (2000) *Language, power and pedagogy: Bilingual children in the crossfire*. Buffalo, NY: Multilingual Matters.

Daniel, M.C. and Ball, A. (2010) 'The Moroccan educational context: Evolving multilingualism', *International Journal of Educational Development*, 30, pp. 230–135.

Danzak, R. and Silliman, E. (2005) 'Does my identity speak English? A pragmatic approach to the social world of an English language learner', *Seminars in Speech and Language*, 26, 3, pp. 1–15.

Droop, M. and Verhoeven, L. (2003) 'Language proficiency and reading ability in first-and second-language learners', *Reading Research Quarterly*, 38, pp. 78–103.

Extra, G. and Yagmur, K. (2002) 'Management of social transformations: Language diversity in multicultural Europe'. MOST Programme, United Nations Educational, Scientific, and Cultural Organization. Available at: http://www.unesco.org/most/dp.3extra.pdf (accessed 3 September 2010).

Fogel, H. and Ehri, L.C. (2006) 'Teaching African American English forms to Standard American English-speaking teachers: Effects on acquisition, attitudes, and responses to student use', *Journal of Teacher Education*, 57, pp. 464–480.

Francis, D., Lesaux, N. and August, D. (2006) 'Language of instruction for language minority learners', in August, D.L. and Shanahan, T. (Eds.) *Developing literacy in a second language: Report of the National Literacy Panel*. Mahwah, NJ: Lawrence Erlbaum Associates, pp. 365–414.

Fry, R. (2007) 'Are immigrant youth faring better in US schools?', *International Migration Review*, 41, 3, pp. 579–601.

García-Sánchez, I.M. (2010) 'The politics of Arabic language education: Moroccan immigrant children's language socialization into ethnic and religious identities', *Linguistics and Education*, *21*, pp. 171–196.

Gersten, R., Baker, S., Shanahan, T., Linan-Thompson, S., Collins, P. and Scarecella, R. (2007) *Effective literacy and English language instruction for English learners in the elementary grades*. Washington, DC: National Center for Education Evaluation and Regional Assistance: Institute of Education Sciences. NCEE #2007–4011. Available at: http://ies.ed.gov/ncee/pubs/20074011.asp. Accessed August 2010.

Grosjean, F. (2010) *Bilingual: Life and reality*. Cambridge, MA: Harvard University Press.

Hakuta, K., Butler, Y. and Witt, D. (2001) 'How long does it take English learners to attain proficiency?', *Policy Report 2001*. Santa Barbara, CA: University of California, Linguistics Minority Research Institute.

Haskins, R., Holzer, H. and Lerman, R. (2009) *Promoting economic mobility by increasing postsecondary education*. Washington, DC: The Brookings Institution and the Pew Charitable Trusts.

Horton-Ikard, R. and Pittman, R.T. (2010) 'Examining the writing of adolescent African American English speakers: Suggestions for assessment and intervention', *Topics in Language Disorders*, *30*, pp. 189–204.

Hua, Z. (2008) 'Duelling languages, dueling values: Codeswitching in bilingual intergenerational conflict talk in diasporic families', *Journal of Pragmatics*, *40*, pp. 1799–1816.

Lewin, T. (2010) 'Many states adopt national standards for their schools', *New York Times*, 21 July 2010. Available at: www.nytimes.com/2010/07/21/education/21standards.html (accessed 30 July 2010).

Lyons, Z. and Little, D. (2009). 'Executive summary: The English language support programme'. Available at: www.tcd.ie/immigration/css/downloads/TIIReport01.07.10.pdf (accessed 3 September 2010).

Migration Policy Institute (2010). 'United Kingdom: Top ten sending countries as a percentage of the total inflow, by country of nationality, 1991 to 2006'. Available at: www.migrationinformation.org/datahub/countrydata/data.cfm (accessed 6 September 2010).

National Center for Education Statistics (2010a) 'Condition of education, 2010'. Available at: http://nces.ed.gov/programs/coe/2010/pdf/4_2010.pdf (accessed 10 September 2010).

National Center for Education Statistics (2010b) 'Digest of education statistics, 2009'. Available at: http://nces.ed.gov/programs/digest/d09/tables/dt09_020.asp?referrer=list (accessed 10 September 2010).

National Center for Education Statistics (2010c) 'The Nation's report card 2010'. Available at: http://nationsreportcard.gov/ (accessed 21 September 2010).

Ravid, D., Dromi, E. and Kotler, P. (2010) 'Linguistic complexity in school-age text production: Expository versus mathematical production', in M.A. Nippold and C.M. Scott (Eds.) *Expository discourse in children, adolescents, and adults: Development and disorders*. New York, NY: Psychology Press, pp. 123–154.

Reyes, I. and Ervin-Tripp, S. (2010) 'Language choice and competence: Code-switching and issues of social identity in young bilingual children', in Shatz, M. and Wilkinson, L. (Eds.) *The education of English language learners: Research to practice*. New York, NY: Guilford Press.

Scheele, A.F., Leseman, P.M.P. and Mayo, A.Y. (2010) 'The home language environment of monolingual and bilingual children and their language proficiency', *Applied Psycholinguistics*, *31*, pp. 117–140.

Schleppregrel, M. (2007) 'The linguistic challenges of mathematics teaching and learning', *Reading and Writing Quarterly*, *23*, 2, pp. 139–159.

Shatz, M. and Wilkinson, L. (Eds.) (2010) *The education of English language learners: Research to practice*. New York, NY: Guilford Press.

Short, D. and Fitzsimmons, S. (2007) *Double the work: Challenges and solutions to acquiring language and academic literacy for adolescent English language learners*. Washington, DC: The Alliance for Excellent Education.

Silliman, E. and Wilkinson, L. (2010) 'Literacy', in Hogan, P. (Ed.) *The Cambridge encyclopedia of the language sciences*. Cambridge: Cambridge University Press, pp. 448–450.

Treffers-Daller, J., Özsoy, A.S. and van Hout, R. (2010) '(In)complete acquisition of Turkish among Turkish-German bilinguals in Germany and Turkey: An analysis of complex embeddings in narratives', *International Journal of Bilingual Education and Bilingualism*, *10*, pp. 248–276.

Verplaeste, L. and Migliacci, N. (2008) (Eds.) *Inclusive pedagogy for English language learners: A handbook of research-informed practices*. New York, NY: Lawrence Erlbaum Associates, Taylor and Francis Group.

Wilkinson, L. and Silliman, E. (2008) 'Academic language proficiency and literacy instruction in urban settings', in Wilkinson, L., Morrow, L. and Chou, V. (Eds.) *Improving literacy achievement in urban schools: Critical elements in teacher preparation*. Newark, DE: International Reading Association, pp. 121–142.

Wilkinson, L. and Silliman, E. (2010) 'Academic language proficiency', in Clauss-Ehlers, C. (Ed.) *Encyclopedia of cross-cultural school psychology*. New York, NY and Berlin: Springer-Verlag Publishers, pp. 573–576.

15

Motivation and behaviour

Simon Ellis and Janet Tod
Canterbury Christ Church University

Overview

Motivation and behaviour are broad constructs. Motivation is a much-used term within educational discourse, with an implication that we know what it is, we can recognise it in an individual and we can, through manipulating variables such as teaching methods and curricular content, develop it. Behaviour tends to be discussed in the context of classroom disruption, though increased emphasis on developing the whole child within school contexts has placed a welcome focus on the development of social and emotional behaviours. Within this chapter the focus is upon those behaviours associated with the development and expression of motivation within school contexts. Drawing on sources from our own context of England and making links to other nations, the stance we adopt is that a focus on the behaviours associated with motivation provides educators with a clear purpose for their practice.

Descriptive introduction

When educators refer to a pupil as motivated, they are essentially saying that the individual is displaying a set of behaviours that they, as the observer, believe are the behaviours of a person who is motivated. Among educators and others, there is likely to be some consensus about the behaviours that represent motivation. Within this chapter the stance we adopt reflects Miller's (1989, p. 69) view that 'Motivation can be understood not as something one *has* but rather as something one *does*'.

Concerns regarding the motivation of children and young people tend to take two forms: an apparent lack of motivation and motivation that is directed towards activities considered by the observer to be problematic. Educators are faced with a challenge. On the one hand, they are seeking to *increase* the motivation that will encourage children and young people to actively engage in *learning* but at the same time *reduce* motivation to engage in behaviour judged to be

136

harmful either to the individual or to the needs of others. It is clear that there are conceptual problems in relation to 'reducing motivation'. If we say 'stop talking' to our students, we do not really mean we want them to be quiet and stare into space – what we mean is 'redirect your attention to your work'. It is understandable therefore that research into motivation and behaviour within educational contexts has mainly been directed towards the search for strategies and approaches that increase motivation for behaviours that are considered to support academic learning. However, it does not follow that simply improving student motivation for learning will suffice to address enduring and emergent concerns about 'behaviour'. As Foster *et al.* (2002, p. 28) note, the link between school learning and behaviour is complex:

> Many of the factors that increase a child's risk for developing behaviour problems affect their behaviour in school and their academic performance. Social and academic problems in school in turn make it even more likely that early problems will persist and become worse over time.

It may be sobering for policy-makers and educators to accept Biehler and Snowman's (1997) cautionary reminders that although context exerts an influence, motivation comes from the person themselves. As such it follows that we cannot *make* someone else motivated to produce particular behaviours that suit *our* purpose. Neither can any one policy, guidance document or set of strategies serve to positively influence the behaviours, and motivation of *all* members of the diverse group of learners that inhabit classrooms. Strategies designed to change the behaviours of groups will necessarily be interpreted and experienced differently by individuals within that group as they actively make sense of their environment from their perspective. On a more positive note, we can seek to understand more about the behaviours to be promoted or changed and the purpose they serve for the individuals who exhibit them. This chapter aims to engage the reader in that process.

Definitions

Although day-to-day terms, it is useful to discuss how 'motivation' and 'behaviour' have been defined within educational settings.

Behaviour in schools continues to be of interest to the media and an ongoing concern for politicians, parents, teachers and sometimes pupils. Interestingly, in spite of these concerns there remains a consistent message from the English government that 'The great majority of pupils enjoy school, work hard and behave well' (Ofsted, 2005, p. 5) and 'the great majority of schools are successfully achieving satisfactory or better standards of pupil behaviour' (DCSF, 2009, p. 4).

Although incidents of violent behaviour make the headlines, English government reports (e.g. DES 1989; DfES, 2005) note that teachers consider low-level disruptive behaviour to be the most wearing and disturbing for learning due to its frequency. Such behaviour is often perceived by teachers to show a lack of respect for them and a lack of interest in their teaching – particularly as such behaviour varies between teachers and across schools.

Reflecting the English government's view that strengthening teaching and learning is an effective route to improving behaviour, the terms 'learning behaviour' and 'behaviour for learning' are now part of educational discourse (e.g. DfES, 2005; DCSF, 2009; DfES, 2004a). However, this does not necessarily imply a common understanding of how learning and behaviour are linked. For example, Elkin (2004) describes a whole-school approach bearing the name Behaviour for Learning that has different principles and priorities to our own (Ellis and

Tod, 2009) behaviour for learning conceptual framework, developed to enable teachers to define the learning behaviours they want to promote in order to improve both learning *and* behaviour.

Motivation within this chapter is considered to be a descriptor given to a set of behaviours a person exhibits that as educators we associate with being motivated. If a person demonstrates these behaviours, we say they have the quality or disposition of motivation.

Most definitions of motivation enshrine the components of direction, persistence and intensity (Capel and Gervis, 2005). For example, Coles and Werquin (2005) defined learner motivation as:

> a range of an individual's behaviours in terms of the way they personally initiate things, determine the way things are done, do something with intensity and show perseverance to see something through to an end.
>
> (cited in Lord and O'Donnell, 2005, p. 4)

Such definitions can be viewed as generic descriptions of motivation. They are applicable in a range of settings and are arguably value-neutral in the sense that they could be demonstrated by an individual in relation to anti-social or self-injurious activities as well as in the context of more positive pursuits.

A further area for consideration in relation to motivation and behaviour is the nature of motivation needed for an individual to *change* their behaviour. The issue of what makes an individual *want* to change is complex. It involves developing the will and/or disposition to change as well as the skills and knowledge needed to enact a change in behaviour. Motivation belongs to one person, yet it can be understood to result from the interactions between the individual and other people or environmental factors. As the US Department of Health and Human Services (1999, p. 19) note:

> Research and experience suggest that motivation is a dynamic state that can fluctuate over time and in relation to different situations, rather than a static personal attribute. Motivation can vacillate between conflicting objectives. Motivation also varies in intensity, faltering in response to doubts and increasing as these are resolved and goals are more clearly envisioned. In this sense, motivation can be an ambivalent, equivocating state or a resolute readiness to act – or not to act.

We can see this definition enacted through the following sequence of events set in the context of the classroom:

1   A pupil is 'off task' and refusing to work: one possible explanation is that the pupil, responding *emotionally*, fears failure and is protected from this by not starting the task.
2   The teacher, judging that motivation is low, explains to the pupil that they have succeeded in this type of task before and further explains what is required of them – the pupil, responding to *reasoning*, starts working on the task.
3   If the pupil's efforts and progress are recognised and valued by the teacher and/or the class, they may persist and continue with their work. At any point in this sequence, for example if peers sought to distract them, the pupil's motivation to stay on task could change due to the influence of *social* factors.

While this is a relatively simplistic example, it can be seen that the pupil's behaviour is influenced by the interaction of social, cognitive and emotional components. Recognising the dynamic interaction between these three components offers the teacher the opportunity to further explore and understand the extent to which the task, the social milieu of the classroom and/or the pupil's emotional state is impacting on their pupil's motivation. This emphasis on looking at motivation from the pupil's perspective should help the teacher to decide which components it is feasible to strengthen, and judge which strategies are likely to be most effective. Teachers have considerable potential to influence motivation through the manipulation of variables such as the delivery and assessment of the curriculum and the quality of social relationships that are fostered. This potential can be harnessed in order to secure improved motivation for developing new positive learning behaviours and/or to change those behaviours that are problematic.

Wider political and social context

Political context

The perceived *causal* link between behaviour and learning in schools continues to inform political agendas. Typically the focus is on securing better behaviour in order that pupils can learn, with an emphasis on externally imposed discipline requirements. A combination of rewards and sanctions tends to be the strategy of choice to motivate pupils to behave. An increased emphasis on discipline may serve to encourage those children who have appropriate behaviours in their repertoire to 'behave to learn' but are likely to be less effective if the pupil has not yet developed the behaviours required for academic learning in group settings and needs to 'learn to behave'.

Within England there have been government initiatives that seek to strengthen teaching and learning in order to better engage and motivate pupils based on the premise that this will secure better behaviour. For example, the Key Stage 3 National Strategy emerged in the wake of concerns regarding dips in motivation and attainment during the early years of secondary education and subsequent detrimental effects on later schooling. One of the four underpinning principles of the Key Stage 3 National Strategy was the promotion of 'approaches to teaching and learning that engage and motivate pupils and demand their active participation' (DfES, 2004b, p. 3). Attempts to make what is on offer to children and young people more appealing are made within the context of an English National Curriculum that prescribes both content and levels of attainment expected at certain ages. Schools and their teachers are therefore seeking to encourage pupils to direct their motivation towards particular content and targets that have been defined as important by others. Some pupils share this agenda, recognising, for example, a good education as opening up employment opportunities and contributing to their social mobility. We might debate whether it is easier to remain motivated towards these things for the individual who regularly and readily experiences success in their school learning. This raises the interesting question of whether the pupil who finds school learning difficult actually requires a higher level of motivation. It may also be the case that some pupils are motivated by the social dimension of schooling rather than the curriculum, the successful meeting of targets or the gaining of qualifications.

Social context

There is an expectation that schools contribute to societal aspirations both to improve social mobility and social cohesion and to reduce welfare dependency, inequality and social exclusion. Education now has an extended remit for producing citizens who will be able to contribute to the economy and take on personal responsibilities for their own health and well being (Illeris,

2002; DfES, 2003). This means that motivation for learning must address two essentially different types of processes, defined by Illeris as:

> external interaction processes between the learner and his or her social, cultural and material environment and internal psychological processes of acquisition and elaboration in which new impulses are connected with the results of prior learning.
>
> (2002, p. 1)

It has always been appropriate that schools contribute to the development of the whole person and do not operate an artificial divide between the academic, social and emotional aspects of learning. However, it needs to be recognised that if schools are required to both raise standards of academic attainment *and* enable pupils to contribute positively in order to address social ills, then pupils will be required not only to develop appropriate behaviours but learn to make *choices* about the use and balance of these behaviours – some of which may be in conflict.

As an example, in order to succeed or excel in particular areas of learning, a person is likely to have motivations that are expressed by focused, tenacious, competitive, persistent, self-directed and possibly self-serving behaviours. It could be argued that such behaviours are necessary if individual excellence is to contribute to knowledge-building, international competition and the creation of jobs. However, while such behaviours support academic and competitive learning, they are often oppositional to the cooperative, responsive, flexible and altruistic behaviours that are required both to manage the complex functions of modern life and to maintain the common and democratic functions of society including those of freedom, fairness and responsibility.

As schools respond to directives to widen the range of learning outcomes for their pupils and cater for increasingly diverse groups within agendas for inclusion, they will have to make decisions about what behaviours it is feasible to prioritise, enhance, develop and change in schools. Such decisions will inevitably influence judgements about the behaviours and dispositions that are assumed to be indicators of motivation in school contexts.

Where and how might these issues of motivation and behaviour develop in the future?

Motivation is a powerful determinant of individual differences in learning behaviour. It is reasonable to assume that motivation will continue to be important within the discourse of teaching and learning. Existing and emerging technology is likely to mean that educators' judgements about pupil motivation will focus increasingly on the extent to which the learner demonstrates the dispositions and academic skills required to pursue and critically engage with a variety of knowledge bases.

The motivation to learn

Clearly motivation is a powerful construct for practitioners seeking to improve pupil behaviour and learning in schools. Its strength as a construct is in its explanatory powers that focus attention on why individual pupils who are exposed to the same curriculum opportunities and teaching strategies often exhibit qualitative differences in their learning behaviours. Such differences affect both what individuals choose to direct their attention towards and the intensity and persistence of their behaviour.

As noted earlier, external conditions exert an influence upon pupils' approaches and responses to learning. It is likely that there will continue to be a strong focus on the influence on pupil motivations of the nature of the curriculum, teacher attitudes, teacher training, approaches to assessment and school organisation (Maehr and Midgley, 1991; Montgomery and Kehoe, 2010; Stern, 2007).

For academic learning it is reasonable to predict that an emphasis on raising standards will be retained, supported by the interpretation and application of research and evidence relating to motivation. There has, quite appropriately, been a move way from simply *implementing* government strategies towards an enhanced focus on the *evaluation* of those strategies at school, class and individual level. Teachers and schools need to be encouraged to identify what learning behaviours and outcomes they expect if a student is to be judged to be motivated and to evaluate the efficacy of their practice against the occurrence of these behaviours in order to build an evidence base.

While evidence-based practice is demanded in all areas of professional practice, educational practice is embedded in social systems and consequently any evaluation of intervention programmes is affected by multiple complexities. We cannot feasibly exert the level of control necessary over the variables that would enable us to simply operate a 'cause' and 'effect' approach and report that a policy or strategy either does or does not work and then either keep it or abandon it. We need instead to identify what works for whom under what conditions and then from this decide upon a course of action (Tilley, 2010).

The motivation to behave well

Given that 'behaviour' in school contexts typically refers to disruption, disturbance, disaffection and disengagement, a useful function of motivational theories is to explain how occasional, often 'normal' (mis)behaviours exhibited at some time by many children and young people, develop in a minority of individuals to a level of frequency and intensity that becomes problematic for schools, parents and pupils. In tackling this issue, there are proactive and reactive approaches that it will be useful for educators to consider.

Proactive approaches

Schools and other educational settings are likely to continue to create contexts and conditions that reduce the frequency and/or intensity of problematic behaviours by developing oppositional (positive) learning behaviours that support learning in school contexts (Ellis and Tod, 2009). This is in line with developments noted earlier that seek to improve motivation for academic learning. Early intervention programmes seek to support the development of positive learning behaviours that harness the social, emotional and cognitive dimensions (e.g. DfES, 2003) and it is reasonable that this will remain a priority for preventative action (Foster et al., 2002). Ongoing and recent initiatives are likely to continue to promote the wider engagement for young people in their community in order to foster increased motivation for the development of skills and dispositions that support social cohesion, and reduce social exclusion.

Reactive approaches

There are some children and young people who are already engaged in activities or locked into particular patterns of behaviours that are harmful either to them or to the needs of others.

141

Educators need to harness what is known about motivation to encourage behavioural *change*. We should continue to provide the context and conditions that promote, encourage and reward the development of behavioural change and in so doing address the *purpose* that the current behaviours are serving for the individual. In order to secure behavioural change in individuals who have exhibited such behaviours over time, it is likely that the demand for services and agencies to work more closely together in order to achieve greater coherence and continuity of experience for the individual (Hodgkinson *et al.*, 2009) will continue to remain on educational agendas.

The individual: the source of motivation and the primary target for change

It is important to remember that although behaviour may seem strange to the observer, for the individual it always has a purpose or function (La Vigna and Donnellan, 1986). Although social and cultural conditions and contexts can have a powerful impact on the development and enactment of pupil motivation, ultimately the pupil owns that motivation. Although it may be a contentious issue for some (e.g. Craig, 2007; Ecclestone and Hayes, 2009) as to whether teachers should get involved in 'emotions' many diverse theories of motivation can be unified by an understanding that:

> emotions and beliefs are thought to elicit different patterns of behaviour such as pursuit of mastery, failure avoidance, leaned helplessness, and passive aggression.
>
> (Seifert, 2004, p. 137)

We know that pupil *perceptions* of themselves influence their motivations to learn. Pupils who perceive themselves as capable are more likely to demonstrate achievement behaviours that we label as 'motivated' (Bandura, 1993) while pupils who perceive themselves as not capable may avoid tasks and exhibit distracting behaviours. This allows pupils to exercise control over stressors that may provoke anxiety (Bandura, 1993).

Another influence on pupil behaviour and motivation is their attributional style (Weiner, 1985). If, for example, a pupil thinks that personal failure can be attributed to causes perceived as 'fixed', such as lack of ability or task difficulty, then they are likely to continue to display behaviours that could be described as 'unmotivated'. Teachers and others have a role to play in exploring, questioning and hopefully changing the attributional styles of those individuals whose motivation, and associated behaviour, is judged to be problematic.

Perceptions of self, such as self-worth and self-esteem, have consistently been used to explain the motivations of some pupils as attempts to protect or enhance self-worth (Covington, 1984). Covington is of the view that in Western culture self-worth is inherently connected to 'being able to do something well'. This resonates with the question raised earlier in this chapter of whether it is easier for the individual who is successful at school to remain motivated. In English schools, for example, children and young people are often learning in a context where national targets have been explicitly and publicly expressed based on the expected attainment of a majority (typically around 80 per cent) at certain ages. Such an approach effectively constructs 20 per cent of pupils to be in a position of 'not being able to do something well'. Within this group there will be pupils who, in spite of making an effort, still 'fail'. It is conceivable that such pupils may be displaying a higher level of motivation for learning than those who can achieve success with less effort. There is a risk therefore if educators judge and reward pupil motivation based solely on successful task completion without reference to variables such as task difficulty, effort required and the extent of self-directed learning. At the broader level of national educational policy, a focus on assessing and rewarding the attainment of learning targets related to national benchmarks rather than progress from the individual's baseline risks contributing to reduced motivation and increased disaffection.

Crucial to the development of thinking in relation to motivation and behaviour is the need to consider how pupils are *experiencing* the policies, strategies and cultures of our education system. Pupils are not passive recipients of our practice but active learners who seek to make sense of their environment and experiences in school from *their* perspective. Individuals are engaged in a dynamic and reciprocal relationship with self (Ellis and Tod, 2009) and this needs to be understood and valued if we are to influence the state we call 'motivation'. In so doing we can further explore and observe what motivates students (Smith *et al.*, 2005), and elicit the *purpose* their behaviour serves for them so that we can continue to improve behaviours for learning in schools and beyond. Such a view is endorsed by Seifert in his review and synthesis of motivational theories. He writes:

> Ultimately the critical factor on the learning process may be how the teacher and students interact. Teachers who are perceived as being nurturing, supportive and helpful will be developing in students a sense of confidence and self determination which will be translated into the learning-oriented behaviours of the intrinsically motivated student.
>
> (2004, p. 148)

Conclusion

Motivation is a multifaceted construct liberally used in education to explain differences in individuals' responses to their learning environment. It is typically judged by others based on behaviours that are considered to display direction, intensity and perseverance. Understandably, within educational contexts, fostering and increasing motivation has been considered a priority in relation to academic learning. However, in contrast, when considering behaviour in education, there is emphasis on reducing motivations for the disruption, disturbance, disaffection and disengagement that is of concern to teachers, parents, pupils and policy-makers.

Importantly, motivation is a dynamic, changeable state that fluctuates over time and in relation to different situations. Whilst motivation comes from the individual, contexts and conditions exert a powerful influence upon it. Research and development related to motivation for learning has much to offer educators in the improvement of student behaviour. This includes an enhanced focus on the nature and delivery of the curriculum, assessment and feedback procedures, and the quality of social relationships that are fostered in the classroom.

Motivation is influenced by the reciprocal interactions that an individual has with themselves, with others and with their material environment. Relationships and interactions are crucial to the development of motivation. The individual learner does not experience the social and academic aspects of learning separately. It follows that a useful area for development is to bridge the divide that separates the research and practice into motivation to *learn* from that concerned with motivation to *behave*. Both involve learning.

Motivational behaviour is broadly based on the attributes of resilience, responsiveness and persistence. These three attributes are relevant in relation to both learning and behavioural change. As with the overarching construct of motivation, there is scope for educators to identify the specific learning behaviours that represent each of these attributes. The clarifying and sharing of what specific learning behaviours and attributes are required from the learner will increasingly allow pupils, parents, teachers, agencies and others to harness their efforts to influence motivation.

Questions for further investigation

1   What behaviours would you look for as evidence that an individual is motivated?
2   What are the limitations of gauging an individual's motivation based on the behaviours they exhibit?
3   To what extent do you think the use of rewards such as housepoints and stickers in schools is counterproductive to the development of pupils' intrinsic motivation to learn and behave?
4   Why is it that some pupils become disaffected or disengaged from school based learning?

Suggested further reading

Brophy, J. and Wentzel, K. (2010) *Motivating Students to Learn* (3rd Ed.). Abingdon: Routledge. This book offers a range of research-based principles for motivating students to learn. Its focus on motivational principles rather than motivation theorists or theories leads naturally into discussion of specific classroom strategies. Guidelines are provided for adapting motivational principles to group and individual differences and for doing 'repair work' with students who have become discouraged or disaffected learners.

McLean, A. (2009) *Motivating Every Learner*. London: Sage. This book explores the interactions between teachers and pupils, presenting a variety of ways to engage young people in learning. It focuses on understand children's learning and the behaviour they bring with them to the classroom. Linking this to specific teaching methods, McLean shows how teachers can shape their teaching to help children learn more effectively.

References

Bandura, A. (1993) 'Perceived self-efficacy in cognitive development and functioning', *Educational Psychologist*, *28*, pp. 117–148.

Biehler, R.F. and Snowman J. (1997) *Psychology Applied to Teaching* (8th Ed.). Boston, MA: Houghton Mifflin.

Capel, S. and Gervis, M. (2005) 'Motivating pupils', in Capel, S., Leask, M. and Turner, T. (Eds.) *Learning to Teach in the Secondary School* (4th Ed.). Abingdon: Routledge.

Coles, M. and Werquin, P. (2005) *The Growing Importance of NQS as a Resource for Lifelong Learning Policy*. Paris: OECD.

Covington, M. (1984) 'The self-worth theory of achievement motivation: findings and implications', *Elementary School Journal*, *85*, pp. 5–20.

Craig, C. (2007) *The Potential Dangers of a Systematic, Explicit Approach to Teaching Social and Emotional Skills (SEAL): An overview and summary of the arguments*. Glasgow: Centre for Confidence and Well-Being. Available at: www.centreforconfidence.co.uk/docs/SEALsummary.pdf (accessed 28 July 2008).

DCSF (2009) *Learning Behaviour: Lessons Learned: Review of behaviour standards and practices in our schools*. Nottingham: DCSF.

DES (1989) *Discipline in Schools* (The Elton Report). London: HMSO.

DfES (2003) *Every Child Matters: Summary*. Nottingham: DfES.

DfES (2004a) *Effective Lessons and Behaviour for Learning*. Nottingham DfES.

DfES (2004b) *Key Stage 3 National Strategy: A Handbook for Consultants*. Nottingham: DfES.

DfES (2005) *Learning Behaviour: The Report of the Practitioners' Group on School Behaviour and Discipline* (The Steer Report). Nottingham: DfES.

Ecclestone, K. and Hayes, D. (2009) *The Dangerous Rise of Therapeutic Education*. Abingdon: Routledge.

Elkin, S. (2004) *Top-performing School Starts by Managing Behaviour*. London: Specialist Schools Trust.

Ellis, S. and Tod, J. (2009) *Behaviour for Learning: Proactive Approaches to Behaviour Management*. Abingdon: Routledge.

Foster, S., Brennan, P., Biglan, A., Wang, L. and al-Gaith, S (2002) *Preventing Behaviour Problems – What Works*. Brussels: International Academy of Education.

Hodgkinson, J., Marshall, S., Berry, G., Newman, M., Reynolds, P., Burton, E., Dickson, K. and Anderson, J. (2009) 'Reducing gang related crime: A systematic review of "comprehensive" interventions' (Technical report). London: EPPI–Centre, Institute of Education, University of London.

Illeris, K. (2002) *The Three Dimension of Learning: Contemporary learning theory in the tension field between the cognitive, the emotional and the social*. Copenhagen: Roskilde University Press.

La Vigna, G.W. and Donnellan, A.M. (1986) *Alternatives to Punishment: Solving Behaviour Problems with Non-Aversive Strategies*. New York, NY: Irvington Publishers Inc.

Lord, P. and O'Donnell, S. (2005) *Learner Motivation 3–19: an International Perspective*. Slough: NFER/QCA.

Maehr, M.L. and Midgley, C. (1991) 'Enhancing student motivation: a schoolwide approach', *Educational Psychologist*, *26*, 3 and 4, pp. 399–427.

Miller, W. (1989) 'Increasing motivation for change', in Hestor, R. and Miller, W. (Eds.) *Handbook of Alcoholism Treatment Approaches*. New York, NY: Pergamon.

Montgomery, A. and Kehoe, I. (2010) 'Reimagining our school system', *The Psychologist*, *23*, 6, pp. 486–487.

Ofsted (2005) *Managing Challenging Behaviour*. London: Ofsted.

Seifert, T.L. (2004) 'Understanding student motivation', *Educational Research*, *46*, 2, pp. 137–149.

Smith, C., Dakers, J., Dow, W., Head, G., Sutherland, M. and Irwin, R. (2005) *A Systematic Review of What Pupils, Aged 11–16, Believe Impacts on Their Motivation to learn in the Classroom*. London: EPPI–Centre, Institute of Education, University of London.

Stern, J. (2007) 'Mattering: what it means to matter in school', *Education 3–13*, *35*, 3, pp. 283–293.

Tilley, N. (2010) 'Realistic evaluation of children's programmes'. Unpublished paper presented at Division of Educational and Child Psychology Annual CPD event, Bournemouth, 13–15 January 2010. Reported in *Debate 135*, June 2010, pp. 9–10.

US Department of Health and Human Services (1999) *Enhancing Motivation for Change in Substance Abuse (Treatment Treatment Improvement Protocol (TIP) Series* 35). Rockville, MD: Department of Health and Human Services. Available at: www.adp.ca.gov/SBI/pdfs/TIP_35.pdf (accessed 23 August 2010).

Weiner, B. (1985) 'An attributional theory of achievement motivation and emotion', *Psychological Review*, *92*, pp. 548–573.

16

Creativity

Robina Shaheen
Regent's College, London

Overview

This chapter is a discussion about what constitutes creativity, why we might need a suitable definition, and existing criticisms of ideas of creativity. The large number of definitions has been grouped, for simplicity, into five broad categories. The meanings of the two most common defining features, originality and usefulness, are also discussed as well as views on how children's creativity should be defined. The chapter ends by presenting findings from existing research on creativity definitions across cultures, by teachers and in the education policy documents.

The need for and views about definitions of creativity

An impression which emerges from the literature is that the debate about what creativity actually means is still ongoing. One of the reasons why there is need for a definition of creativity is because there are many criticisms about how it *has* been defined. It is accused of being 'elusive' a 'puzzle . . . mystery' of a 'fuzzy nature' and a 'chaos' (Schofer, 1975, p. 366). It is also said to be important to have a definition so that it can be enhanced and investigated. The issue of defining creativity is of particular concern to those working in education, especially when in some languages there is not even an equivalent word (Kaufman and Sternberg, 2006).

Creativity is considered to be multidimensional involving different factors. The number of definitions being offered appears to have been increasing over time. Morgan (1953) listed 25 and Rhodes (1961) identified 40. Upon closer examination of these it was found that the contents consisted of characteristics of creative persons, aspects of creative process, creative product and the environments (press) which develop creativity (Puccio, 1999). Treffinger (2000) identified a list of 112 definitions, ranging from 1929 to 1994, arguing that the term can have different meanings for different people. In 2001, Aldrich developed a dictionary of creativity containing 1,400 definitions and related terms.

Categorization of definitions

It is very difficult to categorize the many definitions alluded to above. However, for the sake of gaining a better understanding these have been grouped as: a) production of something original; b) production of something original and of value; c) production of something new, of value and imaginative; d) production of something original, of value and which is accepted by a group. There is also the category for other definitions not fitting these four categories.

Perhaps a good point to start is that creativity does not mean:

> doing whatever you like . . . [behaving in an] undisciplined way . . . impulsive expression . . . [or being] unconventional.
>
> (Cropley, 1967, pp. 20–21)

Creativity as production of something original

Creativity has been defined by some as production of something that is original. The ability to produce something original is considered as central to creativity. The definitions which include the element of originality range in time as well as subjects showing that the concept is widely applicable:

> Creativity to me means mess, freedom, jumbled thoughts, words and deeds each fighting to claim their own space in my mind, and deciding, given the small amounts of free time, whether I shall write, paint, draw, take off to the beach with a camera, run outside, turn my house upside down to create a new environment, plant a garden or plan a new business. Or in a more formal sense it is the original thought, the spark, the ignition, the original design concepts or the blueprint.
>
> (Thorne, 2007, p. 17)

> process of generating new ideas, new concepts, goals, wishes, new perceptions of problems—the output is new thoughts which in themselves do not change anything in the real world until they are implemented in some way.
>
> (Nolan, 2004, p. 45)

The examples given above show that an original outcome implies producing anything be it an idea or a tangible product. This according to Nolan, as indicated in the second definition above, is insufficient in itself. For this author an original outcome means little unless it is put into action and resultantly brings change.

Creativity as production of something original and useful

Some authorities have concluded that 'originality' and 'usefulness' are the 'two defining characteristics of creativity' (Kaufman and Sternberg, 2006, p. 450). These are also used by the United States Patent Office as criteria to issue patents (Huber, 2001). Some examples of definitions in this category are given below:

> a response or an idea that is novel or at least statistically infrequent. But novelty or originality, while a necessary aspect of creativity is not sufficient . . . it must also to some extent be adaptive to reality. It must serve to solve a problem, fit a situation, or

accomplish some recognizable goal. And thirdly, true creativeness involves a sustaining of the original insight, an evaluation and elaboration of it, a developing of it to the full.

(MacKinnon, 1975, p. 68)

A product or response will be judged creative to the extent that (a) it is a novel and appropriate, useful, correct, or valuable response to the task at hand, and (b) the task is heuristic rather than algorithmic (Amabile, 1988, pp. 65–66).

Creativity as something original, useful and imaginative

Some of the current definitions, particularly those coined for use in the educational context, involve three characteristics; imagination, original and useful/valuable. Amongst the most popular is that provided by Robinson (2001):

Imaginative activity fashioned so as to produce outcomes that are both original and of value.

(p. 114)

This outlines four elements of the creative processes which are: thinking or behaving imaginatively, the imaginative activity having some purpose and the outcome generated being original and of value in relation to the objective (NACCCE, 1999). This definition is considered appropriate for education because it recognizes that all children can be creative (Craft, 2001). On the basis of the NACCCE definition, the Qualifications and Curriculum Development Agency (QCDA) in the UK further defined creativity at the classroom level to include the following:

- questioning and challenging;
- making connections and seeing relationships;
- envisaging what might be;
- exploring ideas, keeping options open;
- reflecting critically on ideas, actions and outcomes (2009).

Although there are very few criticisms of the NACCCE definition, Craft (2004) is of the view that it gives the impression that creativity is 'arts-based' and offers the following, what she calls 'little c' or 'everyday life' creativity:

a life-wide resourcefulness which is effective in successfully enabling the individual to chart a course of action by seeing opportunities as well as overcoming obstacles. This may occur in personal and social matters or in undertaking an activity in a curriculum area, such as mathematics or the humanities.

(pp. 143–144)

Creativity as something that is original, useful and the outcome is accepted by a group

There is also a view that something can only be deemed as creative if people judge it to be so. It is believed that people are aware of the conventions of their area of expertise and this enables them to make this judgment. Some examples of definitions which include the criteria of acceptance by a group of people are given below:

Creativity is, in fact, a judgment made by the community, culture or field, be they gallery owners . . . or teachers.

(Gibson, 2005, p. 164)

Creativity is that process which results in a novel work that is accepted as tenable or useful or satisfying by a group at some point in time.

(Stein, 1963, p. 215).

Important elements of a widely used explicit definition of creativity are originality and novelty of ideas, behaviors or products which are accepted and judged as appropriate by a group of people within the specific socio-cultural context.

(Rudowicz, 2003, p. 276).

If, as is being stated by these authors, something can only be deemed creative if there is a group consensus, this then indicates to the subjective nature of the definition of creativity. This, if it continues to exist, would move us further away than we are already from reaching a universally accepted definition of creativity.

Other definitions given within the educational context

Other definitions which have been given in the literature, written within the educational context, are not easily classified with the above, but are as follows.

Claxton (2006) describes what he terms as 'soft creativity' as the:

gentle, long-term cultivation of the psychological skills and attitudes that underpin a wide range of creative projects – all those that involve the gradual emergence of an idea, or a way of thinking or talking, that gives a novel purchase on an interesting and previously intractable problem.

(p. 353)

open-mindedness, exploration, the celebration of differences and originality. It stands for humor and the pleasures of learning.

(Cullingford, 2007, p. 133)

involves ideas, invention, exploration, imagination and risk taking. It is about how we think, learn, have cognition and understanding of the world around us. It is concerned with the potential in everyone to generate imaginative ideas and to explore connections between seemingly unrelated pieces of knowledge.

(Goodwin, 2005, p. 45).

These, contrary to the definitions given in the other sections above, all contain the element 'to learn' which is perhaps appropriate since we are talking about creativity and education.

Meanings of value and originality

Having given examples of definitions under the described categories, the meanings attributed to originality and usefulness deserve further elaboration. Originality is defined as something that does not already exist (Ghiselin, 1963). Stein (1953) explains that the degree of novelty depends upon the degree of divergence from 'the traditional or the status quo' (p. 311). However, Abinun (1981) asks what the extent of this deviation should be and Walberg (1988) asks if the outcome should be original to the person, culture or the world. In this there are two views. Some say that the creative outcome should be new for the person creating it (Johnson-Laird, 1988). This is termed as 'private novelty' (Eysenck, 1994, p. 201), 'subjective novelty' (Kaufmann, 2003, p. 238) and 'personal originality'. For others it should be original for the circumstances in which it occurs, that is 'social originality' (Robinson, 2001, p. 116) and for a patent the product must be new for the world. This is termed as 'objective novelty' (Kaufmann, 2003, p. 238) or 'historic originality' (Robinson, 2001, p. 116). It is the first two categories of originality that are taken to judge general creative work.

For the child it is the 'private' or 'subjective' novelty that is considered to be more appropriate as Storr (1972) states:

> The child who links together in his mind two ideas which have hitherto been separated, and who produces a third as a result of the fusion, may find, disappointingly, that he has not been as original as he had supposed when his teacher points out that someone else has had the same idea before him. None the less, he has been creative in that he has produced for himself something which is new to him.
>
> (p. xi)

The work must be original for the child or in comparison to other children (Robinson, 2001). This is because if it is defined against anything beyond this then much of children's work will be excluded (Runco, 2003).

If something is helpful in solving a problem or achieving something, it is considered as useful (James et al., 2004). The usefulness of an outcome is judged in relation to the purpose of the task (NACCCE, 2009). For children the outcome is valuable if it is 'pleasing or communicative or meaningful' to the child. In the school context, Davies (undated) suggests that the 'value' (p. 3) of a creative work should be judged through negotiation between those who are judging and those whose work is being judged. For a patented product being 'useful' means having an 'economic value' (Huber, 2001, p. 28).

Defining children's creativity

Definitions specifically stated for children are very few; however, in this it is suggested that a 'broad, democratic' (Sharpe, 2001) definition should be adopted because in this way all children can be considered to be capable of being creative. Some of the definitions include:

> adaptive . . . innovative behavior.
>
> (Feldhusen, 2002, p. 179)

> thinking or problem solving that involves the construction of new meaning, [which] relies on personal interpretations, and these are personal and new for the individual, not on any larger scale.
>
> (Runco, 2003, p. 317)

In both of these it is clear that when we consider creativity in relation to children, originality is the foremost factor. The original behavior or output is only required to be so for the child producing it and nothing beyond. This implies that for others it may already exist and therefore may not be deemed as original.

Creativity as defined in policy documents

Educational documents have often included creativity but have failed to define it, or at the most have associated it with problem-solving and thinking skills. There is also inconsistency in the use of terminology within documents across countries. In Japan the word used is 'creativity,' in Sweden it is 'creative skills' (O'Donnell and Micklethwaite, 1999, p. 636) and in Singapore it is 'creative' (MOE, 2009, p. 1).

The inconsistency in terminology is also found across different documents within the same country as documented by Craft (2004) in the case of the UK. For example despite a comprehensive definition being provided in the influential NACCCE report, the National Curriculum describes it as a 'thinking skill' (QCDA, 2009, p. 1). Odena (2001) in this regard sums up in that:

> issues concerning creativity and its interpretation remain nonetheless because they are not resolved by the centralized production of policy . . . Policy makers are being called upon to include in future guidelines an explanation of what is meant by the word 'creativity' so that there are no confusions conceptually.
>
> (pp. 2–8)

Teachers' definitions of creativity

Studies have been conducted to identify how teachers define creativity and some of the findings from various countries around the world have been collated and presented in Table 16.1. It has become evident that teacher definitions are diverse, being defined as a 'general capacity' (Odena, 2001, p. 7), 'general ability' (Diakidoy and Kanari, 1999, p. 225), a 'skill' and 'an element of a child's character, a personal quality' (Goldsmiths and Fasciato, 2005). However, some teachers do not have a specific definition or prefer not to define creativity because it is believed that this will 'limit the extent to which pupils will be encouraged to show a wide range of creative responses' (Craft, 2001, p. 25).

The common definitions of teachers from all the countries given in Table 16.1 include imagination and producing something original. However, imitation and producing something that is not necessarily new are specific to teachers from India and China. In fact Froebel once regarded imitation as a definition of creativity contrary to today's Western view (Feldman and Benjamin, 2006), which shows that definitions are prone to change with time and, as discussed later, with place as well.

As has been shown, teachers have their own ideas about what creativity means and these can affect their approach to teaching and assessment activities that are aimed to develop creativity. It is also important to understand teachers' beliefs about creativity as these may help to improve interventions for their professional development.

151

Table 16.1 Teacher definitions of creativity from various countries around the world

UK (The Creativity Centre, 2006) N=90	UK (Jackson, 2006) N=29	Finland (Rudowicz, 2003)	China (Vong, 2008)	India (Sen and Sharma, 2004)
Imagination (90)	Generating new ideas (100)	Finding new solutions	Imitation	Doing something new/different in contrast to copying
Seeing unusual connections (87)	Thinking outside the box (100)	Using old knowledge in new ways	Gaining social recognition	
Original ideas (80)	Inventing (96)	Hard work		Doing something without it being new
Combining ideas (80)	Adapting already invented things (96)	Humor		Re-creation reproduction of others' work/idea
Innovation (77)	Curiosity (96)	Imagination		
The lowest rated definitions	Experimenting (96)	Flexibility in social situations		Producing something new and original
Mysterious processes				
Tangible products				
Unconscious activities				
Aesthetic products				

(Figures in brackets represent percentage of teachers responding)

Creativity across cultures

Every culture has some concept of creativity but research has shown that there are differences, albeit subtle rather than fundamental. Amongst the very few global agreements on the issue of creativity includes the definition:

> Creativity involves thinking that is aimed at producing ideas or products that are relatively novel and that are, in some respect, compelling.
>
> (Sternberg, 2006, p. 2)

However, while there is a consensus on the creative product being useful, there is a difference on the 'newness' aspect. According to the Eastern view, a creative product can be a 'modification' and 'adaptation' and if a 'new' idea or outcome is generated it must fit into the 'socio-cultural system' (Rudowicz, 2003, p. 276). The emphasis of the Eastern view (Asian) is on producing 'new and applicable responses to the daily challenges of living' rather than something that is 'novel or original' (Sen and Sharma, 2004, p. 153). The Eastern approach places emphasis on 'intuitive experiences' while the Western approach (American and European) is on 'reason . . . logical progression' (Wonder and Blake, 1992, p. 184), individuality and independent thinking (Craft, 2004).

The definitions identified by various authors from across Europe, Africa and India have been collated and given in Table 16.2. These reveal that novelty is a common feature. However, the views from India and Africa include imitation which is similar to teacher views as discussed earlier.

Conclusion

The current creativity definitions are blamed for suffering from American and European influences (Rasekoala, 2004). Their universal nature is therefore questioned and despite studies being conducted into the ways it is perceived in other parts of the world, a common understanding has not emerged. It is argued that its universalization may be 'premature and inappropriate' because there are still strong cultural 'identities' (Craft, 2004, p. 147) as well as different traditions and values. In fact some have been of the view that there is no need for a universal definition (Sprecher, 1963). A culture can influence the way creativity is conceptualized and what is considered as creative in one culture may not be in another.

In conclusion, the evidence indicates that the current understanding of creativity is still evolving, continually being defined and redefined. This is evidence of the fact that a common understanding has not been reached and that there is dissatisfaction. More so the differences between the Eastern and Western countries still persist, which calls for further investigation that may broaden our understanding and lead to resolution of what some call a 'conflict' (Hussain, 2004, p. 96).

Table 16.2 Creativity definitions across countries

Spain (Genovard et al., 2006)	Poland (Necka et al., 2006)	Germany (Preiser, 2006)	Africa (Mpofu et al., 2006)	India (Misra et.al., 2006)
Generating new solutions	Producing a new and valuable outcome	Producing an outcome which is:	Process that aims to transform reality	Newness
Coming up with something that didn't exist		– Novel	Effective solution to a problem or situation	Sociability
Breaking the routine		– Suitable/useful	To produce something using existing resources	Leadership
Being unexpected		– Socially accepted	Adding value to what already exists	Unconventional personality orientation
Novel contribution			To produce something of value to the self and others	Task persistence
Valuable product			A gift from god	
To help society progress			Able to imitate new things	

Questions for further investigation

1 How would you define creativity?
2 How do you think your views differ from those discussed in the creativity literature?
3 Gather other people's definitions of creativity and identify both the common and differing elements.
4 Using the answers to the previous question explain why you think there are similarities and/or differences in people's views over the meaning of creativity?

Suggested further reading

Kaufman, J. and Sternberg, R. (Eds.) (2006) *The international handbook of creativity*. New York, NY: Cambridge University Press. This book provides a detailed account of the views, thinking and research by authors from around the world. It serves as a comprehensive guide for those both starting, or advancing the study of creativity and provides an international perspective of the field across different cultures.

Robinson, K. (2001) *Out of our minds: Learning to be creative*. Chichester: Capstone Publishing Ltd. This book explains why in today's world creativity is so essential and how it is continued to be ignored in our educational systems. The author provides his 'four step' definition of the concept and many of the ideas discussed are easily applicable in any field from the personal to educational and business.

Torrance, E. and Safter, H. (1999) *Making the creative leap beyond . . .* Buffalo, NY: Creative Education Foundation Press. This book is for all those who are interested in identifying and applying ways to enhance creativity. Along the way the authors provide evidence, examples and illustrations to help the reader in understanding at times complex concepts.

References

Abinun, J. (1981) 'Creativity and education: Some critical remarks', *Journal of Aesthetic Education*, 15, 1, pp. 17–29.

Aldrich, G. (2001) *Developing of creativity terms and definitions*. Masters thesis. New York, NY: State University of New York.

Amabile, T. (1988) 'Within you, without you: The social psychology of creativity, and beyond', in Sternberg, R. (Ed.) *The nature of creativity, contemporary psychological perspectives*. Cambridge: Cambridge University Press, pp. 61–88.

Claxton, G. (2006) 'Thinking at the edge: Developing soft creativity', *Cambridge Journal of Education*, 36, 3, pp. 351–362.

Craft, A. (2004) 'Creative thinking in the early years of education', in Fryer, M. (Ed.) *Creativity and cultural diversity*. Leeds: The Creativity Centre Educational Trust Press, pp. 137–151

Craft, A. (2001) *An analysis of research and literature on creativity in education*. London: Qualifications and Curriculum Authority.

Cropley, A. (1967) *Creativity*. Edinburgh: Neil and Company Ltd.

Cullingford, C. (2007) 'Creativity and pupils' experiences of school', *Education 3–13*, 35, 2, pp. 133–142.

Davies, D. (undated) *Creative teachers for creative learners – a literature review*. Available at: www.ttrb.ac.uk/attachments/c3096c7b-da04-41ef-a7ac-50535306e8fb.pdf (accessed 29 January 2010).

Diakidoy, N.A. and Kanari, E. (1999) 'Student teachers' beliefs about creativity', *British Educational Research Journal*, *25*, 2, pp. 225–244.

Eysenck, H. (1994) 'The measurement of creativity', in Boden, M. (Ed.) *Dimensions of creativity*. Cambridge, MA: MIT Press, pp. 199–242.

Feldhusen, J. (2002) 'Creativity: The knowledge base and children', *High Ability Studies*, *13*, 2, pp. 179–183.

Feldman, D. and Benjamin, A. (2006) 'Creativity and education: An American retrospective', *Cambridge Journal of Education*, *36*, 3, pp. 319–336.

Genovard. C., Prieto, M. and Bermejo, M. *et al.* (2006) 'History of creativity in Spain', in Kaufman, J. and Sternberg, R. (Eds.) *The international handbook of creativity*. New York, NY: Cambridge University Press, pp. 68–95.

Ghiselin, B. (1963) 'Ultimate criteria for two levels of creativity', in Taylor, C. and Barron, F. (Eds.) *Scientific creativity: Its recognition and development*. New York, NY: John Wiley & Sons, Inc., pp. 30–43.

Gibson, H. (2005) 'What creativity isn't: The presumptions of instrumental and individual justification for creativity in education', *British Journal of Educational Studies*, *53*, 2, pp. 148–167.

Goldsmiths, M. and Fasciato, M. (2005) *Can creativity be assessed?* Unpublished paper presented at BERA annual conference, 14–17 September 2005, University of Glamorgan.

Goodwin, P. (2005) 'Creative young readers', in Wilson, A. (Ed.) *Creativity in primary education: Theory and practice (achieving QTS cross-curricular strand)*. Exeter: Learning Matters Ltd., pp. 45–57.

Huber, J. (2001) 'A statistical analysis of special cases of creativity', *Mensa Research Journal 46*, *32*, 1, pp. 25–43.

Hussain, Z. (2004) 'Synergy of East and West for greater creativity', in Fryer, M. (Ed.) *Creativity and cultural diversity*. Leeds: The Creativity Centre Educational Trust Press, pp. 90–97.

Jackson, N. (2006) *Developing and valuing students' creativity: A new role for personal development planning*. Scholarly paper 2 (January 2006). Guildford: Surrey Centre for Excellence in Professional Training and Education.

James, V., Gerard, R. and Vagt-Traore, B. (2004) *Enhancing creativity in the classroom*. Available at: www.projects.coe.uga.edu/epltt/index.php?title=Creativity (accessed 24 August 2009).

Johnson-Laird, P. (1988) 'Freedom and constraints in creativity', in Sternberg, R. (Ed.) *The nature of creativity: Contemporary psychological perspectives*. Cambridge: Cambridge University Press, pp. 202–219.

Kaufman, J. and Sternberg, R. (Eds.) (2006) *The international handbook of creativity*. New York, NY: Cambridge University Press.

Kaufmann, G. (2003) 'What to measure? A new look at the concept of creativity', *Scandinavian Journal of Educational Research*, *47*, 3, pp. 235–251.

MacKinnon, D. (1975) 'IPAR's Contribution to the conceptualization and study of creativity' in Taylor, I. and Getzels, J. (Eds.) *Perspectives in creativity*. Chicago, IL: Aldine Publishing Company, pp. 60–89.

Misra, G., Srivastava, A. and Misra, I. (2006) 'Culture and facets of creativity: The Indian experience', in Kaufman, J. and Sternberg, R. (Eds.) *The international handbook of creativity*. New York, NY: Cambridge University Press, pp. 421–455.

MOE (2009) 'Desired outcomes of education'. Available at: www.moe.gov.sg/education/desired-outcomes/ (accessed 17 October 2009).

Morgan, D. (1953) 'Creativity today: A constructive analytic review of certain philosophical and psychological work', *Journal of Aesthetics and Art Criticism*, *12*, 1, pp. 1–24.

Mpofu, E., Myambo K. and Mogaji. A. *et al.* (2006) 'African perspectives on creativity', in Kaufman, J. and Sternberg, R. (Eds.) *The international handbook of creativity*. New York, NY: Cambridge University Press, pp. 456–489.

NACCCE (1999) *All our futures: Creativity, culture and education*. Available at: www.cypni.org.uk/downloads/alloutfutures.pdf (accessed 14 December 2009).

Necka, E., Grohman, M. and Słabosz, A. (2006) 'Creativity studies in Poland', in Kaufman, J. and Sternberg, R. (Eds.) *The international handbook of creativity*. New York, NY: Cambridge University Press, pp. 270–306.

Nolan, V. (2004) 'Creativity: The antidote to the argument culture', in Fryer, M. (Ed.) *Creativity and cultural diversity*. Leeds: The Creativity Centre Educational Trust Press, pp. 45–51.

O'Donnell, S. and Micklethwaite, C. (1999) *Arts and creativity in education: An international perspective*. Available at: www.inca.org.uk/pdf/1999_creativity_and_arts.pdf (accessed 17 October 2009).

Odena, O. (2001) *How do secondary school teachers view creativity? A report on educators' views of teaching composing skills*. Paper presented at BERA annual conference, 13–15 September 2001. Leeds: University of Leeds.

Preiser, S. (2006) 'Creativity research in German-speaking countries', in Kaufman, J. and Sternberg, R. (Eds.) *The international handbook of creativity*. New York, NY: Cambridge University Press, pp. 167–201.

Puccio, G. (1999) *Two dimensions of creativity: Level and style*. Available at: www.buffalostate.edu/orgs/cbir/Readingroom/html/Puccio-99a.html (accessed 25 August 2009).

QCDA (2009) 'National Curriculum'. Available at: http://curriculum.qcda.gov.uk/key-stages-1-and-2/Values-aims-and-purposes/index.aspx (accessed 26 September 2009).

Rasekoala, E. (2004) 'African perspectives on creativity and innovation', in Fryer, M. (Ed.) *Creativity and cultural diversity*. Leeds: The Creativity Centre Educational Trust Press, pp. 11–18.

Rhodes, M. (1961) 'An analysis of creativity', *Phi Delta Kappan*, *42*, pp. 305–310.

Robinson, K. (2001) *Out of our minds: Learning to be creative*. Chichester: Capstone Publishing Ltd.

Rudowicz, E. (2003) 'Creativity and culture: A two way interaction', *Scandinavian Journal of Educational Research*, *47*, 3, pp. 273–290.

Runco, M. (2003) 'Education for creative potential', *Scandinavian Journal of Educational Research*, *47*, 3, pp. 317–324.

Schofer, G. (1975) 'Creativity for the elementary school', *The Elementary School Journal*, *75*, 6, pp. 366–372.

Sen, R. and Sharma, N. (2004) 'Teachers' conception of creativity and its nurture in children: an Indian perspective', in Fryer, M. (Ed.) *Creativity and cultural diversity*. Leeds: The Creativity Centre Educational Trust Press, pp. 153–169.

Sharp, C. (2001) *Developing young children's creativity through the arts: What does research have to offer?* Paper presented to an invitation seminar. London: National Foundation for Educational Research.

Sprecher, T. (1963) 'A proposal for identifying the meaning of creativity', in Taylor, C. and Barron, F. (Eds.) *Scientific creativity: Its recognition and development*. New York, NY: John Wiley & Sons, pp. 77–88.

Stein, M. (1963) 'A transactional approach to creativity', in Taylor, C. and Barron, F. (Eds.) *Scientific creativity: Its recognition and development*. New York, NY: John Wiley & Sons, pp. 217–227.

Stein, M. (1953) 'Creativity and culture', *Journal of Psychology*, *36*, pp. 311–322.

Sternberg, R. (2006) 'The nature of creativity', *Creativity Research Journal*, *18*, 1, pp. 87–98.

Storr, A. (1972) *The dynamics of creation*. London: Secker & Warburg.

The Creativity Centre (2006) *Facilitating creativity in Higher Education: The views of National Teaching Fellows*. Torquay: The Creativity Centre Ltd.

Thorne, K. (2007) *Essential creativity in the classroom: Inspiring kids*. London: Routledge.

Treffinger, D. (2000) *Dimensions of creativity: Idea capsules series*. Sarasota, FL: Centre for Creative Learning, Inc.

Vong, K. (2008) 'Developing creativity and promoting social harmony: The relationship between government, school and parents' perceptions of children's creativity in Macao-SAR in China', *Early Years*, *28*, 2, pp. 149–158.

Walberg, H. (1988) 'Creativity and talent as learning', in Sternberg, R. (Ed.) *The nature of creativity: Contemporary psychological perspectives*. Cambridge: Cambridge University Press, pp. 340–361.

Wonder, J. and Blake, J. (1992) 'Creativity East and West: Intuition vs. logic', *Journal of Creative Behavior*, *26*, 3, pp. 172–185.

17

Assessment

Kathryn Ecclestone
University of Birmingham

Overview

This chapter analyses concerns and debates about the role and nature of assessment as a central aspect of education and schooling. It focuses largely on policy and practice in the English education system, whilst seeking to make links with practice in other nations. At the time of writing (late 2010), new and radical proposals for the organisation of schools and the curriculum are beginning to emerge from a new government. The 'English way of doing things' is therefore an important contextual starting point for this chapter which aims to outline the political and social purposes of assessment over the past 30 years, describe the main features of assessment systems currently on offer, clarify the relationship between formative and summative assessment and summarise some key findings from recent research about the effects of assessment on students' 'learning careers'.

Introduction

Assessment in the British education system, and especially in England, attracts more public and political scrutiny than any other aspect of education, with public and political criticism of inflated pass levels and grades in end of school exams, and the effects of testing on levels of stress and demotivation (Mansell, 2009). Children in Britain are more assessed than those anywhere in the world, and our post-school qualifications system is probably the most complex and most often reformed. Successive British governments have used assessment to change teaching methods, the content and learning outcomes of qualifications, and, more than any other country, to link the outcomes of assessment to accountability, funding and quality control. These changes have added an increasing array of purposes to assessment throughout the education system, where raising levels of achievement and participation is seen to promote social inclusion, motivation for lifelong learning and progression in the labour market.

These developments, and the tensions they create, are not confined to Britain. European Union countries are increasingly using the formal assessment of learning outcomes to create unified qualifications frameworks, with growing homogeneity between assessment content and methods. In the United States, the move towards standardised testing as part of 'No Child Left Behind' legislation is not always easily compatible with individualised and personalised learning, and locally designed teacher assessment. Many national governments are influenced by their performance in key subjects as part of comparative international assessment measures, such as Programme for International Student Assessment (PISA), Trends in International Mathematics and Science Study (TIMSS) and Progress in International Reading Literacy Study (PIRLS).

Governments in a growing number of countries therefore pay more political attention to assessment, attempting to realise an array of social and educational goals and reconcile the tensions these produce. Nevertheless, it might be argued that the United Kingdom has gone furthest over the past 30 years in political control of assessment, with a particular focus on creating 'parity of esteem' between vocational and general learning. Despite these attempts, choices and progression between different 'tracks' (general academic, general vocational and work-based) remain strongly segregated in the UK. At the same time, repeated overhauls to qualification systems, and the huge expansion of learning outcomes deemed essential for assessment, have been exacerbated by lack of public and professional debate about what subject content and learning outcomes across education system as a whole, and what differences there should be between general and vocational learning, and between cognitive and practical demands at different levels.

Intractable problems also arise over how the public and policy-makers understand 'standards'. On the one hand, changes to general qualifications aim to 'stretch' the high achievers so that over-subscribed universities can select from students with the best grades, and reassure the public about 'standards'. On the other, diverse assessment methods aim to encompass a range of authentic learning outcomes and experiences. This tension makes comparison between learners and courses virtually impossible in any meaningful sense. As a result, questions of what count as reliable and valid assessments are not only complicated but are also widely misunderstood by policy-makers and the public. It is probably therefore accurate to describe policy and practice around the whole area of 'standards' as a technical and political quagmire (Black, 2006; Goldstein and Heath, 2000; Baird et al., 2000; Ecclestone, 2002; Newton et al., 2008). Finally, outcome-based systems, and the pressures summarised here, have had a powerful effect on attitudes to learning, choices and opportunities, and on teachers' and students' day-to-day assessment practices (e.g. Ecclestone, 2002; Torrance et al., 2005; Ecclestone, 2010). Although some of these difficulties are similar to those in other countries, and are neither new nor surprising, a particular problem in the UK is 'policy amnesia', where radical, repeated overhauls and adjustments to qualifications take little account of previous attempts. Indeed, there appears to be cynical resignation to what some policy-makers describe as the 'English way of doing things': in education policy generally, and vocational assessment in particular, policy amnesia, fragmentation, confusion and selective use of 'evidence' are seen by policy-makers as 'inevitable' (see Ecclestone, 2002; 2005).

Political and social purposes of assessment

Promoting higher levels of achievement and wider access to qualifications

An abiding pressure behind assessment reform is a perceived crisis of demotivation and 'disengagement' from formal education. Problems of poor achievement have moved from the 'bottom 40 per cent' that left school with no formal qualifications in the late 1970s to the 55 per cent who currently leave school with poor or mediocre grades in the General Certificate of Secondary Education (GCSE), an examination usually studied for by pupils aged between 14 and 16. There is also a discernible and, some argue, growing lack of enthusiasm amongst those achieving formal qualifications, leading authors of a recent major review of the 14–19 curriculum in the UK to call for attention to pedagogy and personal support across the system rather than merely offering 'work-related' activity to those seen as disaffected (Hayward *et al.*, 2005).

Since the mid-1970s, political responses to these problems have focused on overhauls to vocational education and its assessment methods rather than reforms to general education or to the overall curriculum and qualifications system. Three tracks and an ad hoc collection of other certificates currently dominate the national qualifications framework of achievement:

- A workplace-based system centred on the competence-based model of National Vocational Qualifications (NVQs), introduced in 1989, together with a large array of other employer-led qualifications, offered by a very wide range of awarding bodies and providers, including universities and professional associations.
- A general vocational education system for 14–19 year olds, with qualifications accredited by three unitary bodies: Edexcel (owned by Pearson International), the Assessment and Qualifications Alliance (AQA) and the Oxford, Cambridge and RSA group (OCR) and run by schools, sixth form colleges and further education colleges.
- General education for 14–16 year olds through General Certificates of Secondary Education, and for 16–19 year olds through Advanced Certificates of General A-levels. The latter, while much changed, are derived from syllabuses and assessment methods that have endured since the 1950s. These are accredited by the three unitary bodies listed above, and run by schools, sixth form colleges and further education colleges.

There are also many certificates in leisure, general education and work-related activities that do not 'qualify' young people to do anything but which are seen as motivating devices and a way of supplementing a portfolio of achievement.

Until October 2010, the content of qualifications, and their place in the national qualifications framework, together with the work of the unitary bodies, was regulated by the Qualifications and Curriculum Authority. This was abolished in 2010 and, at the time of writing, it is not clear what future arrangements will be put in place. Since 1997, attempts to encourage participation, progression and achievement have rested heavily on formal targets set by policy-makers for 50 per cent of workers to gain at least NVQ level 2, to raise participation and achievement rates at levels 2 and 3, and in adult literacy and numeracy, and for 50 per cent of 18–30-year-olds to progress to higher education.

Conflicting purposes for post-14 education

A series of initiatives to motivate young people to stay on and achieve in formal education at the age of 14 and to progress to further education and work-based training has created assessment systems that must respond to competing demands:

- motivating learners who would otherwise not stay on in post-16 education or who are disaffected earlier in their school careers, by responding to, and rewarding, learners' expressed interests and notions of relevance;

159

- expanding routes into higher education whilst also making sure that expansion does not lead to over-subscription for limited places;
- preparing students for progression into work and job-related qualifications;
- encouraging learners to carry on gaining qualifications;
- keeping students labelled as 'low ability' by defenders of academic, general education from 'undermining' standards in these qualifications;
- convincing learners, teachers, admissions tutors in universities that vocational qualifications have parity of esteem with general ones;
- ameliorating poor levels of achievement in numeracy and literacy;
- unifying post-16 qualification pathways;
- satisfying demands from different constituencies, such as employers' representatives, subject associations etc., to include 'essential' content and skills;
- having credibility in the compulsory school sector which has less experience of mainstream vocational education;
- raising the status of vocational training and education;
- providing a meaningful work-based route.

Features of assessment

Changing ideas about measurement

Different demands and purposes for assessment have produced a growing array of formal certification of achievement, and political attempts to create equivalence between the qualification pathways summarised above. Yet, it is important to note, as authors of a large study of assessment in post-school education observe, that:

> the nomenclature of equivalence ... is always articulated in relation to academic certification. ... By discursive articulation ... academic achievement is established and continually re-established as the known, tried and tested standard to which all others are compared ... each system derives from, and revolves around assessment practices that reflect different beliefs about what counts as 'achievement' and thereby what constitutes 'fair assessment'.
>
> (Torrance *et al.*, 2005, p. 11)

The current system has evolved over the past 50 years to offer diverse forms of certification derived from strong norm-referenced, graded systems, strong criterion-referenced systems, open-ended records of achievement, and non-graded competence-based assessment. In different historical periods, emphasis given to one approach or another reflects changing social and political beliefs about achievement which are rarely debated publicly. Since the late 1970s, ideas about appropriate educational and social purposes for assessment, and appropriate methods to realise them, have eroded notions of meritocracy based on measures to justify selection, and moved meritocracy towards goals for more people to participate and achieve in education. A corresponding impetus is for assessment regimes to certificate a much broader range of life and personal skills than in the past and to engage people with their learning in deep rather than instrumental ways.

Such goals have shifted strong norm-referenced systems developed in the 1950s to strong and weak forms of criterion-referencing (see Baird *et al.*, 2000 for detailed discussion). In theory, criterion-referenced systems can measure a wider range of real-life skills and attributes whilst enabling people to get the grade they deserve, providing they meet the publicly defined criteria. From the late 1980s, these aims have dominated the strong criterion-referenced system of competence-based workplace qualifications, and the application of this approach to general vocational education. In criterion-referenced systems, 'standards' come from raising levels of competence and performance against pre-defined specifications of competence that aim to be more valid and authentic measures of performance, and encourage 'coverage' or 'mastery' of performance. Formative assessment, feedback, setting and reviewing targets not only enable more students to reach the required standard but are also seen to be inherently democratic and motivating (see Jessup, 1991).

In contrast, strong norm-referenced systems are predicated on a view that any cohort contains a limited pool of innate ability that can compare learners and provide reliable assessment as the basis for selection. Until 1972, this idea underpinned competitive examinations and norm-referenced grading at the age of 11 to select children for grammar, technical and secondary modern schools. After 1988, it also informed changes to exams at the end of secondary schooling, on entry to university, and at the end of university. All these assessment systems have moved away from strong norm-referencing, which is now only really used for selection in professional licensing and for recruitment to high-status jobs or over-subscribed university courses. 'Standards' depend on measures of reliability and consistency to compare performance over time, and between individuals within cohorts, and between cohorts. In this approach, failure is an inevitable adjunct to success.

Over the past 30 years, there has been a significant move across the education system towards weak criterion-referencing, where the goal of parity of esteem between vocational and general education combines ideas about meritocracy, differentiated ability, criterion and cohort-referencing. A hybrid model is now increasingly evident in all three qualification tracks, placing strong emphasis on teacher assessment, with some features of recording achievement and portfolio-building, external assessment, moderation by awarding bodies and standardisation of grading. At the time of writing, the new government in the UK is reviewing these tracks and their forms of assessment.

Standards

Emphasis given in assessment systems to validity or reliability or to formative or summative activities is not merely a technical matter: the fate of assessment in general vocational education in the early 1990s was dominated by traditional images of 'rigorous' standards based on reliable, comparable performance between general and vocational students. As one education civil servant pointed out:

> High level ministerial concerns were basically to do with the standard achieved in qualifica-
> tions over time . . . ministers have to constantly juggle with the concern to protect both
> the credibility of standards and to increase levels of participation and achievement . . .
> ministers collectively were concerned what the public impact would be. They didn't like,
> quite rightly, any suggestion that standards were being tweaked to facilitate that increase.
>
> (quoted in Ecclestone, 2005, p. 44)

Yet, standards based on a view that assessment can both measure and differentiate accurately between average and superior ability in a 'typical' cohort, or on a view that achievement against a clearly defined measure of performance is similarly accurate, produce unrealistic political and public expectations that assessments can produce comparable, reliable results across the whole system (see Cresswell, 2000; Murphy, 2004; Black and Wiliam, 2006; Assessment in Education, 2010). As Goldstein and Heath point out:

> Standards have figured prominently in recent debates over education policy and in the UK and elsewhere. Despite this, or even because of it, there is little clarity about the nature of a 'standard', little understanding of how such debates are situated historically, and scant awareness of measurement issues.
>
> (2000, p.xi)

Competing meanings of standards have created a sophisticated, expensive array of specifications, guidance, criteria, testing and recording methods, verification and moderation procedures and statistical monitoring of results. Although there are no clear estimates of the cost of these mechanisms and their various procedures to institutions (and the taxpayer), it is likely to run into millions every year. These systems are hard to understand, even for those inside assessment systems, a problem exacerbated by the large range of groups and organisations trying to design and regulate assessment (see Ecclestone, 2002; West, 2000).

The importance of formative assessment

Defining formative assessment

Formative assessment or 'assessment for learning' is now widely regarded as integral to good teaching, student motivation and engagement and higher levels of achievement. Promoted through the well-known work of Paul Black and Dylan Wiliam, with colleagues from the Assessment Reform Group, it is one of the few academic ideas, supported by sound research evidence, to have had a major influence on policy and practice in the UK, and has been taken up by academics, teachers and policy-makers around the world.

There is currently no watertight definition of formative assessment. It is often described as 'assessment *for* learning' as distinct from 'assessment *of* learning':

> Assessment for learning is any assessment for which the first priority in its design and practice is to serve the purpose of promoting students' learning. It thus differs from [summative] assessment designed primarily to serve the purposes of accountability, or of ranking, or of certifying competence. An assessment activity can help learning if it provides information to be used as feedback, by teachers, and by their students, in assessing themselves and each other, to modify the teaching and learning activities in which they are engaged. Such assessment becomes 'formative assessment' when the evidence is actually used to adapt the teaching work to meet learning needs.
>
> (Assessment Reform Group, 2002)

> In assessment for learning, the learner's task is to close the gap between the present state of understanding and the learning goal. Self-assessment is essential if the learner is to do this. The teacher's role is to communicate appropriate goals and promote self-assessment as pupils work towards the goals. Feedback in the classroom should operate from teacher to pupils and from pupils to teacher.
>
> (Sadler, 1989, p. 119)

In contrast to much everyday practice, feedback is not one way, from teacher to student. Instead, feedback from a student about his or her own performance, or to other students about their performance (self- and peer-assessment) are also important, achieved through peer- and self-assessment, carefully planned discussion work and teachers' written feedback, and from carefully constructed, open-ended classroom questioning (Black, 2007). Nevertheless, even when feedback from teachers is regular, detailed and helpful, students can fail to improve:

> For students to be able to improve, they must develop the capacity to monitor the quality of their own work during actual production. This in turn requires that students possess an appreciation of what high quality work is, that they have the evaluative skill necessary for them to compare with some objectivity the quality of what they are producing in relation to the higher standard, and that they develop a store of tactics or moves which can be drawn on to modify their own work.
>
> (1989, p. 119)

With formative assessment at its heart, a holistic view of pedagogy encompasses 'all those activities undertaken by teachers and/or by their students which provide information to be used as feedback to modify the teaching and learning activities in which they are engaged' (Black and Wiliam, 1998, p. 7). Albeit rather 'medical' in its associations, the idea of 'diagnosis' is central to formative assessment, revealing strengths and weaknesses, gaps in understanding and barriers to learning and enabling teachers to adjust teaching and learning inputs, for whole groups or for individuals. From this perspective, assessment activities cannot be understood as formative unless evidence from feedback is used to adapt teaching and learning activities, in the present, or in future planning. An iteration between feedback and activity can therefore be minute to minute as teachers and tutors think on their feet and respond to individuals or groups during classroom sessions or tutorials, or more considered as teachers plan new activities and lessons.

Yet, in most everyday practice, this holistic view of a 'pedagogy of engagement' is not evident. Instead, formative and diagnostic purposes are widely seen by teachers as confined to processes such as tutorial reviews of progress, using records of achievement, or undertaking initial diagnostic tasks, and marking students' work prevents teachers from developing a 'pedagogy of engagement', where they need to make students engage at a higher level cognitively than students either want to, or would choose to, and capitalising on 'moments of contingency', where learning might go one way or the other. Rather than focusing on what is to be learned, or what happens when learning takes place, a *pedagogic* focus informs teaching decisions better, and encourages teachers to find new ways to break down complex learning activities into small steps (Wiliam, 2008).

The impact of assessment in shaping students' 'learning careers'

Research has highlighted some powerful effects of formative and summative assessment on young people's attitudes to learning and on teaching and assessment methods, particularly in post-14 education. This section summarises some key findings.

Choice and progression

Despite goals to raise levels of participation and achievement in post-14 education, there are large gaps between idealised notions of choice and opportunity and the reality of progression in academic and vocational courses. Students often choose progression routes that reflect their images of themselves as types of learners suited for different types of assessment, thereby creating self-selection of very separate tracks and outcomes and strong beliefs amongst teachers and students that there are types of students suited to particular types of assessment experience. Stereotypes and expectations are reinforced by segregation of vocational and academic teachers who usually teach in the tracks that they themselves have experienced as students (Torrance *et al.*, 2005; Ecclestone, 2002; see also Reay and Wiliam 1999; Ecclestone and Pryor, 2003). Other studies show that choices of a particular assessment system, and the effects of assessment on attitudes to learning and on one's identity as a learner, are highly differentiated, affecting choice of institution and courses. For young people leaving school, decision-making and institutional marketing are both predicated on images of what counts as an appropriate learning identity and culture and these images are class, gender and culturally based (Ball *et al.*, 2000).

Sociocultural analysis suggests that children and young people are socialised in the requirements of formal assessment systems, taking certain attitudes and dispositions about assessment, and their role in it, through compulsory schooling into post-school contexts. Longitudinal, ethnographic studies of primary and secondary school students show how attitudes and activities emerge over time, in a complex interplay between the factors summarised above, where 'pupil career . . . [is] a particular social product deriving from children's strategic action in school contexts [and] strongly influenced by cultural expectation' (Pollard and Filer, 1999, p. 22). The experience of successive formal tests as 'key classification events' have a profound effect on children's identity as successful or failing learners (e.g. Reay and Wiliam, 1998; Torrance and Pryor, 1998).

Students' attitudes and assessment strategies are also affected by the ethos of an educational institution, the official demands of awarding bodies, the written specifications of qualification requirements, inspection criteria, resources, parents' attitudes, and the norms of different peer groups. Studies of learning and assessment cultures in further education colleges show that these interactions and their effects on attitudes and everyday teaching and assessment practices shift erratically over time. They are shaped by crises, transformations and changing images of identity in family life, work and relationships (see Bloomer and Hodkinson, 2000; Ecclestone, 2002; Colley *et al.*, 2003; Ecclestone, 2010).

Images of achievement and failure

Of course, dispositions and attitudes cannot be isolated from structural conditions such as employment prospects or the effects of educational selection and differentiation in a local area, the social class and cultural background of students and the educational institutions they choose or are sent to. In studies of young people and adults in further and adult education, images of achievement and failure not only shape choices but also images of themselves as 'learners', ideas about what they can and will do, and, conversely, cannot and will not do, and the sorts of practices they value or do not value (see Ecclestone, 2002; Torrance *et al.*, 2005; Ecclestone, 2010). Those images, and the assessment practices and outcomes that emerge from them affect students' and teachers' perceptions about the suitability of a vocational or academic qualification, rooted in perceptions about local employment and education prospects.

Ideas about 'achievement' and 'learning' are also influenced strongly by official targets to raise attainment of grades and to increase overall pass rates, retention on courses and progression to formal education at the next level. This has created assessment systems, particularly in vocational tracks, where 'learning' and 'achievement' are synonymous, and where 'assessment' becomes the 'delivery of achievement'. These images are reinforced by awarding body procedures for quality control and national inspection. As a result, instrumental, target-driven practices to improve motivation and raise levels of achievement have become endemic (see Ecclestone, 2010).

Fair, valid and reliable assessment

The interplay between norm-referencing, criterion-referencing and competence-based assessment, and resulting attempts to balance validity and reliability in different assessment systems affect what we regard as 'fair assessment'. At the level of day-to-day assessment, vocational and general education students and teachers have very different views about what counts as 'fair' assessment and these are almost irreconcilable (Torrance *et al.*, 2005). For example, many A-level tutors regard raising grade attainment through coaching and feedback as professionally unethical: fair assessment relies on unseen examinations, marked independently. For vocational tutors, not maximising students' confidence and chances to succeed when they have not done well at school is unethical, making coaching to the criteria entirely unproblematic (see also Ecclestone, 2010). Whichever track they are in, students accept the ethos of each approach, not only because they and their teachers are unaware of the technical and political complexity of assessment, but also because it conforms to their own learning identity and to the 'type' of assessment they expect.

Students therefore accept the assessment systems they experience largely without complaint or dissent and learn to navigate the various demands and processes. Yet, they are far from passive recipients of assessment. Instead, attitudes to learning, ideas about their abilities and 'acceptable' teaching and assessment methods and their strategic approach shape assessment practices just as much as the official specifications and teachers' ideas about what is possible. Assessment cultures and the attitudes and activities that emerge from them cannot therefore be separated from these factors.

The rise of instrumental compliance

In contrast to the idealised goals of formative assessment to enhance motivation and to deepen students' engagement with learning, research shows that there has been a rise in the numbers of post-14 academic and vocational students who work compliantly, strategically and superficially to meet assessment criteria, together with significant numbers working happily in a comfort zone lower than their potential achievement (Ecclestone, 2002; Torrance *et al.*, 2005; Ecclestone, 2010). In the context of targets for higher levels of achievement and concerns about disaffection, one effect of outcome-based/criterion-referenced assessment has been to encourage students to expect high levels of coaching and feedback which enable them to get a 'good grade' easily. A cultural understanding of assessment is useful because techniques such as feedback, explaining the criteria, encouraging student self-assessment and using detailed grade descriptors are seen widely as 'good practice'. Yet, in some assessment cultures they encourage superficial compliance with tasks derived from the assessment criteria, bureaucratic forms of self-assessment against the criteria, and high expectations of coaching and support.

In vocational education, and increasingly in general education too, teachers are coming to see their role as a translator of official criteria. In vocational education, it is now commonplace to break up the strongly framed summative assessment tasks, which are often in the form of assignments, into sequential tasks to meet each criterion. Students prepare their assignments, working to copies of the official criteria specified for grades in each unit, and can submit a completed draft for feedback. One effect is that class contact time is used to introduce students to each assignment and to talk through the outcomes of draft assignments. Typical practice is outlined here by a vocational tutor:

> I talk through the assessment criteria grid with them and the assignment brief, pinpointing the relationships between P, M and D [pass, merit and distinction] and that it does evolve through to D. The students like to go for the best grade possible and discuss how they could go about getting an M. There again, some students just aim for basic pass and those are the ones who leave everything to the last minute. Then I see a draft work, read through it, make notes, talk to each one, show the good areas in relation to the criteria and explain why and how if they have met them, saying things like 'you've missed out M2'. . . some will action it, some won't. It's generally giving them ideas and giving them a platform to achieve the outstanding M or D criteria.
>
> (Torrance *et al.*, 2005, p. 46)

Assessment, achievement and learning have become to a large extent synonymous in post–14 education, where assessment is not merely 'for' learning or 'of' learning but *is* learning, especially in vocational courses:

> The clearer the task of how to achieve a grade or award becomes, and the more detailed the assistance given by tutors, supervisors and assessors, the more likely the candidates are to succeed; but succeed at what? Transparency of objectives, coupled with extensive use of coaching and practice to help learners met them, is in danger of removing the challenge of learning and reducing the quality and validity of outcomes achieved . . . assessment procedures and practices come completely to dominate the learning experience, and 'criteria compliance' comes to replace 'learning'.
>
> (Torrance *et al.*, 2005, p. 46)

Conclusion

Thirty years of assessment reform, particularly in the post–14 system, have not produced any agreement about what might comprise knowledge, skills and outcomes of the three main tracks that make up the UK's qualifications system. The combined effect of lack of consensus, *ad hoc* reform, and prioritising assessment over purpose and content, has led to over-loaded, prescriptive assessment systems where diverse bodies compete to define what curriculum content and outcomes should be included in qualifications at different levels.

Although competing goals have led to growing instrumentalism, academics, policy-makers, educators and the public disagree fundamentally about the extent to which this is progressive because it spreads attainment more widely, or whether it represents an erosion of aspirations for high-quality learning, particularly for those groups who need all the cultural and social capital they can get in order to have any chance of equality of opportunity, and learning outcomes should be included (see Wolf 1995; Ecclestone, 2002; Stanton, 1998).

In a context where it is not possible to identify sound assessment principles and methods without consideration of curriculum content and outcomes across academic and vocational tracks and between different stages and levels, research evidence about the effects of assessment on attitudes to learning is overlooked. There is, therefore, a need for better understanding about both the principles of assessment and the political context in which they are operationalised amongst the various groups who design, implement and evaluate assessment systems. This understanding is crucial since merely redesigning the technical features and implementation of qualifications, with no attention to lessons from the past, will not resolve enduring problems highlighted in this chapter.

Questions for further investigation

1   How can researchers draw together insights and findings about the impact of assessment policy on practice and attitudes to learning, between educational sectors within national contexts, and between countries?
2   How can research inform the training and education of teachers, and raise awareness amongst those designing and regulating qualifications?
3   How can research illuminate the problem of 'policy amnesia' and attempt to resolve it?

Suggested further reading

Black, P. and Wiliam, D. (1998) 'Assessment and classroom learning, principles, policy and practice', *Assessment in education, 5*, 1, pp. 1–78. An influential systematic review of international research evidence about the effects of formative assessment on learning and achievement.

Ecclestone, K. (2002) *Learning autonomy in post-compulsory education: the politics and practice of formative assessment*. London: RoutledgeFalmer. A sociological empirical study of the impact of policy on teachers' and students' assessment practices in advanced level vocational education in the UK.

Ecclestone, K. (2010) *Transforming formative assessment in lifelong learning*. Buckingham: Open University Press. An extensive sociocultural study of teachers' formative and summative assessment practice in vocational education and adult literacy, language and numeracy programmes.

Gardner, J. (Ed.) (2011) *Assessment and Learning* (2nd Ed.). London: Sage Publications. A collection of chapters by leading academics in assessment, exploring the principles, theories and practices of assessment in different contexts of learning.

References

Assessment Reform Group (2002) *10 principles of assessment for learning*. Cambridge: University of Cambridge.

Baird, J., Cresswell, M. and Newton, P. (2000) 'Will the real gold standard please step forward?', *Research Papers in Education, 15*, 2 pp. 213–229.

Ball, S.J., David, M. and Reay, D. (2005) *Degrees of difference*. London: RoutledgeFalmer.

Ball, S.J., Maguire, M. and Macrae, S. (2000) *Choices, pathways and transitions post-16: new youth, new economies in the global city*. London: RoutledgeFalmer.

Bathmaker, A.M. (2003) 'Learners and learning in GNVQs', PhD thesis. Warwick: University of Warwick.

Black, P. and Wiliam, D. (1998) 'Assessment and classroom learning, principles, policy and practice', *Assessment in Education*, 5, 1, pp. 1–78.

Black, P. and Wiliam, D. (2006) 'The reliability of assessments', in Gardener, J. (Ed.) *Assessment and Learning*. London: Sage.

Bloomer, M. and Hodkinson, P. (2000) 'Learning careers: continuity and change in young people's dispositions to learning', *British Educational Research Journal*, 26, 5, pp. 583–598.

Cresswell, M. (2000) 'The role of public examinations in defining and monitoring standards', in Goldstein, H. and Heath, A. (Eds.) *Educational Standards*. Oxford: British Academy/Oxford University Press.

Ecclestone, K. (2000) 'Bewitched, bothered and bewildered: a policy analysis of the GNVQ assessment regime', *Journal of Education Policy*, 15, 5, pp. 539–558.

Ecclestone, K. (2002) *Learning Autonomy in Post-compulsory Education: the Politics and Practice of Formative Assessment*. London: RoutledgeFalmer.

Ecclestone, K. (2004) 'Learning in a comfort zone: cultural and social capital in outcome-based assessment regimes', *Assessment in Education*, 11, 1, pp. 30–47.

Ecclestone, K. (2005) '"The English way of doing things": the implications of GNVQ assessment policy for 14–19 reform', in Whitehead, J. (Ed.) *The 14–19 Reforms: the Contribution of Teacher Educators, An Account of a Joint UCET/HMI Symposium*. Cardiff, December 2004.

Ecclestone, K. (2010) *Transforming Formative Assessment in Lifelong Learning*. Buckingham: Open University Press.

Ecclestone. K. and Pryor, J. (2003) '"Learning careers" or "assessment careers"?: the impact of assessment systems on learning', *British Educational Research Journal*, 29, pp. 471–488.

Goldstein, H. and Heath, A. (Eds.) (2000) *Educational Standards*. Oxford: British Academy/Oxford University Press.

Harlen, W. (2006) 'The role of assessment in developing motivation for learning', in Gardener, J. (Ed.) *Assessment and Learning*. London: Sage.

Jessup, G. (1991) *Outcomes: NVQs and the Emerging Model of Education and Training*. London: FalmerPress.

Murphy, R. (2004) *Grades of Uncertainty: Reviewing the Uses and Misuses of Examination Results*. A report commissioned by the Association of Teachers and Lecturers. London: ATL.

Pollard, A. and Filer, A. (1999) *The Social World of Pupil Career: Strategic Biographies Through Primary School*. London: Cassell.

Reay, D. and Wiliam, D. (1999) '"I'll be a nothing": structure, agency and the construction of identity through assessment', *British Educational Research Journal*, 25, pp. 343–354.

Stanton, G. (1998) 'Patterns of development', in Tomlinson, S. (Ed.) *Education 14–19: Critical Perspectives*. London: Athlone Press.

Torrance, H. and Pryor, J. (1998) *Investigating Formative Assessment: Teaching, Learning and Assessment in the Classroom*. Buckingham: Open University Press.

Torrance, H., Colley, H., Garratt, D., Jarvis, J., Piper, H., Ecclestone, K. and James, D. (2005) *The Impact of Different Modes of Assessment on Achievement and Progress in the Learning and Skills Sector*. Learning and Skills Development Agency. Available at: www.lsda.org.uk/cims/order.aspx?code=052284&src=XOWEB. Accessed December 2010.

Section 3

Organisation and issues in education

18

Early childhood education and care

Sacha Powell

Canterbury Christ Church University

Overview

This chapter provides an overview of contemporary policies and provision for the education of young children in places outside their homes. There is no intention to diminish the learning and development that happens – formally or informally – in family contexts; it is simply not the focus here. Although the chapter refers predominantly to England, there are many ways in which the issues raised stem from and are pertinent to international contexts and references to texts from authors in other countries are included. Chapter 26, 'Comparative education', by Michele Schweisfurth in this volume serves as a useful reminder for the application of cautious approaches to comparisons between different systems and cultures, and readers may wish to consider her methodology when discussing issues raised here.

Introduction

The chapter begins with an exploration of the different terms used to describe provision for early education and discusses their origins and implications. As such, there is a brief account of key historical influences and the impact of current social and political agendas. Having established some of the factors that shape provision, the nature and purposes of different forms of early childhood institutions are considered. The chapter briefly touches on pedagogy and curriculum. Workforce characteristics and judgements about what constitutes 'quality' provision are not covered and so readers are referred to useful texts at the end of the chapter. Readers are also invited to consider and discuss questions concerned with what early years provision might be called, might consist of, and might be intended to do.

Around the world, provision for young children varies for numerous reasons. First, traditionally, 'early childhood' has been defined internationally as the phase from birth to eight years and consequently has included the first years at primary school. More recently, studies of services for young children in 20 member countries by the Organisation for Economic Cooperation and Development (OECD) (2001, 2006) have confined the term to the period from birth to admittance to primary school. Since the age of admittance varies across nations, the term 'early childhood' depends on local circumstances.

Provision of services has also depended upon assumptions and beliefs about babies and young children, their learning (both how they learn and what they should learn), development (whether believed to occur due to nature and maturation or to the interplay between nature and nurture), children's position in society, and the role and responsibilities of the family. In particular, in relation to the last, the role of women and whether a country's policies have been intended to enable mothers to go out to work are a major factor (David et al., 2010).

Early education and care

The separation – and integration – of education and care *services* and their governance is a significant historical feature of early childhood provision in many countries and is discussed later. But the title for this chapter was a deliberate choice, favouring a particular viewpoint about what happens – or, in the author's view, should happen – when very young children experience ECEC provision. Namely, that the *concepts* of education (in its broadest sense) and care are vitally interdependent and inseparable. It could be argued that a caring approach to education negates the need for the word 'care' at all. But this is a statement about early learning and development, about what young children can hope to experience, and also about the roles and responsibilities of early childhood professionals and those who govern provision. In their historically grounded review of early childhood education, Nutbrown et al. (2008, p. 180) say that 'learning is about relationships, and in the early years relationships are key'. This being said, it is not suggested that the use of a range of other terms in policy, academic and professional documents automatically precludes the importance of relationships or separates education and care. But it is important to recognise the different emphases that a particular term may overtly convey as well as the potential for underlying assumptions that are less obvious and often historically significant. One such tension involves multiple perspectives about the value of play and its place in ECEC.

Reporting an international, thematic exploration of early years curricula in 18 countries, Bertram and Pascal (2002) refer throughout their report to early childhood education and care (ECEC) but note that '*Early years* is an imprecise definition. Alternatives such as *pre-school education, preparatory education, pre-elementary education* or *early childhood education* are similarly difficult to define' (p. 5). Even where both education and care are mentioned, the emphasis on one or other of these aspects may vary. The United Nations Educational, Scientific and Cultural Organisation (UNESCO), for example, refers to Early Childhood Care and Education (ECCE) as 'an integral part of basic education and represents the first and essential step in achieving the goals of Education for All'. Its focus on both care and education reflects its perspective that provision should be holistic to reflect the multidimensionality of young children's learning and development (UNESCO, 2010).

An array of terms is also used for the titles of prominent English language journals for early years professionals, academics and policy-makers. An examination of the aims and scope of 13 such publications revealed that all but one (*Education 3–13*) claimed coverage of young children's education *and* care, although not always seeing the two as integrated concepts or provision.

Social and cultural factors – including economic priorities – have influenced the nature and purposes of early childhood provision over time and in different countries. These factors affect how that provision is viewed, governed, managed, funded, used, experienced and judged. Locating provision under the jurisdiction of particular government ministries (e.g. Education, Health, Social or Family Services) conveys messages about their priorities and leads to comparisons between different types of services and different groups of children.

A random snapshot of governments' documentation from five countries shows that policy is often directed at education and care, but this does not always mean that contexts to which the policy is directed have merged the two concepts in their provision or that governance structures are integrated.

> Te Whariki is . . . a curriculum for early childhood care and education in New Zealand. This curriculum statement covers the education and care of children from birth to school entry age.
>
> (New Zealand Ministry of Education, April 2009)

> The EYFS [Early Years Foundation Stage for England] brings together and simplifies the learning and development and welfare requirements . . . ending the distinction between care and learning.
>
> (Department for Children, Schools and Families, 2008, p. 10)

> According to the Party's educational principle and Chairman Mao's instruction 'care for and educate children well', young children will be provided with basic overall development education in order to grow up healthy and happy.
>
> (China Pre-school Education Research Association, 1999, cited in Tang, 2008, p. 16)

> Pre-school integrating early education and care is considered to be the first step in the child's lifelong learning.
>
> (Swedish Ministry of Education and Science, 1998, cited in OECD, 2004, p. 21)

> the [Nigerian] curriculum was reviewed and revised in 2003/4 using an integrated bottom up approach, targeting children age 0–5 years . . . expected to promote the integrated approach and converge all sectoral interventions – health, nutrition, water and environmental sanitation, psycho-social care, early learning, child protection.
>
> (UNESCO, 2006, p. 7)

The recent increase in integrated provision around the world suggests ongoing international debate and dialogue. But some scholars (e.g. Dahlberg and Moss, 2008) have expressed concerns that dominant approaches from economically more developed and powerful nations may have led to hegemonic globalisation of particular models or philosophies. Potentially this view fails to account for the enduring strength of local conditions, traditions and beliefs or acknowledgement that policy may be (re)created in its interpretation by professionals (Powell, 2010) but attendance to the views and needs of local communities is an important consideration in international exchange of ideas.

Interpreting seemingly similar combinations of care and education in policy terms requires caution. Bertram and Pascal (2002) found that terminology such as pre-primary and pre-school conveyed the impression that early education was primarily seen as a preparatory phase for the compulsory school system. Bennett (2003) noted an emphasis in some institutions on formal instruction for very young children where education and care had traditionally been separate. He highlighted differences between early education approaches in Nordic countries that promoted young children's social development with others that worked to improve their readiness for school. In 2010, Bennett co-authored a report on a study of the integration of education and care in five countries in which it was concluded that:

> Locating the responsibility for ECCE within education is important as the education framework highlights access, affordability, concern for a (relatively) well trained workforce, and curriculum as a basic tool for practice. Except in one case country, there is no evidence that integration within education has brought about 'schoolification' of ECCE services.
>
> (Kaga *et al.*, 2010, p. 10)

Despite Kaga *et al.*'s assurances, some vestiges of 'schoolification' may endure and face opposition. This cross-national study included integrated provision in England where concerns have recently been voiced by some about early, formal instruction in the 'Three Rs' (Open EYE Campaign Newsletter, 2010).

The purposes of early childhood education and care

To understand the complex picture that constitutes the purposes of ECEC, it is important to remember that these are constructed by numerous factors and that certain historical figures and events have had lasting effects in both England and other international contexts.

In many countries, advocates of provision for babies and young children have continued to be influential in the field. They include: Froebel, Owen, Montessori and the Macmillan sisters, for example (see Nutbrown *et al.*, 2008). Dame schools were the forerunners of crèches, nursery schools and playgroups and in some countries, such as Trinidad and Tobago this kind of provision existed unregulated and unregistered, as a service to mothers for whom employment has been essential. Meanwhile, services in Sweden were initiated in the 1960s, when the country needed women to participate in the labour force. Children were regarded as belonging to and the responsibility of the whole society. Similarly in China, workplace and collective nurseries allowed mothers to combine a return to paid work with continued breastfeeding. The emphasis in these nurseries was on the babies' welfare at a time of high infant mortality and a drive for economic modernisation (Sidel, 1982).

In other countries, where provision had developed, early education was emphasised; for example, in parts of the United Kingdom where maintained nursery schools and classes were established over 50 years ago, especially in areas where light industry employed large numbers of women. Simultaneously, there was a growth in voluntary provision, such as playgroups, in more affluent areas, where parents wanted their children to have opportunities to play outside their homes with friends. In some of the inner city and 'disadvantaged' areas, day nurseries were set up, generally catering for children whose families were living under difficult circumstances. Childminders (caring for children in their own homes) filled the gaps in provision in some areas and for babies and younger children. More recently, integrated ECEC and family services have been brought together in children's centres. With the increase in knowledge about brain development, interest in young children's learning has become widespread, highlighting the importance of the first few years of life as critical (Gopnik *et al.*, 1999; Eliot, 1999), laying the foundations for lifelong learning and development. Neuroscientific evidence contributed to the OECD's decision to undertake its studies of 20 countries' services and plans for the very young and influenced policy decisions about provision of early education with renewed focus on early learning. It has also increased concerns about social inequalities and the life chances of children from 'disadvantaged' backgrounds. The *Ten Year Childcare Strategy* for England (HM Treasury, 2004), for example, aimed to 'improve child outcomes by giving children the opportunity to attend a high quality early years setting, and to reduce child poverty by facilitating parental employment' (Smith *et al.*, 2010). Accompanied by the introduction of free early education vouchers, the implication was that such free childcare involved early education and that the 'best outcomes' might be realised through children's participation in 'good quality' out-of-home ECEC settings. This has led to some accusations that 'compensatory education' accentuates and relies upon explanations of cultural or social group deficits and plays down structural factors. Criticisms include 'schoolcentric' models that alienate some families (e.g. Tveit, 2009) and favour others (e.g. Angelides *et al.*, 2006), and failure to value households' 'funds of knowledge' (Moll *et al.*, 1992; Comber and Kamler, 2004). The Sure Start programme, established by the British government in 1998, has been described as 'compensatory education'. But despite seeking to bring services to families described as having the highest levels of need and being the 'hardest to reach', the National Audit Office found more targeted work was needed for this aim to be fully realised (NAO, 2006).

Parents' and practitioners' views

In addition to politically driven reasons for ECEC, parents' needs and wishes have affected the amounts and types of provision. Arthur *et al.* (2010) explored parents' perspectives in their study of character formation in the early years. A sample of 180 parents from urban and rural areas in England returned a questionnaire in which they had been asked why their child was enrolled in an ECEC setting. The response options had been derived from parent discussion groups. Analysis involved ordinal logistic regression models and principal component analysis (PCA). The parents most frequently agreed that *meeting other children, learning to be independent, getting ready for school* and *learning to be confident* were the reasons their child attended an ECEC setting. Comparatively fewer parents strongly agreed that their child attended a setting so that they could *go out to work*, suggesting that the majority were less inclined to see the primary purpose of the provision as a form of childcare. The PCA revealed a component of 'social and independence' perspectives versus 'readiness for school' perspectives where the parents were marginally more strongly in agreement with statements like *meeting other children* compared with others who were marginally more in favour of statements that included *get ready for school*.

When the practitioners from the same six settings were asked about the purposes of ECEC, their responses did not always match those of the parents whose children attended their settings. All either strongly agreed or agreed that the main purposes of their provision were to allow *children to meet other children, to help children learn to be confident* and *to help children become more independent*. The statements to *allow parents to go out to work, to give parents a break* and *to allow children to learn to read and write* yielded more disagreement and diversity of responses (Arthur *et al.*, 2010, p. 108). The apparent discrepancy between the views of some of the parents and the practitioners echoes findings from earlier studies (e.g. Ebbeck and Wei, 1996; Mooney and Munton, 1998; Evans and Fuller, 1999). In a large-scale, representative survey of parents in 2009, Smith *et al.* (2010, p. 57) found that fewer parents of children aged from birth to four years cited 'economic reasons' (e.g. to enable parents to work, look for work, or study) than 'child-related reasons' (e.g. for educational or social development, or because the child liked going there) for their childcare arrangements – 58 per cent and 64 per cent respectively. Child-related reasons were also associated with formal care (centre-based) rather than informal care (e.g. with grandparents). The purposes of early childhood education seem to differ according to whose perspective is sought. Published literature lacks young children's views about the *purposes* of their ECEC, although some studies have reported what children liked and disliked (e.g. Mooney and Blackburn, 2003; Rayna, 2007; McAuliffe, 2003).

Pedagogy and curriculum

Debates about the nature and indeed the existence of early childhood education curricula and pedagogies are steeped within sociocultural-historical frameworks as well as closely linked to public, political and professional views about the purposes of ECEC. David (2003, p. 7) has argued that, 'different ideas and beliefs about early childhood result in different pedagogical theories and practices . . . all this means that pedagogy and research on pedagogy can only ever be provisional and all those involved in ECEC research need to examine the assumptions on which their work is premised'. The world-renowned Reggio Emilia nurseries, whose practices are emulated in many countries, claim not to have a curriculum. Their *raison d'être* is to ensure children think for themselves and can reason with others, so as to prevent another Fascist regime being able to hold power again in that region of Italy. Questions arise, therefore, about the possibility to follow a 'Reggio approach' in countries with different political histories.

In England, there have been concerns about a national, statutory framework for the early years, reflecting divergent views about pedagogy and curriculum; the *Early Years Foundation Stage* (EYFS) provides a statutory framework for early learning and welfare requirements for children from birth to five (DCSF, 2007). Its introduction in 2008 was met with vociferous concerns in some quarters that it was target-driven and overly prescriptive (Watson, 2008) and might diminish the autonomy of professionals to interpret young children's learning (Thomson, 2006). At the time, the government department with responsibility for early years, the Department for Children, Schools and Families, vehemently dismissed such criticisms, although its successor, the Department for Education, under a new coalition government from May 2010, launched a review in 2010 just two years after its introduction, suggesting the existence of political anxieties about the EYFS.

The principles that underpin young children's education and/or their care lead to varied structures for governance and delivery of provision. This chapter has sought to highlight the complex web of sociocultural, historical and political issues that inform and shape decisions about the nature of provision and what it aims to do. A range of discourses exists, promoting different priorities in provision for young children (Papatheodorou, 2010). There has not been space to cover functional aspects such as access (especially for babies and children from birth to three); funding; premises; staffing (including qualifications and conditions of service); regulation, particularly safeguarding and definitions of quality; or multi-professionalism and multi-agency working. The recommended texts that follow collectively address all these issues. Questions are included below to support and encourage readers' reflection. But in the midst of the debates, the everyday experiences of babies and young children must be of central concern. Many spend more waking hours in an ECEC setting than they do in their homes each week. Whatever shape and purposes early education and care may adopt, ultimately it is for and about young children; awareness of their views and experiences as well as one's own assumptions about these must be central to reflective practice and drive research on early childhood education and care.

Questions for further investigation

1 What are the purposes of early childhood education and care? Why do you think this?
2 Who should pay for early childhood education? Why do you think this?
3 In your opinion, what is 'good quality' early childhood education like? Why do you think this?

Suggested further reading

Kernan, M. and Singer, E. (Eds.) (2010) *Peer Relationships in Early Childhood Education and Care*. London: Routledge. This book examines children's rights and well-being against a backdrop of increased social movement and migration, changing family structures and work practices.

Nutbrown, C., Clough, P. and Selbie, P. (2008) *Early Childhood Education History, Philosophy and Experience*. London: SAGE Publications Ltd. This book richly illustrates the development of ECE by giving imaginative examples of the influence of early childhood education pioneers on contemporary thinking and practice.

OECD (2006) *Starting Strong II. Early Childhood Education and Care*. Paris: OECD. For an overview of the provision for ECEC in 20 member states of the Organisation for Economic Cooperation and Development, comparisons and suggestions for improvement.

Pugh, G. and Duffy, B. (Eds.) (2010) *Contemporary Issues in the Early Years* (5th Ed.). London: SAGE Publications Ltd. This edited text draws on a range of perspectives from the field of ECEC and highlights contemporary debates and issues.

References

Angelides, P., Theophanous, L., and Leigh, J. (2006) 'Understanding teacher–parent relationships for improving pre-primary schools in Cyprus', *Educational Review*, 58, 3, pp. 303–316.

Arthur, J., Powell, S. and Lin, H.-S. (2010) *Foundations of Character: Developing Character and Values in the Early Years*. Birmingham: University of Birmingham. Available at: www.learningforlife.org.uk (accessed 27 October 2010).

Bennett, J. (2003) 'Persistent division between care and education', *Journal of Early Childhood Research*, 1, 1, pp. 21–48.

Bertram, T. and Pascal, C. (2002) *Early Years Education: An International Perspective*. London: INCA, QCA.

Comber, B. and Kamler, B. (2004) 'Getting out of deficit: pedagogies of reconnection', *Teaching Education*, 15, 3, pp. 293–310.

Dahlberg, G. and Moss, P. (2008) Beyond quality in early childhood education and care – languages of evaluation, *Forum*, 2008/2, pp. 21–26.

David, T. (2003) *What do We Know About Teaching Young Children?* BERA Professional User Review Summary. Available at: www.bera.ac.uk/files/reviews/eyyrsp.1.pdf (accessed 27 October 2010).

David, T., Powell, S. and Goouch, K. (2010) 'The world picture', in Puch, G. and Duffy, B. (Eds.) *Contemporary Issues in the Early Years*. London: SAGE Publications Ltd, pp. 33–46.

DCSF (2008) *Statutory Framework for the Early Years Foundation Stage*. Nottingham: DCSF Publications.

DfES (2007) *Early Years Foundation Stage Statutory Framework*. Nottingham: DfES Publications.

Ebbeck, M. and Wei, Z.G. (1996) 'The importance of pre-school education in The People's Republic of China', *International Journal of Early Years Education*, 4, 1, pp. 27–34.

Eliot, L. (1999) *Early Intelligence. How the Brain and Mind Develop in the First Five Years of Life*. Middlesex: Penguin Books Ltd.

Evans, P. and Fuller, M. (1999) 'Parents' views on nursery education: perceptions in context', *International Studies in Sociology of Education*, *9*, 2, pp.155–175.

Gopnik, A., Metzoff, A. and Kuhl. P. (1999) *How Babies Think*. London: Orion Books Ltd.

HM Treasury (2004) *Choice for Parents, the Best Start for Children. Ten Year Childcare Strategy*. London: HM Stationers.

Kaga, Y., Bennett, J. and Moss, P. (2010) *Caring and Learning Together. A Cross-National Study on the Integration of Early Childhood Care and Education within Education*. Paris: UNESCO.

McAuliffe, A.-M. (2003) *'When are We Having Candyfloss?' Report on a Project to Investigate Consultation with Very Young Children in Early Years Services 2002–3*. London: National Children's Bureau.

Moll, L., Amanti, C., Neff, D. and Gonzalez, N. (1992) 'Funds of knowledge for teaching: Using a qualitative approach to connect homes and classroom'. *Theory into Practice*, *31*, 2, pp. 132–141.

Mooney, A. and Blackburn, T. (2003) *Children's Views on Childcare Quality*. Nottingham, DfES Publications.

Mooney, A. and Munton, A.G. (1998) 'Quality in early childhood services: parent, provider and policy perspectives', *Children and Society*, *12*, 2, pp. 101–112.

National Audit Office (2006) *Sure Start Children's Centres*. London: The Stationery Office.

New Zealand Ministry of Education (2009) *Early Childhood Education. Te Whariki*. 29 April 2009. Available at: www.educate.ece.govt.nz/learning/curriculumAndLearning/TeWhariki (accessed 27 October 2010).

Nutbrown, C., Clough, P. and Selbie, P. (2008) *Early Childhood Education. History, Philosophy and Experience*. London: SAGE Publications Ltd.

OECD (2001) *Starting Strong. Early Childhood Education and Care*. Paris: OECD.

OECD (2004) *Starting Strong Curricula and Pedagogies in Early Childhood Education and Care. Five Curriculum Outlines*. Paris: OECD.

OECD (2006) *Starting Strong II. Early Childhood Education and Care*. Paris: OECD.

OpenEYE (2010) 'Newsletter'. 27 October. Available at: http://openeyecampaign.wordpress.com/ (accessed 27 October 2010).

Papatheodorou, T. (2010) *Being, Belonging and Becoming: Some Worldviews of Early Childhood in Contemporary Curricula*. Forum on Public Policy. Available at: www.forumonpublicpolicy.com (accessed 27 October 2010).

Powell, S. (2010) 'Hide and seek: values in early childhood education and care', *British Journal of Educational Studies*, *58*, 2, pp. 213–229.

Rayna, S. (2007) 'Some 4-year-olds voices on French preschool'. Presentation at the *European Early Childhood Education Research Association Annual Conference*, Prague, 29 August to 1 September 2007.

Sidel, R. (1982) *Women and Childcare in China*. Middlesex: Penguin Books.

Smith, R., Poole, E., Perry, J., Wollny, I., Reeves, A. *et al.* (2010) *Childcare and Early Years Survey of Parents 2009*. Nottingham: DfE Publications.

Swedish Ministry of Education and Science (1998) *Curriculum for the Pre-school*. Stockholm: Fritzes.

Tang, F. (2008) *A Comparative Ethnographic Case Study of the Early Years Curriculum in Chinese and English Settings*. Doctoral thesis. London: Roehampton University.

Thomson, R. (2006) 'Checklist fears in EYFS structure', *Nursery World*, 26 May.

Tveit, A.D. (2009) 'A parental voice: parents as equal and dependent – rhetoric about parents, teachers, and their conversations', *Educational Review*, *61*, 3, pp. 289–300.

UNESCO (2006) *Country Profile Prepared for the Education for All Global Monitoring Report 2007 Strong Foundations: Early Childhood Care and Education. Nigeria Early Childhood Care and Education (ECCE) programmes*. Geneva: UNESCO International Bureau of Education.

UNESCO (2010) *Early Childhood Care and Education*. Overview of programme themes. Available at: www.unescobkk.org/education/appeal/programme-themes/ecce/ (accessed 27 October 2010).

Watson, R. (2008) 'Government vows to fight EYFS critics', *Children and Young People Now*, 17 September 2008.

19

Education and schooling 5–11 years

Hazel Bryan
Canterbury Christ Church University

Overview

This chapter draws on the context of primary schools in England before contrasting this with that of other nations. It opens with an analysis of the most recent reports of the lead inspecting body for schools, the Office for Standards in Education, Children's Services and Skills, on ten of the lowest achieving (based on national Standard Assessment Tests) primary schools in England. The chapter then locates these findings within the gradual politicisation of the English primary curriculum asking 'how did we get to here?' The relationship between teachers, pupils, parents and the State is at the heart of this consideration; education policy in England, as this chapter will demonstrate, has positioned professionals, pupils and parents in terms of expectations and roles. These are sometimes explicitly defined in recent policy documentation and are a new departure in terms of the role of the State in relation to education. Finally, the chapter explores the ways in which other countries (namely Sweden, Norway, France and the Republic of Ireland) monitor the performance of pupils and teachers at the primary phase of education.

Introduction

Primary schools in England have been the recipients, in recent years, of a litany of policies that can be defined by targets, performance criteria and league tables (Ball, 2003; Jeffrey, 2003; Troman and Jeffrey, 2007) and this has resulted, arguably, in a 'performative' culture (Pheysey, 1993). That is, a culture where teachers are required to perform their duties in relation to externally defined targets, and each pupil's performance is judged against these same targets. This performative context is kept under scrutiny and reported upon through inspections by the lead inspecting body for schools, the Office for Standards in Education, Children's Services and Skills (known commonly as, and hereafter, Ofsted). Primary schools in England today are under considerable scrutiny, and the genesis of this surveillance culture is mapped out in this chapter. Ofsted inspects schools on a regular basis and subsequent inspection reports are publicly available online. There are a range of measures used to assess the effectiveness of primary schools in England, amongst which are the Standard Assessment Tests (hereafter SATs), taken by pupils in mainstream state schools at the end of Key Stage 1 (age 7 years) and Key Stage 2 (age 11 years). Pupils are assessed in English, Maths and Science and the scores enable teachers to compare individual pupils. Under the previous Labour government (1997–2010), schools where fewer than 30 per cent of pupils reached Level 4 were considered underperforming. The current Conservative–Liberal Democrat coalition government, elected in 2010, is raising this to 35 per cent of pupils at Key Stage 2. Schools with fewer than 60 per cent of pupils reaching Level 4 at Key Stage 2 are considered underperforming if their pupils are also failing to progress fast enough. The scores also enable the public to make overall judgements about school performance, with the results published on the website of the British Broadcasting Corporation (BBC) website as part of which local authorities (a sub-national level of local government in England which play a large role in educational organisation) are listed in rank order of SATs results. There is also a section dedicated to the lowest-achieving schools in England, in which these schools are named.

An analysis of ten low-achieving English primary schools

After randomly selecting ten of the lowest-achieving schools in the country (according to SATs scores), an analysis of each school's most recent Ofsted report has been undertaken. Following each individual school analysis the following common themes have emerged:

- mobility;
- learning difficulties/disability;
- communication skills on entry to school;
- attendance;
- teaching and learning;
- assessment.

It is important, in the reading of these themes, to keep in mind that they have been identified by Ofsted inspectors within an inspection framework. Nevertheless, these are the pronouncements made upon primary schools in England today and they are the main means by which schools are judged. Importantly, these themes have a wider relevance in that they point to significant issues in the education sector as a whole.

Mobility

From the Ofsted reports analysed, pupil mobility was identified as a problem. Inspectors commented that pupils arriving or leaving school at different times during the school year was disruptive in terms of continuity of learning. But what more do we know about pupil mobility that will help us to understand this issue? In empirical terms, relatively little research has been undertaken in this field. The longtitudinal data source, PLASC (Pupil Level Annual School Census) offers comprehensive data on all state schools which provides information on whether a mobile pupil has changed home address or simply changed school. Machin *et al.* (2006) use the PLASC study to consider the impact of a change of home residence as well as whether there is a change in the school that a pupil attends between two academic years. Their findings show that

> pupils from lower social backgrounds are more likely to switch schools than other pupils, and this is true for pupils at all stages of schooling; pupils who change schools are more likely to have a low previous academic attainment record than pupils who do not change schools; pupils placed in schools with high Key Stage performance levels move less than pupils from lower performance schools; pupils who move school and home simultaneously are typically more socially disadvantaged than otherwise.
>
> (Machin *et al.*, 2006, p. i)

Strand (2002) has undertaken research looking at the association between pupil mobility and attainment at the end of Key Stage 1 (KS1) and has interrogated tests for over 6,000 pupils in an English urban education authority: 'The results indicate that pupil mobility during the early years is associated with significantly lower levels of pupil attainment in reading, writing and mathematics tests at age 7' (p. 63). Strand qualifies this, however by urging the reader to note that

> mobile pupils are more likely than stable pupils to be entitled to free school meals, to have English as an additional language, to require higher levels of support in learning English, to have identified and more severe special educational needs and to have higher levels of absence. When the relative impact of these factors is considered, the effect of mobility, while still statistically significant, is substantially reduced.
>
> (2002, p. 63)

Learning difficulties/disability

Additional learning needs are higher than the national average in all schools analysed. These present as a complex mix of behavioural, social and emotional needs as well as, for example, needs met by expert speech and language provision. It is helpful here to put this within the wider context:

> In 2005 around 18 per cent of all pupils in school in England were categorised as having some sort of special educational need (SEN) (1.5 million children). Around 3 per cent of all children (250,000) had a statement of SEN and around 1 per cent of all children were in special schools (90,000) – which represents approximately one third of children with statements.
>
> (House of Commons Education and Skills Committee, 2006, summary)

Over the last 14 years, governments have introduced a litany of policy initiatives into state schools. The Green Paper *Excellence for All Children: Meeting Special Educational Needs* (DfEE, 1997) was the genesis for a comprehensive review of education for children with special educational needs (SEN) and indicated the Labour government's commitment to the principle of inclusion. Policy initiatives have been relentless since 1997. As one SENCO commented, 'We've got a special needs policy . . . we've got an EAL [English as an Additional Language] policy, we've got an anti-racist policy . . . we've got a vulnerable children policy' (Humphrey and Lewis, 2008, p. 135). Following the Salamanca Statement (UNESCO, 1994) the Index for Inclusion gained European influence and the language of inclusion became adopted: 'inclusion has obtained status as a global description' but there is no 'formally fixed and stable use of the terminology in the literature' (Vislie, 2003, p. 18). Vislie concludes that the issues surrounding inclusive practice are far from resolved and that there is a multiplicity of practice and interpretation across countries.

Communication skills on entry to the school

Lower than average communication skills on entry to the school were reported and one school reported that although there was a nursery, fewer than half of the pupils in Reception had attended. The *Birth to Three Matters* (DfES, 2003) document reminds us that during the crucial years before children start school, they are acquiring the cultural codes of our literacy-dependent society. This includes speaking, listening, reading and writing.

From the very beginning of life, young babies convey messages about what they want and need, as well as how they feel:

- Babies learn that their voice and actions have effects on others and they strive to share meanings.
- Young children use actions and words to make and justify choices and influence the behaviour and responses of others.
- As vocabulary increases, children make sense of the world through bargaining, negotiating, questioning, describing and labelling (David *et al.*, 2003, p. 93).

Language acquisition is not simply a matter of developing a vocabulary and grammar but, rather, it is about understanding how and when to engage – that is, a developmental process of engaging with cultural codes. Learning 'how to be' in a particular culture comes with rich play contexts. David *et al.* make a compelling case for a focus upon the early years (see also Chapter 18, 'Early childhood education and care', by Powell in this volume). Although there are still areas that are contested within this field, such as whether early years education is or should be regarded as a preparation for schooling, or as a state in its own right (David *et al.*, 2000), it seems that the need for rich experiences in the early years are incontestable and are likely to impact positively on the primary stage of education.

Attendance

Most of the schools in the English Ofsted reports had attendance as an area for attention and it was reported that low attendance levels below the national average inhibited pupil progression. Reid (2005) in his comprehensive analysis of the dimensions of attendance found that, 'despite all the good practice which is taking place within schools and local education authorities, the number of pupils missing school continues to resist staunchly the best endeavours of the full range of caring professionals' (p. 59). Reid has also argued that children most likely to be absent are from 'one parent families; families with an above average number of children; families living in council owned housing; and families living in poor quality and/or old housing' (1999). The seriousness of absenteeism is not to be underestimated, as it is a key risk factor for 'violence, injury, substance use, psychiatric disorders, and economic deprivation. Contextual risk factors include homelessness and poverty, teenage pregnancy, school violence and victimization, school climate and connectedness, parental involvement, and family variables' (Kearney, 2008, p. 451).

Teaching and the curriculum

Within the Ofsted reports, Inspectors commented that:

- Teacher expectations were not high enough for all pupils and consequently there was insufficient challenge in lessons. This was found to be the case for high attaining pupils in particular.
- Pupils' ability to work and learn independently was linked to the balance of teacher talk to pupil talk in the classroom. There was an over-reliance on teacher input at the expense of independent working, which compromised the development of pupil resilience and independence.
- There was insufficient focus on progressing pupils in their learning.
- Teachers missed opportunities to capitalise on pupil's mistaken answers.
- The curriculum did not always meet the needs of high attaining pupils – tasks did not match sufficiently pupils' ability.
- There was insufficient stretch that consequently inhibited progress.
- Sometimes topics did not inspire pupils, and where this happened, the curriculum itself de-motivated pupils.

A starting point for addressing the issues above is to consider beliefs about learning. Claxton (2001) argues that 'what you believe learning is, profoundly influences success and failure' (p. 26). He argues that 'learning is impossible without resilience' (p. 331). Pupils will not develop sufficient resilience if they are not immersed in independent learning contexts: 'high self-efficacy creates persistence and resilience; low breeds a brittle and impatient attitude' (p. 332). The learning environment a pupil inhabits will have a profound effect upon their skills and resilience and the balance of teacher dominated space and pupil dominated space is critical.

Assessment/marking

Within the Ofsted reports analysed, inspectors commented that:

- Teachers regularly set targets for pupils, but pupils are often unsure about what they are to do to achieve the target.
- Marking should provide pupils with clear information on how to improve on the learning objective.
- Teachers should use assessment information to adapt planned work for differing pupil need.
- Teachers regularly check pupil progress, but more could be done to use this information to challenge pupils in lessons.
- Data should be more fully understood by teachers and governors in order that they can be used rigorously to improve standards.

The comments made above by Ofsted inspectors provide a clear way forward. But as Wiliam *et al.* (2004) note,

> There is no 'quick fix' that can be added to existing practice with promise of rapid reward. On the contrary, if the substantial rewards of which the evidence holds out promise are to be secured, this will only come about if each teacher finds his or her own ways of incorporating the lessons and ideas that are set out above into her or his own patterns of classroom work. This can only happen relatively slowly, and through sustained programmes of professional development and support.
>
> (p.2)

This then, is a snapshot of some of the barriers identified by the state (i.e. Ofsted inspectors) to high performance in English primary schools today. The journey the primary English education system has travelled to get to this point is one defined by waves of reform underscored by ideological tensions. It is a story worth the telling.

The genesis of a surveillance culture

The Labour government of 1965 began a structural change in the education system, reported in Circular 10/65, 'The Organisation of Secondary Education'. A motion was passed on 21 January 1965 in the House of Commons, stating: 'That this House, [is] conscious of the need to raise educational standards at all levels' (DES, 1965). This circular is extremely significant. In stating this intention, government, for the first time, expressed not only an interest in 'standards' but also a wish to see them (whatever they were) 'raised'. Circular 10/65 did not simply address the structure of the secondary system. The design of the curriculum in the junior school, the appropriate deployment of staff to address differentiation, teaching methods, monitoring, assessment and continuity of experience between junior and senior school were all highlighted by government as important.

The discourse of primary education during the mid-1960s in England was shaped by a focus upon the child; it could be said that this was a period when the explicit link between education and the economy was unconsidered, a time when the ultimate professional goal was a child-centred approach to teaching and learning, influenced by Rousseau's philosophy, Piagetian theory of cognitive development and the Enlightenment ideals of what it is to be human. The values of a child-centred approach were promoted and celebrated in the Plowden Report of 1967. Plowden resisted even the recommendations of the Hadow Report of 1931 with regard to streaming, which, it suggested, could be psychologically damaging to the child. Not all teachers, though, were enamoured with child-centred approaches to teaching and learning. The Black Papers, a collection of writings, published between 1969 and 1977, represented a sustained critique of approaches to teaching and learning. The papers had three central themes; first, the decline in standards of literacy and numeracy; second, the danger of progressive teaching methods and feminist ideology; and third, indiscipline in schools which represented a threat to society (Trowler, 2003). One teacher, writing in the 1969 Black Paper *The Crisis in Education* reflected upon her own recent teacher-training course and commented:

> The 'in-phrase' at that time was 'free expression' and any attempt at formal teaching was strictly taboo. I well remember how appalled my Infant Tutor was when I asked her how

one set about teaching reading. Briefly, her reply was that one must never 'teach' reading. If one's classroom was sufficiently interesting, reading would emerge.

(Cox and Dyson, 1969, p. 87)

The ultimate criticism within the Black Papers was of 'progressive methods', which, to the contributors, meant that 'children will choose to work when they are ready to do so, and need to do so; that children know what is best for them and should never be corrected' (Pinn, 1969, p. 99). And so a line was drawn in the sand between the 'progressives' and those who saw progressivism as inhibiting effective learning. This tension survives in English primary schools to this day.

Government intervention in primary education increases

Government intervention in primary education was limited to structural change until Margaret Thatcher took office in 1979 as the Conservative prime minister. The then secretary of state for education, Sir Keith Joseph, wary of a centrally controlled curriculum (McCulloch *et al.*, 2000), was an 'ideologically non-interventionist Secretary of State' (Jenkins, 1995, p. 113). In his 1984 White Paper *Better Schools*, he sought to determine the principles underpinning the curriculum and the purposes of learning at school. In 1985 the Inspectorate published the rather different paper, *The Curriculum from 5–16* (Curriculum Matters). These two documents were written from differing perspectives in terms of learning, teaching and teacher autonomy. Sir Kenneth Baker, Joseph's successor intervened in the curriculum as soon as he was appointed secretary of state in 1986 and his Education Reform Act of 1988 represents government at the heart of educational systems and curriculum policy, although not yet at the stage of influence or intervention on pedagogical practice. The Education Reform Act is a complex cocktail of tension between centralisation and decentralisation: on the one hand, finance was decentralised with power devolved to schools, and in juxtaposition, a centralised curriculum and assessment system were introduced and rigorously inspected.

In 1992, the Conservative government published *Curriculum Organisation and Classroom Practice in Primary Schools* (DES, 1992) otherwise known as the report of the 'Three Wise Men'. Increased intervention into curriculum design hardened after the publication of the report by Alexander, Rose and Woodhead in 1992. The establishment of an Office for Standards in Education, headed by HMCI Chris Woodhead, created a new era of teacher accountability and increased government influence in curriculum design. Throughout Prime Minister Major's term in office, the 'back to basics' campaign set the tone for the future development of core subject strategies – begun during Prime Minister Major's term of office but ultimately realised by a Labour government in 1997.

The total core curriculum: a corpus of knowledge, a given pedagogy

The implementation of the National Literacy (NLS) and Numeracy Strategies (NNS) (DfEE, 1998) represented the most far-reaching government intervention into the English and Mathematics curriculum to date. The genesis for the NLS came in the form of the bleak findings from the 1993/4 Review of Research Findings in English, and the SATs results in English for

1995/6, which were followed by the harshest criticism of teachers and teaching methods in the publication of *The Teaching of Reading in 45 Inner-London Primary Schools* (Ofsted, 1996). The report was highly critical of teachers' practice in its conclusion that these results were a result of 'the quality of teaching in the classroom, namely, how reading is taught'. In terms of teaching, the report criticised the amount of time given to phonic knowledge and skills, reading beyond the basics, the lack of non-fiction texts and a failure on the part of teachers to address pupil errors in reading. The style of the report was significant in that it moved towards suggesting a need for a given corpus of knowledge and a pedagogy for delivering this corpus. Similarly, the National Numeracy Strategy suggested, in the form of the Numeracy Hour, a pedagogy underpinned by a given corpus of knowledge.

At this point in the primary English education system, with a given corpus of knowledge in Literacy and Numeracy and a suggested pedagogy, government was able to inspect the performance of pupils and teachers against suggested, if not statutory, practice. And so if this is the story of the primary English system, what is the state of play across Europe?

Centralisation, surveillance and the European context

The politicisation of the English primary education system has been charted, if briefly, above. But the question of why nations adopt a centralised system remains unanswered. Unexplored in the chapter above is the role of the Church (or Churches), faith groups and, increasingly, business entrepreneurs in both policy and practice arenas. Interested, influential groups create a hegemonic discourse that arguably marginalises the voice and autonomy of teachers. This is increasingly the case in England, with the emergence of academies sponsored by business entrepreneurs. This growth in monitoring and accountability can be understood within the wider context of neo-liberalism (Olssen *et al.*, 2004), where teachers are held accountable for the successful delivery of external curricula. Kells (2002) argues that quality assurance, quality assessment and quality control are at the heart of this movement. Though, whilst McNamara and O'Hara argue that 'one result of these policies has been that virtually every education system in the developed world and indeed many others elsewhere have been busy creating or where they existed before reforming their school evaluation policies and procedures' (2008, p. 173), they also suggest that lessons learned from the English system are influencing a move towards self-evaluation. Indeed, Ofsted supports self-evaluation through the Self Evaluation Form (SEF). In the Republic of Ireland, McNamara and O'Hara argue that the whole school evaluation system, Looking at Our School (LAOS), is

> effectively predicated on the concept of schools evaluating themselves and producing 'streams of high quality data' on which to base judgements about quality and plans for improvement . . . with the support of external evaluation carried out by the Inspectorate.
>
> (2008, p. 175)

Interestingly, in Sweden, teachers still enjoy a high level of professional autonomy, although Helgoy and Homme (2007) consider this a 'weakness' in that there is a limited opportunity for Swedish teachers to therefore influence national policy. By contrast, they report that Norwegian teachers are 'characterized by old professionalism', with a much tighter control on teacher autonomy. This, however, is presented as a strength in that 'national standards and control in education are accepted as tools for securing professional knowledge and status' (Helgoy and

Homme, 2007, p. 232). The link between influence at policy-making level and lack of autonomy seems counter-intuitive, but is balanced in this Scandinavian context by teachers, as an occupational group, having status in society as a result of their 'professional knowledge'.

By contrast, in France the curriculum is determined by the State – with a 'national standard' (Alexander, 2000) of practice articulated. French education is understood as intellectual engagement, rather than, as is presented in English policy documents of the last decade, a means by which education will strengthen the economy of the future. What is interesting here is that the inspection system in England was presented to the public as a transparent means by which parents could judge the performance of schools, whereas in France there is a different relationship with schools, inspectors, parents and the general public.

It can be seen then, that nation states' education policies construct different relationships between teachers and government. The Norwegian teachers enjoyed enhanced professional status in spite of the fact that curriculum design was not solely in their hands, whereas the Swedish teachers felt that although they were under less surveillance, their collective professional voice was weaker. In England and Eire, the surveillance systems of the past decade are moving towards a self-evaluation model, which suggests a shift in relationship between government and teachers. For an extensive review of international comparisons in primary education, that are beyond the scope of this chapter, readers should turn to *The Cambridge Primary Review Research Surveys* (Alexander, 2009).

Conclusion

This chapter has provided an analysis of the key themes identified within Ofsted inspection reports from ten of the lowest achieving schools in England. By doing so it raises the question of how such an inspection system developed. The chapter went on to chart the gradual politicisation of the primary education system in England thus, almost inevitably resulting in the question of what inspection systems are in place in other European countries. It would seem from an analysis of the literature that whilst there has been a neo-liberal swing across Europe in the last decade, other countries are moving more towards a self-evaluation model of accountability, and indeed, the Scandinavian model presents us with a notion of professionalism that relinquishes autonomy in order to retain status in society.

Questions for further investigation

An analysis of recent primary Ofsted reports on the lowest-achieving schools suggests that high pupil mobility, learning difficulties, poor communication skills, sporadic attendance, inadequate teaching and learning and weak assessment tools and approaches are inhibiting effective learning.

1   What, in your experience, are the key inhibitors to effective learning?
2   In what ways does your school address inhibitors to learning?
3   What opportunities do you have to engage in CPD to enhance your pedagogy?

Suggested further reading

Alexander, R. (Ed) (2009) *The Cambridge Primary Review: children, their world, their education.* London: Routledge. This review represents one of the most important investigations into primary education to date and is most significant. The scale and scope of the review are extensive and as such this is recommended strongly.

Alexander, R. (Ed) (2009) *The Cambridge Primary Review Research Surveys.* London: Routledge. This text accompanies *The Cambridge Primary Review* and presents extensive research across a range of themes relating to primary education, including an international dimension, referenced in the chapter above.

Smyth, J. and Shacklock, G. (1998) *Re-making Teaching: Ideology, Policy and Practice.* London and New York, NY: Routledge. This book is essential reading if you are interested in the relationship between teachers and the role of the State in relation to education. It explores educational ideology and education policy, asking provocative questions about teacher autonomy and professionalism.

References

Alexander, R. (2000) *Culture and Pedagogy*. Oxford: Blackwell.

Alexander, R. (Ed) (2009) *The Cambridge Primary Review Research Surveys*. London: Routledge.

Ball, S.J. (2003) 'The teachers soul and the terrors of performativity', *Journal of Education Policy, 18,* 2, pp. 215–228.

Claxton, G. (2001) *Wise Up*. Stafford: Network Educational Press Ltd.

Cox, C.B. and Dyson, A.E. (1969) *Black Paper Two: The Crisis in Education*. London: The Black Papers.

David, T., Goouch, K., Powell, S. and Abbotts, P. (2003) *Birth to Three Matters: a Review of the Literature*. London: DfES.

David, T., Raban, B., Ure, C., Goouch, K., Jago, M., Barrière, I., Lambirth, A. (2000) *Making Sense of Early Literacy: a Practitioner's Perspective*. Stoke-on-Trent: Trentham Books.

DES (1965) *Circular 10/65*. London: HMSO.

DES (1992) *Curriculum Organisation and Classroom Practice in Primary Schools*. London: HMSO.

DfEE (1997) *Excellence for all Children: meeting special educational needs*. London: HMSO.

DfEE (1998) *The Implementation of the National Literacy Strategy*. London: HMSO.

DfES (2003) *Birth to Three Matters*. London: Queen's Printer.

Helgoy, I. and Homme, A. (2007) 'Towards a new professionalism in school? A comparative study of teacher autonomy in Norway and Sweden', *European Educational Research Journal, 6,* 3 pp. 232–249.

House of Commons Education and Skills Committee (2006) *Education and Skills – Third Report Session 2005*.

Humphrey, N. and Lewis, S. (2008) 'What does 'inclusion' mean for pupils on the autistic spectrum in mainstream secondary schools?', *Journal of Research in Special Educational Needs, 8,* 3, pp, 132–140.

Jeffrey, B. (2003) 'Countering student instrumentalism: a creative response', *British Education Research Journal, 29,* 4, pp. 489–504.

Jenkins, S. (1995) *Accountable to None*. London: Penguin Books.

Kearney, C. (2008) 'School absenteeism and school refusal behaviour in youth', *Clinical Psychology Review, 28,* pp. 451–471.

Kells, H.R. (2002) *Self-regulation in Higher Education: A multinational perspective on collaborative systems of quality assurance and control*. London: Jessica Kingsley Publishers.

Machin, S., Telhaj, S. and Wilson, J. (2006) *The Mobility of English School Children*. London: London School of Economics.

McCullogh, G., Helsby, G. and Knight, P. (2000) *The Politics of Professionalism*. London: Continuum.

McNamara, G. and O'Hara, J. (2008) 'The importance of the concept of self-evaluation in the changing landscape of education policy', *Studies in Educational Evaluation, 34,* pp. 173–179.

Office for Standards in Education (1996) *The Teaching of Reading in 45 Inner London Primary Schools: a report by Her Majesty's Inspectors in Collaboration with the LEAs of Islington, Southwark and Tower Hamlets.* London: Ofsted.

Olssen, M., Codd, C. and O' Neill, A. (2004) *Education Policy, Globalisation, Citizenship and Democracy.* London: Sage.

Pheysey, D. (1993) *Organisational Cultures.* London: Routledge.

Pinn, D.M. (1969) 'What kind of primary school?' in C.B. Cox and A.E. Dyson (Eds.) *Black Paper Two: The Crisis in Education.* London: The Black Papers.

Plowden, B.H. (1967) *Children and their Primary Schools: a report of the Central Advisory Council of Education in England* (Vol. II Research and surveys). London: Department for Education.

Reid, K. (1999) *Truancy and Schools.* London: Routledge.

Reid, K. (2005) 'The causes, views and traits of school absenteeism and truancy: an analytical review', *Research in Education,* *74,* pp. 59–82.

Strand, S. (2002) 'Pupil mobility, attainment and progress during Key Stage 1: a study in cautious Interpretation', *British Education Research Journal,* *28,* 1.

Troman, G. and Jeffrey, B. (2007) 'Creativity and performativity policies in primary school cultures', *Journal of Education Policy,* *22,* 2, pp. 549–572.

Trowler, P. (2003) *Education Policy.* London: Routledge.

UNESCO (1994) *The Salamanca Statement and Framework for Action on Special Needs Education.* Paris: UNESCO.

Vislie, L. (2003) 'From Integration to Inclusion: focusing global trends and changes in the western European societies', *European Journal of SEN,* *18,* 1, pp. 17–35.

Wiliam, D., Lee, C., Harrison, C. and Black, P. (2004) 'Teachers developing assessment for learning: impact on student achievement', *Assessment in Education: Principles, Policy and Practice,* *11,* 1, pp. 49–65.

20

Education and schooling 11–16 years

Andrew Peterson and Ralph Leighton
Canterbury Christ Church University

Overview

This chapter takes as its focus the stage of education and schooling experienced by pupils broadly between the ages of 11 and 16 and referred to generally as secondary, lower secondary or high school education. While age 11 is not an internationally uniform juncture at which the aims, content and organisation of children's education changes, evidence clearly indicates that there is a separation at or near this age in most countries. Following the introduction, three areas are considered. We start by considering the organisation and structure of education and schooling for pupils aged 11–16. Further to this, we consider the range of aims which underpin national curricula and relate these to the third area in a discussion of what nations expect schools to teach and pupils to learn through their curricular policies.

Introduction

From the outset it is both useful and necessary to establish the scope and confines of this chapter. First, the term 'education schooling 11–16' is used broadly to refer to what is generally known in the English-speaking world as secondary, lower secondary or high school education (for the purposes of this chapter we will use the term 'secondary' education). Second, the age-span of 11–16 reflects the current structuring of secondary education in the context in which we write (England), and should be understood by the reader in general terms as indicative of the age of young people who typically engage in secondary education. In using this age-span we recognise, however, that it is not precisely applicable to all nations, with variation identifiable in how different phases are subdivided. Whatever its particular determination and age-span, the stage of education and schooling with which we are concerned in this chapter is that which follows the primary/elementary stage of education and ends with optional progression in non-compulsory tertiary (further and higher) education or direct transition into the world of work.

It is a stage of education deemed so important that some have considered it to be a universal human right (Grover, 2010).

James Tooley (2003, p. 427) reminds us that 'there are three levels at which states can intervene in education: provision, funding and regulation'. In this chapter we draw extensively on two recent reports published by the International Review of Curriculum and Assessment Frameworks Internet Archive (hereafter INCA) which shed light on these areas through surveying curricular structures and policies across a number of nations. These are: Australia, Canada (British Columbia and Ontario), Finland, France, Germany, Hungary, Ireland, Italy, Japan, South Korea, the Netherlands, New Zealand, Northern Ireland, Scotland, Singapore, South Africa, Spain, Sweden, Switzerland, the United States (Kentucky and Maryland) and Wales.

The organisation and structure of education and schooling 11–16

As might be expected, there are clear variations across nations regarding the organisation and structure of schooling in the secondary sector, not least in terms of responsibility and control. In many nations, illustrated by current practice in England, Scotland, Northern Ireland and Wales, control of education represents a combination of centralised national government jurisdiction with a level of sub-national local management. In other nations, such as Ireland, there is currently no intermediary level between national government and institutional school boards of management (O'Donnell et al., 2010). Conversely, in some nations, of which Canada provides a clear example, educational policy and provision is the responsibility of individual provinces and territories. Even in nations where national governments play a comparatively limited role in standard policy and curricular provisions, they may still exert significant influence through particular and specific initiatives. In the USA, educational policy and curricular detail is typically proscribed at a state-level, and is in turn interpreted by local district school boards. However, federal educational policies (such as the No Child Left Behind Act of 2001, which required individual states to establish and conduct standardised assessment tests) fundamentally act upon schools across the nation, reminding us that national governments are able to influence the content and structure of secondary education and schooling. As Schmidt and Prawat (2006, p. 642) point out such legislation 'employs a hybrid . . . approach . . . that supposedly combines federal mandates – in this case [NCLB] accountability mandates – with a high degree of state responsibility and control'.

There is also notable variation regarding the types of schools which exist in respective nations. Recourse to the English context, which has a mixed composition of types of school, highlights how complex such organisation can be. In simplistic terms, and in common with a number of other nations, English secondary schools can be separated into state (i.e. schools which receive direct public funding) and independent/private sectors. The latter comprises schools which are funded outside of national and local government sources, usually by way of fees and donations. Because they are not in receipt of direct government funding, these schools, which include those institutions traditionally referred to in England as 'public' schools, are not subject to the full extent of government control and inspection and are free to operate outside of a National Curriculum compulsory for state-funded schools. The former are those schools which are directly funded by national and/or local government and which, as a result, do not directly charge pupils fees for their tuition.

This distinction between private and state-schools aside, the English state secondary school system is characterised by its multifarious and complex nature, with a plethora of different types of schools existing. These include selective grammar schools (schools in certain areas of England which select pupils at the age of 11 on the basis of perceived academic ability), high schools (schools in those same areas which provide for pupils who do not pass selection tests at the age of 11), comprehensive schools (schools which are open to pupils of all abilities), faith schools (schools which have the religious character of a particular faith, and which usually prioritise places for pupils of the respective religious faith), co-educational schools, single-sex schools, and special schools (schools which meet the needs of pupils with special educational needs). Over the last decade, successive governments have legislated for the establishment of academies in England – state schools funded directly by central government which are given greater freedom in certain areas of curriculum and which are outside the control of local authorities; many of these are also part-funded and part-managed by businesses. Since their election in May 2011 the Conservative–Liberal Democrat coalition government made provision for the formation of Free Schools (similar to Charter Schools in the United States) with the aim of permitting parents, teachers, charities and other organisations to set up their own schools in response to parental demand. The system in England, in which there are a number of types of secondary schools, is predicated on the benefits (or perceived benefits) of choice, with parents given some freedom to select the schools at which their child attends. According to some, this privileges pupils whose parents possess greater capital (economic, cultural and knowledge), in that these parents are able to make greater use of the system of choice to their own benefit (Brighouse, 2000; Taylor, 2001).

Curricular aims and subjects

In this section, we consider two specific questions in turn – what are the aims of national curricula for secondary education and which subjects are pupils taught? Before undertaking this, it is important to make a few points by way of framing our focus and intentions. First, our intention here, and drawing extensively on the INCA reports, is to simply consider those aims and curricular subjects which can be found in key policy documentation. On the basis of this we cannot, however, make any extensive pronouncements or considerations as to what actually is taught in schools and the quality, success and extent of this. As Reid *et al.* (2010, p. 5) make clear, there are likely to be areas of disparity between policy and practice, not least 'there is never a one-to-one correspondence between the state's agenda and its realisation in the classroom'.

Second, there is some disparity regarding the extent to which some nations' curriculum reviews and curricular documentation take account of the whole-school curriculum (i.e. they extend across all of the phases of compulsory education) and practice in other nations in which reviews and documentation are typically undertaken on the basis of individual phase groups. In England, for example, between 2001 and 2010 the New Labour government commissioned separate reviews of the Key Stage 3 curriculum (pupils of 11–14 years of age) and the curriculum for primary schools (pupils of 4–11 years of age), thereby allowing for the discrete needs of each phase of education and schooling to be taken into account. Elected in 2010, the current Conservative–Liberal Democrat coalition government have conversely ordered a review of the entire curriculum for compulsory education (pupils of 5–16 years of age), with the view of gaining greater consistency across all compulsory phases of education. Third, there is a notable difference in practice across the nations regarding the regularity and scheduling of curricular reviews. In some nations, such as Hungary and the Netherlands, school curricula are officially reviewed at legislated periods. In others, reviews of the curriculum occur on a more flexible basis, often owing to either a perceived need for the curriculum to be updated and/or a change in priorities of national or sub-national governments. The condition of England illustrates this latter approach. Shortly after election in 1997, the Labour government announced a review of the National Curriculum (published in 1999 for teaching from August 2002) for schools which, among other changes, led to the establishment of Citizenship Education as a statutory subject for state secondary schools. Following their election in 2010, the Conservative–Liberal Democrat coalition government have similarly announced a review of the curriculum, with the secretary of state for education, Michael Gove (2011), locating the need for this in the following terms:

> We have sunk in international league tables and the National Curriculum is substandard. Meanwhile the pace of economic and technological change is accelerating and our children are being left behind. The previous curriculum failed to prepare us for the future. We must change course. Our review will examine the best school systems in the world and give us a world-class curriculum that will help teachers, parents and children know what children should learn at what age.
>
> (Gove, 2011)

In this quotation, Gove makes reference to some of what O'Donnell *et al.* (2010, p. 9) identify as the most frequent 'drivers' for curriculum review in nations in which such reviews are not statutorily required, namely 'political change, curriculum overload, contributing to an excellent and equitable education system and curriculum modernisation to focus on the skills required for the demands of life and work in the 21st Century'. These remarks are not dissimilar from the views expressed in the preamble to the Melbourne Declaration on Educational Goals for Young Australians, a joint national statement of educational aims in Australia published in 2008 by the Ministerial Council on Education, Employment, Training and Youth Affairs. The preamble begins:

> In the 21st century Australia's capacity to provide a high quality of life for all will depend on the ability to compete in the global economy on knowledge and innovation. Education equips young people with the knowledge, understanding, skills and values to take advantage of opportunity and to face the challenges of this era with confidence.
>
> (MCEETYA, 2008, p. 4)

Following a discussion of these challenges, which include globalisation and technological advancements, the preamble continues '[o]ver the next decade Australia should aspire to improve outcomes for all young Australians to become second to none amongst the world's best school systems' (p. 5).

Similarly to Michael Gove's reasoning behind the curriculum review in England, the Melbourne Declaration explicitly references a desire to strengthen performance in international comparison tests as an important factor in amending the content of national and local education curricula. Over recent years, standardised tests have been used to judge comparative standards across nations. At the level of secondary education, the Programme for International Student Assessment (PISA), overseen by the Organisation for Economic Cooperation and Development (OECD), has since 2000 undertaken three-yearly surveys of student knowledge and skills across 'the principal industrialised countries' in the 'domains of reading, mathematical and scientific literacy' (www.pisa.oecd.org). The Trends in International Mathematics and Science Study

(TIMMS) has assessed standards of mathematics and science knowledge of pupils of 9–10 and 13–14 years of age across more than 40 nations on a four-yearly basis since 1995.

Curricular aims

Every education system, albeit through different processes, predicates its curricular provision on particular aims. In essence these can be understood as a response to the question 'what is the purpose of the curriculum?' In their analyses of educational aims, purposes, goals and principles of education found in key policy documents across the 21 nations cited in the introduction, O'Donnell *et al.* (2010, p. 9) found aims relating to the following categories to be common to all nations surveyed:

- individual development;
- social development;
- equal opportunities/multiculturalism;
- basic skills (literacy/numeracy);
- citizenship/community/democracy;
- health/physical/leisure;
- special learning needs (including gifted).

In addition, they found the following aims to be common to the vast majority of nations surveyed:

- excellence/raising standards;
- values/ethics/morals;
- emotional/spiritual development;
- personal qualities;
- national economy;
- preparation for work;
- scientific/technological skills;
- foundation for further education;
- knowledge and understanding;
- cultural (heritage literacy);
- non-mother tongue language;
- environment/sustainable development;
- lifelong learning;
- parental participation.

Interestingly, whilst there is variation across the nations as to those categories of aims which do and do not appear in key curricular documents, the data presented by O'Donnell *et al.* suggests that England, Ireland, Northern Ireland, Scotland and Wales include *all* of these aims (with the sole exception of England's omission of 'non-mother tongue language') within their documentation. We should also remember that although we have presented these curricular aims in a neutral sense here, no curriculum document, much less any curriculum produced at a governmental level, is neutral in intention and impact. For many, curricular are 'social products that are constituted within historically specific social relations of possession/dispossession and advantage/disadvantage' (Seddon, 2001, p. 309; cf. Young, 1971).

Curricular subjects

Across nations there is variation as to whether there is a proscribed national curriculum for secondary education. In some nations, such as Canada, Germany and the United States, no national curriculum exists, although as suggested previously there may be some level of national coordination through national government initiatives or through inter-governmental practice between sub-national jurisdictions (as in the case of MCEETYA in Australia which brings together the minister with responsibility for education in national government and their state counterparts). In other nations, including England, France, Ireland and Finland, national curricula are in place, with state/publically funded schools required to take such curricular provisions into account in their individual curricular frameworks.

In their analysis of curricular documents across nations, O'Donnell *et al.* (2010, p. 31) found the following subjects to be common to all nations' secondary education curriculum:

- national language (and literature);
- first foreign language;
- mathematics;
- science (either as general science or subdivided as biology, chemistry and physics);
- technology/technical education;
- history;
- geography;
- physical education/sport.

These subjects would appear to reinforce the notion that secondary education is concerned both with ensuring the transmission of socially dominant norms and values, and with preparing pupils with skills and knowledge which will allow them to find employment and thus play a part in the nation's economy. It is worth noting, however, that the School Board Act (1904) in England required broadly the same subjects to be taught, indicating a dedication to the '"traditional" and perhaps somewhat anachronistic' (Bailey, 1996, p. 16) which belies many nationally asserted ambitions to becoming world leaders in the development of education and learning.

The O'Donnell *et al.* (2010) analysis also found a mixture of continuation of the traditional in conjunction with new or adapted subjects, with the following being common to the majority of nations' secondary education curriculum, but not present in all of them:

- alternative language (i.e. a regional or mother tongue);
- environment;
- information technology/computer literacy;
- society/social studies/civics/politics;
- economics/business;
- the arts/crafts/fine arts;
- music/dance;
- health;
- moral education/ethics;
- religious education (usually as optional);
- homemaking/domestic skills;
- social/life skills/sex education;

■ careers;
■ European dimension/multiculturalism.

What this analysis cannot tell us, however, is the extent to which each of these subjects is prioritised, and how each finds expression, at the institutional level of individual schools. Nor does it identify the extent to which subjects with a shared or similar title enjoy a shared, similar or related content. Often, important choices are made at local or institutional levels which affect the time allocation for subjects as well as their respective importance within a schools' curriculum. Schools have a finite time within which they may (and in many nations are compelled to by law) cover a variety subjects, and as such the decision to allocate a given amount of time to one subject brings with it an opportunity cost in regard to the loss of that time for other subjects. Indeed, a concept which has received increasing attention in recent educational discourse is that of 'curriculum overload'. In relation to this, a study of secondary school teachers in England which was undertaken at the University of Cambridge (Macbeath and Galston, 2004, p. 40) reports that '[t]he overloaded curriculum ranked fifth in order of priority among obstacles to teaching. It reflects a view that there is too much content to "cover", too little time for following up pupils' interest and everything is too driven by targets, tests and other external pressures'.

For a number of reasons, some educationalists have been critical of the extent to which subjects (particularly in terms of their content knowledge) have been the key organising principle of education and have argued, instead, for a more flexible, skills-based approach through which pupils typically investigate issues or themes encountering subject-based content knowledge through the overarching topic at hand (usually referred to as cross-curricular or integrated-subject-based approaches). For some critics, subject-based approaches to curriculum organisation can often neglect to develop wider educational objectives. Writing at the time of the preparation of England's first National Curriculum in the late 1980s, Denis Lawton (1987) suggested that 'virtually all enlightened views on curriculum planning are now agreed that subjects should be regarded as important only if they help reach other objectives'. At the heart of such debates is an important question for secondary education which is worth re-stating in clear terms, namely whether pupils should encounter the content of their learning primarily through the content of individual subjects or through cross-subject themes and topics.

Moreover, as Boyle and Bragg (2006) point out in the context of England, even in situations where governments legislate for a broad-based curriculum which includes a number of subjects, schools may choose or be manipulated into focusing primarily on certain subjects (most usually English, maths and science) in order to 'perform' well in high-profile measurements of school effectiveness. An equally important discussion centres on the extent to which what is being taught is also what is being learned. Many of the issues and principles which relate to the theory and practice of assessment are dealt with in detail in other chapters of this book, and it will be clear that most forms of assessment can only identify and possibly measure those things which the assessors deem deserving of identification and measurement. Hahn (2003) clearly demonstrates that teachers and pupils throughout Europe have different understandings – within and between these groups – of what is meant by 'Citizenship/community/democracy', one of the key aims shared by all national curricula as found in the O'Donnell et al. (2010) study. This can only come about through differing perceptions of subject content, variations in teaching approaches and in degrees of teacher autonomy, pupil activity and passivity, and the means and purposes of assessment. What teachers believe they have taught is not necessarily the same as what pupils believe they have learned – a circumstance which transcends international boundaries and curricula.

Conclusion

This chapter has, primarily through drawing on recent work from the International Review of Curriculum and Assessment Frameworks Internet Archive, reviewed the organisation, aims and content of education and schooling for pupils of 11–16 years of age. Whilst it has not been possible to consider the vast remit of policy, curricula and pedagogical practice and issues relating to this stage of education (readers should consult the other chapters of this volume for more detailed analysis of these), it has suggested that at the heart of policy and curricula content are the questions relating to the purpose of education and the content of pupils' learning. As this brief overview highlights, there is some degree of commonality across a number of nations in relation to this, as well as inevitable differences.

In many nations, education is directed through a combination of national government jurisdiction and sub-national local management, although the relative authority of these varies between countries. In other nations, there is no intermediary level between national government and institutional school boards of management, while there is a third group of countries in which educational policy and provision is the responsibility of individual provinces and territories. There is a high level of consistency in nationally stated aims for 11–16 education and schooling, and in the curricula which are required to be followed; the extent of adherence to such curricula and the ways in which they might be delivered were not here discussed but there is evidence to suggest that variation exists within as well as between nations and schools in this regard. At national government level there is a growing emphasis on international assessment procedures such as PISA and TIMMS to enable the facilitation of comparisons which appear to be regarded as indicators of progress or regression. This emphasis relates to raising standards, one of the universally implied shared aims of 11–16 education policies, although clearly measurement is not synonymous with aims, content or organisation. There exists a hierarchy of aims just as there is a hierarchy of subjects, both of which are fairly consistent across nations. As national governments seek to raise their pupils' relative placing in international comparison tables – something which clearly cannot be achieved by all countries – they simultaneously look to each other for effective practice while striving to retain uniquely national characteristics. The different ways in which these aims, organisation and content are brought together ensures that education and schooling 11–16 remains dynamic.

Questions for further investigation

1 Should secondary education be considered as a universal human right?
2 How do the aims and purposes of education reported by O'Donnell *et al.* (2010) relate to the philosophical views presented in the chapters found within the first section of this volume?
3 What are the arguments for and against a statutory curriculum at either a national or sub-national (state/province/territory) level?
4 Can cross-curricular or integrated-subject-based learning ever provide a viable alternative to subject-content for the organisation of curriculum?

Suggested further reading

Brighouse, H. (2000) *School Choice and Social Justice*. Oxford: Oxford University Press. An interesting and insightful philosophical exploration of school choice and social justice, which integrates liberal political philosophy with a critical reading of public policy in education.

Sargent, C., Byrne, A., O'Donnell, S. and White, E. (2010) *Thematic Probe: Curriculum Review in the INCA Countries*. London: QCDA. A clear and accessible review of curriculum across a number of nations, which considers the scheduling and drivers of curriculum reviews. A useful source for an initial comparison of practice across nations.

O'Donnell, S., Sargent, C., Byrne, A. and White, E. with Gray, J. (2010) *INCA Comparative Tables. November 2010 Edition*. London: QCDA. A useful collection of tables which describe national educational policies across a number of nations. The content includes national education aims, recent education reforms, lower secondary curriculum and national assessment and public examination arrangements.

References

Bailey, R. (1996) 'The irony of the National Curriculum', in Hayes, D. (Ed.) *Debating Education: Issues for the New Millennium?* Canterbury: Department of Education, Canterbury Christ Church College.

Boyle, B. and Bragg, J. (2006) 'A curriculum without foundation', *British Educational Research Journal, 32*, 4, pp. 569–582.

Brighouse, H. (2000) *School Choice and Social Justice*. Oxford: Oxford University Press.

Gove, M. (2011) *Speech Made to Launch the Review of the National Curriculum at Twyford School*. Available at: www.education.gov.uk (accessed 10 March 2011).

Grover, S. (2010) 'Secondary education as a universal human right', *Education and the Law, 16*, 1, pp. 21–31.

Hahn, C. (2003) 'Becoming political in different countries' in Roland-Levy, C. and Ross, A. (Eds.) *Political Learning and Citizenship in Europe*. Stoke-on-Trent: Trentham.

Lawton, D. (1987) *Times Educational Supplement*, 18 September.

MacBeath, J. and Galston, M. with Steward, S., Page, C. and Edwards, J. (2004) *A Life in Secondary Teaching: Finding the Time for Learning*. Cambridge: University of Cambridge.

MCEETYA (2008) *Melbourne Declaration on Educational Goals for Young Americans*. Melbourne: MCEETYA.

O'Donnell, S., Sargent, C., Byrne, A. and White, E. with Gray, J. (2010) *INCA Comparative Tables. November 2010 Edition*. London: QCDA.

Reid, A., Gill, J. and Sears, A. (2010) 'The forming of citizens in a globalising world', in Reid, A., Gill, J. and Sears, A. (Eds.) *Globalization, the Nation-State and the Citizen*. London: Routledge.

Schmidt, W.H. and Prawat, R.S. (2006) 'Curriculum coherence and national control of education: issue or non-issue', *Journal of Curriculum Studies, 38*, 6, pp. 641–658.

Seddon, T. (2001) 'National curriculum in Australia? A matter of politics, powerful knowledge and the regulation of learning', *Pedagogy, Culture and Society, 9*, 3, pp. 307–331.

Taylor, C. (2001) 'Hierarchies and "local" markets: the geography of the "lived" market place in secondary education provision', *Journal of Education Policy, 16*, 3, pp. 197–214.

Tooley, J. (2003) 'Why Harry Brighouse is nearly right about the privatisation of education', *Journal of Philosophy of Education, 37*, 3, pp. 427–447.

Young, M. (1971) *Knowledge and Control*. London: MacMillan.

21

Post-compulsory, higher education and training

Marion Bowl
University of Birmingham

Overview

Throughout the industrialised world, tertiary education is at the centre of debates about the link between education and economic competitiveness, and the role of education and training in distributing life chances, economic and social power. This chapter begins by defining the scope of the tertiary sector and the ideological underpinnings of policy and practice in this area. It then presents some key themes and debates in this field which centre on:

- access and participation;
- skills, knowledge and the economy;
- learning and academic engagement.

Introduction: defining the field

The terms *tertiary education*, *post-compulsory education and training* and *higher education* are used in different national contexts to describe formal educational activity taking place beyond primary and secondary school. In this chapter, *tertiary education* describes the whole range of such activity, encompassing training for and at work, community- and institution-based further and higher education and including:

- academic study for sub-degree, undergraduate and postgraduate qualifications;
- institution-based vocational education and training;
- continuing professional development at work and/or college or university;
- on the job training;

- 'second chance' and compensatory education;
- community-based adult education.

Post-compulsory education and training

Post-compulsory education and training (PCET) is sometimes used in the same generic sense as tertiary education. However, the term is used here to describe education and training which take place in institutions known variously as further education colleges (the United Kingdom), technical and further education (TAFE) colleges (Australia), polytechnics (New Zealand) or community colleges (the United States), which are traditionally regarded as providing vocational training opportunities for school leavers but whose scope is far wider.

The expression 'post-compulsory' is misleading. The boundaries between compulsory and voluntary involvement in education and training are not clear-cut: although the statutory school leaving age in most industrialised countries ranges from 16 to 18, it is increasingly expected that young people under the age of 19 remain in some form of education or training after school-leaving age, whether they wish to or not. In a number of countries too, particularly those which are members of the OECD (Organisation for Economic Cooperation and Development), there is an expectation that adults involve themselves in education or training throughout their lives (OECD, 1996) to acquire new skills and knowledge for employment or as a condition of receiving state benefits if unemployed. For others, for example those in the prison system, decisions about whether to participate in education or training may carry rewards or sanctions, rendering educational involvement more-or-less compulsory.

Higher education

Historically, *higher education* has largely been confined to the universities, vested with powers to award undergraduate and post-graduate qualifications in academic and professional fields of study. Historically, too, higher education has been regarded as the preserve of social and academic elites and, in contrast to PCET, as somewhat detached from the world of work. However, there has been considerable change in the role and status of universities. Whilst the notion of 'elite' universities – exemplified by Oxford and Cambridge – remains, there has been a shift towards a mass system, particularly in the richer countries (Osborne *et al.*, 2004; Tapper and Palfreyman, 2005). There has also been increasing differentiation among higher education institutions. University league tables (based on judgements about teaching and research quality, students' qualifications on entry, staff-student ratios, performance in specific subject areas, and graduate employability) are now a common feature of higher education.

Furthermore, the boundaries between PCET and higher education are not firmly fixed. In England, for example, polytechnics, which formerly focused on vocational education at sub-degree level, gained university status in 1992; many further education colleges have become 'dual sector' institutions offering undergraduate as well as sub-degree qualifications; some universities offer sub-degree qualifications, particularly in the field of continuing professional development and preparatory study for university. In Finland meanwhile, a clear divide within higher education has been established between the polytechnics (primarily vocational) and the universities (primarily academic), though the recent trend towards institutional merger may render this divide less clear cut. And across the sector there has been a growing emphasis on tertiary education's contribution to developing the skills and dispositions thought to be required for employment.

Ideologies and tertiary education

A number of contrasting ideological perspectives can be discerned in the discourse of PCET and higher education (Ball, 1990; Williams, 1997). These are neither consistently articulated nor mutually exclusive. They are contested yet overlapping, though at different times in history one perspective may dominate. These ideological positions are played out in debates around tertiary education policy and practice – particularly the balance between the vocational and the academic, the needs of society and the economy and the question of who should be enabled – or compelled – to participate.

Conservatism

A conservative perspective views tertiary education as maintaining the social and economic status quo and preparing adults to assume their 'natural' place in society. It is characterised by a demarcation between training for lower status occupations and education for the elite vocations, through academic study. In this formulation, universities are the preserve of a small section of society possessing the requisite social, economic and cultural capital (Bourdieu, 1997) to enable them to progress into the professional or managerial classes. Social and economic relations are seen as being successfully reproduced by tertiary education. Social engineering in the form of widening participation policies, alternative routes to university, and alternative types of higher education provision is resisted as an attempt to dilute established academic standards and undermine the value of university education.

A liberal-meritocratic perspective

A liberal-meritocratic perspective is informed by the post–Second World War social democratic consensus. Its ideal is to increase educational participation as a force for social inclusion and broaden the base of higher education. Entry to university should therefore be open to those demonstrating the aptitude and diligence required through the acquisition of suitable qualifications. Initiatives to encourage disadvantaged adults to participate in education, including new entry routes, credit transfer systems and schemes to foster the aspirations of 'bright' young people, sit comfortably with this perspective.

Radicalism

The radical strand in post-compulsory education is associated with Freire (1972), Nyerere (1978) and Illich (1973) who took a critical view of dominant (Eurocentric) modes of formal education and regarded informal adult education as a tool for raising consciousness, empowering communities and changing unequal socio-economic structures. Radicalism was discernable in adult education policies of developing countries in the 1960s and 1970s, as they emerged from colonial domination and began to express a counter-hegemonic view of education in reshaping the future. In industrialised countries, radical ideas have influenced community-based and 'second chance' education. This philosophical strand has been weak within formalised tertiary education, although its ideals continue to influence adult educators.

Neo-liberalism

Since the mid-1970s, the dominant ideological thrust in tertiary education across the industrialised world has been a neo-liberalising one (Slaughter and Leslie, 1997; Avis, 2007).

201

Neo-liberalism is underpinned by a belief that the state should have a minimal role in funding educational participation and that the onus should rest on the learner to pay to access educational opportunities. From a neo-liberalising point of view, tertiary education is a commodity, whose value can be estimated through the award of qualifications. Tertiary institutions (particularly higher education institutions) should compete in the teaching and research marketplace, meeting the needs of industry and producing skilled labour for the global economy. A neo-liberalising ideology sees tertiary education operating on a business model, for those with the ability to pay, or the inclination to 'invest' in their future through taking on loans for education. This ideology has impacted on the curriculum in PCET and higher education, shifting the emphasis towards meeting the needs of business, rather than cultural and social utility.

Access and participation

Extending educational opportunities to a wider section of the population has been a concern of industrialised countries since at least the beginning of the nineteenth century. Since the 1990s the issue has taken centre stage in tertiary education policy in Europe, North America, Australia and elsewhere (Osborne *et al.*, 2004). The preoccupation with access and participation is driven by two, contradictory, concerns. On the one hand, seen through a radical or liberal lens, broader access to tertiary education is a matter of social justice. On the other hand, ensuring participation in education and training may be seen, from a neo-liberalising perspective, as a means of optimising human resources and ensuring that young people and adults are work-ready – and compliant.

Promoting access to education

'Second chance' education has been seen as a means of redressing inequalities arising from social and economic disadvantage and discrimination. The identification of under-represented groups has been a preoccupation (McGivney, 1990; Tuckett and Aldridge, 2010). Adult literacy, access to higher education and return-to-learn provision are pedagogical expressions of this concern. Such provision has mainly been offered by PCET institutions, local authorities and community-based adult education organisations, focusing on flexible, student-centred learning environments for adults lacking confidence in their educational ability.

Concern for equal access has shifted to widening the social base of higher education. Whilst female participation in higher education has increased, the expectation that widening participation policies would redress deeply embedded socio-economic inequalities has proved more problematic. Working-class representation in higher education has remained stubbornly resistant to widening participation initiatives. A number of explanations have been advanced to account for this. First, educational inequalities are established early in life (Gorard *et al.*, 2007), impacting on the likelihood of higher education participation. Second, research (Reay, 2001; Bowl, 2003) reveals that educational expectations, choices and experiences are shaped by family and institutional *habitus* (Bourdieu, 1997) which reproduces tacit norms, predispositions and expectations in respect of education. Accessing university (particularly the elite universities) may therefore seem an unrealistic expectation for those who have habitually been excluded; university may feel like an alien environment. Third, class-based differentials in holdings of social and cultural and economic capital (Bourdieu, 1977) benefit the middle classes disproportionately. Finally, as educational opportunities become increasingly stratified, economic inequalities are likely to continue to determine who gets access to the most prestigious opportunities (Avis, 2007). The creation of greater social equality through broadening access to a university education is therefore an elusive goal.

Ensuring participation in education and training

Increasing participation has also been part of an agenda which constructs engagement in education and training as an economic imperative – a means to ensuring that young people and adults contribute to a healthy national or global economy. However, the call to take up training opportunities has been resisted by some. It is scarcely surprising that those least likely to participate in education or training – those with low levels of school achievement, who are unemployed, on low income, or living in areas of deprivation – will feel they have little to gain from participation. This resistance has been constituted as a social problem (Coffield, 2000) and it has become customary to label non-participants in education and training (particularly young school leavers) as unmotivated. The dominance of this view has shifted the discourse of PCET from *enabling* disadvantaged groups to participate to *ensuring* participation though exhortation (appealing to national or individual interests), distancing (characterising the 'non-learner' as deviant), or compulsion (making benefits dependent on participation).

Skills, knowledge and the economy

The *academic/vocational divide* is an enduring theme in tertiary education. However, since the mid-1970s, the language of economic utility, and employer needs, underpinned by *human capital* theory has featured strongly, giving new meaning to vocational education and training and the notion of skills. Whilst the importance of skills – for economic development, for employment and for life – has been the rallying cry of policy documents on tertiary education across the world, and skills and competences for employment – sometimes of doubtful definition and value – have pervaded all levels of tertiary education, academic knowledge gained in the most prestigious universities maintains its social status.

The academic/vocational divide

In order to survive, societies need to develop and pass on knowledge and skills from one generation to the next. Whilst different countries may draw on different cultural and historical traditions and assumptions in shaping their tertiary education systems (Winch and Hyland, 2007), in many countries there is a status divide between the *academic* ('pure' knowledge) and the *vocational* (practical skills). The origins of this divide can be traced back to Greek philosophers Aristotle and Plato (Armitage *et al.*, 2003). And although, historically, schools and universities have had a vocational function in preparing middle- and upper-class 'gentlemen' for the professions through academic study, the academic/vocational separation persists in tertiary education policy, whilst vocationalism has taken on a narrower and less prestigious focus.

Academic education may be defined as the development of knowledge, understanding and judgement. Vocational or skills training involves instruction and practice aimed at producing the skills and attitudes required to perform in defined occupational or operational settings. Although the terms *education* and *training* are often run together, they are also sometimes expressed as binaries. In reality, there is considerable overlap. For example, a nurse or airline pilot would be expected to be trained – proficient in specific technical skills; they might also reasonably be expected to be academically educated – able to make judgements about situations or problems based on their knowledge and understanding and an evaluation of evidence. Yet, on the whole, tertiary education remains hierarchically organised, with vocational training occupying an inferior status. One explanation for this may lie in the stratified nature of societies, where educational segregation maintains the class status quo. Another lies in the tendency to associate training and skills with a limited notion of competence. A third possibility is that in times of high unemployment the 'skills training' label has been attached to schemes to reduce unemployment rates when the problem of unemployment is not lack of skills, but lack of jobs. Such schemes may involve trainees undertaking low paid work placements without the guarantee of a job, leading to scepticism about whether vocational training is developing valuable skills or a political ploy to label the unemployed as unskilled.

Human capital and the 'knowledge economy'

The perceived value of academic knowledge has been undermined by the dominance of human capital theory. The concept of *human capital* has its origins in the work of Schultz (1961) and Becker (1975) in the USA. Its premise is that educational investment serves the economy and that the knowledge and skills of workers are a productive investment, which accounts for the superiority of advanced industrial economies. It is argued that, as educational investment increases, the national economy benefits. Human capital theory carries two imperatives: educational expansion, particularly tertiary education, and the privileging of 'applied', over 'pure' knowledge. An association is made between a successful economy and an education system which develops the skills and knowledge of the workforce. In turn, it is argued, individual prosperity and social well-being are promoted as opportunities and wages for skilled workers to rise.

Human capital theory has been criticised on a number of grounds. First, the assertion that the rate of return on investment in human capital can be measured by increased earnings does not appear well-founded: structural and sector disparities in workers' income, regardless of their qualifications, make it difficult to sustain the claim for the link between human capital investment and social mobility (Avis, 2007). Second, *qualification inflation* (Dore, 1976) increases expectations on workers to train continually, whilst enabling employers to use credentials as a screening mechanism for job applicants where skills and experience would formerly have been the measure of suitability. Third, whilst human capital theory was originally utilised as an argument for increased state and employer expenditure in education, in a neo-liberalising climate the onus for investment has shifted to the individual; those unable or unwilling to invest the time or money in education or training thus become problematised.

Skills and competence

Across the tertiary sector there has been growing emphasis on the acquisition of skills for employment (Esland, 1990; Coffield, 2000). However, it is argued (Hyland, 1994; Winch and Hyland, 2007) that the concept of skills for employment has moved beyond the workplace and has been translated into work-related (rather than work-based) skills, demonstrated through performance in simulated work environments, or integrated into practical and academic assessments. They note too, that the notion of skills has extended from competence in specific practical operations to more vague generic, transferable, key or core skills, and into academic as well as vocational education. This, they suggest, reflects a discourse of individual deficiency, fashioning attitudes to modes of compliance and drawing attention away from structural economic problems.

This focus on skills has been accompanied by the rise of competence-based assessment, informed by 'scientific management' theories and behaviourist psychology. Skills are assessed through:

- prescribing clear standards and definitions of competence in a given context;
- assessing what the learner/trainee can do, rather than what they know;
- collecting observable or measurable evidence of performance.

Whilst competence-based assessment has been influential in the development of vocational qualifications and outcomes-based assessments, it has been criticised (Hyland, 1994) as over-emphasising assessment, over-simplifying learning and sidelining knowledge and understanding in favour of a 'lowest common denominator' view of competence.

Learning and academic engagement

'Learning' has become so central in the discourse of education and training that it has been argued that it has obscured the role of education and teaching (Armitage *et al.*, 2003). Theories of learning are based on psychological explanations of how learning takes place; but learners and teachers are also socially situated. The diverse nature of the tertiary sector also means that no single theory of learning is likely to suffice to explain how education and training should be planned and conducted. Below, we sketch the main theories of learning and academic engagement as they apply to tertiary education.

Theories of learning

Most theories of learning originate from research into children's learning. Whilst these theories are relevant to tertiary education, they may not account for the diversity of motivations, prior knowledge and experience of post-school learners. Learning theories, and their application in tertiary education, have been comprehensively described by Curzon (2004) and are briefly described below:

Behaviourism

Learning is evidenced by observable changes in behaviour and only that which can be measured counts as learning. It proceeds sequentially, building on past knowledge and is reinforced by success. In tertiary education and training, behaviourist theory underpins competence-based assessment and behaviour modification schemes which seek to control or change behaviour.

Gestalt theory

Learning is a holistic process. It involves restructuring perception through the operation of insight: thinking about a problem, rearranging the mental elements into a new structure, thereby arriving at a solution. In tertiary education, Gestalt theory informs problem-solving approaches to teaching, which utilise exploration and interaction to develop understanding.

Cognitive theories

Learning is a developmental process. New learning is constructed on previous knowledge and understanding through interaction with the environment and others (social constructivism). In tertiary education and training, the role of the teacher is to identify an area for the learner's development and to construct (or 'scaffold') learning opportunities accordingly. Formative assessment, for example, may be used by teachers to ascertain the learner's current understanding and to devise learning activities to build from this.

Humanist theories

Humanistic psychology is concerned with learning as a holistic and experiential process. The teachers' role is as facilitator of learning, rather than instructor. A variation on humanistic theory which is relevant to tertiary education is Knowles' (1984) notion of Andragogy. Andragogy assumes that adults' learning is of a different nature from children's: that adults are intrinsically motivated to learn, that their experience is a resource for their own and others' learning and that they have a unique capacity for self-direction. Whilst Andragogy has been influential among adult educators, it has been critiqued for its arbitrary definition of 'adult' and its generalised assumptions about adults' motivation, prior experience and propensity for self-direction.

Academic engagement and approaches to learning

Research on academic engagement has focused on a range of factors affecting learning. Since the 1970s, research on higher education learning has been dominated by *approaches to learning* theories. Marton and Saljo (1976), Ramsden (1984) and others have developed and elaborated notions of *deep and surface* learning to account for academic engagement. Deep learning is associated with understanding, whereas surface learning is characterised as instrumental and pragmatic. Whilst theorists of deep and surface learning stress that they are referring to students' reactions to learning contexts, rather than attributes of individual students, they have been criticised for proposing an over-simplistic dichotomy, for problematising students who do not engage on the academy's terms and for failing to take account of the political, social and cultural contexts in which learning occurs.

Conclusion

This chapter has reviewed the contested terrain of PCET and higher education, and some of the debates about purpose and practices in this rapidly changing field. Theories of learning and teaching provide academics and practitioners with a range of tools for analysing the dynamics of education and training in the tertiary sector. However, as this brief survey suggests, currently no single theory adequately explains the complex interaction between political, social, epistemological and individual factors in tertiary education.

Questions for further investigation

1   What are the long-term social, economic and individual outcomes of participation in tertiary education?
2   How are new technologies and web-based instruction impacting on teaching and learning?
3   What are the impacts of economic recession on widening participation in different national contexts?

Suggested further reading

Armitage, A., Bryant, R., Dunhill, R., Renwick, M. Hayes, D., Hudson, A., Kent, J. and Lawes, S. (2003) *Teaching and Training in Post-compulsory Education*. Maidenhead: Open University Press. A textbook for teachers and trainers, covering key concepts, theories and current debates in PCET.

Osborne, M., Gallacher, J. and Crossan, B. (Eds.) (2004) *Researching Widening Access to Lifelong Learning; Issues and approaches in international research*. Abingdon: RoutledgeFalmer. International perspectives on research in widening access to higher education.

Tapper, T. and Palfreyman, D. (2005) *Understanding Mass Higher Education: Comparative perspectives on access*. Abingdon: RoutledgeFalmer. Focuses on political and policy discourses of access, exploring how industrial economies have experienced a shift from elite to mass higher education.

Winch, C. and Hyland, T. (2007) *A Guide to Vocational Education and Training*. London: Continuum. Critically reviews the 'academic/vocational divide' and vocational education and training policy in the UK and Europe.

References

Armitage, A., Bryant, R., Dunhill, R., Renwick, M. Hayes, D., Hudson, A., Kent, J. and Lawes, S. (2003) *Teaching and Training in Post-compulsory Education*. Maidenhead: Open University Press.

Avis, J. (2007) *Education, Policy and Social Justice: Learning and Skills*. London: Continuum.

Ball, S.J. (1990) *Politics and Policy Making in Education*. London: Routledge.

Becker, G. (1975) *Human Capital*. Princeton, NJ: Princeton University Press.

Bourdieu, P. (1977) *Outline of a Theory of Practice*. Cambridge: Cambridge University Press.

Bourdieu, P. (1997) 'The forms of capital', in Halsey, A.H., Lauder, H., Brown, P. and Stuart-Wells, A. (Eds.) *Education, Culture, Economy, Society*. Oxford: Oxford University Press.

Bowl, M. (2003) *Non-traditional Entrants to Higher Education: 'They talk about people like me'*. Stoke on Trent: Trentham.

Coffield, F. (2000) *Differing Visions of A Learning Society: Volume 1*. Bristol: Policy Press.

Curzon, L.B. (2004) *Teaching in Further Education*. London: Continuum.

Dore, R. (1976) *The Diploma Disease: Education, qualification and development*. London: Allen and Unwin.

Esland, G. (1990) *Education, Training and Employment Volume 2: The educational response*. Wokingham: Addison-Wesley.

Freire, P. (1972) *The Pedagogy of the Oppressed*. Harmondsworth: Penguin.

Gorard, S. with Adnett, N., May, H., Slack, K., Smith, E. and Thomas, L. (2007) *Overcoming Barriers to HE*. Stoke on Trent: Trentham.

Hyland, T. (1994) *Competence, Education and NVQs: Dissenting perspectives*. London: Cassell Education.

Illich, I. (1973) *Deschooling Society*. Harmondsworth: Penguin.

McGivney, V. (1990) *Education's for Other People: Access to education for non-participant adults*. Leicester: NIACE.

Knowles, M. (1984) *The Adult Learner: a neglected species*. London: Gulf Publishing.

Marton, F. and Saljo, R. (1976) 'On qualitative differences in learning: 1 – outcome and process', *British Journal of Educational Psychology*, *46*, pp. 4–11.

Nyerere, J. (1978) 'Development is for Man, by Man, and of Man', in Hall, B. and Kidd, J. (Eds.) *Adult Learning: A design for action*. Oxford: Pergamon.

OECD (1996) *Lifelong Learning for All*. Paris: OECD.

Osborne, M., Gallacher, J. and Crossan, B. (Eds.) (2004) *Researching Widening Access to Lifelong Learning* Abingdon: RoutledgeFalmer.

Ramsden, P. (1984) 'The context of learning', in Marton, F., Hounsell, D. and Entwistle, N. (Eds.) *The Experience of Learning*. Edinburgh: Scottish Academic Press.

Reay, D. (2001) 'Finding or losing yourself: Working-class relationships to education', *Journal of Education Policy, 16*, 4, pp. 333–346.

Schultz, T.W. (Ed.) (1961) *Investment in Human Beings*. Chicago, IL: University of Chicago Press.

Slaughter, S. and Leslie, L.L. (1997) *Academic Capitalism: politics, policies and the entrepreneurial university*. London: Johns Hopkins University Press.

Tapper, T. and Palfreyman, D. (2005) *Understanding Mass Higher Education: Comparative perspectives on access*. Abingdon: RoutledgeFalmer.

Tuckett, A. and Aldridge, F. (2010) *A Change for the Better*. Leicester: NIACE.

Williams, J. (Ed.) (1997) *Negotiating Access to Higher Education: The discourse of selectivity and equity*. Buckingham: SRHE/Open University Press.

Winch, C. and Hyland, T. (2007) *A Guide to Vocational Education and Training*. London: Continuum.

22

Lifelong learning

Peter Jarvis
University of Surrey

Overview

Lifelong learning is a buzzword in the contemporary education vocabulary but it is one with a long history: this chapter presents an overview of the history. However, it came to the fore as a result of the demands of the knowledge economy, although it went by a number of different names as it emerged – each having a slightly different philosophy. Because it was so tied to the knowledge economy, its wider usage was not so widely explored but this chapter examines these briefly in the third section – especially the education of seniors and the learning region. It is, perhaps, in this section that we understand more fully the implications of the concept.

Introduction

Lifelong learning is commonly defined as education from the cradle to the grave and like many common-sense definitions this one hides more than it reveals: when, for instance, does learning begin – at birth, or with the emergence of consciousness, or even with pre-conscious experiences in the womb? Likewise, when does it finish – when we retire from work or when we finally lose consciousness and die? But it hides other ambiguities – does learning encapsulate education or does learning occur within the framework of education? Naturally, in a chapter like this we cannot explore all of these issues and we will initially examine the emergence of lifelong learning within the framework of the knowledge economy and thereafter look at lifelong learning beyond the world of work, but before we do this we will look briefly at the way the term achieved prominence.

The early history of the concept

When this term was adopted by United Nations Educational, Scientific and Cultural Organization (UNESCO) after the Second World War (see Lengrand, 1975), it already had a long history. For instance, Dewey (1916, p. 51) wrote:

It is common place to say that education should not cease when one leaves school. The point of this common place is that the purpose of school organization is to insure the continuance of education by organizing the powers that insure growth. The inclination to learn from life itself and to make the condition of life such that all will learn in the process of living is the finest product of schooling.

While not everyone would agree with Dewey's understanding of the purpose of schooling, they may well agree with the sentiments expressed in the remainder of the quotation:

Since life means growth, a living creature lives as truly and positively at one stage as at another, with the same intrinsic fullness and the same absolute claims. Hence education means the enterprise of supplying the conditions which insure growth, or adequacy of life, irrespective of age.

For Dewey, education is one of the major foundations of a rich life but it is also one that need not be laid at the beginnings of life or in childhood; it may be laid at any stage of life and then built upon. However, in the light of our current understanding, Dewey might actually have used the term 'learning' rather than 'education' to make his point more clearly. Soon after Dewey's book was published, an important document about adult education – the 1919 Report – was published in Britain. A.L. Smith, chairman of the committee wrote:

That the necessary condition is that adult education must not be regarded as a luxury for the few exceptional persons here and there, nor as a thing which concerns only a short span of early manhood, but that adult education is a permanent national necessity, an inseparable aspect of citizenship, and therefore should be both universal and lifelong.

(Smith, 1919, Introductory letter, p. 5)

This far-sighted statement, like many others in the report, was loudly acclaimed but never really implemented, so that the idea of lifelong education remained an ideal. Yeaxlee (1929, p. 31), who served on the committee that drafted the report, returned to the subject in the very first book about lifelong education and claimed that:

The case for lifelong education rests ultimately upon the nature and needs of the human personality in such a way that no individual can rightly be regarded as outside its scope, the social reasons for fostering it are as powerful as the personal.

In this groundbreaking book, Yeaxlee began to point to some of the conceptual problems that arise when we see learning as lying both within and beyond the educational system.

UNESCO, however, continued to focus on lifelong education with the Faure Report (1972) advocating that education should be both universal and lifelong, claiming that education precedes economic development and prepares individuals for a society that does not exist but which may do so within their lifetime. The report also claimed that education is essential for human beings and their development and that, therefore, the whole concept of education needs to be reconsidered. The sentiments of this report were echoed by the Delors Report (1996) in which it was claimed that learning has four pillars – learning: to know; to do; to live together; to be. One pillar, however, was I feel omitted – learning to care for the planet. But it was not really until the knowledge economy began to emerge that lifelong learning become socially and politically significant.

Lifelong education and the demands of the knowledge economy

Lifelong learning gained currency through the demands of the emerging knowledge economy in which professional updating found its place within the educational vocabulary: four terms reflect the way in which lifelong learning developed: continuing professional development, continuing education, recurrent education and human resource development.

Continuing professional development

In the UK, continuing professional development (CPD) was financed a great deal by the government through a number of differing agencies, e.g. the Manpower Services Commission, PICKUP, the local Training and Enterprise Councils and later the Learning and Skills Councils that controlled the budget. In the first instance, CPD was a matter of in-service or education-provided short courses for specific professions, and the term 'development' was beginning to be replaced by 'education'.

Continuing education

The Advisory Council for Adult and Continuing Education in the UK (ACACE, 1979, p. 7) recognised that continuing education has long been a popular idea among those educators concerned with the education of adults but that it had gone under a variety of names. This report also made it clear that continuing education was not the same as further education as it existed in the United Kingdom: further education could be post-compulsory but not necessarily post-initial; it implied a specific level of study, whereas continuing education does not; it was pre-vocational, vocational or academic while, conceptually, continuing education need not be necessarily be directed towards any course assessment or award.

In the US, continuing professional education was the term adopted and defined by the Accrediting Commission of the Continuing Education Council of the United States as:

> The further development of human abilities after entrance into employment or voluntary activities. It includes in-service training, upgrading and updating education. It may be occupational education or training which furthers careers or personal development. Continuing education includes that study made necessary by advances in knowledge. It *excludes* most general education and training for job entry. Continuing education is concerned primarily with broad personal and professional development. It includes leadership training and the improvement of the ability to manage personal, financial, material and human resources. Most of the subject matter is at the professional, technical and leadership training levels or the equivalent.
>
> (Apps, 1979, 68f. emphasis added)

Professions also provided their members with many updating programmes and there has been considerable debate over the past 20 years as to the extent to which continuing education should become mandatory for continued registration as a member of a professional occupation. Whilst it was the professions that emphasised continuing education, global capitalism led by the corporations were much more effective in introducing it. This process began to emerge in the 1980s with Eurich's (1985) book, *The Corporate Classroom*, being one of the earliest studies:

others were to follow quite rapidly (e.g. Castner-Lotto, 1989). At this stage it was recognised that the corporations working with knowledge had to change rapidly to respond to the wider social and competitive forces. By so doing, they had earned the title of learning organisations with studies being conducted in both the UK (Pedler *et al.*, 1997) and the USA (Senge, 1990; Watkins and Marsick, 1993). The learning organisation emerged in the beginning of the 1990s when it was recognised that organisations had to be flexible, adapt rapidly and efficiently to the market conditions and produce new products at competitive prices. Amongst the earliest writers on the subject, Argyris and Schon (1974, 1978) rightly focused upon the need for organisations to change procedures, and while they recognised that power relationships within the organisation prevented the lower hierarchical orders communicating rapidly to the hierarchy about the needs for change without risking their own position, some of the later studies of these organisations tend to be functionalistic and not emphasise power sufficiently. Argyris and Schon (1978, p. 28) suggested that:

> Organizational learning occurs when members of the organization act as learning agents for the organization, responding to the internal and external environments of the organization by detecting and correcting errors in organizational theory-in-use, and embedding the results of their inquiry in private images and shared maps of organization.

Since that time learning in the workplace has become a major topic of research. Thereafter, there followed one other organisational innovation: the corporations founded their own universities (Jarvis, 2001: Meister, 2000) and the idea of corporate knowledge was developed (Tuomi, 1999).

Since continuing education offered no criticism of the structure of education, it is inherently conservative: no such claims may be legitimately made about the next form of education strategy to be discussed.

Recurrent education

This was the concept espoused most frequently by the Organisation for Economic Cooperation and Development (OCED) and, in the United Kingdom from the mid-1970s, through the publications of the Association of Recurrent Education. It was defined in a tautologous manner as 'the distribution of education over the lifespan of the individual in a recurring way' (OECD 1973, p. 7).

One of the most significant features of recurrent education was the belief that individuals should have a right to six years full-time education beyond compulsory schooling. Gould (1979) not only regarded this as a moral argument about the equality of educational opportunity but he also saw it as providing equality of occupational opportunity. But having such a right to full-time education later in life is both inconvenient and expensive to employers and governments and so it is hardly surprising that with the economic stringency and the advent of the 'new right' politics of the 1980s that recurrent education disappeared from the political and educational agendas. Even the Association of Recurrent Education in the United Kingdom adopted a new name—the Association of Lifelong Learning.

One aspect of recurrent education which has survived, however, is paid educational leave. This was recognised in some of the early OECD literature (OECD, 1973, pp. 70–72), where discussion occurred about the extent to which paid educational leave should be a statutory right or whether it should be the result of negotiations between employers and employees. By the time that the OECD had actually published this document, France had already introduced legislation which allowed for up to 2 per cent of a firm's labour force to take leave of absence at any one time and for 1 per cent of the wage bill, rising to 2 per cent by 1976, to be spent on employee education (OECD, 1975, p. 35).

Continuing and recurrent education, then, were two major approaches to lifelong learning: a more radical one that regarded it as a strategy for the reform of the whole education system and perhaps also the wider society, while the more conservative stand was less ambitious in its claims, preferring to regard it as a reformist.

Human resource development

As we noted in the section on continuing education, the corporations began to develop their own education and training during this time. However, there was another conceptual shift just a little earlier when Schultz (1961) introduced the term 'human capital'. He pointed out that economists shied away from the use of this term because, while individuals actually invested in themselves, they might find it offensive to think of themselves in this manner. He wrote:

> Our values and beliefs might inhibit us from looking upon human beings as capital goods, except in slavery, which we abhor. We are not unaffected by the long struggle to society on indentured service and to evolve political and legal institutions to keep men free from bondage. These are achievements we prize highly. Hence, to treat human beings as wealth that can be augmented by investment runs counter to deeply held values.
>
> (cited from Jarvis with Griffin, 2003, vol. 5. p. 246)

However, it was not long before the idea of human capital development arose, and corporations opened their own human resource development (HRD) departments, some of which eventually turned into the corporate universities. HRD seeks to enhance the personal and work-related knowledge and skills of individuals, helping them to achieve their full potential. Training officers, and even some personnel and welfare officers, have become human resource managers and trainers and gradually HRD has assumed its own place in the learning society (see Brinkerhoff, 1987; Jayagopal, 1990; Hargreaves and Jarvis, 2000 inter alia). In 1993 the Academy of Human Resource Development was founded in the United States by adult educators who had undertaken a great deal of their research in organisational settings, and human resource development became a separate profession. The academy runs its own conferences and publishes its own books (see Redmann, 2000).

By the mid-1990s all of these terms were subsumed under the concept of lifelong learning (EC, 1995) for the term 'education' began to take second place to learning, and lifelong learning became the significant term in Europe, although in 2006 the European Commission (EC, 2006) started to use the term 'adult learning' since it recognised that formal schooling, higher education and training had their own identities that could never be subsumed within the all-embracing term 'lifelong learning'.

Lifelong learning and the wider society (life-wide learning)

In this section we will look briefly at the education of seniors, learning cities and learning regions and social capital.

The education of seniors

In the European Commission, lifelong learning was seen to have four aims: to produce an efficient work force, to help generate European citizenship, social inclusions and personal development (EC, 2000, 2001 inter alia) although the dominant focus was vocational. No mention was made of older people until 2006 when the commission's report was entitled *Adult Learning: It's Never Too Late to Learn*. The education of older people was by this time an exceedingly vibrant sector of education with the two most well-known organisations being the Institute for Retired Professionals – founded by Hy Hirsch in 1962 in New York – and the University of the Third Age in Europe – founded by Pierre Vellas in Toulouse in 1972. It took another ten years for the U3A to spread to the United Kingdom and when it did so it assumed a more independent approach than that in France where it was closely tied to its local university. Each of the UK's over 725 U3As is an independent non-governmental organisation (NGO), although there is a Third Age Trust which, in some ways, acts as a coordinating body. The difference in these two types of U3A reflects something of the difference in their approach to their activities: the ones that follow the pattern of the European continental ones are attached to universities and appear to be much more academically orientated, whilst those in the UK tend to emphasise leisure as much as learning.

In the USA, the development of the Institute for Retired Professionals had begun under the sponsorship of the New School for Social Research in New York City but spread slowly. In 1976, however, a conference of interested parties led to these becoming known as Institutes for Learning in Retirement. At roughly the same time (1975), in New Hampshire another movement was born – Elderhostel (*www.elderhostel.org*) and this grew extremely rapidly – offering educational travel. By 2006, it offered some 8,000 programmes throughout the world to about 160,000 members – its success once again reflects the significance of globalisation and the wealth of the current retirees. However, it was in 1988 that 24 Institutes for Learning in Retirement joined with Elderhostel to form the Elderhostel Institute Network. At about the same time locally they adopted the name Lifelong Learning Institute. The network is a voluntary association of Lifelong Learning Institutes funded by Elderhostel. It is significant that the cognitive interest motivation factor is dominant amongst its members, if the small-scale study conducted by Kim and Merriam (2004) is to be taken as representative. In contrast, Elderhostel clearly caters for the many seniors who want to travel and learn local knowledge at the same time. It is also not insignificant that the United Nations should run a network of university departments throughout the world which is involved in educational tourism and which seeks to preserve local knowledge.

Another model that has emerged in Germany and Spain, amongst other places, is where universities open their classes to seniors. The so-called Third Age Classrooms began to function as early as 1978 in Spain (Socias *et al.*, 2004) and by 1993 it was decided to open universities to seniors with the University of the Balearic Islands initiating an Open University for Seniors. There are third age educational movements in most countries of the world now – see, for instance, Shirasha (1995) for Japan and Li Herzhong (1997) for China.

Finally, older people are now living beyond what was generally referred to as the third age into the fourth age – a time when they lose their independence. Learning initiatives have emerged in what Withnall (2010) has called longer life learning in care homes.

The Learning Cities and Learning Regions

One of the outcomes of globalisation has been a growing awareness of the local – a form of glocalisation. Robertson (1995, p. 31) makes the point that 'there is an increasingly globe-wide discourse of locality, community, home, and the like' and so it is not surprising that there should be a focus on the local. The information society and its network counterpart have also assisted in this development as the ideas of the learning region and the learning city have arisen, in which local information networks have been established. In fact, we might see the learning region and learning city as new forms of community education.

In the same way as we noted that the concepts of society and organisation are reified in the above discussions, so we see the same process happening with the learning city:

> A learning city is one which strives to learn how to renew itself in a period of extraordinary social change. The rapid spread of new technologies presents considerable opportunities for countries and regions to benefit from the transfer of new knowledge and ideas across national boundaries. At the same time global shifts in capital flows and production are creating uncertainties and risk in managing national and local economies.
>
> (Department for Education and Employment – DfEE, 1998, p. 1)

The DfEE definition of the learning city actually goes on to explain something of the origins of the idea – both global and local use of capital and technology. While many of the initiatives for learning cities and learning regions have come from adult educators, support is necessary from local government and local business and commerce. In fact, Longworth (1999, p. 114) suggests that the network consists of:

- primary and secondary education;
- universities and tertiary education;
- industry, business and commerce;
- professional bodies and special interest groups;
- adult and vocational education;
- social services and voluntary organisations;
- local government.

The purposes of the learning city are to support lifelong learning and to learn how to promote social and economic regeneration (Department for Education and Employment – DfEE 1998, p. 1). The DfEE document sees the tasks of the learning city as: partnership, participation and performance, and when the first international meeting on the learning city did not happen, one was organised in Barcelona in 1990. Thereafter the idea grew and was supported by the British government from the mid-1990s when the first local governments committed their towns and cities to become a learning city. Thereafter a learning city network evolved and the European Commission supported the development of networks to promote and support lifelong learning locally and regionally (European Commission, 2003). Now there are learning cities and regions in many countries of the world.

Social capital

The development of the learning regions focused interest on social capital rather than human capital: Field et al. (2000, p. 243) suggest that social capital offers 'one way of apprehending and analysing the embeddedness of education in social networks'. But they go on to say that 'it also challenges the dominant human capital approaches . . . which concentrate on narrowly defined, short-term results or tidy analytical devices'. The outset of their argument is that social capital actually provides many opportunities for informal learning but that it is inherently narrowing – which is precisely the same type of argument that has existed for years about the advantages and disadvantages of living in small communities, but they produce considerable evidence.

Social capital takes us back to the ideas of the community and the community spirit, phenomena that have apparently declined tremendously as a result of the division of labour (Putnam, 2000), although the same concern about the decline existed nearly a century ago. It might well be that this reflects the social process of constructing ideal communities but we either see them as utopian and in the future or locate them in a dim and distant past! In both cases their function is to illustrate that we do not live in a perfect society – but then we may never ever do so! What these studies have shown, however, is that there are community resources that can enrich human living, although they might have their drawbacks; these resources might aid informal learning but through planning and learning we can create conditions and structures through which human living may be enriched.

Conclusion

It may be seen from all of this discussion that in many ways lifelong learning is actually a term for learning beyond initial education – however long that lasts. Few conferences have been organised where pre-school educators, school educators, academics from higher education, distance education and educators involved in all other forms of education and training have met. In the same way the European Union has its department responsible for lifelong learning but it has always had separate departments for education and training and higher education.

This overview of lifelong learning has examined the way that it has developed institutionally in the West but there are other ways of researching lifelong education such as: biographical research (e.g. Alheit, 1999; West, 2001) and learning from our lives (Dominice, 2000; the Stirling project (http://www.learninglives.org/); and Jarvis, 2009). In some ways, therefore, lifelong learning is a tautologous term since for as long as the human being has conscious life, learning occurs and so learning is in some way a manifestation of the life force in the human being (Jarvis, forthcoming).

Questions for further investigation

1   To what extent do you consider adult learning to be a more precise concept than lifelong learning for what has been described in this chapter?
2   Why do you think that lifelong learning is better regarded as an umbrella concept than as a national system?
3   Does the term 'adult learning and education' better describe what is happening in some countries, such as the UK, than just 'adult learning'?
4   To what extent does the concept of the learning region capture the essence of lifelong learning?

Suggested further reading

Field, J. (2000) *Lifelong Learning and the New Educational Order.* Stoke on Trent: Trentam Books. This book explores the way in which lifelong learning burst upon the scene in the UK and highlights issues of policy and practice. It provides a clear understanding of the events and illustrates some of the major issues involved.

Jarvis, P. (2007) *Globalisation, Lifelong Learning and the Learning Society* (Vol. 2) London: Routledge. This is a sociological analysis of globalisation demonstrating how the process generated the information society, the knowledge society, the learning society and brought lifelong learning to the forefront of the education of adults.

Jarvis, P. (Ed.) (2009) *The Routledge International Handbook of Lifelong Learning.* London: Routledge. This large handbook contains chapters on almost all aspects of lifelong learning, written by leading scholars and exponents in the field – it has sections on learning throughout life, sites for lifelong learning, modes of learning, lifelong learning policies, social movements, different perspectives on lifelong learning and a geographical dimension.

Withnall, A. (2010) *Improving Learning in Later Life.* London: Routledge. This is a small book that captures the essence of learning in later life – it covers recent research and policy and points to some of the major issues. It is a very good introduction to the topic.

References

Advisory Council for Adult and Continuing Education (1979) *Towards Continuing Education.* Leicester: ACACE.

Alheit, P. (1999) 'On a contradictory way to the "Learning Society": A critical approach', *Studies in the Education of Adults, 31,* 1, pp. 66–82.

Apps, J.W. (1979) *Problems in Continuing Education.* New York, NY: McGraw Hill Book Co.

Argyris, C. and Schon, D. (1974) *Theory in Practice: Increasing Professional Effectiveness.* San Francisco, CA: Jossey Bass.

Argyris, C. and Schon, D. (1978) *Organizational Learning: A Theory of Action Perspective.* Reading, MA: Addison-Wesley.

Brinkerhoff, R. (1987) *Achieving Results from Training.* San Francisco, CA: Jossey Bass.

Casner-Lotto J and Associates (1988) *Successful Training Strategies.* San Francisco: Jossey Bass.

Delors, J. (chair) (1996) *Learning the Treasure Within.* Paris: UNESCO.

Dewey, J. (1916) *Education and Democracy.* New York, NY: The Free Press.

DfEE (1998) *The Age of Learning.* London: Department for Education and Employment.

Dominice, P. (2000) *Learning from our Lives.* San Francisco, CA: Jossey-Bass.

Eurich, N. (1985) *The Corporate Classroom.* Princeton. NJ: Carnegie Foundation for the Advancement of Teaching.

European Commission (1995) *Teaching and Learning: Towards the Learning Society.* Brussels: European Commission.

European Commission (2000) *A Memorandum on Lifelong Learning.* Brussels: European Commission SEC 1832.

European Commission (2001) *Making a European Area of Lifelong Learning a Reality.* Brussels: European Commission COM 678 final.

European Commission (2003) *Compendum: European Networks to Promote the Local and Regional Dimension of Lifelong Learning.* Brussels: European Commission – Education and Culture.

European Commission (2006) *Adult Learning: it is never too late to learn.* Brussels: European Commission COM 614 Final.

Faure, E. (1972) (Chair) *Learning to Be.* Paris: UNESCO.

Field, J., Schuller, T. and Baron, S. (2000) 'Social capital and human capital re-visited', in Baron, S., Field, J. and Schuller, T. (Eds.) *Social Capital*. Oxford: Oxford University Press.

Gould, A. (1979) *Towards Equality of Occupational Opportunity*. Association of Recurrent Education, Discussion Paper 5. Nottingham: Centre for Research into Education for Adults, University of Nottingham.

Hargreaves, P. and Jarvis, P. (2000) *The Human Resource Development Handbook*. London: Kogan Page Limited.

Jarvis, P. (2001) *Universities and Corporate Universities*. London: Kogan Page.

Jarvis, P. (2009) *Learning to be a Person in Society*. London: Routledge.

Jarvis, P. (forthcoming) *Pro-Active and Re-Active Learning*. London: Routledge.

Jarvis, P. with Griffin, C. (Eds.) (2003) *Adult and Continuing Education: Major Themes in Education* (5 vols.) London: Routledge.

Jyagopal, R. (1990) *Human Resource Development: conceptual analysis and strategies*. New Delhi: Sterling Publishers.

Kim, A. and Merriam, S. (2004) 'Motivations for learning among older adults in a learning in retirement institute', *Educational Gerontology*, 30, 6, pp. 441–455.

Lengrand, P. (1975) *An Introduction to Lifelong Education*. London: Croom Helm.

Longworth, N. (1999) *Making Lifelong Learning Work: learning cities for a learning century*. London: Kogan Page.

Meister, J. (2000) *Corporate Universities* (2nd Ed.). New York, NY: McGraw Hill.

Organisation for Economic Cooperation and Development (1973) *Recurrent Education: a strategy for lifelong education*. Paris: OECD.

Pedler, M., Burgoyne, J. and Boydell, T. (1997) *The Learning Company* (2nd Ed.). London: MacGraw-Hill.

Putnam, R. (2000) *Bowling Alone*. New York, NY: Simon and Schuster.

Redmann, D. (Ed.) (2000) *Defining the Cutting Edge*. Academy of Human Resource Development.

Robertson, R. (1995) 'Glocalization: Time-Space and Homogeneity – Heterogeneity', in Featherstone M, (Ed.) *Undoing Culture: Globalization, Postmodernism and Identity*. London: Sage.

Schultz, T. (1961) *Investment in Human Capital*. Basingstoke: MacMillan.

Senge, P. (1990) *The Fifth Discipline*. New York, NY: Doubleday.

Shirasha, I. (1995) 'Japan, a developing country in the field of lifelong learning as well as ageing: its new perspectives and barriers', *Third Age Learning International Studies*, 5, pp. 101–104.

Smith, A.L. (1919) 'Adult Education Committee Final Report', reprinted in 'The 1919 Report'. Nottingham: Department of Adult Education, University of Nottingham.

Socias, C., Brage, L. and Garma, C. (2004) 'University programs for seniors in Spain: analysis and perspectives', *Educational Gerontology*, 30, 4, pp. 315–328.

Tuomi, I. (1999) *Corporate Knowledge*. Helsinki: Metaxis.

Watkins, K. and Marsick, V. (1993) *Sculpting the Learning Organization*. San Francisco, CA: Jossey Bass.

West, L. (2001) *Doctors on the Edge; general practitioners, health and learning in the inner-city*. London: Free Association Books.

Withnall, A. (2010) *Improving Learning in Later Life*. London: Routledge.

Yeaxlee, B.A. (1929) *Lifelong Education*. London: Cassell.

23

Alternative education

Paul Warwick
University of Leicester

Overview

State-defined instrumentalist education continues to dominate across the Western world. But concerns over the sustainability of mainstream Western lifestyles, findings from emerging fields of research such as neuroscience, and worrying trends of disaffection and tension within mainstream schooling systems have led to a burgeoning alternative education movement. This movement can be seen to support increasing levels of freedom and diversity in schooling.

In this chapter we explore some examples of alternative education that are underpinned by a holistic notion of human development; seeking to foster the well-being of young people and support a more just, creative and democratic society through a transformative pedagogy and personalised learning environments. These examples provide an important insight into how the place of school can be envisioned differently and in so doing raise a number of key issues for debate in our consideration of the ethos, purpose and organisation of education today.

Introduction

The service of education has never been a neutral enterprise and has constantly existed in a state of flux across ideologies, politics and insight from educational research. The contested and complex nature of education means that the traditional mainstream conceptualisation of education has continually been debated and criticised. For example, John Dewey in 1897 argued for an alternative model of education based upon a criticism of traditional education that was seen to:

- be disconnected from the experiences that the students brought from their homes and their community;

- be disconnected from the practical and manual activity through which they are engaged with experience;
- ignore the interests that motivated young people to learn;
- treat knowledge as something purely symbolic and formal – organised in textbooks, 'stuck on' without connections to experience or existing ways of understanding;
- maintain discipline through external authority rather than through the engagement of the young people.

(Dewey, cited in Pring, 2007, p. 15)

Interestingly many of these same concerns remain today. As a result, increasing interest is being expressed in alternative models of education that are more holistic in their approach to human development. Renewed interest is being expressed in areas such as moral education and character education (Arthur, 2003). Across many countries, a skills-based and values-based reform has been undertaken in the guise of Citizenship or Civic Education (Kerr, 2002). More recently through the encouragement of the United Nations Decade for Education for Sustainable Development, a worldwide transformative educational agenda has risen in profile seeking to address social justice and environmental degradation issues (Scott and Gough, 2003). So the world of education is immersed in a time of flux with increasing levels of educational experimentation and innovation.

This chapter seeks to outline a number of key examples of alternative education in terms of both vision and practice, and in so doing highlight some of the core features of new learning spaces flourishing in the twenty-first century.

Size matters: the centrality of relationship and a question of scale

A number of key alternative education movements centre around the principle of the primacy of relationships within the learning space.

Originally inspired by the principles of E.F. Schumacher (1974) and his 'small is beautiful' study of economics, Human Scale Education (HSE) was founded in 1985 around the notion of a more personalised educational experience for children. This was seen to require a shift towards small-scaled approaches to schooling. HSE's vision of the good school is essentially based upon putting relationships at the heart of the school's organisation, and recognising the importance of a democratic community and a respect for the individual. Today HSE advocates a practical manifesto for schools consisting of eight key practices:

1   Small size. Schools or learning communities of no more than 250 to 300 students.
2   Small teams of between four to six teachers, learning mentors and learning support assistants who will see no more than between 80 to 90 learners each week.
3   A curriculum that is thematic, cross-disciplinary and holistic.
4   A timetable that is flexible with blocks of time that makes provision for whole-class teaching, small group teaching and individual learning. Teacher planning and evaluation timetabled.
5   Pedagogy that is inquiry based, experiential and supported by ICT.
6   Assessment that involves the 'assessment for learning' approaches of dialogue, negotiation and peer review and develops forms of authentic assessment such as portfolio, exhibition and performance.

7   Student voice. Involving students in the learning arrangements and organisation of the school.

8   Genuine partnership with parents and the community.

(Tasker, 2008, p. 13)

This alternative vision of the purpose and structure of education led in 2006 to a Human Scale Schools initiative where 39 secondary schools across England experimented with how they could develop along human scale lines. As reported by Wallace (2009) and Harland and Mason (2010) this generated a range of student voice innovations and renewed interest in the schools within a school restructuring model whereby a school operates through smaller more personal units but still benefits from economies of scale and shared educational resources.

This issue of school size has also been of concern in many other countries, including America where a five-year research study led by Ted Sizer (1996) resulted in the founding of the Coalition of Essential Schools. This alternative education network drew from the findings of this research and formed around ten common principles for essential schooling that seeks to be personalised, equitable and intellectually challenging.

These ten principles can briefly be described as: students learning to use their mind well; less is more, depth over coverage; apply goals to all students; personalisation of teaching and learning; notions of student as worker and teacher as coach; assessment based on students' demonstration of mastery; a tone of decency and trust; commitment to the entire school; resources dedicated to teaching and learning; and democracy and equity (CES, 2010).

The Coalition of Essential Schools is now a leading network behind the small schools movement in America and currently consists of hundreds of essential schools serving students of all ages in urban, suburban and rural communities (CES, 2010).

So in some examples of alternative education today a core principle is one of ensuring a smallness of scale. This small learning community structure as Wetz (2009) identifies enables a variety of opportunities in terms of relationships, pedagogies, curriculum, assessment and learning space design. In so doing it affords an interpersonal sensitivity to the individual student's talents, passions and learning needs that larger organisational structures find much more difficult to achieve. Such approaches towards 'humanising education' are being increasingly recognised worldwide (Bryon-Meisels et al., 2010). But such a view of school organisation requires a significant paradigm shift for the dominant educational system. For example, it has significant implications with regard to teacher training and professional development with smaller school structures requiring educators to move beyond subject specialism towards adopting much more collaborative and interdisciplinary teaching roles.

Freedom to learn: the issue of student autonomy

Over recent years there have been a number of exemplar schools that have gained an international reputation in their passionate and uncompromising commitment to a maximal democratic structure and in particular to student autonomy.

Perhaps most famously, Summerhill School in Suffolk, England was founded in 1921 by A.S. Neill. This co-educational boarding school commonly referred to as 'the oldest children's democracy in the world' continues to be an internationally renowned model for progressive democratic education. It currently consists of approximately 100 students ranging in age from 5 to 18 years old. Key aspects of the school's ethos are introduced as:

Imagine a school:

- Where kids have freedom to be themselves;
- Where success is not defined by academic achievement but by the child's own definition of success;
- Where the whole school deals democratically with issues, with each individual having an equal right to be heard;
- Where you can play all day if you want to;
- And there is time and space to sit and dream.

(Summerhill, 2004)

In line with Neill's philosophical viewpoint, at Summerhill every student plays their part in a self-governing democratic community (Neill, 1968). This means that attendance at lessons is not compulsory; with learners being free to decide what they study and when. There is a strong commitment to egalitarian relationships between staff and students. This is embodied in the core organisational structure of the school, namely the 'School Meeting', where all pupils and staff decide together how the school will be run, with each person having one vote. Based upon the decisions made in the School Meeting, a series of committees and pupil-appointed functionaries then run certain aspects of the school (Vaughan, 2006).

In this way Summerhill frames the purpose of education as being much more than academic achievement. It is structured around A.S. Neill's greater concern over what 'kind' of people its students will become, their character and qualities such as tolerance and sincerity rather than achievements or status in society (Croall, 1984).

Such a radical experiment in a maximal notion of democratic and participatory education has not been without criticism and challenge from a range of sources including the State. In 2000 the school came under the threat of state-enforced closure, with the British government calling into question a number of the school's central principles and in particular the policy of students' voluntary attendance at lessons. The school was forced to follow a legal process in order to resist this threat that gained worldwide attention. This appeal at the Royal Courts of Justice in London led to a settlement being reached that has allowed the school to continue to operate in line with its foundational principles.

Following a similar vision of the rich capacity of children and the broader purpose of schooling is the Sudbury Valley School model, based in Massachusetts and founded upon the educational philosophy of Philip Greenberg. Here, students of all ages decide what they will do, as well as when, how and where they will do it. This freedom for children to decide for themselves is viewed as being a fundamental human right. The school holds as its central value the principle of the young person as an autonomous learner:

there can be little doubt that self-initiated learning that arises from the internal motivation of the learner is the most efficient and best retained type of learning, least likely to arouse resistance or encounter seemingly insurmountable blocks.

(Ackoff and Greenberg, 2008, p. 11)

More broadly the school is based upon the notion that:

all people are curious by nature; that the most efficient, long-lasting, and profound learning takes place when started and pursued by the learner; that all people are creative if they are allowed to develop their unique talents; that age-mixing among students promotes growth in all members of the group; and that freedom is essential to the development of personal responsibility.

(Sudbury Valley School, 2010)

Through daily life and structures such as the weekly school meeting students are trusted and treated as responsible people able to negotiate the complexities of living in a participatory democratic community. Today the Sudbury Valley model is being implemented by other schools in the US as well as schools in countries such as Japan, Israel, Belgium and Germany, creating an emerging international movement for radical democratic education.

Holistic education: engaging with the whole person

A common characteristic within alternative education is attention towards holistic human development. Outlined below are two educational movements of international significance that have sought to avoid what Rathunde (2009) refers to as 'disembodied education' where too great a focus is placed on the cognitive aspects of the learning process at the expense of contextualising dimensions such as physical and experiential aspects.

Montessori Education, based upon the work of Maria Montessori, is an alternative education movement that gives explicit attention to educating the senses as well as cognitive stimulation and places a particular emphasis upon students' intrinsic motivation for learning. Montessori education seeks to create the space where young people are able to deeply concentrate and immerse themselves in a rich learning experience. The teacher's responsibility therefore becomes to try to create a learning environment that is sensitive to and in tune with a student's interests and curiosity. Consequently, Montessori Education necessitates a high degree of student autonomy where learners are free to choose activities set before them within an ordered educational context and limited by a caring consideration for their peers (Rathunde, 2009). In this way Montessori education seeks to strike the balance between freedom and discipline.

Another central objective of Montessori education is to try to bring embodiment or 'concrete experience' to abstract concepts. One way this is commonly achieved is through seeing the natural environment as being a core educational resource. As summarised by Rathunde:

> It is fair to say that Maria Montessori was far ahead of her time in taking the beauty of nature seriously and emphasising its educational value. Nurturing a sense of awe and wonder through frequent contact with nature was integral to Montessori's philosophy.
>
> (2009, p. 201)

Montessori's legacy of taking learning beyond the classroom and engaging students in nature walks and husbandry is today increasingly being advocated within mainstream education mandates through initiatives such as Environmental Education, Education for Sustainable Development and Forest Schools. This once again highlights the commonality between alternative paradigms of schooling and mainstream educational innovation and reform initiatives.

Based upon the ideas of the Austrian academic Rudolf Steiner (1861–1925) Steiner/Waldorf Education holds as a central principle the goal of student freedom and inclusivity. Steiner/Waldorf Education can be framed as being multi-cultural through its approach to validating each individual child and their cultural background whatever that might be (McEvoy, 1996). The curriculum in Steiner/Waldorf schools is essentially taught in thematic blocks and is designed with the holistic agenda of seeking to give equal attention to the physical, emotional, intellectual, cultural and spiritual needs of each pupil.

A central principle of the Steiner ethos is to:

> provide an unhurried and creative learning environment where children can find the joy in learning and experience the richness of childhood rather than early specialisation or academic hot housing.
>
> (SteinerWaldorf, 2010)

Steiner/Waldorf schools identify their distinct difference to traditional state-funded approaches to education as being:

- Literacy and numeracy being introduced at a later stage to children, with an initial much greater focus on play and a stress free learning environment.
- For the first eight years (age 7–14) children will ideally have the same class teacher, providing what is seen to be an important sense of stability, continuity and security.
- As the children grow older, they adopt increasing levels of autonomy and responsibility with regard to how they present their work.
- Learning is not driven by testing and standardised assessment but instead pupil progress is monitored and supported by the class teacher's close working relationship with each pupil and intimate understanding of their interests and capabilities.
- Steiner/Waldorf schools traditionally operate as collegiate systems with no designated headteacher, instead being managed by the teachers through a collaborative leadership approach.

Steiner/Waldorf schools are commonly organised around a particular understanding of child development. This can be simplistically characterised as framing a child's development towards maturity as having three distinct phases; from birth to 7 years, from 7 to 14 years and from 14 to 21 years (OpenWaldorf, 2003). These distinct phases of child development then inform the structure, curriculum and pedagogy of the Steiner/Waldorf school. Ashley (2009) notes that this theory, as with other forms of developmentalism, such as Piaget's staged theory of cognitive development and Kohlberg's moral stage theory, is not above criticism, with concern being expressed over such a systemic view constricting and predetermining a child's nature. Yet in recognition of its ability to help nurture free thinking individuals, Steiner/Waldorf Education today represents worldwide one of the most strongly established alternatives to state education. Currently there are over 1,000 schools in more than 65 countries including Egypt, Kenya, India, Australia, the US as well as most countries in Europe.

De-schooling society – the rise of homeschooling

In 2001, the Organisation for Economic Cooperation and Development (OECD) published their report *Schooling for Tomorrow: What schools for the future?* In this they identified six different scenarios for the future of schooling in 2020. These descriptive pictures sought to take into consideration the nature of childhood and adolescence today, the emergence of a knowledge-based economy, the persistence of inequality and exclusion, and changing family and community life. Two of the OECD scenarios referred to the possibility of a movement in society towards 'De-schooling'. This is where an increasing dissatisfaction with state-dictated institutionalised provision combines with the increasing possibilities of resources and networks afforded, for example, by inexpensive ICT. This results in growing numbers of individual families as well as cultural and religious community groups coming to the fore and establishing their own learning arrangements for their children. One example of such an educational alternative to mainstream schooling that is already experiencing a growth worldwide is that of 'homeschooling'.

Homeschooling is becoming increasingly popular in countries such as America and in many European countries where it is not prohibited by law including, for example, Cyprus. Increasingly through the use of ICT, homeschoolers are becoming networked, thereby functioning in some ways as informal learning communities. Homeschoolers hold a variety of reasons for joining this movement, some are ideological, some are pedagogical, whilst others take the decision much more along pragmatic lines (Gaither, 2008). So, for example, within America a significant homeschooling group is associated with the ideology of conservative Christianity with parents wishing to take greater control over what their children learn and the context within which they learn it. A recent study in America conducted by Gray (2010) and involving over 11,000 participants has provided some interesting findings with regard to the broad demographics of families and students engaging in homeschooling and the generally exceptionally high academic achievement of home-educated students. But concerns remain over the implications for such an ICT-driven movement and the inequality of provision that this could create through trends such as the digital divide.

The 'networked' home-school movement raises some important questions with regard to the sustainability of existing patterns of institutionalised and centralised school systems and the potential for individualised arrangements for education becoming more widespread. This in turn brings into question the sustainability of the traditional notion of school-based teachers. One possible scenario for the future is an era where new learning professionals emerge, who are increasingly asked to work in more personalised and informal educational settings or as consultants to parents and community leaders who have taken on the role of educating their children much more for themselves (NCSL, 2003).

Conclusion

Across the world, new blueprints for education and schooling continue to emerge and flourish. They bring into question the core purposes of education and encourage the educator to consider afresh their role and image of both the child and the school. The alternative education movement is far from a singular and united endeavour with a wide variety of ideologies, theoretical frameworks and evidence bases informing and shaping a range of provision. This chapter has paid particular attention to a cluster of alternative educations that can be seen to champion to various degrees a number of common educational themes. These include greater levels of partnership and engagement with parents and the community in the schooling of children and young people. They emphasise greater attention to student voice, and the conceptualisation of the learner as a person with innate capacities, potential and interests who needs to be placed at the centre of the educational endeavour. They also give greater recognition to the relational component of education, and sensitivity to the social contextual factors that shape each young person's engagement with the process of learning.

Ultimately these alternative models of education point towards a more holistic and participatory paradigm of learning. They seek to support and sustain notions of human flourishing, active citizenry and community well-being and in so doing go beyond a notion of schooling being primarily concerned with subject-based knowledge transfer or preparation of young people for future employment. There undoubtedly continues to be the need for greater levels of empirical investigation in order to establish a more comprehensive evidence base for these different educational alternatives. But despite this they still present ideas and principles that offer credible and thought-provoking perspectives on the current debates about education and human development. They also offer a fresh lens through which we can reconsider the design of learning spaces that are fit for living and growing up in the twenty-first century.

Questions for further investigation

1   What are the implications for the future of teacher training if the validity of the diversity of educational provision in the twenty-first century were to be acknowledged? Do we need to educate a professional workforce that has greater capacity for creativity, innovation and collaboration?
2   In what ways could a more holistic notion of education influence and shape the design of future schools?

Suggested further reading

Fielding, M. and Moss, P. (2010) *Radical Education and the Common School – a democratic alternative*. London: Routledge. This book takes as its starting point the need to develop a more just, creative and sustainable democratic society. Through this lens it then comprehensively explores the fundamental values of education, how learning is currently understood, and our images of the child and school.

Wetz, J. (2009) *Urban Village Schools: putting relationships at the heart of secondary school organisation and design*. London: Calouste Gulbenkian Foundation. This former headteacher in the UK develops a series of principles for rethinking the way schools are organised and formulates a new more human scale model of schooling for inner city and urban areas in the twenty-first century.

Woods, P. and Woods, G. (Eds.) (2009) *Alternative Education for the 21st Century: Philosophies, approaches, visions*. New York, NY: Palgrave MacMillan. This book provides a review of a wide variety of alternative educations from a number of international contexts including Brazil, Palestine, Canada and Maori education. It also provides important insight into a number of faith-based alternative models of schooling.

References

Ackoff, R. and Greenberg, D. (2008) *Turning Learning Right Side Up*. New Jersey, N.d.: Wharton School Publishing.

Arthur, J. (2003) *Education with Character: The moral economy of schooling*. London: Routledge.

Ashley, M. (2009) 'Education for freedom: The goal of Steiner/Waldorf Schools', in Woods, P. and Woods, C. (Eds.) (2009) *Alternative Education for the 21st Century: philosophies, approaches, visions*. New York, NY: Palgrave MacMillan.

Bryon-Meisels, G., Cooper, K., Deckman, S., Dobbs, C., Francois, C., Nikundiwe, T. and Shalaby, C. (Eds.) (2010) *Humanizing Education: Critical alternatives to reform*. Cambridge: Harvard Educational Review.

CES (2010) 'Coalition of Essential Schools – who we are' Available at: www.essentialschools.org/items (accessed 1 September 2010)

Croall, J. (1984) *Neill of Summerhill. The permanent rebel.* London: Routledge and Kegan Paul.

Gaither, M. (2008) *Homeschooling: An American history.* New York, NY: Palgrave MacMillan.

Gray, B. (2010) 'Academic achievement and demographic traits of homeschool students: A nationwide study', *Academic Leadership,* 8, 1.

Harlan, J. and Mason, B. (2010) *Towards Schools where People Matter: A study of the Human Scale Schools Project.* London: Calouste Gulbenkian Foundation.

Kerr, D. (2002) *England's Results from the IEA International Citizenship Education Study: What Citizenship and Education mean to 14 Year Olds.* London: DfES.

McEvoy, P. (1996) 'Steiner Schools in Ireland – a case study of opting in', in Carnie, F., Large, M. and Tasker, M. (Eds.) *Freeing Education.* Stroud: Hawthorn Press.

National College for School Leadership (NCSL) (2003) *Schooling for Tomorrow: OECD scenarios.* Nottingham: NCSL.

Neill, A.S. (1968) *Summerhill.* Harmondsworth: Penguin.

OpenWaldorf (2003) *Rudolf Steiner's Child Development Theory.* Available at: www.openwaldorf.com/academics.html (accessed 25 October 2010).

Organisation for Economic Cooperation and Development (OECD) (2001) *Schooling for Tomorrow: What schools for the future.* Paris: OECD.

Pring, R. (2007) *John Dewey – A philosopher of education for our time?* London: Continuum.

Rathunde, K. (2009) 'Montessori and embodied education', in Woods, P. and Woods, C. (Eds.) *Alternative education for the 21st century: philosophies, approaches, visions.* New York, NY: Palgrave Macmillan.

Schumacher, W.F. (1974) *Small is beautiful.* London: Abacus.

Scott, W. and Gough, S. (2003) *Sustainable Development and Learning.* London: RoutledgeFalmer.

Sizer, T. (1996) *Horace's Hope.* New York, NY: Mariner Books.

SteinerWaldorf (2010) 'What is steiner education?'. Available at: www.steinerwaldorf.org.uk/whatissteinereducation.html (accessed 4 September 2010).

Sudbury Valley School (2010) 'Independence: creating leaders'. Available at: www.sudval.com/01_abou_01.html (accessed 23 August 2010).

Summerhill (2004) 'Imagine a school'. Available at: www.summerhillschool.co.uk/ (accessed 9 September 2010).

Tasker, M. (2008) *Human Scale Education: History, values and practice.* Bristol: Human Scale Education.

Vaughan, M. (Ed.) (2006) *Summerhill and A.S. Neill.* Maidenhead; Open University Press.

Wallace, W. (2009) *Schools Within Schools: Human scale education in practice.* London: Calouste Gulbenkian Foundation.

Wetz, J. (2009) *Urban Village Schools.* London: Calouste Gulbenkian Foundation.

24

Citizenship education

Ian Davies
University of York

Overview

In this chapter I aim to:

- explore the meaning of citizenship by discussing key concepts;
- discuss recent developments in policy and practice relevant to citizenship education;
- inform the above with reference to classic and recent theoretical and empirical research.

Following a brief introduction there will be three main sections to this chapter. In the first (and longest) part of the chapter I will discuss the definitions and characterisations that have been – and are being – used by those who are involved in debates about citizenship education. I will refer to the trends and issues that affect citizenship education today. In the next main section I will briefly explore what I think will be important in citizenship education in the future. I will provide some summary comments and, additionally, at the end of the chapter there will be some questions for the reader to consider, some recommended reading and a list of the references that have been used. By the end of the chapter I hope that readers will be familiar with the key issues about – and be better able to contribute actively to – debates and the practice of citizenship education.

Introduction

Citizenship, although, of course, being of ancient origin, has been discussed very explicitly in relation to educational contexts, since the 1980s in the UK and elsewhere. It need not be associated only with democracies but it is in that context that I will discuss ideas and practice in this chapter. I mention this link with democracy deliberately as it is necessary, without exploring the obvious existence of citizens of totalitarian societies, to avoid focusing on the negative or perhaps unintended consequences of including citizenship education in schools and elsewhere. Citizenship, unlike something like human rights, is by nature at least in part exclusive. I am a British citizen and, as such, I can very easily identify those who are not. This may help certain potentially unattractive policies to be achieved by narrowly focused nation states at a time when immigration is regarded as a key political issue. However, I do think that citizenship education has huge potential to achieve positive processes and outcomes and in this sense of constructive criticism I will consider the ideas, issues and practices that are (and, perhaps, could and should be) influential today.

Definitions, trends and issues

The Council of Europe has usefully outlined the key aspects of citizenship:

> Democratic Citizenship is a skill that everyone needs. In its most practical form, it is the knowledge about how a country and society works. But democratic citizenship is more than just the ballot box – it is also the skill we need to live well in a family and community. It shows us how to resolve disputes in a friendly and fair way, how to negotiate and find common ground, and how to make sure that our rights are respected. A democratic citizen knows about the ground rules of the society they live in and the personal responsibilities they need to respect.
>
> (Council of Europe, nd)

In an attempt to link citizenship education to democratic citizenship itself, it is necessary to provide some brief historical background. Although the contemporary phase of concern for and about citizenship education began in the 1980s, perhaps the most significant academic foundations were established in the late 1950s and early 1960s by T.H. Marshall (Marshall, 1963). In characterising the growth of citizenship as associated with civil rights (eighteenth century), political rights (nineteenth century) and welfare rights (twentieth century), Marshall was perhaps guilty of underplaying the significance of political struggle, the contributions to citizenship made by women and the emergence of new perspectives with, for example, environmental rights. And yet it is possible to see discussions about rights and duties, regarding liberal and civic republican conceptions, and the latest incarnation of community focused politics as having direct connections with the thinking of Marshall.

The recent history of citizenship education across the world is too broad a canvas to paint in this brief chapter (see a useful overview by Hahn, 2010) but, essentially, a move has been made from a perceived need to tell young people society's rules appropriate to their position within it, to a more wide-ranging sense of what power means to individuals and groups in a diverse democracy. Although there were some professionally useful approaches in the past, it is generally true that prior to the 1970s elite students were prepared in part for future leadership roles through courses about constitutional matters, while others were told to follow the rules of passive social engagement in civics lessons. In part under Crick's influence within England and elsewhere, the 1970s saw the rise of political literacy programmes in which controversial issues were discussed in an attempt to develop a proclivity for action. Throughout the 1980s (and to some extent beyond) the so-called 'new' educations dealt often in a more explicitly politically driven and affective manner with anti-racism and anti-sexism, peace and development. In the late 1980s and early 1990s, governments emphasised a connection between the need to reduce crime and citizenship education with, specifically, the rise of volunteering. According to the home secretary of the UK government in the early 1980s, there was a need for young people to recognise their voluntary obligations and, consequently, a rather narrowly conceived service learning model of citizenship education that was promoted at that time. In 1997 in England, Crick was given a second chance to influence education and in his report in 1998 (QCA, 1998) he declared the constituent elements of citizenship to be social and moral responsibility, political literacy and community involvement.

At times rather fierce debates in which the Crick Report was described negatively (Osler, 2003) were the academic foreground to bombs in London, debates about Britishness (Ajegbo, 2007) and the revision of the National Curriculum for citizenship saw identity and diversity as the fourth dimension (in addition to the original three elements identified in the Crick Report). Elsewhere similar debates occurred as the Australians, for example, struggled with *Discovering Democracy*, the Canadians introduced civics education in Ontario with associated developments in other provinces and the Europeans highlighted work in this field in part through the 2005 Year of Citizenship through Education. Several international projects reviewed the sort of citizenship education that was taking place, the largest of which was the IEA CIVED study (see Torney-Purta *et al.*, 2001). It is not possible in the space of this brief chapter to provide comprehensive coverage of all the themes and issues referred to here but below I attempt to provide some comments in three main sections about key issues relating to citizenship with a particular focus on voting patterns, some reflections of the nature of what teaching and learning about and for a diverse society means, and, finally, a discussion of the nature of global citizenship.

Citizenship and engagement in formal political structures: do we and should we vote and is it the responsibility of teachers to encourage young people to participate in this way?

There have been some rather alarmist commentary, generally, about the perceived crises that afflict society (Sears, 2005) and more particularly about the low turnout in elections for the European and UK parliaments. The data for turnout over recent European elections certainly seems to show less than a wholehearted involvement with the formal political process. In 1979 when the first direct elections to the European parliament took place, 62 per cent of the total European electorate voted. There has been a decline in that figure for every election that has taken place since, with the figure for the most recent election (in 2009) being 43 per cent (and the turnout in the UK for the 1999 European election was a mere 23 per cent). The data for the UK (see www.ukpolitical.info/Turnout45.htm) are similarly not reassuring for those who might wish to see full participation by all those who are eligible to vote. Although there was a slight increase from the turnout recorded in 2005 to that in 2010 (from approximately 61 per cent to 64 per cent), there have been many commentators who have used this evidence to express serious reservations about the health of the UK democracy. However, these figures have not alarmed all (see Pattie and Johnston, 2002). Indeed it may be the case that any expression of concern is rather narrowly based around a negative view of the 59.4 per cent turnout that occurred in 2001, which was the lowest turn out since 1919. These sorts of concerns about the legitimacy of the electoral system are often linked not just to turnout but also to the nature of the ways in which power can be achieved. One of those issues relates to the fact that only 22 per cent of the total electorate voted for the political party that formed the government in 2005 and we could speculate in rather more complicated ways about the figure that would apply for the 2010 UK result (we could either combine the percentages received by both the Conservative and Liberal Democrat parties or suggest that no one actually voted for a coalition government). Similar discussions could be held in relation to many coalition governments established around the world. We could also debate the extent to which (perhaps primarily in the 2000 US presidential election) the number of people voting has actually led to an impact on the formation of the government.

The rather gloomy picture presented so far of a democracy in crisis suggests to some that teachers have a responsibility to encourage young people to vote. There is no question in my mind that voter turnout and the workings of our democratic machinery are absolutely essential parts of any citizenship education programme. However, I am deeply sceptical about the argument that, in essence, tells teachers to 'get the vote out' for established politicians. Crick was right when he suggested that politics was more important than democracy. The simple arithmetic of democratic societies is necessary but not sufficient for healthy political engagement. Karl Rove – who became known as Mr 51 per cent – was not seen in the Bush administration as someone who was always committed to promoting full understanding and democratic participation. The casting of a vote is only one indication (and perhaps at times not a very important one) of democratic citizenship. There is in any case no golden age of democratic participation (Jeffreys, 2008) and young people today may be more likely to engage in new and less formal types of politics than did their predecessors. The fear of a generational shift in political activity seems less likely than a process through which young people grow into the habits of voting. Although there is some evidence to suggest that those who vote from an early age are more likely than others to continue to do so throughout their lives, young people's levels of involvement in associational activity (see Whiteley *et al.*, 2004) may be indicative of a more active engagement than that which will occur later in their lives. Perhaps young people are simply interested in politics and bored by politicians (Haste, 2005) and, if so, it would be wrong to encourage teachers to attempt to persuade them of the supposed virtues of moving away from participatory to the more cursory forms of representative democracy.

Teaching and learning for a diverse society

It is vital to state strongly that a diverse society is to be struggled for and celebrated. There are huge advantages (economically, morally and in many other ways) of a society in which a plurality of cultures engage and interact in ways that are not mutually exclusive but which acknowledge the existence of multiple citizenships. This multiplicity can, of course, be achieved in formal ways. Dual national citizenship, as well as various formulations that exist locally, regionally and in federations, means that the concrete expression of multiple citizenship is widely experienced. Diversity is often also discussed in relation to more affective perspectives and questions of identity are extremely important (Kymlicka, 1995). It is admittedly inadequate to discuss such matters as if they are the same as reflections on the nature of justice but the work of Sandel (2009) is very useful here. He argued that there are, broadly, three ways in which to consider the achievement of justice and I would like to make use of those positions to suggest that the culture wars can be considered constructively in their light. Sandel suggests that utilitarianism in which the greatest happiness of the largest number is insufficient as a means of judging a fair society. The meaning of happiness and the power that is available to certain individuals and types of people would be insufficiently addressed when using only this perspective. Sandel is also resistant to the notion of blind process models of justice as put forward by Kant and, more recently,

Rawls. The determination to avoid being explicit about the intended goal of a just society and how precisely it should be formulated and impacted is not persuasive for Sandel. Instead he suggests that there needs to be awareness of both the process of decision-making and the intended outcomes of such a process in order to achieve justice. Certain things are better than others and we should not be afraid of characterising justice clearly. Of course there are risks in such an approach and, to repeat, all aspects of a diverse society are unlikely to be brought into the compass of a consideration of justice. But a consideration, in appropriately complex ways, will help teachers and learners to engage in dialogue in which the key concepts associated with a just diverse society and the ways to attempt to achieve it will be made explicit. Should it be thought that this would be too complex for 'ordinary' learners in state schools, it should be recognised that good educational materials that target political concepts and skills already exist (e.g. see Huddleston, 2004).

Global and international citizenship education

Global citizenship education is an attractive label. Who would not want to see themselves engaged positively with others across the globe in efforts to make the world a better place? And yet, of course, like all good slogans there is a considerable amount hidden within a simple phrase. For some it is very generally about ensuring that educational standards in all subjects are developed through the acquisition of skills and dispositions that are appropriate to an increasingly interconnected world. For others it might be more about something that is expressed through or emerges from comparative education that essentially seeks to understand policies and practices in different countries. Often, however, in the contexts which relate most directly to the issues pursued in this chapter, it is about a particular form of social studies education in which a wide-ranging, often politically focused, affectively oriented education is promoted for the development of cosmopolitan perspectives in which the nation state is not seen as the final arbiter of our destinies. The distinctions between global education and citizenship education have been discussed in some detail elsewhere (Davies et al., 2005) and will not be repeated here but it is necessary to look beyond the mutually exclusive positions that are at times adopted for citizenship education and global education. The former's focus on promoting cognitive understanding about state structures and positive participation in community activities has the attractions of allowing for exploration of concrete rights and responsibilities. The latter's highly motivating, ambitious, affective approach to matters of peace and justice for people, animals and the environment is similarly vitally important (and has some excellent classic as well as contemporary educational resources, e.g. Pike and Selby, 1988).

The future

Crystal ball gazing is an uncertain business but perhaps three areas can be highlighted: national policy; global economic developments; academic and professional initiatives. The shape of the national government is always influential on what is taught and learned in schools (or at least on the development of policy which signals official preferences). In the UK, for example, the coalition government led by a Conservative prime minister in 2010 is likely to put greater emphasis than the previous administration on history education, parent power and the distinctiveness of schools rather than emphasising the integration of children's services. Global economic developments will probably give rise to further intensification of international links with national identities being seen increasingly as something that exists alongside and as an integral part of several overlapping identities that exist below and above the nation state. In this respect it is likely that citizenship education that relates to migration and explores cultural identity for many including indigenous peoples is likely to grow across the world. The work that has and will take place in specific regions is likely to become more explicitly recognised. East Asia is perhaps particularly significant. The debates within China about the nation and the sort of citizenship education necessary for the preferred form of democracy will attract more attention globally (and, more particularly, in areas such as Hong Kong). There is likely to be continuing debate within Japan about citizenship. And, in the long term, there will be much more heard about the possibility of religious (especially Muslim) forms of citizenship and forms of education for citizenship in various African countries (including connections with development education and post-conflict education). Finally, the characterisation of academic and professional frameworks will be influenced by the preference for the 'big society' by national politicians and the workings of global markets to encourage still more managed individually oriented enterprise. Despite the older versions of community action that were at times seen to be dependent on direct management by central government, more fluidity – perhaps fragmentation – is likely in the future. Citizenship education will continue to be important as a means of encouraging young people to have the knowledge, understanding and skills to provide social glue and to innovate although it may not be as explicitly formulated in the curriculum as it once was when Crick's influence was at its height. In short, we will see attempts to strengthen the national centre which will nevertheless be increasingly forced to recognise global networks within which citizens will be expected to be individually enterprising. In this context, perceived academic aspects of citizenship education will be located in traditional subjects such as history; there will be a clearer resolution of the current divisions between personal and social education and citizenship with the latter being seen as the key site for messages about personal responsibility and the need for enterprising activity locally, nationally and in the global economic market. In light of the recently achieved increasingly secure position of citizenship education in schools in England (Keating *et al.*, 2009; Ofsted, 2010), this rumination on what might come to pass may not be entirely comforting to those – including me – who felt that for all his faults Crick had got things about right.

Conclusion

In his classic book *In Defence of Politics*, Crick argued that politics is vitally important and essentially concerned with engaging with others in order to pursue ways forward that are necessary for the attempted resolution of public issues. This is obviously a necessary task and given the engagement that is an intrinsic part of educational institutions and educational processes, it is an unavoidable part of what teachers and learners do. As such we do not have a choice of avoiding politics and we decide to approach matters explicitly and hopefully professionally or to leave it to chance (which means allowing those who are already established as opinion formers and decision-makers to continue to exercise control). Teachers and students and others must decide not whether to engage in citizenship education but what sort of citizenship education they wish to develop. This chapter has outlined some of the influences that act upon us and encourages educators to develop forms of understanding and engagement that enhance political engagement for a diverse, just democratic society.

233

Questions for further investigation

1   It is obvious that citizenship is contested and often seen as being controversial. Consider why this is by reflecting on three fundamental challenges: citizenship is intrinsically contradictory; it has the potential to be used in programmes of indoctrination; and/or it has the appearance of common sense while hiding very complex matters.
2   New technology initially allowed for more people to receive more information more quickly than they had before. The most recent types of new media (commonly referred to as Web 2.0) allow for greater interactivity. Does this mean that the potential for the realisation of citizenship education has been strengthened?
3   What would an effective programme of teacher education for promoting young people's democratic practice look like?

Suggested further reading

Arthur, J., Davies, I. and Hahn, C. (Eds.) (2009) *The Sage International Handbook of Education for Citizenship and Democracy.* London: Sage. No book with this sort of title could ever hope to be comprehensive but this publication does bring together the foremost scholars and practitioners in citizenship education in the world today. It contains discussion of key philosophical perspectives, approaches to citizenship education, as well as national and transnational case studies of policy and practice.

Coleman, S. (2009) *The Internet and Democratic Citizenship.* Cambridge: Cambridge University Press. The rhetoric associated with the power of so-called 'new media' for enhancing democratic understanding and practice may need to be viewed critically and constructively. But these media cannot be ignored and all educators should consider their potential and the ways in which policy and action could be developed. This book (awarded a prize for book of the year by the American Political Science Association) discusses key issues and makes suggestions for how government and others can help realise the 'vulnerable potential' of the internet for enhancing democratic societies.

Davies, I. (2011) *100+ Ideas for Citizenship.* London: Continuum. An attempt has been made in this very brief book to outline the key ideas, organisations and issues about citizenship with many practical suggestions that will help develop teachers' thinking and practice.

Pike, G. and Selby, D. (1988) *Global Teacher, Global Learner.* London: Hodder and Stoughton. Although this book is more than 20 years old, it is still a fascinating example of what many global educators feel is important. It contains very many practical examples that may be used in and beyond the classroom. Readers should ask whether and, if so, to what extent this global education book may be seen as something that is centrally relevant to citizenship education.

References

Ajegbo, K., Kiwan, D. and Sharma, S. (2007) *Curriculum Review: Diversity and Citizenship.* London: DfES.
Council of Europe (nd) *Education for Democratic Citizenship and Human Rights (EDC/HRE): Questions and Answers.* Available at: www.coe.int/t/dg4/education/edc/1_what_is_edc_hre/edc_q&a_EN.asp (accessed 28 April 2010).

Crick, B. (2000) *In Defence of Politics* (5th Ed.). Harmondsworth: Penguin.

Davies, I., Evans, M. and Reid, A. (2005) 'Globalising citizenship education? A critique of "global education" and "citizenship education"', *British Journal of Educational Studies*, 53, 1, pp. 66–89.

General Election Turnout 1945–2010. Available at: www.ukpolitical.info/Turnout45.htm (accessed 23 June 2010).

Hahn, C. (2010) 'Comparative civic education research: what we know and what we need to know', *Citizenship Teaching and Learning*, 6, 1, pp. 5–23.

Haste, H. (2005) *My Voice, My Vote, My Community*. Nestle Social Research Programme and ESRC.

Huddleston, T. (2004) *Citizens and Society: Political Literacy Teacher Resource Pack*. London: Citizenship Foundation.

Jeffreys, K. (2008) *Politics and the People*. London: Atlantic Books.

Keating, A., Kerr, D., Lopes, J., Featherstone, G. and Benton, T. (2009) *Embedding Citizenship Education in Secondary Schools in England (2002–08): Citizenship Education Longitudinal Study Seventh Annual Report* (DCSF Research Report 172). London: DCSF

Kymlicka, W. (1995) *Multicultural Citizenship*. Oxford: Oxford University Press.

Marshall, T.H. (1963) 'Citizenship', in Marshall, T.H. (Ed.) *Sociology at the Crossroads and Other Essays*. London: Heinemann.

Osler, A. (2003) 'The Crick Report and the future of multiethnic Britain', in Gearon, L. (Ed.) *Learning to Teach Citizenship in the Secondary School*. London: RoutledgeFalmer.

Ofsted (2010) *Citizenship Established? Citizenship in Schools 2006/9*. Available at: www.ofsted.gov.uk/publications/090159 (accessed 24 June 2010).

Pattie, C. and Johnston, R. (2002) 'A low turnout landslide: abstention at the British General Election of 1997', *Political Studies*, 49, 2, pp. 286–305.

Pike, G. and Selby, D. (1988) *Global Teacher, Global Learner*. London: Hodder and Stoughton.

Qualifications and Curriculum Authority (QCA) (1998) *Education for Citizenship and the Teaching of Democracy in Schools* (Crick Report). London: QCA.

Sandel, M. (2009) *Justice: What's the Right Thing To Do?* London: Allen Lane.

Sears, A. (2005) 'Citizenship: education or indoctrination?', *Citizenship and Teacher Education*, 2, 1, pp. 3–17.

Torney-Purta, J., Lehmann, R., Oswald, H. and Schulz, W. (2001) 'Citizenship and education in twenty-eight countries: civic knowledge and engagement at age fourteen'. Amsterdam: The International Association for the Evaluation of Educational Achievement.

Whiteley, P., Seyd, P. and Pattie, C. (2004) *Citizenship in Britain: Values, Participation and Democracy*. Cambridge: Cambridge University Press.

25

Social class and education

Jon Davison
Canterbury Christ Church University

Overview

This chapter outlines the historical and global nature of social class in society and how membership of a class may determine educational attainment. It discusses the concepts of cultural capital and cultural reproduction and the part these play in maintaining inequalities in society. Finally, the chapter considers some of the reasons for the underachievement of working-class children as a group in school.

There are no two ways about it: social class is a difficult idea. Sociologists in whose discipline the concept emerged, are not of one mind about its value or validity.

(Coleman, 1983)

Introduction

Class is not a new phenomenon. It may be distinguished as a facet of almost all societies. Ancient Greek and Roman societies were hierarchical. Adult males, who were not slaves but citizens, were divided into several classes both by ancestry and by property. However, there were also several classes of non-citizens with fewer legal rights, such as married women, children and slaves – who had no rights – and might be killed legitimately, ejected, or sold by the head of their household. Aztec society comprised a hierarchy of the nobility, warriors, traders, artisans, peasants and slaves. The feudal system in pre-Confucian China divided the population into six classes: the king, the dukes, the great men and the scholars (these four classes known collectively as 'the nobles'), the commoners and the slaves. Historically, in slave, feudal and colonial societies, examples of social classes were found in Inca, Japanese, Iranian, Indian and Latin American societies. Following the Industrial Revolution analysis of society by social class has been applied to modern capitalist systems in the UK, USA, Africa, Australia, the Middle East, New Zealand and Europe.

For anthropologists, economists, political scientists, social historians and sociologists, class is an essential object of cultural analysis. Classes are often distinguished in relation to, for example, differences in power, knowledge and wealth: the social stratification of a society. Indeed, sociologists such as Durkheim (1964) saw inequalities, which were due to differences in talent and ability, as a functional necessity of a society.

However, in Marxist theory (see, for example, MacLellan, 2008), two fundamental class divisions are identifiable from the economic structure of work and property: the proletariat and the bourgeoisie. In *The Communist Manifesto* published in 1848, Marx notes that although French peasantry may not be united but dispersed:

> In so far as millions of families live under economic conditions of existence that separate their mode of life, their interests and their culture from those of the other classes, and put them in hostile opposition to the latter, they form a class.
>
> (Giddens, 1971, p. 37)

At several points, Marx notes how a class defines itself and that it is possible that it might do so only as it acts in opposition to other classes. Marx notes how, in the emergence of the bourgeoisie as a class in early capitalist Europe, both competition and unity may characterise a class:

> separate individuals form a class only insofar as they have to carry on a common battle against another class; otherwise they are on hostile terms with each other as competitors.
>
> (Giddens and Held, 1982, p. 20)

In 1904, Max Weber published his seminal essay *The Protestant Ethic and the Spirit of Capitalism*, which became the basis for much later research into economic systems and cultures. Whereas Marx proposed that the economic basis of society determines the other facets of it, Weber maintained that the predominance of Protestants among technical, industrial and wealthy classes indicated that the development of capitalism had been influenced by Calvinist ethics of work, virtue and happiness. Weber proposed a three-component theory of societal stratification wherein class, status and party (or politics) are subordinate to the means of production, but stated that how these facets interact will vary from society to society.

Models of society

More modern sociological analysis might be said to draw less upon the analytical Marxian and Weberian concepts of class and be founded more upon empirical traditions by considering socio-economic factors such as education, income and wealth and their relation to social outcomes.

In *Social Class in America*, Warner *et al.* (1949) proposed an early stratum class model of American society comprising three main divisions: upper, middle and lower classes. Each of these were further subdivided into upper and lower segments: upper upper class – people with inherited wealth; lower upper class – people who had become wealthy in their own lifetime; upper middle class – well-educated professionals, artists, writers, etc.; lower middle class – lower paid white collar workers, middle managers, teachers, clerical workers, technicians; upper lower class (working class) – blue collar workers, manual labourers; lower lower class – the working poor, permanently unemployed, homeless.

For over half a century, US sociologists have developed and refined Warner's model. In 1978 sociologists Coleman and Rainwater conceived the 'Metropolitan Class Structure' consisting

Table 25.1 Social grades based upon social class and the chief income-earner's occupation in a household

Grade	Class	Occupation
A	Upper middle class	Higher management, administrative, professional
B	Middle class	Intermediate management, administrative, professional
C1	Lower middle class	Supervisory, clerical and junior managerial, administrative or professional
C2	Skilled working class	Skilled manual workers
D	Working class	Semi- and unskilled manual workers
E	Subsistence	Casual or lowest grade workers, pensioners, welfare state dependents

of three social classes (upper Americans, middle Americans, lower Americans), each with a number sub-classes: in the first upper-upper class, lower-upper class and upper-middle class; in the second middle class and working class, and in the third semi-poor and 'the bottom'. More recently, further refinements of a stratified model of society may be found in the works of Gilbert (2002), Beeghley (2004) and Thompson and Hickey (2005) each of whom proposes a model comprising five or six sub-classes.

In the United Kingdom, market research has made use of the demographic classification within the National Readership Survey (NRS) social grades based upon social class and the chief income-earner's occupation in a household (Table 25.1).

Often grades A, B, C1 are grouped and taken to reflect middle-class attributes while C2, D, E are seen as broadly reflecting the working class. It should be noted that with less than 2 per cent of the population identified as upper class, this group is not represented in the NRS model. Such a model needs to be treated with caution in the light of the social, economic and demographic changes of the past three decades as these classifications have become less reliable, especially in terms of security of employment, disposable income and education.

Cultural markers

Put simply, social classes comprise economic or social groups in a society: an individual's class status is a form of group membership. Although theorists disagree about the elements determining membership of a class, as may be seen in the brief examples at the beginning of this chapter, a number of common features appear in many accounts that include an individual's:

- family, kinship or tribal group structures and membership;
- relationships to means of production, ownership and consumption;
- legal status and rights;
- acculturation and education.

Undoubtedly, distinct lifestyles emphasise class differences. The most powerful, or dominant, class in a society often uses markers such as dress and styles of grooming. Particular manners and language codes mark insiders from outsiders. Members of the dominant class will acquire unique political and social rights. However, each class has distinctive features that define elements of personal identity and behaviour. French sociologist Pierre Bourdieu suggests a notion of high and low status classes characterised by distinct differences between bourgeois tastes and sensitivities and working–class tastes and sensitivities. Inequalities in a society come to be normalised and reproduced through cultural ideology.

Cultural capital and cultural reproduction

The terms 'cultural capital' and 'cultural reproduction' stem from the work of Bourdieu (see, for example, Bourdieu, 2007). Put simply, cultural reproduction is the process through which existing cultural values and norms are transmitted from generation to generation thereby ensuring continuity of cultural experience across time. Bourdieu proposes that different social groups have different 'cultural capital', which may be seen as the knowledge, experience and connections an individual has, and develops, over time that enable a person to succeed more so than someone with knowledge, experience and connections that is seen in society as being of less value.

Further, particular groups of people, notably social classes, act to reproduce the existing social structure in order to legitimise and preserve their social and cultural advantage. Cultural reproduction, therefore, often results in 'social reproduction' – the process through which facets of society, such as class, are transferred from generation to generation.

Education as an agent of cultural reproduction

Brown (1973), Bourdieu (1973) and Bowles and Gintis (1976) propose that it is the stratification of school knowledge that reproduces inequalities in 'cultural capital'. Bourdieu argues that the structural reproduction of disadvantages and inequalities are caused by cultural reproduction and are recycled through the education system, as well as through other social institutions. The education system, therefore, is an agent of cultural reproduction biased towards those of higher social class, not only in the curricular content of subjects taught, but also through what is known as the 'hidden curriculum', which includes the language, values and attitudes located in, and which an individual acquires from, the discourse of curricular subjects and all aspects of school life that contribute to an individual's socialisation through the education process. An individual's success or failure within the formal education system is determined by the ability to achieve formal educational qualifications *and* to acquire the appropriate language, values, attitudes and qualities through the process of socialisation within the system. The ability to complete successfully all aspects of schooling correlates strongly to an individual's capacity subsequently to enjoy high cultural capital such as inter alia, adequate pay, occupational prestige and social status in adult life. Lankshear sums up:

> Dominant social and cultural groups have been able to establish their language, and their knowledge priorities, learning styles, pedagogical preferences, etc., as the 'official examinable culture' of school. Their notions of important and useful knowledge, their ways of presenting truth, their ways of arguing and establishing correctness, and their logics, grammars and language as institutional norms by which academic and scholastic success is defined and assessed.

> (1997, p. 30)

At this point it would seem appropriate to consider what are believed to be some specific causes of educational underachievement related to social class.

239

Social class and underachievement

> Longitudinal studies across the world indicate that education success rates at school and post-school are in good part determined by social class origin – in particular parents' wealth, occupational status, education and aspirations.
>
> (Argy, 2007)

It is apparent from an examination of the achievement of children from lower social classes in any modern society that they fair less well in a country's education system. While results from the Programme for International Student Assessment (PISA) studies (Organisation for Economic Cooperation and Development, 2005, 2009) indicate that the level of educational attainment by students in European schools is high compared to that of children and young people in emerging Latin American or African countries, they also show that in many European countries there are significant differences between the achievement of pupils from privileged backgrounds and those from poorer backgrounds (for a detailed discussion of social inequality in education in Europe, see, for example, Van Zanten, 2005). Research in Australia into progression to university education shows 'The large and possibly growing under-representation of students from low social backgrounds and from government schools' (Argy, 2007).

> PISA 2000 showed that even some of the best performing countries in the world have gaps between high and low performers and between students from socially advantaged and socially disadvantaged backgrounds. In the UK's case, for instance, these gaps were much greater than in many other countries.
>
> (McGaw, 2004)

In a chapter of this length, it would be impossible to consider educational achievement in all societies. Therefore, this chapter will now use the United Kingdom as a case study to illustrate the relationship between social class and educational underachievement that typifies the central issues related to social class and underachievement in most modern societies.

The United Kingdom

> In 2001, only a fifth of pupils in schools with the poorest intakes achieved five GCSE passes at grades A★–C, compared with 50 per cent nationally.
>
> (Lupton, 2004)

In the latter half of the twentieth century a variety of aspects of school life were examined in the UK in order to identify the causes of pupil underachievement, such as access, institutional structures and the nature of school knowledge. For example, Hargreaves (1967), Lacey (1970) and Ball (1981) cited the institutional structures of schools, such as streaming and banding, as being influential in determining the performance of working-class pupils: a disproportionate number of whom were found to be represented in the lower streams and bands.

It is well documented that, despite the intentions of Education Acts from 1944 to 1988, children from the working class in the UK have continued to underachieve at school. The '11 plus' test was created by the 1944 Education Act, which proposed the establishment of a tripartite system of secondary schooling comprising 'grammar', 'technical' and 'modern' schools, which some have seen as a reflection of the class structure itself. Success or failure in the '11 plus' determined the type of school an individual attended. The test became the gatekeeper of an individual's educational progress. Floud *et al.* (1966) exposed massive under-representation of working-class boys at grammar schools. Key to the process of selection for grammar school places was the '11 plus' examination, which included an Intelligence Quotient (IQ) test (see below). Douglas (1964) showed how working-class pupils with the same IQ scores as middle-class children were failing to gain grammar school places, because of the class bias of teachers in primary schools.

The '11 plus' and IQ tests were criticised for a middle-class bias in their content, their use of middle-class cultural references, their vocabulary and language register. The '11 plus' was seen as culturally biased towards the middle-class children (e.g. a question might refer to the name of a classical composer, something a middle-class child would be more likely to answer correctly than would a child from the working class because of social and cultural differences in their home backgrounds). Additionally, in *Class, Codes and Control*, Basil Bernstein (1971) showed marked differences in the language use of members of different social classes, with middle-class children having access in their language to a more formal 'elaborated code' while working-class language was characterised as operating within a simple 'restricted code'. However, many researchers including Trudgill (1974), Boocock (1980), and Bennett and LeCompte (1990) criticised Bernstein as a proponent of 'deficit theory'.

This is not to say that working-class pupils are simply passive recipients of a dominant culture, for studies by Gaskell (1985) and Willis (1977, 1981), for example, have shown how pupils resist school culture – although Abraham's (1993) study reveals that resistance comes more from 'anti-school' pupils whatever their social background. Abraham (1993, p. 136) goes on to argue that:

> the organising and processing of school knowledge provides a setting which is not sufficiently critical of social class and gender divisions to discourage their reproduction in further schooling and out into the occupational structure.

Social class and educational policy-makers

If there are such determinants that militate against success of working-class children in the education system, how were these structures and systems put in place? The answer, of course, is that they are, inter alia, the results of a combination of national and local education policy, which is espoused in the discourse of dominant social and cultural groups.

An examination of twentieth-century official government education documentation highlights the antipathetic attitudes to the working class displayed by educational policy-makers. (For a full account of class bias in government documents, see Davison, 2010.)

> Many persons, most prominently social and economic leaders and social reformers, grasped the uses of schooling and the vehicle of literacy for the promotion of values, attitudes and habits considered essential to the maintenance of social order and the persistence of integration and cohesion.
>
> (Graff, 1987, p. 7)

For Gossman (1981, p. 82) state education, introduced by the 1870 Education Act (The Forster Act), was 'advocated in a hard-headed way as a means of social control'.

241

Literacy

State education acts on behalf of employers and manufacturers by providing a functionally literate workforce of active consumers. There is a strong link here with the perceived needs of industry and commerce for individuals who are able to function in the workplace and to earn an income.

A report of the Organisation for Economic Cooperation and Development (OECD) found eight million adults in the United Kingdom to be 'functionally illiterate': 'one in five of all adults had poor literacy and numeracy skills. The proportions were around 10 per cent higher for women than men' (United Nations Educational, Scientific and Cultural Organization (UNESCO), 2003). Therefore, much of the drive for the introduction of the National Literacy Strategy came from a belief that workers in the UK were less literate than their European counterparts – most notably those in Germany – and were, as a consequence, not only a symptom but also part of the cause of the decline in British manufacturing industries.

There were many cries from employers that the level of literacy among school leavers was in steady decline. This perception is, however, hardly surprising, considering the social changes that have occurred since, say 1960, and the growth in the literacy demands on individuals. For example, exponential growth in advertising has led to a need to decode sophisticated, complex advertisements in print alone; increasingly, the demands made upon applicants for even the lowest status jobs have increased during a periods of high unemployment; as a consumer, the individual has had to develop complex skills brought about by the transition of corner grocery shops into out-of-town supermarkets filled with a plethora of signs and aisle guides, with shelves containing an abundance of groceries in sophisticated packaging bearing complex instructions. Similarly, the 'packaging' of political messages in the 'infomercial' on television, increasing delivery into the home of political pamphlets through the use of the mail-shot (both print-based and electronically via email) and sophisticated enigmatic poster campaigns, all have placed increasing literacy demands on the individual. While in the home, every major electrical appliance comes complete with its 48-page installation and user guide in six languages. Lankshear observes:

> Even if schools improved their current performance to the point where they matched the functional demands of the present day, changes occurring *outside* the school – in technology, economic production, commerce, communications, consumerism, cultural life, etc., – would tend towards creating a rate of illiteracy in the future by simply continuing to raise the minimum required level of print competence.
>
> (1987, p. 135)

Conclusion

> International comparisons show that the gap in attainment between children from higher and lower socio-economic groups in the UK is wider than that in almost every other OECD country.
>
> (Her Majesty's Treasury, 2004, p. 86)

Social class and education are inextricably linked. From Bourdieu's perspective the structural reproduction of societal social and cultural disadvantages and inequalities are caused by cultural reproduction and are recycled through the education system, as well as through other social institutions. In over one hundred years of state education in the UK, various aspects of schooling have disadvantaged children from lower socio-economic classes: access, institutional structures, the nature of school knowledge, testing and examining; cultural contexts; language and discourse, as a result of the fact that the discourse of dominant social and cultural groups determines the nature of schooling and the curriculum. The language, the cultural references, attitudes and values of the middle class underpin the official examinable culture of the school.

Furthermore, the dominant discourse of government documents that established and maintains the education system in England and Wales was, and remains, high cultural and has displayed an antipathy to working-class children and to popular culture (see Davison, 2010). Since 1990 the central metaphor of the National Curriculum has been 'delivery'. Eisner (1984) notes that the metaphors we use shape our understanding of the concepts we study. A curriculum to be 'delivered' by a teacher is disempowering of pupils and teachers alike. It is a view of knowledge that is hierarchical, top-down and is characterised by prescription and direction. Consequently, it is unsurprising that the 'official examinable culture' of school – the language, knowledge priorities, learning styles, pedagogical preferences – is that of dominant social and cultural groups. Without a radical change to the curricula and structures of state schooling it is likely that children from the working class will continue to underachieve as a group compared to middle-class children: even with the Coalition Government's announcement in the May 2010 Queen's Speech of the proposed creation of a 'pupil premium' for the most disadvantaged. In the introduction to the report *Who Cares about the White Working Class?*, Runnymede Trust vice chair Dr Kate Gavron provides an overview of the report's findings:

> working-class people of whatever ethnic background, roughly the poorest fifth of the population, are increasingly separated from the more prosperous majority by inequalities of income, housing and education. By emphasizing the virtues of individual self-determination and the exercising of 'choice', recent governments have in fact entrenched the ability of the middle and upper classes to avoid downward social mobility and preserve the best of life's goods for their own children . . . life chances for today's children are overwhelmingly linked to parental income, occupations and educational qualifications – in other words, class.

(2009)

Questions for further investigation

1   Are continued differences in attainment between children of different social classes the product of a conscious process by dominant groups in society, or just what tends to happen?
2   Is it appropriate to regard Literacy as political as well as cultural?
3   Are all types of culture equally valid? Should cultural studies cross class divisions?

Suggested further reading

Freire, P. (2000) *Pedagogy of the Oppressed* (trans. M. Ramos). London: Continuum. Inspirational, groundbreaking and revolutionary examination of the part played by education in the economic, social and political domination of the poor in developing countries. Freire's pedagogy has helped to empower countless impoverished and illiterate people throughout the world.

Jenkins, R. (2002) *Pierre Bourdieu* (2nd Ed.). London: Routledge. A clear, insightful introduction to Pierre Bourdieu's contributions to theory and methodology in his studies of education, social stratification and culture.

Lankshear, C. with Lawler, M. (1987) *Literacy, Schooling and Revolution*. London: Falmer Press. An exploration of the politics of education in relation to the way in which reading and writing are shaped and transmitted within dominant discourses. The inherently political character of literacy is argued and assumptions about the nature and value of reading and writing are challenged.

Shannon, P. (Ed.) (1992) *Becoming Political: Readings and Writings in the Politics of Literacy Education*. Portsmouth, NH: Heinneman. A collection of seminal readings on the politics of literacy education by authors such as Gee, Brice Heath, Bloome and Giroux and is an excellent starting point for anyone interested in the issues related to literacy and power.

References

Abraham, J. (1993) *Divide and School: Gender and Class Dynamics in Comprehensive Education*. London: Falmer Press.

Argy, F. (2007) 'Education inequalities in Australia', *The New Critic*, 5, May.

Ball, S. (1981) *Beachside Comprehensive: A Case Study of Secondary Schooling*. London: Cambridge University Press.

Beeghley, L. (2004) *The Structure of Social Stratification in the United States*. Boston, MA: Pearson, Allyn & Bacon.

Bennett, K.P. and LeCompte, M.D. (1990) *How Schools Work: A Sociological Analysis of Education*. London: Longman.

Bernstein, B. (1971) *Class, Codes and Control*. London: Paladin.

Boocook, S. (1980) *Sociology of Education: An Introduction* (2nd ed.). Boston: Houghton Mifflin.

Bourdieu, P. (1973) 'Cultural reproduction and social reproduction' in Brown, R. (Ed.) *Knowledge, Education and Cultural Change*. London: Tavistock.

Bourdieu, P. (2007) *Distinction: a Social Critique of the Judgment of Taste* (trans. R. Nice). Cambridge, MA: Harvard University Press.

Bowles, S. and Gintis, H. (1976) *Schooling in Capitalist America: Education and the Contradictions of Economic Life*. London: Routledge and Kegan Paul.

Brown, R. (Ed.) (1973) *Knowledge, Education and Cultural Change*. London: Tavistock.

Coleman, R.P. (1983) 'The continuing significance of social class to marketing', *The Journal of Consumer Research*, 10, 3, pp. 265–280.

Davison, J. (2010) 'Literacy and social class' in Davison, J., Daly, C. and Moss, J. *Debates in English Teaching*. London: Routledge.

Douglas, J. (1964) *The Home and the School*. London: MacGibbon and Kee.

Durkheim, E. (1964) *The Division of Labour in Society* (Reprint Ed. 1997) New York, NY: Free Press.

Eisner, E. (1984) *Cognition and Curriculum*. London: Longman.

Floud, H., Halsey, A. and Martin, F. (1966) *Social Class and Educational Opportunity*. Bath: Chivers.

Gaskell, J. (1985) 'Course enrollment in high school; the perspective of working class females', *Sociology of Education*, 58, pp. 48–59.

Gavron, K. (2009) 'Introduction' in Runnymede Trust *Who Cares about the White Working Class?* London: Runnymede Trust.

Giddens, A. (1971) *Capitalism and Modern Social Theory: An Analysis of the Writings of Marx, Durkheim and Max Weber.* Cambridge: Cambridge University Press.

Giddens, A. and Held, D. (1982) *Classes, Power, and Conflict: Classical and Contemporary Debates.* Berkeley, CA: University of California Press.

Gilbert, D. (2002) *The American Class Structure: In An Age of Growing Inequality.* Belmont, CA: Wadsworth.

Graff, H.J. (1987) *The Labyrinths of Literacy: Reflections on Literacy Past and Present.* New York, NY: Falmer.

Gossman, L. (1981) 'Literature and education', *New Literary History, 13,* 341–371.

Hargreaves, D. (1967) *Social Relations in the Secondary School.* London: Routledge and Kegan Paul.

Her Majesty's Treasury (2004) *Comprehensive Spending Review.* London: Stationery Office.

Lacey, C. (1970) *Hightown Grammar.* Manchester: Manchester University Press.

Lankshear, C. (1987) *Literacy, Schooling and Revolution.* London: Falmer Press.

Lankshear, C. (1997) *Changing Literacies.* Buckingham: Open University Press.

Lupton, R. (2004) *Do Poor Neighbourhoods Mean Poor Schools?* London: Centre for Analysis of Social Exclusion/ESRC.

MacLellan, D. (Ed.) (2008) *The Communist Manifesto by Marx, K. and Engels, F.* Oxford: Oxford University Press.

McGaw, B. (2004) 'Quality education: Is the sky the limit?' in *OECD Observer* No. 242, March 2004. Paris: OECD Publishing.

Organisation for Economic Cooperation and Development (2005) *Education at a Glance: Education Indicators 2005.* Paris: OECD Publishing.

Organisation for Economic Cooperation and Development (2009) *Education at a Glance: Education Indicators 2009.* Paris: OECD Publishing.

Thompson, W. and Hickey, J. (2005) *Society in Focus.* Boston, MA: Pearson, Allyn & Bacon.

Trudgill, P. (1974). *Sociolinguistics: An Introduction to Language and Society.* London: Penguin Books.

Van Zanten (2005) 'New modes of reproducing social inequality in education: the changing role of parents, teachers, schools and educational policies', *European Educational Research Journal, 4,* 3, 155–169.

Warner, W.L., Meeker, M. and Eells, K. (1949) *Social Class in America: A Manual of Procedure for the Measurement of Social Status.* Chicago, IL: Science Research Associates.

Willis, P. (1977) *Learning to Labour: How Working Class Kids Get Working Class Jobs.* Sheffield: Saxon Press.

Willis, P. (1981) 'Cultural production is different from cultural reproduction . . .', *Interchange, 12,* 2–3, pp. 48–67.

UNESCO (2003) *Education for All: United Kingdom Perspectives.* Paris: UNESCO.

26

Comparative education

Michele Schweisfurth
University of Birmingham

Overview

Comparison is a natural human activity and arguably 'the basis of all knowledge' (Hughes, 1901). So, for as long as people have travelled and education has existed, it is likely that travellers have noticed similarities and differences, and thought about their implications. However, the first *systematic* comparative studies in education are traditionally considered to be the surveys of European forms of education undertaken by Marc-Antoine Jullien de Paris in the early nineteenth century. Using a questionnaire as a framework, he produced comparable data on issues such as ages of starting and leaving primary school, entrance and diagnostic examinations, and class sizes (Jullien, 1817). Since that time, the field of comparative education has grown along with interest in educational studies, and has expanded particularly in the current context of globalisation.

This chapter will survey some key aspects of comparative education. It will offer a brief overview of the purposes and methods of comparison, and conclude with a future-oriented look at contemporary developments in the field.

Introduction – why compare?

Over 100 years ago, Michael Sadler famously stated:

> The practical value of studying . . . the working of foreign systems of education is that it will result in our being better fitted to study and understand our own.
>
> (Sadler, in Higginson, 1979).

This quotation captures the essence of one of the key purposes of comparative education. We all take for granted the education systems we have experienced, but these norms look very different in the light of other possibilities. Someone who grew up in England, for example, is likely to assume unquestioningly that school uniforms, transition from primary school to secondary after Year 6, and high-stakes common examinations are all normal and therefore desirable – but to someone who grew up in Ontario, Canada, all of these could come as some surprise, and they would raise questions about the purposes these serve.

Comparative religion, comparative anatomy and comparative law help us to understand the nature of religion, anatomy and law. Similarly, knowledge of the essential nature of education can be extended by comparatively examining the range of possibilities as found in different contexts and systems. This can lead to the creation of theory, which can be tested against further cases. One example is Human Capital Theory, which draws causal relationships between schooling, individual's life chances and a nation's economic health, and which was developed from studies of educational investment and expansion in different countries. A further example is the study of education in what Cowen has called 'transitologies': contexts where dramatic political change has taken place within a short space of time (e.g. from communism to capitalism or from authoritarian regime to democracy) (Cowen, 1999). Studies of how education has responded to, and shaped, these changes have led to a range of theories including Bîrzea's seven-stage transition process, based on comparative analysis of Eastern and Central European countries in the period following the collapse of the Soviet Union (Bîrzea, 1994).

And so comparative education 'is of intrinsic interest as a scholarly activity' (Phillips, 2000, p. 298). This still begs the 'so what?' question. Much comparative education is undertaken in an ameliorative spirit, with a view to improving education provision by looking for models for reform or innovation. Comparative studies can facilitate 'indirect experimentation' (Durkheim, 1982/1901), in allowing us to see how different models work in different contexts and to observe the effects of a particular policy or practice. For example, a researcher or policy-maker interested in knowing the effects of increased investment in prescribed textbooks can research what happened when this policy was pursued in different countries, before risking a major policy change or conducting costly and ethically questionable experiments.

In a similarly pragmatic vein, large-scale international surveys of achievement, such as the Trends in International Mathematics and Science Survey (TIMSS) or the Programme for International Student Assessment (PISA), set benchmarks by which the performance of different systems can be judged. These surveys result in a sort of 'league table' of results, ranking different countries according to how well their students perform on the same test at set ages. Inevitably, education systems in countries which perform well are scrutinised, with a view to learning from their success, and even to transferring policies and practices in the hope that these will lead to success elsewhere. Finland's strong performance in recent PISA surveys has led to policy, academic and popular media interest internationally. Equally, when countries perform poorly, especially if results are a surprise (as in Germany's 'PISA-Shock' after the survey in 2000), the results are often used to scandalise and to drive a government reform agenda in a direction they wish to pursue. More sophisticated analyses of these data can also reveal in-country variations which are informative – for example, not only has Finland performed well overall but the results are also relatively less stratified than in many countries, indicating that in the Finnish case the best students are not succeeding at the expense of the worst, and that socio-economic factors do not determine educational chances.

Equally, one of the great practical applications of comparative education is to call into question misguided policy decisions. As intimated above, comparative studies have on occasion been misused by governments who have a pre-determined agenda which they wish to promote; comparative evidence is open to selective usage. So, for example, in the late 1990s in the UK a significant policy discourse about pedagogy was in favour of whole-class teaching rather than learner-centred individualised or group work. The claimed basis for this promotion was the success of certain Pacific Rim nations in international tests of achievement, and the use there of teacher-directed, whole-class methods. This stance ignored, however, the fact that whole-class methods are also used in most countries where standards are the lowest (Alexander, 2000).

Methods

A glance at any journal of comparative education will reveal the eclectic range of methods and perspectives that comparativists use. Policy-oriented statisticians, Marxist ethnographers and historians specialising in particular countries all co-inhabit the comparative education world, if not always agreeably. While there is no particular comparative method, a number of frameworks have been developed to assist researchers in making valid comparisons, and we will consider one of these here, with a view to highlighting some of the central issues that are fundamental to the comparative process. Figure 26.1 shows a possible structure for comparing education in two different contexts.

The process in Figure 26.1 begins with conceptualisation. This is where the all-important issue of ethnocentrism first raises its head, as researchers often carry with them a set of normative perspectives about education based on their own backgrounds, which can lead to bias. In order to make a valid comparison, it is important that the concepts are carefully scrutinised. Virtually any unit of analysis is appropriate for comparison – Bray and Thomas identify seven possible levels, from individual people through world regions (1995). So one could, for example, compare a teacher in Botswana with a teacher in Brazil; a classroom in Germany with a classroom in Indonesia; a school in Australia with a school in the US, etc. But attention to the *nature* of the unit of analysis is crucial, so that we are comparing like with like, or at least are aware of essential differences. For example, research which starts with a question about quality nursery schooling in two countries may seem clear enough. But is such schooling the same thing in both places, in terms of its age cohort, purposes, relationship to the state, to parenting practices and to formal schooling, and so on? It might be more neutral (if more awkward) to use a term such as 'state-regulated education for children between three years old and the commencement of primary school'. Even more challenging: how is the concept of quality to be understood? A globally recognised definition of quality – such as those found in UNESCO frameworks – might be a suitable defining concept for the study, given the value-laden nature of the word and the range of definitions used internationally. Nowak (1977) identifies four key 'equivalences' (among others) which can guide the process of conceptualisation: cultural, contextual, structural and functional.

The next stage aligns to what Bereday in his classic work (1964) calls 'juxtaposition'. Having tried to 'neutralise' research questions in the first stage, it is an essential tenet of comparative education to bring context back into the process. Full attention needs to be paid to the 'historical, geographical, cultural, political, religious, linguistic (etc.) features of each context' (Phillips and Schweisfurth, 2008). Sadler famously and poetically described the organic relationship between education and its context:

> In studying foreign systems of Education we should not forget that the things outside the schools matter even more than the things inside the schools, and govern and interpret the things inside. We cannot wander at pleasure among the educational systems of the world, like a child strolling through a garden, and pick off a flower from one bush and some leaves from another, and then expect that if we stick what we have gathered into

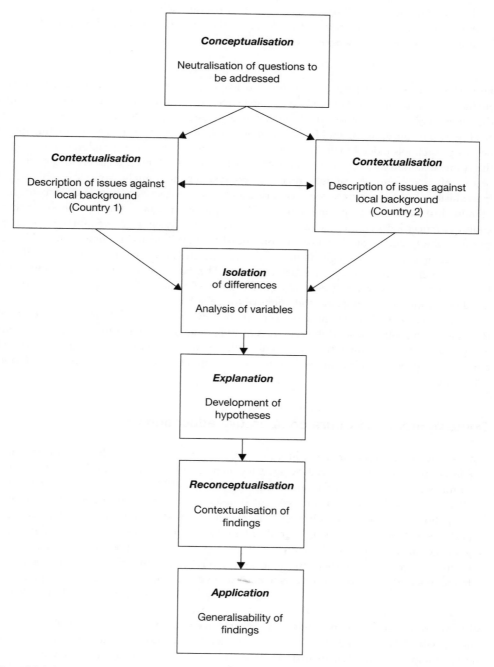

Figure 26.1 A structure for comparative inquiry (from Phillips and Schweisfurth, 2008 p. 100)

the soil at home, we shall have a living plant. A national system of Education is a living thing, the outcome of forgotten struggles and difficulties, and 'of battles long ago'. It has in it some of the secret workings of national life.

(Sadler in Higginson, 1979).

From this process of juxtaposition and contextualisation, differences will become apparent, and are then subject to analysis. This leads to the next stages, where the researcher attempts to explain the differences. Any hypotheses that emerge at this stage need to be set in context, and this can lead to a reconceptualisation. In the example in Figure 26.1, for instance, one finding might be that pre-schools judged to be high quality in country *a* have far fewer children in each class than those in country *b* (see Tobin *et al.*, 1989 and Tobin *et al.*, 2009 for an interesting discussion of this phenomenon). A careful process of contextualisation might point to a culture of individualism and competitiveness in country *a*, and a more collective culture and a discouraging of individual attention-seeking in country *b*. The hypothesis might be that pre-schools in these countries reflect local culture and are used as a vehicle for learning and reinforcing particular cultural values, which could lead to a reconceptualisation of 'quality' in these contexts. In the final stage, generalisations might (with great care!) be attempted about this function of pre-schools generally, for testing in other contexts. The fact that this particular finding and hypothesis resonate with a well-established theory on the functions of schools generally – cultural socialisation theory – strengthens the potential for generalisation.

This structure makes the process seem quite tidy, but it is of course very complex. Realistically, it is often beyond the resources of an individual researcher to come to terms with every possible relevant contextual factor, unless they spend many years in the country and speak the language fluently. This is an idealised process to aim for: reality is usually messier and more expedient.

Contemporary and future comparative educations

there are several comparative educations. We still have, for example, a 'comparative education' of solutions offered by agencies such as the OECD or the World Bank; a 'comparative education' of international evaluation – IEA studies and PISA and the effective and efficient schools movement is not yet dead; a 'comparative education' of the politically sanctified or politically correct dichotomised binaries (traditional/modern; developed/developing; capitalist/socialist; East/West; North/South); and a specialist and good 'comparative higher education' literature. Nevertheless, it is possible to suggest what is rarely suggested – that there are some basic and relatively invisible assumptions which frame much of the academically driven comparative education in any given time period.

(Cowen, 2010, p. 1285)

What are some of the frameworks and drivers of contemporary comparative educations? Much of what has been said so far in this chapter has focused on the nation state as the central unit for comparison or contextualisation. It remains important in comparative education, not least because that is typically where educational goals are set, in line with national development priorities, and where education policy is made. There are notable exceptions, such as Canada, where education is a matter decentralised to provinces for historical reasons. But the context which is receiving intensive attention within contemporary comparative education is the global one.

On the one hand, the global consensus around key educational priorities, and the work of international agencies to promote these, makes the global level an increasingly significant one in the provision of education, especially in poorer parts of the world. The United Nations Millennium Development Goals, for example, include two related to education specifically, with particular implications for developing countries:

Goal 2: Achieve universal primary education
. . . ensure that, by 2015, children everywhere, boys and girls alike, will be able to complete a full course of primary schooling.
Goal 3: Promote gender equality and empower women
. . . Eliminate gender disparity in primary and secondary education, preferably by 2005, and to all levels of education no later than 2015.
(UN Resolution A/56/326, quoted in UNESCO, 2002)

These, and other global agreements regarding education, are supported and monitored by multilateral aid agencies, and are used as a policy framework for many bilateral agencies from national governments, such as the Department for International Development in the UK. Note the rapid approach of the deadlines for achieving these goals – while there has been considerable progress, despite the global agreements and levels of support, they are almost certainly not going to be met. While consensus can be a force for good, it is also worth pointing out that powerful and controversial global hegemonies are generated by the work of some such agencies, such as the World Bank, and the much-critiqued neo-liberal agenda in education is one of these.

On the other hand, the compression of space and time created by the technologies, movements and attitudes of globalisation sometimes make the country x to country y comparative process and the language of x to y policy 'borrowing' seem old-fashioned (although they are still highly relevant analyses). Technology makes it harder and harder even for authoritarian governments to control learning. Minorities and other special interest groups, as well as working at the local level, are forming global coalitions that unite them across borders in promoting particular forms of education. What Carney has called the 'globalisation optique' (quoted in Steiner Khamsi, 2010) reveals how individuals in far-flung parts of the world share perspectives on education, and educate each other, in a manner that used to be controlled by the state and by their teachers.

Beyond the obvious importance of globalisation, what follows is a rather personal discussion of what is increasingly important in comparative education, from a fairly informed but admittedly biased perspective. I have argued elsewhere (e.g. Phillips and Schweisfurth, 2008) that comparative education should have a moral purpose as well as an academic and practical one, and there is an evident increase in attention to the questions of research ethics, the nature of research partnerships, and social and global justice in education. The prevailing model of research relationships was traditionally that partners with more resources had the power to set the research agenda, define priorities and methods, guide policy lessons, and reap the rewards of publication. In the developing world, this meant that local people were subjects of research, or occasionally acted as on-the-ground researchers to gather data, but were not equal partners in the process. This is shifting and is itself an important topic within comparative education (e.g. Crossley and Watson, 2003; Mason, 2008). There is active promotion of combining insider and outsider perspectives in research, and attention to integrity in how the 'other' is conceptualised and included. Similarly, young people's rights are being promoted in the research process; for example, by including them as researchers, not merely as respondents (Cox et al., 2010).

The topics of comparative research also reflect a growing concern for social justice in education. Some examples of the themes of recent special issues of key comparative education journals in the past two years attest to this: learning in conflict and post-conflict contexts (Davies and Talbot, 2008); access to education in Africa (Lewin and Akeampong, 2009); gender and education (Unterhalter and North, 2009; Arnot and Fennell, 2008); and migration and socio-economic mobility (Rao, 2009).

In conclusion, contemporary comparative education is a well-established and flourishing field. It has its own national and international societies, such as the North American Comparative and International Education Society (www.cies.us), the British Association of International and Comparative Education (www.baice.ac.uk), the China Comparative Education Society (www.compe.cn/) and the World Congress of Comparative Education Societies (www.wcces.net). It also has well-regarded journals such as *Comparative Education, Compare* and *Comparative Education Review*, and a vast literature. It is taught as a specialist subject at selected universities internationally, at undergraduate, post-graduate and doctoral levels. But regardless of whether a scholar of education chooses personally to use the 'comparativist' label, what has been called a 'comparative sensibility' (Turner, 2010) is useful to anyone interested in education in a globalising world.

Questions for further investigation

1 If you could learn more about education in one other country, what country would that be and why?
2 Which aspects would you wish to research? Design a comparative inquiry, based on the model in this chapter, which could be used to compare this other country with your own, focusing on one of these aspects.
3 How have education policies in other countries, and globalisation, affected education in your own context?

Suggested further reading

Alexander, R.J. (2000) *Culture and Pedagogy: international comparisons in primary education.* Oxford and Boston: Blackwell. This book was winner of the 2002 American Educational Research Association Outstanding Book Award, and awarded first prize in the Society for Educational Studies Book Awards for 2002. As well as exploring primary education in the US, UK, India, France and Russia, it provides an excellent discussion of comparative methodology.

Cowen, R. and Kazamias, A. (2009) *International Handbook of Comparative Education.* Heidelberg: Springer Dordrecht. This is a comprehensive and up-to-date compendium, organised thematically, which provides both depth and breadth of coverage of the field. Entries, written by authors from around the world, are analytical and sophisticated but accessible. A good resource for exploring a particular theme or to learn more about the field itself.

Phillips, D. and Schweisfurth, M. (2008) *Comparative and International Education: an introduction to theory, method and practice.* London: Continuum. This text provides a useful and accessible overview of key concepts and approaches with reference to extensive literature. It includes chapters on issues particular to developing countries, on large-scale surveys, and on themes that have been explored comparatively.

References

Alexander, R.J. (2000) *Culture and Pedagogy: international comparisons in primary education.* Oxford: Blackwell.

Arnot, M. and Fennell, S. (2008) 'Gendered education and national development: critical perspectives and new research', *Special Issue of Compare, 38,* 5, pp. 515–523.

Birzea, C. (1994) *Education and the Policies of the Countries in Transition.* Strasbourg: Council of Europe Press.

Bray, M. and Thomas, M.R. (1995) 'Levels of comparison in educational studies: different insights from different literatures and the value of multilevel analyses', *Harvard Educational Review, 65,* 3, pp. 472–490.

Cowen, R. (1999) 'Late modernity and the rules of chaos: an initial note on transitologies and rims', in Alexander, R., Broadfoot, P. and Phillips, D. (Eds.) *Learning from Comparing: new directions in comparative education research, Vol. 1.* Oxford: Symposium.

Cowen, R. (2010) 'Then and now: unit ideas and comparative education', in Cowen, R. and Kazamias, A. (Eds.) *International Handbook of Comparative Education.* Heidelberg: Springer Dordrecht, pp. 1277–1294.

Cox. S., Dyer, C., Robinson-Pant, A. and Schweisfurth, M. (Eds.) (2010) *Children as Decision Makers in Education: sharing experiences across cultures.* London: Continuum.

Crossley M. and Watson, K. (2003) *Comparative and International Research in Education.* London: Routledge.

Davies, L. and Talbot, C. (2008) 'Special issue on education in conflict and post-conflict societies', *Comparative Education Review, 52,* 4.

Durkheim, E. (1982/1901) in Lukes, S. (Ed.) *The Rules of Sociological Method and Selected Texts on Sociology and its Method.* London: Macmillan.

Higginson, J.H. (Ed.) (1979) *Selections from Michael Sadler.* Liverpool: Dejall and Meyorre, p. 49.

Hughes, R.E. (1901) *Schools at Home and Abroad.* London: Swan Sonnenschein.

Jullien, M.A. (1817) *Esquisse d'un Ouvrage sur l'Education Comparée.* Ann Arbor/London: University Microfilms Inc.

Lewin, K. and Akeampong, K. (2009) 'Special issue on access to education in Sub-Saharan Africa', *Comparative Education, 45,* 2, pp. 151–174.

Mason, M. (2008) 'The philosophy and politics of partnership', *Norrag News, 41,* pp. 15–19.

Nowak, S. (1977) 'The strategy of cross-national survey research for the development of social theory', in Szlai, A. and Petralla, R. (Eds.) *Cross-National Comparative Survey Research: theory and practice.* Oxford: Pergamon Press, pp. 3–47.

Phillips, D. (2000) 'Learning from elsewhere in education: some perennial problems revisited with reference to British interest in Germany', *Comparative Education, 36,* 3, pp. 297–307.

Phillips, D. and Schweisfurth, M. (2008) *Comparative and International Education: an introduction to theory, method and practice.* London: Continuum.

Rao, N. (2009) 'Special issue on migration, education and socio-economic mobility', *Compare, 40,* 2, pp. 137–145.

Steiner-Khamsi (2010) 'The politics and economics of comparison', *Comparative Education Review, 54,* 3, pp. 323–342.

Tobin, J., Wu, D. and Davidson, D. (1989) *Preschool in Three Cultures: Japan, China, and the United States.* New York, NY: Yale University Press.

Tobin, J., Hsueh, Y. and Karasawa, M. (2009) *Preschool in Three Cultures Revisited: China, Japan and the United States.* Chicago, IL: University of Chicago Press.

Turner, D. (2010) 'The twin fields of comparative and international education', in Masemann, V., Majhanovich, S., Truong, N. and Janigan, K. (Eds.) *A Tribute to David N. Wilson: clamouring for a better world.* Rotterdam: Sense Publishers.

UNESCO (2002) *EFA Global Monitoring Report: Education for All – is the world on track?* Paris: UNESCO.

Unterhalther, E. and North, A. (2009) 'Special issue on gender mainstreaming in education', *Compare, 40,* 4, pp. 389–404.

27

Development education

Douglas Bourn
Institute of Education, University of London

Overview

Development education has been a feature of educational practice in most industrialised countries for the past 25 to 30 years. It has sometimes gone under the names of global education or global citizenship, or themes such as the global dimension in education, and more recently, global learning. It may not be a well-known term but is an area of educational practice that has had contradictory influences and strong political and funding support in some countries, alongside a potentially radical and transformative agenda from non-governmental organisations (NGOs).

This chapter will outline the evolution of development education and its relationship to the other terms cited above. It will demonstrate why development education has emerged and what are its distinct features. It will conclude by suggesting that development education can potentially be seen as more than just a response to support development, but as an approach that has connections to critical pedagogy.

Introduction: the emergence of a global and international approach to education

Learning about the wider world has been part of formal education in many industrialised countries for more than a century. Knowledge in Europe and North America about other continents, such as Africa, in the nineteenth and for most of the twentieth century was, however, influenced by colonial and missionary traditions. A major influence on the break from that mould came in the post-Second World War period with the emergence of a number of international institutions including the United Nations, and later UNESCO, who recognised the need for education to have a more international outlook (Tye, 1999). This encouragement of education to have a more international outlook gained influence in a number of European countries and also in Japan (Ishii, 2003). In the United States, through Hanvery, Merryfield and Tye (Kirkwood-Tucker, 2009) and in the UK, through Richardson (1990), Pike and Selby (1988) and Hicks (2003), an approach towards learning under the heading of 'global education' emerged. It had a practice-based focus around a child-centred and world-minded approach to education that stressed the importance of attitude and skill development as well as the exploration of a range of global issues. Above all it saw education as a vehicle for some form of personal and social transformation. A variation on this concept of global education also emerged in Europe in the 1990s, promoted by the Council of Europe, which has closer linkages to development education but includes reference also to human rights, sustainability, citizenship, inter-cultural and peace education. It emphasises the opening of people's eyes and minds to 'the realities of the world, and awakens them to bring about a world of greater justice, equity and human rights for all' (see Osler and Vincent, 2002; Hoeck and Wegimont, 2003).

The development agenda and development education

These traditions were influential to development education because they had similar goals and objectives around promoting a broader worldview with an emphasis on participatory forms of learning. Terms were used interchangeably. What in one country might be called global education or global learning might in another be called development education. In some cases this was for linguistic reasons and in others political, but it was also because of a general lack of conceptual clarity as to what these terms meant. What came to distinguish development education, however, was its relationship to development and consequent support from aid ministries and international non-governmental organisations, with an emphasis on linkages between learning and action within a social justice-based perspective.

Development education emerged in the late 1960s and 1970s in Europe and North America in response to the de-colonisation process and the emergence of development as a specific feature of government and NGO policies and programmes. Resources began to be given to ensure the public was supportive through educational programmes, production of resources and general awareness-raising. These programmes had in many cases a strong international outlook with, as Harrison (2008) notes in regard to the work of Oxfam in the UK, 'a desire to open up hearts and minds, as well as the purses', to the problem of poverty in countries overseas. However, much of this practice, as Hammond (2002) and others have commented, was located within an approach that served to educate for support a 'largely ignorant or disinterested public' through an information-delivery model of learning.

The emergence of a more critical stance and a movement for radical change

From the late 1970s there was an emergence within this development education practice of more critical approaches. Practitioners were beginning to question the aid industry, and often as a result of personal experience and volunteering were seeing the need for a more social justice-based approach (Harrison, 2008). In a number of countries, solidarity groups emerged, partly as a response to political events in Latin America, for example, or to the struggles of peoples against continued Portuguese colonisation in Africa, but also in response to hearing about radical educational approaches, notably the work of Paulo Freire. By the 1990s, in countries such as UK, Canada, Germany, Netherlands and Japan there were movements of educationalists, mainly working with NGOs, but with some support from teachers and academics, who were promoting an approach that was influenced by critical perspectives on development combined with the pedagogy of Freire (1972) and progressive classroom practices. But as McCollum noted, the 1990s were still dominated by the efforts of individual enthusiasts with the emphasis on producing materials for practitioners but with little consideration of theoretical influences (McCollum, 1996, p. 22).

The changing role of the media and emergence of a campaigning focus

Earlier in this chapter it was stated that development education first emerged in terms of raising awareness and support for aid and development but that it gradually began to take a more critical stance. This critical stance has at various times since the 1970s been challenged and in some cases diverted by media campaigns on development issues, often generated by crises such as famine or other disasters. This has meant that whilst development education has often strived to promote appropriate and positive images of people in continents such as Africa, media images have reinforced traditional stereotypes. The media has also reduced issues to simple messages that might have helped NGOs and governments but not necessarily educationalists.

Peter Adamson writing in 1993 (Adamson, 1993) stated that whenever he gave a talk in a school or college, the dominant views of children were of poverty and starvation in the developing world because of the influence of the media. The perceptions of Africa, for example, as a continent of helplessness and 'starving babies' was still evident in the school classroom in the first decade of the twenty-first century (Lowe, 2008). The need to challenge dominant and negative views about the developing world following the Live Aid campaign and events in the 1980s became a major concern of development and development education organisations. VSO (2002) noted in its report on public perceptions of development that the Live Aid legacy was still very prevalent in UK society. Whilst at one level this led to resources and materials being produced for schools, it also led to increased emphasis being given to what became known as public education or communications strategies focused on promoting messages and visual representations. From the 1990s onwards therefore, around Europe there has been increased emphasis on resources being given to media-related materials and initiatives encouraging the public to be supportive and engaged in development. As a consequence, less attention and resources were given to debating from a more critical perspective the role and contribution of aid and development to combating global poverty. This move from education to awareness-raising, communicating messages, public engagement and campaigning can be seen in both the practice of NGOs and the focus of governments culminating in activities around the Make Poverty History initiative of 2005 and since then around climate change.

Growing influence of globalisation and learning in a global society

During the 1990s, the term 'global' became to be seen as more appropriate than 'development' in the education sector. Programmes, projects, resources and initiatives began to refer more to global than development. This was in part for tactical reasons: people no longer understood, if they ever did understand, what development education actually meant. There was also increasing use of the term 'global' in response to recognition by policy-makers and practitioners of the influence of globalisation. In Germany, for example, Klaus Seitz in 1991 used the term 'global learning' in response to globalisation and the needs of a global society. He argued against the 'third world' being added to the curriculum. There was a need, he said, for a wider horizon for the promotion of a world that had global connections (Hartmeyer, 2008, p. 45). Annette Scheunpflug (2008; Scheunpflug and Asbrand, 2006), a key influential figure in this field, has challenged the value of the term 'development education'. She states that with the moves towards a more global society, development is no longer an appropriate term. For her, there are still power centres in the world but their location is less and less defined. The world is much more complex and for her a more appropriate term is 'global learning', which she defines as the pedagogical reaction towards a world society with social justice at its heart (Hartmeyer, 2008).

In a number of countries, such as Canada, Australia, Finland, Germany and Netherlands, the terms 'global education' or 'global learning' were, by the first decade of the twenty-first century, the dominant terms within which discourses around learning and understanding about international development could be found. In the UK terms such as 'Learning in a Global society' became common (QCA, 2008). By 2008, the Development Education Association (DEA), the umbrella body for this sector, was increasingly questioning the use of the term 'development'. They decided to use the term 'global learning', which to them puts learning in a global context, fostering:

> critical and creative thinking; self-awareness and open-mindedness towards difference; understanding of global issues and power relationships; and optimism and action for a better world.

> (DEA, 2008)

Other influences that led to some partial re-alignments have been the rise in influence of sustainable development as one of the adjectival educations, bringing together environment and development; and the increasing emphasis on global citizenship.

These evolving debates around terminology were also increasingly influenced by closer proximity in thinking and practice to similar traditions in global education alongside linkages to sustainable development and global citizenship. Education for Sustainable Development (Scott and Gough, 2003) has in a number of countries (notably Japan, Germany, Sweden, Netherlands) become a major influence in re-aligning development and global education. 'Global citizenship' is another term that has become a popular manifestation of these practices, particularly in North America (see Abdi and Shultz, 2008) and the UK (Oxfam, 2006). This term is often used to make connections with rights and responsibilities and also to demonstrate the global and interconnected lifestyles of many people in the Global North.

Moving from the margins to the mainstream

Regardless of discussions around terminology, it cannot be denied that the first decade of the twenty-first century witnessed the biggest ever expansion of interest in and engagement with learning about global and development issues in the leading industrialised countries (Hoeck and Wegimont, 2003). There were four main reasons for this. First, at a policy level the launch of the UN Millennium Development Goals in 2000, an onus was put on governments to demonstrate impact and influence. The support of the public for these goals became a political priority for many countries. This drive for support for development goals was given a major boost by the 2005 campaign Make Poverty History. Second, the wider world and developing countries in particular no longer seemed in the Global North to be far away. Globalisation, instant communications, the impact of climate change and the support for campaigns around fair trade, for example, made learning about global issues part of everyday learning. Examples can be found from a number of countries of educational programmes that recognise the globalised nature of societies and the need for education to respond, through changes to the curriculum and in new approaches to learning (Mundy, 2007; Rasanen, 2009). Third, policy-makers and practitioners were beginning to demonstrate the value of learning about development issues not only in terms of public support for development but also in educational terms. Therefore in countries such as Australia (AusAid, 2008), Austria (Forghani-Arani and Hartmeyer, 2010) and Portugal (IPAD, 2010) strategies emerged under the label of 'development awareness', 'global learning' or 'global education' that were owned not only by ministries responsible for aid, but also by ministries of education, with engagement of civil society bodies. Fourth, educational institutions were referring to equipping learners for living and working in a global society (Abdi and Shultz, 2008). Schools, for example, referred to learning about global issues through links with schools in developing countries as part of creating a global mindset.

What remains less clear is what constitutes the main elements of development education today and whether the use of other terms such as 'global learning', 'global citizenship' or 'global education' suggests a radical shift in the focus and forms of delivery of this area of learning. Above all, has the ever-changing terminology been simply a response to a tactical or political need to communicate a body of practice more effectively? Or does it represent a fundamental re-alignment of practice linked to the challenges of globalisation? It is suggested here that regardless of the twists and turns in the use of terminology, and alignments to broader educational traditions and social influences, there is a need to explore the key principles and practices that could constitute a distinctive pedagogy of development education.

Development education and critical pedagogy

Development education could be seen as an area of education such as the environment or human rights, if you see it as an area of educational practice located within and around discourses of development. It could also be seen as an approach towards learning that once had value but should now be subsumed within concepts such as global learning, global education, global citizenship or education for sustainable development. There is another interpretation of development education, which is that it includes methodology and approach that has relevance to broader theories of learning, particularly critical pedagogy. If one looks at the practices of organisations in many countries in the Global North, there are some common factors that suggest that development education still has connections to the ideas of Paulo Freire and his emphasis on continuing reflection, questioning of knowledge and dominant orthodoxies, of empowerment and social change (Darder et al., 2009).

Henry Giroux suggests that critical pedagogy needs to create new forms of knowledge and to break down disciplinary boundaries (Giroux, 2005). Mclaren (2009) in defining critical pedagogy emphasises not only the importance of forms of knowledge but also dominant and subordinate cultures and consequent influences of power and ideology. This questioning of dominant myths and ideas, to go beneath the surface and look at root causes and social contexts, lies at the heart of critical pedagogy (Shor, 1992). These theoretical viewpoints relate closely to the practical manifestations of a 'critical development education' in terms of making sense of understanding the global forces that shape one's life. A key theme of development education practice is the promotion of the interdependent and interconnected nature of our lives, the similarities as well as the differences between communities and peoples around the world. A second theme is about ensuring the voices and perspectives of the peoples of the Global South are promoted, understood and reflected upon along with perspectives from the Global North (Ohri, 1997). This means going beyond a relativist notion of differing voices to one that recognises the importance of spaces for the voices of the oppressed and dispossessed (Andreotti, 2006). Third, development education seeks to encourage a more values-based approach to learning with an emphasis on social justice, fairness and the desire for a more equal world (Abdi and Shultz, 2008). Finally, development education promotes the linkage between learning, moral outrage and concern about global poverty, and wanting to take action to secure change (Oxfam, 2006).

If you went into a school classroom in many European countries, at some stage during a school year, there would be examples of learning about development issues or some form of activity or project about global issues. What would first distinguish this activity as a 'development education' activity would be the extent to which it was moving beyond a traditional view of seeing the Global South as 'just about poor people' who were helpless and needed aid and charity. Positive examples would be where learning questioned, challenged assumptions and stereotypes, and located poverty within an understanding of the causes of inequality and what people were doing for themselves. This move from a 'charity mentality' to one of social justice remains an underlying theme of development education in practice in schools. A development education perspective would question the emphasis a school might give to raising money unless it was located within broader learning. It would also mean that central to learning would be the promotion of positive images, often through the use of photographs and personal stories.

Second, development education practice would often include giving space to stories and perspectives from people from the Global South. This would lead on to looking at issues through different lenses. Examples of this are two web-based programmes that have emerged from the work of Vanessa Andreotti (2006). Open Spaces for Dialogue and Enquiry (OSDE, 2006) is a methodology produced by UK-based development educationalists that supports the creation of open and safe spaces for dialogue and enquiry about global issues where 'people are invited to engage critically with their own and different perspectives' (OSDE, 2008). Through Other Eyes, a development of this approach, aims through a range of educational methods to 'enable educators to develop an understanding of how language and systems of belief, value and representation affect the way people interpret the world' (Andreotti and De Souza 2008, pp. 23–24). Third, development education learning would, as Oxfam (2006) has suggested, encourage 'a sense of moral outrage', of wanting to take the learning forward through some form of follow up activity. Finally, and central to all development education practice, would be the encouragement of participatory learning methodologies (DEA, 2000) with clear echoes of the influence of Freire and other radical educationalists from the 1970s and 1980s.

Conclusion

This chapter has suggested that development education has become an important component of learning for the twenty-first century. However, the funding-driven agenda has resulted in a chequered history within many industrialised countries and a consequent tendency to operate within dominant discourses of development. While political influences and NGO agendas have contributed to the slow development of (or failure to develop) an independent discourse, there is evidence from the practice of many organisations that a more open and independent approach can be undertaken.

At a time when societies are increasingly globalised and interdependent, learning and understanding about the causes of increased divisions in the world could be argued to be even more important than ever before. As international bodies such as the UN, G8 and the

European Commission put increased emphasis on 'combating global poverty', the need to engage the public in these debates becomes ever more important. However, unless this engagement is based on opportunities for critical reflection on development and global inequalities, development education could be reduced to being the 'mouth piece' of policy-makers or large NGOs; and a major learning opportunity will be missed.

What cannot be denied is that around the world, educational bodies are addressing global themes and issues more directly. The challenge for proponents of development education is whether it merely follows and responds to these opportunities or sees its engagement as part of a broader ideological debate, challenging the influences of dominant neo-liberal agendas in education. If proponents of development education look to theories related to 'critical pedagogy', then there is the opportunity of linking to a theoretical framework that could take the practice beyond the agendas of policy-makers and NGOs.

Questions for further investigation

1   Does development education as a discourse have a future, or should it be re-conceptualised around themes of global education or sustainability?
2   What and where are the potential openings and opportunities for development education within the school curriculum?
3   What role can and should education play in relation to promoting a wider world or more global outlook with children and young people?

Suggested further reading

Bourn, D. (Ed.) (2008) *Development Education: Debates and Dialogues*. London: Bedford Way Papers. This edited volume brings together writings by some of the leading international academics in this field notably Vanessa Andreotti, Annette Scheunpflug and David Hicks alongside two research based chapters from Barbara Asbrand on role of adolescents in learning about globalisation and Alison Leonard on school linking and a more activist-based chapter from two former workers within Oxfam UK, Gillian Temple and Anna Laycock.

Bourn, D. (Ed.) *International Journal of Development Education and Global Learning*. Stoke-on-Trent: Trentham Books. This journal first published in 2008 has included articles looking at both theory and practice in development education and related fields from North America, Europe and the Global South. Key themes have included influence of postcolonial thinking on developing a theory of development education and the continuing influence of 'charity mentalities'. It is published three times a year.

Kirkwood-Tucker, T.F. (Ed.) (2009) *Visions in Global Education*. New York, NY: Peter Lang Publishers. This volume includes chapters looking at history and aspects of global education in North America and Russia and includes some excellent examples of practice particularly relevant to teacher education.

Hartmeyer, H. (2008) *Experiencing the World – Global Learning in Austria: Developing, Reaching Out, Crossing Borders*. Munster: Waxmann. Helmuth Hartmeyer is a leading figure within Global Learning in Europe and this volume is a re-working of his doctorate and covers the history, conceptual basis and examples of different approaches to global learning in Austria.

References

Abdi, A. and Shultz, L. (Ed.) (2008) *Educating for Human Rights and Global Citizenship*. Albany, NY: State University of New York Press.

Adamson, P. (1993) 'Charity begins at home', *The Independent*, 18 May.

Andreotti, V. (2006) 'Soft versus critical global citizenship education', *Policy and Practice*, 3, pp. 40–51.

Andreotti, V. and de Souza, L.M. (2008) 'Translating theory into practice and walking minefields: lessons from the project "Through Other Eyes"', *International Journal of Development Education and Global Learning*, 1, 1, pp. 23–36.

AusAid, GEP, Curriculum Corporation, Asia Education Foundation (2008) *Global Perspectives: A framework for global education in Australian schools*. Available at: www.globaleducation.edna.edu.au/globaled/go/engineName/filemanager/pid/122/GPS_ForWeb_150dpi.pdf?actionreq=actionFileDownload&fid=24877. Accessed September 2010.

Bourn, D. (Ed.) (2008) *Development Education: Debates and Dialogue*. London: Institute of Education.

Darder, A., Baltodano, M.P. and Torres, R.D. (Eds.) (2009) *The Critical Pedagogy Reader*. New York, NY: Routledge.

DEA (2000) *Principles and Practices of Development Education in Schools*. London: DEA.

DEA (2008) *Global Matters Learning – Case Studies*. London: DEA.

Forghani-Arani, N. and Hartmeyer, H. (2010) 'Global learning in Austria', *International Journal of Development Education and Global Learning*, 2, 2, pp. 45–58.

Freire, P. (1972) *Pedagogy of the Oppressed*. London: Penguin.

Giroux, H. (2005) *Border Crossings*. New York, NY: Routledge.

Hammond, B. (2002) *DFID's Invisible Hand – A Challenge to Development Education?* Unpublished MA dissertation. UEA.

Harrison, D. (2008) *Oxfam and the Rise of Development Education in England from 1959 to 1979*. Unpublished PhD. London: Institute of Education, University of London.

Hartmeyer, H. (2008) *Experiencing the World – Global Learning in Austria: Developing, Reaching Out, Crossing Borders*. Munster: Waxmann.

Hicks, D. (2003) 'Thirty years of global education', *Education Review*, 55, 3, pp. 265–75.

Hoeck, S. and Wegimont, L. (2003) *National Structures for the Organisation, Support and Funding of Development Education*. Lisbon: Council of Europe North-South Centre.

Instituto Portugues de Apoio ao Desenvolvimento (IPAD) (2010) *National Strategy for Development Education 2010 – 2015: Portugal*. Lisbon: IPAD.

Ishii, Y. (2003) *Development Education in Japan*. New York, NY/London: Routledge.

Kirkwood-Tucker, T.F. (Ed.) *Visions in Global Education*. New York, NY: Peter Lang.

Lowe, B. (2008) 'Embedding global citizenship in primary and secondary schools: developing a methodology for measuring attitudinal change', *International Journal of Development Education and Global Learning*, 1, 1, pp. 59–64.

McCollum, A. (1996) *On the Margins? An Analysis of the Theory and Practice of Development Education in the 1900s*. Ph.D. Thesis, Open University.

Mclaren, P. (2009) 'Critical pedagogy: a look at the major concepts', in Darder, A., Baltodano, M.P. and Torres, R.D. (Eds.) *The Critical Pedagogy Reader*. New York, NY: Routledge, pp. 61–83.

Mundy, K. (2007) *Charting Global Education in Canada's Elementary Schools*. Toronto, ON: Ontario Institute for Studies in Education (OISE)/UNICEF.

Ohri, A. (1997) *The World in Our Neighbourhood*. London: DEA.

Open Space for Dialogue and Enquiry (OSDE) (2006) *OSDE Introductory Booklet*. Nottingham: Nottingham University. Available at: www.osdemethodology.org.uk/keydocs/osdebooklet.pdf. Accessed September 2010.

Osler, A. and Vincent, K. (2002) *Citizenship and the Challenge of Global Education*. Stoke-on-Trent: Trentham Books.

Oxfam (2006) *Education for Global Citizenship*. Oxford: Oxfam.

Pike, G. and Selby, D. (1988) *Global Teacher, Global Learner*. Sevenoaks: Hodder & Stoughton.

Qualification and Curriculum Authority (QCA) (2008) *The Global Dimension in Action*. London: QCA.

Rasanen, R. (2009) 'Transformative global education and learning in teacher education in Finland', *International Journal of Development Education and Global Learning*, 1, 2, pp. 25–40.

Richardson, R. (1990) *Daring to be a Teacher*. Stoke-on-Trent: Trentham Books.

Pike, G. and Selby, D. (1998) *Global Teacher, Global Learner*. Sevenoaks: Hodden and Stoughton.

Scheunpflug, A. (2008) 'Why global learning and global education? An educational approach influenced by the perspectives of Immanuel Kant', in Bourn, D. (Eds.) *Development Education: Debates and Dialogue*. London: Institute of Education.

Scheunpflug, A. and Asbrand, B. (2006) 'Global education and education for sustainability', *Environmental Education Research*, 12, 1, pp. 33–46.

Scott, W.A.H. and Gough, S.R. (2003) *Sustainable Development: Framing the Issues*. London: Routledge.

Shor, I. (1992) *Empowering Education: Critical Teaching for Social Change*. Chicago, IL: University of Chicago Press.

Tye, K. (1999) *Global Education – A Worldwide Movement*. Orange, CA: Interdependence Press.

VSO (2002) *The Live Aid Legacy*. London: VSO.

Cultural-linguistic diversity and inclusion

Robin L. Danzak, Louise C. Wilkinson
and Elaine R. Silliman
University of South Florida Sarasota-Manatee, Syracuse University
and University of South Florida

Overview

The two purposes of this chapter are to: 1) define cultural and linguistic diversity and inclusion among school-age children; and 2) review the current policy context for research on diversity and inclusion, as well as their relationships to successful schooling for culturally and linguistically diverse learners. The case of the United States is highlighted and considered within a global context. The chapter includes a discussion of current issues and trends in this area, and suggests how future research is likely to develop.

The current context for education in Europe

Cultural and linguistic diversity in the European context

Nearly ten years ago, the European Commission conducted an analysis of educational programs for immigrant children in seven countries (Italy, Greece, Great Britain, France, Sweden, Belgium, and Israel) (Collicelli, 2001). Three major conclusions were arrived at: 1) how European countries classify immigrant minors and minors of immigrant origins is unsatisfactory, varies from country to country, and makes coordination of educational policy at a European level difficult; 2) immigrant minors are too often portrayed in the media as a security problem for the host country, which then discourages attempts at educational integration and reinforces beliefs of social isolation on the part of immigrants and their children; and 3) immigrant children, because they struggle with academic language acquisition (see Chapter 14, "Language," Wilkinson and Silliman in this volume), tend to chose, or be advised to select, vocational or technical schools over high schools, which often do not have high standards; the result is limited higher education or job prospects. A total of 17 European policy recommendations were made to establish common definitions and regulations among countries.

While progress in bilingual education policy has been made on a country-by-country basis, and even a region-by region basis within countries, the European Commission recommendations for a more unified policy approach seem to remain in abeyance. England and Wales provide contrasts in this respect. The European Union (EU)-funded project, TEL2L (Teacher Education by Learning through Two Languages) (2000), which is oriented to mainstream bilingual education (MBE), reports that the integration of experimental bilingual education projects in England, the pre-professional education of bilingual teachers, and the availability of teaching materials are not national priorities. (Note: MBE aims are not directed to bilingualism, but rather to the teaching of content in a second language.) In contrast to England, the purpose of bilingual education in Wales is to protect the minority language, Welsh, from becoming extinct. Under the 1993 Welsh Language Act, Welsh and English were to be treated "on a basis of equality" (Jones and Martin-Jones, 2004, p. 52) in primary and secondary public sector schools.

Students with special needs in the European context

The European Agency for Development in Special Needs Education (2009) is an independent organization that collects and disseminates country-specific information and encourages collaboration among its 27 European Union (EU) member states along with Iceland, Norway, and Switzerland. The organization's website affords the opportunity to compare the educational policies of member countries for providing education to students with special education needs and to evaluate teacher preparation requirements to support this endeavor. As might be expected, there is major variation among countries as to: 1) legal protections for special needs students and their families (e.g. both England and France have such laws), 2) how students with physical, cognitive, or learning problems are identified and assessed (see Florian *et al.*, 2006; McLaughlin *et al.*, 2006), and 3) the scope of teacher training (whether specialized preparation is required or is optional).

Despite variations, the members of the European Agency for Development in Special Needs Education all agree at a philosophical level that, as a matter of equality of opportunity, students should receive an inclusive education in the general education classroom.

Inclusive education in England and Scotland

From a practical perspective, inclusion is an educational placement. Within the European context, implementation of the inclusion philosophy into actual practices is still confronted with many challenges, not the least of which is whether or not current inclusive education is more than "social justice" inclusion.

England and Scotland are instructive cases where educational policy supports the teaching of children with and without disabilities in the same neighborhood schools. In both United Kingdom (UK) countries, debate continues on at least five complex aspects of inclusion. These include (Allan, 2010; Hodkinson, 2010), 1) how inclusion is defined or even if it can be defined; 2) whether it should apply only to children with special educational needs or encompass as well children whose "differences" extend to race, ethnicity, culture, social class, and gender; 3) the extent to which inclusive education meshes with the national curriculum, which stresses whole-class teaching of literacy and numeracy; 4) how inclusive practices can work successfully when mainstream children still hold a negative view of disability and children with disabilities, and teachers believe that inclusion should apply only to those with mild mobility or sensory problems; and 5) the limited impact of inclusion when there is a long-standing shortage of teachers prepared in meeting special education needs combined with "the economically driven imperative" (Allan,

2010, p. 206) for general education teachers to raise achievement levels. These challenges, which reflect competing government policies and the current economics of educational funding, have compromised the promise of inclusive education in England and Scotland.

The current context for education in the United States

Two trends define contemporary US education in the first decade of the twenty-first century: 1) the persistent achievement gap among students of varied backgrounds; and 2) the emphasis on accountability in public education, with a particular focus on teacher efficacy. Both of these trends make clear the immediate, critical need for better teacher preparation and continuing professional development with respect to multicultural competence, including improving academic outcomes for bilingual and English language learner (ELL) students, as well as students who are African American.

The achievement gap

The current policy context in the United States differs in many ways from the European context. A major reason is the achievement gap, which currently drives national policy in both the general and the special education systems.

The achievement gaps among groups of children with varying socio-economic status, first language preference, and race and ethnicity represent the major challenge for US education in the early twenty-first century. Stable for decades, these gaps appear early and become amplified from first grade through high school, and even extend to higher education (Aud *et al.*, 2010). Ultimately, the negative consequences of the attainment gaps in higher education between rich and poor, and between whites and minorities, may lead to a downturn in economic mobility, making it more difficult for today's poor to move up the income ladder (Haskins *et al.*, 2009). Finally, students in the United States have not fared well on international comparisons. For example, on the Program for International Student Assessment (PISA) and the Progress in International Reading Literacy Study (PIRLS) assessment, the number of countries outperforming the US on PIRLS increased from three in 2001 to seven in 2006, among the 28 nations that participated in both tests (Organisation for Economic Cooperation and Development, 2001).

The educational impacts of cultural and linguistic diversity

The cultural and linguistic diversity of students attending public schools in the United States continues to grow. In 2008, approximately 21 percent of all school-age students were classified as English Language Learners (ELL); that is, they possessed less-than-adequate skills in English for schooling. Although Hispanic children who speak Spanish as their first language comprise the majority of the ELL population (75 per cent, Aud *et al.*, 2010), many other heritage backgrounds are represented, including students from various Asian, Middle Eastern, European, and African nations. African American school-age children comprised 16 percent of the school-age population (Aud *et al.*, 2010), a figure that represented minimal growth since 1998. The 2009 poverty rates for African American and Hispanic families remained high: 25.8 percent and 25.3 percent, respectively. Moreover, these rates increased from 2008, as did the poverty rate for Americans in general. These increases can be at least partially attributed to current economic and unemployment conditions in the US.

In addition to the varied languages spoken in US classrooms, many dialects of English are also present, from regional dialects to African American English (AAE), which can also vary by geographic area and with socio-economic status (SES) (Van Hofweven and Wolfram, 2010). The term, *dialect*, therefore, does not refer to an improper way of speaking, since every person has a dialect, but "a variety of language associated with a regionally or socially defined group of people" (Adger, Wolfram, and Christian, 2007, p. 1). Furthermore, consider the existence of regional varieties of Spanish as well, and the cultural and linguistic diversity in almost any US public school is impressive.

It is notable that 83 percent of public school teachers across the country represent white, non-Hispanic ethnic backgrounds (Coopersmith, 2009), which is inconsistent with the diversity of the student body. A positive note, however, is that the fastest growing group of non-white public school teachers are persons of Hispanic origin (National Center for Education Information (NCEI), 2005). Still, there is a growing crisis in US schools: a primarily non-diverse teacher workforce must educate an increasingly diverse student population. Although teachers, in many ways, are held accountable for student outcomes, few educators have been prepared to understand and address the strengths and challenges of culturally and linguistically diverse students and their families, as well as students with disabilities and their families, situations also found in the European context in general.

No Child Left Behind (NCLB, 2001) and teacher accountability

NCLB, a federal law, was a two-fold legislative response to the achievement gap in the United States, a crisis that included the overrepresentation of African American and ELL students in special education programs, especially in the learning (or reading) disability and oral language disability categories. This legislation was also the first time since Sputnik in the late 1950s that the federal government played such an extensive role in US education (see Chapter 14, "Language" in this volume for brief discussion of education as a function belonging to the 50 states). The legislation was propelled by the recognition that inappropriate diagnoses and placement in special education could no longer be tolerated as an inevitable outcome for many African American and ELL students who came from poor families. NCLB was also intended to raise educational expectations for students with disabilities by requiring that their learning be embedded in the general education curriculum. A basic assumption was that, by requiring all students to master learning to read, there would be reduced identification of children for special education services and fewer children with disabilities who could not read or write.

The NCLB Act also represented a radical departure from previous national practice for parents in the education of their children. Parents were provided increased educational choices, including public charter schools and private school vouchers, as well as, depending on the performance of their children's school, the option of supplemental instructional services. Never before had national legislation tied school failure so closely to parental choice. Ultimately, there was no shelter for non-performing schools, which were to be "reorganized" out of existence after consistent failure.

Since the passage of NCLB in 2001, the call for teacher accountability in the US is strong. School districts are under pressure to guarantee a skilled, "highly qualified" teacher in every public education classroom. Effective teachers are considered those whose students can demonstrate learning in a variety of venues including, most importantly, standardized tests. However, simply demanding that teachers, even "highly qualified" ones, be accountable for students' achievement on standardized tests is not enough to overcome the achievement gaps. Students with effective teachers should also be capable of achieving at each grade level, be prepared to learn the curriculum at the next level, and, eventually, graduate from high school with the skills necessary to seek higher education and/or employment. All teachers, regardless of the grade level or content area they teach, should have sufficient knowledge about language – including academic English language, to be discussed shortly – and the research-based instructional strategies to assist all students to comprehend and produce academic discourse and content (Wilkinson and Silliman, 2008).

As an example of this need, according to NCLB provisions, the assessment of ELL students' progress in English language development must align with state standards. However, in many states, current assessments in the area of English language proficiency are not necessarily designed to measure progress in language acquisition. Instead, as García and colleagues (2008) noted, very often the intended purpose of these measures is to determine students' classification into ELL services or, in contrast, their reclassification as fluent English proficient (R-FEP) status. Thus, teachers instructionally responsible for these reclassified ELL students in their classrooms are often unaware of their English language abilities, other than a percentile score. In this case, the accountability standard is negatively impacted by assessment procedures that fail to yield meaningful instructional information about the students' English language needs.

Students with special education needs

Educational policy and legal foundations

The Individuals with Disabilities Education Act (IDEA, 2004), initially passed by the US Congress in 1975 (under a different name), is a civil rights act in that it mandates that all children with handicapping conditions must be provided a free appropriate public education in the least restrictive educational setting. IDEA, therefore, provides the educational policy and legal foundations for how individual states may identify, assess, and provide instructional and intervention services for students with disabilities. Students must be formally identified as eligible to receive special education and related services (e.g. speech-language pathology intervention, occupational therapy, physical therapy, etc.) in one of the 13 existing categories of handicaps. These classifications, unlike England's needs-based approach, are categorical and based on the medical model. The categories range from specific learning disabilities, speech/language impairment, mental retardation, and emotional disturbance to other health impairments (i.e. attention deficit hyperactivity disorder), autism, hearing impairment, and deaf-blind. Each student receiving special education and related services must have an Individual Educational Plan (IEP), which parents or the legal guardian must approve.

Since 2004, IDEA has been aligned with the core premises of NCLB along two strategic principles: 1) to replace the long-standing "wait to fail" model of special education with a model of prevention through early identification and intervention in the general education classroom using "scientifically based reading instruction"; and, 2) to decrease the number of inappropriate referrals for IDEA services, particularly for the learning disabilities category. In 2007–08, 13.4 percent of school-age children were receiving special education services across the 13 categories compared with 13.8 percent in 2004–05 (US Department of Education, NCES, 2010a).

It is notable that ELL students were overrepresented in the learning disabilities category (McCardle *et al.*, 2005). In addition, language minority children with language and learning impairments are often diagnosed late as compared to their language-dominant peers. For example, while most monolingual children who were diagnosed with a learning disability were identified in 2nd or 3rd grade, ELL students tended not to receive this identification until

4th–6th grade (Wagner *et al.*, 2005). Late identification likely results in deleterious implications for the language and literacy development of these students. One challenge in effectively assessing and servicing the needs of ELL students is the great variation in this population; another is that NCLB requires ELL students to take state standardized achievement tests after only one year of English language instruction. If they perform below grade level expectations, this is erroneously taken as evidence of inadequate instruction or even of a learning disability, when the real issue is insufficient English language knowledge (Cummins, 2009).

Moreover, a process of "resegregation" (Blanchett, 2009, p. 379) may occur with African American students in urban settings who have been appropriately (or erroneously) identified with special needs under IDEA. Across the 13 disability categories, approximately 80 percent of students are mainstreamed into general education classes for 40 to 80 percent of the school day (US Department of Education, NCES, 2010b). In Blanchett's analysis, however, African American students with disabilities from poor families were more likely to receive their education full time in self-contained (segregated) classrooms, which marginalized them further and resulted in a low-quality education (Blanchett, 2009).

Response to intervention

The policy decision to reduce the unnecessary referral of students from cultural and linguistic minority groups led to an alternate model for decision-making about whether a child might need referral for a pre-existing disability. This model is a response to intervention (RTI), which accentuates how students actually respond to early reading instruction at various tiers of support. However, states still have the option of employing standardized testing rather than RTI to determine children's need for special education, especially in the areas of learning disability and speech/language impairment, which are often intertwined. Federal data (US Department of Education, NCES, 2010a) also show that, as a proportion of the total public school enrollment, the percentage of students classified with a learning disability under IDEA decreased from 6.1 percent in 2001–02 (the point at which NCLB was implemented) to 5.2 percent in 2007–08, suggesting that the prevention model as represented in RTI may have had some positive effects on beginning reading ability. However, the speech/language disability category showed no decrease, while the autism and other health impairment categories (attention deficit hyperactivity disorder) increased over the same period. Growth in the autism category, for example, has been attributed to earlier identification (Lord and Bishop, 2010). A critical issue that has not been addressed, however, is the validity of the diagnostic criteria applied either in RTI programs or to standardized testing for determining special education eligibility (Silliman and Berninger, 2011).

Inclusive education

In contrast to inclusion as an educational philosophy and policy in many countries of the European context, IDEA does not mention inclusion as an educational placement. Instead, IDEA requires that decisions must be made first on a child's educational needs and only then can an educational placement be considered based on a flexible continuum of services, from the least restrictive setting (mainstreaming in the general education classroom, a form of partial integration, with support services provided on a "pull-out" basis) to more restrictive settings (self-contained classroom to a separate residential facility).

In practice, the US inclusion literature on academic outcomes for students with disabilities (and mainstreaming in general) has been mixed. Difficulties in comparing inclusion studies are hampered by marked variations in (Klingner *et al.*, 1998; Salend and Duhaney, 1999): 1) the individual differences of students selected for inclusive classrooms, such as the type and severity of their disabilities; 2) the extent to which special education support is provided in inclusive classrooms; and 3) teacher attitudes, degree of expertise, and consultative support available for working effectively with students with disabilities.

Trends and issues

The challenge of academic language proficiency

Notwithstanding their linguistic, cultural, or educational backgrounds, ELL and African American students, as well as students with language and learning disabilities, who are struggling with literacy must acquire academic English language proficiency – including the various tasks of literacy – in order to succeed in school. The task confronting ELL students is more complex because many have not yet fully acquired conversational English language skills. Distinct from everyday conversational skills, academic English language skills include, among others (Bailey, 2008; Carhill *et al.*, 2008): 1) active knowledge of both generalized academic vocabulary and specialized (discipline-specific) vocabulary; 2) the ability to comprehend and produce varied text structures and functions including discourse that compares, explains, describes, or argues; and 3) the ability to make inferences, summarize, and critique information.

For these three groups of struggling students, academic language skills may require years to develop (Cummins, 2009). In fact, in a longitudinal study on the development of academic language proficiency of adolescent, newcomer ELLs, Carhill *et al.* (2008) found that, after residing in the US for nearly seven years, only 19 out of 274 students (7.4 per cent of the sample) scored at or above norms for age-equivalent English speakers on a standardized English language proficiency test. Less is known about closing the academic language gap for African American students and even less about bridging this chasm for students with language and learning disabilities.

Frameworks for educating diverse learners

Over a decade ago, Valenzuela (1999) used the term "subtractive schooling" (p. 27) to describe how assimilatory models of language-majority schools can be detrimental to culturally and linguistically diverse students. For example, practices of subtractive schooling include the tracking of ELL and African American students into "regular" or even remedial courses (rather than honors/AP), devaluation of the students' cultural and linguistic resources, stereotypical beliefs, and low expectations, including minimal expectations for students in special education. From a subtractive perspective for ELLs, their first language and culture are perceived as "difficulties," or "problems," that must be overcome. This perspective aligns with a deficit construct and frames traditional, sink-or-swim, English-only strategies for ELLs, as well as early-exit transitional bilingual programs whose goal is rapid assimilation. That is, early on, students' L1 is supported, but it is phased out, usually within the first three years, in favor of English-only instruction.

Although bilingual models have been shown to be more effective in promoting ELL achievement than English-only programs (Francis *et al.*, 2006), bilingual education is not always available or feasible due to funding, staffing, or policy, issues. Therefore, school districts often adapt a sheltered approach to English-only education (García and Kleifgan, 2008). Ideally this occurs through language arts classes specifically designed for ELLs, as well as through the application of ELL instructional strategies across the content areas. This model is best supported by quality teacher professional development for educators at all levels and disciplines.

A goal to reach for is buttressed by empirical findings that support an additive language-learning environment. This language-learning context embraces ELLs' home language and experiences as resources (i.e., their funds of knowledge; Moll *et al.*, 1992), which can both enrich the classroom/school community and support the students' academic English language acquisition. This perspective is put into practice by late-exit bilingual programs, heritage language programs (e.g. a Spanish for Spanish-speakers class), and the two-way (dual-language) immersion model. Unfortunately, these kind of additive programs are few in number in US schools.

In summary, in the context of school, academic language and literacy serve as means to acquire access and experience; therefore, they represent sources of symbolic capital in the classroom/school community (Christian and Bloome, 2004; Toohey, 2000). This implies that, similar to monolingual English-speaking students, culturally and linguistically different students who possess the experience, tools, and resources to acquire academic language proficiency early on are more likely to successfully meet the demands of school. Unfortunately, those who do not are more likely to lack the necessary symbolic capital and, thus, become excluded from the cultural practices of schooling (i.e. literacy instruction) that they do not identify with (Danzak and Silliman, 2005). Culturally and linguistically diverse students and students with disabilities are more likely to experience this disconnect. Without strong support to engage and develop their academic English language proficiency, these students are at risk of diminished interest in school and falling through the cracks.

Conclusion

This chapter has summarized the current policy context for the education of culturally and linguistically diverse learners in Europe and the US. While educational policy and trends differ in many respects within the European Union and certainly vary in comparison with the US, there are many similarities. Shared trends include: 1) increasing diversity in public school classrooms leading to achievement gaps related to SES and race/ethnicity as students fail to acquire the level of academic language proficiency required to succeed in school; 2) a move toward higher levels of teacher accountability for student achievement, including ELL (or immigrated) students and students with disabilities; and 3) philosophical and practical commitments in difficult economic times to inclusive education for students with disabilities, more so in the European Union than in the US.

In the face of these gaps, it becomes clear that a focus of instruction for all students, including ELLs and students with disabilities, should be on the acquisition of the academic English language skills that support students' success in school. However, this being said, literacy – and other school subjects – cannot be taught as decontextualized, instructed practices. Reducing the cultural practice of literacy to an autonomous set of discrete skills does little to improve the achievement of culturally and linguistically diverse students (Gee, 2004). Instead, educators, whatever their country of residence, must work to discover and integrate students' meaningful life experiences with language and literacy practices. This process involves the rejection of a deficit perspective in exchange for a focus on students' strengths. These strengths can include understanding of cultural and linguistic diversity as resources that contribute to learning and development, not only for the ELL student, but also for the entire classroom and school community.

Questions for further investigation

1 How can we develop and implement valid, practical assessments that effectively portray the language and academic abilities of English language learners? There is a critical need for continuous assessment of the English language and literacy development of ELLs after they are placed in this category (Bailey, 2010).
2 How might we better identify and serve ELL students with language learning disabilities?
3 What changes need to be made in teacher preparation programs to empower all teachers to successfully work with culturally and linguistically diverse students?

Suggested further reading

Hodkinson, A. (2010) 'Inclusive and special education in the English educational system: Historical perspectives, recent developments, and future challenges', *British Journal of Special Education, 37*, pp. 61–67. This article presents a detailed discussion of the promises and pitfalls of inclusive education against a historical backdrop.

Lenski, L., Mack, C. and Esparza, J. (2008) 'Critical elements for literacy instruction in urban settings', in Wilkinson, L., Morrow, L. and Chou, V. (Eds.) *Improving literacy achievement in urban schools: Critical elements in teacher preparation*. Newark, DE: International Reading Association. This chapter reviews the significance and mechanics of how understanding of linguistics-cultural diversity is essential or optimal teacher effectiveness.

Wilkinson, L. and Silliman, E. (2008) 'Academic language proficiency and literacy instruction in urban settings', in Wilkinson, L., Morrow, L. and Chou, V. (Eds.) *Improving literacy achievement in urban schools: Critical elements in teacher preparation*. Newark, DE: International Reading Association, pp. 121–142. This chapter defines academic language in the context of linguistics-cultural diversity of contemporary schools and shows the connections to improving student achievement.

References

Adger, C.T., Wolfram, W. and Christian, D. (2007) *Dialects in schools and communities* (2nd Ed.). Mahwah, NJ: Lawrence Erlbaum Associates.

Allan, J. (2010) 'Questions of inclusion in Scotland and Europe', *European Journal of Special Needs Education, 25*, pp. 199–208.

Aud, S., Fox, M. and Kewal Ramani, A. (2010) *Status and trends in the education of racial and ethnic groups* (NCES 2010–015). US Department of Education, National Center for Education Statistics. Washington, DC: US Government Printing Office.

Aud, S., Hussar, W., Planty, M., Snyder, T., Bianco, K. and Fox, M. (2010) *The condition of education 2010* (NCES 2010–028). US Department of Education, National Center for Education Statistics, Institute of Education Sciences. Washington, DC: US Government Printing Office.

Bailey, A. (Ed.) (2008) *The language demands of school: Putting academic English to the test*. New Haven, CN: Yale University Press.

Bailey, A. (2010) 'Implications for assessment and instruction', in Shatz, M. and Wilkinson, L. (Eds.) *The education of English language learners: Research to practice*. New York, NY: Guilford, pp. 222–247.

Blanchett, W.J. (2009) 'A retrospective examination of urban education: From Brown to the resegregation of African Americans in special education – it's time to "go for broke"', *Urban Education*, 44, pp. 370–388.

Carhill, A., Suarez-Orozco, C. and Paez, M. (2008) 'Explaining English language proficiency among adolescent immigrant students', *American Education Research Journal*, 45, pp. 1155–1179.

Christian, B. and Bloome, D. (2004) 'Learning to read is who you are', *Reading and Writing Quarterly*, 20, pp. 365–384.

Collicelli, C. (2001) *Integrating immigrant children into Europe, briefing paper 17*. Available at: www.pjb.co.uk/npl/bp.17.pdf (accessed 15 September 2010).

Coopersmith, J. (2009) *Characteristics of public, private, and bureau of Indian education elementary and secondary School Teachers in the United States: Results from the 2007–08 schools and staffing survey* (NCES 2009–324). US Department of Education, National Center for Education Statistics, Institute of Education Sciences. Washington, DC: US Government Printing Office.

Cummins, J. (2009) 'Literacy and English-language learners: A shifting landscape for students, teachers, researchers, and policy makers', *Educational Researcher*, 38, pp. 382–385.

Danzak, R.L. and Silliman, E. (2005) 'Does my identity speak English? A pragmatic approach to the social world of an English language learner', *Seminars in Speech and Language*, 26, pp. 1–15.

European Agency for Development in Special Needs Education (2009). Available at: www.european-agency.org/about-us (accessed 23 September 2010).

Florian, L., Hollenweger, J., Simeonsson, R.J., Wedell, K., Riddell, S., Terzi, L., and Holland, A. (2006) 'Cross-cultural perspectives on the classification of children with disabilities: Part I: Issues in the classification of children with disabilities', *The Journal of Special Education*, 40, pp. 36–45.

Francis, D.J., Lesaux, N.K. and August, D.L. (2006) 'Language of instruction for language minority learners', in August, D.L. and Shanahan, T. (Eds.) *Developing literacy in a second language: Report of the National Literacy Panel*. Mahwah, NJ: Lawrence Erlbaum, pp. 365–414.

Garcia, O. (2008) 'From English language learners to emergent bilinguals', *Equity Matters*, 1. New York, NY: Teachers College.

Garcia, O. and Kleifgen, J. (2008). *Educating Emergent Bilinguals: Policies, Programs, and Practices for English Language Learners*. New York: Teachers College Press.

Gee, J.P. (2004). *Situated language and learning: A Critique of traditional schooling*. New York, NY: Routledge.

Haskins, R., Holzer, H. and Lerman, R. (2009) 'Promoting economic mobility by increasing postsecondary education'. *The Brookings Institution and the Pew Charitable Trusts*. 2 May. Available at: www.pewtrusts.org/uploadedFiles/wwwpewtrustsorg/Reports/Economic_Mobility/PEW_EM_Haskins%207.pdf (accessed 11 October 2010).

Hodkinson, A. (2010) 'Inclusive and special education in the English educational system: Historical perspectives, recent developments, and future challenges', *British Journal of Special Education*, 37, pp. 61–67.

Jones, D.V. and Martin-Jones, M. (2004) 'Bilingual education and language revitalization in Wales: Past achievements and current issues' in Tollefson, W. and Tsui, A. (Eds.) *Medium of instruction policies: Which agenda?* Mahwah, NJ: Lawrence Erlbaum Associates, pp. 43–70.

Klingner, J.K., Vaughn, S., Hughes, M.T., Schumm, J.S. and Elbaum, B. (1998) 'Outcomes for students with and without learning disabilities in inclusive classrooms', *Learning Disabilities Research & Practice*, 13, pp. 153–161.

Lord, C. and Bishop, S.L. (2010) 'Autism Spectrum Disorders: Diagnosis, prevalence, and services for children and families', *Social Policy Report of the Society for Research in Child Development*, 24, 2, pp. 1–26.

McCardle, P., Mele-McCarthy, J., Cutting, L., Leos, K. and D'Emilio, T. (2005) 'Learning disabilities in English language learners: Identifying the issues', *Learning Disabilities Research and Practice*, 20, pp. 1–5.

McLaughlin, M.J., Dyson, A., Nagle, K., Thurlow, M., Rouse, M., Hardman, M., Norwich, B., Burke, P.J. and Perlin, M. (2006) 'Cross-cultural perspectives on the classification of children with disabilities: Part II. Implementing classification systems in schools', *Journal of Special Education*, 40, pp. 46–58.

Moll, L.C., Amanti, C., Neff, D. and González, N. (1992) 'Funds of knowledge for teachers: Using a qualitative approach to connect homes and classrooms', *Theory into Practice*, 31, pp. 132–141.

National Center for Education Information (NCEI) (2005) 'Profile of teachers in the U.S 2005'. Available at: www.ncei.com/POT05PRESSREL3.htm (accessed 21 September 2010).

No Child Left Behind Act (2001) L. No. 107–110, 115 Stat. 1425 (enacted 8 January 2002).

Organisation for Economic Cooperation and Development (2001) 'Knowledge and skills for life: First results from PISA 2000'. Paris: OECD.

Salend, S.J. and Duhaney, L.M.G. (1999) 'The impact of inclusion on students with and without disabilities and their educators', *Remedial and Special Education, 20*, pp. 114–126.

Silliman, E. R. and Berninger, V.W. (2011) 'Cross-disciplinary dialogue about the nature of oral and written language problems in the context of developmental, academic, and phenotypic profiles', *Topics in Language Disorders, 31*, 6–23.

Teacher Education by Learning through Two Languages (2000). Available at: www.unavarra.es/tel2l/eng/menu.htm (accessed 18 September 2010).

Toohey, K. (2000) *Learning English at school: Identity, social relations and classroom practice*. Clevedon: Multilingual Matters.

US Department of Education, National Center for Education Statistics (2010a) '*Conditions of education 2010, Table A-6-1*'. Available at: http://nces.ed.gov/programs/coe/2010/section1/table-cwd-1.asp (accessed 20 September 2010).

US Department of Education, National Center for Education Statistics (2010b) '*Conditions of education 2010, Table A-6-2*'. Available at: http://nces.ed.gov/programs/coe/2010/section1/table-cwd-2.asp (accessed 20 September 2010).

Valenzuela, A. (1999) *Subtractive schooling: US-Mexican youth and the politics of caring*. Albany, NY: State University of New York Press.

Van Hofweven, J. and Wolfram, W. (2010) 'Coming of age in African American English: A longitudinal study', *Journal of Sociolinguistics, 14*, 427–455.

Wagner, R.K., Francis, D.J. and Morris, R.D. (2005) 'Identifying English language learners with learning disabilities: Key challenges and possible approaches', *Learning Disabilities Research & Practice, 20*, pp. 6–15.

Wilkinson, L. and Silliman, E. (2008) 'Academic language proficiency and literacy instruction in urban settings', in Wilkinson, L., Morrow, L. and Chou, V. (Eds.) *Improving literacy achievement in urban schools: Critical elements in teacher preparation*. Newark, DE: International Reading Association, pp. 121–142.

29

Neuroscience and education

Jodi Tommerdahl
University of Texas at Arlington

Overview

This chapter will discuss the emergence of a field of study currently being created through the interaction between neuroscience and education. It will briefly present commonly used tools and techniques before discussing important existing research trajectories in educational studies. A host of vibrant debates as well as accepted difficulties in this new domain will then be explored before examining possible future directions of the field.

Introduction

The press is awash with reports of how the brain functions and learns. Colourful brain images showing hotspots of activity linked to mental manipulations have become commonplace in our daily lives. Neuroscience has made an impression on language and culture with most of us being familiar with expressions such as "being right or left brained". Neuroscience has branched out in several areas such as ethics (Gazzaniga, 2005; Glannon, 2006) and economics (Lee *et al.*, 2007) as we humans hunger not only to understand ourselves, but also to understand *how* we understand ourselves. It is not surprising that advances in neuroscience's understanding of the brain have led many to ask whether this knowledge will provide insight into our own learning processes which will allow us to develop more effective, evidence-based teaching practices.

Brain-based research existed for centuries, but this has radically intensified in recent decades. This is reflected by the number of institutions developing specialization in education linked to the neurosciences. Harvard University developed a Masters level programme in Mind, Brain and Education and a sister programme is under development at the University of Texas in Arlington. The American Educational Research Association (AERA) has a special interest group in neuroscience and education and both Cambridge and Oxford universities have laboratories dedicated to the use of neuroscience in education.

The 1990s were officially declared the decade of the brain by the US government. In 2007, the Organisation for Economic Cooperation and Development (OECD) published a 250-page report on brain research in education, stating that although there is a lack of consensus on applications of brain research to education, that "there are strong various reasons for fostering the pioneering brain and learning centres and promoting the creation of more bridges between the two research communities" (OECD, 2007, p. 3).

The above quote makes clear that not all is settled in the courtship between education and the neurosciences. This is also shown by the fact that no one name for this emerging field has become accepted. Amongst the many monikers put forward so far are 'Educational neuroscience' (Pettito and Dunbar, 2004), 'Neurolearning' (Bruer, 2003) and 'Neuroscience and Education' (Goswami, 2004). This chapter will present the accomplishments of this fledgling field along with its challenges, actual and potential.

Tools

Techniques such as reaction times, preferential looking and the study of patients with brain lesions have allowed researchers to make inferences about brain function for decades. However, the progress in our ability to monitor the biological activities of the brain in response to particular stimuli has rapidly expanded with the development and improvement of neurological tools. An overview of some of these follows. Tools will be categorized by their membership into one of two groups: one that focuses on identifying the physical location of brain activity, thereby providing spatial information, and the other which provides information about the timing of brain activity, or temporal information (not to be confused with the *temporal* lobe of the brain). Both spatial and temporal information about brain activity are useful. Spatial information provides information about what areas of the brain are active during specific tasks. This can lead to insight regarding which areas work together in complex tasks. Temporal information, on the other hand, shows exactly how long after a stimulus a certain type of processing is carried out. This allows us to make inferences about whether a certain aspect of processing is carried out before or after another. Ideally, both spatial and temporal information are used in conjunction to build a fuller picture of where, when and in what order aspects of cognitive processing are carried out. Unfortunately, neuroscientific techniques that monitor brain activity tend to have either high spatial *or* temporal accuracy, but not both.

Amongst the tools most commonly used in the research of cognitive activity are the fMRI (functional Magnetic Resonance Imaging), PET (Positron Emission Tomography), MEG (magnetoencephalogram) and the EEG (electroencephalogram), the first two being primarily spatial tools and the last two being mainly temporal. The fMRI and the PET both provide images of the working brain, but using different sources of measurement. In a PET scan, a radioactive isotope is injected, allowing the amount of glucose being metabolized in the brain to become visible. The metabolization of glucose indicates the amount of blood used in each part of the brain which in turn represents brain activity. Despite the high-quality images that PET provides, the need for radioactive material, its poor temporal resolution and high cost are all disadvantages (Otte and Halsband, 2006).

The fMRI provides images of the brain by measuring bloodflow. As with PET, higher blood flow indicates greater neural activity. The fMRI performs better on both the spatial (1–3mm) and temporal fronts (1 or more seconds) than the PET scan and is less expensive to operate. Its major drawback is the noise produced, making it inappropriate for certain kinds of studies.

The MEG and EEG are both commonly used for exploring the time course of cognitive processing due to their high-quality temporal resolution with measurements in milliseconds. Both give detailed information about the time course of studied activities. Both give some indications of locations, but not with the degree of accuracy of the spatial instruments described above. However, the MEG has much better spatial resolution than the EEG because the EEG measures the electrical fields of the cortex which are greatly distorted when passing through the convolutions of the brain matter and then the skull. The MEG, on the other hand, is measuring magnetic fields which are less prone to this distortion. The disadvantages of the MEG in relation to the EEG, however, are its lack of mobility and its cost.

Debates

Controversy existing within the hybrid field linking neuroscience and education has already been alluded to. At the most basic level, the question of the usefulness of this new combination has been repeatedly put forward. The range of opinions is broad. Bruer (1997) acknowledges that educators should rightly be interested in how the brain functions but goes on to clearly state "Neuroscience has discovered a great deal about neurons and synapses, but not nearly enough to guide educational practice". The author advises a 'wait and see' attitude towards applying neural findings to the classroom. Davis (2004) writes that medical models of cognition "have only a very limited role in the broader field of education", and argues that the brain sciences cannot investigate the intentional states of the individual related to learning. In opposition, Pettito and Dunbar (2004) go as far as to say that this new discipline "provides the most relevant level of analysis for resolving today's core problems in education". Several other articles published on the topic fall somewhere in between these examples (Goswami, 2004; Ansari and Coch, 2006; Wasserman, 2007; Willingham and Lloyd, 2007; Tommerdahl, 2010).

An important variation of this argument can be made by those who admit that neuroscientific findings are indeed applicable to better understanding and manipulating the learning process, but who note the lack of an existing pathway between the laboratory findings and classroom applications. The importance and difficulty of linking these two ends of a trajectory have been noted (Huttenlocher, 2003; Szűcs and Goswami, 2007; Tommerdahl, 2010). Given that most neuroscience researchers are not experts in education and that educators are equally unlikely to be competent in accurately understanding findings published in neuroscience journals, the melding of the areas calls out for a (or more possibly, several levels of) go-between. These go-betweens or *translators*, if you will, need to encompass the language, philosophies and epistemologies of the two fields (Samuels, 2009) as well as specific bodies of research and particular areas of need. Although people with this knowledge are likely to exist in some fields such as cognitive and educational psychology, the appetite of some for neuroscience to fill in educational holes has led to the phenomenon of the *neuromyth*, or unsubstantiated links made between neurological findings and ideas of how people learn such as the idea that people are 'right-brained' or 'left-brained' or that learning two languages at the same time will confuse a child as the languages compete for brain resources (OECD, 2007). Some neuromyths have even been packaged as brain-based educational material, used in today's classrooms with no evidence of efficacy. This has the potential to be disastrous to the burgeoning field of education and neuroscience as educators lose faith in taking the brain into consideration in the classroom as they see mismarketed products that fail to support child learning. An appropriate bridge between neuroscience and education will be not only one relating the theories and needs of two fields, but also of educational design and rigorous testing of those designs.

Several topical debates such as whether neuroscience is appropriate for studying the individual as opposed to groups, whether there are critical timeframes for learning, and to what extent neuroscience will influence teaching and learning, also exist, but possibly the most important question to answer is how the two fields will communicate and work together.

Current state

An interesting question to ask of a new field, one too young to yet even have a name, regards its current state of achievement. Ideally, the mixture of the brain sciences and education would result in a wide array of teaching and learning methods with a rigorously tested, scientific evidence base stemming from knowledge of brain processing. How far have we come towards this goal? Has the surface yet been scratched? This section aims to answer this question and to give some snapshots of studies that exemplify both the accomplishments and the possibilities of this emerging field.

Mathematics

Our understanding of how the human brain processes numbers has expanded rapidly in recent years. An article by Dehaene *et al.* (2003) is notable in that it uses earlier research findings in numerosity to develop a new hypothesis of brain circuits used in arithmetic before linking this new model to education. In the article, Dehaene describes how his model is built on findings from areas including developmental behavioural testing, animal cognition, neuroimaging, neuropsychology and brain stimulation experiments. The article then presents a model of a three-part system for carrying out arithmetic processes. They propose three separate mechanisms or circuits housed in different areas of the brain which can work together to manipulate numbers. The first proposed circuit is said to carry out quantity processing and takes the form of an internal number line. A second circuit is responsible for number manipulation in a verbal form and is connected to the linguistic system and a third is accountable for the orientation of attention onto the number line.

The article then makes predictions about expected types of developmental dyscalculia or trouble in the representation and/or manipulation of numbers that should be seen in some children. The first type would regard difficulties with the first circuit described above which would hinder the processing of quantity while the second would be due to a breakdown in the linguistic system which carries phonological and semantic information about numbers. While evidence from consecutive research has had varying results (Temple and Sherwood, 2002; Landerl *et al.*, 2004), predictions such as those put forward here allow for the creation of educational theories which can be tested in children learning arithmetic. This article is an excellent example of neuroscience's ability to take a complex skill such as arithmetic or reading and to better understand it by breaking it down into subcomponents which can then be studied both independently and in cooperation.

Literacy

Literacy is probably the area with the greatest overlap between the neuroscientific and educational fields. We will not go into great detail in this section as thorough reviews of the area already exist. These will be referred to in the *suggestions for further reading* section at the end of this chapter. What is special about literacy is that not only has much been learned about the reading process from neuroscience studies, but also the research results from literacy have contributed to our more general knowledge of how the brain develops. Furthermore, educational interventions in the area of literacy have used neuroscience, along with behavioural methods, to verify their efficacy.

The representative paper chosen for presentation here is McCandliss *et al.*'s (2003) development of a model of written word perception. This is closely related to the proposed existence of a brain region called the Visual Word Form Area (VWFA), said to be responsible for recognition of commonly experienced words in their written form. The process of recognizing a written word necessarily begins with visual aspects of processing marks on a page before moving to phonological and semantic processing. An area in the left fusiform gyrus has been shown to be responsive to both real words and made-up words that fit the spelling rules of the language in question as opposed to pseudowords that break orthographic principles (Cohen *et al.*, 2002). The existence of this VWFA explains how competent readers recognize common words as quickly and efficiently as they do. It may also explain why it does not take readers longer to recognize a word made of six letters than one of three letters (Nazir *et al.*, 1998). McCandliss *et al.* discuss the fact that people with dyslexia have been shown to have a less active VWFA than normal readers and refers to the educational study (Temple, 2003) where a targeted intervention correlates with increasing brain activity in the vicinity of the VWFA while also significantly improving reading ability.

What is particularly interesting about McCandliss *et al.*'s paper is that it asks the question of how this VWFA could come into being considering the relatively recent development of reading compared to the amount of time required to develop circuits through evolution. The answer proposed is a developmental process where experience in reading drives the specialization of a pre-existing system. This fits well with findings that the VWFA is not limited strictly to word forms, but is also used for the visual processing of other objects. This is an interesting notion regarding the plasticity of our brains and our ensuing ability to become experts in certain areas due to relatively rapid cortical adaptation. It is clear that our learning capacities are not completely constrained by evolutionary development. We are of course limited by the limits of our brain matter and its degree of plasticity, but it also appears that we can call upon brain areas which came into being for very specific demands and bootstrap new abilities onto them.

Special education

Perhaps the most promising area for the near future is the impact that neuroscience could have on the education of students with special educational needs such as dyslexia, dyscalculia and learning difficulties. It is not surprising that scientists learn about cognitive systems of learning by comparing normally functioning systems with those that are different in some way. This is true for those who study behaviour as well; for example, much can be learned about normal interactional skills by comparing typically developing children with those on the autistic spectrum. Furthermore, much has been learned about normal language processing by studying people with aphasia, or language loss due to acquired brain damage. It is perhaps only natural for the first product of this knowledge to be therapy for aphasics although general language learning applications for the mainstream population may also be eventually developed.

Using neuroscience in a way that may be influential to special education is exemplified by a study carried out by Molfese (2000). Using evoked response potentials (ERPs), the author was able to make predictions within the first 36 hours of infants' lives whether they would later fit into one of three reading groups: normal, poor or dyslexic readers. The difference between the poor and dyslexic readers were that while poor readers have a below average IQ, dyslexic readers have a normal IQ. His predictions were then followed up eight years later with IQ (Wechsler, 1991) and reading tests (Wilkinson, 1993).

The testing paradigm examined children's ability to discriminate between particular elements in sound combinations while electrodes recorded brain activity. Analyses showed early auditory processing responses which allowed the researcher to place the infants into the three groups. Final results showed predictions to be 81.25 per cent accurate as seven out of seven poor readers, 13 of 17 children with dyslexia and 19 out of 24 normal readers were correctly identified. Although the initial predictions were imperfect, the author points out that from an educational point of view, had language/reading interventions been put into place as early as possible based on the early ERP predictions, 22 out of 24 requiring support could have received it while five out of 24 children would have received support unnecessarily. ERPs therefore identified 92 per cent of the children needing early intervention.

Although research findings such as these do not tell us explicitly how to teach literacy, it provides a necessary first step in identifying children at risk of developing educational difficulties. While current practices might be able to identify poor reading or dyslexia around the age of nine or ten years (Molfese, 2000), methods such as the one described above would identify children at risk at a much earlier age, thereby allowing appropriate interventions to be put into place. Of course, this implies that information gleaned from the brain sciences is only a beginning. Several stages such as the development of interventions and their rigorous testing remain for educationalists to carry out.

Looking towards the future

Current work shows the neurosciences to be methodically exploring the neurological substrates of various aspects of cognition. Although this chapter has discussed only a few of these, other areas such as attention, emotional regulation and reasoning abilities are under study as well. One roadblock to advancing our knowledge of these systems is the difficulty in using neuroimaging equipment on children. Hopefully, technological advances in this area along with continued work with children in other modalities will allow researchers to build a cognitive map identifying brain circuits, their function and their ability to interact with each other in a way that will model our basic cognitive capacities.

As the above research continues, educationalists have the challenging task of developing interventions designed to support learning based on findings from the brain-based sciences and subjecting them to rigorous testing. It seems likely that early interventions will focus on the support of children with special needs, based on cognitive maps which pinpoint circuits or mechanisms that could be damaged and leading to processing breakdowns. Simultaneously, researchers must pay close attention to whether a difference in a particular brain area (such as the VWFA discussed earlier) is a cause of a learning difficulty or is simply correlated with it.

Connections between the laboratory results and the learning of children are still fragile. The direction of current research, matched with the interest in the brain sciences shown by professional educators, shows much promise for teachers and learners of the future.

Questions for further investigation

1 Consider the teaching methods that you are currently using or studying. Can you find the source of these methods? Is there an evidence base for their efficacy? If not, how could one be developed?
2 Think about your main subject area that you hope to teach. How much do you know about neuroscientific research in that area? Attempt to find the major works in your field.
3 Does the emerging field of neuroscience and education reduce children to heaps of neurons or can it be used while taking the individual characteristics of the child into account?

Suggested further reading

Gabrieli, J. (2009) 'Dyslexia: a new synergy between education and cognitive neuroscience', *Science, 325*, pp. 280–283. This article discusses causes, screening and treatment of dyslexia.
OECD (2007) *Understanding the Brain: The Birth of a Learning Science*. This book is a free web download from *www.oecd.org/dataoecd/39/53/40554190.pdf* which provides a clear introduction to several topics such as how the brain learns, literacy and numeracy and the existence of 'neuromyths'.
The Journal of Mind, Brain and Education. This journal began in 2007 to provide a forum for the presentation of research in cognitive science and education. It won the 2007 award of Best New Journal in the Social Sciences & Humanities by the Association of American Publishers' Professional & Scholarly Publishing (PSP) Division.

References

Ansari, D. and Coch, D. (2006) 'Bridges over troubled waters: education and cognitive neuroscience', *Trends in Cognitive Sciences, 10*, pp. 146–151.
Bruer, J.T. (1997) 'Education and the brain: a bridge too far', *Educational Researcher 26*, pp. 4–16.
Bruer, J.T. (2003) 'Learning and technology: a view from cognitive science', in H.F. O'Neil and R.S. Perez (eds) *Technology Applications in Education: a Learning View*. Hillsdale, NJ: Lawrence Erlbaum Associates, pp. 159–172.
Cohen, L., Lehéricy, S. Chochon, F., Lemer, C., Rivaud, S. and Dehaene, S. (2002) 'Language-specific tuning of visual cortex? Functional properties of the Visual Word Form Area', *Brain, 125*, 5, pp. 1054–1069.
Davis, A. (2004) 'The credentials of brain-based learning', *Journal of Philosophy of Education, 38*, pp. 21–36.
Dehaene, S., Piazza, M., Pinel, P. and Cohen, L. (2003) 'Three parietal circuits for number processing', *Cognitive Neuropsychology, 20*, pp. 487–506.
Gazzaniga, M.S. (2005) *The Ethical Brain*. New York, NY: Dana Press.
Glannon, W. (2006) *Bioethics and the Brain*. New York, NY: Oxford University Press.
Goswami, U. (2004) 'Neuroscience, education and special education', *British Journal of Special Education, 31*, pp. 175–183.
Huttenlocher, P. (2003) 'Basic neuroscience research has important implications for child development', *Nature Neuroscience, 6*, p. 541.

Landerl, K., Bevan, A. and Butterworth, B. (2004) 'Developmental dyscalculia and basic numerical capacities: a study of 8–9-year-old students', *Cognition*, *93*, pp. 99–125.

Lee N., Broderick A.J. and Chamberlain, L. (2007) 'What is "neuromarketing"? A discussion and agenda for future research', *International Journal of Psychophysiology*, *63*, 2, pp. 199–204.

McCandliss, B., Cohen, L. and Dehaene, S. (2003) 'The visual word form area: expertise for reading in the fusiform gyrus', *Trends in Cognitive Neurosciences*, *7*, 7, pp. 293–299.

Molfese, D. (2000) 'Predicting dyslexia at 8 years of age using neonatal brain responses', *Brain and Language*, *72*, pp. 238–245.

Nazir, T.A., Jacobs, A.M. and O'Regan, J.K. (1998) 'Letter legibility and visual word recognition', *Memory and Cognition*, *26*, pp. 810–821.

OECD (2007) *Understanding the Brain: The Birth of a Learning Science*. Paris: OECD Publishing.

Otte, A. and Halsband, U. (2006) 'Brain imaging tools in neurosciences', *Journal of Physiology-Paris*, *99*, pp. 281–292.

Pettito, L.A. and Dunbar, K. (2004) 'New findings from educational neuroscience on bilingual brains, scientific brains and the educated mind', *MBE/Harvard Conference*. October 6–8, 2004.

Samuels, B. (2009) 'Can the differences between education and neuroscience be overcome by mind, brain, and education?', *Mind, Brain, and Education*, *3*, 1, pp. 45–55.

Szűcs, D. and Goswami, U. (2007) 'Educational neuroscience: defining a new discipline for the study of mental representations', *Mind, Brain, and Education*, *1*, 3, pp. 114–127.

Temple, E. (2003) 'Neural deficits in children with dyslexia ameliorated by behavioral remediation: evidence from functional fMRI', *Proceedings of the National Academy of Sciences, USA*, *100*, pp. 2860–2865.

Temple, C.M. and Sherwood, S. (2002) 'Representation and retrieval of arithmetical facts: developmental difficulties', *Quarterly Journal of Experimental Psychology*, *55A*, 3, pp. 733–752.

Tommerdahl, J. (2010) 'A model for bridging the gap between neuroscience and education', *Oxford Review of Education*, *36*, 1, pp. 97–109.

Wasserman, L.H. (2007) 'The correlation between brain development, language acquisition, and cognition', *Early Childhood Education Journal*, *34*, pp. 415–418.

Wechsler, D. (1991) *Wechsler Intelligence Scales for Children*. New York, NY: The Psychological Corporation.

Wilkinson, G.S. (1993) *Wide Range Achievement Test*. Wilmington, NC: Wide Range.

Willingham, D.T. and Lloyd, J.W. (2007) 'How educational theories can use neuroscientific data', *Mind, Brain, and Education*, *1*, pp. 140–149.

30

Gender

Vanita Sundaram
University of York

Overview

The rationale for this chapter is to:

- examine the significance of gender to education in an international perspective;
- examine competing explanations for differences in educational opportunity, participation and attainment between men and women;
- explore the future development of the field of gender and global education, with specific reference to ongoing monitoring and evaluation of gender equality in national contexts.

Introduction

This chapter is divided into four parts. It begins with a brief outline of the nature of gender, seeking to introduce readers to predominant explanations for behavioural, and other, differences between boys and girls/men and women. Second, the chapter introduces key scholarship within the field of gender and global education, focusing specifically on issues of access, participation and outcomes in education. Third, we explore the future development of gender and global education, paying particular attention to the definitions of gender equality employed in international policy and scholarship, and the implications for combating gender-based discrimination in education. Last, we consider the need for ongoing monitoring of progress towards achieving gender equity in education, including the development of appropriate measures and indicators with which we can document and evaluate gender equity. This is particularly important in terms of the accountability of high-level stakeholders, such as governments and international aid agencies.

What is gender?

Men and women tend to behave in different ways across society as a whole, as well as in education in particular. Many theorists have sought to explain these patterns of behavioural difference, as well as the many instances where individual men and women behave atypically, or where groups of men and women behave similarly. Explanations for the differences observed between men and women mainly address two theoretical perspectives: the position that behavioural differences between men and women are due to inevitable biological distinctions between them, and the position that differences observed between men and women are socially constructed, or rooted in social expectations and representations of appropriate male and female behaviour.

Biological difference between men and women

Differences between men and women have been attributed to their specific and different biologies. The physiological differences between men and women have thus been used to explain intellectual, emotional, behavioural and sexual differences. The view that men and women are 'naturally different' is widely held across disciplines. Advocates of the innate differences perspective often refer to variation between men and women as 'sex' difference. Evolutionary development, hormones and brain structure are thought to underlie oppositional patterns of behaviour in men and women. Thus, the biology of men produces more aggressive behaviour, more logical patterns of thinking and linear communication, which naturally predisposes them to particular roles in society. Conversely, women's biology renders them more peaceful, emotional, intuitive and nurturing, in accordance with the primary roles they occupy. Such innate qualities are seen to present a 'natural' obstacle to full gender equality and have thus been used to explain inequalities between men and women in education, as well as in wider society.

Socially constructed difference between men and women

In contrast, some theorists view differences between men and women as socially developed, or constructed. Gender difference thus describes a social (rather than natural) division between men and women, and one that positions them in hierarchical opposition to one another. In other words, what is viewed as 'male' or masculine behaviour is defined not only as different, but also as opposite, to behaviour which is regarded as 'female' or feminine. Further, qualities that are represented as 'male' (e.g. rationality) are positioned as superior to those represented as 'female' (e.g. emotion). A defining feature of 'gender' is that is while the division itself is fixed, modes of being 'male' or 'female' may vary (Delphy, 1993). Thus, gender identities may be diverse within the separate categories that men and women are seen to belong to. This view on gender difference therefore does not see any one property (or set of properties) as naturally belonging to a female or male body, as behaviours, qualities and characteristics (physical or otherwise) can be adopted varyingly by actors in different situations. Differences in roles, behaviours and attributes of men and women are reinforced through social structures, cultural representations, social and political discourse, and in individuals' own practices (Jackson, 2005). Gender inequalities, including those in education, thus arise from specific social and structural processes.

Gender inequality in global education

On a global level, gender differences in education manifest themselves in three primary areas: access to education at primary, secondary and tertiary levels; participation in education, including enrolment, attendance and access to curricula; and outcomes of education in terms of achievement on standardised tests, entry to higher levels of education and career trajectories. Inequality in access to and participation in education is justified by biological, as well as social perspectives on differences between boys and girls (although the two often intertwine). Girls are argued to be intellectually less capable than boys, and money spent by relatively poor families on educating girl children is thus seen as wasteful. Girls and women are also viewed as being reproductive in function, rather than productive, and education for future employment is therefore not considered necessary (UNICEF, 2007). The social roles of girls also determine their limited participation in education; in many contexts, girls marry 'out' of their parental family, so any financial gains to be made from educating them would not benefit their parents. Further, the organisation of teaching, including curricula and the attitudes of teachers, has been argued to disadvantage girls across national contexts. The gender bias in education has been acknowledged in international conventions and declarations aimed at eliminating this inequality (e.g. Convention on the Elimination of all Forms of Discrimination Against Women, 1981; Beijing Declaration and Platform for Action, 1995; Millennium Declaration, 2000).

There has been much attention paid to the exclusion of girls from all levels of education in sub-Saharan Africa in particular. An increased focus on the role of external aid organisations in funding initiatives for, and monitoring, gender equality have led to wider debates about the meaning of 'gender equality' in global education, the mechanisms by which this can be achieved and sustained, and responsibility/accountability. These discussions can similarly be applied to other developing contexts in which action for gender parity is largely reliant upon external aid and political support. The primary focus of this chapter is thus gender and education in sub-Saharan Africa.

Access to education

The UNESCO Education for All conferences – Jomtein in 1990 (UNESCO, 1990) and Dakar in 2000 (UNESCO, 2000) – and the Millennium Declaration (United Nations, 2000) committed countries to universalising primary education and to achieving gender equity in school enrolments by 2015. On a global level, an estimated 93 million children are not in school and of these, 52 per cent are girl children (UNICEF, 2008). Dropout at the earliest stages of education disproportionately affects girls and the supposed gains in enrolment and participation made at lowest levels of schooling are not always sustained or reflected at higher levels. Numerous factors impinge on girls' access to basic schooling, including cultural norms, concerns regarding their safety (particularly in fragile or unstable contexts) and limited resources. Of the 113 million children of primary school age in sub-Saharan Africa, over 32 million remain out of school (Lewin, 2009; Arnot and Fennell, 2008). Compared with a world average of 92 per cent enrolment for girls and 95 per cent enrolment for boys, enrolment in sub-Saharan Africa is half of this (UNICEF, 2006). However, it must be noted that within this region access to education does differ markedly between countries with some countries maintaining high levels of enrolment from primary through to secondary education, while others have overinflated enrolment rates at the lowest levels of schooling, which decline to below 50 per cent at the highest levels of primary schooling (and which thus has implications for the transition into secondary schooling).

Similarly, while gender differences may appear negligible on an aggregate level, it is important to consider intra-national variations, such as those between rural and urban areas – even where figures for enrolment look relatively equal (Raynor, 2008). For example, in some

South-Asian countries, boys under-enrol compared to girls and they are more likely to drop out beyond a certain level of schooling due to opportunities to take on unskilled, low-earning labour. The Millennium Development Goals, which focus largely on universal access to education, have been regarded as comprehensive markers of gender equality in education. However, access to education can be conceptualised in many ways: admission and progression by age, attendance, appropriate access to post-primary schooling opportunities and age or level-appropriate achievement. It has been argued that it is necessary to have an expanded definition of access because the prevailing criteria for having achieved gender parity can be mutually exclusive (Lewin, 2009). For example, many children of school-going age in sub-Saharan Africa are enrolled in school but may not be participating in the appropriate age range for school. Enrolment at non-appropriate levels of education can result in increased dropout, poor attendance and under- or non-achievement. Further, enrolment does not always signify attendance at school and enrolment data does not reveal dropout or compromised attendance. The mere enrolment of girls in school may not necessarily reflect their actual attendance and research indicates that they are likely to be taken out of school to contribute to household labour (Raynor, 2008; Unterhalter, 2008). Teachers and officials may not enforce compulsory attendance, perhaps due to their own lack of engagement with the necessity for gender equity in schooling, or stereotypes about the practices of rural and poor families, who are most likely not to send their girl children to school (Sundaram et al., 2010).

The three primary explanations for girls' lower attendance, retention and attainment in school are lack of resources (family and school); cultural norms and expectations for girls; and the presumed and real heightened vulnerability of girls. The salience of biological explanations for differences between the treatment of boys and girls and the educational opportunities afforded to them is evident in predominant explanations for girls' lower participation in education.

Lack of resources

Clearly, economic resources are scarce in many developing contexts. Primary education is not universally free of cost and, in many instances, only some family members can attend school. The cost of education as well as the need for young members of the family to supplement the family income and contribute to household labour mean that regular attendance at school is impeded for many children. Where only few children in a given family are able to attend school, the male children are usually favoured. This is due to a number of reasons (UNICEF, 2008; Subramaniam, 2005; Bingham, 1992). First, young women marry (or are expected to marry) out of the family. Prevailing kinship practices dictate that girls become members of their husband's family on marriage and therefore their labour and eventual earnings will not benefit the natal family. Naturalised beliefs about women's role as reproductive, as responsible for family and childcare, determine that investing in girls' education is less likely to result in a good return for natal families. Beliefs about biological differences in appropriate roles for women and men in this way act as a barrier to girls' participation in education. Second (and accordingly), young men are viewed as the primary economic providers for their parental families. The socially differentiated roles for men and women are largely premised on biological truths about the most 'natural' and therefore, appropriate functions for each gender. So, a family's choice to prioritise the education of their male children serves as a more secure investment as their future earnings will benefit the natal family, and this choice reflects prevailing cultural beliefs about appropriate future tasks for males as differentiated from females.

Cultural norms

In societies where girls are marginalised in education relative to boys, differences in the value accorded to girls and boys are apparent. This includes the devaluation of their socially constructed roles as carers, home-makers, less ambitious, less intelligent and so on. An emphasis towards analysing gender relations in the household has increasingly been seen as key to understanding gender inequality in education, social and economic life. Cultural norms in many developing contexts dictate that girls and women primarily need domestic and agricultural skills. Women are mainly engaged in household labour, childcare and provision of care for older relatives. Their work outside the home involves tending animals, caring for vegetable crops, fetching water and firewood and assisting their husbands in farming work (Raynor, 2008; UNICEF, 2006; Bingham, 1992). Further, girls are viewed as being less intelligent than boys. Therefore, their enrolment in education may be seen as a waste of resources (human and financial) and the innate skills of girls can be used more effectively to support other areas of community, social or family life. Lastly, girls are viewed as needing protection from the dangers and temptations of the public (male) world (e.g. Chege, 2008). This concern is two-pronged: there is the concern that girls will succumb to the temptations of the freedoms associated with the male world, including men themselves; second, there is a fear that girls will be abused by men on entry into the public sphere and that their virtue and honour (and that of their family) should be protected. The differential experiences and opportunities of education experienced by men and women are based on naturalised differences between them, which have in turn been used to legitimate their differential treatment. Subramaniam (2005) names the unequal division of labour to situate girls as responsible for reproductive activities, including the maintenance of the family home as a powerful example – a role which is based on assumptions about women's natural instincts and appropriate roles. Thus, it is not the physical or biological differences between men and women, so much as the socially dictated aspects of gender that lead to the different ways in which men and women are constrained during their lives.

Heightened vulnerability of girls

Threats to the physical safety of girls and young women may prevent them from participating regularly in education in some developing contexts, which are frequently settings of fragility resulting from political instability and/or natural disaster. The heightened vulnerability of girls is not only entrenched in gender-specific assumptions about morality, sexuality and honour, but is borne out in practice. In reality, the increased exposure of girls to violence and abuse is not limited to the public sphere, and a vast body of research demonstrates the prevalence of abuse towards girls and women in the home and at the hands of relatives (WHO, 2002; Watts and Zimmerman, 2002; Heise, 1994). The commercial exploitation and abuse of women is also an emerging concern, and the ILO (2005) estimates that 98 per cent of young people forced into commercial sexual exploitation are women and girls. Girls are also more vulnerable to discriminatory practices, such as sexual harassment and assault in educational and social settings. In contexts characterised by natural and socio-political instability, cultural and gendered norms may become more firmly entrenched and act as strengthened barriers to girls' education (UNICEF, 2008). Girl children may be needed to support the household and rebuild homes, cultural norms regarding the appropriate gender roles and behaviour for men and women become reinforced, and where children become displaced and orphaned, they become easier targets for violence, child prostitution and trafficking – which disproportionately affects girl children. Education generally is more likely to be neglected as it is viewed as something of a luxury compared with more basic and immediate needs that need to be met, and the education of girls in particular is deprioritised due to specific sociocultural beliefs and practices about gender. Schools may not be safe places for girls to inhabit, and following armed conflict, girls are particularly exposed to abuse even within schools (Sundaram *et al.*, 2010).

How will the issue develop in the future?

Measuring progress in gender equality

There is a clear need to continue striving for gender equality and equity in access to, participation in and outcomes of education. Available data about patterns of enrolment, attendance and attainment, including official national statistics, often conceal patterns of gender discrimination at the micro or classroom level. Focusing solely on macro-trends in these areas of education overlooks the reproduction of gender norms by teachers, parents and young people themselves. In some sub-Saharan contexts, official data reveal that girls out-enrol boys at higher levels of education. However, in terms of indicators of gender equality, these countries fare poorly and girls are underrepresented at higher levels of attainment, employment and society. Therefore, it is increasingly argued that outcomes-focused measures or indicators of gender parity need to be further developed and expanded in order to capture multiple facets of gender inequality in education.

The commitments made by the Millennium Declaration to tackle gender inequality in education are specific and time-bound. From the point of view of international donors and aid agencies, the Millennium Development Goals provided a series of 'hard' and quantifiable objectives and outcomes to illustrate and monitor what progress has been made towards achieving education for all. However, the Millennium Development Goals are very difficult to use for monitoring gender equality in a broader sense, due to the outcomes–oriented focus of the progress indicators (Barakat *et al.*, 2009; Lewin, 2009). Official data on enrolment is insufficient and does not reflect a shift in gender norms, gender roles or gender equality. Clearly, what is *meant* by 'equality' in any statements agreed upon by the international community is central to monitoring progress in achieving equality and evaluating whether it can be achieved at all.

Gender equality versus gender equity

The concepts of 'equity' and 'equality' are often used interchangeably in educational policy and interventions, and 'equality' is typically taken to be a favourable outcome in education. While the former refers to the principle of equality of opportunity, the latter refers to the principle of 'sameness', which we should not always assume to be a preferable goal. If we take the example of access to education, then we could argue that it is favourable that equal numbers of girls and boys have access to school. Girls and boys should also have equal access to the same curricula, so, for example, girls should be equally encouraged to study science subjects as are boys. If we look to achievement though, striving for equality or 'sameness' may be more problematic. In the UK, there is a current concern that girls are performing much better than boys on standardised tests in secondary school (e.g. Francis and Skelton, 2005). If achieving gender equality is the favoured goal in this case, then this could imply supporting boys to achieve at the same standard as girls, or reducing the performance of girls to be more in line with that of boys. In both cases, we would achieve gender *equality*. Similarly, gender parity in enrolment could be achieved by increasing the enrolment of girls to reach the level of boys, or by bringing the enrolment rates of boys down to be in line with that of girls. The latter is clearly an undesirable outcome in terms of achieving education for all, but could be used by governments to claim that equality had been achieved. It is therefore imperative that there is transparency around the definitions of terms employed in international and national policies, and that appropriate differentiation is made between the removal of social and structural barriers to achieve parity between the genders, and a blanket desire to make everything 'the same'. We also need to think beyond a sole focus on quantitative outcomes as illustrative of progress, and analyse the processes by which these outcomes are secured, as well as other, simultaneous indicators of a more gender equal society or culture.

What does 'gender equality' mean?

Subramaniam (2005) argues that full equality would denote achievement of equality of opportunities to participate in education, equality of learning processes in school, equality of outcomes and equality of external results, such that job opportunities and earnings for men and women with similar educational qualifications would be equal. In current gender parity and human development indices, gender equality is largely measured by gender parity values for primary and secondary education (the relative proportion of girls to boys enrolled in either stage of education) and therefore does not necessarily reflect accurately gender equality in the country in a broader sense. Colclough (2005) and Subramaniam (2005) have both argued for the need to conceptualise gender equality in a more strategic, rather than practical sense. More emphasis needs to be given to process, structure and the rights of individuals to fundamental freedoms and choice about their lives, rather than the more needs-based approach that has frequently characterised gender and education work. A consideration of whether men and women are equally able to do valuable acts and reach valuable states of being (Sen, 2002) necessitates an analysis of the position of men and women in a given context, gender-normative roles, the value given to girls and boys and the investments made in them – clearly more than a descriptive and decontextualised analysis of enrolment figures for girls and boys.

Using gender parity as a measure of gender equality having been achieved represents only 'formal equality' as it is termed by Subramaniam (2005). Formal equality can be used to deny socio-structural differences between men and women and that disadvantage women. In this sense, 'equality' measured primarily in terms of outcomes (rather than process) is premised on an assumption of 'sameness' between men and women and a denial of socially constructed differences in power, roles, value, opportunities and possibilities between men and women. Understanding *how* differences between men and women arise is key to conceptualising, addressing and monitoring gender inequality and it has been argued that indicators such as equality of treatment in education and quality of experience in education are more useful representations of equality of process and therefore of equality in a wider, social sense (Unterhalter, 2008). What Subramaniam refers to 'substantive gender equality' is therefore a more useful guide on which to base indicators of progress in achieving goals of gender equality in education. A first step towards assessing progress towards substantive gender equality entails exploring what it means to be a man or woman in a given context, including what roles are considered appropriate for men and women to perform in a given context and how these are valued socially and economically. These may determine the opportunities to which they have access. So, while schools may be available in theory for both boys and girls, barriers imposed by the socially differentiated gender roles – for example, work in the home for girls – may prevent them from accessing education fully.

Data and tools for measuring gender equality and equity in education

Despite an almost global consensus on the need to make education universally available and not to discriminate on the basis of gender, the simple ratification of numerous international treaties does not, of course, imply the upholding of these obligations to protect and secure the rights of men and women. To help secure countries' observance of these obligations, UN organisations and international donors require national reports to monitor and evaluate the progress made towards diminishing inequalities. Tomasevski (2003) points out that far from all countries (or even the majority of countries) have submitted any such reports however. With regard to combating exclusion from education and girls' marginalisation in particular, monitoring and evaluation systems remain sparse and inconsistent.

In order to monitor and evaluate the progress being made towards achieving the Millennium Development Goals, Education for All objectives and the Dakar goals, we must ensure an appropriate conceptualisation of 'gender equality' as well as rigorous data on which to base any conclusions about gender equality. This necessitates the development of robust and context-appropriate indicators, systems and tools for data collection. As discussed above, an exclusive focus on numbers in measuring equality in education can, on the one hand, present real progress such as equality in enrolment figures, and, on the other hand, give a very partial account of gender equality in education (by ignoring classroom processes, factors which influence attendance, participation and dropout and wider social factors which impact on educational outcomes) and can also conceal patterns of gender-based discrimination. A full consideration of gender equality in education needs then to analyse gender equality in terms of rights *to* education, rights *in* education and rights *through* education (including a recognition that education equality links with wider equality goals) (Colclough, 2005). Reliable data which reflects these areas of equality in education is necessary for progress in a fuller sense to be measured and evaluated.

Single indicators or measures cannot tell us much about the quality of education being received, the equality of treatment and the value attributed to girls' educational achievement relative to that of boys. Equal numbers of boys and girls enrolled in school do not tell us about attendance through the school day, participation in lessons or dropout during the school year. Similarly, equal numbers of male and female teachers do not tell us whether processes of teaching, teacher–pupil interactions, and curricula employed, are gender-aware and seek to disrupt discriminatory gender norms, beliefs and practices. For example, textbooks and the attitudes of teachers may reinforce social norms that deem it more appropriate for girls to take responsibility for household chores and boys to participate actively in the public world and to become primary economic providers. Equality in achievement alone does not tell us whether community norms regarding gender roles are shifting or whether this equality translates to equality of employment opportunities or reward for young men and women. As was argued above, equality is not always a desirable outcome in education and more emphasis should therefore be given to measuring equality of opportunities to engage with education.

Conclusion

Gender inequalities within education are likely to reinforce wider social inequalities, including those women face in employment, political representation and the public arena generally. Thus, measures of gender equality should not only be gender-aware but also gender-transformative in challenging and disrupting gendered power relations that constrain the possibilities available to women and men through education.

Questions for further investigation

1   How are different approaches to explaining gender difference used to justify differential access to, participation in and outcomes of education?
2   Why might it be important to define access to education more broadly than simply enrolment in school?
3   What are the primary criticisms of current measures of gender equality in developing contexts?
4   Why is the way in which gender difference is explained important to considering how gender equality should be monitored?

Suggested further reading

Fennell, S. and Arnot, M. (2008) *Gender education and equality in a global context*. London and New York, NY: Routledge. This research-based book discusses the need to reconceptualise 'gender equality' in a global context and provides case studies of local action towards gender equality in education in a range of settings in the developing world. The studies provide excellent examples of the numerous pathways for achieving gender equality and explore the interrelation between gender, poverty and education.

UNESCO (2003). *Gender and education for all: the leap to equality*. EFA Global Monitoring Report 2003/4. Paris: UNESCO. This report summarises the state of gender equality in education in the international community. It emphasises the need to look beyond numbers in measuring and monitoring gender equality and suggests that national governments focus on securing equality in classroom processes, as well as transitions into higher education and employment.

Unterhalter, E. (2005) 'Global inequalities, capabilities, social justice and the Millennium Development Goal for gender equality in education', *International Journal of Education and Development*, 25, pp. 111–122. This paper argues for a consideration of the capabilities approach in conceptualising gender equality. It argues that more emphasis needs to be given to well-being and conditions for human flourishing in governmental policies for measuring gender equality, in pursuit of the Millennium Development Goal.

References

Arnot, M. and Fennell, S. (2008) '(Re)visiting education and development agendas: contemporary gender research', in Fennell, S. and Arnot, M. (Eds.) *Gender education and equality in a global context*. London and New York, NY: Routledge, pp. 1–16.

Barakat, S., Connolly, D., Hardman, F., Sundaram, V. and Zyck, S. (2010) *UNICEF's education in emergency and post-crisis transition programme: programme review cum evaluability study. Final Report*. New York, NY: United Nations Children's Fund.

Bingham, M. (1992) 'Gender and education in a global context', in Lynch, J., Modgil, C. and Modgil, S. (Eds.) *Cultural diversity and the schools: human rights, education and global responsibilities*. London: Falmer Press, pp. 51–68.

Chege, F. (2008) 'Researching gender: explorations into sexuality and HIV/AIDS in African contexts', in Fennell, S. and Arnot, M. (Eds.) *Gender education and equality in a global context*. London and New York, NY: Routledge, pp. 102–116.

Colclough, R. (2005) 'Rights, goals and targets: how do those for education add up?', *Journal of International Development*, 17, pp. 101–11.

Delphy, C. (1994) 'Rethinking sex and gender', *Women's Studies International Forum*, 16, 1, pp. 1–9.

Francis, B. and Skelton, C. (2005) *Reassessing gender and achievement*. London: Routledge.

Heise, L.L., Pitanguy, J. and Germain, A. (1994). *Violence against women: the hidden health burden*, World Bank discussion papers (225). Washington, DC: World Bank.

Jackson, S. (2005) 'Sexuality, heterosexuality and gender hierarchy: getting our priorities straight', in Ingraham, C. (Ed.) *Thinking straight: new work in critical heterosexuality studies*. London: Routledge, pp. 15–38.

ILO (2005) *Human trafficking and forced labour exploitation*. Geneva: ILO.

Lewin, K.M. (2009) 'Access to education in sub-Saharan Africa: patterns, problems and possibilities', *Comparative Education*, 45, 2, pp. 151–174.

Raynor, J. (2008) 'Schooling girls: an inter-generational study of women's burdens in rural Bangladesh', in Fennell, S. and Arnot, M. (Eds.) *Gender education and equality in a global context*. London and New York, NY: Routledge, pp. 117–130.

Sen, A. (2002) 'Response to commentaries', *Studies in Comparative Development*, 37, 2, pp. 78–86.

Subramaniam, R. (2005) 'Gender equality in education: definitions and measurements', *International Journal of Educational Development*, 25, pp. 395–407.

Sundaram, V., Connolly, D. and Hardman, F. (2010) *UNICEF's education in emergency and post-crisis transition programme: programme review cum evaluability study. Kenya Country Study Report*. New York, NY: United Nations Children's Fund.

Tomasevski, K. (2003) 'School fees as hindrance to universalising primary education', Background paper for *EFA Global Monitoring Report 2003/4*.

UNESCO (1990) Online: http://unesdoc.unesco.org/images/0019/001919/191931E.pdf. Accessed August 2010.

UNESCO (2000) *The Dakar Framework for Action*. Online: http://unesdoc.unesco.org/images/0012/001211/121147e.pdf. Accessed August 2010.

UNICEF (2008) *State of the world's children: child survival*. New York, NY: United Nations Children's Fund.

UNICEF (2007) *A human-rights based approach to education for all*. New York, NY: United Nations Children's Fund.

UNICEF (2006) *State of the world's children: excluded and invisible*. New York, NY: United Nations Children's Fund.

United Nations (2000) *United Nations Millennium Declaration*. Online: http://www.un.org/millennium/declaration/ares552e.htm. Accessed August 2010.

Unterhalter, E. (2008) 'Global values and gender equality in education: needs, rights and capabilities', in Fennell, S. and Arnot, M. (Eds.) *Gender education and equality in a global context*. London and New York, NY: Routledge, pp. 19–34.

Watts, C. and Zimmermann, C. (2002) 'Violence against women: global scope and magnitude', *Lancet*, 359, pp. 1232–1237.

World Health Organisation (2002) *World report on violence and health*. Geneva: World Health Organisation.

31

Globalization

Nick Peim
University of Birmingham

Overview

This chapter considers current accounts of globalization, its political and cultural implications. The educational dimension is considered including global institutions promoting education as a human right, but also in terms of the dissemination of a hegemonic model involving the management of populations and the formal ordering of knowledge. Specific vignettes are offered – from Qatar, South Africa and Mexico – indicating some of the complexities of globalized education in practice. Globalized education is then explored in terms of the contest between performativity and enlightenment ideals, especially in relation to the university. Finally, some reflections are offered on the extent that education has become a globalized force permeating all stages and aspects of contemporary life.

What is globalization?

The ontological status of globalization is uncertain, a matter for ongoing definition and dispute. Is globalization an actual state of affairs or a way of describing the world? Some claim globalization is simply the ongoing condition of modernity, a feature of the world since Henry the Navigator first sponsored forays along the west coast of Africa in 1415 (Parry, 1990). Others cite the cosmopolitan condition of the Roman Empire as a conglomerate of different identities brought together into a pragmatic unity. Others insist that globalization is specifically a postmodern phenomenon, a product of the destabilization of the world in the shift from a 'solid' to a 'liquid' modernity (Bauman, 2000). As such, globalization is a radical transformation of the world. This version of globalization – as recent, rapid and beyond any controlling power – is represented as fraught with dangers. The very identity of things is destabilized as familiar borders shift, as time and space are compressed and as information flows at the speed of light.

Recently globalization has been used to describe the order of things: geopolitics, geo-communications system, geo-economics and geo-culture, including education. It is frequently given negative implications, associated with the dominance of multi-national companies, with the Americanization of global culture and the demise of indigenous modes of being. Deterritorialization has undermined traditional cultures, stable values and forms of conduct, unmooring communities from the stabilities that have historically guided them in the long, slow processes of cultural adaptation. According to Zygmunt Bauman, 'negative globalization' is the driving force behind the heightened forms of anxiety that define contemporary human life (Bauman, 2000, 2005, 2006a, 2006b). Such anxieties invade the most intimate domains of our collective and individual lives (Bauman, 2003).

Bauman's dystopic globalized world is a far cry from Marshall McLuhan's cosier 'global village' (1964). According to McLuhan, among the first to articulate relations between global time-space and modern, electronic communications systems: 'Today, after more than a century of electric technology, we have extended our central nervous system in a global embrace, abolishing both space and time as far as our planet is concerned' (1964, p. 3). Since McLuhan, a powerful discourse concerning communications technologies and their effects has heightened a sense of danger in terms of both identity and security. The new 'plug and play' world order, comprising radical shifts in the capacities of communications systems, including global satellite coverage, digitalization, fibre optic cabling, high-definition television and the exponential growth of computer processing power, has meant a dizzying proliferation as well as an uncontrolled and perhaps uncontrollable domain of 'media' (Demac, 1990). In conjunction with numerous population migrations of modernity, these information technologies seem to seriously threaten national borders and local ways of being in the world.

The movement of people has strongly contributed to the mingling of cultures and the condition of hybridity (Lyotard, 1986), complicating relations between global, national and local, and changing these dimensions of 'being-in-the-world'. Location is no longer simply a question of topography. Where we are is a complex matter involving multiple aspects of being. Globalization involves meta-regional convergences: integrated world markets; global system of communications, knowledge and culture; accelerated mobility of people; and the export and import of policy norms. Global flows are transformative of practices and institutions as well as identities. According to Arjun Appadurai, it now makes more sense to divide the world into spheres of operation than geographic continents. The world can thus be defined in terms of (a) the ethnoscape; (b) the mediascape; (c) the technoscape; (d) the financescapes; and (e) the ideoscapes. The suffix 'scape' refers to 'fluid, irregular shapes' (1996, p. 52).

Time-space compression and consciousness wrought by globalization have transformed both our sense of the world and in our experience of it (Harvey, 1991; Hoogvelt, 1997). Time-space compression refers both to physical travel and to communications connectivity. A major effect is the disruption of the local by presence of the 'Other'. Cosmopolitanism is no longer the special condition of particular locations, but is dispersed. It is visible in supermarkets, audible on radio channels, and generally palpable in the material substance of our lives, wherever we are. Global consciousness promotes an increased awareness of the 'world'. Discourses concerning world politics, world culture and world ecology proliferate. 'Globe-talk' heightens uncertainty. Faraway, 'alien' forces are no longer faraway. They impinge on our world while still remaining beyond our control. Our fate is not in our own hands but is subject to distant political, economic and cultural forces, processes and institutions (Holton, 1998).

For some, dark political forces are at work in the new morphology of globalized economic powers; at the same time, new resistant political forces arise in the agonistics of conflict between the forces of 'empire' and the manifold, self-organizing identities of 'multitude' (Hardt and

Negri, 2000). Communities may have died, but the new force of networks – by no means all on the side of the rich and the powerful – have given rise to a new articulation of politics, how it works and where it is (Hardt and Negri, 2005, 2009). David Harvey's influential account of *The Condition of Postmodernity* proposes a global shift in the very nature of economics and culture and seeks to identify a new political world order (Harvey, 1991, 2005). Jean François Lyotard in *The Postmodern Condition* offers a radical critique of metaphysics rethinking the very nature of identity, meaning and history. Lyotard indicates that totalizing descriptions must be handled with care. After Nietzsche, all 'global' descriptions must acknowledge the provisional and positioned nature of their premises. Postmodernism – a self-professedly anti-totalizing position – both makes claims about the 'new' condition of the world while recognizing that no such descriptions can claim transcendental authority (Lyotard, 1986).

Educational dimensions

Globalization has given rise to the idea of education as a generalized human right, drawing on the 1948 Universal Declaration of Human Rights, the United Nations' 1959 Convention on the Rights of the Child, and the UN International Covenant on Economic, Social, and Cultural Rights (1976). All of these declare education a fundamental human right. In recognition that universal access to education remains unrealized, further discussion has continued at the Education for All conferences held in Thailand in 1990 and Senegal in 2000 as well as in the International Commission on Education for the twenty-first century's report (1996). There is, however, no universal agreement on what amounts to an education to meet the minimum requirements to fulfil that right. Questions arise about who should provide what form of education to whom and about how the right to education might be claimed or enforced (Lindahl, 2006).

For some, globalized education is a function of neo-liberalism, imposing governmental education policies and practices, while eroding 'proper' enlightenment ideals. Education has been distorted into a tool for managing the social division of labour and for promoting market ideology, an arena for ideological forces on a global scale. The impact of supra-national institutions such as the OECD on national education systems, promoting convergence, is seen to be hostile to local identity and community (Burbules and Torres, 2000). On this view, 'world education' represents the opposite of equal access. Powerful institutions dominate education in a new, competition-driven hierarchy. A deficit discourse identifies poorer national contexts as deprived. At the same time, all national contexts strive to enforce a national system as education is represented as an economically necessary form of governance. The school has become globalized as a key institution of population management. The university, similarly, partakes of the global knowledge economy – and the form of that economy is remorselessly on the side of capital and accumulation (Hatcher, 2001).

The school as an instrument of globalization

Globalization can be seen at the very origins of schooling in modernity, where the school becomes the paradigm institution of socialization in the so-called 'West': Europe, North America, Australasia and Japan. The UK example is instructive given the colonial and postcolonial dimensions of globalization. In her account of education in India under the British Raj, Gauri Viswanathan points to an interesting relation between colonial and home practices.

Examining the rise of English as a school curriculum subject, Viswanathan notes that the English curriculum first took shape in India as a vehicle for the enculturation of the subaltern population in the process of education for administration of British rule. Ironically, she claims, English was imported 'back' into the 'home' country after the First World War as a way of re-enculturating the working-class population. Fears of the contagion of Bolshevism, a concern for the cultural integrity of the nation, a fear of the 'corrupting' influence of popular culture and a moral panic about the corruption of the English language impelled this reformation. National coherence, it was felt, was at stake in this project to construct a national culture through the now well-established education system (Newbolt, 1921; Viswanathan, 1989).

This vignette illustrates that the global dimension of education has long been a feature of geopolitical relations. As the modern form of the school took shape in the nineteenth century, it began to permeate national borders (Green, 1997). As modernity took shape with the division between developed and developing sectors, the level of schooling became a significant measure of development for nations, and an index of prosperity, economic potential and relative well-being. In national contexts of relative poverty, access to schooling became and remains a powerful political issue. The meaning of access, however, continues to complicate the issue as excluded or disadvantaged ethnic, class or gender groups struggle not only to 'receive' education, but also to shape its content and form. In Foucault's terms education is the most powerful example of 'bio-power' – a far-reaching social technology (Castells, 2004, p. 86; Spivak, 2009).

The form of the school is an interesting index and aspect of globalization. This institution has been adopted, and adapted, as the key instrument for development in virtually all global contexts. A number of significant points arise from this metastasis. As schooling becomes ubiquitous, so the model of education it carries with it also disseminates. While the specific form of the school may vary, some consistent elements of the institution and its purposes will have become pandemic. These may include benefits for children that would be hard to contest, such as systematic pastoral care, concern for personal development, a degree of freedom from labour and access to non-local knowledge. But it may also carry with it loss or negation of local identity, linguistic domination, subjection to regimes of knowledge and collusion with the social division of labour that may systematically discriminate against significant segments of the population (Bernstein, 1971). Education is never simply a gift: it always enacts governance. In contemporary terms, education has become a dominating concept in terms of development, prosperity and well-being at local, national and global levels. Formal, systemized education is seen as an absolutely essential dimension of any nation state. The implication of this apparently natural state of affairs will be briefly addressed in some vignettes below but will also be addressed towards the end of this chapter with some reflections on the current world domination of education as a mode of 'Being'.

An example from the oil-wealthy Middle East may illustrate the impact of educational development on national life. Recently, the Supreme Education Council in Qatar, established by decree of the Emir, has made educational reform a main government priority, referring to the need to modernize. The iconography of its public literature juxtaposes traditional references with hypermodern images of hi-tech learning environments: 'Best practices from around the world combined with Qatar's unique culture are ensuring a bright future for every child.' 'Best practices' in this case include the intervention of the RAND Corporation, a Californian-based NGO. In terms of the structure of school governance, the form of the curriculum, assessment systems, the dominant model of professional development and ideas about learning, the new, reformed Qatari education system now follows a Western model. It is hard in this case to see how RAND-led modernization has enabled 'local' identity into the 'new era' initiative. The curriculum includes Arabic, but is dominated by English, mathematics and science. The public message promoted by the Supreme Education Council emphasizes global competition, giving prominence to 'performance levels' and 'scale scores' to drive 'school improvement' with publicly published results and cohort comparisons.

The salience of English in Qatari education signifies a characteristic aspect of global education issues. South Africa after apartheid furnishes a problematic and illustrative case of complexities in the force field of globalization. One of the first decrees of the post-apartheid government was to recognize 11 official national languages. Nevertheless, English soon became recognized, and disputed, as the dominant language of government and education. Arguments about the rights of minority languages against the de facto hegemony of English indicated the global, local, national torsions at work in the arguments the policy engendered (de Kadt, 2007). Neville Alexander, currently a member of the Interim Governing Board of the African Academy of Languages, has focused recent work on the tension between multilingualism and the hegemony of English in the public sphere. Alexander, an educationist with impeccable ANC credentials, fellow prisoner on Robben Island with Nelson Mandela, has become a champion of alternative education arguing for resistance to any simple acceptance of the hegemony of English. Alexander's independent organization, PRAESA (Project for the Study of Alternative Education in South Africa), argues that while accepting 'the immediate and obvious economic and social benefits of English', it is vital to sustain 'home languages' for cultural and political reasons as well as for economic and social reasons (PRAESA, nd). In this case, the hegemonic form of education has met with some powerful resistance, for urgent sociocultural and political reasons. The outcome of this resistance remains to be seen, but it is worth noting that the form of educational reform in South Africa after apartheid, in terms of institutions and curricula, has followed a globally hegemonic model often in spite of explicit policy intentions.

Indigenous education may struggle to retain its indigeneity, impelled to follow the hegemonic model of powerful nation states (Green, 1997). Manuel Castells offers an example of a struggle over education arising with the Indian insurgency in Mexico. Hitherto 'an absent actor' in the current Latin American modernization process, constitutional reform granted rights of access to education to Indians. Castells claims that health and education services improved for Indian communities, and that 'limited self-government was in the process of implementation' (Castells, 2004, p. 86). What this apparently cheerful story indicates is that hitherto excluded communities may gain 'access' to education through political intervention and changes in rights legislation within national contexts. But what is also indicated is that entry into the sphere of education is not necessarily empowering. Local populations are included within the norm-related practices of national institutions of socialization. An excluded population in being brought within the ambit of education becomes subjected to – and subjugated by – the institutionalized ordering of identity. Such processes – including the excluded, in order better to manage them and their potentially disruptive presence – occur in wealthy and powerful nations to the less wealthy and powerful population segments (Peim, 2006).

Higher education

In contemporary philosophy there is a strand of thinking suggesting that the very idea of the university is under threat from forces driven by globalization. According to this narrative, the liberal enlightenment ideal is what is in danger. This ideal of the university, as essentially a place of freedom, demands independence from national governments and global economic powers. This independent university, guaranteeing academic freedom, stands for 'communicative rationality': its task is to promote the values of scientific thinking as a model for the public sphere and as a mechanism for the production of objective and politically neutral knowledge. This story claims that it is essential that key knowledge producing institutions in modern societies affirm and enact the values of freedom, objectivity and integrity (Habermas, 1987; Derrida, 2004). While universities in all national contexts face pressures to be or become more economically efficient and 'relevant', the counter-discourse seeks to reclaim the special educational role of the university against the dominance of 'technological enframing' (Heidegger, 1993). Such discourses have seriously questioned the proliferating tendency to orient research and teaching towards a programmable and profitable end.

One problem is that there are many ideas of what the university and higher education should be. The university, as we know it, is largely a product of modernity. As modernity mutates, so our understanding of this powerful institution will have to take into account the global dimension. Universities are increasingly globalized institutions: with networks, flows of students, a global hierarchy, as well as global convergence of practices, aspirations and orientations to knowledge. For Jacques Derrida, the question is how can the university develop the legacy of its enlightenment ideal in the face of globalized lines of force and operate as a properly cosmopolitan, 'hospitable' institution, open to 'Others' in both the form of cultural identities and the forms of knowledge. How might the classic functions of the institution – teaching, research, training, transmission of culture – sustain both rigour and hospitality in the face of rationalizing tendencies and competition that have taken on a globalized character?

The history of the university as we know it is aligned with the history of the rise of the modern nation state. Universities have been seen as key institutions in the construction of the nation state, in the development of secularization, industrialization, in the promotion of public culture, influencing civil society, and creating significant forms of citizenship along with the emergence and development of the 'knowledge society'. Neo-liberal market forces have been seen to influence this history and to have given rise to a new era of globalized higher education dominated by market forces and an instrumental, managerialism, displacing the classic form of the institution with its monstrous new progeny, the 'multiversity' (Sun-keung Pang, 2006). According to some, on the other hand, 'higher education remains a primary source of cultural and social innovation in modern societies' (Rhoads and Torres, 2006, p. xviii).

The enlightenment version of the university promoted by Kant and von Humboldt, the liberal vision articulated by Newman, Eliot, Jaspers and the more recent 'radical' visions of Dewey, Habermas and Gouldner, have all had to come to terms with the functionalist perspective that dominates much of the impact of global market forces on higher education. The university remains central to what remains of the project of modernity, including both its rationalizing and its liberalizing tendencies, but also to the postmodern, globalized, university of 'liquid modernity'. While it may be that the university retains a degree of 'relative autonomy' from the state and from the pressures of the neo-liberal hegemony (Ball, 2004), new regimes of university governance – including emphasis on financial accountability, formal audits, and rankings for research, internal review, appraisal schemes and self-assessment – all impact as constraints on the productivity of academics. Current measures of professional competence, including peer review, citation indexing and the new emphasis on impact, draw their power to define the work of universities from global forces (Rhoads and Torres, 2006; Delanty, 2005). Such performative pressures are symptomatic of the global self-consciousness of the university and its standing in the global education market (Brown and Lauder, 2004).

The three main exporters in the global knowledge economy – the US, the UK and Australia – promote their educational exports as part of their foreign trade interests. Government departments in these countries encourage, represent and even coordinate activities that enhance the global reach of their HE institutions. Quality, status and cultural questions arise in relation to the double flow of exported courses and programmes and imported students (van Der Wende, 2001). Larger cultural effects of such global educational flows might be understood in terms of some of the work done in media theory. The simple thesis of cultural domination is challenged by detailed ethnographic work indicating that aspects of the local 'life-world' are not necessarily negated as cultural products, such as forms of knowledge, pedagogical relations and the production of identities, get exported from one – frequently more dominant – cultural context to another (Tomlinson, 1991).

The ontological dimension

Most accounts of globalization emphasize the 'new global disorder' as a process to be resisted, demanding a critical stance towards 'neo-liberal' reorganization of global capital and power. Hence the rise of the anti-globalization movement, an alliance of disparate forces and itself, paradoxically, a globalized force. For many theorists, globalization carries with it a duality of power and possible resistances. Derrida (2001) has identified the ten 'plagues' of globalization, but has also proposed the idea of a 'new international', as an informal association with common interests and purposes coming together in the name of social, cultural, political and economic justice. For Michael Hardt and Antonio Negri, the new hegemonic global force of 'empire' is balanced by the rising force of 'multitude' informed by a series of democratically oriented concepts they refer to as 'commonwealth' (Hardt and Negri, 2000; 2005; 2009). In both these cases, education is identified as caught up with the flow of powers and the struggles between forces, as an instrument on the side of the forces of 'empire' *and* as a means for resisting 'negative globalization'.

The term 'globalization' must always be problematic and in need of deconstruction. To describe 'the world' all at once is the impossible dream of metaphysics. The world as a totality can only be apprehended, or surmised, from a specific position, as both Wittgenstein and Heidegger articulated at length in the first half of the twentieth century. At the current point of the twenty-first century, the borders between the 'global', the national and the local, and between the overarching structures and the possibilities of play remain areas for exploration. Heidegger, Wittgenstein, Derrida, Spivak and Foucault, among many others, have all problematized the idea of 'the world' as a Eurocentric construction. In the context of education, the fact of the convergence of curricula, institutions, hierarchies and values must be seen against the specificities of local practices and cultures that invariably operate against any simple, one-way flow of 'cultural imperialism'.

It is now generally agreed that the bold enunciation of 'the end of history' and the triumph of liberal democracy and market capitalism made by Francis Fukuyama was not just premature but also misguided (1992). The question of the condition of the 'world' is not settled but remains in play. Similarly, the question concerning education is very much alive. Education appears in an increasingly 'ontotheological' mode, a globalized force defining both 'lifelong' personal development and fuelling the global economy. Education is seen as the driving force to redress corrosive inequalities and solve the practical problems facing the human species. In this elevation of education to a powerful principle of being, enlightenment versions of education struggle against the general culture of performativity. One aspect of future debate may be to address the present hegemony of the idea of education as the solution to all the world's problems. While globalization has sold education as the dominant ontological principle and has made the reach of education ubiquitous, questions may still be asked about the rights of this hegemony.

Conclusion

This chapter has examined globalization as a contested way of describing the current condition of the world in the wake of space-time compression, postcolonialism and the rapid rise of powerful communications technologies: all forces that have changed relations between national, local and global dimensions of existence and impacted on cultural identities. Education has been globalized as systems have experienced convergence, institutions have been imported and exported and what counts as effective knowledge has been defined beyond local contexts. Globalized education seems to carry with it a double movement of (i) the extension and amplification of hegemonic power and of (ii) the counter-movement of globalized forces of resistance. Local contexts have expressed some resilience in the face of global incursions. The reign of performativity has yet to entirely displace the enlightenment ideals of objectivity and freedom for education. The still growing geographic and cultural reach of education as a governmental force, however, may encourage educationalists to rethink the current emphasis given to education as global ontological principle.

Questions for further investigation

1 What different effects of globalization can be seen in the context of national school systems?
2 How does globalization impact on the ordering of knowledge in academic institutions and what effect does this ordering have on the determination of knowledge in general?
3 How have global technologies affected the flow of information across national boundaries and what are the effects of these flows?
4 Consider the concept of the global university. What does this idea signify and what do examples reveal about the globalization of HE?
5 Does globalization inevitably imply a convergence of ideas, structures and practices in education and a consequent loss of local identities?

Suggested further reading

Bauman, Z. (2000) *Liquid Modernity*. Cambridge: Polity. This text examines globalization and its effects on social systems and individual experiences from five key perspectives – emancipation, individuality, time-space, work and community.

Burbules, N. and Torres, C. (Eds.) (2000) *Globalization and Education. Critical Perspectives*. London: Routledge. This is a collection that offers multiple views. It can be usefully read in terms of changes that have occurred since its 2000 publication date.

Green, A. (1997) *Education, Globalization and the Nation State*. London: Palgrave Macmillan. Provides a classic and detailed account of the history of the global development of modern education.

References

Appadurai A. (1996) *Modernity at Large. Cultural Dimensions of Globalization*. London: University of Minnesota Press.

Appadurai, A. (2008) 'Disjunction and difference in the Global Cultural Economy' in Inda, J. and Rosaldo, R. (Eds.) *The Anthropology of Globalization: a Reader*. Oxford: Blackwell.

Ball, S. (2004) 'Performativities and fabrications in the education economy' in Ball, S. (Ed.) *The RoutledgeFalmer Reader in Sociology of Education*. London: RoutledgeFalmer, pp. 143–155.

Bauman, Z. (2000) *Liquid Modernity*. Cambridge: Polity.

Bauman, Z. (2003) *Liquid Love*. Cambridge: Polity.

Bauman, Z. (2005) *Liquid Life*. Cambridge: Polity.

Bauman, Z. (2006a) *Liquid Fear*. Cambridge: Polity.

Bauman, Z. (2006b) *Liquid Times Living in an Age of Uncertainty*. Cambridge: Polity.

Bernstein, B. (1971) *Class, Codes and Control*. London: Routledge and Kegan Paul.

Brown, P. and Lauder, H. (2004) 'Education, globalisation and economic development' in Ball, S. (Ed.) *The RoutledgeFalmer Reader in Sociology of Education*. London: RoutledgeFalmer, pp. 47–71.

Burbules, N. and Torres, C. (2000) 'Globalization and education: an introduction' in Burbules, N. and Torres, C. (Eds.) *Globalization and Education. Critical Perspectives*. London: Routledge, pp. 1–26.

Castells, M. (2004) *The Power of Identity*. Oxford: Blackwell.

de Kadt, E. (2007) 'Attitudes towards English in South Africa', *World Englishes*, *12*, 3, pp. 311–324.

Delanty, G. (2005) 'The sociology of the university and higher education: the consequences of globalization' in Calhoun, C., Rojek, C. and Turner, B. (Eds.) *Handbook of International Sociology*. London: Sage, pp. 530–545.

Demac, D. (1990) 'New communication technologies: a plug 'n' play world?' in Downing, J., Mohammadi, A., Sreberny, A. (Eds.) *Questioning the Media: a critical introduction*. London: Sage.

Derrida, J. (2001) *On Cosmopolitanism and Forgiveness*. London: Routledge.

Derrida, J. (2004) *The Eyes of the University: the Right to Philosophy 2*. Stanford, CA: Stanford University Press.

Fukuyama, F. (1992) *The End of History and the Last Man*. Harmondsworth: Penguin Books.

Green, A. (1997) *Education, Globalization and the Nation State*. London: Palgrave Macmillan.

Habermas, J. (1987) 'The idea of the university: learning processes', *New German Critique*, *41*, pp. 3–22.

Hardt, M. and Negri, A. (2000) *Empire*. Cambridge, MA: Harvard University Press.

Hardt, M. and Negri, A. (2005) *Multitude: War and Democracy in the Age of Empire*. Harmondsworth: Penguin.

Hardt, M. and Negri, A. (2009) *Commonwealth*. Cambridge, MA: Harvard University Press.

Harvey, D. (1991) *The Condition of Postmodernity*. Oxford: Blackwell.

Harvey, D. (2005) *A Brief History of Neoliberalism*. Oxford: Oxford University Press.

Hatcher, R. (2001) 'Getting down to the business: Schooling in the globalized economy', *Education and Social Justice*, *3*, 2, pp. 45–59.

Heidegger, M. (1993) 'The question concerning technology' in *Basic Writings*. London: Routledge, 31–34.

Holton, R. (1998) *Globalization and the Nation-State*. London: MacMillan.

Hoogvelt, A. (1997) *Globalisation and the Postcolonial World*. London: MacMillan.

Lindahl, R. (2006) 'The right to education in a globalized world', *Journal of Studies in International Education*, *10*, 1, pp. 5–26.

Lyotard, J.-F. (1986) *The Postmodern Condition*. Manchester: Manchester University Press.

McLuhan, M. (1964) *Understanding Media*. New York, NY: Mentor.

Newbolt Report, The (1921) *The Teaching of English in England*. London: HMSO.

Parry, J.H. (1990) *The Establishment of the European Hegemony: 1415–1715*. New York, NY: Harper Collins.

Peim, N. (2006) 'The children's fund and schooling: changes in the governance topography', *State of Knowledge Paper 7 on Governance and Engagement*. The Joseph Rowntree Fund.

PRAESA (nd). Available at: www.praesa.org.za/ (accessed 15 July 2010).

Rhoads, R. and Torres, C. (2006) *The University, State, and Market: the Political Economy of Globalization*. Stanford, CA: Stanford University Press.

Spivak, G. (2009) 'They the people: Problems of alter-globalization', *Radical Philosophy*, *158*, pp. 31–36.

Sun-keung Pang, N. (Ed.) (2006) *Globalization: educational research, change and reform*. Hong Kong: Chinese University Press.

Tomlinson, J. (1991) *Cultural Imperialism: a critical introduction*. London: Continuum.

Viswanathan, Gauri. (1989) *Masks of Conquest: Literary Study and British Rule in India*. New York, NY: Columbia University Press.

Wende, M.C. van der (2001) 'Internationalisation policies: about new trends and contrasting paradigms', *Higher Education Policy*, *14*, 3, 249–259.

32

Well-being and education

Kathryn Ecclestone
University of Birmingham

Overview

This chapter considers well-being and education through a focus on policy and practice in the UK, whilst making some links with concerns about well-being in other nations. It draws on an inter-disciplinary seminar series funded by the Economic and Social Research Council in Great Britain between 2007 and 2009. The series was the first time that research, policy and practice around emotional well-being had been explored from different disciplinary perspectives, by academics, representatives from policy groups and practitioners in welfare and education, and the first time that developments in Britain had been related to other countries and historical contexts (see Ecclestone, 2011). The chapter summarises key concerns driving policy and practice, and the interventions that arise from them, identifies implications for educational purposes and highlights some contested questions.

Introduction

The well-being and emotional well-being of populations are now seen as central to problems facing developing countries and addressed through the World Bank's poverty reduction approaches and humanitarian aid programmes. In British social policy, for example, government departments such as International Development, Environment and Rural Affairs, and Education have the 'well-being' of individuals and communities in their official remits and there is widespread agreement that government attention to individual and communal well-being is economically, socially and educationally progressive. Former adviser to the British prime minister's strategy unit, Geoff Mulgan, said in February 2008 that 'well-being' would come to be as important in the goals of national governments as military prowess was in the nineteenth century.

Of course, the idea that educational institutions should place more emphasis on emotional aspects of life and learning is hardly new. Nor is it confined to developments in Britain. Yet, current consensus in the United Kingdom is especially strong and provides a useful illustrative case study, drawing in diverse interests and associated initiatives from numerous organisations, creating different meanings of well-being and various assumptions that justify interventions which are largely unchallenged. In addition, while contemporary ideas about emotional well-being are rooted in old religious and philosophical insights about physical, mental and spiritual health and the idea of educating the emotions, current developments are dominated by psychological ideas and practices (see Ecclestone, 2010).

Concerns about emotional well-being

Defining well-being and emotional well-being

Academic discussions of well-being in educational contexts acknowledge confusion about the term in education policy and practice (see Coleman, 2009). Well-being is rooted in spirituality and religious beliefs and widely associated with spiritual, mental and emotional health in the rapidly expanding field of complementary therapies and alternative medicine (Corrywright, 2009). A policy-based meaning is the World Health Organisation's definition of 'a state of complete physical, mental and social well-being and not merely the absence of disease or infirmity'. In a report about the benefits of lifelong learning, well-being is:

> A dynamic state, in which the individual is able to develop their potential, work productively and creatively, build strong and positive relationships with others, and contribute to their community. It is enhanced when an individual is able to fulfil their personal and social goals and achieve a sense of purpose in society.
> (Government Office for Science, quoted by Field, 2009, p. 9)

Mental health is integral to most depictions of emotional well-being, and widely seen to be central to the everyday work of education and welfare services. In the UK, for example, organisations concerned with mental health have long campaigned to promote the voice of people with mental health problems, not only to make them feel less marginalised and stigmatised but also to contribute to improvement or cure. According to a recent government project in the UK, supporting mental well-being is a significant change from a sickness model of mental health and 'no longer seen simply as the absence of mental illness, but as encompassing emotional health and well-being' (Spratt et al., 2007). Under the previous British government, policy initiatives encouraged schools to destigmatise mental health problems, design strategies and systems to identify children and young people 'at risk' of mental ill-health and also prevent their emergence through activities that encourage the expression and sharing of emotions before they become debilitating. For the Inquiry into the Future of Lifelong Learning, a focus on well-being as an outcome of both participating and achieving in adult education could reduce costs to the economy of stress, depression and other forms of mental ill-health (Field, 2009).

A recent powerful influence in education policy and practice in growing numbers of countries, including Australia, Canada, the UK and America, is positive psychology which has created a significant shift from individual psychopathology towards social and individual characteristics of subjective well-being (see Eid and Larsen, 2008; Seligman et al., 2009). A special edition of *American Psychologist* defines positive psychology and its significance as follows:

A science of positive subjective experience, of positive individual traits, and of positive institutions promises to improve the quality of life and also to prevent the various pathologies that arise when life is barren and meaningless. The exclusive focus on pathology that has dominated so much of our discipline results in a model of the human being lacking the positive features, which make life worth living. Hope, wisdom, creativity, future mindedness, courage, spirituality, responsibility, and perseverance are either ignored or explained as transformations of more authentic negative impulses.

(Seligman and Csikszentmihalyi, 2000, p. 1)

From this perspective, emotional well-being is a set of psychological 'constructs' in the form of dispositions, attitudes and attributes that encompass stoicism, resilience, optimism, altruism, being in the moment, emotional literacy (managing and expressing one's emotions and those of others constructively) and self-esteem (see Huppert, in Sharples, 2007). According to British supporters, genetic factors account for about 40 per cent of these constructs in individuals and material factors for 15 per cent: interventions are therefore effective, both in preventing future problems and enhancing educational and life achievement in the present (Layard, 2005, 2007; Huppert, 2009a; 2009b; Seligman *et al.*, 2009).

Emotional intelligence

Emotional well-being encompasses emotional intelligence, defined in early work by John Mayer and Peter Salovey as the ability to combine reason with emotion through being able to perceive, understand and manage emotion (1997). Yet it is Daniel Goleman's best-selling book which has brought the idea that measurable psychological constructs comprise emotional intelligence into popular and political thinking in America and Britain and that these are more important to life and work success than traditional academic intelligence. Drawing together personal and intra-personal 'intelligences', Goleman identifies 'abilities such as being able to motivate oneself and persist in the face of frustrations; to control impulse and delay gratification; to regulate one's moods and keep distress from swamping the ability to think; to empathise and to hope' (1996, p. 43). A recent study argued that children with traits of low impulsivity and self-motivation do better in exams in certain subjects, thereby requiring schools to provide interventions for emotional intelligence and to design institutional indicators to show its development (see Rodiero *et al.*, 2009).

There is disagreement amongst psychologists about whether emotional intelligence is 'trait-based' or socially constructed, or both, and whether it exists as a separate aspect of intelligence (Matthews *et al.*, 2002; Craig, 2007). Nevertheless, Goleman has managed to persuade millions of readers, including policy-makers, that the skills of emotional intelligence can be taught and learned. This resonates with Howard Gardener's popular idea of 'multiple intelligences', and although Gardener has distanced himself from Goleman's ideas, the combination of emotional intelligence as a powerful determinant of social and educational achievement with an inclusive view that everyone is a unique mix of separate abilities appears to offer a more holistic, humane view of how children learn and also what they should learn.

Emotional literacy

Objections that 'intelligence' is a divisive and discredited psychometric construct are reflected in promotion of 'emotional literacy' as a broader range of behaviours, attitudes and dispositions, thereby side-stepping discussions about whether psychometric constructs can be 'measured', and whether they are 'learned' or 'inherited'. An influential organisation that campaigns in Britain for more attention to emotional literacy in policy and practice defines emotional literacy as: 'the practice of interacting with others in ways that build understanding of our own and others' emotions, then using this understanding to inform our actions' by enabling people to:

- find ways to feel connected to each other and of using their relationships to deal with emotions that might otherwise cause them to lash out in rage or withdraw in despair;
- deal with the emotions that can render them unable to take in new information, access emotional states such as curiosity, resilience and joy that lead to a rich experience of learning;
- engage in activities that promote physical and emotional well-being and broaden the range of what they can talk about with each other in ways that make it less likely that they will abuse drugs and alcohol, bully their peers, or engage in other forms of self-destructive activity (Antidote, 2001).

The previous British government formalised concerns and claims about emotional literacy and well-being in its Social and Emotional Aspects of Learning (SEAL) strategy for primary and secondary schools, citing ideas from emotional intelligence and literacy in its rationale (DfES, 2005).

Developing personal capital and capabilities

Partly as a response to disagreement about the extent to which emotional intelligence is genetic and the respective effects of individual and social factors in its development and significance, some researchers emphasise 'capabilities'. Studies from the British government-funded Wider Benefits of Learning research centre claim that high levels of socio-psychological capital (self-esteem, self-efficacy, low levels of stress, and strong self-concept about one's potential to develop ability (as opposed to a tendency to 'learned helplessness')) correlates with the emotional/psychological climate of schools, good social capital and the importance of good relationships with significant others, feeling included, valued and listened to (see www.learningbenefits.net; Stevens et al., 2007). It is also widely agreed that the skills and capabilities of emotional well-being are integral to the creation of 'emotionally literate' citizens, and to preparation for a changing labour market, particularly in service and public sector jobs, that require 'emotional labour'.

From this perspective, building personal and social capital is particularly important for 'vulnerable' groups, and includes dispositions, attitudes and behaviours associated with 'reflective learning', 'self-awareness', 'collaborative learning' and 'learning to learn'. Following this argument, if schools can develop strategies that do both, they will raise achievement and develop capabilities and attitudes that lead to a lifelong 'love of learning' (see also Sodha and Guglielmi, 2009).

Combating exclusion and disadvantage

In Britain, concerns about the effects of low educational achievement and participation on particular groups, such as young people and single mothers, emanate mainly from liberal-Left political ideas. These focus on low self-esteem, feelings of vulnerability, risk and exclusion amongst particular groups in a cycle of deprivation. From this perspective, breaking out of this cycle depends on educational and welfare initiatives to identify those 'at risk', address the emotional impact of deprivation, and offer practical strategies for leading people back into work and education. Educational institutions, working with other agencies and organisations, have been the prime focus for initiatives that aim to change parents' and family behaviours as much as individual children's (e.g. SEU, 1999; DfES, 2003).

The idea that social exclusion is inextricably linked to destructive influences that damage self-esteem and emotional well-being suggests that government agencies, particularly in education and welfare, need to address the effects of poverty, unemployment and social exclusion on personal and emotional capabilities (e.g. Giddens, 1998). In this scenario, emotional or mental ill-health, low self-esteem and feelings of exclusion are not only part of a cycle of deprivation passed onto subsequent generations, but are also 'treatable'. Although policy-makers have been careful not to elide environmental and structural causes of social and personal cycles of deprivation with individual 'traits' or attributes of low self-esteem and emotional vulnerability, the view that emotional dysfunction both arises from and contributes to inequality enables government to emphasise the emotional, individual and social outcomes of inequality rather than material causes and effects (see Ecclestone, 2011).

More recently, there has been a shift away from notions of communal and individual risk, vulnerability and need and personalised responses by government agencies, towards positive, 'asset-based' approaches that build on psychological and material resources and social capital already present in communities (IDEA, 2010).

Engaging 'disaffected' children and young people

One of the most powerful arguments for educational institutions to pay more attention to emotion comes from widespread agreement that disengagement, disaffection and poor achievement arise, in large part, from lack of social and emotional competences as foundational skills, associated with positive attitudes to learning, enjoyment, engagement and active participation and inclusion. A report by DEMOS, a highly influential political think tank in the United Kingdom, covered widely in the media, exemplifies this view, arguing that while lack of these skills is especially problematic for children from disadvantaged backgrounds, notably white working-class boys, schools should develop the emotional well-being and associated competences of all children (Sodha and Gugleilmi, 2009). Following this argument, tackling the rising problem of 'disengagement' from formal education requires a transformation of educational goals and processes that will instil a lifelong love of learning, enjoyment and better attitudes to learning. In this scenario, social inequality and poor educational achievement are inextricably linked, addressed through interventions run locally through partnerships between government, schools and other organisations, such as charities, to support parents and children.

DEMOS' analysis reflects a widespread and growing view that the education system is not merely unjust in reproducing social inequality but also increasingly irrelevant as preparation for successful work and personal lives and for combating disaffection and alienation:

> It is not too fanciful to see, behind the youth culture of raves and drugs, sport and celebrity, the rise of teenage pregnancy and fundamentalism, the shadow of insecurity: the feeling of not being able to get a grip on the miasma of choices and opportunities . . . It's not so much that young people live in poverty . . . as they do not know where to turn for direction and value. In such a state, algebra and parts of speech can seem a little beside the point.
>
> (Claxton, 2002, p. 48)

In a similar vein, Matthew Taylor, chief executive of the Royal Society of Arts, argues that interest in emotional well-being is a response to a school system where growing numbers of children and young people are 'mind-numbingly bored' with traditional subjects and teaching (Taylor, 2008; see also Layard and Dunn, 2009; Rodiero et al., 2009).

Interventions for emotional well-being

In different ways, all the perspectives summarised above draw on growing popular interest in psychology and neuroscience for evidence about the importance of emotions and effective interventions. Matthew Taylor argues that concern about emotional well-being, and our ability to intervene effectively to enhance or develop it, are both logical outcomes of better political and public understanding about the extent to which emotional well-being is 'hard wired' and how far it is socially determined, creating the possibility that we will become more sophisticated at managing our emotions reflexively, and in intervening in it pro-actively.

In Britain, a consensus that educational institutions should develop and assess psychologically or emotionally based 'skills' created a large growth in specialist, generic and universal interventions. At a seminar hosted by the Research Centre for Therapeutic Education at Roehampton University in December 2006, 70 representatives from mental health organisations, children's charities, education psychologists, psychiatrists and therapists could not agree how many people needed interventions but they all agreed that the scale of emotional problems was huge and growing. Education was seen as a key site of influence:

> If we are to stand a chance of our children and ourselves leading good lives, it may be vital for psychotherapists amongst others to examine how we can influence education in general . . . Perhaps, therefore, those of us who are psychotherapists need to look at psychotherapy as an educational practice, not only in the consulting room but to see the wisdom for both children and adults to learn from each other and for our society to continue to attempt to ensure that scientific and technical learning, whilst important, is secondary to the resources of the human soul . . . thus, education and therapy might be seen not so much abut knowledge but rather about awakening . . . by imparting and acquiring through the relational.
>
> (Lowenthal and House, 2009)

Specialist interventions for children and young people diagnosed with behavioural and emotional problems include 'nurture groups', group counselling for children with family and personal problems, formal psychological assessments of individual children and accompanying strategies such as 'circle of friends'. The largest provider of these assessments and interventions have been local authority educational psychology services, but charities and other organisations also offer specialist services or interventions within and outside educational institutions.

There has also been an increase in support provided by counsellors, retention officers, learning managers and classroom assistants, disability support officers and internal and external mentors. Some schools combine a universal approach with more targeted interventions, involving charities and other organisations. For example, Place2Be is a British school-based counselling organisation that advertises its services in the following way:

> We take an holistic approach, offering school-based counselling services to children and their parents or carers, accredited training to school staff members, and professional

qualifications for those who wish to become child counsellors. Our services address the problems of individual children and adults and help to build 'mentally healthy' schools where all children can thrive. Children who can resolve their emotional and behavioural difficulties are less likely to go off the rails, whilst parents who are equipped to tackle their own issues are able to form more positive relationships with their children. The result is happier children with better prospects and that benefits everyone.

Every Child a Chance Trust is a British charity working with schools, offering programmes that aim to improve everyday classroom teaching, provide 'light-touch' intervention for those with moderate needs and one-to-one tuition for those with greatest difficulties (see Sodha and Guglielmi, 2009).

Through the previous British government's SEAL strategy for primary and secondary schools, generic interventions include circle time, the use of Philosophy for Children classes, peer and non-peer mentoring and buddy schemes, mediation and anti-bullying schemes, drama workshops for transition between sectors and stages, special assemblies and the harnessing of traditional and new subject areas (the latter include personal, social and health education and citizenship) as vehicles for emotional well-being and emotional literacy (see Ecclestone and Hayes, 2008, chapters 2 and 3; DfES, 2005).

Strategies derived from American initiatives in state schools, based on positive psychology, have also been imported into British schools, through programmes of pre-designed materials and activities for teaching resilience, stoicism, optimism, altruism and 'being in the moment'. These have been recommended in a recent Children's Society report as effective for all children (Dunn and Layard, 2009; see also Seligman *et al.*, 2009).

Outside specialist and universal interventions, supporters of 'learning to learn', 'thinking skills' and some strands of 'assessment for learning' argue that changes to curriculum content, pedagogy and assessment can foster self-awareness, collaborative learning, reflective learning, group work and flexibility, not just as a matter of learning techniques such as mind mapping or brain gym but, instead, developing attitudes, values, self-image and relationships as well as skills and strategies (e.g. Claxton, 2002). In a similar vein, advocates of emotional literacy argue that subject teachers can develop positive self-concept, social skills, emotional sensitivity and empathy (e.g. Weare, 2004).

More broadly, James Park, chief executive of Antidote, believes that schools need to offer a humane, democratic and inclusive response to the real and growing emotional needs of children alienated and stressed by school and/or external factors. While formal interventions are important, a better approach is to embed emotional literacy and well-being in management and school council, support services, curriculum content and teaching, thereby encouraging genuine inclusion, voice and engagement. This enables a school to deal with individual children with specific problems without stigmatising them whilst developing emotional well-being amongst all pupils (Park, 2008).

Implications for the purposes of education

Many of the imperatives driving current developments, and the cultural, psychological and political concerns that underpin them are far from new. In earlier periods, behavioural psychologists and child guidance experts both encouraged and responded to very similar images of children and concerns about their behaviour and well-being as those we see now (e.g. Hendrick, 2009; Stewart, 2009). Arguments summarised above reflect the inexorable rise of ideas from behavioural and cognitive psychology over the past hundred years, and the corresponding demise of sociological, religious and philosophical understandings of emotion (see Stewart, 2009; Dixon, forthcoming; Hendrick, 2009). In this respect, the psychologisation of the curriculum and ideas about learning is hardly new and historical insights point to the impact of different psychological fashions on ways of understanding human character and identity amongst educationalists, bureaucrats, health professionals, parents and young people (Thomson, 2006).

Yet, the contemporary dominance of psychology and the prevalence of a view that growing numbers of children and young people need emotional intervention obscure incompatible images of the human subject, or self, that underpin how various interest groups in this area regard the purposes of education. These images are largely implicit in debates and practices around emotional well-being. First, the idea that formal education is a prime site for intervention challenges political and social commitment to the idea that a school's main purpose is to foster a rational, autonomous self through a firm grounding in humanity, based on subject disciplines, that enable children to locate themselves in a wider world and to become autonomous (see Cummings, 2009; Heartfield, 2002). In contrast, much support for emotional intervention comes from a view that there is no coherent, single self or sense of 'myself', but a shifting, fragmented set of different 'senses of myself'. Not only is there no coherent self, but the attempt to educate one is at best irrelevant and at worst oppressive. Instead, to navigate one's way in a fragmented and uncertain world, children need to be reflexive and self-aware, with particular dispositions and attitudes as part of a flexible, adaptable personality that both understands how one behaves and why, and can manage emotional responses and actions.

These two positions raise old questions about whether the primary purpose of formal education is to socialise people into a body of knowledge about the world from which a sense of self emerges: from that perspective, teachers' educational authority in that process comes from political and social agreement about what that body of knowledge comprises and about the importance of getting students to learn it. In contrast, an emphasis on emotional well-being places the self and knowledge about the self (or selves), and its feelings and emotions, at the heart of education, where teachers' authority comes increasingly from being able to engage and motivate students, and relate to them emotionally. Advocates of the second position are sceptical that we can agree about a body of external knowledge whilst regarding it as increasingly irrelevant (see Ecclestone, 2011; Young, 2008 for discussion).

Philosophical questions also emerge from the dichotomous thinking that splits emotion and reason. For some philosophers, shaping a meaningful life requires us to deal with disillusionment and despair, requiring a pessimistic engagement with reality and therefore a more authentic, subtle account of the possibilities of human life that counters the tyranny of optimism and the current equation of well-being with individual autonomy (Dienstag, 2009). For other philosophers, the psychologisation of emotional well-being as a set of trainable skills is both normative and troubling because it does not help children and young people consider the moral questions that lie behind these skills, and, instead, develop resources for a meaningful life (Cottingham, 2009; Clack, 2012; Suissa, 2008). From this perspective, current developments are a far cry from educating the emotions, reflecting, instead, new versions of old tensions between subject-based education and skills-based training.

Some critics have argued that preoccupation with emotional well-being responds to profound political and social pessimism about discipline and behaviour. According to Frank Furedi, a long-running crisis of motivation and engagement and concerns about self-esteem, coupled with doubts about the poor quality of teachers (doubts that, according to Furedi, cannot be voiced) lead to attempts to intervene in emotional well-being instead of confronting a crisis of authority that makes adults increasingly uncertain about motivating and socialising children. Uncertainty and lack of moral purpose leads to repeated failed attempts to find technical solutions to behaviour and motivation (see Furedi, 2009).

Other critics argue that children and their families are being exposed to state attempts to 'educate the emotions' in a form of what Foucault called 'bio-politics' – a subtle form of behavioural, psychological and emotional regulation to maintain order that is gradually internalised by its targets. From this perspective, countering this requires educating children's needs and desires in more radically utopian ways, even to educate *un*happiness, the dissatisfaction with the prevailing order that has always been the driver of progressive social change (Amsler, 2009). Following this argument, emotional well-being is not a subjective state to be accomplished by individuals *in spite* of or within their social circumstances, but an inter-subjective one that emerges as a result of becoming a person with others, in conditions that enable human fulfilment and through processes to create these conditions. In contrast to seemingly value-free psychological skills, this pedagogy emphasises what advocates see as resistance, critical hope and transcendence. Although projects in critical pedagogy are marginal within formal education in Britain, supporters argue that they present alternatives and raise questions about underlying assumptions behind taken-for-granted practices (Amsler, 2009).

Other objections to government intervention argue that presenting people as 'vulnerable' or 'at risk' or, conversely, potentially 'emotionally well', leads the state to regard the human subject as psychologically 'reformable'. From this perspective, current policy and practice reflect an unprecedented authoritarian political turn (e.g. Jones, 2008, 2009a, 2009b).

Conclusion

There is strong, widely held agreement that problems with emotional well-being are increasing and need attention. However, there is disagreement about whether it is a problem for all children, young people and adults or for a growing minority. Evidence is cited to show rising levels of dissatisfaction, mental ill-health and emotional barriers to learning, hindering educational and social progress. Within this viewpoint, some argue that dispositions, attitudes, skills and capabilities are largely 'trait-based', others that they are socially constructed. There are also different views about the nature of the problems that require support or intervention. Some argue that definitions of mental ill-health and poor well-being are expanding through an increase in self-reported and official diagnoses of problems, and a loosening of diagnostic measures for conditions such as depression, ADHD, Asperger's syndrome and dyslexia. Others argue that official constructs of well-being reflect a narrow, cultural perspective that distorts informal and formal diagnosis and interventions, and that meanings of stress, depression, anxiety and trauma (for example) change over time and between cultures (e.g. de Abreu, 2009; Summerfield, 2004).

From a philosophical perspective, there are challenges to the widespread view that negative emotions hinder social and educational achievement. Whilst there is a recognition that debilitating clinical depression or anxiety is not desirable, depression and anxiety, as well as general dissatisfaction, pessimism or anger, might fuel positive aspirations for achievement, creativity and individual and social change. Educational questions also arise from John Stuart Mills' famous observation that explicit attention to happiness destroys it, and that it is best developed as a by-product of doing meaningful, intrinsically good or interesting things. Whilst 'happiness' is not synonymous with emotional well-being, Mills' observation raises a fundamental question about the role of educational institutions in developing it.

Questions for further investigation

1 What imperatives drive policy and practice around well-being in different countries?
2 How are meanings of emotional well-being and 'social justice' connected, both academically and politically?
3 How do contemporary concerns and developments differ from other historical periods?
4 What images of the human subject are implicit and explicit in these developments?
5 What are the implications of current policy-led developments for educational subject content, activities and outcomes, and for the state's role in interventions for emotional well-being?

Suggested further reading

Coleman, J. (Ed.) (2009) 'Special issue on "well-being in schools"', *Oxford Review of Education*, 35, 3, pp. 281–405. An important article on 'well-being' in this established journal.

Craig, C. (2007) *The Potential Dangers of an Explicit, Systematic Approach to Teaching Social and Emotional Skills (SEAL)*. Glasgow: Centre for Confidence and Well-Being. A controversial paper offering a counterpoint to the arguments given on the benefits of SEAL.

Ecclestone, K. and Hayes, D. (2008) *The Dangerous Rise of Therapeutic Education*. London: Routledge. A controversial critique of the ways in which concerns about emotional well-being are changing ideas about social justice, inclusion and the goals of education.

Ecclestone, K. (2010) 'The rise of an epistemology of the emotions?: educational implications of emotional well-being', *International Journal of Sociology of Education*. Recent and up-to-date article submitted to this established journal.

Layard, R. (2005) *Happiness: lessons from a new science*. London: Allen Lane. This key text discusses the paradox at the heart of our lives, and that with sophisticated ways of measuring people's happiness, evidence suggests people's happiness has not increased in the last fifty years.

References

Amsler, S. (2009) 'Educating the emotions: the new bio-politics of critical pedagogy', paper given to *ESRC Seminar Series, Emotional Well-being and Social Justice*, 3 February 2009, Oxford Brookes University.

Antidote (2001) *Manifesto: developing an emotionally literate society*. Available at: www.antidote.org. Accessed December 2010.

Clack, B. (2010) 'Philosophy and well-being: implications for education and practice', *Research Papers in Education*, 27, Special Edition.

Claxton, G. (2002) *Building Learning Power*. Bristol: TLO.

Coleman, J. (Ed.) (2009) 'Special issue on "well-being in schools"', *Oxford Review of Education*, 35, 3, pp. 281–405.

Corrywright, D. (2009) 'Well-being and spirituality', paper for *ESRC Seminar Series, Emotional Well-being and Social Justice*, 22 July 2009, Oxford Brookes University.

Cowie, H., Boardman, H., Barnsley, J. and Jennifer, D. (2004) *Emotional Health and Well-being: a practical guide for schools*. London: Paul Chapman.

Craig, C. (2007) *The Potential Dangers of an Explicit, Systematic Approach to Teaching Social and Emotional Skills (SEAL)*. Glasgow: Centre for Confidence and Well-Being. Accessed December 2010.

Cummings, D. (2009) 'Knowing me, knowing you: therapeutic education and the human subject', *Culture Wars*. Available at: www.culturewars.org.uk.

de Abreu, G. (2009) 'Identity and children's well-being: a cultural perspective', paper given to *ESRC Seminar Series, Emotional Well-being and Social Justice*, 10 June 2009, Canterbury Christ Church University.

DfES (2003) *Every Child Matters*. London: Department for Education and Schools.

DfES (2005) *Social, Emotional Aspects of Learning Strategy for Schools*. London: Department for Education and Schools.

Dienstag, J. (2009) 'Pessimism and well-being', paper given to *ESRC Seminar Series, Emotional Well-being and Social Justice*, 22 April 2009, Canterbury Christchurch University.

Ecclestone, K. (2010) 'Changing the subject?: Emotional well-being and social justice', *End of Award Report for the Economic and Social Science Research Council*. Birmingham: University of Birmingham.

Ecclestone, K. (2011) 'The rise of an epistemology of the emotions?: educational implications of emotional well-being', *International Studies in Sociology of Education*.

Ecclestone, K. and Hayes, D. (2008) *The Dangerous Rise of Therapeutic Education*. London: Routledge.

Field, J. (2009) *Well-being and Happiness: thematic paper 4, Inquiry into the Future for Lifelong Learning*. Leicester: National Institute of Adult and Continuing Education.

Furedi, F. (2009) *Wasted: Why Education is Not Educating*. London: Continuum.

Goleman, D. (1996) *Emotional Intelligence: why it matters more than IQ*. London: Bloomsbury Press.

Heartfield, J. (2002) *The 'Death of the Subject' Explained*. Sheffield: Sheffield Hallam University.

Hendrick, H. (2009) 'The coming of the child as an emotional subject, c. 1900–1950', paper given to *ESRC Seminar Series, Emotional Well-being and Social Justice*, 8 July 2009, Oxford Brookes University.

Huppert, F. (2009a) 'The science of well-being: causes, benefits, and approaches to its enhancement', Presentation to *ESRC Seminar Series, Emotional well-being and social justice*, 10th June 2009, Canterbury Christ Church University.

IDEA (2010) *A Glass Half Full: how an asset approach can improve community health and well-being*. London: Improvement and Development Agency/Department of Health.

Jones, L. (2008) 'Resisting emotional education', *Culture Wars*. Available at: www.culturewars.org.uk. Accessed December 2010.

Jones, L. (2009a) 'Adapting to alienation', *Culture Wars*. Available at: www.culturewars.org.uk. Accessed December 2010.

Jones, L. (2009b) 'Historicising the therapeutic turn', *Culture Wars*. Available at: www.culturewars.org.uk. Accessed December 2010.

Layard, R. (2005) *Happiness: lessons from a new science*. London: Allen Lane.

Layard, R. and Dunn, J. (2009) *A Good Childhood: searching for values in a competitive age*. Harmondsworth: Penguin Books.

Lowenthal, D. and House, R. (Eds.) (2009) *Childhood, well-being and a therapeutic ethos*. London: Routledge.

Matthews, G., Zeidner, M. and Roberts, R. (2002) *Emotional Intelligence: science and myth*. Cambridge, MA: Massachusetts Institute of Technology Press.

Mayer, J.D. and Salovey, P. (1997) 'What is emotional intelligence?', in Salovey, P. and Sluyter, D. (Eds.) *Emotional Development and Emotional Intelligence: implications for educators*. New York, NY: Basic Books, pp. 3–31.

NEF (2008) *A Well-being Manifesto for a Flourishing Society*. London: NEF.

Rodiero, C., Bell, J.F. and Emery, J. (2009) 'Can trait Emotional Intelligence predict differences in attainment and progress in secondary school?', Research Report. Cambridge: Cambridge Assessment.

Seligman, M., Randal, E., Gilham, J., Reivich, K. and Linkins, M. (2009) 'Positive education, positive psychology and classroom interventions', *Oxford Review of Education*, 35, 3, pp. 293–313.

Sharples, J. (2007) 'Well-being in the classroom', transcript of a keynote seminar of the All-Party Parliamentary Group on scientific research in learning and education, Portcullis House, 23 October 2007.

Social Exclusion Unit (1999) *Bridging the Gap: new opportunities for 16–19 year olds not in education or training*. London: SEU.

Sodha, S. and Guglielmi, S. (2009) *A Stitch in Time: tackling educational disengagement*. London, DEMOS.

Spratt, J., Shucklesmith, J., Philip, K. and Wilson, C. (2007) 'Embedded yet separate: tensions in voluntary sector working to support mental health in state-run schools', *Journal of Education Policy*, 22, 4, pp. 411–429.

Stevens, P., Lupton, R., Mujtaba, T. and Feinstein, L. (2007) *The Development and Impact of Young People's Social Capital in Secondary Schools*, Wider Benefits of Learning Research Report No.24. London: Institute of Education.

Stewart, J. (2009) 'The "normal" child and the "maladjusted" child: the case of British child guidance 1918–1955', paper given to *ESRC Seminar Series, Emotional well-being and social justice*, 8 July 2009, Oxford Brookes University.

Taylor, M. (2008) 'A clumsy road to well-being', presentation to *ESRC Seminar Series, Emotional well-being and social justice*, 9 December 2008, Oxford Brookes University.

Weare, K. (2004) *Developing the Emotionally Literate School*. London: Paul Chapman.

33

Leadership and school effectiveness

Christopher Rhodes and Tom Bisschoff
University of Birmingham

Overview

In this chapter we commence by exploring the relationship between leadership and school effectiveness. We place this exploration in an international context and introduce the parameters of national policy expectations and socio-economic influences, such as poverty, upon the nature and extent to which schools and school leaders can make a difference in the lives of children. Given that leaders and leadership are important in advancing school effectiveness, the chapter highlights the importance of good leadership development and the problem of recruiting good leaders in some countries as influential in the school improvement journey. The chapter offers focus on the central role of leaders in fostering high-quality teaching and learning within their schools and explores how they might help to translate this into better outcomes for all pupils in their care. We include recent examples of evolving approaches to leadership in some countries intended to better serve pupils, their families and their communities. Finally the chapter asks what of the future for continued school improvement, what kind of futures can be envisaged and what kinds of visions should be pursued?

Introduction

For many decades, school effectiveness research has sought to identify those characteristics of schools which can impact positively or adversely upon the educational achievement of pupils from all backgrounds (Muijs, 2006). The desire to raise the effectiveness of schools, as indicated by improving pupil outcomes has, over time, become bound up with a wide variety of change initiatives in many parts of the world. It is perceived that the now well-established international focus on continuous school improvement is driven at national policy level by a combination of prevailing political, social, cultural and economic imperatives. Thus the details of national focus and how this is understood and implemented in schools varies from context to context but typically it has involved the establishment of a variety of external and internal audit regimes, consideration of the effectiveness of teaching and learning, the influence of communities from which pupils are drawn and the quality of leadership and management in schools. School effectiveness research has repeatedly identified the importance of 'school leadership' as an important element in helping to bring about change, improvement and greater school effectiveness. It is highly unlikely that any school is completely effective in all of its endeavours; however, a firm belief has been established that good leadership is linked to school effectiveness and that good leaders are necessary for school improvement to occur. This linkage has been reflected in many studies (e.g. Teddlie and Reynolds, 2000; Hallinger and Snidvongs, 2005) and a document presented to the UK parliament by the secretary of state for education and skills (DfES, 2005) emphasises that good leadership is at the heart of every good school.

Trying to make a difference

The extent to which schools make a difference in the lives of pupils has been shown to depend upon factors such as the levels of wealth and social capital that the families of pupils' possess (West-Burnham, 2009). Hopkins *et al.* (2005) further reveal that what learners learn in school is at least in part determined by the levels of socio-economic advantage or deprivation they experience in daily life. Whilst initiatives to improve schools are commonplace in many parts of the world, in some countries limited access to schooling and equity issues caused by family, community and cultural considerations blight the lives of many children. For example, in rural Africa, Saunders (2000) reports on the lack of connection between schools and communities, poor health and nutrition, inappropriate teaching materials and a depleted teaching force due to AIDS as removing or diminishing educational opportunity for large numbers of children. In the UK, Busher (2006) locates schools within their socio-political environments and lists the impacts of local and national policy contexts on the day-to-day working of schools and the resultant influence upon the way in which teachers can and are expected to act. It is concluded that such enforced operating environments have consequences for the improvement journeys of schools and may serve to direct or deflect improvement efforts being played out in particular local contexts. Nevertheless, the appointments of senior and middle leaders in schools, particularly heads, are some of the most significant events in the life of a school as these events may help to strengthen a current improvement journey or bring a discontinuity and a new and hopefully successful and sustainable direction for the future (Hargreaves and Fink, 2006).

Given that human resources are essential in school improvement journeys, there has been considerable international interest in the professional development of staff and in the development of leaders themselves. There is a rapidly growing international focus upon leadership development (Brundrett and Crawford, 2008) as it has been identified as an important component of school improvement (Bush, 2008). For example, in the US, Crow (2006) has recognised the importance of the good preparation of school leaders as it may well make a difference to their subsequent leadership practices. If leaders learn to do their jobs well, they may well be better equipped to address their school improvement journey and make a bigger difference in identifying and serving the needs of their learners. Rhodes and Brundrett (2008) contend that the establishment of schools as effective training grounds for leadership development represents a major challenge for incumbent school leaders. Although more work is needed in order to establish the best way to identify and enhance the leadership talent of individuals, it is timely for leaders to ask the questions, 'what creative mechanisms can we use to encourage staff to aspire to leadership roles?' and 'how do we know we really are a good training ground for leadership development?'

A leadership crisis and the improvement journey

Given their importance, the quality and supply of leaders in schools has attracted much international attention. Shortages of school leaders, especially headteachers, have been reported in Australia (Gronn and Rawlings-Sanaei, 2003; Barty et al., 2005; Cranston, 2007), Canada (Williams, 2003), New Zealand (Brooking et al., 2003) and in the United States (Thompson et al., 2003). In the UK, a dwindling supply of school leaders has been reported in the educational press (Ward, 2004; Griffiths, 2005; Shaw, 2006), by the National College for School Leadership (NCSL, 2006a, 2006b, 2007) and in annual reports on the state of the labour market for senior staff in schools in England and Wales (Howson, 2007). In contrast, MacBeath (2006a) points to the lack of leadership shortages in most Asia-Pacific countries especially those with a sense of leadership succession planning which includes an early identification of those with leadership talent and its continued and systematic development. There is increasing evidence to suggest that high levels of workload and bureaucracy in UK schools serve to deter individuals from aspiring to leadership posts (Draper and McMichael, 2003; Hayes, 2005; Bedford, 2006; Hargreaves and Fink, 2006; Fink and Brayman, 2006; Hargreaves and Goodson, 2006; NCSL, 2006a; 2006b).

The challenging nature of headship and particularly early headship is well documented in the literature. Hobson et al. (2003) emphasise the difficulties awaiting new heads in terms of their professional isolation and loneliness; the legacy, practice and style of the previous head; managing time and priorities; managing the school budget; dealing with ineffective staff; accommodating new government initiatives and problems with site management. Briggs et al. (2006) also list the many day-to-day pressures and changing demands unsettling to new heads. These difficulties can be exaggerated by the context new heads can find themselves in, especially if they have moved to a new school to take up their post (Holligan et al., 2006). One of the most significant challenges facing heads is that the enactment of their leadership is a very public performance which can attract success or failure on a day-to-day basis. Although heads may feel that they can accommodate the emotional cost involved with this as well as the likely need to repeatedly internalise their own feelings during the enactment of their leadership, the protracted control of emotions by heads could lead to feelings of stress and disenchantment. Nevertheless, incumbent heads have accepted a duty to become the lead professional in their school and to fix learning as the central mission of their school. Heads can have no more important role than seeking to enhance the outcomes for pupils in their care.

Leadership and learning

The quality of teaching and learning in schools has long been associated with the achievement of pupils and was one of the key characteristics identified by school effectiveness researchers as contributing to an effective school (see Sammons et al., 1995; Mortimore, 1998). However, following the decentralisation of education management in many parts of the world (see Brundrett and Rhodes, 2010) concerns were expressed by both researchers and practitioners that heads' time may be unduly deflected towards human and financial management to the detriment of a full focus on teaching and learning within their schools. There is now much renewed interest in leadership for high-quality teaching and learning in schools. Indeed, the relationship between leadership and learning is increasingly identified as one of the most important factors in improving the effectiveness of schools. Although the conceptualisation of the relationship between leadership and learning is likely to vary internationally, MacBeath and Dempster (2009) have argued that five principles underlie the notion of 'leadership for learning'. These principles include: shared or distributed leadership; a focus on learning; creation of the conditions favourable for learning; creation of a dialogue about leadership and learning; and, the establishment of a shared sense of accountability. The question emerges as how can leaders best impact upon learning within their schools?

The notion of becoming a more 'learning-centred' school suggests that new forms of leadership may be required, emphasising structural and cultural change to enable greater collaboration and distribution of power and authority between staff so that they may contribute more fully to improvement (Burton and Brundrett, 2005). The importance of learning-centred leadership in schools has received much attention in the literature and it has been seen to have great potential in promoting and sustaining school improvement journeys (Benson, 2002; Hollinsworth, 2004; Webb, 2005). Dimmock (2000) sees a learning-centred school as one whose mission, organisation, curriculum and leadership are wholly focused on providing successful learning experiences and outcomes for pupils. Dimmock and Walker (2004) suggest that the starting point for leadership should be to identify the nature and quality of learning outcomes sought by the school. If school leaders seek to promote high-quality teaching and learning within their schools, teachers need to be enabled to provide the best possible learning experiences for their pupils so as to inspire and bring about the engagement and inclusion of a wide diversity of learners. Leadership for diversity and social justice in schools is seen as essential to ensure that all pupils from all groups represented within the school have access to all available opportunities. Leaders in schools have a duty to exert their power, authority and influence to best effect in addressing any structural and cultural changes necessary to improve inclusion and dismantle barriers wherever they exist. Indeed, inclusion has emerged as an important element of school improvement in many schools as they seek to reduce the gap between the highest and lowest achievers (Cruddas, 2005).

Because teachers are leaders of learning in their own classrooms, senior leaders need to help teachers improve their own practice by enabling teachers to learn. In short, a learning-centred school places both pupil and staff learning at the core of its work. Links between leadership and learning may, for example, involve enabling others to learn (Swaffield and MacBeath, 2009), empowering middle leaders and teachers to take a direct lead in teaching and learning (Fitzgerald and Gunter, 2006), using outcome data as a basis for improvement and rewarding good teacher performance (Blasé and Blasé, 2004) or skilfully understanding and working with the immediate sociocultural context of the school so as to best foster desired change and school improvement (Busher, 2002).

In leading for learning it is certain that productive partnerships with both internal and external stakeholders who have an interest in the school, such as pupils, staff, parents and community, will need to be secured and directed towards improvement efforts. The reconciliation of a variety of expectations as well as engaging the focus of diverse groups of stakeholders clearly demands high commitment and emotional resilience on the part of heads and other leaders in schools and this cost may be further exaggerated in schools facing challenging circumstances. For example, in the United States, Van Voorhis and Sheldon (2004) have explored the importance of the school principal in developing partnerships with pupil families and the community in order to obtain positive effects on pupil outcomes and behaviour. Attempts have been made in some schools, through mechanisms such as parents' consultation groups, pupils' councils and the engagement of pupil voice, to involve learners and their parents in a variety

317

of decision-making and school improvement activities. Despite improvements in many schools, the notion of parental choice of a preferred school within a framework of market accountability in the UK, intended to cause unpopular schools to improve, has met with mixed success. Day (2003) contends that the drive to secure school improvement and school effectiveness in this way has been more readily assimilated by middle-class communities to the continued disadvantage of many socially and economically deprived and migrant communities.

Learning communities and school improvement

There has been much debate concerning the possible benefits to schools in adopting the characteristics of a learning community. These benefits have been associated with improved response to change (Stoll and Louis, 2007), enabling staff development (Stoll *et al.*, 2006) and increased effectiveness as evidenced by better pupil outcomes (Roberts and Pruitt, 2003). Busher (2006) suggests that a school learning community involves the voice of leaders, teachers, pupils, support staff and other adults with the purpose of working together to foster pupil learning. Despite the notion that if a school wishes to improve teaching and learning, the recipient pupils may be able to add to this debate, in some schools 'pupil voice' has generally remained limited to letting pupils 'have a say' within the bounds of school constraints (MacBeath, 2006b). In an Australian study, Lewis and Burman (2008) have elaborated areas of decision-making about classroom management in which teachers would not feel comfortable in negotiating with pupils. Power and maturity differences between teachers and pupils do exist; however, it is open to leaders to consider if pupil voice can have a positive effect on the improvement of teaching and learning (see Angus, 2006) and whether or not they wish to encourage pupil leadership as part of their vision for leadership for learning within their own schools.

Changing models of leadership and school effectiveness

The research literature shows the emergence and consideration of many types and models of leadership thought to be influential in enhancing teaching and learning. For example, Harris (2004) suggests that those heads who distribute leadership responsibilities amongst staff are more likely to build capacity for change and realise desired improvements. Whilst leadership distribution is seen by many as an important means of realising improved pupil outcomes (Gronn, 2000; Wallace, 2002; Hargreaves and Fink, 2006; Spillane, 2006), presently there is no conclusive evidence that such distribution impacts directly on pupils' achievements (see Hartley 2007, 2009). Notwithstanding this, the pragmatic approach of allowing teachers more involvement in decision-making about their work would seems to make sense in many circumstances. For example, in South Africa, Grant (2006) has shown that in some schools where teacher leadership is underdeveloped there is a consequent limitation on the impact teachers can have in effecting improvements in teaching and learning. Increasingly, the improved management of teaching and learning is being seen as a key role of school principals in South Africa and an important element in raising school effectiveness (Bush and Glover, 2009).

The Every Child Matters (DfES, 2003) agenda in the UK recognises that schools have an important role to play in raising pupil educational achievements, including those disadvantaged groups who consistently underachieve. A leading principle of the Every Child Matters Agenda is that greater integration of schools with their communities should enable more effective provision of services to meet the needs of children and families. Coupled with this, the DfES

(2005) Extended Schools Prospectus suggests that by 2010 all schools should offer extended services including access to childcare, parenting skills and other specialist services. This requires school leaders to be able to collaborate effectively with a wide range of agencies and to integrate their work into the work of the school. In England, the emergence of 'Federations', which are groups of schools that have formally agreed to work together with the intention of improving pupil inclusion and raising achievement, reflect a trend to address school improvement via networking, collaboration and knowledge sharing. Federations are reported to increase possibilities for sharing not only ideas, but also resources, staff development opportunities and leadership and management. Despite variations in the way leadership is put in place in different federations, findings drawn from a number of case studies reported by Chapman et al. (2010) show that the quality of the heads' leadership is highly influential in the creation of successful collaboration within federations and hence the possibility to better serve the needs of all learners.

The future

The linkage between high-quality leadership and effective schools has been well documented. Although the leadership effect in bringing about improvement is difficult to quantify, it is clear that leaders can and do make a difference. In this chapter, some of the direct and indirect effects of leadership on change, improvement and effectiveness have been considered. The chapter offers suggestions that, despite the many challenges facing leaders, leadership and the effective school are related via strategy and vision, understanding and developing people, fostering enabling cultures and communication, managing the teaching and learning programme and helping to balance bureaucracy with passion. Wrigley (2008) reminds us that in our search for improvement we should not lose sight of the kind of future we would like to see and who will be the beneficiaries of any changes proposed. Despite successes, Wrigley (2008) argues that the predominant paradigm of school improvement is too uncritical of the 'givens' of curriculum and pedagogy and still fails to accommodate a full understanding of the potential mismatch between school culture and the communities in which pupils live. He suggests a paradigm shift away from an education 'market', as in the case of England, driven to improve by league tables, privatisations and forms of accountability which may constrain creativity, to a future where more open debate about these such 'givens' would contribute to a new vision for school improvement and notions of school effectiveness that had meaning for all learners, their parents and their communities. Whilst details of the relationship between leadership and the effective school will vary internationally, school leaders should never lose sight of their role in securing the life chances of all pupils within the debates, policies and enactment yet to come.

Conclusion

High-quality school leadership has been repeatedly identified with the establishment of effective schools. Although the conception of effectiveness may vary internationally, and is subject to the influence of prevailing policy contexts, heads and other school leaders have an important role to play in promoting the best possible teaching and learning experiences for pupils in their care. Incumbent school leaders may establish a focus on teaching and learning in a variety of ways. These include structural and cultural changes to foster staff collaboration, shared leadership, creativity in pedagogy and curriculum planning, the use of data to inform continued progress, teacher development and hearing the voices of stakeholders such as parents, community representatives, other caring agencies and perhaps the voice of pupils themselves. School leaders should not forget their own learning as part of their improvement efforts and their continued motivation, even in the face of leadership recruitment difficulties in some countries, needs to be maintained and energised if improvement journeys are to be successfully made. The literature shows that leadership creativity is still alive, for example, many schools have benefitted from leadership actions to effect networking with other schools in order to share ideas, resources and good practices that can be tailored to meet their school's own unique circumstances and the needs of their pupils. Finally, leadership for diversity, inclusion and social justice remains essential in all countries if all pupils are to have a better chance of achieving their potential and pursuing a chosen life agenda with dignity and success.

Questions for further investigation

1   What are the sources of professional learning for teachers in a school? What actions could a head take to foster teacher learning and its transference to the classroom experience of pupils?
2   What factors might limit the raising of learner achievement in a school?
3   To what extent can pupil voice and pupil leadership contribute to school improvement and effectiveness?
4   What cross-boundary transactions can occur between a school and the local community? How could a head harness these to contribute to school improvement and effectiveness?

Suggested further reading

Blasé, J. and Blasé, J. (2004) *Handbook of Instructional Leadership: How successful principals promote teaching and learning*. Thousand Oaks, CA: Corwin Press. This book is for those interested in establishing what successful leaders do to enhance teaching and learning. It offers an examination of instructional leadership in relation to the development of a professional learning community.

Brundrett, M. and Rhodes, C.P. (2010) *Leadership for Quality and Accountability in Education*. Abingdon: Routledge. Set within the 'Leadership for Learning Series' this book explores the place of leadership in developing high-quality teaching and learning set against a backdrop of stakeholder expectations and accountability measures. It is based upon the premise that learning is at the heart of leadership and leaders themselves should also be learners.

Coleman, M. and Earley, P. (2005) *Leadership and Management in Education: Cultures, Change and Context*. Oxford: Oxford University Press. This edited text provides international perspectives on leadership and management in relation to the improvement of educational organisations. It offers an exploration of how leadership and management can contribute to the enhancement of student learning and staff development.

MacBeath, J. and Dempster, N. (Eds.) (2009) *Connecting Leadership and Learning: Principles for Practice*. London: Routledge. This book examines the nature of learning and the qualities of leadership that make schools places of learning. The relationship between leadership and learning is presented to enable the reader to see how this can work in schools and in classrooms.

References

Angus, L. (2006) 'Educational leadership and the imperative of including student voice, student interests, and students' lives in the mainstream', *International Journal of Leadership in Education*, 9, 4, pp. 369–379.

Barty, K., Thomson, P., Blackmore, J. and Sachs, J. (2005) 'Unpacking the issues: researching the shortage of school principals in two states in Australia', *Australian Educational Researcher*, 32, 3, pp. 1–18.

Bedford, S. (2006) 'Workload: the real turn-off for would-be heads', *Times Educational Supplement*, 5 May, p. 7.

Benson, S. (2002) *Leading Learning: Instructional Leadership in Infants Schools*, Full Practitioner Report. Nottingham: National College for School Leadership.

Blasé, J. and Blasé, J. (2004) *Handbook of Instructional Leadership: How successful principals promote teaching and learning*. Thousand Oaks, CA: Corwin Press.

Briggs, A.R.J., Bush, T. and Middlewood, D. (2006) 'From immersion to establishment: The challenges facing new school heads and the role of "New Visions" in resolving them', *Cambridge Journal of Education*, 36, 2, pp. 257–276.

Brooking, K., Collins, G., Court, M. and O'Neill, J. (2003) 'Getting below the surface of the principal recruitment crisis in New Zealand primary schools', *Australian Journal of Education*, 47, 2, pp. 146–158.

Brundrett, M. and Crawford, M. (Eds.) (2008) *Developing School Leaders: An International Perspective*. London: Routledge.

Brundrett, M. and Rhodes, C.P. (2010) *Leadership for Quality and Accountability in Education*. London: Routledge.

Burton, N. and Brundrett, M. (2005) *Leading the Curriculum in the Primary School*. London: Paul Chapman Publishing.

Bush, T. (2008) *Leadership and Management Development in Education*. London: Sage.

Bush, T. and Glover, D. (2009) *Managing Teaching and Learning: A Concept Paper*. Johannesburg: Matthew Goniwe School of Leadership and Governance.

Busher, H. (2002) 'Managing change to improve learning', in Bush, T. and Bell, L. (Eds.) *The Principles and Practice of Educational Management*. London: Sage.

Busher, H. (2006) *Understanding Educational Leadership: People, Power and Culture*. Maidenhead: Open University Press.

Chapman, C., Lindsay, G., Muijs, D., Harris, A., Arweck, E. and Goodall, J. (2010) 'Governance, leadership, and management in federations of schools', *School Effectiveness and School Improvement*, 21, 1, pp. 53–74.

Cranston, N.C. (2007) 'Through the eyes of potential aspirants: another view of the principalship', *School Leadership and Management*, 27, 2, pp. 109–128.

Crow, G. (2006) 'Complexity and the beginning principal in the United States: Perspectives on socialization', *Journal of Educational Administration*, 44, 4, pp. 310–325.

Cruddas, L. (2005) *Learning Mentors in Schools: policy and practice*. Stoke on Trent: Trentham Books.

Day, C. (2003) 'Successful leadership in the twenty-first century', in Harris, A., Day, C., Hopkins, D., Hadfield, M., Hargreaves, A. and Chapman, C. (Eds.) *Effective Leadership for School Improvement*. London: RoutledgeFalmer.

DfES (2003) 'Every Child Matters' (CM5860). Norwich: HMSO.

DfES (2005) *Higher Standards, Better Schools for All: more choice for parents and pupils*. London: Stationery Office.

Dimmock, C. (2000) *Designing the Learning Centred School: a cross-cultural perspective*. London: Falmer Press.

Dimmock, C. and Walker, A. (2004) 'A new approach to strategic leadership: learning-centredness, connectivity and cultural context in school design', *School Leadership and Management*, 24, 1, pp. 39–56.

Draper, J. and McMichael, P. (2003) 'The rocky road to headship', *Australian Journal of Education*, 47, 2, pp. 185–196.

Fink, D. and Brayman, C. (2006) 'School leadership succession and the challenges of change', *Educational Administration Quarterly*, 42, 1, pp. 62–89.

Fitzgerald, T. and Gunter, H. (2006) 'Leading learning: middle leadership in schools in England and New Zealand', *Management in Education*, 20, pp. 6–8.

Grant, C. (2006) 'Teacher leadership: emerging voices on teacher leadership – some South African views', *Educational Management Administration and Leadership*, 34, 4, pp. 511–532.

Griffiths, S. (2005) 'Schools without heads in staff crisis', *Sunday Times*, 18 December, p. 16.

Gronn, P. (2000) 'Distributed properties: a new architecture for leadership', *Educational Management and Administration*, 28, 3, pp. 317–338.

Gronn, P. and Rawlings-Sanaei, F. (2003) 'Recruiting schools principals in a climate of leadership disengagement', *Australian Journal of Education*, 47, 2, pp. 172–184.

Hallinger, P. and Snidvongs, K. (2005) *Adding Value to School Leadership and Management: A review of trends in the development of managers in the education and business sectors*. Available at: www.ncsl.org.uk/publications (accessed 10 December 2009).

Hargreaves, A. and Fink, D. (2006) *Sustainable Leadership*, San Francisco CA: Jossey-Bass.

Hargreaves, A. and Goodson, I. (2006) 'Educational change over time? The sustainability and non-sustainability of three decades of secondary school change and continuity', *Educational Administration Quarterly*, 42, 1, pp. 3–41.

Harris, A. (2004) 'Distributed leadership and school improvement: leading or misleading?', *Educational Management Administration and Leadership*, 32, 1, pp. 11–24.

Hartley, D. (2007) 'The emergence of distributed leadership in education: why now?', *British Journal of Educational Studies*, 55, 2, pp. 202–214.

Hartley, D. (2009) 'Paradigms: how far does research in distributed leadership "stretch"?', *Educational Management Administration and Leadership*, 38, 3, pp. 271–285.

Hayes, T. (2005) *Rising Stars and Sitting Tenants: a picture of deputy headship in one London borough and how some of its schools are preparing their deputies for headship*, Summary Practitioner Enquiry Report. Nottingham: National College for School Leadership.

Hobson, A., Brown, E., Ashby, P., Keys, W., Sharp, C. and Benefield, P. (2003) *Issues for Early Headship – problems and support strategies*. Nottingham: National College for School Leadership.

Holligan, C., Menter, I., Hutchings, M. and Walker, M. (2006) 'Becoming a head teacher: the perspectives of new head teachers in twenty-first-century England', *Journal of In-Service Education*, 32, 1, pp. 103–122.

Hollinsworth, A. (2004) *The School as a Learning Community*, International Research Associate Perspective Report. Nottingham: National College for School Leadership.

Hopkins, D., Reynolds, D. and Gray, J. (2005) *School Improvement – Lessons from Research*. London: DfES.

Howson, J. (2007) *The State of the Labour Market for Senior Staff in Schools in England and Wales 2006–2007*. Available at: www.educationdatasurveys.org.uk (accessed 21 April 2007).

Lewis, R. and Burman, E. (2008) 'Providing for student voice in classroom management: teachers' views', *International Journal of Inclusive Education*, 12, 2, pp. 151–167.

MacBeath, J. (2006a) 'The talent enigma', *International Journal of Leadership in Education*, 9, 3, pp. 183–204.

MacBeath, J. (2006b) 'Finding a voice, finding self', *Educational Review*, 58, 2, pp. 195–207.

MacBeath, J. and Dempster, N. (Eds.) (2009) *Connecting Leadership and Learning: Principles for Practice*. London: Routledge.

Mortimore, P. (1998) *The Road to Improvement: Reflections on School Effectiveness*. Lisse: Swets and Zeitlinger Publishers.

Muijs, D. (2006) 'New directions for school effectiveness research: towards school effectiveness without schools', *Journal of Educational Change*, 7, pp. 141–160.

National College for School Leadership (2006a) 'Leadership succession: an overview'. Available at: www.ncsl.org.uk/publications (accessed 5 December 2009).

National College for School Leadership (2006b) 'Succession planning: formal advice to the secretary of state'. Available at: www.ncsl.org.uk/publications (accessed 5 December 2009).

National College for School Leadership (2007) 'Recruiting headteachers and senior leaders: overview of research findings'. Available at: www.ncsl.org.uk/publications (accessed 12 April 2009).

Rhodes, C.P. and Brundrett, M. (2008) 'What makes my school a good training ground for leadership development?', *Management in Education*, 22, 1, pp. 21–27.

Roberts, S. and Pruitt, E. (2003) *Schools as Professional Learning Communities*. London: Sage.

Sammons, P., Hillman, J. and Mortimore, P. (1995) *Key Characteristics of Effective Schools: A Review of School Effectiveness Research*. London: Institute of Education and Ofsted.

Saunders, L. (2000) *Effective Schooling in Rural Africa Report 2: Key issues concerning school effectiveness and improvement*. Washington, DC: World Bank.

Shaw, M. (2006) 'New signs of crisis in leadership recruitment', *Times Educational Supplement*, January 13, p. 2.

Spillane, J.P. (2006) *Distributed Leadership*. San Francisco, CA: Jossey-Bass.

Stoll, L. and Louis, K.S. (2007) *Professional Learning Communities: divergence, depths and dilemmas*. Maidenhead: Open University Press.

Stoll, L., Bolam, R., McMahon, A., Thomas, S., Wallace, M., Greenwood, A. and Hawkey, K. (2006) *What is a Professional Learning Community? A summary*, DfES-0187–2006. London: DfES.

Swaffield, S. and MacBeath, J. (2009) 'Leadership for learning', in MacBeath, J. and Dempster, N. (Eds.) *Connecting Leadership and Learning: Principles for Practice*. London: Routledge.

Teddlie, C. and Reynolds, D. (Eds.) (2000) *The International Handbook of School Effectiveness Research*. London: Falmer Press.

Thomson, P., Blackmore, J., Sachs, J. and Tregenza, K. (2003) 'High stakes principalship – sleepless nights, heart attacks, and sudden death accountabilities: reading media representations of the United States principal shortage', *Australian Journal of Education*, 47, 2, pp. 118–132.

Van Voorhis, P. and Sheldon, S. (2004) 'Principal's roles in the development of US programs of school, family, and community partnerships', *International Journal of Educational Research*, 41, pp. 55–70.

Wallace, M. (2002) 'Modelling distributed leadership and management effectiveness: primary school senior management teams in England and Wales', *School Effectiveness and School Improvement*, 13, 2, pp. 163–186.

Ward, H. (2004) 'Is head's exodus starting already?', *Times Educational Supplement*, 6 February, p. 16.

Webb, R. (2005) 'Leading teaching and learning in the primary school: from educative leadership to pedagogical leadership', *Educational Management Administration and Leadership*, 33, 1, pp. 69–91.

West-Burnham, J. (2009) *Rethinking Educational Leadership: From improvement to transformation*. London: Continuum.

Williams, T.R. (2003) 'Ontario's principal scarcity: yesterday's abdicated responsibility – today's unrecognised challenge', *Australian Journal of Education*, 47, 2, pp. 159–171.

Wrigley, T. (2008) 'School improvement in a neo-liberal world', *Journal of Educational Administration and History*, 40, 2, pp. 129–148.

34

Multicultural education

Dina Kiwan
Birkbeck College, University of London

Multiculturalism is not about difference and identity per se but about those differences that are embedded in and sustained by culture; that is a body of beliefs and practices in terms of which a group of people understand themselves and the world and organise their individual and collective lives. Unlike differences that spring from individual choices, culturally derived differences carry a measure of authority and are gathered and structured by virtue of being embedded in a shared and historically inherited system of meaning and significance.

(Parekh, 2000, p. 23)

Overview

What is clearly evident on reading the vast literature on multiculturalism and 'multicultural education' is that these are contested terms with no agreed-upon definitions. Below, I briefly outline a number of approaches to conceptualising 'multiculturalism' before locating these approaches within the educational context with respect to theory, research, policy and practice. Using the case study example of the relatively recent development of citizenship education in England, I examine how discourses of multiculturalism are utilised and positioned in relation to the policy debates on 'integration', 'diversity' and 'identity'.

Introduction: what is 'multiculturalism'?

The conceptions of 'hodgepodge' vs. 'mosaic' multiculturalism distinguish two approaches to multiculturalism (Joppke and Lukes, 1999) where 'hodgepodge' multiculturalism is conceptualised in terms of hybridity and mixing, conceiving of culture as in a state of flux rather than as static. In contrast, 'mosaic' multiculturalism is conceptualised in terms co-existing different 'bounded' groups, where differences are kept distinct, therefore producing the phenomenon of different groups living separately. In this conception of multiculturalism, culture is conceptualised in a more deterministic, bounded way, where culture is linked directly to territory.

Another conceptualisation presents multiculturalism as a critique of Western universalism and liberalism, where multiculturalism is conceptualised as a reaction against the dominant discourse of universalism, and where universalism is conceptualised as the ethnocentrism of the dominant group (Joppke and Lukes, 1999). This was exemplified, for example, in the UK, when David Blunkett, home secretary in 2001, called on ethnic minorities to adopt British 'norms of acceptability', when he said: 'and those that come into our home – for that is what it is – should accept those norms' (2001, p.1).

A third conceptualisation of multiculturalism utilises the notions of 'thick'/'strong' and 'thin'/'inclusive' (Spinner-Halev, 1999). 'Thick' multiculturalism refers to groups wanting to maintain and protect their separateness; for example, the Amish, or the ultra-Orthodox Jews in the USA. In contrast, 'thin' or 'inclusive' multiculturalism refers to where groups wish to have their cultural practices accepted by the dominant culture. In the thick/strong model, the focus is on the issue of intergroup justice, rather than focusing on the rights of the individual and the relationship to the state. In contrast, the 'thin' model of multiculturalism is concerned with individual rights, and hence addresses the intragroup dynamics to a greater extent. In this model, group rights supplement individual human rights. This is the form of multicultural citizenship being advocated by Kymlicka (1995).

Multicultural approaches in education

Discourses of multiculturalism can be seen in educational policies and practices dominant from the 1980s onwards. In the UK, many teachers were primarily concerned with two issues: the educational underachievement of ethnic minorities, and including non-British culture, literature and history within the British curriculum (Grillo, 1998). Likewise in the United States, there has been pedagogical and curriculum reform in the name of multiculturalism. James Banks, recognised as a leading scholar and founder of the field of multicultural education in the United States, conceives of its main aims as transformative, in terms of improved outcomes for marginalised students (Banks, 2006). Concerns relating to balancing 'unity' and 'diversity' are clearly evident in the US, the roots of which can be traced back to the nineteenth century, evidenced in debates about the notion of the 'melting pot', the teaching of history in schools, and whether the English language should be the official language (Nieto, 2009). Over the last 50 years, Australia has moved from a model of assimilating immigrants to – like Canada – officially adopting multiculturalism as its guiding policy, in particular in the domain of education (Inglis, 2009). This has included a focus on language provision ('community' languages), and cultural maintenance (Inglis, 2009). In the UK and also Australia, anti-racist advocates typically perceived some of the 'softer' multicultural approaches as tending to exoticise ethnic minorities and presenting only a superficial characterisation of minority cultures – what Troyna (1984) referred to as 'the three S's – saris, samosas and steelbands'; as such, multicultural approaches were deemed to be relatively ineffective, and tokenistic, rather than effectively addressing structural disadvantage and inequalities. As a consequence, human rights and anti-racist education approaches have often been embraced in light of such criticisms. It has been argued that multicultural approaches in education tend to use 'softer' terms such as 'culture', 'equality' and 'prejudice', as opposed to anti-racism's link with 'harder' language, such as 'conflict', 'oppression' and 'exploitation' (Gillborn, 2004).

325

However, it is important to take into account that multiculturalism emerged in Europe – in contrast to the US – as an 'extension of liberal tolerance rather than aiming at participation' (Delanty, 2003, p. 93); as such it was not primarily intended as a model for bringing about societal change. In countries that had formally been colonial powers (e.g. France, Belgium, UK, Netherlands), the integration of these immigrants was the context of such educational initiatives, although approaches varied from the negation of difference in France, with its civic republican approach, to the celebration of difference in the UK and the Netherlands (Allemann-Ghionda, 2009). Banks' (2004) transformative model of multiculturalism in the US outlines five dimensions: 1) content integration – where teachers used contextualised examples, 2) knowledge construction processes – uncovering implicitly held assumptions, 3) prejudice reduction, 4) equity pedagogy – facilitating achievement of students from different backgrounds, and 5) empowering school culture and social structures. Anti-racist movements in the UK can be historically contextualised in relation to the dual movements from 'Black' and working-class solidarities (Virdee and Cole, 2000). In addition to these different contextualisations and aims, it has also been argued that there is terminological confusion: that 'multiculturalism' is not merely a *descriptor* of a given society, but rather refers to (or should refer to), the society's *response* to a given multicultural setting (Parekh, 2000). Similarly, Sen (2006) argues that typically what tends to be erroneously labelled as multiculturalism – where different communities live separately side by side – is in fact 'plural monoculturalism'.

Proponents of multiculturalism have attempted to respond to anti-racist criticisms by re-inventing and re-naming multiculturalism as 'critical' multiculturalism (May, 1994, 1999; Watson, 2000), which aims to be more pro-active and less 'celebratory' in its emphasis. UK examples of 'critical' multiculturalism include the revision of curricula, and the establishment of faith schools (Watson, 2000). The British state has historically funded Christian and Jewish faith schools, and this has been extended for Islamic schools (Grillo, 1998). However, government support has resulted in much debate, with those supporting the maintenance of faith-based schools arguing in terms of equality of treatment between different religious groups (Pring, 2005), parents' rights to a diversity of choice with respect to the education of their children, that such schools provide a strong moral framework, and also that they are often academically successful (Parker-Jenkins, 2005). Although the number of requests for such stated-funded Islamic schools are very small (Gates, 2005), critics argue that separate faith schools are divisive and not conducive to community cohesion (Mason, 2005), and indeed antithetical to the liberal aims of education (Brighouse, 2005; Pring, 2005). In the US, examples of critical multiculturalism include bilingual and bicultural programmes, prejudice reduction programmes and equality promotion programmes (Banks, 2009).

Yet in response to anti-racist critiques of multiculturalism and its aims, anti-racist approaches have been critiqued as falling into a 'racial dualism' with their prioritisation and emphasis on 'race' or 'colour' (Gillborn, 2004). Indeed, it has been argued that anti-racist approaches neglect the importance of culture and ignore political, religious and socio-economic differences within groups (Modood, 1996; Parekh, 2000). Whilst acknowledging the laudable anti-oppressive aims of anti-racist movements, it is asserted that these approaches, albeit unintentionally, essentialise groups (Gilroy, 1987).

Taking account of, and acknowledging such critiques, more 'critical' theories of race have been developed. Omi and Winant (2004), for example, outline key features of a critical theory of race where they propose that it must be politically and historically contextualised and globally applicable. Coming from the United States, there has been the development of critical race theory (CRT) – originally developed by legal theorists, and now being applied to the field of education (Ladson-Billings, 2004; Gillborn, 2008; Taylor *et al.*, 2009). CRT defines racism as 'not the acts of individuals, but the larger, systemic, structural conventions and customs that uphold and sustain oppressive group relationships, status, income, and educational attainment' (Taylor, 2009, p. 4). As such, the focus is not on culture or identity, but rather on the political and legal structures 'rooted in the ideology of White European supremacy and the global impact of colonialism' (Taylor, 2009, p. 4). In terms of the methodological approach of CRT, narrative plays an important role, emphasising the importance of the perspectives of those traditionally excluded. It also implies a theory of knowledge, grounded in the way in which reality is interpreted, influenced by the understandings of those experiences (Taylor, 2009).

CRT in education is a relatively new methodological endeavour, where it is believed that 'racial analysis' can be utilised to examine and challenge the educational barriers that non-white people face. Notions of meritocracy, objectivity and knowledge are also interrogated through pedagogical tools such as dialogue and participation through a variety of stakeholders (Taylor, 2009).

More recently, multicultural approaches have also increasingly come under attack from those concerned with a perceived emphasis on diversity and difference at the expense of unity, national identity and common values (Schlesinger, 1992; Huntington, 2004). This has been evident in the UK over the last decade, where there has been a growing discontent in media and policy discourses with the term 'multiculturalism' (e.g. Alibhai-Brown, 2000; Blunkett, 2001, p. 4; Phillips, 2004; Toynbee, 2004; Commission on Integration and Cohesion, 2007). The UK's policy emphasis on integration, community cohesion, common values and 'Britishness' has become an increasingly dominant theme since 9/11, evident in a number of policies across a number of different government departments, relating to community cohesion, citizenship education and naturalisation (Home Office, 2001a, 2001b, 2002, 2003; Rammell, 2006; Ajegbo *et al.*, 2007; Commission on Integration and Cohesion, 2007). A review of diversity and citizenship in the curriculum was launched by the UK government in 2006 to examine 'how we can incorporate modern British cultural and social history into the curriculum within our secondary schools', framed in terms of community cohesion (Rammell, 2006). Since November 2006, a new statutory requirement (Education and Inspections Act 2006) has been introduced putting a duty on schools to promote community cohesion with a concomitant requirement for schools to be officially inspected for this since September 2007.

Citizenship education policy in the UK: a case study

The United Kingdom is both a 'multination' state – made up of England, Scotland, Northern Ireland and Wales – and a 'polyethnic' state, with a large number of different ethnic and religious groups, largely, although not exclusively a result of mass immigration since the Second World War. British national identity has historically been formulated implicitly rather than explicitly (Grillo, 1998); also it has not managed to supersede Scottish, Welsh or Irish nationalism (Rex, 1991). With regard to English nationalism, despite England's dominant position within the Union, the English did not, to the same extent, develop a distinct English identity, although there has been a reclamation by the political mainstream of 'English' identity in the last few years from the far-right (e.g. Blunkett, 2005). This lack of a unified concept of 'Britishness' has been explained in terms of globalisation, Britain's declining economic power coupled with the collapse of the Empire, Britain's changing relationship with Europe, devolution and increased pluralism (Runnymede Trust, 2000).

Grillo (1998) proposes that 'Britishness' has been defined by means of contrast with an 'other' – historically, Catholic France – as well as through reference to certain civic values and institutions. Racialised discourses have been implicitly coupled to discourses on national identity, which can be understood in the context of post-war mass immigration predominantly from the former colonies of the British Empire (Runnymede Trust, 2000), and more recently, perceived threats to liberties arising from international terrorism (Pattie *et al.*, 2004).

The history of citizenship education in England can be traced back to the nineteenth-century Victorian context where education had clear social and moral purposes (Batho, 1990; Lawton, 2000). 'Public' schools (which refer to private or independent schools in the UK as opposed to state schools) prepared the upper classes for leadership in England and the Empire, in contrast to education for the poor – teaching them to accept their position in society. Until 2002, citizenship education was never a statutory requirement in schools, although its history can be traced over the last century (Batho, 1990). In the 1970s, a programme of political literacy committed to developing active participation was developed by Sir Bernard Crick, long-time campaigner and public intellectual advocating political education in schools, however, this did not take hold with the Conservatives coming to power in 1979, and a raft of new social justice programmes in education were developed in the 1980s – for example, 'peace education', anti-sexist education' and anti-racist education' – reflecting public debates of the time (Davies, 1999).

A historic shift occurred with the policy review of citizenship education undertaken in 1998 by the Advisory Group on Education for Citizenship and the Teaching of Democracy in Schools, chaired by Bernard Crick (QCA, 1998). The conceptualisation of citizenship was defined in terms of the three strands of social and moral responsibility, community involvement and political literacy, referring to T.H. Marshall's conceptualisation of citizenship as being made up of three elements – civil, political and social citizenship – (Marshall and Bottomore, 1992), although it lacked Marshall's emphasis on rights.

Although the Crick Report takes T.H. Marshall as its starting point for his conceptualisation of citizenship (QCA, 1998), the issue of social inclusion is not substantively addressed; in particular, issues relating to ethnic and religious diversity were relatively neglected (Kiwan, 2008). In the text of the Crick Report itself, diversity is referred to as a potential barrier to citizenship, rather than as an integral aspect of citizenship. Diversity is seen as a potential problem linked to the loss of a values consensus and linked to 'dissent and social conflict' (QCA, 1998, p. 44). The dominant conception of citizenship is a 'participative' conception, based on equipping pupils with the skills for active participation, with the implicit assumption that if the knowledge and training is provided, that this necessarily translates into active and inclusive participation for all. However, such an approach does not consider what motivates or acts as a barrier to participation; I have proposed that identity plays a significant role in motivation to participate, as one must be able to *identify* with the larger community – therefore I have advocated a 'multicultural' conception of citizenship (Kiwan, 2008).

In 2006, a Diversity and Citizenship review was commissioned by the government Department of Education and Skills, to review teaching of ethnic and religious diversity across the curriculum and, in particular, within the citizenship curriculum. A review report recommended the addition of an additional 'fourth' strand, entitled 'Identity and Diversity: Living together in the United Kingdom' (Ajegbo *et al.*, 2007). The addition of this fourth strand aimed to broaden the focus on citizenship education predominantly in terms of skills, to contextualising pupils' skills of active participation in relation to the historical as well as contemporary socio-political context in the UK, Europe and globally. This has been incorporated into the Programmes of Study (QCA, 2007), and was introduced in schools in

England in September 2007. Key concepts include 'democracy and justice', 'rights and responsibilities' and 'identities and diversity: living together in the UK', juxtaposed in relation to the key processes of 'critical thinking and inquiry', 'advocacy and representation' and 'taking informed and responsible action'. This case study exemplifies the tensions between 'unity' and 'diversity' – between multicultural approaches to education and national conceptions of citizenship and the promotion of shared values, in the context of perceived internal division and potential conflict.

Conclusion

In this chapter, I have outlined different conceptions of multiculturalism, and traced some of the key debates between multicultural and anti-racist approaches in education. Using the case study example of citizenship education policy and curriculum development in England, I examine how multiculturalism is negotiated in relation to the increased emphasis on national identity witnessed in the UK, as well as in Europe and indeed globally.

Questions for further investigation

1 To what extent does 'multiculturalism' look similar and different across different societal contexts; for example, USA, Canada, Europe?
2 How are discourses of multiculturalism mediated in relation to public debates on immigration, integration and national identity?
3 How do discourses of multiculturalism and 'race' intersect with gender, class, disability, sexuality?

Suggested further reading

Kiwan, D. (2008) *Education for Inclusive Citizenship*. London and New York, NY: Routledge. This book examines the extent to which ethnic and religious diversity is accommodated in the citizenship education policy and curriculum development process in England, based on original accounts from interviews with the key players involved. It outlines four main models of citizenship, examining the theoretical and practical implications for ethnic and religious diversity.

Schiffauer, W., Baumann, G., Kasoryano, R. and Vertovec, S. (Eds.) (2004) *Civil Enculturation: Nation-state, schools, and ethnic difference in four European countries*. Oxford: Berghan Books. This book explores the changing dynamics in different nation-state contexts in four European multicultural societies. The authors conduct original empirical research in four countries, examining school curricula, texts and pedagogical practices.

Verma, G.K., Bagley, C.R. and Jha, M.M. (Eds.) (2007) *International Perspectives on Educational Diversity and Inclusion: Studies from America, Europe and India*. London and New York, NY: Routledge. This book explores the impact of globalisation on the challenge of including minorities within mainstream education, with examples from the USA, Europe and India.

References

Ajegbo, K., Kiwan, D. and Sharma, S. (2007) *Curriculum Review: Diversity and Citizenship*. London: DfES.

Alibhai-Brown, Y. (2000) *After Multiculturalism*. London: Foreign Policy Centre.

Allemann-Ghionda, C. (2009) 'From intercultural education to the inclusion of diversity: theories and policies in Europe', in Banks, J. (Ed.) *The Routledge International Companion to Multicultural Education*. Abingdon and New York, NY: Routledge, pp. 134–145.

Banks, J. (2004) 'Multicultural education: historical development, dimensions, and practice', in Banks, J.A. and Banks, C.A.M. (Eds.) *Handbook of Research on Multicultural Education* (2nd Ed.) San Francisco, CA: Jossey-Bass, pp. 3–29.

Banks, J. (2006) *Race, Culture and Education: The selected works of James A. Banks*. London and New York, NY: Routledge.

Banks, J. (2009). 'Multicultural education: dimensions and paradigms', in Banks, J. (Ed.) *The Routledge International Companion to Multicultural Education*. Abingdon and New York, NY: Routledge, pp. 9–32.

Batho, G. (1990) 'The history of the teaching of civics and citizenship in English schools', *The Curriculum Journal*, 1, 1, pp. 91–100.

Blunkett, D. (2001) 'Blunkett's "British test" for immigrants', *The Independent on Sunday*, 9 December, p. 1.

Blunkett, D. (2005) *A New England: An English Identity within Britain*. Speech to the Institute for Public Policy Research (IPPR), 14 March.

Brighouse, H. (2005) 'Faith-based schools in the United Kingdom: an unenthusiastic defence of a slightly reformed status quo', in Gardner, R., Cairns, J. and Lawton, D. (Eds.) *Faith Schools: Consensus or Conflict?* Abingdon: RoutledgeFalmer.

Commision on Integration and Cohesion (2007) *Our Shared Future*. Crown Copyright.

Davies, I. (1999) 'What has happened in the teaching of politics in schools in England in the last three decades, and why?', *Oxford Review of Education*, 25, 1&2, pp. 125–140.

Delanty, G. (2003) *Community*. London and New York, NY: Routledge.

Gates, B. (2005) 'Faith schools and colleges of education since 1800', in Gardner, R., Cairns, J. and Lawton, D. (Eds.) *Faith Schools: Consensus or Conflict?* Abingdon: RoutledgeFalmer.

Gillborn, D. (2004) 'Anti-racism: from policy to praxis', in Ladson-Billings, G. and Gillborn, D. (Eds.) *The RoutledgeFalmer Reader in Multicultural Education*. London: RoutledgeFalmer.

Gillborn, D. (2008) *Racism and Education: coincidence or conspiracy?* London and New York, NY: Routledge.

Gilroy, P. (1987) *There Ain't No Black in the Union Jack*. London and New York, NY: Routledge.

Grillo, R.D. (1998) *Pluralism and the Politics of Difference*. Oxford: Clarendon Press.

Home Office (2001a) *Community Cohesion: A Report of the Independent Review Team* (Cantle Report). London: Home Office.

Home Office (2001b) *The Report of the Ministerial Group on Public Order and Community Cohesion* (Denham Report). London: Home Office.

Home Office (2002) *Secure Borders, Safe Haven: Integration with Diversity in Modern Britain*. London: Home Office.

Home Office (2003) 'The New and the Old: the Report of the "Life in the United Kingdom" Advisory Group'. London: Home Office.

Huntingdon, S.P. (2004) *Who are we? America's Great Debate*. London: Simon and Schuster, UK Ltd.

Inglis, C. (2009) 'Multicultural education in Australia: Two generations of evolution', in Banks, J. (Ed.) *The Routledge International Companion to Multicultural Education*. Abingdon and New York, NY: Routledge, pp. 109–120.

Joppke, J. and Lukes, S. (1999) 'Introduction: multicultural questions', in Joppke, C. and Lukes, S. (Eds.) *Multicultural Questions*. Oxford: Oxford University Press.

Kiwan, D. (2008) *Education for Inclusive Citizenship*. London and New York, NY: Routledge.

Kymlicka, W. (1995) *Multicultural Citizenship*. Oxford: Oxford University Press.

Ladson-Billings, G. (2004) 'Just what is critical race theory and what is it doing in a nice field like education?', in Ladson-Billings, G. and Gillborn, D. (Eds.) *The RoutledgeFalmer Reader in Multicultural Education*. London: RoutledgeFalmer.

Lawton, D. (2000) 'Overview: citizenship education in context', in Lawton, D., Cairns, J. and Gardner, R. (Eds.) *Education for Citizenship*. London: Continuum.

Marshall, T.H. and Bottomore, T. (1992) *Citizenship and Social Class*. London: Pluto Press.

Mason, M. (2005) 'Religion and schools – a fresh way forward? A rights-based approach to diversity in schools', in Gardner, R., Cairns, J. and Lawton, D. (Eds.) *Faith Schools: Consensus or Conflict?* Abingdon: RoutledgeFalmer.

May, S. (1994) *Making Multicultural Education Work*. Clevedon: Multilingual Matters.

May, S. (Ed.) (1999) *Critical Multiculturalism: rethinking multicultural and anti-racist education*. London and New York, NY: RoutledgeFalmer.

Modood, T. (1996) 'The changing context of "race" in Britain', *Patterns of Prejudice*, *30*, 1, pp. 3–13, cited in Gillborn, D. (2004) 'Anti-racism: from policy to practice', in Ladson-Billings, G. and Gillborn, D. (Eds.) *The RoutledgeFalmer Reader in Multicultural Education*. London: RoutledgeFalmer.

Nieto, S. (2009) 'Multicultural education in the United States: historical realities, ongoing challenges and transformative possibilities', in Banks, J. (Ed.) *The Routledge International Companion to Multicultural Education*. Abingdon and New York, NY: Routledge, pp. 79–95.

Omi, M. and Winant, H. (2004) 'On the theoretical status of the concept of race', in Ladson-Billings, G. and Gillborn, D. (Eds.) *The RoutledgeFalmer Reader in Multicultural Education*. London and New York, NY: Routledge.

Parekh, B. (2000) *Rethinking Multiculturalism*. Basingstoke and London: MacMillan Press Ltd.

Parker-Jenkins, M. (2005) 'The legal framework for faith-based schools and the rights of the child', in Gardner, R., Cairns, J. and Lawton, D. (Eds.) *Faith Schools: Consensus or Conflict?* Abingdon: RoutledgeFalmer.

Pattie, C., Seyd, P. and Whiteley, P. (2004) *Citizenship in Britain: Values, Participation and Democracy*. Cambridge: Cambridge University Press.

Phillips, T. (2004) 'I want an integrated society with a difference', Tom Baldwin: interview with Trevor Phillips, *The Times*, 3 April. Available at: www.timesonline.co.uk/printFriendly/0,,1-2-1061080,00.html (accessed 21 July 2010).

Pring, R. (2005) 'Faith schools: can they be justified?', in Gardner, R., Cairns, J. and Lawton, D. (Eds.) *Faith Schools: Consensus or Conflict?* Abingdon: RoutledgeFalmer.

Qualifications and Curriculum Authority (QCA) (1998) *Education for Citizenship and the Teaching of Democracy in Schools* (Crick Report). London: QCA.

QCA (2007) 'Programmes of Study: Citizenship. (KS3 and KS4) at the secondary curriculum review'. Available at: http://curriculum.qcda.gov.uk/uploads/QCA-07-3329-pCitizenship.3_tcm8-396.pdf (accessed 25 October 2010).

Rammell (2006) 'Speech to Community Cohesion Event, Southbank University', 16 May. Available at: dfes.gov.uk/speeches/search-detail.cfm?ID=340 (accessed 16 February 2007).

Rex, J. (1991) 'Ethnic identity and ethnic mobilisation in Britain', *Monographs in Ethnic Relations*, *5*. Warwick: Centre for Research in Ethnic Relations.

Runnymede Trust. Commission on the Future of Multi-Ethnic Britain (2000) *The Future of Multi-Ethnic Britain: Report of the Commission on the Future of Multi-Ethnic Britain*. London: Profile Books.

Schlesinger, A.M. (1992) *The Disuniting of America*. London and New York, NY: W.W. Norton & Company, Inc.

Sen, A. (2006) *Identity and Violence: the illusion of destiny*. London: Allen Lane.

Spinner-Halev, J. (1999) 'Cultural pluralism and partial citizenship', in Joppke, C. and Lukes, S. (Eds.) *Multicultural Questions*. Oxford: Oxford University Press.

Taylor, E. (2009) 'The foundations of critical race theory in education: an introduction', in Taylor, E., Gillborn, D. and Ladson-Billings, G. (Eds.) *Foundations of Critical Race Theory in Education*. New York, NY and London: Routledge.

Taylor, E., Gillborn, D. and Ladson-Billings, G. (Eds.) (2009) *Foundations of Critical Race Theory in Education*. New York, NY and London: Routledge.

Toynbee, P. (2004) 'Why Trevor is right', *The Guardian*, 7 April. Available at: www.guardian.co.uk/Columnists/Column/0,5673,1187233,00.html (accessed 21 July 2010).

Troyna, B. (1984) 'Multicultural education: emancipation or containment?', in Barton, L. and Walker, S. (Eds.) *Social Crisis and Educational Research*. Beckenham: Croon Helm.

Virdee, S. and Cole, M. (2000) 'Race, racism and resistance', in Cole, M. (Ed.) *Education, Equality and Human Rights*. London and New York, NY: RoutledgeFalmer.

Watson, C.W. (2000) *Multiculturalism*. Buckingham: Open University Press.

35

Education policy

Anne West
London School of Economics and Political Science

Overview

This chapter focuses on education policy. It examines selected policies that have been introduced in three different jurisdictions – England, Sweden and the United States – and the policy goals that underpin them. Three specific goals are explored: equality of opportunity, increased educational standards and school choice. The historical context, policy and goals relating to equality of opportunity in the mid-twentieth century are outlined. More recent goals and policies that can be seen to have been influenced by neo-liberal ideas are then discussed. There are some similarities in terms of the goals in the three countries, but given the differing contexts it is unsurprising to find that the policy instruments vary. In all cases, there are tensions and contradictions between policy goals, in particular between equality of opportunity and goals relating to school choice and increased educational standards.

Introduction

School-based education is significant for society and for the individual. For society, it has a key role in terms of increasing human capital and economic competitiveness; it is important in terms of socialisation and fostering social cohesion. For the individual, it plays a key role in terms of cognitive development, skill development and personal and social development. This multiplicity of purposes and its compulsory nature – at least in developed countries – means that policy-makers have given education a high priority. Education policy is of fundamental importance given its role in relation to school structures, access, what is taught and how it is assessed. It is formulated by policy-makers and is heavily dependent on politics. Whilst the process of implementation is crucial to the policy process, being subject to interpretation by policy-makers at different levels of government and practitioners at school level, the focus here is on education policy at a national level and its varying goals.

The policies and goals of particular interest in this chapter are equality of opportunity (a goal relating to children's access to education, for example to schools, curriculum), school choice (a goal relating to parents' role in the education process) and increased educational standards (a goal relating to children's educational outcomes). It is important to stress that policy goals are varied and can be construed in many different ways. From the perspective of policy-makers goals may shift, whilst from the perspective of those outside the policy arena they may remain constant; for example, a focus on equality of opportunity may not be a stated goal of policy-makers, but may be seen as a crucial goal by those outside. It may also be seen as a goal from a normative perspective. Some goals may be seen as both goals and instruments of policy; for example, choice may be seen as a goal in its own right or as a means to another goal, such as improved educational outcomes. Given the multiplicity of goals, conflicts may result.

This chapter examines selected goals of education policy in England, Sweden and the US. A key goal in all three countries by the middle of the twentieth century was equality of opportunity. More recently other policy goals have been given a high profile, in particular, increasing educational standards and increasing parental choice. In all three cases, recent policies have been heavily influenced by neo-liberal ideas. There have been some similarities in terms of goals pursued, but how these are interpreted and the means adopted to seek to achieve them are varied. There are also tensions between the goals pursued, and indeed contradictions, particularly between equality of opportunity and other goals. Significantly, the outcomes of policies aimed at increasing choice may jeopardise the realisation of the goal of equality of opportunity.

The next section provides a historical context and focuses in particular on the goal of equality of opportunity and associated policies. This is followed by an examination of policy over the past three decades with respect to all three countries, with particular reference on the role played by neo-liberal ideas and two particular policy goals: increasing school choice and increasing educational standards. The final section examines the tensions and conflicts that exist between differing education policy goals: equality, choice and increasing educational standards.

Historical context

In England and Wales, the church historically played an important role in the provision of education. The state took on an increasing role in the late nineteenth century. The 1870 Elementary Education Act aimed to help schools to fill the gaps in existing provision. The 1918 Education Act abolished fees for elementary schools and education became compulsory until the age of 14 (Gordon et al., 1991). The 1944 Education Act set up a universal system of free, compulsory education from 5 to 15 years (and increased to 16 in 1972) with a system of primary and secondary schools, some with a religious character. A key policy goal was equality of opportunity (see Lowe, 1993). The Act enabled the implementation of a 'tripartite' system of secondary education, with grammar schools for the most academically able, technical schools and 'secondary modern' schools for the remainder. The prevailing view was that every child was born with a certain amount of intelligence, that this remained constant, and that children could be sorted into schools of different types that would meet their differing needs (Chitty, 2009). However, concerns were expressed about intelligence testing and the system itself as a disproportionate number of places were allocated to children from middle-class backgrounds (Gordon et al., 1991). Moves towards comprehensivisation followed the election of a Labour government in 1964, and in 1965, local education authorities were requested to submit plans

333

for the introduction of comprehensive education. Although withdrawn by the Conservative government elected in 1970 (Simon, 1991), proposals for comprehensive reorganisation continued to be submitted and by the early 1980s comprehensive education was almost universal (Gordon *et al.*, 1991). The system was not similar across the country: local authorities had the power to decide what type of system to introduce and some grammar schools were retained.

In Sweden as in England, the church historically played a key role in the provision of schools. In 1842, legislation required every parish to establish at least one elementary school. The head of every school board was the parish minister and schools were administered by the church. Children from wealthy families either had tutors or went to private schools which led to élite institutions. In 1880, school attendance became compulsory between the ages of 7 and 13 (Fägerlind and Saha, 1989). In 1948, a proposal was made by the social democratic prime minister for a compulsory nine-year comprehensive school that would replace all schools catering for pupils between 7 and 16 (Fägerlind and Saha, 1989). One of the key goals of the comprehensive reform was equality of opportunity (Husén, 1986). The Swedish parliament in passing the 1950 Education Act provided for a ten-year pilot programme whereby elementary and lower secondary schools were integrated during the whole nine-year period of compulsory education. The outcomes of pupils educated in the comprehensive schools and those in selective academic schools were compared and revealed that pupils in comprehensive schools had the same achievement levels as those in selective grammar schools. In 1962 the decision was taken to implement a nine-year comprehensive school across the whole country and by 1972 comprehensivisation was fully implemented (see Fägerlind and Saha, 1989; Husén, 1986).

The US borrowed a number of ideas relating to educational provision from Europe 'but tailored them in particularly American ways' (Goldin, 1999, p. 1). The transformation to mass primary schooling (amongst the free population) was completed in the middle of the nineteenth century; in this common school period, 'democratic equality was the dominant goal of American education' (Labaree, 1997), which aimed to prepare people for political roles.

Historically, two broad goals of education policy in the US have been identified – the promotion of individual attainment and 'the collective purpose of promoting democracy through the teaching of democratic values and practices, and the *provision of equal opportunity for all children* [italics added]' (McDonnell, 2007). The US system of education was from the beginning more egalitarian than in much of Europe: 'Americans eschewed different systems for different children, and embraced the notion that everyone should receive a 'common', unified, academic education' (Goldin, 1999, p. 2). This excluded slaves who received little formal instruction particularly after southern states passed legislation prohibiting the teaching of reading to slaves. All states passed compulsory education laws but before the late 1920s there was not generally a binding maximum age (Goldin, 1999). In terms of equality of educational opportunity, the issue of segregation is significant. The *Brown v Board of Education* (1954) case was fundamental to *de jure* desegregation in the school system: 'Segregation of children in public schools solely on the basis of race deprives children of the minority group of equal educational opportunities, even though the physical and other "tangible" factors may be equal'. By the 1960s and 1970s 'the national movement for racial equality infused schooling and spilled over into efforts to provide an education that was socially inclusive and offered equal opportunity along lines of class, gender, and handicapping condition as well as race' (Labaree, 1997, p. 58). However, although access has been seen as the key to opportunity, the capabilities of schools to equalise opportunity have been uneven (Cohen *et al.*, 2007).

Era of neo-liberal ideas

Neo-liberal ideas have been highly significant in debates about policy in recent decades. Neo-liberalism has been associated with a range of different policy goals including the conversion of the public education system into markets and privatisation of educational services. A further goal is the promotion of 'personal responsibility through individual choice within markets' (Hursh, 2007, p. 4):

> Increased efficiency can only be attained, argue neoliberals, if individuals are able to make choices within a market system in which schools compete . . . Further if individuals are to make decisions, they must have access to quantitative information, such as standardized test scores, that presumably indicate the quality of the education provided. Neoliberals believe competition leads to better schools, and hence better education for all students, closing the achievement gap between students of color and White students.
>
> (Hursh, 2007, p. 498)

In all three countries, neo-liberal ideas have influenced education policy and the education system. However, the policies introduced and the specific goals have differed. In the following sections selected policies and goals are outlined.

England

Education policy in England shifted markedly with the election of a Conservative government in 1979. The reforms were largely driven by a desire to increase educational standards and so economic competitiveness (Chitty, 2009). As a result of the 1980 Education Act and the 1988 Education Reform Act, a 'quasi-market' in the publicly funded school system was created (Le Grand and Bartlett, 1993). Across England, parents were able to make 'choices' (preferences) for schools; schools became funded predominantly on the basis of pupil numbers; and public examination and national test 'league tables' were published. Schools were thus given incentives to maximise their levels of funding and pupils' test and examination results (West and Pennell, 2000). Underpinning the reforms was the view that parents would choose the 'best' schools for their child, based on the information available – in particular, examination results – and that the ensuing competition between schools would result in educational standards increasing. The precise goals of government varied. The 1992 White Paper *Choice and Diversity* (Cm 2021, 1992) gave as the themes of the Conservative administrations since 1979: quality, diversity, parental choice, greater school autonomy and greater accountability. These themes provided 'the framework for the Government's aims and together define our goal for Britain's education system' (p. 5). More specifically the White Paper stated: 'The Government's goal is to ensure that we have an education system that is second to none in helping to liberate the talents of our children while at the same time ensuring that they get the same high quality common grounding' (p. 11).

With the election of a Labour government in 1997 there was continuity in terms of the main tenets of the quasi-market. 'League tables' continued and there was an increase in school diversity: 'independent' schools, known as academies, were introduced, with most of the costs being covered by the government (see West and Currie, 2008); these new schools tended to be located in disadvantaged areas. The White Paper, *Higher Standards Better Schools For All* (Cm 6677, 2005) gave as stated goals 'excellence' and 'equity'. Thus, one stated aim was 'to transform the school system so that every child receives an excellent education – whatever their background and wherever they live' (p. 7) and another related to a new duty for local authorities to 'promote choice, diversity and fair access' (p. 105). (The notion of fairness is that of procedural as opposed to substantive fairness (Noden and West, 2009).)

In 2010 a Conservative–Liberal Democrat coalition government took office. Its goals include tackling inequality, and increasing choice by means of new providers being encouraged to enter the market (Cabinet Office, 2010). Schools deemed as 'outstanding' can convert and become state-funded academies and other schools may apply to become academies; in addition, interested groups (including parents) have been given the opportunity to set up new state-funded 'free' schools under the Academies Act 2010. There is thus continuity with the previous administrations, accompanied by an element of change.

Sweden

Education policy in Sweden underwent a significant change in the 1990s following the election of the non-socialist government in 1991. Funding was decentralised to municipalities and market-oriented reforms introduced. In 1992, a speech delivered by Swedish School Minister, Beatrice Ask (1992), stated: 'The work with developing and expanding freedom of choice carries on both in the government and out in the municipalities' (p. 48) and a 'school system – based on the free choice of students and parents – is far better tha[n] the pacifying school monopoly that we have had' (p. 46). The state monopoly was broken and market-oriented reforms implemented.

The key policy instrument was the establishment of independent (free) schools, set up by different providers. Policy goals comprised freedom of choice, higher quality education and greater cost-effectiveness (Skolverket, 2009). First, by creating a wider range of schools (including those with a religious profile and those run by private for profit companies) freedom of choice would be increased: freedom of choice was seen as a goal in its own right and a means of achieving other aims. Second, by allowing different providers and schools with different specialisations (profiles) into the system, schools would compete with one another so improving the quality of the school system. A third goal was a more cost-effective school system, via the more effective use of resources such as disseminating cost-effective working methods (Skolverket, 2009). As noted by Lundahl (2002), 'even if the equality goal of education was never abandoned it may be questioned to what extent it was actually at the core of the education reforms of 1990s' (p. 696). The social democrats, elected in 1994, continued these policies, but also expressed the desire for the integration of pupils from different backgrounds and stressed the need for an 'equivalent' school system.

US

In *A Nation At Risk* (National Commission on Excellence in Education, 1983) major concerns regarding publicly funded education were raised: the view was expressed that the educational foundations of US society were 'being eroded by a rising tide of mediocrity' and that this was a threat to the nation. The two key goals proposed were equity and high-quality schooling. The Goals 2000: Educate America Act built on this with the aim of improving education and ensuring that all children reached high academic standards (US Department of Education, 1998). National assessment became part of the thinking, along with measures of performance and 'report cards' (akin to league tables). Federal legislation including the 2001 No Child Left Behind

(NCLB) Act required states to implement standards-based reform in order to receive funds for education programmes for disadvantaged pupils; under this Act schools and districts in which pupils' test scores do not show 'adequate yearly progress' are subject to sanctions (e.g., loss of some federal funds, intervention, school closure) (see McDermott, 2004). The purpose of the legislation was: 'to ensure that all children have a fair, equal, and significant opportunity to obtain a high-quality education' (US Department of Education, 2002).

Another key instrument aimed at improving the quality of education and enabling greater choice has been the charter schools legislation. Charter schools are independently run but publicly funded schools; they are not subject to the same regulatory framework as other public schools. 'While not every new school is extraordinarily innovative and some school operations may mirror that of traditional public schools, policymakers, parents, and educators are looking at chartering as a way to increase educational choice and innovation within the public school system' (US Charter Schools, 2010). Education is primarily a state responsibility in the US and thus charter schools vary between states: individual charters have their own mission and goals and moreover, state charter laws vary significantly (US Charter Schools, 2010). Bulkley (2005), for example, found that the goals of charter school legislation varied between three states she investigated. In all three – Arizona, Georgia and Michigan – quality was a key goal, in Arizona and Michigan, choice was also a goal and in Arizona, efficiency a goal.

Equality, choice and standards: conflicting goals?

Different policy goals have had different salience in the three countries at different points in time. Equality of opportunity was a clear policy goal in the mid-twentieth century in all cases, although the means to realise this goal differed, with pupil sorting into different school types in England and schools for pupils of all abilities in Sweden and the US. Over the past three decades, neo-liberal ideas can be seen to have influenced policy goals and policies. Goals have tended to focus on improving educational standards and school choice, with choice also being seen as a means to increase educational standards.

Whilst the influence of neo-liberal ideas is clear in each jurisdiction, the goals have been different as have the policies implemented. Key policy goals across countries are common, particularly in relation to increasing educational standards. Although equality may remain a goal, in England and Sweden the profile given to this goal is muted, with notions of 'fairness' having prevailed in England and 'equivalence' in Sweden.

There is, however, a conflict between goals relating to choice in a market-oriented system and to equality of opportunity. By definition, if schools compete with one another, a hierarchy will ensue. Schools will seek to enhance their position in the 'market'. Given the strong links between social background and educational attainment, schools are likely, given the opportunity, to select some pupils as opposed to others. Parents from different social groups are also likely to be better able to make choices because of their higher levels of education, their ability to access information and their ability to navigate the system. This has implications in terms of equality of access. Moreover, if schools become more segregated following the implementation of policies designed to increase choice, there will be additional conflicts with the goal of equality of opportunity: in the US the concerns relating to segregation and equality were clearly identified in *Brown v Board of Education*. With a hierarchy of schools offering what is likely to be a different quality of education, equality of access and hence opportunity is likely to be hindered.

Segregation has been a concern in all three countries. In England, concerns have been raised about segregation by ethnicity, ability and poverty, particularly with respect to faith schools (Allen and West, 2011). In Sweden, there have been concerns about segregation between pupil backgrounds as a result of the choice policies: independent schools, compared with municipality schools, have a larger proportion of girls, a larger proportion of pupils with parents who have continued with education following upper secondary school, and a larger proportion of pupils with a foreign background. In relation to the latter, pupils attending compulsory independent schools have parents who are better educated than pupils with a foreign background attending municipal schools (Skolverket, 2006). In the US, charter schools have been shown to have more extensive segregation than other publicly funded schools; in particular, black pupils in charter schools are much more likely than those in traditional public school to be educated in highly segregated settings, and higher percentages of pupils in charter schools of 'every race attend predominantly minority schools' than do peers of the same race in traditional public schools (Frankenberg et al., 2010).

Is it possible for the goals of choice and equality of opportunity to be realised in a market-oriented system? There is an inherent tension. Regulation can be used to try to ensure equality of access. In England, regulation and quasi-regulation have been used in an attempt to increase fair access to schools (West et al., 2011). In Sweden where market-oriented reforms have been the strongest of all three countries, the 2010 Education Act has moved in the direction of making for a level playing field in terms of the regulations to which schools of different types have to adhere. However, regulation is unlikely to have a major impact on school segregation (see Allen et al., 2010). Additional problems relate to geographical segregation, the will and capacity to implement reform by policy-makers, finance (McDermott, 2004) and indeed to parents' own preferences where choice is a primary goal of policy. In conclusion, although the context varies between countries, choice policies appear likely to lead to the separation of children into different types of schools; this, in turn, is likely to lead to equality of educational opportunity not being achieved because of the intangible negative consequences of segregation.

How issues will develop

In the coming years, policy goals are likely to focus on increasing educational standards given their association with economic competitiveness. Equality of educational opportunity is likely to remain a clearly stated goal in the US; it is less clear that this will remain the case in either England or Sweden. Choice as a goal or as a means to other goals is likely to continue; the belief that choice can improve educational standards remains. In England, the Coalition government elected in 2010 stated its aim to 'tackle educational inequality' and also to break open the state school monopoly via new independent schools akin to Swedish independent (free) schools and US charter schools. An aim is that the poorest pupils can 'get to go to the best schools not the worst' (Cabinet Office, 2010). However, it is not clear to what extent this is likely to be achieved even with new policy instruments such as the 'pupil premium'. Interestingly, in Sweden, where market-oriented reforms have been the most pronounced, the Education Act 2010 has sought to put independent schools and municipal schools on a more equal footing in terms of their regulatory context. Significantly, the fact that in all three jurisdictions other providers are entering 'the market' means that the role of the state is likely to continue to change. In particular, it is likely to continue to finance schools but increasingly less likely to provide. The extent to which this will result in 'privatisation' of the education system, a key aim of neo-liberalism, remains to be seen.

Conclusion

In conclusion, there are multiple goals of education policy. In the three countries, there are similarities in terms of the policy goals: equality of opportunity for individual children was apparent from the mid-twentieth century. However, the means by which it was to be achieved varied as different school systems developed in different countries. Over the past three decades, a greater emphasis, it would appear, has been given to increasing educational standards overall. The influence of neo-liberal ideas has also been apparent. In all three countries, choice is a means if not a goal of education policy.

Some of these policy goals are contradictory, some are not. Whilst the goal of increasing equality of opportunity was overt and explicit in all countries, this appears to be less apparent now, at least in England and Sweden. Instead, goals tend to be more general – for example, increasing standards for all. Moreover, when related goals are espoused it is not necessarily clear how they can be achieved given conflicts with other goals. Thus, a goal of increasing choice in a competitive environment will ultimately result in a hierarchy of schools – some 'better' than others – with equality of educational opportunity remaining as elusive as ever.

Questions for further investigation

1   To what extent are the goals of equality of opportunity and choice compatible?
2   Can equality of opportunity be achieved via market-oriented reforms?
3   Examine continuity and change in relation to education policy goals over time and associated policy instruments.

Suggested further reading

Chitty, C. (2009) *Education Policy in Britain*. Basingstoke: Palgrave Macmillan. This book is invaluable for those interested in education policy in England.

Fuhrman, S.H., Cohen, D.K. and Mosher, F. (2007) *The State of Education Policy*. New York, NY: Routledge. This book is of particular interest for American readers as it focuses on the US context.

Hursh, D. (2007) 'Assessing No Child Left Behind and the rise of neoliberal education policies', *American Educational Research Journal*, 44, 3, pp. 493–518. This paper provides an original account of the role played by neo-liberal education policies in the US, with specific reference to No Child Left Behind.

References

Allen, R., Coldron, J. and West, A. (2010) *The effect of changes in published secondary school admissions on pupil composition*. London: Department for Education.

Allen, R. and West, A. (2011) 'Why do faith secondary schools have advantaged intakes? The relative importance of neighbourhood characteristics, social background and religious identification amongst parents', *British Educational Research Journal*.

Ask, B. (1992) 'Freedom of choice and independent schools: A speech by the Government's School Minister', in Miron, G. (Ed.) *Towards Free Choice and Market-Oriented Schools: Problems and Promises*. Stockholm: Institute of International Education and Skolverket.

Brown v. Board of Education, 347 US 483 (1954) (USSC+) Supreme Court of the United States. Available at: www.nationalcenter.org/brown.html. Accessed October 2010.

Bulkley, K. (2005) 'Understanding the charter school concept in legislation: The cases of Arizona, Georgia and Michigan', *International Journal of Qualitative Studies in Education*, 18, 4, pp. 527–554.

Cabinet Office (2010) 'The Coalition: Our programme for government'. London: Cabinet Office.

Chitty, C. (2009) *Education Policy in Britain*. Basingstoke: Palgrave Macmillan.

Cm 2021 (1992) *Choice and Diversity: A new framework for schools*, CM 2021. London: HMSO.

Cm 6677 (2005) *Higher Standards Better Schools For All*. London: The Stationery Office. Available at: http://publications.education.gov.uk/eOrderingDownload/Cm per cent206677.pdf. Accessed October 2010.

Cohen, D.K., Moffitt, S.L. and Goldin, S. (2007) 'Policy and practice', in Fuhrman, S.H., Cohen, D.K. and Mosher, F. (Eds.) *The State of Education Policy*. New York, NY: Routledge.

Fägerlind, I. and Saha, L.J. (1989) *Education and National Development*. London: Pergamon Press.

Frankenberg, E., Siegal-Hawley, G. and Wang, J. (2010) *Choice without Equity: Charter school segregation and the need for civil rights standards*. Los Angeles, CA: The Civil Rights Project/Proyecto Derechos Civiles at UCLA. Available at: http://civilrightsproject.ucla.edu/research/k-12-education/integration-and-diversity/choice-without-equity-2009-report/frankenberg-choices-without-equity-2010.pdf. Accessed October 2010.

Goldin, C. (1999) 'A brief history of education in the United States', Historical Paper 119. Cambridge, MA: National Bureau of Economic Research.

Gordon, P., Aldrich, R. and Dean, D. (1991) *Education and Policy in England in the Twentieth Century*. London: The Woburn Press.

Husén, T. (1986) 'Why did Sweden go comprehensive?', *Oxford Review of Education*, 12, 2, pp. 153–163.

Labaree, D.F. (1997) 'Public goods, private goods: The American struggle over educational goals', *American Educational Research Journal*, 34, 1, pp. 39–81.

Le Grand, J. and Bartlett, W. (Eds.) (1993) *Quasi-Markets and Social Policy*. London: Macmillan.

Lowe, R. (1993) *The Welfare State in Britain Since 1945*. Basingstoke: Macmillan.

Lundahl (2002) 'Sweden: decentralization, deregulation, quasi-markets – and then what?', *Journal of Education Policy*, 17, 6, pp. 687–697.

McDermott, K.A. (2004) 'Incentives, capacity, and implementation: evidence from Massachusetts Education Reform', *Journal of Public Administration Research and Theory*, 16, pp. 45–65.

McDonnell, L.M. (2007) 'The politics of education: Influencing policy and beyond', in Fuhrman, S.H., Cohen, D.K. and Mosher, F. (Eds.) *The State of Education Policy*. New York, NY: Routledge.

National Commission on Excellence in Education (1983) 'A nation at risk'. Washington, DC: National Commission on Excellence in Education. Available at: www2.ed.gov/pubs/NatAtRisk/index.html. Accessed October 2010.

Noden, P. and West. A. (2009) *Secondary School Admissions in England: Admission forums, local authorities and schools*. London: Research and Information on State Education Trust. Available at: www.risetrust.org.uk/forums.pdf. Accessed October 2010.

Skolverket (2006) *Schools like any other? – Independent schools as part of the system 1991–2004*, Stockholm: Skolverket. Available at: www.skolverket.se/sb/d/355. Accessed October 2010.

Simon, B. (1991) *Education and the Social Order*. London: Lawrence and Wishart.

US Charter Schools (2010) 'US Charter Schools'. Available at: www.uscharterschools.org/pub/uscs_docs/o/movement.htm. Accessed October 2010.

US Department of Education (1998) 'Goals 2000: reforming education to improve student achievement'. Washington, DC: Department of Education. Available at: www2.ed.gov/PDFDocs/g2kfinal.pdf. Accessed October 2010.

US Department of Education (2002) 'Title I—improving the academic achievement of the disadvantaged'. Washington, DC: Department of Education. Available at: www2.ed.gov/policy/elsec/leg/esea02/pg1.html#sec101. Accessed October 2010.

West, A., Barham, E. and Hind, A. (2011) Secondary school admissions: Impact of legislation on policy and practice, *Oxford Review of Education*, 37, 1, 1–20.

West, A. and Currie, P. (2008) 'The role of the private sector in publicly-funded schooling in England: Finance, delivery and decision making', *Policy and Politics*, 36, 2, pp. 191–207.

West, A. and Pennell, H. (2000) 'Publishing school examination results in England: Incentives and consequences', *Educational Studies*, 26, 4, pp. 423–436.

West, A., Barham, E. and Hind, A. (2011) 'Secondary school admissions: Impact of legislation on policy and practice', *Oxford Review of Education*, 37.

36

Religion and education

Alan Sears and Theodore Michael Christou

University of New Brunswick

Overview

This chapter will:

- examine the interconnections between religion and education;
- describe various approaches to religion as the context for education;
- describe various approaches to religion as content for education;
- argue that to be comprehensive education must include significant attention to religion.

Introduction

An Italian mother who was concerned that Roman Catholic symbols, particularly crucifixes, adorning the walls of Italian public schools violated her children's right to a secular education went to court to argue her case. In November 2009, the European Court of Human Rights found in her favour in a judgement that stated non-Christians might find the symbols disturbing and that state-run schools 'observe confessional neutrality in the context of public education' where attendance is compulsory (Associated Press, 2010). The court ordered the Italian government to remove the crucifixes from state schools.

Over the past 15 years the government of the Canadian province of Québec has been moving steadily to secularise state supported schools both from fully public schools and from private schools that receive state subsidies. A constitutional amendment in 1997 changed public school boards from being religiously based (Catholic and Protestant) to being linguistically based (French and English). A law in 2005 removed parents' right to choose from among Catholic and Protestant religious instruction or moral education for their children. These were replaced by a single, compulsory ethics and religion course for all grades. The course is designed to be taught from a secular and relativist perspective.

A Jesuit-run school in the province argued that its own world religions course taught from a Roman Catholic perspective was a reasonable alternative to the ethics and religion course and asked to be exempted from the new requirement. The government refused the exception and the school went to court. In June of 2010, a justice of the Québec Superior Court found in the school's favour stating in his judgement that forcing the school to teach from a secular perspective 'assumes a totalitarian quality essentially equivalent to the order given to Galileo by the Inquisition to renounce Copernican cosmology' (quoted in Hamilton, 2010).

These cases are from two democratic jurisdictions with similar human rights laws but resulted in very different judgements. In one case, a panel of judges found the state was oppressive in allowing the presence of Christian symbols in schools and, in the other, a judge found the state oppressive in trying to remove Christian influence from schools.

These cases demonstrate some of the ways in which religion and education are inextricably intertwined and the tensions and uncertainties often raised by those interconnections. In this chapter we provide an overview of some of the ways in which religion and education are connected, the issues raised by those connections, some of the policy and practice solutions attempted in various jurisdictions and, finally, argue that explicit recognition of and attention to religion in schooling is essential for democratic education. While we will draw some examples from the rest of the world, our focus is on how this plays out in Western democracies.

Religion as the context for education

Gates (2007, p. 165) argues that, through history, religion has often provided the context in which education takes place with religious organisations and institutions being the primary providers of educational services. Today, he contends, constitutional arrangements about the place of education in schooling range from 'established singularity', where one religion dominates to the exclusion of all others, to 'secular pluralism', where religion and education are rigorously separated.

Contemporary Pakistan is an example of 'established singularity'. Dean (2010, p. 64) argues that Pakistan was originally conceived as 'a secular democratic state in which there would be civic equality regardless of the religious identity of its citizens'. An aggressive programme of 'Islamization of the state' (p. 68) in the 1970s and 1980s, however, resulted in state institutions, including schools, being mandated 'to inculcate in accordance with the Quran and *Sunnah*, the character, conduct and motivation expected of a true Muslim' (p. 68). So while the state and not Islamic institutions provide public education, the context is thoroughly Muslim. Minorities and minority religions lack both status and attention in this system.

In virtually all Western societies, common public schooling was first provided by whatever part of the Christian Church was dominant in the relevant jurisdiction. The reason there are crucifixes in most Italian public schools is that the Roman Catholic Church originally built, maintained, and provided the teachers for those schools. The same was true of the Anglican Church in England, the Christian Reformed Church in the Netherlands, and a variety of churches in the more religiously diverse (or tolerant) immigrant nations of Canada and the United States. In fact, religious organisations in these societies not only built, maintained, and ran schools but they also did the same for a range of social institutions including universities, hospitals, and welfare agencies of various kinds.

Religious organisations of one kind or another, for example, began virtually all pre-twentieth-century universities in North America. As the ruling from the European Court of Human rights discussed above illustrates, there has been a move across the Western world towards secular pluralism as the context for education. The expansion of the welfare state in the twentieth century across much of the democratic world saw public institutions to one degree or another largely taken out of the hands of religious organisations and brought under the authority of the state.

The extent of this secularisation of public institutions varies greatly across jurisdictions. France, for example, is among the most aggressively secular of Western states following a policy of 'laïcité' which is the 'strict separation between church and state' (Gereluk, 2008, p. 15). Recent laws banning the wearing of religious symbols, including head coverings or obvious jewellery, by teachers and students in state schools is an illustration of this policy in action. The US also attempts to strictly separate religion from publicly supported education with court rulings eliminating prayer and other confessional activities from official practice in schools.

Other Western jurisdictions take a rather different approach. Canada and England, for example, both use a mixed system. For the most part, public schools in Canada resemble those in France and the US in that they are state funded and strictly (even aggressively) secular. However, several Canadian provinces maintain fully state-funded Roman Catholic school systems alongside public schools. While these schools are responsible for teaching the provincially mandated curriculum, they have relative autonomy in their governance and can include religious instruction and practice as part of their programmes. For the most part, they require teachers to be practising Roman Catholics. In England, Voluntary Aided schools receive most of their funding from the state but are largely run by private foundations that are often religious organisations of one sort or another. As in Canada, these schools are public in that they do not charge fees and are expected to teach the state-mandated curriculum, but in addition to that they maintain a religious character and include religious instruction and practice in their offerings.

The precedent set by the European Court of Human Rights' ruling on removal of religious symbols in Italian schools has evoked serious debate across Europe, which has united countries with both Roman Catholic and Greek Orthodox majorities (Vella, 2010). The question of the crucifix in the school has thus galvanized Christians across contexts with a 1000-year history of sometimes-contentious religious debate in common advocacy for religious symbols in schools (Brabant, 2010). Complicating the question is the matter of formal recognition of religion in state constitutions, as the arrangement of church and state is not monolithic across Europe. While Italy has been constitutionally secular since 1984, other countries have entrenched a religion in their constitutions; for instance, the Greek constitution recognises Greek Orthodoxy as the national faith, and Roman Catholicism is entrenched in Malta's constitution. In the case of Greece, the Greek Orthodox Church has claimed that the Italian precedent threatens to both obfuscate the role that Christianity played in the formation of Europe's identity and deprive children of noble symbols that remind them of that heritage. Groups such as the Helsinki Monitor that have appealed to the precedent in calling for the removal of icons in Greek schools are in fact opposing the national constitution (ZENIT, 2010).

Even with the often-aggressive secularisation of Western democracies (Arthur et al., 2010), religion still forms a key part of the context of public education in many of these states. Virtually all, including the most secular of states, allow parents to meet the statutory requirement for their children's education by sending them to privately funded religious schools. These schools often require state approval to operate but represent a full range of religious expression and have considerable autonomy.

We offer one final word about religion as a context for education before moving on to consider religion as content. One of the reasons nations in the West have moved to secularise public institutions including schools is an assumption that religious institutions are inherently narrow- and closed-minded. This assumption belies much of religious history. It is particularly curious when promoted by scholars who work in universities given that members of religious orders originally created Western universities as places of scholarly exploration. Lindberg (2006, p. 93), for example, traces the intellectual tradition of Saints Augustine, Thomas Aquinas, and Anselm through to the scholastic monks of the thirteenth century in the Dominican and Franciscan orders who 'unleashed an intellectual energy that transformed universities from trade schools for training clerks into centres of intellectual ferment and creativity'. This heritage is often forgotten even in places such as Harvard University, itself founded by a religious community, where a distinguished professor recently argued that 'universities are about reason, pure and simple. Faith – believing something without good reasons to do so – has no place in anything but a religious institution' (Pinker, 2006).

Wilken (1989, p. 710) counters the characterisation of faith as 'believing something without good reasons to do so' arguing that in Judaism, Christianity and Islam 'conviction and rational justification have been complementary, seldom adversarial'. All, he contends, have a considerable history of engaging in open and public disputation and it is the 'enlightenment, and historiography since that time, that promoted the idea that "traditional" religion was based solely on "faith" independent of the claims of reason'. A key example of faith rooted in reason and exploration is the Jewish Talmud, which includes as marginal notes the discussion of the Rabbis about texts across time 'so that the contemporary student can enter into a discussion that has been going on for centuries'.

In more contemporary contexts, educators from a range of Christian traditions affirm the importance of reason to the development of the complete person. Groome (1980, p. 59), for example, outlines the long commitment to holding together faith and reason in Roman Catholicism claiming that 'when it is at its best, the tradition is to maintain a partnership between reason and revelation'. Writing from a Christian Reformed perspective, Wolterstorff (Wolterstorff et al., 2002) rejects a Christian education narrowly focused on catechisms and devotional life in favour of an approach that develops thoughtful study of and engagement with the world.

Religion as the content of education

Religion connects with education, not only in terms of providing the context for it, but also as important content for understanding human history and contemporary societies. Gates (2007) points out that there is a range of approaches across the world to religious education as part of the curriculum from sectarian religious instruction to rigorous exclusion of religion as a subject of study. He contends that England and Wales, where religious education is a compulsory subject, have the most balanced approach in the world. He emphasises the distinctiveness of the approach in this jurisdiction including a non-sectarian focus on world religions, a high degree of professionalism and specialisation expected of educators, and extensive input in curriculum design from faith communities. While specific approaches are locally developed, there is a central national framework that 'incorporates two attainment targets: "learning about" religion and belief (AT1) and "learning from" religion and belief (AT2)' (Ofsted, 2010, p. 9). As a recent report from school inspectors makes clear, the actual delivery of religious education in England and Wales is of mixed quality but there are many clear examples of good practice (Ofsted, 2010).

For the most part, a more secularist approach dominates curriculum policy and practice in Western democracies. In a national examination of religious education in Canada, for example, Sweet (1997, p. 235) found it was simply absent from most public school classrooms even when it was included or allowed in policy and curricula. This, she argues was largely due to fear on the part of educational leaders:

> Fear of indoctrination. Fear of offending. Fear of conflict. Fear of lawsuits. Fear of curriculum hassles, administrative hassles. Fear of dumping yet one more thing onto teachers who haven't been educated in this area themselves. Fear of the unknown.

Nash (2005) and Noddings (2008) argue the same is true of the USA where in-depth, critical consideration of religion or religious ideas is almost non-existent in schools.

Where religion and culture are dealt with in public schools, the treatment is often superficial using a food, fun and festivals method, which Nash (2005, p. 94) describes as 'a folkloric approach' characterised by 'superficial and ceremonial sharing'. This method of teaching about religion does avoid some of the potential conflicts that terrify policy-makers and practitioners, but it does not do justice to the topic and leaves students ignorant and confused. It does little to achieve the outcomes outlined in the English curriculum.

We contend that religion is an essential area of study in a balanced curriculum for several reasons. Can we imagine engaging in the study of ancient Egypt without examining the various ways that faith, religion and ceremony shaped the culture or way of looking at the world in that context? It would be impossible to develop any robust understanding of, for instance, the great pyramids without appreciation for how the pharaohs for whom they were constructed would have answered the grand questions that we may still ask ourselves. What are the nature and purpose of life? What happens after death? In what do we have faith, and to what beliefs shall we cling when all reason fails? Those grand wonders of the ancient world, architecturally and aesthetically awing, were tombs. Similarly, how might we possibly approach a subject such ancient Greek theatre without implicating a careful study of faith, religion, and ceremony in the context of the Athenian polis? Dramatic festivals, where the beliefs and myths were interpreted and enacted, began with the sacrifice of a goat upon an altar that was omnipresent to audience and actors alike. So foundational were these religious roots of drama in its development that the word *tragedy*, in Greek, *tragodia*, means *goat's ode*.

In teaching history the importance of introducing religion as a key element of contextual study is crucial. Why then might we presume that religion and faith are not vital to the study of our own context, locally and broadly? Where we as educators are charged with developing habits of mind in our students that will enable them to think critically about the world in which they live so that they may act with a moral sense of responsibility, religion cannot reasonably be marginalised in schools. Any articulation of educational aims, which aspires to foster open or critical mindedness in social studies must implicate religion. The alternative is to nip in the bud an aspect of social life that gives meaning and substance to diverse aspects of society. It is ethically indefensible to foster contexts in which the discussion and study of religion is imbued with fear, as our faiths and beliefs are vital to the ways we can explore and describe what it means to be human.

Pragmatically, attention to diversity, particularly contentious aspects of it, often gets subverted because it is complex, difficult to deal with and has the potential to generate conflict. In studies of policy and practice in several Canadian provinces, Bickmore (2005a, p. 165) found that schools and teachers generally avoided difficult issues with high potential for conflict including those involving ethnicity and identity. Instead, they focused on what she calls 'harmony building' and 'individual skill building' approaches rooted in conflict avoidance. The first includes attention to the 'appreciation of diverse cultural heritages' but does not explore the real difference between and among those heritages. Similarly, Kiwan (2008, p. 49) found that in England 'identity and diversity are being presented as something that pupils learn about, as opposed to actively engage with'. She calls this a 'pedagogy of acceptance', which entails 'being passive rather than active, engaging or challenging' (p. 49). Bickmore (2005b) argues that teachers largely avoid more difficult approaches to citizenship inherent in opening up and exploring identity partly because their own background, preparation and opportunities for professional development have not provided them with the tools needed:

> To teach for democratization, in the context of student diversity and globalization, requires more substantive knowledge, more skills, and more comfort with openness and uncertainty than to teach for unquestioned dominant 'common sense.' This can feel overwhelming, especially for novice teachers.
>
> (p. 3)

Finally, difference is sometimes dealt with by engaging in the culture wars. Fortunately in schooling this approach almost never shows up directly at the classroom level but it certainly does in the so-called curriculum wars that fester at the level of policy and planning. Social education, in general, and citizenship education, in particular, have been central areas of conflict in these wars which are often characterised by 'name-calling, insult, ridicule, guilt by association, caricature, innuendo, accusation, denunciation, [and] negative ads' (Guinness, 2008, p. 84).

The first two of these approaches (ignoring religion, and trivialising it) do nothing to build the kind of deep understanding mandated in curricular outcomes, and the last (a culture wars approach) alienates and does nothing to build understanding. In terms of the latter, Noddings (2008, p. 78) reflects on the implications of the 'new outspoken atheism', implicating the works of writers such as Richard Dawkins and Christopher Hitchens for schooling. While she has definite sympathies for many of the points made in these works, she concludes that their polemical nature makes them unsuitable as vehicles for education. About Hitchens, for example, she writes, 'his language is more likely to inflame than to persuade those with whom he disagrees. In that sense his book is unlikely to spread critical religious literacy among those who do not already possess it' (p. 372). As a general technique, she argues, 'approaching the topic of belief with scorn and ridicule is almost certainly a mistake' (p. 377).

In reflecting on the culture wars around the scholarship and teaching of history in Australia, MacIntyre (Macintyre and Clark, 2004, p. 243) contends that 'the object of war is to vanquish the enemy. The duty of the scholar is to seek understanding.' In this observation he points a way forward for education, which is, at least substantially, a scholarly activity. To develop the kind of intercultural understanding desired in virtually every democratic state around the world, educators must deal with religion and religious ideas in a substantial way: neither coddling religion nor vilifying it.

Space does not allow for a full discussion of how this might be done, but it has been well articulated by a range of writers from a number of national contexts (Sweet, 1997; Nash, 2005; Gates, 2007; Noddings, 2008). All argue that the consideration of religion in schools should be open, scholarly and respectful. That is, education should allow for consideration of multiple points of view; claims emanating from those points of view should be subjected to investigation and critique; and students should feel safe in expressing their opinions and making arguments. Because we are dealing with people's most cherished beliefs and traditions and in an open society these will differ greatly, the process of balancing scholarly investigation with respect will be difficult. Nash (2005, p. 105) outlines five principles for doing this rooted in 'the supposition that a genuine attempt to understand another's religious views must always be a prerequisite for critique and judgment of those views'.

Social cohesion is an important outcome of education in most jurisdictions around the world (Reid *et al.*, 2010). In Western democracies we have engaged in an experiment with pluralism premised on the idea that we can both learn from each other and learn to work with each other in a civic community even when we have important differences. A key purpose of civic education is to lay the groundwork for that enterprise. Dealing with the sensitive and nuanced issues around religion in the classroom will be difficult but if we cannot do it there, we probably cannot do it anywhere. As Gates (2007, p. 62) points out, 'readiness to engage with religion in the context of publicly funded education is more than ever a necessary prerequisite for community cohesion and political health'.

Conclusion

In his *School and Society* (1907), the chapters of which initially constituted lectures to parents of children at the laboratory school founded at the University of Chicago, John Dewey expressed great concern for the dissipation of unity of life within educational administration. Beyond the school, in society and in everyday living, many of the distinctions that we entrench in our schools are non-existent. The organisation of the day into various subjects and courses, for instance, imposes distinctions in the ways of study that are artificial and not representative of the way we think and act in life outside the schoolhouse; as a consequence, Dewey explained:

> The unity of education is dissipated, and the studies become centrifugal; so much of this study to secure this end, so much of that to secure another, until the whole becomes a sheer compromise and patchwork between contending aims and disparate studies. The great problem in education on the administrative side is to secure the unity of the whole.
>
> (p. 86)

Bringing schools – pedagogically, administratively, and culturally – into greater correlation with social life and reality is, for Dewey, a means of reaching for a more authentic and sound vision for education. Where religion is and has been intrinsically intertwined in the fabric of our cultural and social lives, the expurgation and restriction upon religion in schooling might justifiably be seen as a disintegration of the unity of life. Where religion is made illicit in schools, education is rendered less relevant to social and cultural life and, consequently, more artificial.

Jürgen Habermas (2003) has argued that the secularisation thesis, which presupposed and insisted on a strict separation of the religious sphere from the political realm, has lost its explanatory power. We are, he argues, in a 'post-secular' world, where our ongoing interpretation of notions such as democracy and citizenship in life depend upon relations of mutual dependence between faith and knowledge (Reder and Schmidt, 2010, p. 7). Because religious and secular thinking are interdependent – often overlapping in their interests and always complementary in their explanations – public discourse should silence the utterances of neither fountainhead or understanding. Habermas offers the process of mutual translation as a working model, suggesting that secular institutions seek to understand and incorporate religious ideas into terms comprehensible to them, and vice versa. Becoming aware of the cultural, intellectual and educational traditions binding religion and education is thus a process of understanding 'what is missing' (Habermas, 2010) when aggressive religious or secular institutions impose a broad divide between the two, which is ultimately counterproductive to the social aims of schooling.

347

Questions for further investigation

1 What has been your own experience of religion and education? Have you attended religious schools or schools established and run by religious organisations? What role has the study of religion played in your own education?

2 What is the relationship between religion and education in your jurisdiction? Are there religious schools or state schools run by religious organisations? What approach to teaching religion or teaching about religion is taken in these schools? What approach is taken in secular state schools?

3 What role do you think religion should play in education? Is there a place for religious schools? Should religious organisations be involved in the running of state schools? Should religion be a subject of study in the curriculum? If so, what form should that study take?

Suggested further reading

Arthur, J., Gearon, L. and Sears, A. (2010) *Education, Politics and Religion: Reconciling the Civic and the Sacred in Education*. London and New York, NY: Routledge. This book traces the interconnections between religion and education in the Western tradition from ancient to contemporary times. With a particular focus on democratic civic education it pushes back against the post-Enlightenment secularisation agenda of the West arguing that religion has been and can be a positive force in democratic societies.

Gates, B. (2007) *Transforming Religious Education*. London: Continuum. This book traces the development of Religious Education as a school subject in England and Wales from the 1960s to the present through a retrospective examination of the work of prominent religious educator Brian Gates. It provides a nice overview of the development of policy and practice in the field.

Noddings, N. (1993) *Educating for Intelligent Belief or Unbelief*. New York, NY: Teachers College Press. Nel Noddings is one of the best-known philosophers of education in the United States. In this book she laments the absences of the study of religion in American curricula and argues that fundamental beliefs, religious or otherwise, are an important component of human life and ought to be the subject of rigorous academic study in schools. She presents a coherent overview of how to go about this.

Prothero, S.R. (2010) *Religious Literacy: what every American needs to know – and doesn't*. San Francisco, CA: HarperCollins. This book documents the pervasive ignorance about religion and religious ideas in the United States and argues this should be of serious concern. Prothero contends that understanding religious people and religious ideas is essential for a mature understanding of local and world affairs.

References

Arthur, J., Gearon, L. and Sears, A. (2010) *Education, Politics and Religion: Reconciling the Civic and the Sacred in Education*. London and New York: Routledge.

Associated Press (2010) 'Plea to Overturn Ban on School Crucifixes'. Available at: www.guardian.co.uk/world/2010/jul/01/italy-crucifix-ban-human-rights (accessed 1 July 2010).

Bickmore, K. (2005a) 'Foundations for Peacebuilding and Discursive Peacekeeping: Infusion and Exclusion of Conflict in Canadian Public School Curricula', *Journal of Peace Education*, 2, 2, pp. 161–181.

Bickmore, K. (2005b) 'Teacher Development for Conflict Participation: Facilitating Learning for "Difficult Citizenship" Education', *Citizenship Teaching and Learning*, 1, 2, pp. 2–16.

Brabant, M. (2010) 'Greek Church Acts on Crucifix Ban'. Available at: http://news.bbc.co.uk/2/hi/europe/8358027.stm (accessed 12 July 2010).

Dean, B. (2010) 'Citizenship Education in Pakistan: Changing Policies and Practicies in Changing Social-Political Contexts', in A. Reid, J. Gill and A. Sears (Eds.), *Globalization, the Nation-State and the Citizen: Dilemmas and Directions for Civics and Citizenship Education*. New York and London: Routledge, pp. 64–79.

Dewey, J. (1907) *The School and Society*. Chicago, IL: University of Chicago Press.

Gates, B. (2007) *Transforming Religious Education*. London: Continuum.

Gereluk, D. (2008) *Symbolic Clothing in Schools: What Should be Worn and Why*. London: Continuum.

Groome, T.H. (1980) *Christian Religious Education: Sharing Our Story and Vision*. San Francisco: Jossey-Bass.

Guinness, O. (2008) *The Case for Civility And Why Our Future Depends on It*. New York, NY: HarperOne.

Habermas, J. (2003) *The Future of Human Nature*. Cambridge: Polity Press.

Habermas, J. (2010) 'A Reply', in Habermas, J. *An Awareness of What is Missing*. Cambridge: Polity Press, pp. 72–83.

Hamilton, G. (2010) 'Quebec to Appeal Ruling on "Totalitarian" Ethics and Religion Course'. Available at: http://life.nationalpost.com/2010/06/22/quebec-to-appeal-court-ruling-on-totalitarian-ethics-and-religion-course/ (accessed 1 July 2010).

Kiwan, D. (2008) 'Citizenship education in England at the Crossroads? Four models of citizenship and their implications for ethnic and religious diversity', *Oxford Review of Education*, 34, 1, 39–58.

Lindberg, C. (2006). *A Brief History of Christianity*. Malden, MA: Blackwell Publishing.

Macintyre, S. and Clark, A. (2004) *The History Wars* (New Ed.). Melbourne: Melbourne University Press.

Nash, R.J. (2005) 'A Letter to Secondary Teachers: Teaching about Religious Pluralism in the Public Schools', in Noddings, N. (Ed.) *Educating Citizens for Global Awareness*. New York, NY: Teachers College Press, pp. 93–106.

Noddings, N. (2008) 'The New Outspoken Atheism and Education', *Harvard Educational Review*, 78, 2, pp. 369–390.

Ofsted. (2010) *Transforming Religious Education: Religious Education in Schools 2006–2009* (No. 090215). Manchester: The Office for Standards in Education, Children's Services and Skills.

Pinker, S. (2006). Less Faith, More Reason. *The Harvard Crimson*. Available at: www.thecrimson.com/printerfriendly.aspx?ref=515314 (accessed 2 November 2009).

Reder, M. and Schmidt, J. (2010) 'Habermas and Religion', in Habermas, J. *An Awareness of What is Missing*. Cambridge: Polity Press, pp. 72–83.

Reid, A., Gill, J. and Sears, A. (Eds.) (2010) *Globalization, the Nation-State and the Citizen: Dilemmas and Directions for Civics and Citizenship Education*. New York and London: Routledge.

Sweet, L. (1997) *God in the Classroom: The Controversial Issue of Religion in Canada's Schools*. Toronto, ON: McClelland & Stewart.

Vella, F. (2010) 'To Tolerate or not to Tolerate the Crucifix'. Available at: www.independent.com.mt/news.asp?newsitemid=108430 (accessed 12 July 2010).

Wilken, R.L. (1989) 'Who Will Speak For the Religious Traditions', *Journal of the American Academy of Religion*, 57, 4, 699–718.

Wolterstorff, N., Stronks, G.G. and Joldersma, C.W. (2002). *Educating for Life: Reflections on Christian Teaching and Learning*. Grand Rapids, MI: Baker Academic.

ZENIT (2010) 'US Professor's Testimony in Europe's Crucifix Trial'. Available at: www.zenit.org/article-29769?l=english (accessed 12 July 2010).

37

Social justice and inequalities in education

Emma Smith
University of Birmingham

Overview

This chapter considers a role for education in improving social justice and reducing inequality. While the issues that are explored here are relevant for education systems across the world, this chapter has a particular focus on what is happening at present in the UK; a country which, in 2010, has a new government with a new agenda for educational change and along with this a new ideology for how a fairer and more equitable society might be achieved. The discussion which follows considers two ways in which schools might reduce inequalities and enhance social justice. It begins by looking at the outcomes of schooling in terms of examination success at age 16 before considering the role of schools as micro-societies in their own right and at the function they may have in promoting a fair and just society.

Introduction – social justice and education

Without good education there can be no social justice.

(David Cameron, 2007, p. 84)

It is education which provides the rungs on the ladder of social mobility.

(Gordon Brown, 2010)

As the above quotations from UK politicians demonstrate, the role of education in reducing inequalities and promoting social mobility and social justice is a favourite topic among politicians seeking to share their vision for a fair and just society. Firmly in 'the front line against poverty and inequality' (Cameron, 2009) the nation's schools and colleges have been charged with producing a skilled and competent workforce capable of ensuring the nation's economic competitiveness in an increasingly globalised community. However, while politicians from various parties may agree that education has a key role in promoting social justice, they do differ in their views on the best way to achieve it. Consider this from the former British Prime Minister Gordon Brown:

> fairness can be advanced by but cannot, in the end, be guaranteed by charities, however benevolent, by markets, however dynamic, or by individuals, however well meaning, but guaranteed only by enabling government.

> (Brown, 2005)

Brown's notion that only the state can 'guarantee fairness' is in contrast to present Prime Minster David Cameron's view of a 'Big Society' where power and control are redistributed from the state to individuals and local communities; in other words, a movement 'from state action to social action' (Cameron, 2009). For the new UK Coalition government, limiting the role of the state in matters to do with education is exemplified by plans to expand the Academy schools programme and the establishment of new Swedish-style Free Schools (The Conservative Party, 2010). Both initiatives will mean a lessening of the control that government and local authorities have over how schools are administered. In the case of Academies this will involve allowing the most 'outstanding' schools increased autonomy over the curriculum, admissions policies as well as teachers' pay and conditions. For critics who consider the role of the state to be crucial in ensuring educational equity, such proposals are tantamount to privatisation (e.g. Bousted, 2010).

Whatever their differing ideologies on how best to achieve a more just society, the political consensus that education is at the heart of social justice issues does give rise to the question: what are schools for? For many policy-makers the answer would seem to lie in the economic imperative of education being the cornerstone of an effective economy, a perspective which might be characterised by three words: efficiency, effectiveness and accountability. This view, however is not uncontroversial. In her excellent book *Does Education Matter?*, Alison Wolf suggests that 'our preoccupation with education as an engine of growth has . . . narrowed – dismally and progressively – our vision of education itself' (2000, p. 254). A perspective which finds support among philosophers of education who argue that schools 'should orient themselves to the needs of the children who will have to deal with the economy, and not to the needs of the economy itself' (Brighouse, 2006, p. 28).

This more holistic view of education would require greater emphasis on the role of schools in helping shape the next generation of 'socially and morally responsible citizens'. This presents a view of education which is arguably at odds with the current preoccupation with academic standards as the key output from schooling and suggests a notion of schooling which brings us closer to Pring's (2010) conception of an educated 19-year-old who:

> has a sufficient grasp of those ideas and principles to enable him or her to manage life intelligently, who has the competence and skills to tackle practical tasks including those required for employment, who has a sense of community and the disposition to make a contribution to it, who is morally serious in the sense that he or she cares about fairness and responsibility to others, who is inspired by what has been done by others and who has a sense and knowledge of self-confidence and resilience in the face of difficulty . . . Such an aim should shape the education for the future.

> (p. 63)

What do we mean by social justice?

Before considering how educational inequalities manifest themselves and the extent to which schools, and education more widely, can reduce these inequalities and promote educational, and even social, justice, it is worth pausing very briefly to consider what it is that we mean by social justice and equality in the first place. This is not necessarily straightforward and is an issue which has preoccupied philosophers since the time of Aristotle and Plato. Here we will focus on three concepts of justice as described by Ruitenberg and Vokey (2010).

We start with Plato's conception of what Ruitenberg and Vokey (2010) call *Justice as Harmony*. This approach argues that people have different talents and that these differences when put together will strengthen the community as well as society more widely. Education should seek to support these different talents and by doing so would help enable individuals to reach their (different) potentials. This particular notion of justice therefore requires that people are treated differently and accepts that educational opportunities are inherently unequal. For example, we can see this principle in use throughout the education system in the UK – in the post-Second World War tripartite system of Grammar and Secondary Modern schools, in the school diversification programmes of today and in debates over parity of esteem between vocational and academic qualifications.

A somewhat different concept of justice is one of *Justice as Equity*, possibly the most well-known proponent of which is John Rawls. Rawls argues for an egalitarian notion of justice, the key aim of which is to reduce inequalities. To understand how Rawls' notion of justice might be applied to education, consider the following vignette:

> Jacinta has difficulty reading and finds it hard to keep up in class. The teacher has to spend a lot of time helping Jacinta and gives her a lot of attention. Sometimes the other students have to wait for the teacher to stop helping Jacinta and to come and help them.

One's response to the fairness of such a situation might be:

1 That Jacinta needs extra help so it is fair that the teacher should spend more time helping her.
2 That the teacher should spend equal time with all the students. It is not fair that others should have to wait.

A supporter of the *Justice as Equity* argument would say that scenario 1) is the fairest. In other words, that it is justifiable for the teacher to treat the students differently in order that their opportunities for success become more equal. So here we have two different approaches to ensuring justice, both of which advocate different treatment but one where different (and possibly unequal) outcomes are expected and the second where the principle is to equalise an individual's opportunity in order to facilitate more equal (and arguably more just) outcomes.

One further principle of justice – *Justice as Equality* – takes a slightly different approach. This argues that although people are not the same, they are equally deserving, so equal treatment is essential even if the eventual outcomes are themselves unequal. This would favour the situation 2) response in the scenario above: Jacinta's teacher ought to devote the same amount of attention to all her students, even if this means that some students will achieve lower grades.

Whatever one's view about the most appropriate way of ensuring that educational opportunities are as fair as possible, it is nevertheless the case that there are many diverse ways in which inequalities can and do manifest themselves within schools. For example, some pupils achieve better examination results than others, attend more 'effective' schools, have longer school careers – thus educational opportunities and outcomes are not distributed equally. It is useful to remind ourselves that it is those pupils who are academically the least successful who tend to have the shortest school careers and who may end up leaving school without even the most basic skills. This is not to argue that those who aspire to a career in medicine should not have longer educational careers than those who aspire to arguably less skilled jobs, but it is worth reflecting upon how we, as a society, choose to allocate our educational resources.

In the next section we consider two dimensions of schooling and the role they play in enhancing social justice: first, academic attainment and then schools as fair societies.

Academic emphasis of schooling

Increased scrutiny of examination performance as the most tangible outcome of schooling has led to sections of the school population being labelled as failing or underachieving. The emergence of sophisticated international comparative tests such as the Programme for International Student Assessment (PISA) and the Trends International Maths and Science Study (TIMSS) have enabled nations to look critically at the achievement of their students in the international arena. This has led to many nations re-examining their education systems in light of perceived failings in these comparative assessments. In some countries, this has been used to further justify dissatisfaction with the domestic school system and has led to accusations of underachievement and a 'crisis account' of falling academic standards and failing pupils. Within this context sit contemporary 'moral panics' about the purported failure or underachievement of large sections of the school population.

In the UK, for example, concerns about falling standards have tended to focus on the relative attainment of different social groups. There will be few readers who have not heard of the 'underachieving boys' crisis for example (see Epstein et al., 1998; Francis and Skelton, 2005). However, commentators also raise concerns about the relative attainment of certain young people from certain ethnic minority groups (e.g., Gillborn, 2008), and, to a seemingly lesser extent, those who come from the least wealthy homes (for example, Gorard, 2000; Smith, 2005). The relative lack of examination success among some social groups can be considered by looking at attainment in national tests (for instance, the GCSE examinations which are taken by most 16-year-old students at the end of compulsory schooling). Table 37.1 shows the proportions of male and female students who achieve five or more GCSE passes at grades A★–C, as well as those who achieve at least a grade C in English language. In both sets of results, the performance of boys is consistently lower than that of girls. Trends such as these are often used to suggest that 'boys have failed to build upon their performance at the same rate as girls in recent decades' (Arnot et al., 1999, p. 23) and have helped give rise to the phenomenon of the 'underachieving' boy.

Similar inequalities can be seen in the academic attainment of young people from different ethnic groups (Table 37.2). Indeed the relatively poorer academic attainment of young people from Pakistani, Bangladeshi and Black Caribbean backgrounds has been the focus of considerable recent concern (e.g., Gillborn, 2008). Although it is important to note that the attainment of all young people is improving.

Perhaps the most pronounced inequalities are apparent in the relative attainment of young people from the poorest homes – here characterised by those who are eligible for free school meals (Table 37.3). These inequalities persist at each level of education.

So in terms of 'who gets what?' from education it would appear that there are some social groups who get less than others and that the educational credential game is not a fair one,

Table 37.1 Percentage of students achieving 5+ A★–C grades at GCSE according to sex, England

| Year | 5+ A★–C grades | | English | |
	Boys	Girls	Boys	Girls
2009	66	74	57	72
2008	61	70	56	70
2007	57	66	56	70
2006	54	64	55	69
2005	51	62	54	69
2004	48	58	53	67
2003	48	58	52	68
2002	46	57	52	67
2001	45	55	51	66
2000	44	55	51	66
1999	43	53	50	66
1998	41	51	48	64
1997	40	50	46	63
1996	40	49	47	64

Source: DfES (1996–2009)

certainly in terms of academic outcomes. However, these inequalities are not limited to the UK and are apparent in many other nations with different school systems and cultural priorities. Take the United States, for example.

The National Assessment of Educational Progress (NAEP) is a large-scale national test used to monitor achievement trends across the USA. Also known as the *Nation's Report Card*, NAEP has been undertaking nationwide annual assessments of student achievement in various subjects since 1969. In addition, the NAEP long-term trends assessment has been administering the same set of tests to 9, 13 and 17 year olds since 1971 in reading and since 1973 in mathematics, so making it possible to track educational progress over extended periods of time (NAEP, 2008). Figure 37.1 shows the trends in average reading scores for 13-year-old students between 1971 and 2008. The same pattern in attainment in reading occurs here as in national examinations at age 16 in England and Wales – with white and female students attaining the highest grades – and reflects achievement gaps that appear to have existed over the last three decades.

Notwithstanding the technical and conceptual problems of comparing test data across different years, cohorts and nations, it does appear that achievement gaps between different social groups are relatively well established across time, as well as appearing resistant to various cultural and educational settings. It may also be unsurprising to learn that these same inequalities which are apparent in our school system are also evident in wider society. Consider Figure 37.2. It shows that health inequalities, here exemplified by life expectancy, are apparent between people from different occupational groups. Those from professional backgrounds (such as doctors and chartered accountants) are likely to live around eight years longer than those from unskilled backgrounds (such as labourers and messengers). For a fuller discussion about the consequences of social inequalities internationally, see Wilkinson and Pickett (2009).

Table 37.2 Percentage of students achieving 5+ A⋆–C grades at GCSE according to ethnicity, England

	2005	2006	2007	2008	2009
White	55	58	60	64	70
White British	55	57	60	64	70
Irish	63	61	64	69	73
Traveller of Irish Heritage	22	19	17	18	24
Gypsy/Romany	15	10	14	16	20
Any Other White Background	59	60	60	62	67
Mixed	55	56	58	64	70
White and Black Caribbean	44	47	49	56	63
White and Black African	55	57	58	64	70
White and Asian	67	69	70	73	77
Any Other Mixed Background	59	57	62	67	72
Asian	59	61	63	67	73
Indian	70	72	75	79	82
Pakistani	48	51	54	59	66
Bangladeshi	53	57	59	63	70
Any Other Asian Background	64	65	65	67	72
Black	45	48	53	59	67
Black Caribbean	42	45	50	55	63
Black African	48	51	57	62	70
Any Other Black Background	42	47	51	57	64
Chinese	81	80	84	85	87
Any Other Ethnic Group	54	56	58	61	68
Unclassified	50	53	53	59	67
All pupils	55	57	60	64	70

Source: DCSF (2004, 2010)

Table 37.3 Percentage of students achieving 5+ A⋆–C grades at GCSE according to receipt of free school meals, England

	2005	2006	2007	2008	2009
Free School Meal	30	33	36	41	50
Non-Free School Meal	59	61	63	68	73
All pupils	55	57	60	64	70

Source: DCSF (2004, 2010)

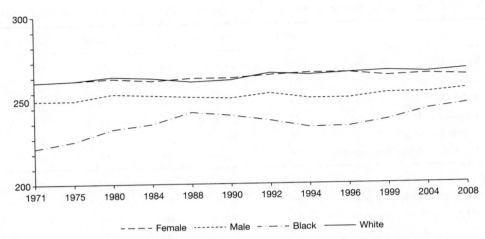

Figure 37.1 Average reading scores among 13-year-old students, by sex and ethnic group

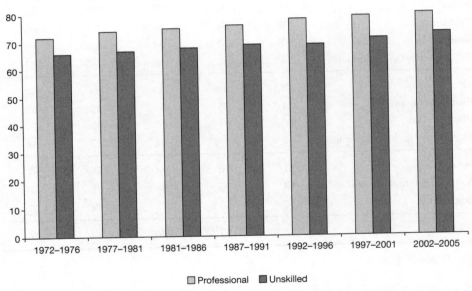

Figure 37.2 Life expectancy from birth for men from England and Wales, 1972–2005

As this section shows, for some social groups their experiences of education, in terms of the qualifications that they receive, are anything but fair. These inequalities are important because they can directly influence an individual's life chances: their opportunities for further study or for securing successful employment, as well as their well-being. However, as we discussed earlier, school, and education more broadly, can serve another function which goes beyond straightforward accreditation, and this is its role in helping shape the next generation of 'socially and morally responsible' citizens.

Schools as fair societies

This discussion draws upon the findings of a series of studies into the views and experiences of fairness of young people in five European countries as well as in Japan. The research took the form of a questionnaire survey of around 15,000 14- and 15-year-old pupils. It asked them about their experiences of being treated fairly by their teachers, peers, parents as well as by the adults they encounter outside school. The focus here is on the school experiences of the young people from England but for further detail on the experiences of those from other nations see Gorard and Smith (2010).

For most pupils school is a positive experience: they enjoy their education, feel that they are well treated and that their learning has purpose. However, our research also points to instances when their reported experiences appear to be less than fair. One recurring example of this comes with pupils' observations that teachers are inconsistent and unfair when punishing students; that teachers had favourites and that certain groups of students (for example, hard working students) were treated better, or more differently, than others. These views are reflected in some of the comments below:

> At this one incident I got a detention for looking at the clock by Ms T. I think that is unfair because it was a harsh punishment and in most peoples' opinion I did nothing wrong.
>
> (male pupil)

> My chemistry teacher sent me out of the classroom for the whole lesson for sitting in the wrong seat.
>
> (male pupil)

> How the naughty children get more attention and get highly praised when they manage to produce the same amount of work as the rest of the class which they should be doing anyway.
>
> (female pupil)

> I had finished some work and asked my teacher to read it and see if I could improve, but she said 'no' because she was dealing with other students who were misbehaving.
>
> (male pupil)

> I try really hard in all my tests and homework, but I don't get grades which reflect the effort I put into it. Also some teachers have their favourites and ignore others.
>
> (female pupil)

That teachers were not always perceived to be treating students fairly and consistently is an important, but perhaps not surprising, finding with important implications for citizenship education in schools (see also Osler, 2010). For example, how can a citizenship curriculum which embraces issues of fairness and democracy be effectively implemented if the students themselves do not mostly believe that their teachers are generally capable of such behaviour?

The views of more 'vulnerable' students

In addition to analysing the opinions of all the young people, we were also interested in gathering the views of more 'vulnerable' students. As we saw earlier, one of the recurring themes in the sociology of education is that there are certain groups of young people who are academically less successful in school. At the aggregate level, these tend to be students from less wealthy homes, or whose families may have experiences of generations of unemployment or low waged work as well as those recently arrived in the country. Here our interest is in the extent to which these inequalities might persist in the young people's experiences of fairness in school.

Table 37.4 shows the proportion of students who agree with the statements about the extent to which they experience fair treatment by their teachers in school. It also compares the responses of pupils from minority social and cultural backgrounds with those of the majority of students who, in this study, were born in the UK, spoke English at home and whose parents had higher status jobs.

Because of the diversity of the countries that participated in this study, it was not possible to use standard measures of ethnic groups to characterise the sample. Therefore, in order to have some indication of the ethnic background of the young people involved in the study, we asked them two questions: the first was about the main language they spoke at home and the second about the country in which they had been born.

Around 13 per cent of the sample spoke a language other than English at home. When asked about their experiences of fairness in school, pupils who spoke English at home and those that did not reported similar experiences; for example, that their teachers treated them fairly (Table 37.4). With regards to country of birth, around 5 per cent of pupils told us that they had been born outside the UK. Their responses to the questionnaire suggests that their experiences were generally little different to those who were native born. For example, 42 per cent of pupils from both groups thought that their teachers were interested in their well-being. It may surprise some readers that less than half the pupils held this view and also that only around 40 per cent felt that they had been treated fairly. However, the point here is that both groups of students share similar (albeit somewhat negative) experiences.

We also compared the experiences of young people whose parents either had no job or were occupied in what might be deemed to be a 'lower status' job (such as a factory worker or labourer) with the views of the rest of the sample. Once again our analysis showed that there was little difference between the experiences of pupils in the majority and minority groups: similar proportions thought their teachers treated them fairly and respected their views and opinions.

Of particular interest in this study were the experiences of those young people who were considered to be the most vulnerable; for example, those from less wealthy homes and recent

Table 37.4 Percentage of students agreeing with statements about treatment in school

	Main home language		Social class		Country of birth	
	English	Other	Lower status job	Other	UK	Other
Teachers treat me fairly	40	40	39	40	40	40
Teachers are interested in my well-being	42	46	41	44	42	42
Teachers treat my opinions with respect	43	42	43	43	43	36
School has been a waste of time	7	7	10	6	7	8

immigrants. That their experiences of school might not be as fair as those of their peers is summed up by one of the respondents when asked to report any instances when they had been treated unfairly: 'Personally no! As I am Caucasian middle class and well spoken. If I was not however, this section might be rather different.' However, examining the responses of the more vulnerable students does suggest that their experiences of fair treatment are not appreciably more negative than their peers. So here we have a situation where young people who tend to be among the lowest attaining and are potentially the most vulnerable in the school population report experiences which are little different to the majority school population – an example perhaps of where schools are successfully reducing inequalities.

Conclusion

Using examples drawn mainly from the UK system, this chapter has tried to show the importance of thinking about issues of social justice and inequality in education. The experience of young people in school is fundamental to shaping their expectations of adult life and in helping to prepare them to live their lives in a 'spirit of peace, tolerance and equality' (Osler, 2010, p. 87). However, as we have seen here, for some groups of students the current emphasis on academic attainment has served only to reinforce educational inequalities. This of course is not to say that good examination results are not important, it is instead to remind ourselves of the other functions of a successful school system. This is a school system where all young people, including the academically least successful, are able to flourish, where they can learn to trust and help each other and to develop positive attitudes towards learning, their peers and themselves. As Gorard (2010, p. 62) argues:

> Schools, in their structure and organisation, can do more than simply reflect the society we have; they can try to be the precursor of the kind of society that we wish to have.

Perhaps this ought to be the basis upon which effective schools are judged.

Questions for further investigation

1 According to the philosopher Basil Bernstein, 'education cannot compensate for society'. Given the huge amount of popular attention that is devoted to educational issues today, to what extent do you think that this statement is true?

2 One of the key complaints of the students who participated in the research that was summarised here is that teachers treat students differently which they feel to be unfair. What are your views on this, do you think that teachers ought to treat all students in the same way?

3 The data that is presented in this chapter shows how some educational inequalities persist over time as well as in different education systems. What are your views on the current emphasis on examination outcomes and how do you think we should decide which schools are the most effective?

Suggested further reading

Gorard, S. and Smith, E. (2010) *Equity in Education: An International Perspective*. Basingstoke: Palgrave MacMillan. This book reports the findings from an international research study into young people's views and experiences of fairness in school and in wider society.

Sandel, M.J. (2009) *Justice: What's the Right Thing to Do?* London: Penguin Books. This is a highly accessible introduction to some of the philosophical ideas behind issues of fairness and justice. The following link will take you to Michael Sandel's popular 'Justice' course website at Harvard University: *www.justiceharvard.org/*.

Wilkinson, R. and Pickett, K. (2009) *The Spirit Level: Why Equality is Better for Everyone*. London: Penguin Books. This book has attracted a great deal of recent attention and provides a compelling account of the inequalities that persist in many developed nations.

Wolf, A. (2000) *Does Education Matter? Myths About Education and Economic Growth*. London: Penguin Books. Another very readable book which looks at the post-compulsory education sector and its role in the economic and social development of the UK.

References

Arnot, M., Gray, J., James, M. and Rudduck, J. (1998) *Recent Research on Gender and Educational Performance*. London: The Stationery Office.

Bousted, M. (2010) 'For flexibility and freedoms, read "chaos"', *Times Education Supplement*, 18 June.

Brighouse, H. (2006) *On Education*. London: Routledge.

Brown, G. (2005) 'Gordon Brown on liberty and the role of the state'. Speech delivered by the chancellor, Gordon Brown, at Chatham House, *The Guardian*, 13 December. Available at: www.guardian.co.uk/politics/2005/dec/13/labour.uk. Accessed August 2010.

Brown, G. (2010) *Gordon Brown 'This election will be about social mobility'*. Speech given to the Fabian Society New Year conference, January 2010. Available at: www.publicservice.co.uk/feature_story.asp?id=13530. Accessed August 2010.

Cameron, D. (2007) *Social Responsibility: The Big Idea for Britain's Future*. London: The Conservative Party.

Cameron, D. (2009) 'David Cameron: The Big Society'. Speech made on 10 November. Available at: www.conservatives.com/News/Speeches/2009/11/David_Cameron_The_Big_Society.aspx. Accessed August 2010.

The Conservative Party (2010) *Invitation to Join the Government of Britain, The Conservative Party Manifesto 2010*. London: The Conservative Party. Available at: http://media.conservatives.s3.amazonaws.com/manifesto/cpmanifesto2010_lowres.pdf. Accessed August 2010.

DCSF (2004) *National Curriculum Assessment GCSE and Equivalent Attainment and Post-16 Attainment by Pupil Characteristics, in England 2004*. Department for Children, Schools and Families. Available at: www.dcsf.gov.uk/rsgateway/DB/SFR/s000564/index.shtml. Accessed August 2010.

DCSF (2010) *GCSE Attainment by Pupil Characteristics, England 2009*. Department for Children, Schools and Families. Available at: www.dcsf.gov.uk/rsgateway/DB/SFR/s000900/index.shtml. Accessed August 2010.

Epstein, D., Elwood, J., Hey, V. and Maw J. (1998) *Failing Boys? Issues in Gender and Achievement*. Buckingham: Open University Press.

Francis, B. and Skelton C. (2005) *Reassessing Gender and Achievement: Questioning Contemporary Key Debates*. Abingdon: Routledge.

Gillborn, D. (2008) *Racism and Education Coincidence or Conspiracy?* London: Routledge.

Gorard, S. (2000) *Education and Social Justice*. Cardiff: University of Wales Press.

Gorard, S. (2010) 'Education can compensate for society – a bit', *British Journal of Educational Studies*, 58, 1, pp. 47–65.

Gorard, S. and Smith, E., (2010) *Equity in Education: An International Perspective*. Basingstoke: Palgrave MacMillan.

NAEP (2008) *National Assessment of Educational Progress Long-term Trend Data*. Available at: http://nationsreportcard.gov/ltt_2008/. Accessed August 2010.

ONS (2007) *Variations Persist in Life Expectancy by Social Class: 2002–2005 Data Released*. London: Office for National Statistics. Available at: www.statistics.gov.uk/pdfdir/le1007.pdf. Accessed August 2010.

Osler, A. (2010) *Students' Perspectives on Schooling*. Buckingham: McGrawHill.

Pring, R, (2010) 'The philosophy of education and educational practice', in Bailey, R., Barrow, R., Carr, D. and McCarthy, C. (Eds.) *The Sage Handbook of Philosophy of Education*. London: Sage.

Ruitenberg, C. and Vokey, D. (2010) 'Equality and justice', in Bailey, R., Barrow, R., Carr, D. and McCarthy, C. (Eds.) *The Sage Handbook of Philosophy of Education*. London: Sage.

Smith, E. (2005) *Analysing Underachievement in School*. London: Continuum.

Wolf, A. (2000) *Does Education Matter? Myths About Education and Economic Growth*. London: Penguin Books.

Wilkinson, R. and Pickett, K., (2009), *The Spirit Level: Why Equality is Better for Everyone*, London: Penguin Books.

38

Sustainable development

John Huckle
University of York

No single thinker, party or school of thought offers a complete answer, or anything like it. Answers will have to be hammered out in open-minded dialogue, between all those who accept that tinkering is not enough, across lines of party and creed. The need, in fact, is for a realignment of the mind, socialist in economics and republican in politics. In such a realignment the Green movement must surely have a central place, along with radicals and dissenters from all parties and none.

(Marquand, 2010)

Overview

In the wake of the third great capitalist crisis of modern times, David Marquand joined other commentators to suggest that the neo-liberal paradigm that has dominated policy-making in much of the world in recent decades, not least in institutions of global governance, had failed after proving itself monstrously unjust and unsustainable. While mainstream politicians sought a return to a modified version of business as usual, radicals predicted that such measures would fail to revive the profits system (Shutt, 2010). They urged a realignment of minds as a first step towards more rational, sustainable, and politically acceptable forms of political economy.

This chapter argues that education has a key role to play in such a realignment of minds. It should engage learners in open-minded dialogue about those values, forms of political economy, and models of democracy and citizenship, that may allow us to live more sustainably with one another and the rest of nature. Such dialogue should consider the merits of greener forms of socialism, alongside those of greener forms of capitalism, and should prompt reflection and action on existing and emergent models of democracy and citizenship.

Unsustainable development

The global economy that underpins all our lives depends on finding profitable sources of investment for ever greater quantities of capital. This requires resource-intensive economic growth that yields profits for companies, tax revenues for governments, and rising standards of living for the majority of citizens. All have an interest in an accelerating treadmill of production and consumption, but this periodically comes up against limits when it is impossible to sell all that is produced at a profit and productive capacity has to be scrapped. The speculative boom that preceded the current crisis was an attempt to prevent the treadmill slowing. The de-regulation and liberalisation of the financial sector created housing, credit, and asset bubbles to absorb excess capital, but when these burst many assets proved worthless (financial crisis), sources of credit dried up (credit crisis), and many countries went into recession (Gamble, 2009; Harvey, 2010).

While recurring crises mean that current forms of capitalist development are not economically sustainable or able to continue in a stable state indefinitely, they are also, to varying extents, ecologically, socially, politically, culturally, personally, and morally unsustainable. They degrade the ecological resources and services on which they depend; fail to meet everyone's social needs; foster corrupt politicians and passive citizens; erode local knowledge and cultural diversity; damage people's physical and mental health; and undermine those values that underpin the realisation of human rights and democracy. This argument is developed by, amongst many others, Myers *et al.* (2005) who provide an overview of the planet's problems and prospects; Kovel (2007) who links ecological crisis to capitalism and its domination of nature; Watts (2010) who focuses on the stark choices currently facing China that, he suggests, will affect us all; and Barber (2007) who explores 'how markets corrupt children, infantalize adults, and swallow citizens whole'.

Sustainable development

Pressure for more sustainable forms of development grew out of social movements, concerned about damage to the bio-physical environment and the extent of world poverty, originating in the 1960s. Early tensions between these movements (development is needed to lift people out of poverty yet it damages the environment) were addressed by the World Commission on the Environment and Development in the 1980s. It offered a definition of sustainable development as 'development that meets the needs of the present without compromising the ability of future generations to meet their own needs' (WCED, 1987, p. 43). Subsequent UN conferences on the environment and development, termed Earth Summits, in 1992 and 2002 led to related declarations and conventions on such issues as biodiversity and climate change, together with action plans at international, national, and local levels. In an era of neo-liberalism, existing forms of global governance were unable to deliver what was essentially a socially democratic agenda (Park *et al.*, 2008), but with the onset of the financial crisis it regained attention when there was widespread advocacy of green new deals (UNEP, 2009).

Sustainable development is contested with competing discourses providing the vocabularies and conceptual frameworks that condition the different ways in which people and institutions understand and act on issues of the environment and development. These discourses may act ideologically to explain away apparent contradictions and hide problems in society making solutions more difficult to obtain, function hegemonically to gain consent for particular positions of power, and/or operate as 'regimes of truth' or rules that govern what can be said

Table 38.1 Two discourses of sustainable development

Sustainable development as the greening of capitalism	*Sustainable development as the greening of socialism*
Continued capital accumulation requires greater attention to environmental protection and social justice.	Due to technological change the capitalist treadmill can no longer provide sufficient sources of capital investment or worthwhile jobs for all. It should be replaced with a socialist economy.
Doing more with less (ecological modernisation) is the key to new green enterprises. Efficiency.	Coordinated and participatory economic planning to meet social needs is the key to development within ecological limits. Sufficiency.
It is often worth sacrificing critical ecological capital (rare species and habitats) for long-term economic and social gain (weak sustainability).	It is never worth sacrificing critical ecological capital (strong sustainability).
Favours market instruments to cut pollution and conserve the environment rather than regulation.	Favours coordinated planning and regulation alongside market instruments.
Encourages sustainable consumption.	Meaningful work for all and shorter working hours provide time for forms of self-development that reduce the attractions of consumerism.
Key roles for experts and expert knowledge.	Key roles for local people and local knowledge.
Favours representative forms of democracy and passive citizenship.	Provides work and a social wage for all in return for active citizenship.
Promotes global welfare through institutional reform and redistribution.	Provides global welfare through redistribution and new forms of global governance and democracy.
Values are strongly anthropocentric and technocentric.	Values are weakly anthropocentric and ecocentric.
Supported by mainstream liberals and social democrats.	Supported by greens, green socialists, and anti-capitalists.
Rogers *et al.*, 2008; Turner, 2001	Dickenson, 2003; Little, 1998

and what must remain unsaid, who can speak with authority and who must listen (Walsh, 2009). While it grossly simplifies an array of relevant discourses (Dryzak, 1997) and ignores others, and is less relevant in many parts of the world than it is in the UK, Table 38.1 summarises the key divide. This is between reformists and radicals: between those seeking the greening of capitalism and those seeking the greening of socialism.

Education for sustainable development (ESD)

ESD emerged in the 1990s, largely shaped by the discourses and practitioners of environmental education and development education. By the start of the UN Decade of ESD (DESD) in 2005, it had a well-developed theory and practice with innumerable texts and articles, pedagogic approaches, toolkits, curriculum resources, and courses for teachers (Huckle, 2005). A review published as a result of the DESD monitoring and evaluation process (Wals, 2009) suggests that since ESD is being developed around the world in ways that are locally relevant and culturally appropriate, it is not necessary to seek consensus over its meaning. Nevertheless analysis of definitions shows that the following keywords appear frequently: creation of awareness; local and global vision; responsibility; learning to change; participation; lifelong learning; critical thinking; systemic approach and understanding complexity; decision-making; interdisciplinarity; problem-solving; and satisfying the needs of the present without compromising future generations.

The review suggests that there is a greater consensus over the following key principles covering the scope, purpose, and practice of ESD:

- A transformative and reflective process that seeks to integrate values and perceptions of sustainability into not only education systems but one's everyday personal and professional life.
- A means of empowering people with new knowledge and skills to help resolve common issues that challenge global society's collective life now and in the future.
- A holistic approach to achieve economic and social justice and respect for all life.
- A means to improve the quality of basic education, to reorient existing educational programmes, and to raise awareness (Wals, 2009, p. 26).

Such principles can clearly be applied and implemented in different ways since ESD reflects the politics both of sustainable development and of education. Much mainstream ESD serves as a hegemonic form of educational discourse, supporting the greening of capitalism, and dealing uncritically with issues relating to the environment and development. Selby and Kagawa (2010) suggest that neglect of politics and a readiness to take on increasingly instrumentalist purposes means that impetus in the field has been conceded to the neo-liberal ideology now tacitly embedded in international agendas. Mainstream ESD thus uncritically embraces economic growth, globalisation and consumerism, an instrumentalist and utilitarian view of nature, the skills agenda in education, and, via targets and indicators, a preoccupation with the tangibles of standardisation and measurement.

Sustainable schools

The greening of schools, colleges, and universities is a key element of ESD (Terry, 2008; Corcoran and Wals, 2004) and the UK Labour government's strategy for sustainable schools provides an example of how mainstream ESD discourse functions ideologically and hegemonically. It aimed for all schools to become models of sustainable development by 2020 'guided by the principle of care: for oneself, for each other (across cultures, distances and time) and for the environment (far and near)' (DfES, 2006, p. 2). This principle is to shape integrated efforts to address eight 'doorways' to sustainability across the curriculum (teaching and learning), campus (values and ways of working), and community (wider information and partnerships). These include food and drink, travel and traffic, buildings and grounds, inclusion and participation, and local well-being.

While the strategy provides opportunities for teachers and pupils to reflect and act on different discourses or approaches to sustainability, there is no encouragement to do this in the related guidance. This urges teachers to use the curriculum to cultivate the knowledge, values, and skills needed to address the 'doorways' but there is no attempt to expand on these learning outcomes and the illustrative case studies suggest that sustainable development is simply a matter of pupils, schools, and communities developing the 'right' attitudes and behaviours and so becoming more caring green consumers and citizens. The strategy functions ideologically by concealing contradictions in government policy for at the same time as it was promoting sustainable schools, it was continuing to introduce greater competition, individualism, and choice into education, so eroding the principle of care and part closing most of the doorways. Greater choice for those parents able to exercise choice of school does, for example, part close the doorway of travel and traffic as journeys to school lengthen.

Values and sustainability as a frame of mind

Viewing schooling, or nature, instrumentally as part of a wider policy to promote sustainable development is an indication of the extent to which the market and state have encouraged us to accept what is expedient, profitable, feasible or possible, rather than what is right. This leads the philosopher Michael Bonnett (2004) to suggest that sustainability should not be fostered as an aspect of policy (as in the example of sustainable schools above) but as a frame of mind that is alive to relationships within and between bio-physical and social systems that allow their mutual development to take place in sustainable ways. ESD requires teachers and learners to be open and engaged with the complexity and meaning of things in the manner of great art or literature, attuned to harmony and discord in the world via a heightened sense of attachment, and capable of viewing nature in ways that are essentially poetic and non-manipulative. The kind of knowledge that learners require will not be exclusively or even predominantly scientific, for the natural and social sciences need to be set in a broader context provided by the arts and humanities. These can encourage learners to recognise the aesthetic, existence, and spiritual values of nature alongside its ecological, scientific, and economic values. They can express the virtue of sufficiency over excess and of sustaining things not in order to have something in hand for the future, but in order to let things be true to themselves, unalienated from their own essence and development.

The Earth Charter and ecopedagogy

A further challenge to mainstream ESD as policy is offered by the Earth Charter and ecopedagogy. At the Earth Summit in 1992, an attempt was made to draw up a statement about the interrelationships between humanity and the Earth that would address the environmental concerns of education once and for all in both ethical and ecological (as opposed to technocratic and instrumentalist) terms. The resulting Earth Charter, launched in 2000, offers 16 principles for building a global society based on respect for nature, universal human rights, economic justice, and a culture of peace. It was hoped that the 2002 Earth Summit would adopt and endorse this 'holistic, pointedly socialist in spirit, and non-anthropocentric' charter (Kahn, 2008, p. 7), but pressure from US delegates and others meant that this did not happen. Nevertheless the Earth Charter Initiative continues to prompt significant ESD initiatives (see Corcoran, 2005, and the Earth Charter website).

In Brazil the principles in the Earth Charter were merged with a future-orientated ecological politics, and the critical pedagogy of Paulo Freire, to create ecopedagogy (Gadotti, 2008) that seeks to develop three complementary forms of ecoliteracy throughout society. Technical/functional ecoliteracy involves understanding the basic science of the bio-physical world as far as it is relevant to social life; knowing how societies can affect ecological systems; and appreciating the potential and limitations of a community's location in place. Cultural ecoliteracy involves understanding the different epistemological relationships to nature found in diverse cultures; knowing why cultures centrally predicated upon Western individualism tend to produce ecological crisis through pervasive homogenisation, monetisation, and the privatisation of human expression (Bowers, 2007), and valuing indigenous and traditional knowledge that allows communities to live in sustainable ways. Critical ecoliteracy, after Freire, involves understanding sustainable development in the ways outlined in the first part of this chapter; recognising the role of ideology in shaping people's understanding of such concepts as those of nature, development, democracy, and sustainability, and acknowledging the role of radical workers' and citizens' movements in realising forms of political economy that reflect Earth Charter principles. Ecopedagogy is essentially a movement of the global South that challenges the mainstream ESD orthodoxies of the global North.

Knowledge and curriculum integration

The composite nature of ecopedagogy reminds us that ESD will inevitably be interdisciplinary, combining academic knowledge from the natural and social sciences, the arts and humanities, with people's everyday knowledge. Dickens (2006) suggests that academic divisions of labour, or the separation of knowledge into specialist subjects, serve to alienate people from nature by denying them a comprehensive understanding of how their own natures and the nature that surrounds them are socially constructed in more or less sustainable ways. He offers critical realism as a foundational philosophy for ESD that can hold relevant knowledge together and provide insights into how social systems should evolve alongside bio-physical systems. It can incorporate dialectical materialism, the 'new' science of complexity, critical theory, systems thinking, and postmodernism, while avoiding the idealism and moral relativism inherent in some postmodern ideas. Forsyth (2003) and Huckle (2004) have examined its potential for curriculum integration in higher education.

Others offer a more idealist approach to curriculum integration by arguing that ESD should promote relational or connected thinking that moves beyond such modernist assumptions as reductionism, analysis, and determinism by emphasising holism, synthesis, and uncertainty or the tolerance of ambiguity. Sterling (2001) outlines a new educational paradigm underpinned by such an ecological worldview and considers its radical implications for the organisation of educational institutions and the learning that takes place within them. His thinking influences several of the contributors to *The Handbook of Sustainability Literacy* (Stibbe, 2009) in which contributors from diverse disciplines (e.g. literature, business studies, climatology, and engineering) consider the twenty-first-century skills that people need in challenging times and how institutions of higher education can best provide these. Webster (2007) also regards an ecological worldview as the best foundation for ESD and has written classroom activities which explore how economy and society can 'go with the flow of nature' as revealed by complex systems science (Webster and Johnson, 2008).

Democracy and citizenship education

Democracy is the means by which citizens call power to account, agree ways of regulating relations between people (and between people and the rest of nature) and so realise their interests in sustainability. Sustainability needs democracy to expose complex issues to the widest possible scrutiny and debate, give government real support and power to regulate corporations and markets, and revitalise interest in politics and trust in politicians. Unfortunately the classical concept of democracy which provides citizens with continually expanding opportunities to participate in public life and bring economic, political, and social institutions under popular control, has largely been replaced by a contemporary concept which leaves decisions to a political elite and renders citizens essentially passive. At the same time, a democratic concept of education which seeks to prepare young people to participate in social life has been largely replaced by a vocational concept that equips them as compliant workers and consumers (Carr and Hartnett, 1996).

ESD should not only examine such developments but should also link with citizenship education to allow learners to reflect and act on existing and emergent forms of environmental, ecological, and global citizenship (Huckle, 2008). While environmental citizenship involves claiming environmental rights against the state in the public sphere, ecological citizenship involves the exercise of ecologically related responsibilities, rooted in justice, in both public and private spheres (Dobson, 2003). Global citizenship involves the exercise of rights and responsibilities in all spheres of one's life (economic, political, and cultural) that impact at all scales from the local to the global (Monbiot, 2003).

Learning as sustainable development

Education for democracy and citizenship brings us back to issues of discourse, ideology, and hegemony. Those practitioners of ESD working in the tradition of critical education claim that it is possible to engage in discourse analysis and educate for democracy and citizenship without indoctrinating learners with the ideas of the green movement or green socialism. After outlining three approaches to sustainable development, learning, and change, Scott and Gough (2003) disagree. In their view, both mainstream and critical ESD are too ready to assume we have the knowledge and tools for the transition to sustainable development and to discount the uncertainty and complexity that characterise the contemporary world. Learning as sustainable development should be an open-ended process, building the capacity to think critically about (and beyond) expert knowledge enshrined in conventional wisdoms. It is for readers to explore the ways in which Scott and Gough's notion of critical thinking differs from that of espoused by critical educators, perhaps by using resources on the Open Spaces for Dialogue and Enquiry website (OSDE, 2010).

It is in the sphere of informal, community-based, and lifelong education that the theory and practice of social learning as sustainable development have made most progress. Blewitt (2006) explores the possibilities for such learning in everyday settings, while Wals (2007) provides case studies from around the world.

The future

An understanding of the potential of ESD to shape the future can be gained by considering Harvey's co-evolutionary theory of social change (Harvey, 2010). He argues that the development of capitalist societies over time takes place as capital moves through seven inter-related activity spheres in search of profit: technologies and organisational forms; social relations; institutional and administrative arrangements; production and labour processes; relations to nature; reproduction of daily life and of the species; and mental conceptions of the world. Each sphere evolves in dynamic interaction with others, none is dominant or independent, and each is subject to perpetual renewal and transformation. Tensions and contradictions between the spheres, at a particular place and time, allow us to say something about the likely future social order but all change is contingent rather than determined.

Education plays a role in the contested reproduction of capitalist societies and their activity spheres. This chapter has argued for forms of ESD that question the dynamics of capitalism and examine alternative ways of carrying out the activities needed to sustain life. Such education should draw on the experience of movements seeking more sustainable forms of development throughout the world. These contain both reformist and radical elements and include non-governmental organisations, grass-roots organisations, organised labour and left/green political parties, movements resisting dispossession via privatisation and the erosion of social services, and movements seeking emancipation around issues of identity (Kingsnorth, 2003). Such concepts in sustainability as a frame of mind, critical realism, eco-pedagogy, and education for ecological and global citizenship, allow ESD to explore the values, ideas, and actions of these movements in ways that can readily be defended against critics, many of whom would confine ESD to outlining and justifying the greening of capitalism.

The latest crisis of capitalism has not been resolved. As austerity measures are introduced in many parts of the world to address economic debt and enable a return to business as usual, the costs are likely to fall disproportionately on the poor and the environments that sustain them. In these circumstances, educators who question prevailing mental conceptions of the world and examine movements seeking alternatives are vital to the realignment that David Marquand and others seek.

Questions for further investigation

1 What evidence would you need to support or dismiss the claim that current forms of development are unsustainable (see last paragraph)? In what ways do current forms of education sustain an unsustainable society?

2 Does ESD necessitate the re-design of curricula, teaching, and learning, and indeed the way an entire educational institution operates, or merely minor adjustments to existing arrangements?

3 Which of the following has the strongest claim to lie at the heart of ESD: ecological education, education in the humanities, or education for citizenship?

Suggested further reading

Jackson, T. (2009) *Prosperity Without Growth*. London: Earthscan. Prompts consideration of the role of education in moving society beyond growth and the profits system.

Scott, W. (2009) 'Judging the effectiveness of a sustainable school', *Journal of Education for Sustainable Development*, 3, 1, pp. 33–39. This article argues that school effectiveness in this area needs to be judged on what young people are learning rather than on, say, the amount of energy they have saved or waste they have recycled. (Further summaries of research on ESD available at: http://naaeeresearch.wordpress.com/.)

Shutt, H. (2010) *Beyond the Profits System*. London: Zed Books. Also prompts consideration of the role of education in moving society beyond growth and the profits system.

Symons, G. (2008) *Practice, Barriers and Enablers in ESD and EE: A Review of the Research*. Preston Montfort: SEEd. A review of research on practice, barriers and enablers of ESD in schools in England.

Winter, C. (2007) 'Education for sustainable development and the secondary curriculum in English schools: rhetoric or reality?', *Cambridge Journal of Education*, 37, 3, pp. 337–354. This article provides an analysis of policy documents relating to ESD in English secondary schools that supports the arguments in this chapter.

References

Barber, B.R. (2007) *Consumed: How Markets Corrupt Children, Infantalize Adults, and Swallow Citizens Whole*. London: Norton.

Blewitt, J. (2006) *The Ecology of Learning: Sustainability, Lifelong Learning and Everyday Life*. London: Earthscan.

Bonnett, M. (2004) *Retrieving Nature: Education in a Post-humanist Age*. Oxford: Blackwell.

Bowers, C.A. (2007) *Critical Essays on the Enclosure of the Commons: The Conceptual Foundations of Today's Mis-Education*. Eugene: Ecojustice Press.

Carr, W. and Hartnett, A. (1996) *Education and the Struggle for Democracy*. Buckingham: Open University Press.

Corcoran, P. (Ed.) (2005) *The Earth Charter in Action*. Amsterdam: KIT Publishers.

Corcoran, P. and Wals, A. (2004) *Higher Education and the Challenge of Sustainability*. Dordrecht: Kluwer Academic.

DfES (Department for Education and Skills) (2006) *Sustainable Schools For Pupils, Communities and the Environment*. Nottingham: DfES Publications.

Dickens, P. (2006) *Reconstructing Nature: Alienation, Emancipation and the Division of Labour*. London: Routledge.

Dickenson, P. (2003) *Planning Green Growth: A Socialist Contribution to the Debate on Environmental Sustainability*. London: CWI Publications and Socialist Books.

Dobson, A. (2003) *Citizenship and the Environment*. Oxford: Oxford University Press.

Dryzek, J. (1997) *The Politics of the Earth: Environmental Discourses*. Oxford: Oxford University Press.

Forsyth, T. (2003) *Critical Political Ecology: The Politics of Environmental Science*. London: Routledge.

Gaddoti, M. (2008) 'Education for sustainability: a critical contribution to the decade of education for sustainble development', *Green Theory & Praxis*, 4, 1, pp. 15–64.

Gamble, A. (2009) *The Spectre at the Feast: Capitalist Crisis and the Politics of Recession*. London: Palgrave Macmillan.

Harvey, D. (2010) *The Enigma of Capital and the Crises of Capitalism*. London: Profile Books.

Huckle, J. (2004) 'Critical realism: a philosophical framework for higher education for sustainability', in Corcoran, P. and Wals, A. (Eds.) *Higher Education and the Challenge of Sustainability*. Dordrecht: Kluwer Academic, pp. 33–47.

Huckle, J. (2005) *Education for Sustainable Development: A Briefing Paper for the Teacher Training Agency*. Available at: www.ttrb.ac.uk/ViewArticle2.aspx?Keyword=sustainable+development+huckle&SearchOption=And&SearchType=Keyword&RefineExpand=1&ContentId=11324 (accessed 21 June 2010).

Huckle, J. (2008) 'Sustainable development' in Arthur, J., Davies, I. and Hahn, C. (Eds.) *The Sage Handbook of Education for Citizenship and Democracy*. London: Sage, pp. 342–354.

Kahn, R. (2008) 'From education for sustainable development to ecopedagogy: sustaining capitalism or sustaining life?', *Green Theory & Praxis*, 4, 1, pp. 1–14.

Kingsnorth, P. (2003) *One No, Many Yeses: A Journey to the Heart of the Global Resistance Movement*. London: Free Press.

Kovel, J. (2007) *The Enemy of Nature: The End of Capitalism or the End of the World?* London: Zed Books.

Little, A. (1998) *Post-industrial Socialism*. London: Routledge.

Marquand, D. (2010) 'Green, socialist, republican: the new politics needs a realignment of mind', *The Guardian*, 28 May, p. 27.

Monbiot, G. (2003) *The Age of Consent: A Manifesto for a New World Order*. London: Harper Perennial.

Myers, N., Kent, J. and Wilson, E.O. (2005) *The New Gaia Atlas of Planet Management*. London: Gaia Books.

OSDE (Open Spaces for Dialogue and Enquiry) (2010). Available at: www.osdemethodology.org.uk (accessed 21 June 2010).

Park, J., Conca, K. and Finger, M. (Eds.) (2008) *The Crisis of Global Environmental Governance*. London: Routledge.

Rogers, P., Jalal, K. and Boyd, J. (2008) *An Introduction to Sustainable Development*. London: Earthscan.

Scott, W. and Gough, S. (2003) *Sustainable Development and Learning*. London: RoutledgeFalmer.

Selby, D. and Kagawa, F. (2010) 'Runaway climate change as challenge to the "closing circle" of education for sustainable development', *Journal of Education for Sustainable Development*, 4, 1, pp. 37–50.

Shutt, H. (2010) *Beyond the Profits System*. London: Zed Books.

Sterling, S. (2001) *Sustainable Education: Re-visioning Learning and Change*. Dartington: Green Books.

Stibbe, A. (2009) *The Handbook of Sustainability Literacy*. Dartington: Green Books.

Terry, S. (2008) *The Green School*. Norwich: Adamson.

Turner, A. (2001) *Just Capital*. London: Macmillan.

UNEP (United Nations Environment Program) (2009) *Global Green New Deal: Policy Brief*. Available at www.unep.org/greeneconomy/ (accessed 28 September 2009).

Wals, A. (Ed.) (2007) *Social Learning: Towards a Sustainable World*. Wageningen: Wageningen Academic.

Wals, A. (2009) *Review of Context and Structures for Education for Sustainable Development*. Paris: Unesco.

Walsh, J. (2009) 'The critical role for discourse in education for democracy', *Journal for Critical Education Policy Studies*, 6, 2, pp. 54–76.

Watts, J. (2010) *When a Billion Chinese Jump: How China Will Save Mankind – Or Destroy It*. London: Faber & Faber.

WCED (World Commission on Environment and Development) (1987) *Our Common Future*. Oxford: Oxford University Press.

Webster, K. (2007) 'Hidden sources: understanding natural systems is the key to an evolving and aspirational ESD', *Journal of Education for Sustainable Development*, 1, 1, pp. 37–43.

Webster, K. and Johnson, C. (2008) *Sense and Sustainability*. Available at: www.ellenmacarthurfoundation.org/education/publications (accessed 20 September 2010).

39

Technologies and learning

Michael Hammond
University of Warwick

Overview

This chapter provides an overview of the application of new technologies in education by:

- presenting a picture of the past use of new technology;
- identifying why policy-makers have supported the use of ICT;
- exploring the association between technology and curriculum reform;
- highlighting contributions of new technology to pupil engagement;
- considering constraints on the take up of new technology;
- outlining future prospects for teaching and learning with new technology.

Introduction

One of the most striking developments within educational systems around the world has been the introduction of new technology very often in the shape of computers and associated peripherals. Technology seems to offer not only tangible contributions for teaching and learning but also the promise of curriculum reform. However, in practice the use of technology has not had the impact some have predicted and hoped for. This chapter explores the varying rationales which lie behind the use of technology and considers the association of new technology with curriculum reform. The chapter is divided into sections: past use of computers in education; rationales for using technology; barriers to using technology; future prospects. A note at the end of the chapter provides an explanation of key terms.

Past use of computers in education

There have been identifiable stages in the adoption of computers in education. The first use of computers goes right back to the early 1970s with the teaching of programming and experiments in using mainframe computers for learning support. However, it was with the introduction of the 'micro' in the early 1980s that computers found a way into schools and into individual teaching rooms (Hammond *et al.*, 2009). This led to designers, often working closely with teachers, to author their own programs to support teaching and learning. These were necessarily 'small programs' as the machines were unable to handle anything but rudimentary graphics. The pedagogical thinking was mixed. Some programs supported exploratory learning; for example, a text revelation program 'Developing Tray' allowed pupils to work together to reconstruct a hidden text through trial and error guessing of letters and words. This very simple idea was seen as supporting pupil talk and developing predictive reading skills in an engaging game-like environment. At the same time, simple drill and practice programs were introduced allowing one commentator at least to warn that using new technology could lead to a giant step backwards in educational thinking (Chandler, 1984). Computing continued to be taught as a subject and many schools developed a special interest around 'Logo' – of which the most well-known application was a 'turtle', an on-screen cursor or physical robot, which could be programmed to produce movement and so create patterns. The rationale behind 'Logo' was much wider than providing an introduction to programming or supporting young learners in understanding concepts of measurement and angle. Rather, to its many supporters it was seen as a means of developing learners' generic problem-solving skills and giving them control over computer environments (Papert, 1980).

In time, computers became better able to process large amounts of data and it became the norm to run networks of computers allowing learners to access a consistent set of software and to store work securely. It became possible to run industry-standard software such as word processing, spreadsheets and desk-top publishing, albeit for educational rather than office activities, and larger content free packages such as dynamic geometry software within mathematics (Ball, 1990). The idea of networking of computers was later enhanced through wide-scale access to the Internet allowing 'anywhere, any time' access to resources and to lines of communication between learners and learners and tutors. More recently, technological advances have meant that Interactive Whiteboards (IWBs) have become affordable to schools in more economically advanced educational systems. A host of peripheral devices including digital video recorders, data loggers, sound recorders and robots have also become widely used.

It is striking just how many countries 'bought into' the idea of using computers in teaching (Plomp *et al.*, 2009) notwithstanding the contrasts in both the priority given to technology and the resources available in less economically developed countries (Ottestad and Quale, 2009). Another contrast between systems is that while nearly all have promoted the use of technology, the teaching of Informatics/Information Technology (IT)/Information Communication Technology (ICT) as a curriculum subject has differed in nature and scope with, for example, greater emphasis put on the teaching of programming in some countries, in particular East European ones (Anderson and Plomp, 2009; Chlopak, 2003). A further point of contrast is between sectors within educational systems. In higher education (HE) virtual learning environments (VLEs) gained ground much earlier than in schools, probably because HE teachers were more likely to work with large, geographically dispersed groups, with restricted opportunity for face-to-face teaching. This provided a context in which out-of-classroom access to materials and to discussion had more obvious benefits (Hunt *et al.*, 2003) and so it is not surprisingly that the first forays into online discussion again took place within HE (Mason and Kaye, 1989).

Rationales for using new technology

The rationale for using new technology for teaching and learning tends to be taken for granted and rests on a simple intuitive idea – education should keep up with changes in a wider world. This is nicely encapsulated in a quote from Kenneth Baker, UK minister of information technology in 1981, who argued for the use of computers in education on the grounds that:

> I want to ensure that the kids of today are trained with the skills that gave their fathers and grandfathers jobs. It's like generals fighting the battles of yesteryear . . . and that is the reason why we've pushed ahead with computers into schools. I want youngsters, boys and girls leaving school at sixteen, to actually be able to operate a computer.
>
> (quoted in Wellington, 2005, p. 6)

It was the kind of statement in favour of a vocational agenda that could have been made again and again by policy-makers over the following years (Wellington, 2005). Yet such an agenda may lead into different directions – to a narrow practice of pre-specified skills or to a 'progressive vocationalism' (Hodkinson, 1991) centred on relevance, authentic learning and practical problem-solving. The latter has thrived among innovators in the field of technology who have drawn attention to the gulf between the curriculum and the knowledge, skills and attitudes needed for work and for participation in society more generally. The rapid development of technology has been seen as central to widely discussed concepts such as the information society (e.g. Eraut, 1991), post modernity (e.g. Hargreaves, 1994) and the knowledge society (e.g. Hargreaves, 2003). There is an implication, readily taken up in policy documentation, that exposure to technology is essential if young learners are to be ready to participate in these new social and economic structures and this seems a common concern within many educational systems (e.g. Baskin, 2006; Looi, 2001; Mastrangelo and Loncarevic, 2004; Plomp et al., 2009). A new agenda for education should highlight the importance of learning to access and evaluate sources of digital information and to make judgments about the value of that information and draw relevant conclusions for different audiences. Learners should, it is further argued, experience online collaboration to help them understand the importance of social capital in personal and professional development (e.g. Tomai et al., 2010; Zinnbauer, 2007). Learners need to develop a new relationship with knowledge and one point of reference here is the contrast proposed by John (2005) between the traditional view of knowledge as 'sacred' (something reified and passed down across generations) and 'profane' (unbounded and continually recreated) or developed 'just in time' (Bonamy and Haugluslaine-Charlier, 1995). Technological innovation provides both the means and the rationale for curriculum reform and this is a prospect that has excited innovators in many different subjects and contexts over the past few years (e.g. De Corte et al., 2003; Leu and Zawilinski, 2007; Papert, 1980; Voogt and Pelgrum, 2005). Reform provides the lens through which to view the purpose of professional development with technology (Sandholtz et al., 1999).

Notwithstanding the association with curriculum reform, technology has been seen as having a pragmatic impact on attainment in teaching and learning as it is presently measured (Harrison et al., 2002) even if the search for such an impact is beset by methodological difficulty and variation (Eng, 2005). Not least of these difficulties is the problem of comparison: how can learning with technology, say involving the search for electronic resources or collecting data over long or very short time frames, be contrasted with learning though manual pen and paper methods? And how can skills learnt in computer environments be expected to impact on attainment in traditional pen and paper timed examinations, the main purpose of which appears to be recall of information? It can further be asked what time frame is needed to provide a fair test for the introduction of computer technologies such as the IWB when teachers themselves may have to spend time learning how to use new systems and develop fluent routines. In spite of these and other difficulties, a great deal of evidence has been collected on the use of new technology and consequent championing of the opportunities which new technology throws up. For example, new technology has been widely seen as impacting on pupils' motivation (Passey, 2004) and this seems to be associated with opportunities for interactivity and for working within media-rich environments. Learners frequently take greater pride in work created at the computer, seeing it as more professionally produced. New technology appears to support greater personalisation meaning greater choice over what is studied, greater independence and autonomy in how it is studied and a better fit of learning to preferred 'learning styles' (Underwood *et al.*, 2009). There is, in addition, a vast literature on the use of technology in particular curriculum contexts including the impact of data loggers and other software in science (Webb, 2005), robotics in design education (e.g. Nourbakhsh *et al.*, 2003), spreadsheets, graphing and other software in mathematics (Oldknow and Taylor, 2000) and discussion of more generic opportunities provided by VLEs (Becta, 2008) and IWBs (Higgins *et al.*, 2007). Of course the impact of using computers will vary according to context but a general theme is that there are features of technology, say, the capacity to easily access huge amounts of multimedia material, the interactivity between learners and machine, and the ease with which products can be amended and communicated to different audience which support experimentation, independence and a stronger focus on higher-order thinking by taking away the grind of producing and amending work by hand.

Barriers to using ICT

Given the discussion of its benefits, why have schools been slow to embrace new technologies and new paradigms for teaching and learning? In part this is a problem of perception. It is perhaps because such high hopes for curriculum reform have been invested in technology that outcomes are bound to disappoint (Nichol and Watson, 2003; Reynolds *et al.*, 2003). In fact, technology has impacted on teaching and learning: computers have entered schools and schooling; teachers have invested time and sometimes their own money in learning to use computers; many teachers use new technology extensively for planning of lessons; many treat the use of the IWB as a normal part of everyday practice; schools manage without undue difficulty to use software for administration and learner tracking; learners use the internet routinely for personal and study use. At the same time, the limits on this are clear: outside of special circumstances, pupils' direct use of technology is not routine in school. There are several reasons for this as discussed, for example, by Scrimshaw (2004) with particular emphasis on the UK and Hodgkinson-Williams *et al.* (2007) with a focus on South Africa. One fundamental problem is insufficient access not only to machines and software but also to technical support in all but special cases such as one-off projects or well-endowed schools. Of course problems of access are more marked when using technology in economically developing countries – for example, Wells and Wells (2007) describe reliable access to electricity as an additional problem for using computers in some Ugandan schools and Gudmundsdottir (2010) describes how differentiated access out of school creates a digital divide for young people in South Africa. Another constraint is the routinised nature of teaching so that schools may not be ready to embrace reform. Many teachers may lack confidence in using IT or they may simply find it difficult to fit technology into their preferred teaching approaches (e.g. Becker, 2000; Veen, 1993). At a more basic level teachers may not see the use of technology as making a difference (Jamieson-Proctor *et al.*, 2006) – this is particularly marked as educational systems have remained largely unreformed (see, amongst others, Coogan, 2003, Cuban, 1993 and Somekh, 2008, drawing largely on evidence in USA, UK and New Zealand respectively). Teachers may further lack necessary support (Condie *et al.*, 2007). Appropriate training is required and the top-down imposition of technology into schools seems unlikely to engage teachers beyond a superficial level (see amongst other cases that of Smart schools in Malaysia, Thang *et al.*, 2010). The barriers have been and continue to be immense.

The future curriculum with new technology

The use of new technology offers opportunities but has been constrained by barriers at many different levels, so what do future prospects look like? If the past is a guide it can be predicted that:

- There will be continual development of computing power in terms of storage, processing speed and greater portability. This may lead to eye-catching developments such as low-cost three-dimensional (3D) printing and creating deeply immersive virtual worlds but will also include more prosaic, but perhaps more significant, developments such as ubiquitous access to the internet or universal low-cost computers in 'developing' countries. Inevitably the use of technology in education systems will lag behind that in the wider world.
- Technological development can be expected to continue to attract the interest of policy-makers and curriculum reformers though there will be tensions within these and other groups arguing for the greater use of technology.

The barriers to the adoption of new technology in education will remain as long as access is constrained and assessment of teaching and learning goes unreformed. Those supporting innovation with new technology will need to view its application through a wider framework which takes in the competing goals of educational system and the wider culture in which reform is expected to take place (e.g. Somekh, 2008; Hennessy and Deaney, 2004).

A note on terminology

Terms in this field change repeatedly. *New technology* provides a catch-all to refer to computer hardware and software and other electronic devices. In the wider literature other general terms include *E-learning, Technology Enhanced Learning* (TEL) and *M-learning* (learning with mobile electronic devices). *Computer Assisted Learning* (CAL) is a further general term but with a more dated feel. *Blended learning* has been popular to describe a mix of online and face-to-face teaching and learning support. There are a range of terms to cover specialist interests within the general field of new technology; for example, the use of communication tools between students is sometimes referred to as *Computer Supported Collaborative Learning* (CSCL) or more widely as *networked learning*. An older tradition of creating instructional or tutorial materials has been referred to as *Computer Assisted Instruction* (CAI) and sometimes as *Courseware*. A specific interest in teaching about technology has often been described as *Informatics or Computer Studies*.

Within this chapter, a *Virtual Learning Environment* (VLE) is seen as a single item of software allowing: the storage of learning materials; communication tools such as chat and forums; quizzes, testing and assessment tracking; learner-authored content. A *learning platform* is sometimes used to describe a combination of these features but not necessarily within a single item of software. *Information technology* (IT) and the broader notion of *Information Communication Technology* (ICT) have been used to describe both the teaching of a new technology as a specialist subject and the use of electronic tools to support teaching and learning across the curriculum. An *Interactive Whiteboard* (IWB) is a large interactive display which allows the projection of previously prepared resources (e.g. multimedia presentations), interactivity (e.g. selecting menu options), and annotations and free-hand writing at the screen.

Questions for further investigation

1   Which technologies do you see as having had the most impact on teaching and learning in recent years and why?
2   Should the use of new technology be seen as a special case or part of a wider problem of curriculum reform?
3   New technology has been described by some as a fix for the irrelevancy of the present curriculum, who might believe this?

Suggested further reading

Cuban, L. (1986) *Teachers and Machines: the classroom use of new technology since 1920*. New York, NY: Teachers College Press. Larry Cuban was one of the first to offer a historical take on the use of technology. Also see the paper Cuban, L. (1993) 'Computers meet classroom: classroom wins', *Teachers College Record*, 95, 2, pp. 185–210.

McDougall, A., Murnane, J., Jones, A. and Reynolds, N. (Eds.) (2010) *Researching IT in Education Theory, Practice and Future Directions*. Routledge: London. A recent international perspective on the use of ICT in education.

'Beyond Current Horizons Project' available at: *www.beyondcurrenthorizons.org.uk/*. Discusses the future curriculum with technology in the UK. See also Perrotta, C., Hague, C. and Williamson, B. (2010) *Expertise Report Maintaining Futures*. Bristol: Futurelab.

References

Anderson, R. and Plomp, T. (2009) 'Introduction' in Plomp, T., Anderson, R. and Law, N. (Eds.) *Cross-National Information and Communication Technology Policies and Practices in Education*. Charlotte, NC: Information Age Publishing.

Ball, D. (1990) 'What is the role of IT within the National Mathematics Curriculum?', *Journal of Computer Assisted Learning*, 6, 4, pp. 239–245.

Baskin, C. (2006) 'ICT integration in schools: Where are we now and what comes next?', *Australasian Journal of Educational Technology*, 22, 4, pp. 455–473.

Becker, H. (2000) 'How exemplary computer-using teachers differ from other teachers: Implications for realizing the potential of computers in schools', *Contemporary Issues in Technology and Teacher Education*, 1, 2, pp. 274–293.

Becta (2008) *Learning Platforms in Action*. Coventry: Becta.

Bonamy, J. and Haugluslaine-Charlier, B. (1995) 'Supporting professional learning: beyond technological support', *Journal of Computer Assisted Learning*, 11, 4, pp. 196–202.

Chandler, D. (1984) *Young Learners and the Microcomputer*. Milton Keynes: Open University Press.

Chlopak, O. (2003) 'Computers in Russian schools: current conditions, main problems, and prospects for the future', *Computers & Education*, 40, 1, pp. 41–55.

Condie, R., Munro, B., Seagraves, L. and Kenesson, S. (2007) *The Impact of ICT in Schools – A landscape review*. Coventry: Becta.

Coogan, P. (2003) 'Forum: The rhetoric of educational achievement and ICT: the reality of implementation', *Education, Communication & Information*, 3, 2, pp. 309–316.

Cuban, L. (1993) 'Computers meet classroom: Classroom wins', Teachers College Record, 95, 2, 185–210.

De Corte, E., Verschaffel, L., Entwistle, N. and van Merriënboer, J. (Eds.) (2003) *Powerful Learning Environments: unravelling basic components and dimensions (advances in learning and instruction)*. Oxford: Pergamon.

Eng, T-S (2005) 'The impact of ICT on learning: A review of research', *International Education Journal*, 6, 5, pp. 635–650.

Eraut, M. (Ed.) (1991) *Education and the Information Society: a challenge for European policy*. London: Cassell.

Gudmundsdottir, G. (2010) 'From digital divide to digital equity: Learners' ICT competence in four primary schools in Cape Town, South Africa', *International Journal of Education and Development using ICT*, 3, 2. Available at: http://ijedict.dec.uwi.edu/viewarticle.php?id=989. Accessed September 2010.

Hammond, M., Younie, S., Woollard, J., Carwright, V. and Benzie, D. (2009) 'What does our past involvement with computers in education tell us?' Available at: www.itte.org.uk/node/35. Accessed September 2010.

Hargreaves, A. (1994) *Changing Teachers, Changing Times: teachers' work and culture in the postmodern age*. London: Cassell.

Hargreaves, A. (2003) *Teaching in the Knowledge Society*. Buckingham and New York, NY: Open University Press and Teachers College Press.

Harrison, C., Comber, C., Fisher, T., Haw, K., Lunzer, E., McFarlane, A., Mavers, D., Scrimshaw, P., Somekh, B. and Watling, R. (2002) *ImpaCT2: The impact of information and communication technologies on pupil learning and attainment*. Coventry: Becta.

Hennessy, S. and Deaney, R. (2004) *Sustainability and Evolution of ICT-Supported Classroom Practice*. Cambridge: University of Cambridge Faculty of Education. Available at: www.educ.cam.ac.uk/research/projects/istl/SAE041.doc. Accessed September 2010.

Higgins, S., Beauchamp, G. and Miller, D. (2007) 'Reviewing the literature on interactive whiteboards', *Learning, Media and Technology*, 32, 3, pp. 213–225.

Hodgkinson-Williams, C., Sieborger, I. and Terzoli, A. (2007) 'Enabling and constraining ICT practice in secondary schools: case studies in South Africa', *International Journal of Knowledge and Learning*, 3, 2/3, pp. 171–190.

Hodkinson, P. (1991) 'Liberal Education and the New Vocationalism: a progressive partnership?', *Oxford Review of Education*, 17, 1, pp. 73–88.

Hunt, M., Parsons, A. and Fleming, A. (2003) *A Review of the Research Literature on the Use of Managed Learning Environments and Virtual Learning Environments in Education and a Consideration of the Implications for schools in the United Kingdom*. Coventry: Becta.

Jamieson-Proctor, R., Burnett, P., Finger, G. and Watson, G. (2006) 'Teachers' confidence in using ICT for teaching and learning in Queensland', *Australasian Journal of Educational Technology*, 22, 4, pp. 511–530.

John, P. (2005) 'The sacred and the profane: subject sub-culture, pedagogical practice and teachers' perceptions of the classroom uses of ICT', *Educational Review*, 57, 4, pp. 471–490.

Leu, D. and Zawilinski, L. (2007) 'The new literacies of online reading comprehension', *New England Reading Association Journal*, 43, 1, pp. 1–7.

Looi, C.K. (2001) 'Regional editorial: IT programmes and policies in the Asia-Pacific region', *Journal of Computer Assisted Learning*, 17, 1, pp. 1–3.

Mason, R. and Kaye, A. (Eds.) (1989) *Mindweave: Communication, computers and distance education*. Oxford: Pergamon.

Mastrangelo, J-G. and Loncarevic, M. (Eds.) (2004) *UNESCO's Basic Texts on the Information Society*. Paris: UNESCO. Available at: http://portal.unesco.org/ci/en/ev.php-URL_ID=12845&URL_DO=DO_TOPIC&URL_SECTION=201.html. Accessed September 2010.

Nichol, J. and Watson, K. (2003) 'Editorial: Rhetoric and reality – the present and future of ICT in education', *British Journal of Educational Technology*, *34*, 2, pp. 131–136.

Nourbakhsh, I., Crowley, K., Wilkinson, K. and Hamner, E. (2003) *The Educational Impact of the Robotic Autonomy Mobile Robotics Course*. Pittsburgh, PA: The Robotics Institute. Available at: www.ri.cmu.edu/pub_files/pub4/nourbakhsh_illah_2003_1/nourbakhsh_illah_2003_1.pdf. Accessed September 2010.

Oldknow, A. and Taylor, R. (2000) *Teaching Mathematics with ICT*. London: Continuum Press.

Ottestad, G. and Quale, A. (2009) 'Trends in instructional ICT infrastructure', in Plomp, T., Anderson, R. and Law, N. (Eds.) *Cross-National Information and Communication Technology Policies and Practices in Education*. Charlotte, NC: Information Age Publishing.

Papert, S. (1980) *Mindstorms: Children, Computers, and Powerful Ideas*. New York, NY: Basic Books.

Passey, D., Rogers, C., Machell, J. and McHugh, G. (2004) *The Motivational Effect of ICT on Pupils*. Lancaster: Department of Educational Research, University of Lancaster.

Plomp, T., Anderson, R. and Law, N. (2009) *Cross-National Information and Communication Technology Policies and Practices in Education*. Charlotte, NC: Information Age Publishing.

Reynolds, D., Treharne, D. and Tripp, H. (2003) 'ICT – the hopes and the reality', *British Journal of Educational Technology*, *34*, 2, pp. 151–167.

Sandholtz, J., Ringstaff, C. and Dwyer, D. (1999) *Teaching with Technology: Creating Student-centered Classrooms*, New York, NY: Teachers College Press.

Scrimshaw, P. (2004) *Enabling Teachers to Make Successful Use of ICT*. Coventry: Becta.

Somekh, B. (2008) 'Factors affecting teachers' pedagogical adoption of ICT', in Voogt, J. and Knezek, G. (Eds.) *International Handbook of Information Technology in Primary and Secondary Education*. New York, NY: Springer, pp. 449–460.

Thang, S-M., Hall, C., Azman, H. and Joyes, G. (2010) 'Supporting Smart School teachers' continuing professional development in and through ICT: A model for change', *International Journal of Education and Development using Information and Communication Technology*, *6*, 2. Available at: http://ijedict.dec.uwi.edu/viewarticle.php?id=813. Accessed September 2010.

Tomai, M., Rosa, V., Mebane, M. E., D'Acunti, A., Benedetti, M. and Francescato, D. (2010) 'Virtual communities in schools as tools to promote social capital with high schools students', *Computers & Education*, *54*, 1, pp. 265–274.

Underwood, J., Baguley, T., Banyard, P., Dillon, G., Farrington-Flint, L., Mary Hayes, L., Hick, P., Le Geyt, G., Murphy, J., Selwood, I. and Wright, M. (2009) *Personalising Learning*. Coventry: Becta.

Veen, W. (1993) 'How teachers use computers in instructional practice – Four case studies in a Dutch secondary school', *Computers & Education*, *21*, 1, pp. 1–8.

Voogt, J. and Pelgrum, H. (2005) 'ICT and curriculum change', *Human Technology*, *1*, 2, pp. 157–175. Available at: www.humantechnology.jyu.fi/articles/volume1/2005/voogt-pelgrum.pdf. Accessed September 2010.

Webb, M.E., (2005) 'Affordances of ICT in Science learning; Implications for an integrated pedagogy', *International Journal of Science Education*, *27*, 6, pp. 705–735.

Wellington, J. (2005) 'Has ICT come of age? Recurring debates on the role of ICT in education', *Research in Science and Technological Education*, *23*, 1, pp. 25–39.

Wells, R. and Wells, S. (2007) 'Challenges and opportunities in ICT educational development: A Ugandan case study', *International Journal of Education and Development using ICT*, *3*, 2. Available at: http://ijedict.dec.uwi.edu/viewarticle.php?id=296. Accessed September 2010.

Zinnbauer, D. (2007) 'What can Social Capital and ICT do for Inclusion?', *European Commission Directorate*. Luxembourg: General Joint Research Centre. Available at: http://ftp.jrc.es/EURdoc/eur22673en.pdf. Accessed September 2010.

40

Values education

Terence Lovat
University of Newcastle, New South Wales

Overview

Values education represents an ancient tradition that focuses on education as an essentially moral enterprise. While mass and universal education in the twentieth century tended to reduce this focus in favour of more instrumentalist approaches, modern educational research has illustrated the wider and indispensable effects on student learning and well-being rendered by the well-constructed values education programme.

Introduction

Values education is known internationally by a number of names, including moral education, character education and ethics education. Each variant has a slightly different meaning, pointing to one or other distinctive emphasis. Overriding these differences, however, is a common belief that entering into the world of personal and societal values is a legitimate and important role for teachers and schools to play. In that sense, values education represents an old tradition in education, being traceable to Confucius and Aristotle, among other ancient doyens of thought. It is also to be found in classical medieval education thinking, be it of Abu al-Ghazzali in the Muslim world, or Thomas Aquinas and Thomas More in Christendom. This tradition found voice in modern educational theory through the works of John Dewey, Lawrence Kohlberg, Richard S. Peters and Jürgen Habermas, among others, whose insights highlighted for educators that, for all the greater mass and politicization of education in the nineteenth and twentieth centuries, the same essential moral parameters obtain around the pursuit of knowledge. While much educational thought of the later twentieth century drove systems towards more instrumentalist ends, in recent times, cognitive, behavioural, social and pedagogical theories have coalesced to shed new light on values education as a means of addressing all the needs of education in a comprehensive and most effective way.

The ancient and medieval traditions

The notion that morality is inherent to all human endeavour, including that related to effective learning, is an idea well embedded in the history of thought. Confucian and Aristotelian philosophies, and the various Eastern, Middle Eastern and Western traditions that have emanated from them, serve as testimony to the notion. Confucius' pedagogy centred on the 'Six Arts', including a range of practical arts but, at the centre of any content, lay morality (Brooks and Brooks, 1998). For Confucius, education was above all about facilitating ethical judgement and practical morality. In similar vein, Aristotelian philosophy is replete with notions of practical action being at the heart of all that we hold to be moral and humane and that practical virtue was the true end of education. Aristotle's (1985) characterization of virtue was of someone who took action to put into effect their beliefs about right and wrong. It was what he referred to as 'education of the heart', rather than merely of the mind.

The medieval Muslim Sufi Abu al-Ghazzali (1991) would echo these sentiments a millennium and a half later in remarking that God (Allah) finds nothing as distasteful as the one who stores up knowledge but fails to take commensurate practical action. In effect, such lack of practical virtue made a mockery of the education provided by the *Ummah of Allah* (Community of God) as a practical expression of the innate justice championed by Islam. This essential conjoining of intention with action would go on to constitute the heart of Christian ethics, as defined by Thomas Aquinas ([1274] 1936) in his notion of *synderesis*, that inborn facility that urges the Christian not only to seek truth but also to express it in practical action. For him, the only authentic goal of education was therefore to be realized in practical virtue, in the manner of Aristotle. Thomas More ([1516] 1989), similarly, saw education as being principally about achieving personal integrity and conforming one's actions to the common good. He contrasted this true education with the piling up of facts and figures that was mere instruction. True education was 'transformative', bringing to life what was a hidden seed in each person.

Hence, from ancient and medieval times, a tradition was inherited that distinguished instrumentalist from holistic education. Central to the latter has been the notion that education is a moral quest in terms both of its addressing of the full range of individual needs and of its role in enhancing the good of society. In that sense, values education has potential to go to the heart of the notion of education being ultimately for the common good, designed both to build individual character and therefore to enhance morality in the citizenry. The earliest forms of education in Islam were about creating this kind of positive, supportive learning environment geared towards redressing the natural inequities to be found in society. Christendom followed suit in the later Middle Ages with many of contemporary Europe's most exclusive schools and universities having their origins in learning centres for those with limited opportunities from birth. The origins of education are inevitably and irretrievably built on moral foundations.

The 'modern' tradition

For John Dewey (1964) education was principally a means of producing moral judiciousness and, in that sense, all education was effectively moral education. Hence, moral education was seen as the means by which students could engage most effectively in the business of learning itself. Dewey spoke of the overarching need for a way of knowing in schooling that cultivated a mindset on the part of teachers that was, at one and the same time, self-reflective and directed towards instilling reflectivity, inquiry and moral capacity in students.

Lawrence Kohlberg (1963) proposed that all of human development was impelled by and rested on the moral challenges that beset all people. His six-stage theory of moral development became a popular way in which all human development could be conceived, taking in stages of childhood motivation via punishment, reward and instrumental purpose, through conventional stages of conformity and social maintenance, and aspiring to an ideal stage where human beings could be motivated by commitment to social contracts and universal principles. Kohlberg's influence on education and teacher education was profound, leading to moral development being seen as central to all human growth, including intellectual development. For him, it was impossible to separate the skills that lay most overtly at the heart of school goals, namely academic skills, from those related to moral development.

Like Dewey, Richard S. Peters (1981) was a major force in proposing that moral education lay at the heart of all authentic education. His concern was with the notion of the 'educated man' and how this might be best conceived and safeguarded in a world of competing demands and politics. The central plank of his argument for being 'educated' in the true sense was in the conjunction of what he described as the 'knowledge condition' and the 'value condition'. In a sense, he was arguing, like many of those above, for a distinction to be made between instrumentalist education (what More would call 'instruction') and holistic education, in which the distinguishing feature was around values. It was only education related to 'what is of value' that allowed education to be of value at all:

> According to R.S. Peters, education implies that something worthwhile is being intentionally transmitted in a morally acceptable manner . . . despite the diversity of values and the culturally dependent interpretation of well-being, some values are conducive to and deducible from the aforementioned definition of development. These values should be present in all educational practices . . . I agree with John Dewey that all education is, and should be, moral education.
>
> (Raulo, 2002, p. 507)

Jürgen Habermas' (1972, 1974) theory of knowing, reminiscent of the core of Deweyian thought, has the added value of an attached theory of social engagement. Habermas (1984, 1987) spoke of authentic knowing leading to 'communicative capacity' and ultimately 'communicative action', a concept about personal commitment, reliability and trustworthiness that spills over into practical action that makes a difference, or what Habermas describes as *'praxis'*. This is the kind of education that aims to transform thought and practice and so make a difference to the way the human community coheres. It is a supremely moral education.

As with the educational theory of all the afore-mentioned scholars, Habermasian epistemology renders the notion of values neutrality in education inappropriate and non-viable. Habermasian epistemology challenges the authenticity of an education conceived of solely in instrumentalist outcomes-based or competencies terms. Habermasian epistemology impels for any legitimate education a values-laden pedagogy that saturates the learning experience both in a values-filled environment and in explicit teaching that engages in discourse about values-related content, transacts practical and personalized values, and in turn inducts students into personal empowerment over their own stated and lived out values. Habermasian epistemology also challenges therefore the notion that values education connotes merely a moral option among various approaches to education, perhaps more suitable to religious than to public systems of schooling. On the contrary, Habermasian epistemology confirms the views of all the scholars noted above that values education is best understood as holistic pedagogy aimed at the full range of developmental measures. Rather than connoting a mere moral or, least of all religious option, values education connotes an effective and indispensable way in which learning should proceed in any school setting.

Updated research findings

The educational perspectives of the scholars above have been vindicated by modern research into quality teaching and effective pedagogy. In a variety of ways and across vastly different research regimes, it has been demonstrated that a values approach to education is no mere option if the fullest effects of learning are to be achieved, including but not limited to academic learning. The Carnegie Corporation's 1994 Task Force on Learning (Carnegie Corporation, 1996) acted as a watershed in impelling the modern era of quality teaching, representing a conceptual turning-point in views about the power of teaching to effect change in student achievement. Carnegie drew on new research in a variety of fields to refute the instrumentalism of conventional educational approaches to assert that effective learning requires a response that is as much about affect, social dynamics and morality as it is about matters of mere cognition. In so doing, it spoke of 'intellectual depth' as the true goal and measure of effective learning. Reminiscent of Habermas, 'intellectual depth' implied that matters of communicative competence, empathic character and self-reflection were at least as significant to learning as the indisputably important technical skills. They were as significant because they represented an education engaged in holistic development, what More would have called true education, rather than merely instruction, and what Peters would have referred to as the 'value condition' that must be allied to the 'knowledge condition' for true education to proceed. Hence, through the Carnegie definition of learning, a values orientation was deemed to be indispensable to any learning if student achievement was to be optimized.

Fred Newmann (Newmann and Associates, 1996) is rightly regarded as an architect of modern quality teaching but could also be seen as one who contributed to the notion of there being a nexus between values and effective learning. Newmann's work centred on identifying the 'pedagogical dynamics' required for quality teaching. These dynamics ranged from the instrumental (e.g. sound technique, updated professional development) to the more aesthetic and values-filled. For instance, 'catering for diversity' was quite beyond more conventional notions of addressing individual differences. Newmann was referring to the centrality of the respectful and sensitive relationship between teacher and student, so ensuring an ambience where the student feels accepted, understood and valued. Similarly, Newmann's concept of 'school coherence' was of the school that is committed unswervingly to the good of the student, a values-rich concept connoting dedication, responsibility, generosity and integrity on the part of all stakeholders. This led naturally to the ultimate pedagogical dynamic of the 'trustful, supportive ambience', deemed to be so indispensable that it would render all teaching ineffective if not attended to. The notion conforms well to Peters' idea of education being an enterprise where something worthwhile is being intentionally transmitted in a morally acceptable manner and as a site where the 'value condition' is indispensably allied to the 'knowledge condition'.

Philosophical and pedagogical research of the kind noted above has been further confirmed by developments in a number of human sciences, including the neurosciences (Immordino-Yang and Damasio, 2007) where the central focus is on those neural systems that underpin reason, memory, emotion and social interaction. The insights effectively re-conceive cognition as entailing affect and social impulses working together to impel action, including moral behaviour. Findings from such work are causing educationists to re-think many of their assumptions about a range of developmental issues, including that of learning itself. The taxonomic notion that cognitive learning outcomes can somehow be separated from affective, social and moral ones comes to be seen as inadequate. For educators, Damasio's work has confirmed the need for new pedagogy that engages the whole person in all dimensions of human development, including moral development.

Research insights and findings from the neurosciences, philosophy and pedagogy have coalesced in illustrating the importance of education being holistic in its focus. The learner is a whole person, impelled by cognitive, emotional, social, spiritual, aesthetic and moral drives, not as separable features but in holistic connection with each other. Pedagogy that ignores such connectionism is coming to be seen increasingly as irrelevant and ineffective for learners in the twenty-first century. Such holistic perspectives are beginning to be seen in public education regimes that have previously been marked by instrumentalist approaches. In Australia, where late twentieth-century education was characterized by its attention to instrumentalist competencies and outcomes, a gathering of the senior political and bureaucratic forces in education designed to set the objectives for twenty-first-century education based on the most updated research findings available proffered:

> Australia's future depends upon each citizen having the necessary knowledge, understanding, skills and values for a productive and rewarding life in an educated, just and open society. High quality schooling is essential to achieving this vision . . . Schooling provides a foundation for young Australians' intellectual, physical, social, moral, spiritual and aesthetic development.
>
> (MCEETYA, 1999)

There is now an increasing store of argumentation and evidence from values education research that the establishment of such ambiences of learning, together with explicit discourse about values in ways that draw on students' deeper learning and reflectivity, has power to transform the patterns of feelings, behaviour, resilience and academic diligence that might once have been the norm among students (cf. Noddings, 2002; Arthur, 2003; Rowe, 2004; Campbell et al., 2004; Benninga et al., 2003, 2006; Carr, 2006, 2007; Nucci and Narvaez, 2008; Lovat and Clement, 2008a, 2008b; Hawkes, 2009; Lovat and Toomey, 2009; Lovat et al., 2009, 2010; 2011). Much of this kind of evidence has been captured in the research and practice of the projects emanating from the Australian Values Education Programme.

The Australian Values Education Programme

The Australian Values Education Programme was a federally funded venture, beginning with a pilot study in 2003 (DEST, 2003), followed by the development of a National Framework for Values Education in 2005 (DEST, 2005) and a range of attached research and practice projects from 2005 to 2009, the most crucial of which were the two stages of the *Values Education Good Practice Schools Project* (VEGPSP) (DEST, 2006; DEEWR, 2008) and the *Project to Test and Measure the Impact of Values Education on Student Effects and School Ambience* (Lovat et al., 2009).

Within the two stages of VEGPSP, 316 schools organized into 51 clusters across the country engaged in a variety of approaches to values education, all based on the central premise that values education and good practice pedagogy are inextricably interrelated. Findings from stage 1 (DEST, 2006) illustrated that a sound values education can be a powerful ally in the development of effective pedagogy, with positive effects being demonstrated across the range of measures, including greater student reflectivity and deeper thinking, improved communicative capacity between teachers, students and each other, broadening students' sense of social justice issues, greater student resilience and social skills, improved relationships of care and trust, and a range of items associated with improved academic diligence, such as strengthened intellectual engagement and students settling into work more readily and calmly as routine effects of the ambience created by the programme.

The Stage 2 Report (DEEWR, 2008) identified strengthened and more sophisticated links between the rollout of values education and the effects on student behaviour and performance. These links included a greater recognition of the centrality of the teacher's role, the explicitness of the pedagogy around values being seen to be determinative, and the role of an experiential (or service learning) component coming to be seen as a particularly powerful agency in enhancing student behaviour and strengthening intellectual engagement.

Consistent with Newmann's thesis that the key to effective teaching was in the ambience of learning, VEGPSP results seemed to provide evidence that a well-constructed, clear and intentional values education programme being integrated into the fabric of the school has the potential to bring transformational changes in the learning environment of the school and its classrooms, influencing student and teacher behaviour, and leading to beneficial effects on student motivation to learn and improved academic diligence.

Testing and measuring the impact of values education

Across the three years in which the VEGPSP projects rolled out, the nature of the resulting evidence was shifting from being purely qualitative to having a quantitative edge, albeit lacking formal instrumentation and measurement. These latter were brought to bear in the *Project to Test and Measure the Impact of Values Education on Student Effects and School Ambience* (Lovat *et al.*, 2009). In this study, there was interest in all of the claims being made around student effects, with a dedicated focus on arguably the most contentious claims, namely those around student academic improvement. Granted the high stakes around this claim, the study was characterized by intensive quantitative as well as qualitative methods of analysis. The items of measurement included school ambience, student-teacher relationships, student and teacher well-being, and student academic diligence.

Concerning the matter of school ambience, evidence was elicited from students, teachers and parents that spoke of a '"calmer" environment with less conflict and with a reduction in the number of referrals (of behaviour problems)' (Lovat *et al.*, 2009, p. 8). Of student-teacher relationships, there was evidence of a 'rise in levels of politeness and courtesy, open friendliness, better manners, offers of help, and students being more kind and considerate . . . (and) greater respect' (p. 9). About student well-being, the report provided evidence of 'the creation of a safer and more caring school community . . . self-regulation and enhanced self-esteem' (p. 10). Arguably, the most contentious evidence was that concerned with the factor of student academic diligence. Here, the report spoke at length about students 'putting greater effort into their work and "striving for quality", "striving to achieve their best" and even "striving for perfection" . . . taking greater pride in their work and producing quality outcomes' (p. 6). The report concluded:

Thus, there was substantial quantitative and qualitative evidence suggesting that there were observable and measurable improvements in students' academic diligence, including increased attentiveness, a greater capacity to work independently as well as more cooperatively, greater care and effort being invested in schoolwork and students assuming more responsibility for their own learning.

(Lovat *et al.*, 2009, p. 6)

385

Conclusion

Values education represents an ancient tradition that focuses on education as an essentially moral enterprise. While mass and universal education tended to reduce this focus in favour of more instrumentalist approaches, modern educational research has illustrated the wider and less dispensable effects on student learning and well-being rendered by the well-constructed values approach to education.

Questions for further investigation

1   In what ways should the notion that all education is a moral venture influence the policies of educational systems, the strategic planning of schools and the dispositions and practical pedagogies of teachers?
2   To what extent do the systems, schools and teachers with which you are most familiar reflect the above characteristics? Why is this so?
3   How might a values education perspective influence one's thinking about issues such as student-teacher relationships, curriculum content, behaviour management, and testing and measuring?
4   What are the practical ramifications for the idea that values education should be seen as holistic pedagogy for all schools rather than a moral option for some schools?

Suggested further reading

Hawkes, N. (2009) 'Values and quality teaching at West Kidlington Primary School', in Lovat, T. and Toomey, R. (Eds.) *Values Education and Quality Teaching: The Double Helix Effect* (International Edition). Dordrecht, Netherlands: Springer, pp. 105–120. A 'best practice' values education case study in a UK schools written by the former headteacher.

Lovat, T., Dally, K., Clement, N. and Toomey, R. (2011) *Values Pedagogy and Student Achievement: Contemporary Research Evidence*. Dordrecht, Netherlands: Springer. A book that captures the most recent international research focused on the impact of values education on student achievement.

Lovat, T., Toomey, R. and Clement, N. (Eds.) (2010) *International Research Handbook on Values Education and Student Wellbeing*. Dordrecht, Netherlands: Springer. Fifty-five chapters of the most updated theoretical, empirical and applied research in values education, with holistic student well-being as the driving theme.

Nucci, L. and Narvaez, D. (Eds.) (2008) *Handbook of Moral and Character Education*. New York: Routledge. Updated research findings in the related area of moral and character education.

Peters, R.S. (1981) *Moral Development and Moral Education*. London: George Allen & Unwin. A modern classic that captures much of the values education tradition and sets the scene for modern research findings.

References

Al-Ghazzali, A. (1991) *The Book of Religious Learnings*. New Delhi: Islamic Book Services.

Aquinas, T. (1936) *Summa Theologica* (trans. L. Shapcote). London: Burns & Oates.

Aristotle (1985) *Nicomachean Ethics* (trans. T. Irwin). Indianapolis: Hackett.

Arthur, J. (2003) *Education with Character: The moral economy of schooling*. London: Routledge.

Brooks, E. and Brooks, A. (1998) *The Original Analects*. New York: Columbia University Press.

Benninga, J.S., Berkowitz, M.W., Kuehn, P. and Smith, K. (2003) 'The relationship of character education implementation and academic achievement in elementary schools', *Journal of Research in Character Education*, 1, 19–32.

Benninga, J., Berkowitz, M., Kuehn, P. and Smith, K. (2006) 'Character and academics: What good schools do', *Phi Delta Kappan*, 87, pp. 448–452.

Campbell, R.J., Kyriakides, L., Muijs, R.D. and Robinson, W. (2004) 'Effective teaching and values: Some implications for research and teacher appraisal', *Oxford Review of Education*, 30, pp. 451–465.

Carnegie Corporation (1996) *Years of Promise: A Comprehensive Learning Strategy for America's Children* (Executive summary). New York: Carnegie Corporation of New York.

Carr, D. (2006) 'Professional and personal values and virtues in education and teaching', *Oxford Review of Education*, 32, pp. 171–183.

Carr, D. (2007) 'Character in teaching', *British Journal of Educational Studies*, 55, pp. 369–389.

DEEWR (Department of Education, Employment and Workplace Relations) (2008) *At the Heart of What We Do: Values education at the centre of schooling*. Report of the Values Education Good Practice Schools Project – Stage 2. Melbourne: Curriculum Corporation. Available at: www.curriculum.edu.au/values/val_vegps2_final_report,26142.html. Accessed June 2010.

DEST (Department of Education Science and Training) (2003). *Values Education Study* (Executive summary final report). Melbourne: Curriculum Corporation. Available at: www.valueseducation.edu.au/verve/_resources/VES_Final_Report14Nov.pdf. Accessed June 2010.

DEST (2005) *National Framework for Values Education in Australian Schools* (Canberra, Australian Government Department of Education, Science and Training). Available at: www.valueseducation.edu.au/verve/_resources/Framework_PDF_version_for_the_web_left_column_file_link.pdf. Accessed June 2010.

DEST (2006) *Implementing the National Framework for Values Education in Australian Schools: Report of the Values Education Good Practice Schools Project – Stage 1: Final report, September 2006*. Melbourne: Curriculum Corporation. Available at: www.valueseducation.edu.au/values/default.asp?id=16381. Accessed June 2010.

Dewey, J. (1964) *John Dewey on Education: Selected Writings*. New York: Modern Library.

Habermas, J. (1972) *Knowledge and Human Interests* (trans. J. Shapiro). London: Heinemann.

Habermas, J. (1974) *Theory and Practice* (trans. J. Viertal). London: Heinemann.

Habermas, J. (1984) *Theory of Communicative Action* (vol. I) (trans. T. McCarthy). Boston: Beacon Press.

Habermas, J. (1987) *Theory of Communicative Action* (vol. II) (trans. T. McCarthy). Boston: Beacon Press.

Hawkes, N. (2009) 'Values and quality teaching at West Kidlington Primary School', in Lovat, T. and Toomey, R. (Eds.) *Values Education and Quality Teaching: The double helix effect* (International Edition). Dordrecht, Netherlands: Springer, pp. 105–120.

Immordino-Yang, M.H. and Damasio, A.R. (2007) 'We feel, therefore we learn: The relevance of affect and social neuroscience to education', *Mind, Brain, and Education*, 1, pp. 3–10.

Kohlberg, L. (1963) 'The development of children's orientation towards moral order: Sequence in the development of moral thought', *Vita Humana*, 6, pp. 11–13.

Lovat, T. and Clement, N. (2008a) 'The pedagogical imperative of values education', *Journal of Beliefs & Values: Studies in Religion & Education*, 29, pp. 273–285.

Lovat, T. and Clement, N. (2008b) 'Quality teaching and values education: Coalescing for effective learning', *Journal of Moral Education*, 37, pp. 1–16.

Lovat, T. and Toomey, R. (Eds.) (2009) *Values Education and Quality Teaching: The double helix effect*. Dordrecht, Netherlands: Springer.

Lovat, T., Toomey, R. and Clement, N. (Eds.) (2010) *International Research Handbook on Values Education and Student Wellbeing*. Dordrecht, Netherlands: Springer.

Lovat, T., Toomey, R., Dally, K. and Clement, N. (2009) *Project to Test and Measure the Impact of Values Education on Student Effects and School Ambience*. Report for the Australian Government Department of Education, Employment and Workplace Relations (DEEWR) by The University of Newcastle,

Australia. Canberra: DEEWR. Available at: www.valueseducation.edu.au/values/val_articles,8884.html. Accessed June 2010.

Lovat, T., Toomey, R., Dally, K. and Clement, N. (2011) *Values Pedagogy and Student Achievement: Contemporary Research Evidence.* Dordrecht, Netherlands: Springer.

MCEETYA (1999) *Adelaide Declaration on National Goals for Schooling in the Twenty-first Century.* Canberra: Ministerial Council on Education, Employment, Training and Youth affairs. Available at: www.curriculum.edu.au/mceetya/nationalgoals/. Accessed June 2010.

More, T. (1989) *Utopia* (trans. R. Logan and G. Adams). Cambridge: Cambridge University Press.

Newmann, F. and Associates (1996) *Authentic Achievement: Restructuring schools for intellectual quality.* San Francisco: Jossey Bass.

Noddings, N. (2002) *Educating Moral People: A Caring Alternative to Character Education.* New York: Teachers College Press.

Nucci, L. and Narvaez, D. (Eds.) (2008) *Handbook of Moral and Character Education.* New York: Routledge.

Peters, R.S. (1981) *Moral Development and Moral Education.* London: George Allen & Unwin.

Raulo, M. (2002) 'Moral education and development', *Journal of Social Philosophy, 31,* pp. 507–518.

Rowe, K.J. (2004) 'In good hands? The importance of teacher quality', *Educare News, 149,* pp. 4–14.

Index